Faust:

My Soul be Damned for the World

Volume I

By

E.A. Bucchianeri

Batalha Publishers
Maxieira, Portugal

Hardback First Edition, Revised 2010
ISBN: 978-989-96844-0-9

Library of Congress Subject Headings

Bucchianeri, E.A.
    Faust: My Soul be Damned for the World, Volume 1
    Bibliography.

    1. Faust, d. ca. 1540. 2. Faust, d. ca. 1540—Appreciation. 3. Faust, d. ca. 1540—Drama. 4. Faust, d. ca. 1540—Fiction. 5. Faust, d. ca. 1540—In literature. 6. Faust, d. ca. 1540—Legends. 7. Faust, d. ca. 1540—Legends—History and criticism. 8. Faust, d. ca. 1540—Legends—Influence. 9. Faustus, Georg, d. ca. 1540. 10. Marlowe, Christopher, 1564-1593.—Biography. 11. Marlowe, Christopher, 1564-1593—Criticism and interpretation. 12. Marlowe, Christopher, 1564-1593. Doctor Faustus. 13. Marlowe, Christopher, 1564-1593. Doctor Faustus—Criticism, Textual. 14. Marlowe, Christopher, 1564-1593. Doctor Faustus—Sources. 15. Lessing, Gotthold Ephraim, 1729-1781—Faust Fragment—Criticism and interpretation. 16. Puppet plays—Faust—History and criticism.

British Library Subject Headings

Bucchianeri, E.A.
    Faust: My Soul be Damned for the World, Volume 1
    Bibliography

    1. Devil — Drama. 2. English literature History and criticism. 3. Faust, d. ca. 1540 — Drama. 4. Faust, d. ca. 1540 — In Literature. 5. Faust, d. ca. 1540 — Legends — History and Criticism. 6. Germany — Drama. 7. Magicians — Drama. 8. Magicians in Literature. 9. Marlowe, Christopher, 1564-1593 Doctor Faustus. 10. Tragedy

Books by the same Author:

A Compendium of Essays:
Purcell, Hogarth and Handel, Beethoven, Liszt, Debussy, and Andrew Lloyd Webber

Handel's Path to Covent Garden: A Rocky Journey

"The praise of the wicked is short, and the joy of the hypocrite but for a moment. If his pride mount up even to heaven, and his head touch the clouds: in the end he shall be destroyed like a dunghill, and they that had seen him, shall say: Where is he?"
(Job 20: 5–7)

శుభ ❖ శుభ

౫౮ ❖ ౮౫

Chapter 1

The Historical Faustus: the Man behind the Myth

Faust, the notorious reprobate who willingly forfeited his immortal soul to the devil in exchange for the fleeting illusory pleasures of the world as depicted and recounted in famous works of art, literature, drama and music, did not originate as the imaginary brainchild of a literary genius. A *historical* figure named 'Faust' did exist, but with the passage of time, this individual faded into semi-obscurity, gradually becoming immortalised as a mythical character — the original name, *Faustus*, became confused in a barrage of theological, philosophical, political, and artistic literature that continually reshaped his legend through the centuries up to the present day.[*]

Retracing the life of Faustus is not a simple task; the facts are shrouded and distorted in the mists of time and speculation, presenting a formidable challenge for any dedicated researcher who endeavours to compile an accurate biography. The proof of his existence survives in university and city records, letters, private journals, chronicles and other similar documents. Furthermore, the meagre historical documentation referring to him is limited and often tainted, it contains partial and oftentimes inaccurate information, or is permeated with the subjective opinions of the chroniclers. For example, the important details pertaining to the time and place of Faustus' birth and death remain subject to scholarly conjecture. Nevertheless, through these various sources we discover the nature of the career he embarked upon, and in certain documented instances, where he travelled. We also discover through these diverse accounts contemporaries whom he influenced or who regarded him with contempt and derision; an important point to observe, for these individuals affected the opinions of those affiliated with their particular social and intellectual circles. As time progressed, these scholars enhanced, magnified and embellished the original accounts — a process that ultimately encouraged the proliferation of the Faustian legend. Our search for the real Faustus must also commence with these existing documents, for they are all that remain of this enigmatic and sinister individual.

One particular bibliography by Hans Henning presents a list of one hundred and eighty-three references[1] documenting the historical Doctor Faustus; however, many of these documents are considered unreliable due to the obvious assimilation of legendary folklore with historical facts. Therefore, scholars found it necessary, for practical purposes, to limit the number of documents in their research to records that originated during his lifetime and certain events recorded by close contemporaries. This condensed criterion generally commences with documents that first mention Faustus, for instance, Trithemius' letter dated 1507, branching to various accounts dated after the assumed year of Faustus' death, (c. 1539 or 1540), extending to

---

[*] **Editorial Policy**: this study is presented in British spelling. Material with braces, { }, indicates editing or comments made by the present author. Material with brackets, [ ], also marks editing and comments of the present author, with the exception of stage directions in the succeeding Chapters.

[1] Hans Henning, *Faust–Bibliographie* (Berlin: Aufbau, 1966), I, 87–105, in Frank Baron, *Doctor Faustus: From History to Legend* (München: Wilhelm Fink Verlag, 1978), p. 7.

1617 with an excerpt from Fynes Moryson's *Itinerary*. In 1913, Karl Schottenloher presented an additional document to Faustus scholars for their consideration, an entry from the registration records of Heidelberg University dated January 9, 1483.[2] Frank Baron discovered a new Faustus document in 1989.[3] Hence, by following a time-line method of categorisation using these same records, we have approximately twenty-nine documents for our particular study. (See Appendix One.)

We may consider twenty-nine sources of information a substantial number to commence with, however, difficulties begin to emerge as we study each respective document. For example, not one, but *two* Faustus figures surface: one who entitled himself "Master Georgius Sabellicus, the younger Faustus", and a second individual recognised as "Johann Faust" (or Johann Faustus / Faustum). This revelation generated significant confusion: who is the real Faustus? Baron identifies the academic culprit who initiated this anomaly — Johannes Manlius, a student from the University of Wittenberg and a pupil of Martin Luther's successor, the famous Philipp Melanchthon.[4] Manlius edited a book entitled *Locurum communium collectanea* (1562), a compilation of anecdotes transcribed from Melanchton's lectures; it is here for the first time that we note the name "Johann" associated with Faustus, nearly twenty-five years after the assumed year of his death.[5] Apparently, Manlius employed artistic licence in his editorial endeavour, for Baron notes that "[...] Manlius did not handle the original material from his teacher very scrupulously; he changed it and added to it to make his presentation more interesting reading."[6]

Further compounding this confusion, we observe the name "Johannes Faust" in an entry dated 1509 in the matriculation records of Heidelberg University. Therefore, discovering the true identity of this infamous magician becomes complex: was Manlius referring to this individual? Eminent scholars have suggested that possibly two Faustus-figures existed and were simultaneously practising the occult. Will-Erich Peuckert presented a controversial argument suggesting these two men, Gerog and Johann, were father and son — an explanation not generally accepted.[7]

Baron's response to this Faustian dilemma was to isolate these two individuals and concentrate on George in particular, basing his argument on the observation that the earliest sources record the name "Georg" in both German and Latin accounts, while "Johann", as mentioned, appeared many years later.[8] Baron states the earliest sources are perhaps the most

---

[2] Karl Schottenloher, *Münchener neuste Nachrichten*, July 5, 1913 (no. 338), in *Doctor Faustus: From History to Legend*, pp. 17–22. Baron observed this particular document was not previously registered in serious scholarly articles.

[3] I wish to thank Prof. Frank Baron for bringing his discovery to my attention. See 'Faustus his Life and Legend', (November 12, 2009) *Historicum.net*:
http://www.historicum.net/themen/hexenforschung/lexikon/personen/art/Georg_Faustus/html/artikel/7114/ca/693f7c07ad/   See also Frank Baron, 'Who was the Historical Faustus? Interpreting an Overlooked Source', *Daphnis* 18, (1989), S. 297–302.

[4] *Doctor Faustus, from History to Legend*, p. 12.

[5] Ibid.

[6] Ibid.

[7] Will–Erich Peuckert, 'Dr. Johannes Faust,' *Zeitschrift für deutsche Philologie*, 70 (1947), pp. 55–74, in *Doctor Faustus, from History to Legend*, p. 11.

[8] See *Doctor Faustus, from History to Legend*.

reliable due to the fact they were recorded before the phantasmagorical aspects of the legend gained momentum. He also highlighted an important detail, the earliest sources, in Latin *and* German, included the Latin word "Faustus" (meaning 'fortunate' or 'auspicious'), and not the German word "Faust" (translated 'fist'); a distinction people of the sixteenth century would be cognizant, yet is not generally recognised in this era, particularly when the works of Lessing and Goethe blurred this nomenclature.[9] Baron states that earlier research incorporating the Heidelberg entry "Johann Faust ex Simern" is a direct result of this erroneous assumption that the Latin appellation was synonymous with the German word "Faust", hence he elected not to include this entry in his argument.[10]

For his study, Baron concentrated on the following nine[11] documents:

January 9, 1483:	Heidelberg University: "Georgius Helmstetter"
August 20, 1507:	Johannes Trithemius: "Magister Georgius Sabellicus Faustus iunior"
October 3, 1513:	Conrad Mutianus Rufus: "Georgius Faustus Helmitheus Hedelbergensis"
February 12, 1520:	Hans Müller: "Doctor Faustus philosoph(us)"
June 17, 1528:	An Ingolstadt scribe: "Doctor Jörg Faustus von Haidlberg"
July, 1528:	Kilian Leib: "Georgius Faustus Helmstet(ensis)"
May 10, 1532:	Hieronymus Holzschuher (Junior Burgomaster of Nuremberg): "Doctor Fausto" (i.e. Doctor Faust[us])
August 13, 1536:	Joachim Camerarius: "Faustus"
January 15, 1540:	Philipp von Hutten: "Philosophus Faustus"

These nine sources of information are of particular importance: they either record the name "George" and / or "Faustus", disclose his place of origin, and reveal the social circles he

---

[9] Ibid. p. 13.
[10] Ibid. p. 12.
[11] Ibid. pp. 13, 17.

was affiliated with. A number of these authors became acquainted or associated through their scholastic studies in humanism and the occult. Baron therefore declared, "On the basis of these sources it is possible to make reliable generalizations about the name, birthplace, and studies of Faustus."[12] As mentioned, Baron discovered an additonal manuscript describing how a certain 'Magister Georgius Helmstette[r]' drafted a horoscope in 1490 for a student named Peter Seuter, (also spelled Suitter), in Heidelberg. For our study of the historical Faustus, we will focus initially on these ten documents.[13]

Baron notes from the onset of the magician's career, Faustus was reluctant to disclose his family name. If "Faustus" was indeed his name, its Latin origin implies it was an assumed identity as humanists adopted the custom of creating pseudonyms by modifying their appellations upon Latin names or Latin phonetics.[14] For an academic occupied in the practise of divination, this Latinised name, 'Faustus', would be advantageous as a method of self-promotion. Supporting this theory is the fact that George also used the name "Sabellicus" according to one of the earliest sources. Baron emphasises the name "Sabellicus" is not German in origin but Latin, and therefore this indicates Faustus designed an affiliation with the land of the Sabines, a region north of Rome that from ancient times became infamously associated with occult practises. By adopting the title "Sabellicus", Faustus claimed an ancestral lineage descending from magicians of antiquity, an appropriate name "[…] for one who claimed to be a *magus*," as Baron observes.[15]

An additional and equally questionable title Faustus assumed was "junior", or "the younger Faustus" depending on the translation of the source. As "Faustus" is evidently not his true family name, George deliberately intended contemporaries to associate him with some personage in particular. It is possible George desired a connection with the famous humanist, Pomponius Laetus (d. 1508), who first promoted the ideal that humanists should adopt Latin names. This desired affiliation may also have extended to the students of Laetus: Marcus Antonius Sabellicus (d. 1506) and Publius Faustus Andrelinus (d. 1518).[16] Marcus Antonius Sabellicus, a famous contemporary Italian historian and poet, adopted the name "Sabellicus" as he was born in the Sabine region. Faustus Andrelinus, a professor of rhetoric in Paris, lectured on astronomy with emphasis on astrology. Baron supports Gustav Schwetschke's thesis that George Faustus was therefore directly or indirectly influenced by the new humanist practise of adopting names, and perhaps "Faustus junior" was inspired by Faustus Andrelinus.[17]

While Faustus may be reluctant to disclose his family name, he was obviously proud to proclaim his place of origin. Early sources list two separate locations, Helmstadt and Heidelberg, however Baron notes there is no contradiction — both are in the same geographical area, and for the sake of convenience, Faustus on occasion may have simply referred to the larger town, Heidelberg, as his birthplace.[18] Baron observes this practise of generalisation was common for

---

[12] Ibid. p. 13.
[13] 'Faustus his Life and Legend'.
[14] *Doctor Faustus, from History to Legend*, p.14.
[15] Ibid.
[16] Ibid. p. 91.
[17] Gustav Schwetschke, "Wer was Faustus senior? Ein Beitrag zur Faustgeschichte," *Deutches Museum*, Oct. 11, 1855, pp. 548–551, in *Doctor Faustus, from History to Legend*, pp. 32–33, 91.
[18] *Doctor Faustus, from History to Legend*, p. 15.

the sake of clarity, when people would not be familiar with smaller geographical townships. In addition, Mutianus Rufus' letter (1513) featuring Faustus' curious title of "Helmitheus Hedelbergensis" may in fact be misspellings for "Helmstadius / Helmstetius" and "Heidlebergensis". Baron therefore concludes, "[...] the primary sources indicate clearly that the place where the historical Faustus was born was not Kundling or Knittlingen, as it was asserted in later sources, but rather Helmstadt near Heidelberg."[19]

From this evidence, it is obvious George Faustus of Helmstadt deliberately fabricated a reputation to reflect his occult knowledge and academic learning. In addition, there are several academic titles associated with Faustus that indicate a university education in the faculty of arts; master (*magister*), philosopher (*philosophus*), and *doctor*. While the master's degree was the foremost qualification a student could attain in philosophy at that time, masters in this field were on occasion referred to as *doctor*, hence this title is not an inaccurate self-proclamation invented by Faustus.[20] Attempts to discover the extent of Faustus' academic studies, as previously discussed, are obstructed by the entry of "Johann Faust" in the records of the University of Heidelberg. Baron observed this student commenced his studies in December 1505 and graduated with a bachelor's degree in 1509, while George Faustus already claimed the title of Master a considerable period before this timeframe, and therefore this particular source cannot refer to the historical Faustus.[21] Of immediate interest is the 1483 entry naming a certain "Georgius Helmstetter" as Baron relates:

> "It is reasonable to assume that a young man who lived in Helmstadt would choose Heidelberg rather than another place for his university studies. [...] Although the name Faustus is not linked anywhere in the records with the name Georgius Helmstetter, there are certain indications that this Heidelberg student was the same Faustus referred to in the primary sources. [...] Students of that time usually indicated their surnames, and during the semester in which Helmstetter registered at Heidelberg, only one other student from a total of sixty-seven elected not to do so. Thus the young Helmstetter demonstrated the same reluctance to reveal his surname that Faustus later consistently displayed.
>
> Very few young men from small villages like Helmstadt ever had the chance to attend the university. During the years 1460 to 1520 a total of thirteen students came from Helmstadt, four graduating with bachelor's degrees and only two obtaining master's degrees. There is no trace of another Georgius Helmstetter at this time. Under these circumstances it is unlikely that the exact correspondence of name and scope of academic training is simply a coincidence. Moreover, the kind of education the Heidelberg graduate of 1487 had received manifests

---

[19] Ibid.
[20] George Kaufmann, *Geschichte der deutschen Universitäten* (Stuttgart, 1888), II, pp. 274–5, in ibid., p. 16.
[21] *Doctor Faustus, from History to Legend,* p. 16.

itself in a number of ways in the subsequent activities of the historical Doctor Faustus."[22]

The University Years

Georg Helmstetter registered at the university on January 9, 1483 and graduated with a bachelor's degree on July 12, 1484. However, he encountered a minor complication when he applied to partake in the final examination for this degree. At the end of June 1484 (*ultima mensis Junii*), the Faculty of Arts examination commission deliberated his application as he apparently lacked several of the prescribed requisites, preventing him from proceeding with the final examination.[23] His attendance record was one particular issue as the statutes of the university required at least one and a half years of study. Baron notes Helmsetter actually completed the minimum time specified, and therefore suggests the unfulfilled requirements referred to may be the result of Helmstetter's late arrival in the academic year of 1482–1483. It is reasonable to assume the young student did not attend all the obligatory lectures at the commencement of this term, and therefore was absent for the introductory segments of this course.[24] A certain Magister, Johannes Hasse, supported Helmstetter and vouchsafed for the student's ability to complete the requirements within a reasonable period. The faculty finally permitted Helmstetter to proceed with the examination and he graduated sixteenth of the seventeen students who participated in July 1484.[25] He subsequently commenced studies for the master's degree: a course that may require a further three years. Prior to receiving this higher degree, Helmstetter, for a second time, came under the scrutiny of the examinations committee concerning his non-fulfilment of the expected requirements — he participated in two of the three prescribed disputations, and was informed of the necessity to complete the third before the faculty would permit him to graduate.[26] On March 1, 1487, he graduated second in his class of ten candidates.[27]

On closer inspection, Helmstetter's erratic attendance at the university reveals valuable information that requires further analysis. Baron observes that the prodigious speed by which this student earned his bachelor's degree is unusual as Heidelberg required an average study period of two years for the first degree.[28] Paradoxically, Helmstetter invested a considerable length of time to acquire his master's degree (1484–1487): in general, students obtained this degree within one year, or one year and nine months.[29] Baron offers two possible explanations

[22] Ibid.
[23] University of Heidelberg Archives (UHA) I, 3, No. 49, fol. 113v. (Akten der Artistenfakultät, vol. 2, 1445–1501), in ibid., pp. 17, 92.
[24] *Doctor Faustus, from History to Legend,* p. 17.
[25] UHA I, 3, No. 49, fol. 114r. (Akten der Artistenfakultät, vol. 2, 1445-1501), in ibid., pp. 92–93.
[26] *Doctor Faustus, from History to Legend,* p. 17
[27] Ibid.
[28] Ibid. p.18.
[29] Ibid.

for this apparent temporal irregularity; Helmstetter may have been absent for a certain period, or, was prevented from applying for the master's examination due to his age.[30] The second theory would appear in character with Helmstetter who had previously opted to spend the minimum amount of time possible in pursuit of his first degree. In this timeframe in Germany, a minimum age policy existed[31] for those aspiring to achieve a master's degree, for example, the minimum age stipulated by the Universities of Ingolstadt and Greifswald was twenty years.[32] Other universities cited twenty-one years as the accepted minimum.[33] Despite the fact that an age criterion was not recorded in the statutes of Heidelberg for this period, Baron assumes a similar desideratum of age must have been upheld. He observed the study periods several scholars had committed to during the 1450s and 1460s share similarities with that of Helmstetter. Baron presents the humanist Hartmann Schedel as one example, who "[...] having registered at Leipzig in 1456, obtained his bachelor's degree one year later, after which time he spent three years in pursuit of a master's degree before graduating in 1460 at the age of twenty."[34] If a similar age restriction was specified at Heidelberg resulting in Helmstetter's delay in obtaining his master's degree, it is possible to assume the year of this student's birth was either 1466 or 1467[35] — a considerable period before the previously accepted supposition of 1480 as the birth date of George Faustus.[36]

Focusing on Helmstetter's character and temperament, we may deduce he was an ambitious student who displayed a profound confidence in his academic abilities. This observation may be denoted by his application to take the bachelor's examination with the support of Hasse before the specified time; Hasse certainly must have been convinced of the student's competence before taking his position of recommendation. Helmstetter's proficiency is also evident in his leap from the penultimate rank for the bachelor's degree to his rating as second in his post-graduate class. This was a noteworthy accomplishment and reflects an assiduous effort on his part to become an adept academic, particularly when we consider that in addition to his studies as a master student, he was expected to fulfil the remaining curriculum required to complete his undergraduate degree. Helmstetter's tenacity is evident in his application for the master's degree having completed only two disputations — perhaps he was notably accomplished in this area and therefore his peers' admiration encouraged him to assert that he had adequately presented his debating abilities on these two occasions. Alternatively, one might hypothetically suggest that he had audaciously presumed he could circumvent this stipulation for the master's degree as simply as he had manipulated the time specified to allow him to partake in the bachelor's examination. According to the university statutes, all newly graduated masters were

---

[30] Ibid.

[31] From Georg Kaufmann, *Geschichte der deutschen Universitäten* (Stuttgart, 1888), II, p. 304, in ibid, p. 18.

[32] *Doctor Faustus, from History to Legend*, p. 18.

[33] Ibid.

[34] Wilhelm Wattenbach, "Hartmann Schedel als Humanist," *Forschungen zur deutschen Geschichte*, 11 (1871), pp. 351–374, in *Doctor Faustus, from History to Legend*, p. 18

[35] Ibid.

[36] Baron: "Hans Henning assumes that Faustus was born in approximately 1480. He does not explain the reasons for making this assumption. In fact, Faustus could have been born much earlier." Baron, n. 8, p. 93.

required to teach for two years in the Faculty of Arts, [37] and Helmstetter may have unilaterally decided that at a later date, during his teaching tenure, he could accomplish the third disputation. These observations concerning Helmstetter's character display an interesting parallel with accounts of George Faustus. Faustus publicly boasted of his acumen in philosophy and academia by which he proclaimed to have surpassed other scholars, and on various occasions displayed an attitude of non-compliance with social morals and a certain defiance regarding civil authority, as recorded in the city records of Ingolstadt. This source documents the occasion of his banishment from the town, and his pledge not to take vengeance on the city officials for their order. The Nuremberg records document a separate occasion when the council decided to refuse him safe conduct through the city due to an accusation of sodomy. We may also presume this refusal referred to his dubious profession, for he proclaimed to practise certain forms of divination that his contemporaries acknowledged as dabbling in the Black Arts.

Continuing with the postulation Helmstetter was indeed George Faustus, then let us first examine the extent of his university education and the subjects that influenced him academically. Perhaps we may discover what occasioned his decision to elect the controversial career of a wandering scholar and diviner. In the era of Helmstetter's attendance at the university, a choice between two methods was offered as part of the curriculum interpreting the philosophy of Aristotle: the *via antiqua* (or *realism*), and the *via moderna* (or *nominalism*).[38] The *via antiqua*, based upon the interpretations of St. Thomas Aquinas (1225–1274), maintained that the truths of faith are compatible with Aristotle's philosophy of sense experience. The knowledge of certain truths recognised as mysteries of faith, e.g. the nature of the Incarnation of Christ, required divine revelation, other truths based on material creation required sense experience. In other instances, a number of truths are manifest through *both* principles equally, e.g. the knowledge of God's existence, disclosed through divine revelation *and* personal experience in the physical world.

However, St. Thomas Aquinas also maintained that the Platonic idea of Forms, or *universals*, had credence. Plato's theory maintains true knowledge comes from that which is permanent and therefore 'real', and does not originate from sense experience based on observations of an ever-changing, visible world. As this 'true' knowledge must be constant, it therefore can only be acquired through the use of reason. Plato believed when reason is employed correctly, intellectual insights are assured and the attainment of true knowledge a certainty. He maintained the *universals*, or Forms that constitute the 'real' world, actually formed the basis for this reasoning. For instance, we in the physical world know what a circle, or a square looks like, and can attempt to draw them although we have never experienced their 'ideal' or 'perfect' forms. However, we could not have understood these concepts or learned *how* to draw these objects unless we employed our power of reasoning to understand that these shapes already existed in principal in changeless *universals* (i.e. 'circularity' or 'squareness') in the unseen world of Idea or Form, and therefore universals are more 'real' than objects in the physical world. A square or circle may be drawn, carved, or observed in the physical world, but it will never be as perfect or exist perpetually as its model — the Form or Idea from which it is distinguished. The same concept is applicable in other areas, for example, the Form of 'Justice'; the word 'just' or 'justice' may describe separate actions if these actions resemble the Form of

---

[37] *Doctor Faustus, from History to Legend*, p . 18.
[38] Ibid.

'Justice'. How man in the physical world practises justice is seldom as perfect as the Idea from which it originates and obtains its definition.

In contrast, the scholastic Roscelin (c.1050 –1125) expounded an alternative theory that later became known as the *via moderna,* or nominalism, based upon Aristotle's philosophy that all reality consists of individual objects. According to his reasoning, Roscelin declared that *universals,* such as *beauty, nation, triangle,* etc., were simply class names and therefore concluded these terms were abstractions without substantive reality. During the eleventh and twelfth centuries, this interpretation of Aristotle became extremely controversial due to the heretical implications it introduced to theology; for example, challenging the Christian doctrine of the Holy Trinity. According to this doctrine, God exists as three separate persons, the Father, Son, and Holy Spirit, but they are united as one in being, or substance. Roscelin applied his theory of nominalism to the doctrine of the Holy Trinity and maintained that each person of the Trinity was separate in substance, and that the unity traditionally associated with the Trinity was simply a verbal, or nominal, classification; an interpretation that was declared heretical in 1092 at the Synod of Soissons. Roscelin fled to England to avoid persecution, but eventually travelled to Rome and once again became reconciled with the Church. During the fourteenth century the nominalist position was defended by William of Ockham (1285?–1349?), an English Franciscan. His philosophy was considered dangerous to the faith by Pope John XXII, and he was detained under house arrest at Avignon while his writings were examined by the Church. Embroiled in a dispute concerning Franciscan property, he escaped to Munich in 1328 and joined the anti-Papal emperor Louis IV who refused to acknowledge the authority of the pope concerning political matters. Ockham was therefore excommunicated, nevertheless, he continued to write in defence of the emperor. Before his death, he sought reconciliation with Pope Clement VI. Ockham's fame rests on the philosophical rule known today as "Ockham's Razor", i.e. that in the process of explanation, one should not assume the existence of more objects than simple logic requires.

Prior to 1452, the *via moderna,* as expounded under the authority of Ockham, was the sole interpretation of Aristotle taught at Heidelberg until reformers of the *via antiqua* regained academic recognition.[39] Helmstetter (Faustus?) opted to study the *via moderna:* a course that remained the popular choice of the two schools of thought at Heidelberg.[40] Baron states that Helmstetter's "[…] graduation as a *magister* near the top of his class demonstrates that he had the intellectual ability to cope with the intricacies of logic and philosophy."[41] Although Helmstetter decided on a philosophical course founded upon idealism denounced as heretical in earlier times, this choice does not present substantial evidence that he was determined to become an apostate or elected to follow the occult realm as vividly recounted in later sources. There remains the possibility he was intrigued by the controversial aspect of nominalism — the temptation to associate this philosophy with his future career as a *magus* is unavoidable — yet to ascertain to what extent nominalism actually influenced him would constitute a vague speculation. It would be logical to assume that Helmstetter simply made an educational choice in electing the *via moderna* as a medium to learn both traditional and contemporary interpretations of philosophy. The *via moderna,* despite its controversial history, would facilitate a well-rounded approach to

---

[39] Ibid. pp. 18–19.
[40] Ibid.
[41] Ibid. p. 18.

philosophy. It is reasonable to presume that an introduction to the *via antiqua*, i.e. the idea of *universals*, would be a prerequisite to understanding nominalism that argued *against* the ideology of *universals*. In addition, Baron observes that the nominalist course in Heidelberg "[…] with its insistence on extensive use of commentaries as developed by Marsilius von Inghen, the [Roman Catholic] founder of the university, could be said to have been the more conservative group of the students and faculty."[42] Baron also noted the two schools, the *via antiqua* and the *via moderna*, did not deviate significantly from the traditional scholastic curriculum.[43]

Upon reviewing the nature of his philosophical education, one might expect Helmstetter to decide on the career of an esteemed theologian; however, on further analysis of the traditional university curriculum, we discover compelling evidence that other specific subjects may have lured him from the path of vocational respectability to study occult mysticism. During the Middle Ages, education in the liberal arts consisted of seven subjects divided into two categories, the *trivium* and the *quadrivium*, a curriculum that remained popular throughout the Renaissance period. The *trivium* centred on Latin encompassing grammar (including the study of literature), dialectic or logic, and rhetoric (the art of written and spoken eloquence that also included the study of law). When a student completed the *trivium* he was entitled to a bachelor's degree. If at this point a student elected to pursue a master's degree, he would advance to the *quadrivium* that consisted of arithmetic, geometry (including geography and natural philosophy), astronomy (to which astrology was often appended), and music. The main purpose of this specific curriculum was to develop erudite scholars who would ultimately benefit society as these courses in most instances led to a career in theology, philosophy, law, or medicine.

The *quadrivium* section of the curriculum, the mathematic disciplines of the liberal arts as designated by Boethius (c. A.D. 430–525), is of particular interest. One of the first Medieval Scholastics, Boethius, a compiler and translator of ancient Greek texts, was influenced by Pythagorean, Platonic and Aristotelian philosophy. Boethius elaborated on the virtues of the *quadrivium* in his series of treatises as a means of "[…] preparing people for higher good, the love of wisdom, and abstract reasoning," as Wayne Bowman states.[44] These works became the cornerstone of medieval academic disciplines and continued to influence the methodology of philosophical education in the universities. Therefore the study of arithmetic, geometry, astronomy and music, signifying the study of the universe and its proportions, was essential for a student who aspired to master a proficiency in pure philosophy. Arithmetic and the study of numbers was deemed important from the time of the Greek philosopher Pythagoras (582?–500? BC) and his disciples who extensively studied the characteristics of even, odd, prime and square numbers. From these studies, the Pythagoreans concluded that the concept of number and ratio was the essence of all proportion, order, and harmony in the universe. The Pythagoreans also delved into the science of geometry and discovered the hypotenuse theorem that determined the square of the hypotenuse of a right triangle is equal to the sum of the squares of the other two sides — a rule that mathematic students continue to learn to this day. No doubt, the singularly visible science of geometry constituting the study of space and dimension, was considered

---

[42] Ibid. p. 19.

[43] Ibid.

[44] Wayne D. Bowman, *Philosophical Perspectives on Music* (New York: Oxford University Press, 1998), p. 24.

important evidence of number being the essence of proportion before and during the time of Faustus.

Although it is credible that Faustus learned astronomy / astrology, it is perhaps amusing for us to consider he would have studied music; however, we must realise it was the *science* of music associated with astronomy that was taught, not necessarily the *art* of music for entertainment purposes. The importance of number, according to the Pythagoreans, pervaded the study of astronomy / astrology and music collectively. This is the first ancient Greek school to propose the earth was globular in shape and that it revolved with the other planets around a central fire according to a numerical order. With regard to music, they discovered that vibrating strings of different lengths (as seen on a harp for example) produced varied pitches, i.e. the shorter the string, the higher the pitch, and that note or pitch intervals could be described as ratios between the various lengths of string. According to this discovery in music, the Pythagoreans concluded that the planets were distanced at intervals similar to the harmonic length of the strings, and therefore produced an unheard and mathematical "cosmic music" as they revolved in the heavens.[45] Bowman states that to the Pythagoreans, "[…] sound and music attained important status as clues to the nature of the universe, each in turn being inextricably and mysteriously associated with number and ratio, which, as if by magic, could exist apart from material things. Numbers and ratios were the presumed essence of concrete, sense-perceived reality."[46] Boethius, promoter of the *quadrivium*, also believed in the music of the spheres, and that the source of music lay in the divine realm of numbers. Bowman states that for Boethius: "The true *musicus* is one who reasons, who understands. […] The philosopher is the true *musicus*, and philosophy the one true consolation in the face of death."[47]

The concept of combining the science of mathematics with astronomy for the Medieval and Renaissance philosopher proved a valid method of mapping a mystical blueprint of the corporal and supernatural world. Hence, numerology and astrology would become obvious subjects of interest to scholars and philosophers. In ancient Greek texts, a scholar could present convincing evidence to defend an interest in 'acceptable' numerology and the validity of astrology, e.g. the Greek myth of Prometheus, one of the Titans entrusted with the task of creating humanity who was punished by Zeus for endowing the divine gift of fire to mankind. According to the Greek tragedy *Prometheus Bound* by Æschylus (525 B.C.– 456 B.C.), Prometheus disclosed to mankind the secret of using celestial portents to determine the seasons, revealed the science of numbers and invented the art of writing:

> "[…] They [mankind] dwelt
> In hollowed holes, like swarms of tiny ants,
> In sunless depths of caverns; and they had
> No certain signs of winter, nor of spring
> Flower-laden, nor of summer with her fruits;
> But without counsel fared their whole life long,
> Until I showed the risings of the stars,

---

[45] *Philosophical Perspectives on Music*, p. 24.
[46] Ibid. pp. 24–25.
[47] Ibid. p. 64.

And settings hard to recognize. And I
Found Number for them, chief device of all,
Groupings of letters, Memory's handmaid that,
And mother of the Muses. [...]"[48]

Therefore, Prometheus bestowed gifts that ultimately distinguished mankind as the superior being over all other created life forms. Scholars recognised the similarity in Christian theology with regard to the use of reason and the gifts the pagan Greeks identified, i.e. that astronomy, numbers and writing, were intellectual skills requiring this use of reason, a gift bestowed by God to humans made in His image and likeness.

An additional example of an ancient Greek text with similar themes is the discourse of Socrates with his disciples, as recounted in Plato's *Phædo.* (See Appendix Two.) One particular topic discussed was the nature of opposites; Socrates effectively uses the example of odd and even numbers, particularly the number three, to demonstrate that opposites exclude each other. From three topics, i.e. his conclusion using number, the characteristics of hot and cold, and the terms *musical* and *justice,* Socrates and his disciples expound upon the nature of the soul, which they concluded to be immortal. Finally, they discuss the importance in living a virtuous life to secure the eternal well being of the human soul. Scholars would certainly be intrigued on how the ancient Greeks employed number, particularly the number three later associated with the Trinity, in their philosophy concerning theological matters on immortality and the creation of the soul; *the* gift God gave exclusively to mankind.

It is logical to assume that scholars recognised a parallel with the book of Genesis in these Greek texts:

> "And God said: Let there be lights made in the firmament of heaven, to divide the day and the night, and let them be for signs, and for seasons, and for days and years. To shine in the firmament of heaven, and to give light upon the earth. And so it was done." (1:14–15)

> "And God created man to his own image: to the image of God he created him: male and female he created them. And God blessed them saying: Increase and multiply, and fill the earth, and subdue it, and rule over the fishes of the sea, and the fowls of the air, and all living creatures that move upon the earth." (1: 27–28)

> "And the Lord God formed man of the slime of the earth: and breathed into his face the breath of life, and man became a living soul." (2:7)

According to Genesis, the first statement relating the creation of the stars and planets describes their function as the heralds of signs and seasons. In addition, there are many celestial

---

[48] Æschylus, "Prometheus Bound ", in Charles W. Eliot, ed., *Nine Greek Dramas, The Harvard Classics, vol. 8* (New York: P.F. Collier and Son Corp., 1963), pp.182–183

signs recounted in the Bible, e.g. the star over Bethlehem that the three Magi recognised and followed, and the prophecy of the Second Coming to be foretold by the sun, moon and stars. The importance of number is also reflected in the act of Creation according to Genesis, i.e. the first seven days, the creation of the lights that would divide the passage of time on earth, which in turn is measured by number. In Sacred Scripture numbers have particular significance, i.e. the Ten Commandments, the twelve tribes and apostles, the seven spirits before the throne of God, the forty days Christ fasted in the wilderness, the three days before Christ's Resurrection — this list could continue *ad infinitum.* All of these references in Sacred Scripture indicated to scholars the importance of numerology, astronomy and astrology as legitimate academic and philosophical methods in man's endeavour to comprehend the Creator and His creation. Hence, these areas of mysticism were cautiously classified as 'natural magic' to distinguish them from prohibited subjects considered 'black magic'.

During the Renaissance period, translations of the Egyptian Hermetic books, or *Corpus Hermeticum,* by the Italian philosopher and theologian Marsillio Ficino (1433–99) facilitated the acceptance of the "natural" occult among European scholars. These works, attributed to a legendary writer named Hermes Trismegistus, contain metaphysical dialogues and treatises dating from the first to the fourth century A.D. once believed by the ancient Egyptians to be divine revelations disclosed by the god of wisdom, Thoth.[49] Baron states that:

> "Ficino saw Hermes as one of the earliest and greatest sources of wisdom, from which there was a direct link to Plato's philosophy. He considered Hermes as a prophet who foresaw the coming of Christ, as well as an ancient practitioner and teacher of philosophical magic, which was not forbidden by the Church. Under the influence of Hermetic writings Ficino popularized the concept of natural magic, which embraced a very wide scope of scientific, philosophical, and religious ideas, but which claimed not to resort to evil spirits."[50]

Ficino also contributed to the revival of Platonic philosophy with his first complete Latin translation of Plato's works (1463–1469) and the foundation of the Platonic Academy outside Florence.

One scholar emphatically impressed by Ficino's work was Conte Giovanni Pico della Mirandola (1463–1494), a prodigious humanist philosopher born near Ferrara. At the age of twenty-three, he settled in Rome (1486) and publicly posted nine hundred theses, which he offered to defend. Many of these theses featured discussions on magic and Jewish mysticism, or *cabala.* Pico was convinced that natural magic ought not to be popularised for the masses, i.e. the ignorant, not capable of comprehending this wisdom. He believed the masses could misconstrue its secrets out of context, and thereby misuse it; this knowledge must remain an esoteric art for those intellectually competent to appreciate its value. He also wrote a mystical account of the Creation entitled the *Heptaplus* (1489). The Church denounced a number of his

---

[49]   The Egyptian god, Thoth, also identified with the Greek god Hermes; "Hermes Trismegistus" is Latin for "Thrice-greatest Hermes."
[50]   *Doctor Faustus, from History to Legend*, p. 26.

theses as heretical and prohibited him from continuing his disputations. However, a year before his death, Pope Alexander VI absolved him from the charge of heresy. Baron states that, "There was no science, according to Pico, that made us more certain of the divinity of Christ than magic and cabala. [...] Pico's arguments in defence of this particular conclusion made an impression on contemporaries and found a strong echo in Germany."[51]

At the University of Heidelberg, research in the occult burgeoned in popularity with the humanist philosophers and scholars before and during the time of Faustus. Baron remarks:

> "It is evident that the entire humanistic school at Heidelberg was very much under the influence of the neoplatonic and hermetic writings of Ficino and Pico in Florence. The revival of Hermes Trismegistus made magic respectable in the scholarly world, although Renaissance thinkers were careful to define their area of interest as 'natural magic,' in contrast to prohibited black magic. The scholarly interest in natural magic gave a strong impetus to the flourishing of all occult science. Hence, at the University of Heidelberg, where the interest in astrology and magic were never totally absent, students had the opportunity to learn a great deal about the occult. [...]
>
> For the master's degree the Heidelberg statutes prescribed two astronomical works that had been used in the universities since the thirteenth century: *De sphaera* [*The Spheres*] by Johannes Sacrobosco and the *Theorica Planetarum* [*Theory of the Planets*] by Gerhard of Cremona. In the higher ranks of the *via moderna* the study of astronomy was considered valuable to the fame of the faculty and the university. This fact comes to light in the rules of the *Collegium Dionysium*, an association of masters in the field of theology, which promoted this field of study with particular vigor, although it was found necessary to warn against the prohibited arts. In his autobiographical notes a certain Conrad Buitzius states that in his bachelor's examination he questioned the legality of believing in, or practicing, and studying the arts of magic. The same autobiographical notes show that Buitzius spent some time copying information about astronomy, necromancy, and geomancy. Jodocus Eichmann, one of the founders of the *via antiqua* in Heidelberg, studied the occult sciences; he wrote (or copied?) a tract on chiromancy. Numerous surviving manuscripts from the old university library in Heidelberg indicate that the interest in astrology was particularly

---

[51] Frances A. Yeats, *Giordano Bruno and the Hermetic Tradition* (Chicago: University of Chicago Press, 1964), pp. 13–80, in ibid., p. 26.

strong.   Many tracts of Arabic astrologers were copied, and the prognostications for particular years were recorded.[52]"[53]

Notwithstanding the immense interest in occult studies during Helmstetter's (Faustus?) time at Heidelberg, Baron once stressed that any attempt to determine the extent of its influence on him remains a matter of conjecture; however, he suggests that Helmstetter "[...] must have sensed that these mysterious subjects were acquiring a new image of respectability as well as popularity. [...] The age during which Faustus lived and became famous experienced a great renaissance of the ancient occult sciences. [...] The beginnings of this significant development were already taking shape at Heidelberg in the 1480s."[54]

However, Baron's new discovery of a Paris manuscript describing 'Magister Georgius Helmstetter' and the horoscope he drafter for Peter Seuter in 1490 shows the ambitious student was not only interested in the occult, but formed his own unique style by combining 'natural' magic with unorthodox methods of divination, such as chiromancy, i.e. palm-reading.[55] Seuter had just commenced his studies in Heidelberg and left that same year, i.e. 1490, but in the interim had commissioned Helmstetter to draft the prognostication. Seuter was obviously impressed with the unusual chart for he held on to it for over four decades, eventually passing it on in 1534 to Nicolaus Ellenbog, a close acquaintance knowledgeable in astrology:

> "[...] I am now sending to you, with the aforementioned Benckius as my messenger, an oration, in the name of the University of Heidelberg, that Doctor Pallas Spangel delivered to Maximilian, the invincible ruler of the empire. I am sending this along with my horoscope, which Magister Georgius Helmstette[r] prepared for me on the basis of astrology, physiognomy, and chiromancy (Baron 1989, S. 301)[56]

Despite Seuter's apparent admiration for Helmstetter, Ellenbog was confused by the astrology-cum-chiromancy format of his chart and sent it back to Seuter without further ado:

---

[52] Baron's footnote, ibid., n. 17, p. 94: "Karl Bartsch, Die altdeutschen Handschriften der Universitätsbibliotek Heidelberg (Heidelberg: koester, 1881), see especially nos. 7, 9, 265, 285, 313, 316, 330, 331 in vol. 1 and nos. 12 and 298 in vol. 2. One of the early representatives of the humanistic movement in Heidelberg, Matthias von Kemnat († 1476), court chaplain of the Elector, was an active astrologer, and a number of his astrological manuscripts have survived. In the Bayerische Staatsbibliothek, Munich, Clm. 1817 and in the Bibliotheca Vaticana Cod. Pal. Lat. 1370. Conrad Celtis also studied what he referred to as "mathematics," and in Vienna he became the head of the so-called *collegium poetarum et mathematicarum*, an association that brought together humanism, astronomy, and astrology. Further evidence of interest in astrology is found in the correspondence of Celtis, Dalberg, and Reuchlin."

[53] *Doctor Faustus, from History to Legend*, pp. 20–21.

[54] Ibid. p. 21.

[55] 'Faustus: His Life and Legend.'

[56] Ibid. (Baron's source: 'Who was the Historical Faustus?' *Daphnis* 18, 1989).

"I read the oration of Doctor Pallas with interest. I am returning the horoscope prepared for you by a certain Helmstetter, for I was unable to make it out fully and even less to understand it, especially since I am ignorant of chiromancy. He indicated the position of the stars with twelve houses, but he omitted the degrees of the signs (which are definitely necessary here). Nor did he show the planets with their signs and degrees. To sum up, I am unable to learn from his work, and I took care to return it to you immediately (Baron 1989, S. 301)."[57]

Why would Helmstetter attempt to combine these various forms of divination? While astronomers and astrologers believed the stars were given by God to manifest divine signs and mark the seasons, perhaps Helmstetter concluded that astrology was insufficient when providing a unique horoscope for an individual as there could be many people born at or near the same time. There had to be some way of discerning the specific stellar influences destined for every person. He obviously found a solution by comparing the unique lines of his clients' hand with the paths of the stars and planets in their horoscopes. We note that like astrology, the divination practised in chriomancy also centres on the planets. Certain sections of the hand have lines associated with Venus, the sun and Mercury. Other sections of the hand are divided into 'mounds' also named after gods and planets, e.g. Jupiter, Saturn, Mars, Apollo, the moon, etc. If Helmstetter was concentrating on Seuter's hand for his prediction, it would explain why he did not include the signs and degrees of the planets expected in traditional astrology charts. Not satisifed with palmistry, Helmstetter also introduced physiognomy to his forecast, i.e. the 'art' of judging character from facial expressions and features. This also had several advantages as Baron notes: "Complementing astrological evidence with an evaluation of personality features may have been a way for Helmstetter to employ psychological insights in making a prediction."[58]

We continue to discover an indication of Helmstetter´s interest in the humanistic / occult training offered at Heidelberg if we return to the subject discussing his decision to fabricate a new identity. His name "Faustus", as previously mentioned, was possibly inspired by his deliberate attempt to create an association with the humanist Publius Faustus Andrelinus. Faustus Andrelinus, although based in Paris, was well known in Germany; in 1490, it was reported he lectured specifically on the *De sphaera* — one of the prescribed works at Heidelberg.[59] Of interest, Seuter's letter demonstrates that Helmstetter, by then a graduate, was present in Heidelberg at this time.

The calibre of the occult education Faustus may have received is reflected in the sciences he professed: necromancy (divination through communication with the dead), chiromancy, pyromancy (divination with fire), and hydromancy (divination with water). Faustus therefore based his profession as a magician upon sciences that during the Middle Ages were classified as esteemed methods of acquiring esoteric knowledge.[60] Baron also observes that while Faustus, in

---

[57] Ibid.
[58] 'Faustus: His Life and Legend'.
[59] *Doctor Faustus, from History to Legend* , p. 33.
[60] Ibid. p. 31.

a pretence of modesty, alludes to famous predecessors who excelled him, he was in reality ostentatiously advertising the pedigree of his occult education:

> "Another unique element is that Faustus referred to himself as the 'second' magus and the 'second' in the divination from water. He was willing to concede, consequently, in these two areas at least (in necromancy and alchemy Faustus claimed to be the first!), that there were those who were superior to him. Who were they? According to a long literary tradition in the Middle Ages, going back to the authority of Isidor and Augustine, the first magus was Zoroaster. Similarly, the first famous practitioner of hydromancy was the Roman king Numa Pompilius, from the land of the Sabines. This, too, had become a popular idea in the literature of the Middle Ages, again largely on the authority of Augustine. Thus, under the guise of modesty, by recognizing superiors, Faustus was actually boasting about his learning, showing that he was aware of the literary tradition relating to magic and divination."[61]

Therefore, when we consider the appellations Faustus adopted and the particular arts he professed, it is obvious he intended to convey the full extent of his university education in the occult. Of particular importance is the blatant recklessness of this action. Faustus' contemporaries, scholars and philosophers of the humanist tradition, were very cautious when admitting they had studied these forms of divination. Immediately recognised as tools of the demon, these sciences reputedly practised by Faustus were frequently researched for the sole purpose of differentiating these subjects as 'dangerous arts' in an attempt to defend the cause for 'natural magic' as a legitimate field of academic and philosophical inquiry. Many individuals were ignorant of, or refused to acknowledge the differences denoting 'natural magic' as opposed to 'black magic'; hence, several prominent scholars were branded as magicians in league with Satan due to their familiarity in both fields and their attempts to defend this distinction.

Johannes Trithemius (1462–1516), an abbot at the Benedictine monastery of Sponheim and a contemporary of Faustus, is one example of a Renaissance scholar who suffered the repercussions of these particular hostile rumours. He was a zealous researcher of natural magic in the hermetic tradition according to Ficino and Pico. He believed that natural magic, numerology in particular, was the only academic science by which man could attempt to comprehend the divine nature of God.[62] Trithemius claimed on many occasions to have received revelations and mystical visions during his quest for knowledge through the medium of natural magic. Apprehensive that his 'divinely revealed' secrets could fall into the wrong hands, and fearing the unavoidable accusation of practicing the black arts should this scenario occur, Trithemius disclosed these manifestations to only a select number of his trusted contemporaries whom he believed to be sympathetic to his cause in accordance with Pico's prudent counsel that magic should not be divulged to the masses. In his correspondence, Trithemius continually

---

[61] Ibid. p. 32.

[62] Ibid. p. 24. See Chapter III "Faustus and His Contemporaries: Johannes Trithemius" in *Doctor Faustus, from History to Legend* for a more detailed account of Trithemius and his interests.

stressed his position was that of a philosopher and not a magician; his 'magic' was purely spiritual in nature and required intellectual meditation as he explained: "Study generates cognition; cognition gives birth to love, love to similitude; similitude to communion; communion to virtue; virtue to dignity; dignity to power, and power produces miracle. This is the sole path to the perfect magic, divine as well as natural [...]."[63]

Despite his precautions, Trithemius' fears were realised — one of his letters addressed to Arnold Bostius dated March 25, 1499 was opened and circulated, for the recipient had died before the letter was delivered.[64] In his letter, Trithemius disclosed his future plans to study occult wisdom, and stated that his personal enlightenment was imparted by mystical revelation. He recounts an incident whereby a mysterious entity appeared at his bedside while he slept and imparted to him all the knowledge he had sought in vain for several days.[65] For the remainder of his life, Trithemius suffered from a slandered reputation. On August 16, 1507 he wrote to an acquaintance, Johannes Cappelarius: "[...] I have accomplished nothing stupendous, and yet I have to contend with the opinion of the masses, many thinking that I am a magus; they claim seriously that I have raised the dead, brought up demons from the underworld, foretold the future, and captured thieves with incantations."[66]

In several of his letters and various other writings, Trithemius attempted to defend his occult interest and restore the lustre to his tarnished name. Adopting the strategy employed by Pico, he attacked the occult arts that he deemed either questionable or outright demonic to differentiate and justify his preoccupation with natural magic. Subjects he categorised as black demonic arts included necromancy, pyromancy, acromancy (divination from heights), hydromancy, geomancy (divination with earth), chiromancy (palm-reading), orincomancy, sic. (a possible misspelling for *oneiromancy*, divination from dreams, *onychomancy*, divination from fingernails, or *ornithomancy*, divination from birds), sortilegium (sorcery, casting or drawing lots from cards or other items), aeromancy (divination from the air), and malfeasance (the wishing or of doing evil, perhaps this also refers to the "Evil Eye").[67] In an earlier letter written to Germanus de Ganay dated August 24, 1505, Trithemius also questioned the validity of astrology and alchemy, the philosophical pseudo-science of turning base metals into gold:

> "[...] the alchemists make promises with reference to compound bodies, but they err; they are deceived, and they deceive everyone who willingly listens to them. They want to imitate nature and to divide what is exclusively whole, since they do not understand the basis of virtue and nature [...]. Our philosophy is not earthly but rather celestial so that we might perceive the highest principle, which we call God. [...] Let unadvised men depart, idle men, the lying astrologers,

[63] Johannes Trithemius, *Epistolarum familiarum libri duo* (Hagenau: P. Brubach, 1536) p. 92, in ibid. pp. 27–28.

[64] *Doctor Faustus, from History to Legend*, p. 24.

[65] Ibid.

[66] Trithemius, *Epistolarum*, p. 303, in ibid. p. 28.

[67] Trithemius, *Nepiachus*, published in J. G. Eckhard, ed., *Corpus historicum Medii Aevi* (Leipzig, 1723), col. 830, in *Doctor Faustus, from History to Legend*, n. 28, p. 97.

deceivers, frivolous babblers. For the disposition of the stars does not contribute anything to the immortal mind, nothing to natural science, and nothing to supercelestial wisdom. [...]"[68]

Faustus: the Wandering Sorcerer

Faustus, in contrast to his apprehensive contemporaries, embarked upon a conspicuous public career in the Black Arts — an audacious undertaking. The first surviving historical account of his career is revealed in a letter written by Trithemius on August 20, 1507 to a fellow humanist, Johannes Virdung von Hasfurt. In this letter, Trithemius vehemently attacked Faustus whom he dismissed as a "fool":

"[...] That man, about whom you wrote me, Georgius Sabellicus, who dared to call himself the foremost of the necromancers, is an unstable character, a babbler, and a vagabond. He deserves to be thrashed in order to prevent him from heedlessly and continuously asserting in public things that are abominable and contrary to the teachings of the Holy Church. What are his assumed titles if not the manifestations of an extremely muddled mind, showing him to be a fool rather than a philosopher? For he composed a calling card to suit his taste: Magister Georgius Sabellicus. Faustus junior, the inspiration of the necromancers, astrologer, the second magus, palmist, practitioner of divination with the use of *argomantica* [= high places?] and fire, and the second in the art of divination with the use of water. Behold the foolishness of this man; with what great madness does he dare to call himself the inspiration of necromancers. One who is ignorant of all good arts should call himself a jester rather than a master of the arts. But I am not blind to his wickedness. When I returned from the Mark Brandenburg last year, I came upon this man in the town of Gelnhausen. In the inn I received reports of the many worthless things he had promised with great rashness. As soon as he heard that I was present, he fled from the inn, and he could not be persuaded by any means to come and meet me. The same foolish calling card he gave to you, and which I mentioned, he also sent to me by means of someone in town. Certain priests in the town reported to me that in the presence of many people he claimed to have acquired such comprehensive wisdom and memory that if all the works of Plato and Aristotle with the whole body of their philosophical thought completely disappeared from the memory of man, he himself, like another Ezra, could restore all things with a greater degree of elegance. Later,

---

[68] Trithemius, *Epistolarum,* pp. 90–3, in *Doctor Faustus, from History to Legend,* p. 27.

while I stayed in Speyer, he travelled to Würzburg, and, driven by the same foolishness, he is reported to have said in the presence of many people that the miracles of Christ were not so amazing; he himself could do all the things Christ had done, as often as and whenever one desired. Towards the end of Lent this year he came to Kreuznach, and, boasting with similar folly, he promised even more remarkable things, contending that in alchemy he surpassed all previous masters and that he understood and could accomplish whatever people wished. In the meantime, a teaching position became vacant in Kreuznach and he was appointed to it on the recommendation of Franz von Sickingen, an official of your prince and a man very fond of the occult. With the most nefarious kind of fornication he soon began to seduce the boys, and when this behaviour was suddenly brought to light, he eluded certain punishment by fleeing. These things are known to me through the most reliable evidence about the man whose arrival you await with such ardent desire. When he comes to you, you will find that he is not a philosopher but rather a very rash fool. Greetings. Remember me to the Prince if the opportunity arises. From Würzburg on the twentieth day of August in the year of our Lord 1507."[69]

This letter is one of the most important documents recounting the official activities of Faustus for it records the precise nature of his career as he promoted it through the use of calling cards — no other surviving document contains information that could be reliably credited as having been personally penned by Faustus. As Virdung also received the same calling card, Baron deduces that "[...] Trithemius must have been all the more careful not to harm his own credibility by inaccuracy."[70] As mentioned previously, Faustus rashly declared he was a master in several forms of divination considered diabolically dangerous, in fact, these are the only subjects he lists on his card of introduction. On first inspection of this letter, we note he conspicuously omitted other titles that he could have used similar to 'learned scholar of philosophy' or 'alchemist' as he previously boasted of these skills in the towns he visited. We observe these two titles would be considered respectable in comparison to the myriad of occult practises he professed — it would appear Faustus was deliberately forging and proclaiming his own evil reputation. Making no effort to conceal or defend his vocation as a *magus*, he blatantly affirmed that he practised the Black Arts.

Baron observes that Faustus was not officially connected "with the devil" in primary written documents until Martin Luther's comments were published in the *Tischreden* (1566); however, this association would be explicitly implied according to the sinister arts Faustus proclaimed to practise. Scholars, particularly theologians, would be thoroughly familiar with the Bible. For university disputations, i.e. debates presented through the medium of Latin, a student

---

69 Trithemius, *Epistolarum familiarum*, pp. 312–314., in *Doctor Faustus, from History to Legend,*. pp. 29–30. See also Philip Mason Palmer and Robert Pattison More, *The Sources of the Faust Tradition: From Simon Magus to Lessing* (New York: Octagon Books Inc., 1966), pp. 83–86.
70 *Doctor Faustus, from History to Legend*, p. 30.

was expected to competently defend or argue specific philosophical or theological topics that may have required evidence from sacred scripture to support their case in theory. Therefore, to acutely develop the ability for total recall and coherent reasoning would be essential for these disputations. In addition, the Church played a prominent role in daily life and influenced culture to a considerable degree; hence, the educated classes were well versed in scripture for spiritual and educational purposes, particularly when the invention of the Gutenberg press (c.1450) with its movable type heralded the mass production of books — the first major publication made widely available for the public was the Gutenberg Bible completed circa 1450–1456.

In accordance with Judeo-Christian scared scripture, all forms of divination practised by magicians are deserving of condemnation as these arts are a direct abomination to Almighty God. There are many passages in the Bible absolutely denouncing idolatry, divination, witchcraft and devil-worship as collective transgressions — when the choice of free will to be obedient to God, the source of all good, is rejected, there is only one remaining option: Satan, the origin of all evil, his dominions, and the limited powers they are permitted to wield.

God created mankind in His own image, and scripture declares we are destined to be spiritually united with Him as one, in a mystical union similar to the prophesy of Adam concerning the physical world that "[...] the two shall be made one flesh." Accordingly, Christ is mystically described as the 'Bridegroom of the Church'. Therefore, when one is disobedient to God, that predestined spiritual union is broken and we adulterate ourselves with Evil by which we are defiled. For instance, in the book of Numbers (14: 33) God describes the spiritual disobedience of the children of Israel as "fornication", manifesting the heinousness of this sin. In the book of Judges (2: 17) those of Israel who fell into idolatry are described as having committed "[...] fornication with strange gods." This is also evident in the Apocalypse (2:20) where the church of Thyatira is rebuked for falling into the sin of idolatry and heresy: "[...] thou sufferest the woman Jezabel, who calleth herself a prophetess, to teach, and to seduce my servants, to commit fornication, and to eat things sacrificed to idols." Continuing with the book of Psalms, Psalm 95 (v. 5) declares that all gods of the Gentiles are "devils". Psalm 105 (vs. 35–37) describes how the children of Israel fell into the practise of idolatry and therefore had "[...] sacrificed their sons and their daughters to devils". St. Paul in 1 Corinthians (10:20–21) declares that all things offered to idols are offered to demons, and one cannot partake of the Lord's table and also that of the devils. In Leviticus (17:7), the Lord stipulates that the children of Israel are not to sacrifice "[...] their victims to devils, [i.e., the heathen Egyptian gods] with whom they have committed fornication." We also observe this term is associated with idolatry and the practise of magic and divination in Leviticus (20:5–6):

> "I will set my face against that man and his kindred, and will cut off both him and all that consented with him, to commit fornication with Moloch, out of the midst of the people. The soul that shall go aside after magicians and soothsayers, and shall commit fornication with them, I will set my face against that soul, and destroy it out of the midst of the people."

A further example is found in the book of Nahum (3: 4–5) where the destruction of Nineveh is foretold:

"Because of the multitude of the fornications of the harlot [i.e. Nineveh] that was beautiful and agreeable, and that made use of witchcraft, that sold nations through her fornications, and families through her witchcrafts. Behold I come against thee, saith the Lord of hosts: and I will discover thy shame to thy face, and will shew thy nakedness to the nations, and thy shame to kingdoms."

In several instances, the names of heathen deities are used synonymously in reference to arch-demons. In the fourth book of Kings, chapter one, King Ochozias sends servants to consult the god of Accaron, named Beelzebub, to inquire if he will recover his health. Beelzebub, signifying the name "Lord of the Flies" in Hebrew, is recognised as one of the infernal princes of the arch-demons, (see Matt. 12:24) although Satan is also referred to as "Beelzebub" according to the Greek translation "Beelzeboul" which means "the devil". The idol Belial, whose name signifies "without yoke", is also considered a princely arch-demon; those who refused the law, i.e. the "yoke" of God are often called in scripture "the children of Belial". In the third book of Kings (21: 10,13) Jezabel finds two men to bear false witness against Naboth who refused to sell his vineyard to King Achab. The two men agree to accuse Naboth of a crime worthy of death — the two false witnesses are described as "sons of the devil" and "sons of Belial".

Therefore, to consult with magicians, soothsayers, and diviners was to consort with the powers of evil, rejecting the One, True God as stated in Deuteronomy, verses 10,11, and 14:

"[v. 10] Neither let there be found among you any one that shall expiate his son or daughter, making them to pass through fire: or that consulteth soothsayers, or observeth dreams and omens, neither let there be any wizard, [v. 11] Nor charmer, nor any one that consulteth python spirits, or fortune tellers, or that seeketh truth from the dead. [v. 14] These nations, whose land thou shalt possess, hearken to soothsayers and diviners: *but thou art otherwise instructed by the Lord thy God.*"

Continuing with the first book of Kings (15:22–23) the prophet Samuel rebukes King Saul for his failure to comply with God's command to strike the king of Amalec, Agag, and all his possessions, saying: "Doth the Lord desire holocausts and victims, and not rather the voice of the Lord should be obeyed? [...] Because it is like the sin of witchcraft to rebel: and like the crime of idolatry, to refuse to obey." In Chapter 28, Saul is rejected by God for his disobedience, and God commands Samuel to anoint David as the future king of Israel. Therefore, Saul did not receive counsel from the Lord when preparing to combat the Philistines. However, Saul refused to repent of his sin, adding insult to injury, he resorted to consulting a woman possessed with a *python*, or divining spirit. He demanded that the woman use her power of necromancy to summon the prophet Samuel, who had died shortly after anointing David. With God's permission, Samuel ascended from the region of the dead and decreed the punishment that Saul had merited by his grievous sins (1 Kings 28: 16–18):

"Why askest thou me, seeing the Lord has departed from thee, and is gone over to thy rival: For the Lord will do to thee as he spoke by me, and he will rend thy kingdom out of thy hand, and will give it to thy neighbour David: Because thou didst not obey the voice of the Lord, neither did thou execute the wrath of his indignation upon Amalec. Therefore hath the Lord done to thee what thou sufferest this day."

Saul resorted to necromancy, an act of absolute disobedience, adding further to the sins he had already committed. This action would imply that Saul initially intended, by his own free will, to rely on the powers of the demons, had not God prevented it by His intervention. Many demons ascended at the woman's command as observed in 1 Kings (28:13): "[...] I saw gods [i.e. devils] ascending out of the earth." However, God did not allow one of the demons to appear as his holy prophet, Samuel.

Hence, to practise any form of divination specifically prohibited in scripture, or that originated from pagan ritual, signified an allegiance with the devil. Therefore, when Faustus unreservedly displayed the skills he practised, he revealed to those of discernment he was not of God, but of Satan. Trithemius believed in order to acquire the art of necromancy, a pact with the devil was an automatic prerequisite.[71] St. Augustine declared that hydromancy, the form of divination employed by the first Roman king, was a demonically influenced skill; this sentiment continued into Faustus' time.[72] It is possible that pyromancy was associated with the pagan ritual of expiating children through fire, and was therefore condemned for this reason. While chiromancy is not mentioned in the Bible, soothsaying in general was prohibited. Baron states Faustus practised one skill that is difficult to recognise, i.e. agromancy, which he argues may be a misspelling for acromancy.[73] In scripture, we also detect evidence of acromancy, or divination in high places; several passages record that idolaters erected abominable high altars, pillars, or monuments to their deities called *excelsa,* commonly mistranslated as *high places.*[74] Hence, due to its pagan origins, acromancy could be categorised as a prohibited art. Alternatively, the word agromancy may also indicate a manner of divination which took place in a field as *agros* is the Greek word for *field.* If this was also a noted form of divination, no doubt it was associated with pagan rituals that were held in sacred groves. Therefore this would also be numbered among the prohibited arts as seen in 4 Kings (17:10–11): "And they [the children of Israel] made them statues and groves on every high hill, and under every shady tree: and they burnt incense there upon altars after the manner of the nations which the Lord had removed from their face: and they did wicked things, provoking the Lord." Astrology could also be questioned as a suspect practise if it was associated with the idolatrous act of worshipping the "host of heaven", i.e. the sun, moon, and stars, as seen in 4 Kings (23:5): "And he [Josias] destroyed the soothsayers, whom the

---

[71] Trithemius, *Liber octo questionum ad Maximilianum Caesarem* (Oppenheim: J. Hasselberg, 1515), fol. Fi-v – Fii-v, in *Doctor Faustus, from History to Legend,* p. 33.

[72] St. Augustine, *De civitate Dei,* VII, xxxv., in *Doctor Faustus, from History to Legend,* p. 32, and nn. 30–31, p. 97.

[73] *Doctor Faustus, from History to Legend,* p. 31.

[74] *The Holy Bible: Douay Rheims Version* (Old Testament translation, 1609, New Testament translation 1582: reprint Illinois: Tan Books and Publishers, Inc., 1989), 1 Kings (9: n. 12).

kings of Juda had appointed to sacrifice in the high places in the cities of Juda, and round about Jerusalem: them also that burnt incense to Baal, and to the sun, and to the moon, and to the twelve signs [the Zodiac], and to all the host of heaven." In addition, the term "host of heaven on high" frequently refers to the demons of the air permitted by God to wander through the lower celestial regions.[75] St. Paul in Ephesians (6:12) employs this term interchangeably with *high places*: "For our wrestling is not against flesh and blood; but against principalities and powers, against the rulers of this world of darkness, against the spirits of wickedness in the high places."

When we consider these points, it is apparent Faustus made no effort to conceal the spiritually dubious path he had chosen. While it is possible to identify the criteria denoting the infernal aspect of Faustus' occult practises, nevertheless it may be argued that there is no evidence in Trithemius' letter suggesting he personally considered Faustus a conscious follower of the devil despite his convictions concerning necromancy and the related black arts. For example, a reader on first inspection of Trithemius' letter may assume that the monk did not take Faustus seriously as he described the wandering scholar to be a babbler and a fool. In addition, the tone of the letter would suggest Trithemius merely viewed Faustus as a blasphemous, amoral hoaxer worthy of scorn who was nothing more to him than a grievous sinner refusing to see the error of his ways. Baron holds with this opinion stating that "[…] in the letter to Virdung, [Trithemius] condemned the foolishness of one who claimed to be the source of all wisdom in necromancy. But Trithemius did not speak of Faustus' connection with the devil. For Trithemius a man who made such claims was not a philosopher but a fool."[76] However, if we re-examine the language of the text, we discern that Trithemius did indeed see Faustus as one who had freely chosen the lot of the damned.

Baron describes Trithemius as a spiritual man notwithstanding his occult interests; "A strong current of religious fervor underlies [his] speculations. Trithemius contemplated the ascent to magical power and miracle just as the mystics contemplated the ascent to the union with God. There is no reason to doubt the sincerity of Trithemius' religious feelings."[77] Continuing with our observations, if we analyse the word "philosopher" we recognise it originates from the Greek *philosophos* signifying "lover of wisdom". To the theologian of any era this term finds its full expression and meaning in the book of Job (28:28): "And [God] said to man: Behold the fear of the Lord, that is wisdom: and to depart from evil, is understanding." In this statement lies the key to unlocking the mysteries written by King Solomon whom God had granted unprecedented wisdom. In Proverbs (1:7) it is written, "The fear of the Lord is the beginning of wisdom. Fools despise wisdom and instruction." We discover in Proverbs (24:7–9): "Wisdom is too high for a fool, in the gate he shall not open his mouth. He that deviseth to do evils, shall be called a fool. The thought of a fool is sin: and the detractor is the abomination of men." Hence, those who are overtly evil are regarded as 'fools' according to scripture and are numbered among the damned in contrast to repentant sinners who may be saved as seen in Proverbs (24:11,16,19–20):

> "Deliver them that are led to death: [i.e. those who are tempted
> and fall into sin], and those that are drawn to death forbear not to deliver.

---

[75] Ibid. Isaiah (n. 24: 21).
[76] *Doctor Faustus, from History to Legend*, p. 33.
[77] Ibid. p. 28.

[...] For a just man shall fall seven times and shall rise again: but the wicked shall fall down into evil. [...] Contend not with the wicked, nor seek to be like the ungodly: For evil men have no hope of things to come, and the lamp of the wicked shall be put out."

It is apparent Trithemius intended this theological inference when he described Faustus as a babbler and a fool, particularly when he referred to the calling card listing the black arts, e.g.: "What are his assumed titles if not [...] showing him to be a fool rather than a philosopher? For he composed a calling card to suit his taste [...]. The same foolish calling card he gave to you [...] he also sent to me by means of someone in town." In addition, Trithemius may have intended to use similar theological metaphors and therefore referred to spiritual "fornication" as described in sacred scripture when he accused Faustus of committing "the most nefarious form of fornication" with the schoolboys of Kreuznach (... *mox nefandissimo fornicationis genere cum pueris videlicet voluptari cepit* ...) based upon certain reports he had heard.[78] For Trithemius, a theologian who yearned to attain the heights of "supercelestial wisdom", it is possible to conceive that the most horrendous form of fornication to him would be the spiritual connotation that clearly signified complete severance from God and an allegiance with the devil. As we have observed earlier, to consult with wizards and soothsayers, and therefore with the infernal powers, was to commit the sin of spiritual fornication. It is probable that Faustus may have attempted to impart his knowledge in the black arts to the students or to sway them with his heretical boasts. If this theory is acceptable, the harsh accusation of "nefarious fornication" confirms the extent Faustus had scandalised Trithemius: obviously, Trithemius believed he was corrupting the young boys with his arts and was thereby severing their souls from God. Under these circumstances, Trithemius did not deem it necessary to state explicitly that Faustus was in allegiance with the devil and trusted that the recipient of his letter would be familiar with theological language and its inherent significance.

It is also possible that Trithemius purposely formatted his letter in this semi-ambiguous fashion to allow for the presumption of other implications, sodomy in particular, and thereby attack Faustus' reputation two-fold in order to justify his own interest regarding accepted 'natural magic'. Baron states that levying accusations of perversion to justify persecution or discrimination was a routine course of action from antiquity:

> "An accusation of sexual perversion levelled at a man with bold, unorthodox religious opinions is not surprising. [...] The Romans accused the first Christians of participating in sexual orgies. Throughout the Middle Ages very similar charges were consistently made against heretics and witches. The authorities in Nürnburg referred to Faustus as a sodomite. But since they did not give evidence, we cannot simply assume that the latter source is a confirmation of the first one. In both instances

---

[78] Trithemius declares that his information on this matter is second-hand, but that his sources were reliable. We may consider this statement to be accurate; although he resigned from his position as abbot in Sponheim 1506, it is probable he did not lose contact with acquaintances from the area, which, coincidentally, is close to Kreuznach. *Sources of the Faust Tradition*, n. 4, p. 83.

overzealous opponents of Faustus may have felt justified in accusing him of acts that men like him were generally thought to commit. It is also conceivable that the later source [i.e. the Nürnburg / Nuremberg document] was based on the story circulated by Trithemius."[79]

Why a learned scholar, Faustus, who had pursued and received an extensive higher education at Heidelberg, would freely choose a profession that would utterly ruin his reputation is bewildering. Not content with composing an infamous calling card, Faustus blatantly made preposterous claims that would be interpreted as either heretical or diabolical, according to the information Trithemius received and recorded. In the town of Gelnhausen it was reported Faustus boasted he was capable of restoring, by his singular gift of recollection, all the collected works of Plato and Aristotle with greater eloquence if wiped from living memory. In the text, Faustus is compared with the priest Ezra, who according to Ireneus,[80] was inspired by God to restore the Scriptures completely destroyed during the Babylonian captivity. Baron offers the possibility that the phrase "like another Ezra" may be a parenthetical comment inserted by Trithemius into the original report. Subsequently in 1508, Trithemius placed Ezra's feat as an important event in his mystical chronology of world history, an action that Baron perceives as convincing evidence Trithemius compared Faustus with Ezra to substantiate his contempt with this claim made by the soothsayer.[81] If Baron's theory is possible, we may interpret this comment "like another Ezra" as a sarcastic observation on the part of Trithemius — for if Faustus claimed to be a practitioner of the black arts, how could it be possible that God would grant him the ability of total recall in the same manner that He had graced Ezra? Therefore, this skill Faustus claimed to have perfected may in fact be perceived by Trithemius to be emanating from the devil. However, if Trithemius did *not* include a sarcastic comparison with Ezra in his letter, and Faustus actually uttered this phrase, his contemporaries would recognise this statement as undeniably heretical — that he, a soothsayer, would have the audacity to compare himself with a priest of Levi God so favoured.

Subsequently, Faustus would make further strides down the path of blasphemous impudence. According to the news Trithemius received, Faustus had travelled to Würzburg,[*] where he remarked somewhat impassively, that the miracles of Christ were not so wondrous, that he was capable also of accomplishing all the miracles of Christ whenever he desired. Hence, Faustus inferred he could turn water into wine, raise the dead, heal the sick, cast out devils at his command, read the thoughts of men, ascend to the heavens, alter his appearance to a divine-like being in parody of Christ's Transfiguration, etc. Baron observes that this information concerning these boasts may be considered reliable, for Trithemius was in Würzburg when he wrote his letter and therefore "[…] had the opportunity to learn about Faustus' visit very soon after it had taken place."[82] Apparently, Faustus was undaunted by the consequences his remarks would precipitate

---

[79] *Doctor Faustus, from History to Legend*, p. 37.

[80] Recorded in *The Ecclesiastical History* of Eusebius, trans. K. Lake (London: Heinemann, 1926), I, p. 461, in ibid., p. 34.

[81] *Doctor Faustus, From History to Legend*, p. 34.

[*] Trithemius was in Speyer after June 2, 1506; Faustus was in Würzburg at this time. Ibid. p. 35.

[82] Ibid. p. 35.

— or was he? Having already generated an ominous and infernal self-introduction with his cards, was Faustus embellishing his reputation to create an ungodly *curriculum vitae*? With a certain degree of confidence, we may deduce his remarks encouraged several of his contemporaries to regard him as an Antichrist. As stated in 1 John (4:1,3) the Antichrist and his precursors are easily recognised if the doctrines preached by them are prudently searched for errors:

> "Dearly beloved, believe not every spirit, but try the spirits if they be of God: because many false prophets are gone into the world. [...] And every spirit that dissolveth Jesus, [i.e. deny His humanity or His divinity] is not of God: and this is Antichrist, of whom you have heard that he cometh, and he is now already in the world [i.e. through his precursors]."

By claiming the miracles of Christ were not particularly amazing and that he could also accomplish them as a mortal man, Faustus denied the Christian doctrine of Christ's divinity by reducing Him to the same level as an ordinary human incapable of performing miracles, unless permitted by an external spiritual source. In addition, if Faustus considered Christ a mere mortal, his remark also suggests further serious implications: by stating he could achieve the same feats as Christ, Faustus, who had publicly declared his practise in the infernal arts, also grievously suggested Christ was equal with *him*, thereby inferring Christ's power was not divine in nature nor of a heavenly origin.

Faustus later boasted in Kreuznach he had surpassed all previous masters in alchemy, the ancient practise devoted to discovering a substance capable of turning base metals into gold, also fabled to possess a mysterious property that had the power to prolong life indefinitely — the legendary 'philosopher's stone'. Hence, Faustus not only boasted he could turn base metal into gold, he also claimed he had the power to grant earthly immortality, (or at least was on the verge of discovering the philosopher's stone). In Kreuznach he also reiterated that he was capable of reading the thoughts of man and accomplishing whatever a person had telepathically suggested to him. In this manner, he was parodying Christ: therefore, these boasts at Kreuznach magnified the Antichrist image he had previously projected. In conclusion, Faustus' claims did not merely border on blasphemy as Baron[83] suggests: they crossed the line absolutely.

As mentioned, this flagrant attitude towards the occult on Faustus' part with apparently little or no regard for his reputation, nor the possible threat of punishment or ostracism, defies comprehension on first inspection. However, when we reconsider the cultural and social climate of the time, we may discover his hellish madness had a hidden agenda — it certainly attracted immediate attention. Baron observes that Faustus attempted to appear learned by his willingness to discuss Plato and Aristotle, and in addition, adopted the terms used by the humanists for this purpose. By stating he would restore the lost works of Plato and Aristotle with "a greater degree of elegance", Faustus was identifying himself with contemporary humanist scholars who aspired to develop an elegant Latin style.[84] However, these remarks display a certain limit in his

---

[83] Ibid.
[84] Ibid.

achievements suggesting Faustus had not progressed beyond the typical university education he received, placing him at a disadvantage with his learned contemporaries as Baron relates:

> "Trithemius was a prolific writer with a solid humanistic background in classical languages. In contrast, Faustus' academic competence probably did not go far beyond Aristotelian logic or its interpretation according to the scholastic method of the *via moderna*. The fact that he did not leave behind teachings, writings, or publications lends support to Trithemius' claim that Faustus had very little to contribute as a genuine philosopher. In an actual face-to-face confrontation, Trithemius would certainly have shown himself superior to Faustus. At Heidelberg, where Faustus had presumably studied, no student could have been unaware of Trithemius' awesome scholarly reputation. Thus, it is not surprising that Faustus was reluctant to confront him in Gelnhausen."[85]

Therefore, if Faustus had opted to follow a career in the popular and less controversial field of natural magic, it is reasonable to assume that his attempt to attract respected patrons, aspire to achieve a university chair or a teaching position, would prove to be too difficult with the added monumental challenge of competing with renowned academics. In an age when the demand for humanists in Germany was increasing, it is possible Faustus realised if he had to compete for a position with the many learned and more advanced scholars, it was imperative he devise a strategy with a sabre-sharp cutting edge that would gain him public recognition as expeditiously as possible. The most obvious strategy would be to act contrary to the accepted norm and in the process scandalise or intrigue the popular imagination, thereby capitalising on the mercurial spread of his infamous reputation by word-of-mouth. We propose Faustus was astutely aware of the consequences when he shunned the more respected and prudent career of the 'natural magic' humanist in favour of the unnatural dubious life of a wandering soothsayer. He embellished his sinister reputation by lending credence to the belief he had joined the forces of darkness. He attracted singular recognition with little effort on his part by his deviant behaviour and reckless arrogance; a simple, but extremely effective introductory card and a few nights of outrageous verbosity were all that was required to promote his name and forge a career. Obviously, Faustus understood the advantages and magnetic power of bad publicity contrary to praiseworthy recognition. It did not matter if he scandalised the world, for it fulfilled his personal agenda.

The fact Faustus had one of his cards delivered to Trithemius at Gelnhausen, while at that time he was not prepared to meet with the famous scholar as we have observed, displays Faustus was primarily concentrating on self-promotion. For instance, Faustus must have realised that his card listing his diabolically associated crafts would have occasioned a definite negative reaction from Trithemius who disapproved of these practises. Apart from the possibility that Faustus *was* academically limited and did not dare risk an intellectual confrontation, there could be no other motive for him to send Trithemius his card provoking his condemnation, unless he expected Trithemius to spread reports of him, infamous or otherwise, to fellow humanists. Accordingly,

---

[85] Ibid. pp. 38–39.

he elicited a negative account from Trithemius, who advises the overenthusiastic Virdung, another calling card recipient, not to be swayed by his empty procrastinations. Trithemius takes it upon himself to patiently reiterate the contents of the card to Virdung in an effort to call his attention to the sinister nature of its origin, and the dubious career of its author.

We must also take into account many philosophers, including Trithemius, disapproved of appealing to the masses, an unconventional tactic Faustus used to his greater advantage. As observed, philosophy and natural magic were to be esoteric arts for the select few capable of comprehending these fields of study and who could be trusted not to misuse their knowledge. It is possible Faustus recognised that by appealing to the general populace he would be, as described in modern terms, venturing into an untapped market. Yet, his willingness to reveal philosophical knowledge in a sensational manner in public places, i.e. a common inn, Faustus acted contrary to the accepted protocol practised by this elitist academic circle, thereby evincing he was a deliberate nonconformist displaying boorish ignorance and a complete lack of professional refinement to his contemporaries. It is not surprising Trithemius deemed it necessary to warn Virdung to avoid any association with Faustus; Virdung was in service as mathematician and astrologer to the Elector of the Palatinate and therefore had a reputation to maintain and a prominent position to uphold. On reflection, we may deduce Faustus was a master showman, assuming a diabolical identity to attract attention by employing the information he acquired to impress the general public who may not be in possession of this occult knowledge, yet simultaneously endeavoured to hide his academic deficiencies from the learned humanists.

However, Virdung was eager to meet with Faustus, demonstrating not all his contemporaries viewed him in an unfavourable light. They may have elected to give Faustus the benefit of the doubt, despite his exaggerated claims, electing to believe he had made significant strides in the sciences and natural magic, perhaps with the expectation to share in his discoveries. Virdung, according to Baron's description, undoubtedly would be eager to meet with Faustus for the purpose of sharing knowledge in a professional academic exchange:

> "[…] Since 1493 he [Virdung] had been in the service of the Elector of the Palatinate in Heidelberg. He had studied at the Universities of Cracow and Leipzig. Manuscripts at the Bibliotheca Vaticana preserve astronomical as well as astrological texts written by his hand. Here one finds evidence of a strong interest in magic. Virdung wrote down information about imprisoning the planets in rings, and he copied magical images ascribed to Hermes. In 1503 he travelled to England for the express purpose of studying magic. Virdung was the author of numerous astrological works; he was accustomed to publishing annual predictions. Philipp Melanchthon was an admirer of Virdung's astrological skills and consulted him in matters relating to his future."[86]

Furthermore, we already discovered that Faustus managed to secure a teaching position in Kreuznach; in this instance, he was recommended by Franz von Sickingen (1481–1523), an

---

[86] *Doctor Faustus, from History to Legend*, p. 30.

astrology devotee and an avid admirer of Virdung's horoscopes and advice, who also held a position in service to the Elector of the Palatinate. Baron notes that:

> "There is no reason to doubt that Franz von Sickingen had been a supporter of Faustus. As Trithemius indicated, in Kreuznach Sickingen served as a district administrator (*balivus*) for the Elector [...], and in this capacity was the patron of the local school. His residence was on the nearby Ebernburg. His father Schwiekart von Sickingen had practised astrology. Sickingen became famous in later years as a militant supporter of unorthodox causes in the persons of Reuchlin, [Ulrich von] Hutten, and Luther. [...] According to a report of a historian of the seventeenth century, Sickingen was dedicated to the study of magic from the time of his youth.[87] [... He] was not accustomed to undertaking anything important without Virdung's prognostications and advice. Moreover, he generally acted according to Virdung's recommendation."[88]

Evidently, Faustus succeeded in obtaining the attention and admiration of several members of an elite humanist circle and secured a position notwithstanding the sinister nature of his publicity methods.

In addition to the vocational and character revelations we glean from Trithemius' letter, this correspondence also discloses rare information concerning the locations Faustus had sojourned at that time. Subsequent to his graduation from Heidelberg with a Master's degree in March 1487, we may presume he remained to fulfil the two-year teaching requirement stipulated by the Faculty of Arts. Baron proposes that if Faustus had not already left Heidelberg after this prescribed duty was accomplished c. 1489, he may have departed sometime in June of 1490 when an outbreak of plague threatened the city, as the faculty of the university received permission to evacuate the vicinity due to this epidemic.[89] As mentioned previsouly, Peter Seuter's letter shows that Magister Georgius Helmstetter was present in Heidelberg in 1490. Subsequently, the name Faustus disappears from written records for an approximate period of seventeen years, until it resurfaces again in Trithemius' letter dated August 1507. We discover in this letter, Faustus visited the town of Gelnhausen situated between Frankfurt and Fulda sometime in May of 1506. Trithemius arrived at Gelnhausen not long after his visit with Elector Joachim of Brandenberg in Berlin,[90] "[...] When I returned from the Mark Brandenburg last year, I came upon this man in

---

[87] Baron's footnote, n. 45, p. 98: "Huis vestigial secutus usque ab adolescentia prima filius rei magicae deditus, ne ulla re patris esset dissimilis, inter alia maleficia, quae ipse Reipublicae iniussit, haec sane literis ac omnium sermonibus celebrata." Because of the late date of this report, it is conceivable that its ultimate source was Trithemius. P. Christopher Brower and Jacob Masen, *Antiquitatum et annalium Trevirensium libri XXV* (Liège, 1670), p. 337.

[88] *Doctor Faustus, from History to Legend*, p. 36.

[89] Ibid. n. 4, p. 93. Baron's source: Gustav Toepke, *Die Matrikel der Universtät Heidelberg* (Heidelberg, 1884–1893), I, p. 397.

[90] Ibid. p. 31. Baron apparently acquired his chronological information of Trithemius' journey in Isidor Silbernagl, *Johannes Trithemius* (Regensburg, 1885) pp. 109–110, and Klaus Arnold, Johannes Trithemius (1462–1516), in *Quellen und Forschungen zur Geschichte des Bistums und Hochstifts*

the town of Gelnhausen. [...]". One month later, after June 2, Faustus travelled to Würzburg, while Trithemius continued to Speyer.[91] Later, towards the end of Lent 1507, Faustus arrived in Kreuznach where he was appointed schoolteacher for a brief period when this position fell vacant. We also learn from Trithemius' letter that Virdung was expecting Faustus in Heidelberg during August 1507. Baron observes the following regarding this possible trip to Heidelberg:

> "The close relationship between Sickingen and Virdung has another possible significance for the biography of Faustus. The time between Faustus' appearance in Kreuznach (towards the end of Lent, 1507) and the time Virdung was awaiting a visit from him in Heidelberg (ca. August, 1507) is not great, considering the fact that Faustus probably resided in Kreuznach for a number of weeks before abandoning his post as teacher there. It is, therefore, possible that Faustus made his way to Heidelberg directly from Kreuznach and that his impending visit to Virdung was inspired by the recommendation of Sickingen."[92]

Armed with this information, significant clues surface, allowing for further speculation. First, there is an obvious pattern to the wanderings of Faustus during this brief period; when we plot this particular journey on a map, we discover that his course formed a definite triangle in an area not far from Heidelberg, before his journey apparently concluded there sometime in August 1507. Second, the context of Trithemius' letter, and the period of documentary oblivion preceding it, suggests Faustus was not accustomed to sending out calling cards before this time. It is reasonable to deduce that a card of this ominous magnitude would have elicited a response proximate to the time of its dissemination. Although we must take into account there may be other sources that are lost, of the nine credible historical documents listed by Baron during the presumed time Faustus was still living, ten when we inlude Seuter's letter to Ellenbog, only Trithemius' letter mentions this card and its contents in specific detail. The Nürnburg (Nüremburg / Nuremberg) document of 1532 describing Faustus' art of necromancy and the accusations of sodomy may have been influenced by Trithemius' letter that possibly circulated privately before publication, and therefore is suspect as a separate document in respect to this calling card. The other accounts written during Faustus' lifetime lack the specific details as printed on the card, for instance, his surname in these later documents is "Faustus" and not "Faustus junior", nor "the younger Faustus" as printed on the card. In addition, these later sources divulge information not included on the card, i.e. his title of Doctor, and his place of origin, Helmstetensis / Heidelberg, which suggests the authors of these documents received their information second hand and did not receive or obtain direct knowledge concerning this card. One particular record of interest is a mention of Faustus in Philip Begardi's *Index Sanitatis* (1539) that presents a definite list of his skills corresponding with the contents of the calling card and emphatically states Faustus *signed himself* with these titles. Additionally, Begardi resided in

---

Würzburg (Würzburg: Schöningh, 1971), p. 207.
[91]   Ibid.
[92]   *Doctor Faustus, from History to Legend*, pp. 36–37.

the city of Worms,[93] circa thirty kilometres (c.18.5 miles) *from Heidelberg*. While Baron did not include Begardi's document in his list of reliable sources, he observes that the expressions used in the account suggests Faustus had died not long before its date of publication; a topic that will be discussed later in greater detail. In conclusion, as Trithemius' letter is the only evidence of the circulation of these personal calling cards while Faustus *was still living*, we may speculate that this was the first, and perhaps the only time they were disseminated by him, i.e. circa 1506–1507.

If this theory is acceptable, this would indicate Faustus did not write or print these cards for continuous use, possibly, he had just embarked upon his career as a wandering magician-scholar and intended the cards to serve solely as publicity for his public debut. This may also explain his endeavour to remain close to the vicinity of Heidelberg during this brief period — as Faustus received his third level education in this locality, it would be an appropriate area to launch his career. Heidelberg was not only the town of his *alma mater*, but also a famous centre for humanist study and culture. During the 1480s, several famous German humanists resided in Heidelberg while Faustus attended the university: Rudolph Agricola, Conrad Celtis, Johannes von Dalberg, Dietrich von Pleningen, Johannes Reuchlin, and Trithemius.[94] Baron observes while humanism was not included in the traditional curriculum, its influence affected every sphere of university life.[95] In addition, the court of the Elector of the Palatinate became a magnet for humanist scholars; in 1482, Dalberg became Bishop of Worms and Chancellor to the Elector.[96] Pleningen was employed at the court as the Elector's advisor.[97] Baron relates students of the university possibly did not have the opportunity to converse directly with these humanists, namely Dalberg and Pleningen, who "[…] spent more time at the court of the elector than in the lecture halls. Nonetheless, this court was within walking distance of the university, and the students could not fail to notice how greatly the intellectual achievements of these men were respected at the courts as well as at the universities throughout Germany."[98] Heidelberg therefore became an attractive location for a scholar who aspired to obtain a patron. Undoubtedly it was for this purpose Faustus was motivated to boast of his knowledge of Plato and Aristotle, adopting the clichés employed by the humanists as previously discussed, i.e. the phrase "an elegant Latin style". Reviewing the calling card Faustus distributed, it is interesting to note that of the known recipients, two were humanists in service to the Elector, i.e. Virdung and Sickingen. Trithemius, an associate of this exclusive circle, was also closely affiliated with the Elector. Hence, we may deduce Trithemius' letter reveals that from the onset of his roving career, Faustus particularly chose the Heidelberg region to initiate his publicity-seeking campaign with the objective to attract recognition at the Elector's court and thereby secure a noteworthy position.

If this was indeed his original motive, there are new and intriguing observations that may be offered. Assuming Faustus was born in either 1466 or 1467, this indicates he was thirty-nine or forty years old when he embarked on this nefarious career. What induced him to decide on this drastic change in his life and in this blatant manner? As there is a sixteen to seventeen-year

---

93 Ibid. p. 69.
94 Ibid. p. 19.
95 Ibid.
96 Ibid.
97 Ibid.
98 Ibid. p. 21

undocumented period between the time he finished his teaching obligation at the university c. 1489-90 until his reappearance, (or public debut) in 1506, we may presume Faustus attempted to follow a respectable career up to this point, but his unorthodox style of combining horoscopes with questionable forms of divination as displayed by Seuter was proving ineffectual in helping him to acquire the wealthy patrons he expected. Perhaps his lack of progress in advancing beyond the level he achieved in college hindered him from becoming the success that he intended. Theoretically, Faustus may have sensed a growing urgency to become successful as he was advancing in years, realising that he would not have an indefinite period to accomplish this goal; hence, his apparent desperation for public recognition. We must also take into account if he was considered unsuccessful in his initial career endeavours when he graduated from the university, it is possible the humanist elite did not deem him worthy of their consideration. This would explain his outrageous conduct — he would attract their attention by declaring an allegiance with the dark side in a manner that flouted accepted social and academic conventions, scandalising many of his contemporaries. If they would not accept him legitimately, he would force them to acknowledge him through his diabolical, infamous fabrication that would be impossible for them to ignore. No doubt, he resorted to an illogical, yet calculated professional gambit, risking whatever legitimate reputation he may retain for any future career possibilities.

We may question why he was determined to continue on this path in Heidelberg when he seemed desperate to be recognised by its academic elite, for the consequences of his actions were definitely causing his professional reputation more harm than good — as a past pupil of their illustrious university, would they not consider he was in disgrace, dishonouring his *alma mater* by conducting his affairs in this manner? Evidently, Faustus had considered all of the above; we reiterate the calling card *did not* disclose his place of origin, nor the city where he studied: it is in the *latter sources* that we discover Faustus revealed this information to his contemporaries. Apparently, it is solely in the vicinity of Heidelberg he did not intend to publicly reveal his past affiliations with the area. In other words, while drawing attention to his scandalous career debut, it was not his intention to tarnish the reputation of the university in the slim hope they would accept him professionally. Hence, we have additional proof that Faustus devised his card of introduction specifically for his debut in the Heidelberg region, if he intended to use the card in other areas indefinitely, he would have included the particulars of his origins from the beginning. This desire to remain anonymous in Heidelberg may explain why he evaded a personal encounter with Trithemius notwithstanding he sent him a card in an effort to promote his name. It is possible Faustus was apprehensive Trithemius would recognise him and reveal his true identity in Heidelberg.

As we discovered, Faustus did secure a position as schoolteacher in Kreuznach on Sickingen's recommendation. No matter how despicable his methods, one could declare Faustus' mission to find employment accomplished. However, he felt compelled to abandon this position when accused of committing the "most nefarious form of fornication" as Trithemius phrased his transgression. As previously discussed, this may not indicate sodomy as there is no substantial evidence surviving supporting this accusation, but this expression could signify 'spiritual fornication', i.e. Faustus' practise or promotion of black magic contrary to God's law. Hence, despite all his well-laid plans, Faustus torched his own bridges and was forced to wander for employment.

Following his presumed visit to Virdung in Heidelberg, Faustus and his activities fade into obscurity for a period of six years. The next documented encounter with him is a letter written by the humanist Conrad Mutianus Rufus, (Konrad Muth), to Heinrich Urbanus dated October 9, [*nonas* (nonus?) *Octobris*], 1513:

> "Eight days ago [October 1] there came to Erfurt a certain chiromancer by the name of Georgius Faustus Helmitheus of Heidelberg, [Helmitheus, (Helmstetius? Helmstheus?), Hedebergensis] a mere braggart and fool. His claims, like those of all diviners, are idle, and this kind of character has not more weight than a water spider. The ignorant marvel at him. Let the theologians rise against him and not try to destroy the philosopher Reuchlin. I heard him babbling at an inn, but I did not reprove his boastfulness. What is the foolishness of other people to me?"[99]

Mutianus had not heard of Faustus prior to their meeting according to his expression "[…] there came […] a certain chiromancer by the name of Georgius Faustus […]". He disapproved of Faustus' bragging, described him as a "fool", and ostensibly indignant at his attempts to appeal to the "ignorant" populace. Mutianus' opinions of Faustus reflect the contempt and indifference Trithemius penned to Virdung, this is not surprising as Mutianus and Trithemus were close friends and shared common interests.

Mutianus (1471–1526) was a canon of St. Mary's church in the town of Gotha near Erfurt.[100] He had studied in Ferrara and Bologna, and although he was a talented teacher, he preferred a humble and quiet monastic lifestyle, sharing ideas with a close circle of humanist friends and not attracted to a public career at a university.[101] His preoccupation, as Baron writes, was "[…] peaceful study and contemplation."[102] Albeit Mutianus did not publish his works, he earned a renowned reputation as a humanist and philosopher — his contemporaries ranked him with Desiderius Erasmus (1466?–1536) and Reuchlin.[103] His few extant works comprise only a small number of poems and personal letters, the survival of which may be credited to a friend who copied them, Heinrich Urbanus,[104] a past pupil who became steward of the Cistercian cloister of Georgenthal in Erfurt c. 1505.[105] Baron denotes the importance of Mutianus' surviving letters:

> "Although much has not been preserved, the correspondence gives certain hints about what one might expect from a confrontation

---

[99] Ibid. p.41. See also *Sources of the Faust Tradition*, pp. 87–88.
[100] *Sources of the Faust Tradition*, n. 10, p. 87.
[101] *Doctor Faustus, from History to Legend*, p. 39.
[102] Ibid.
[103] *Sources of the Faust Tradition*, n. 10, p. 87.
[104] *Doctor Faustus, from History to Legend*, p. 39.
[105] *Sources of the Faust Tradition*, n. 11, p. 87.

between Mutianus and Faustus. The exchange of letters with Trithemius and Reuchlin is particularly significant."[106]

In one letter to Reuchlin dated 1503, Mutianus declared his admiration for his work, expressing the hope that he would accomplish what Pico had only promised — to advance occult knowledge.[107] In a separate letter to Trithemius, Mutianus addresses the recipient as *preceptor ter maximus,* i.e. another Hermes Trismegistus. Baron suggests these comments are evidence Mutianus shared the ambitions of Reuchlin and Trithemius, i.e. their interests in natural magic and cabala according to the humanist tradition of Pico.[108] However, Baron also observes that Mutianus was extremely conservative:

> "If he [Mutianus] himself pursued the study of natural magic seriously, he was very careful to conceal it. Like the great majority of contemporaries, Mutianus believed in astrology. He expressed admiration for Pico, more because of Pico's interpretation of the Psalms than because of his writings on magic. Moreover, when Mutianus referred to Pythagoras, he conjured up praiseworthy customs associated with his school, but did not reveal any interest in numerology. He explained that he intended to take from poets, philosophers, historians, and lawyers only what was compatible with Christianity. Mutianus considered it impious to want to know more than the Church knew. Trithemius, Reuchlin, and Pico were, of course, much bolder."[109]

Perhaps the most revealing documentation that enables us to understand Mutianus' judgement of Faustus is his correspondence to Trithemius in August of 1513, which he composed only a month before his encounter with the soothsayer and the subsequent inscription of this experience to Urbanus. In this preceding letter, Mutianus recommended a friend to Trithemius, a man by the name of Peter Eberbach, who apparently was interested in Hebrew studies and also, in the "[…] more honourable mysteries of the magicians with which Trithemius was very well acquainted."[110] Apparently, Mutianus indicated his support of Pico and the legitimate study of natural magic and cabala. It is of interest to note that Mutianus describes Eberbach as a man who possessed a quiet disposition and could be discreet, unlike the typical vagrant braggadocios that boasted to the masses.[111] Obviously, Mutianus believed in preserving the esoteric aspect of philosophical, natural magic. Baron observes, "Like Trithemius, Mutianus saw philosophy as an occupation for a select few. The attempt to appeal to the masses implied for him the

---

[106] *Doctor Faustus, from History to Legend*, pp. 39–40.
[107] Ibid. p. 40.
[108] Ibid.
[109] Ibid.
[110] "Delectatur etiam magorum honestioribus mysteriis, que tibi penitus perspecta sunt et cognita." Gillert, pp. 382–3. Ibid. p 41. Klaus Arnold, p. 99, in ibid., p. 41.
[111] *Doctor Faustus, from History to Legend*, p. 41.

abandonment of philosophy."[112]   When Mutianus crossed paths with Faustus in October 1513, he obviously perceived him to be an antithesis of Eberbach. To Mutianus, Faustus was a "foolish" man and a "babbler" who made idle promises, a charlatan who demonstrated he was not a true philosopher — opinions that Baron believes "[…] confirm the general reliability of the reports Trithemius had received second-hand."[113]   In comparison, Mutianus' letter to Urbanus is less subjective than Trithemius' account (1507), however, Mutianus also has an ulterior motive and uses his condemnation of Faustus to support his friend, the humanist Johann Reuchlin.

Reuchlin (1455–1522) was born in Pforzheim and educated at the University of Basel, Switzerland. A Greek and Hebrew scholar, he acquired a distinguished reputation as a translator of these languages. He was the first Christian to write a Hebrew grammar, *De Rudimentis Hebraicis* (1506), a text that became an invaluable research companion for biblical scholars. When the Inquisition initiated an anti-Semitic movement, beginning with the burning of Hebrew books brought into the empire, including the Talmud, Reuchlin advised the Holy Roman Emperor, Maximilian I, to publicly denounce this myopic course of action, advice the Emperor followed in 1509. In 1511, Reuchlin became embroiled in a bitter dispute with the faculty of theology in Cologne. Reuchlin's liberal philosophy assisted the Protestant cause, however, he did not personally endorse the Reformation notwithstanding his nephew, Melanchthon, was one of the primary promoters for this religious insurrection.

In 1512, Mutianus emerged from his quiet, monastic seclusion to defend Reuchlin's scholarship by praising him as a humanist.[114] Regarding the letter to Urbanus, Baron concludes:

> "The reference to Faustus is for Mutianus a convenient way of showing that Reuchlin was a genuine philosopher who was unjustly attacked (and whom Mutianus had defended with great vigor in the rest of the letter), while Faustus, practicing the fraudulent occupation of palm reading (*chiromanticus*…), deserved to be punished."[115]

There is evidence that Mutianus considered Faustus more sinister than his letter would lead us to believe when we carefully reconsider its context. The fact that Mutianus calls upon the theologians to direct their attacks to discredit Faustus and not Reuchlin, displays an attitude of intolerance we would expect to encounter in the persecutions of heretics and blasphemers of the first magnitude — not a simple palmistry peddler. Unfortunately, we do not know what marvels Faustus 'revealed' while in Erfurt, but let us study the misspelling for "Helmstetius". Christian August Heumann had concluded this word should read "Hemitheus", meaning "demigod" or "half-god", a theory that was generally accepted until 1913 when Schottenloher[116] argued in favour of the "Helmstetius" (Helmstadt) interpretation, supported by Franz Babinger in 1914.[117] Baron offers an additional explanation that Urbanus may have intended to copy an 's' and not an

---

[112] Ibid.
[113] Ibid.
[114] Ibid. p. 40
[115] Ibid. p. 41.
[116] Ibid. n. 19, p. 91.
[117] *Sources of the Faust Tradition*, n. 13, p. 87–88, also ibid.

'i', so that the exact word could be "Helmstheus" (See also the entry for Mutianus' letter in Appendix One):

> "The original letter of Mutianus Rufus was copied by Heinrich Urban, to whom it was addressed. A careful examination of the manuscript indicates that the corrupted form Helmithius could have arisen because Urban was unable to decipher the letter at this point. In Urban's handwriting the difference between the letters i and s is a matter of length, and therefore one may even suspect that he was actually approximating an s as it appeared in the original letter (i.e., Helmstheus)."[118]

While it is apparent Mutianus intended to refer to Faustus' origins of Helmstadt near Heidelberg, we cannot dismiss the reference to "theus" in the original spelling (from the Greek "theos" meaning "god"). If Urbanus had transcribed an 's', Mutianus' intention may be a sarcastic witticism; "Helmstheus Hede(l)bergensis " = the "Helmstadt-god of Heidelberg", additional evidence that Faustus continued to claim powers beyond those of a mere mortal, similar to his boasts that infuriated Trithemius years earlier due to their blasphemous significance. As the letter to Urbanus was written as a deliberate attempt to demonstrate that Reuchlin was an authentic philosopher by contrasting him with Faustus, it is possible Mutianus was also employing the terms "fool" and "foolishness" with the same theological inference as Trithemius intended in his letter to Virdung. If Faustus was not a true philosopher, or "a lover of wisdom", he was a "fool" who deliberately chose the path to damnation and was beyond repentance or conversion. While Trithemius had attempted to meet with Faustus, Mutianus decided not to approach him, regardless of his Christian duty to correct him, even for the salvation of his soul. We may discover the reason for this seeming indifference in the book of Proverbs:

> "A reproof availeth more with a wise man, than a hundred stripes with a fool." (17: 10) A fool receiveth not the words of prudence: unless thou say those things which are in his heart. (18:2) As an earring of gold and a bright pearl, so is he that reproveth the wise, and the obedient ear," (25: 12)

Mutianus may have prejudged the effort to correct Faustus as throwing rare gems of wisdom before swine: "[…] I did not reprove his boastfulness. What is the foolishness of other people to me?" In addition, the practise of chiromancy would have highlighted the apostate image Faustus coloured with the brushstrokes of his ostentatious claims. If Mutianus would accept from scholars and artists only those theories "compatible with Christianity", it is obvious Faustus could offer nothing of value to him.

In summary, this document displays that Faustus' promotion methods had changed little in seven years. As discussed, Faustus may have ceased to issue his infamous card by this time, and was now revealing his place of origin possibly to intimate the place of his third-level

---

[118] *Doctor Faustus from History to Legend,* n. 19, p. 91.

education — yet, he continued to frequent the taverns, attracting the 'ignorant' with his outrageous and overtly blasphemous claims of magic power in defiance to the esoteric norm established by the theologians and academics.

We have discovered in the case of Virdung and von Sickingen, not all Faustus' contemporaries viewed him in the same negative light. Other accounts prove that Faustus, in later years, had acquired influential patrons and acquaintances impressed with his skills.[119] One of these patrons would include a high-ranking Church official: Georg III Schenk von Limburg, the Bishop of Bamburg.

According to an entry by a Hans Müller in the annual accounts of the bishop, Faustus received ten gulden, or gold pieces, on February 10, 1520 for a horoscope he drafted:

> "The annual accounts of Hans Müller, chamberlain, from Walpurgis [May
> 1] 1519 to Walpurgis 1520.
> Entry on February 12, 1520 under the heading "Miscellaneous."
>
> 10 gulden given and presented as a testimonial [*zuuererung* (rf. to
> Zeugnis?)] to Doctor Faustus, the philosopher, who made for my master a
> horoscope or prognostication. Paid on the Sunday after St. Scholastica's
> Day [February 10] by the order of his reverence."[120]

The circumstances of Faustus' introduction to the bishop remain ambiguous; however, Ulrich von Hutten, a member of the academic circle patronised by the bishop, was associated with those acquainted with Faustus, and may have facilitated his introduction to the court.

Ulrich von Hutten (1488–1523) was born near Fulda and obtained his education at several German and Italian universities. He served as a knight under Emperor Maximilian I who proclaimed him poet laureate in 1517. A staunch supporter of Martin Luther, Ulrich was a fierce patriot advocating German nationalism and the liberal cause to subject the papacy to imperial rule and the nobility. He was acquainted with Franz von Sickingen, the man responsible for securing the teaching position for Faustus in Kreuznach, who coincidentally was a fellow Imperial knight supporting Luther's cause.[121] In addition, Ulrich may have heard of Faustus through his collaboration on the famous satire *The Letters of Obscure Men* (1515–1517), for as Baron states, "It is well known that *The Letters of Obscure Men* [...] originated in the circle of humanists close

---

[119] William Rose observes "[...] There is a legend that Faust [Faustus] was given asylum at the monastery of Maulbronn by the Abbot Entenfuss in the year 1516, and that he there pursued his alchemistic activities. The well-known 'Faust tower' which is still shown there was, however, not built until nearly a hundred years later." William Rose, ed., 'Forward to the First Edition,' *The Historie of the Damnable Life and Deserved Death of Doctor John Faustus: 1592* (Reprint; Indiana: University of Notre Dame Press, 1963), p. 7. As there is a question regarding the tower where Faustus allegedly resided, this legend is suspect as a credible source and therefore is excluded in our discussion of the historical documents.

[120] *Sources of the Faust Tradition*, pp. 88–89.

[121] Baron writes, "Ulrich von Hutton maintained that [Sickingen] was not knowledgeable in Latin." We may assume Ulrich would be well acquainted with Sickingen in order to report this information. *Doctor Faustus, from History to Legend*, p. 36.

to Mutianus [Rufus]. [Mutianus'] own efforts in support of Reuchlin represented a significant catalyst in the publication of this work."[122] As we previously discovered, Mutianus had encountered Faustus in 1513. It is probable that Sickingen and / or Mutianus introduced Faustus to Ulrich, and in turn promoted Faustus during one of his visits to Bamberg facilitated by his close association with the city officials. Ulrich aided the chief administrative official of Bamberg, Johann von Schwarzenberg, with his publication of several books in German in co-operation with the lawyer and humanist Lorenz Beheim.[123] Ulrich was also acquainted with Andreas and Jacob Fuchs, brothers who became Church officials in Bamberg and consequently had connections at the bishop's court.[124] Ulrich was particularly close to Jacob and visited him on two occasions between 1517 and 1520.[125] Baron also observes, "Hutten himself had the opportunity of entering the service of the bishop. In 1518 he dedicated the printed volume of his speech about the Turkish danger to Bishop Georg."[126]

Following his introduction to the Bishop's court, Faustus' audience proved lucrative. Ten gulden was a munificent payment to Faustus as other artists and scholars received less than half this amount for their services. Johannes Schöner, a geographer and astrologer in service as bookbinder to the bishop, was paid less than four gulden for binding Erasmus' work *De regimine principium* only a year before Faustus was handsomely rewarded.[127] The artist Hans Wolf received two gulden for assisting the famous Albrecht Dürer with his portrait of the bishop.[128] Of particular interest is the phrase, "presented as a testimonial to [...] Faustus, the *philosopher*". The term "as a testimonial" implies the bishop was declaring his endorsement of Faustus. We may presume that in addition to Ulrich von Hutton's promotion of Faustus, rumours of the diviner's dubious vocation in the black arts had reached the bishop and he decided to meet with Faustus to ascertain whether or not he was acting contrary to the magisterium of the Church. It would seem the bishop was affirming his approval of Faustus, his generous payment was offered as a public 'testimonial', i.e. an endorsement, in his belief that Faustus was skilled in the arts he practised. In this instance, the record indicates the bishop recognised Faustus as a philosopher. The word 'horoscope' suggests Faustus had offered a 'legitimate' prognostication that as yet, was not absolutely condemned by the church, i.e. an astrological chart. It is possible Faustus was aware he was penetrating dangerous territory and refrained from acting in a manner that would connect him directly with the nefarious occult practises that he willingly admitted to in previous years. He had escaped persecution from church authorities to this point in time; undoubtedly, he was deliberately avoiding the risk of precipitating a witch-hunt that could ultimately lead to his execution. Faustus must have recognised the advantage of gaining approval from a centre of

---

[122]   Ibid. p. 40.

[123]   *Allgemeine Deutche Biographie*, vol. 33, pp. 305–6, in ibid., p. 43.

[124]   Gustave C. Knod, *Deutche Studenten in Bologna* (Berlin: Decker, 1899), pp. 141–2. Johannes Kist, *Die Matrikel des Bistums Bamberg. 1400-1556* (Würzburg: Schöningh, 1965), nos. 1874 and 1878, in *Doctor Faustus, from History to Legend*, p. 43.

[125]   *Doctor Faustus, from History to Legend*, p. 43.

[126]   Leitschuh, pp. 14–6, in ibid.

[127]   *Faustus, from History to Legend*, p. 44.

[128]   Franz Friedrich Leitschuh, *Georg III., Schenk von Limpurg, der Bischof von Bamberg in Goethes Götz von Berlichingen* (Bamberg: F. Züberlein, 1888), pp. 77, 90, in *Doctor Faustus from History to Legend*, pp. 43–44.

religious authority, as this sanction would prevent the rumours he had deliberately initiated during the onset of his career from escalating past that point which he could not control. Alternatively, Faustus may have decided it was expedient to conceal his evil reputation at this time until it would prove advantageous for him to reveal his notorious character sometime in the future if it suited his purpose.

Certainly, we can understand the reasoning behind Faustus playing the role of the chameleon, attempting to appear respectable at this point in his career upon our reflection on one of the most controversial events in German history. Three years before Faustus would be granted an audience with the Bishop of Bamberg, Martin Luther (1483–1546) had initiated the Reformation in Germany on October 31, 1517 with the publication of his *Ninety-Five Theses*. In this publication, Luther challenged the theory and practise of indulgences granted by the Church — only one of the many issues concerned with the necessity of reforming the perceived abuses proliferating unchecked within the Church at that time. To Luther, the perverted practise of selling indulgences, i.e. buying the remission of the temporal punishment due to sin, was the final proof that the Church had crumbled into a state of utter decay. In 1514, Luther remarked, "Never before has the church been so desolate."[129] According to his interpretation of Scripture, and the prophesies of St. Augustine and St. Bernard of Clairvaux, Luther believed that this corruption within the Church was a sign that the Last Days, and therefore the attacks of the devil and the Antichrist, were already unleashed upon the world.[130] Hence, the faithful were to prepare for the establishment of God's kingdom on earth, and he continually stressed that they were to be ever vigilant in detecting the deceits of the devil, who would do all in his power to impede the coming of the Kingdom.[131] Luther's 'Doomsday' approach is clarified when we examine the eschatology preceding his times.

For centuries, *chiliasm*, i.e. the concept of Christ establishing a corporeal kingdom of peace on earth for a thousand years, was a popular topic of speculation with medieval Scholastics. This theory emerged from literal interpretations of Chapter 20 in the Apocalypse, which describes the epoch before the Last Day and the General Judgment:

> "And I saw an angel coming down from heaven, having the key of the bottomless pit, and a great chain in his hand. And he laid hold of the dragon the old serpent, which is the devil and Satan, and bound him for a thousand years. And he cast him into the bottomless pit, and shut him up, and set a seal upon him, that he should no more seduce the nations, till the thousand years be finished. And after that, he must be loosed a little time. And I saw seats; and they sat upon them; and judgement was given unto them; and the souls of them that were beheaded for the testimony of Jesus, and for the word of God, and who had not adored the beast nor his image, nor received his character on their

---

[129] *D. Martin Luthers Werke: Kritische Gesamtausgabe, Abteilung Werke*, vols. I – (Weimar, 1883 -), 3.422,5. in Heiko A. Oberman, tr. Eileen Walliser-Schwarzbart, *Luther: Man between God and the Devil*, (New York: Yale University Press, 1989), p. 72
[130] *Luther, Between God and the Devil*, pp. 57–81.
[131] Ibid. gen.

foreheads or in their hands; and they lived and reigned with Christ a thousand years. The rest of the dead lived not, till the thousand years were finished. Blessed and holy is he that hath part in the first resurrection. In these the second death hath no power; but they shall be priests of God and of Christ; and shall reign with him a thousand years. And when the thousand years shall be finished, Satan shall be loosed out of his prison, and shall go forth, and seduce the nations, which are over the four quarters of the earth, Gog and Magog, and shall gather them together to battle, the number of whom is as the sand of the sea. And they came upon the breadth of the earth, and encompassed the camp of the saints, and the beloved city. And there came down fire from God out of heaven, and devoured them; and the devil, who seduced them, was cast into the pool of fire and brimstone, where both the beast and his prophet shall be tormented day and night for ever and ever. And I saw a great white throne, and one sitting upon it, from whose face the earth and heaven fled away, and there was no place found in them. And I saw the dead, great and small, standing in the presence of the throne, and the books were opened, which is the book of life, and the dead were judged by those things which were written in the books, according to their works. And the sea gave up the dead that were in it, and death and hell gave up their dead that were in them; and they were judged every one according to their works. And hell and death were cast into the pool of fire. This is the second death. And whoever was not found written in the book of life, was cast into the pool of fire. (Apoc. 20)

In the twelfth century, Joachim of Fiore (1132?–1202) a Cistercian abbot, presented a controversial interpretation of this chapter in which he calculated that the course of history followed a Trinitarian cycle. The age of the Father occurred during the Old Testament, followed by the age of the Son and the clerical Church, to be completed in the third age, i.e. the age of the Spirit and the spiritual church, an age that would commence with the year 1226 and endure for a thousand years. The controversy surrounding Fiore's theory concerns his prediction of the third age as Heiko Oberman relates:

> "This third age would [...] put an end to hierarchy and papal rule. The church would be governed by those who dedicate their lives to meditating on the mysteries of God — in short, the time of the friars [the Franciscans] would come. [...] The very expectation of a time when the ruling hierarchy would no longer exist was a basic challenge to the papacy. This dream spoke loud and clear: contrary to all claims, Rome is not the foundation of the Church for all times. The New Age of the Spirit will build upon new foundations and put an end to the rule of the successor to Peter!"[132]

---

[132] Ibid. p. 58.

In summary, this eschatological interpretation of scripture was considered profoundly heretical as it contradicts Christ's declaration concerning the papacy: "And I say to thee: that thou art Peter; and upon this rock I will build My church, and the gates of hell shall not prevail against it. And I will give to thee the keys of the kingdom of heaven. And whatsoever thou shalt bind upon earth, it shall be bound in heaven: and whatsoever thou shalt loose on earth, it shall be loosed in heaven."(Matt. 17:18–19).

Why would the Franciscans be heralded as the leaders of the new Spiritual Church? The answer lies with their rule of voluntary poverty and their vocation to preach the Gospel in imitation of Christ. There could be no greater sign of spirituality than the renouncement of all earthly goods for the greater glory of God's kingdom. Hence, "[…] the struggle for poverty was connected with the hope for the millennium," Oberman explains. When Pope John XXII (c.1245–1334) began to question, (and finally condemned in 1323), a strict interpretation of poverty as personally expressed by St. Francis in his first rule and last will, it was perceived that the old hierarchy was in its death throes, and the New Age was about to commence:

> "The pope's refusal to respect this last will corresponded precisely with the 'new' way the uncompromising wing of the [Franciscan] order, known as Fraticelli or Spirituales, [whose heritage is traceable to Fiore], read history. The 'depraved' papacy is soon to be replaced because of the great reformation, the millennium of peace, is about to begin. The fact that Pope John XXII is battling St. Francis and his devoted followers is not surprising at all; it is the final desperate attempt to delay by any means the inevitable fall from power." (Obermann)[133]

This belief was championed by a Franciscan Bible scholar from Languedoc, Petrus Johannes Olivi (d. 1298) who maintained in his commentary, the *Postilla super Apokalypsim*, that the Franciscans were to reign during the New Age.[134] Olivi believed that St. Francis, entrusted directly by God to proclaim the eternal Gospel ("Evangelium aeternum"), was the authentic successor of Christ.[135] Therefore, the pope and the hierarchy of the Church were now a redundant faction in God's plan for the salvation of mankind and were thereby transgressing the period of time God had granted them. Olivi dared to advance this heretical thought, declaring the hierarchy had outlived their time as servants of Christ and were now His enemies due to their opposition to the new prophets sent to usher in the Era of the Spirit. Finally, in 1326, Pope John XXII condemned the *Postilla,* but the contentions unleashed by this document continued to rage as the Church entered times of crisis:

> "After Olivi's days, criticism was no longer just levelled at the wealth of the Church, but increasingly at wealth as a sign of a Church

---

[133] Ibid. p. 57.
[134] Ibid. p. 59.
[135] Ibid.

poor or even barren in spirit. As critics of the official Church were subjected to ever greater persecution, [...] suspicion [grew] into the conviction that in Rome the harbingers of the Antichrist had invaded and taken over the leadership of the Church. [...] Since 1378 it had seemed evident that the Church of the priests must be in its final throes. One pope in Rome and another in Avignon, each denouncing the other and using excommunication and interdict to call the Devil down upon his opponent! The Council of Pisa was summoned in 1409 to put an end to the havoc, but instead of fulfilling hopes and restoring Christian unity, it bestowed a third pope on Christianity. It is true that the Council of Constance succeeded in reuniting the Western Church in 1415, but hopes of a new age, of the millennium of peace, remained a dream pursued well into the sixteenth century." (Oberman.)[136]

Luther also anticipated the arrival of this Utopia upon Christianity, but his personal experiences convinced him that the Last Days had already come upon them. In 1505 Luther abandoned his studies in law, entered the monastery of the Augustinian Eremites at Erfurt in fulfilment of a vow made to St. Anne, and was ordained a priest in 1507. There is no reason to question Luther's scrupulosity concerning the welfare of his soul. He admitted he was tormented by the thought that God was far from him: "In the monastery I did not think about women, money, possessions; instead my heart trembled and fidgeted about whether God would bestow His grace on me."[137] He was also extremely pious, he recalled he was filled with awe and trembled when celebrating his first Mass, for he came face to face with the majesty of God.[138] In 1511, he travelled to Rome on behalf of the Augustinians to seek an audience with the Pope for the purpose of settling a dispute between the Observant and the Conventual branches of the order. However, the scrupulous Luther was scandalised by the abominations he witnessed in the Eternal City as Oberman states:

> "[Luther] remembered clearly the shock and horror he had felt in Rome upon hearing for the first time in his life flagrant blasphemies uttered in public. He was deeply shocked by the casual mockery of saints and everything he held sacred. He could not laugh when he heard priests joking about the sacrament of the Eucharist [...] now in Rome he had to stand by while servants of God thought it funny to blaspheme the most sacred words of the institution [...i.e. this is My Body, this is My Blood]."[139]

These experiences convinced him the Church was sinking into a quagmire of moral corruption that required immediate reforms, yet he did not doubt or challenge the authority of the

---

[136] Ibid. p. 60.
[137] *D. Martin Luthers Werke*, 47.590, 6–10, in *Luther: between God and the Devil*, p. 128.
[138] *Luther: between God and the Devil*, p. 137.
[139] Ibid. p. 149.

Pope until the indulgence controversy of 1518–1519. It was possible to gain an indulgence by offering alms as an act of charity for sins already absolved, but to set prices for particular indulgences was condoning simony. As mentioned, Luther turned to the scriptures and the writings of St. Augustine and St. Bernard to decipher the significance of this depravity within the Church. According to his interpretation, these abuses manifested the prophecy that the devil who was bound would be "turned loose for a little time" to vent his fury on the faithful. St. Augustine wrote in the *City of God* that at the appointed time Satan would be set free, Christianity would experience a period of unparalleled turmoil, but he was undecided if Satan's last attacks would commence with the founding of an Antichurch, or originate within the Church itself.[140] St. Bernard believed the most alarming predicament that could occur during the last days would be the Antichrist attacking the faith from within — a situation that only Christ could dispel.[141] Luther compared these texts with St. Mathew's Gospel when Christ foretells the coming of the Last Days and the signs that precede them:

> "And Jesus answering, said to them: Take heed that no man seduce you: for many will come in my name and saying, I am Christ: and they will seduce many. And you will hear of wars and rumours of wars. See that ye be not troubled. For these things must come to pass, but the end is not yet. For nation shall rise against nation, and kingdom against kingdom; and there shall be pestilences, and famines, and earthquakes in places: Now all theses things are the beginnings of sorrows. Then shall they deliver you up to be afflicted, and shall put you to death: and you shall be hated by all nations for my name's sake. And then shall many be scandalized: and shall betray one another: and shall hate one another. And many false prophets shall rise and shall seduce many. And because iniquity hath abounded, the charity of many shall grow cold. But he that shall persevere to the end, he shall be saved. And this gospel of the kingdom, shall be preached in the whole world, for a testimony to all nations, and then shall the consummation come. When therefore, you shall see the abomination of desolation, which was spoken of by Daniel the prophet, standing in the holy place: he that readeth let him understand. [...] For there shall be great tribulation, such as hath not been from the beginning of the world until now, neither shall be. [...] And immediately after the tribulation of those days, the sun shall be darkened and the moon shall not give her light, and the stars shall fall from heaven, and the powers of heaven shall be moved: and then shall appear the sign of the Son of man in heaven: and then shall all the tribes of the earth mourn: and they shall see the Son of man coming in the clouds of heaven with much power and majesty." (Matt. 24:4–15, 21, 29–30)

---

[140] Ibid. p. 67.
[141] Ibid. p. 69.

Luther finally deduced that the "[...] Gospel of St. Matthew counts such perversions as the sale of indulgences among the signs of the Last Days."[142] Convinced the Church had "never been so desolate", it is possible he perceived this period to be the "abomination of desolation" Christ had predicted. Luther shared the same hope for the coming of God's kingdom, a time of renewal and reformation, but contrary to the chiliast ideology, he did not believe any human kingdom could declare this period by force, Christ had already explained that to Pilate, "My kingdom is not of this world. If my kingdom were of this world, my servants would certainly strive that I should not be delivered to the Jews."(John 18:36).[143] Hence, Christ would assume responsibility for the establishment of His kingdom, but it was the duty of the faithful to prepare for His coming. Oberman observes that "[...] it is not a question of Luther initiating or bringing on the reformation. From his point of view, all he or any Christian can do is to initiate reforms to better the world to such an extent that it can survive until the moment when God will put a final end to our chaos."[144]

The obvious preparation that required immediate action was the evangelisation of the Gospel, for Christ foretold it would be preached to every nation before the consummation of time. However, in 1519, Luther believed he had discovered the answer to this apocalyptic dilemma from his personal interpretation based upon St. Paul's teaching that the "just shall live by faith," (Rom.1:17). To him, this implied that sinful humans could not achieve salvation by accomplishing good works alone, but only by their faith in the grace of God freely given, for Christ died on the cross in atonement for sin, the sole Victim who could appease Divine Justice. One could not merit heaven or save their souls by any act they could hope to accomplish, but only by their belief in Christ; therefore, accomplishing good works is a consequence of faith, and is simply part of the duty to prepare the world for Christ's return. This new ideal, "justification by faith alone" without the absolute necessity of performing good or charitable works for eternal salvation was part of the "rediscovered" gospel that Luther believed Christ commanded His apostles to preach to the world. However, as the 'Last Days' were now upon them, the faithful were also required, as soldiers of Christ, to remain in readiness to do battle with the devil and his legions. Wherever the Gospel is preached, the devil is not far behind waiting to destroy the good that burgeons from it. Oberman states after 1514, Luther continued to stress the dangers the world faced from the evil one:

> "The prince of darkness will not content himself with the collapse of the Church, he wants to rule the world as well, so that — as he planned from the beginning — he can destroy God's creation and produce chaos again. Now that the Last Days have actually come, not only is steadfastness of faith called for, survival in the world is at stake as well. [...] Christians are threatened, but not helpless, under attack, but not defenceless. Where the Gospel is preached, Satan's destructive assaults can be survived. Where Christian teachings tear the authorities from the clutches of the Antichrist, the world can once again come into its own.

---

[142]   *D. Martin Luthers Werke*, 3.425, 7f., in *Luther, between God and the Devil*, p. 71.
[143]   *Luther, between God and the Devil*, pp. 63–64.
[144]   Ibid. p. 58.

Luther regarded this emancipation of the world, the restoration of its secular rights and its political order, as both necessary and possible."[145]

On June 15, 1520, Pope Leo condemned forty-one statements from Luther's works as heretical in the bull *Exsurge Domine*. The most glaring heresy was his concept of 'justification by faith alone'—Luther was correct that good works alone could not save souls as only Christ could make satisfaction to the Father for sinful humanity; however, faith alone without action implies spiritual presumption in a 'guaranteed' salvation. Christ had warned that not everyone who cried out "Lord, Lord," would be saved, but those who kept His commandments. St. James also warned: "But some man will say: Thou hast faith, and I have works: shew me thy faith without works; and I will shew thee, by works, my faith. [...] But wilt thou know, O vain man, that faith without works is dead?" (James. 2: 18, 20) Luther had a grace period of sixty days to recant, but refused to submit; consequently, he was excommunicated on January 3, 1521. Until this time, Luther's trust in the papacy had remained unshaken. He regarded his efforts to address the indulgence controversy his Catholic obligation towards the Pope and the Church. However, the order of excommunication forced him to painfully conclude that the papacy was no longer capable of caring for the flock, the corrupt hierarchy had left Rome wide open to be triumphantly occupied by the Antichrist — the time of the Second Coming was nigh.[146]

Faustus would have much to fear from this new public awareness of the devil, stirred up by Luther's interpretation of eschatology. Luther graduated with a doctorate in theology at the University of Wittemberg in 1512 and therefore was entitled to many privileges, including the right to freely dispute matters concerning scriptural interpretation without fear of punishment or reprimand. However, Luther's ideology was not restricted to the educated circles for an anonymous supporter translated his *Theses* into German and printed them in Nuremberg.[147] While Luther did not intend his *Theses* to be circulated in the vernacular, and in fact was accused of abusing his academic privileges in this regard, he acknowledged the immediate success they achieved throughout Germany, in as little as two weeks subsequent to their posting on the door of the Castle Church in Wittenberg.[148] In fine, Luther came to acknowledge in later years the importance of disseminating his writings in the German language, and thereby instructed and enlightened those not privileged in the study of Latin with his theology that addressed the true nature of the devil — in effect, he encroached upon that territory of the general populace that Faustus once held secure. As Oberman relates:

> "[To Luther,] this was no longer the Devil who, in a triple alliance with 'sin' and 'world,' seduces the voluptuous flesh of man against his better 'self.' The medieval poltergeist is virtually harmless in comparison with this adversary, who, armed with fire and sword, spiritual temptations and clever arguments, has now risen up against God to prevent the preaching of the Gospel. As long as the righteous God reigns

---

[145] Ibid. pp. 73–74.
[146] Ibid. p. 186.
[147] Ibid. pp. 23, 191
[148] Ibid, p. 191.

far away in Heaven, waiting for the end of the world, the Devil, too, will remain at the edge of world history. But the closer the Righteous One comes to us on earth through our belief in Christ, the closer the Devil draws, feeling challenged to take historically effective countermeasures. The Reformation symbol of Christ's presence is not the halo of the saint, but the hatred of the Devil."[149]

As previously discussed, Faustus may have deemed it necessary for self-preservation to seek protection and the sanction of an ecclesiastical patron as these contemporary events unfolded. He presented himself as a philosopher, drafted a 'licit' academic horoscope chart, was handsomely rewarded by the bishop, and assumed a façade of respectability. A point of interest, no record exists indicating the Bishop of Bamberg ever consulted the astrologers of his court, i.e. his bookbinder Johannes Schöner, or other known astrologers within the city, including the lawyer Lorenz Beheim, an acquaintance of the humanist Willibald Pirckheimer.[150] We may presume his Eminence did not commission horoscopes on a regular basis, or he preferred to treat these consultations as private affairs. Hence, the public recognition Faustus received is noteworthy; it supports the theory Faustus was tested by the bishop, surpassed his expectations, and therefore endorsed him as a legitimate scholar.

The predictions Faustus presented remains subject to conjecture. It is possible Faustus drafted a horoscope that reflected events and issues the bishop wanted to hear or expected to occur — it would not be too difficult to fabricate an acquiescent prediction of this nature if he had knowledge of the bishop's personal phobias and his opinions relating to current events. Baron surmises the bishop's premonitions of death and the current ecclesiastical and political turmoil may be the primary topics Faustus employed for this consultation:

> "In the years 1518–1519 [the bishop] assigned Loy Hering the task of preparing his epitaph and gravestone. In fact, the bishop was to die soon thereafter, on May 31, 1522. The political crisis, brought by Luther's conflict with the Church of Rome, was also of great concern to Georg at this time. Many of his advisors leaned strongly in favor of Luther. Lazarus Spengler wrote to Pirckheimer that the bishop was on Luther's side. But in another letter, written just a few weeks later, on November 5, 1520, Spengler, who was threatened by a papal bull, expressed disappointment in Georg's attitude. Certainly the bishop was careful not to undertake actions that were in conflict with the Roman church."[151]

---

[149] Ibid. p. 155.
[150] *Doctor Faustus, from History to Legend*, p. 43.
[151] Ibid. p. 44.

In addition, Baron observes while the bishop was a man of learning, for he had attended the Universities of Ingolstadt and Basel, he did not achieve the extensive academic acumen compared to Trithemius and Mutianus.[152] Therefore, it would be a simple matter for Faustus to conceal his academic deficiencies from the bishop by manipulating information he already possessed and therefore he could sustain the illusion of his rumoured genius. The bishop's public approval ultimately validated Faustus as an accurate astrologer and a learned philosopher, for a brief period, he could assume a legitimate profile that would afford him a degree of respectability.

Eight years later, we discover Faustus travelled close to the vicinity of Rebdorf in Bavaria. The Augustinian prior of the monastery in the town, Kilian Leib, recorded this event in his journal on July 1528:

> "Georgius Faustus of Helmstetensis said on the fifth of June that when the sun and Jupiter are in the same constellation, prophets are born (presumably such as he). He asserted that he was the commander or preceptor of the Order of the Knights of St. John at a place called Hallestein [sic.] on the border of Carinthia."[153]

Of all the documents that record the activities of the historical Faustus, Baron observes this account is unique for Leib displayed little faith in astrology, nor was he interested in the occult, therefore his observations are more objective.[154] Baron states Leib "[…] was much more sophisticated and modern in that [he] actually attempted to test the accuracy of astrological claims by a persistent method of observation and comparison."[155] When astrologers inaccurately predicted a flood of biblical proportions in 1524 due to the rare convergence of the sun, moon and the planets in the sign of Pisces, Leib made it his duty to record meteorological changes. Over a fifteen-year period, he daily monitored the state of the weather in an attempt to investigate the validity of making predictions through astrology.[156] This pioneering, scientific approach explains Leib's semi-objective observations regarding his encounter with Faustus. Apart from his parenthetical comment, Leib merely recorded the statements and the date on which Faustus delivered them. According to this comment, Faustus was insinuating his skill in divination bordered on the prophetic. This source also implies he did not impress Leib, who remained sceptical of his career in astrology. In addition, Leib conveyed an apparent lack of interest regarding his religious title that may or may not be fraudulent.

Notwithstanding Leib's semi-impartiality, this document offers two important pieces of information relating to Faustus' ongoing attempt to veneer the nefarious reputation he had originally created by varnishing his image with credible academia and noble affiliations. First,

---

[152] Ibid. p. 42.
[153] Ibid. p. 47. See also *Sources of the Faust Tradition*, p. 89.
[154] *Doctor Faustus, from History to Legend*, p. 45.
[155] Ibid.
[156] Ibid. p. 46.

Faustus revealed a sample of his knowledge in astrology, a more respected branch of foretelling the future due to its perceived foundation in philosophy. Similar to the account of his audience with the Bishop of Bamberg, this document did not associate Faustus with the black arts he professed earlier in his career. However, the information Faustus offered did not reveal an earth-shattering discovery, nor did it prove to be a rare diamond of wisdom as Baron explains:

> "The opinion that the conjunction of the great planets, especially of Jupiter, indicated the birth of heroic men and prophets was widespread among the astrologers of the early sixteenth century. This view went back to Hellenistic and Arabic sources and became very popular in the Renaissance through some of the earliest products of the printing press. [...] Thus, what Faustus asserted was consistent with popular astrological opinion of the time."[157]

We observe Faustus was adept at intriguing those around him, creating the impression he was particularly learned by sharing fascinating, but basic information his attendees may not be familiar with. As discussed previously, Faustus possibly employed this tactic to win the approval of the Bishop of Bamberg.

Second, Faustus claimed he joined a prestigious militant order of the Church, the Knights of St. John of Jerusalem, also known as the Hospitalers. Founded before the First Crusade (1095–1099), the Hospitalers were the oldest of the three militant orders in the Roman Catholic Church that included the Knights Templar and the Teutonic Knights. The original vocation of the Hospitalers centred on works of charity, namely the care of sick pilgrims in the Holy Land. The order followed the rule of St. Augustine in their daily routine that consisted of prayer, study, and work. However, the order assumed military duties in later years, by the year 1200, their charitable works became secondary to their military campaigns to defend the Holy Land. Membership in the Hospitalers was originally restricted to men of noble birth. A grand master presided over an internal hierarchy of knights, chaplains and servants, divided into four categories. The order appended a fifth rank in later years:

1) Knights of noble birth, to defend the pilgrims and the hospital(s).
2) Servants-at-arms, military brethren, but not necessarily of noble birth.
3) Servants-at-office: who nursed, fed and washed the sick.
4) Chaplains, who acted as clerks and administered to the spiritual needs of the Brothers and injured.
5) The fifth rank: the Knights-of-Grace, which was conferred on persons who had offered exceptional service to the order.

When the Muslims finally conquered the Crusader States in 1291, the Hospitalers retreated to Cyprus, and re-established their headquarters on the island of Rhodes, which they

---

[157] Aby Warburg, "Heidnisch-antike Weissagung in Wort und Bild zu Luthers Zeiten, "in *Gesammelte Schriften* (Leipzig, 1932), II, pp. 487–558, in *Doctor Faustus from History to Legend*, p. 47.

held secure for two centuries. During that period, they were referred to as the Knights of St. John of Rhodes. Following the capture of Constantinople by the Ottoman Turks in 1453, the Knights of Rhodes were the only Christian militant order present in the Eastern Mediterranean to stand as the primary resistance to the Muslim invasions. They were successful in defending Rhodes until invading forces weakened and finally defeated them following a long siege in 1522. In 1530, Emperor Charles V granted the Knights the island of Malta for their new headquarters where they remained undefeated until Napoleon's invasion in 1798. As in previous times, the name of their order changed to reflect their new base of operation; hence, they became recognised as the Knights of Malta, a title they hold to this day.

There is no logical reason to believe that Faustus was actually a member of the Hospitalers, membership remained generally restricted to those of noble birth who chose a monastic way of life with the obligatory vows of poverty, chastity and obedience. Before an aspiring member was permitted to join the order, the candidate was required to prove he came from a virtuous Catholic family without any blemish on their family name. Obviously, the order would refuse to admit anyone who was a known practitioner of the black arts, or accused of sodomy, unless that person publicly renounced their former way of life, embraced the laws of the Church, and had accomplished the due penance required. According to the historical sources, Faustus had not renounced his soothsaying career; therefore, there is no evidence of a true reconciliation with the teachings of the Church. The rank that Faustus claimed, commander or preceptor, were predominantly held by knights, or chaplains and serving brothers at arms,[158] who held positions as superiors over small houses where the brethren lived with a central church known as a *commanderie*.[159] While the serving brothers were not all necessarily of noble lineage, Faustus' history would certainly have excluded him from this order. In addition, the archives of the Knights in Prague and Malta do not record any entries that mention Faustus as a commander or preceptor during this time.[160] The only facet of his claim that contains any element of truth is the fact the Knights once controlled Heilenstein, located in the province of Styria in southeastern Austria.[161] It is possible Faustus may have travelled through that region in the years preceding the entry date of Leib's account when the Knights had no permanent headquarters (1522–1528), and readily obtained this information. In summary, we may speculate that Faustus was attempting to fortify the religious sanction he previously acquired with the approval of the Bishop of Bamberg. Those familiar with the Hospitalers undoubtedly knew the conditions set forth for admittance, i.e. that a prospective member would be of virtuous character before admission to the ranks of this prestigious order. Faustus may have decided to profit from the assumptions entertained by the populace regarding the Knights, confident they would not take the time, nor had the resources or connections, to verify the truth of his alleged affiliation.

---

[158] E. J. King, *The Knights of St. John in the British Empire* (London: St. John's Gate, 1934), p. 82, in *Doctor Faustus, from History to Legend*, n. 14, p. 100.

[159] Jonathan Riley-Smith, *The Knights of St. John in Jerusalem and Cyprus* (London: MacMillan, 1967), p. 341, in *Doctor Faustus, from History to Legend*, n. 14, p. 100.

[160] *Doctor Faustus, from History to Legend*, p. 47.

[161] *Sources of the Faust Tradition*, n. 20, p. 89. Baron states Heilenstein is located in northwestern Yugoslavia. (Now northwestern Solvenia), *Doctor Faustus, from History to Legend*, p. 47.

If this speculation is acceptable, Faustus' decision to falsely associate with an order that required a vow of chastity as an additional front to promote his façade of respectability is intriguing. His attempt to forge a connection with the Knights of St. John evinces that Faustus was already experiencing difficulties with accusations of perversion *before* the council of Nuremberg declared it openly. As discussed, the accusation of sodomy pronounced by the council of Nuremberg, which refused Faustus safe conduct at Fürth on May 10, 1532, was possibly fostered by the private circulation of Trithemius' letter to Virdung written twenty-five years prior to the notice of rejection issued by the Nuremberg council.

In addition, the very fact that membership to the Hospitalers was generally restricted to the nobility offers a new insight into his psychological profile. Returning to the years he attended the university, we recall Faustus attempted to exempt himself from the third disputation required for his master's examination. Baron observes it was not customary for the nobility who attended the universities to "[...] submit themselves to the unpleasantries of academic requirements and examinations, they pursued their studies through private tutors."[162] Did Faustus from an early age aspire to elevate his status above that of his humble origins in Helmstadt, deluding himself by entertaining grandiose ideas, and in the process attempted to deceive his associates he was numbered among the aristocracy? *Or, was he attempting to claim noble lineage as his lawful right?* Could it be possible he was an illegitimate heir to a noble family who refused to publicly recognise him? Perhaps this may explain the reason Faustus was reluctant to disclose his family name, as the name he was raised with was not his true identity. If this hypothesis holds any validity, it is intriguing to recall he organised his career *debut* to occur in the Heidelberg locale, and attempted to attract the Elector of the Palatinate and form an allegiance with his court. Could Faustus be illegitimately related to the noble family of Heidelberg? Also, this could explain the close friendship Faustus enjoyed with the Imperial knights Franz von Sickingen and Ulrich von Hutten, it is possible they had knowledge of his noble connection. Unsubstantiated as this theory may be, we cannot help but observe his seeming obsession in assuming associations with the elite and yearning for the privileges reserved solely for the aristocracy, forcing them and his contemporaries to recognise him as such.

However, it is possible Faustus was not simply dropping casual information about the planet Jupiter when he visited Rebdorf. During that summer when Lieb eventually recorded Faustus' remark, there was a major conjunction of Mercury, Mars, and Jupiter in Cancer while the sun was in the constellation. Mercury also signifies a 'herald' or a 'prophet', while Mars represents war. The planet Jupiter is also associated with kingly rule. Considering his reference to the Hospitalers, Faustus may have predicted a new clash with the Ottoman Empire was forthcoming, a remarkably accurate forecast when we note the first siege of Vienna led by Suleiman the Magnificent occurred not long after in 1529 marking the furthest offensive into Europe undertaken by the invading Ottomans.

Following Faustus' visit to Rebdorf, the authorities expelled him from the city of Ingolstadt ten days later, twenty kilometres away (c.12 miles), on June 17, 1528:

Minute on the actions of the city Council in Ingolstadt.

---

[162] *Doctor Faustus, from History to Legend,* p. 42.

"Today, the Wednesday after St. Vitus' Day, 1528. [Monday 15ᵗʰ] The soothsayer shall be ordered to leave the city and to spend his penny elsewhere."

Record of those banished from Ingolstadt.
"On Wednesday after St. Vitus' Day, 1528 a certain man who called himself Dr. Jörg Faustus of Heidelberg was told to spend his penny elsewhere and he pledged not to take vengeance on or make fools of the authorities for this order."[163]

Baron observes Faustus' occupation as a fortune-teller provoked the hostility of the council in Ingolstadt, as this is the only offence listed in the records. This questionable occupation earned him numerous enemies in the humanist circles, as with Trithemius and Mutianus, for his practises discredited their own interests in the 'natural' academic braches of the occult. They denounced Faustus, portraying the diabolical or charlatanistic nature of his arts in their efforts to justify and defend their own studies and research. History obviously repeated at Ingolstadt, yet in this instance, there is no particular informant or competitor recorded. We can, however speculate on the identity of an opponent who possibly reported Faustus to the authorities in order to have him evicted from their territory, Johann Eck.

Johann Eck (1486–1543), whose surname was originally Mayer, was born in the town of Eck (Egg), and later changed his name to reflect the geographical origin of his birth. He commenced his studies at the age of twelve for one year at the University of Heidelberg, before transferring to Tübingen for a further year of study, whereupon he relocated to Cologne to avoid a current outbreak of the plague, and continued on to Freiburg-im-Breisgau. In 1508, he was ordained to the priesthood, and graduated two years later with a doctorate in theology. He became professor of theology in Ingolstadt (1510), and in 1512, the university council raised him to the position of prochancellor (Prokanzler), a post he held until his death in 1543. During that time, he used his considerable influence in the jurisdiction of Ingolstadt to stamp an indelible impression of right-wing Catholicism on the city, making it a bastion of traditional faith in Germany.

Eck became an ardent opponent of the Reformation and its defenders following his denunciation of Luther and Carlstadt (Karlstadt), his conflict with the reformers began when Luther dispatched a copy of his *Ninety-Five Theses* to him in 1517. The next year, Eck circulated his refutation of Luther's theses entitled *Oblisci* (Obelisks) in which he accused Luther of defending the Hussite heresies and promoting anarchy within the Church. While Luther counter-attacked these accusations in his *Asterisci adversxes obeliseos Eccii,* Carlstadt rose to Luther's defence, challenging Eck to a public disputation, which took place at Leipzig during the months of June and July 1519. This confrontation lasted for twenty-three days: Eck first disputed with Carlstadt regarding the nature of grace and free will, followed by a dispute with Luther concerning the authority of the pope, indulgences, penance and the existence of Purgatory. Notwithstanding the arbitrators of these disputations did not render a public verdict on the proceedings, the theologians of the University of Leipzig hailed Eck as the victor. He also had

---

[163] *Sources of the Faust Tradition*, p. 90.

the support of a noted persecutor of heretics, Hoogstraten, and the universities of Cologne and Louvain. He continued to do battle with the harbingers of the heretical Reformation that year (1519) by attempting to persuade Elector Frederick of Saxony to publicly burn Luther's writings, coinciding with his publication of eight new refutations opposing the new movement that now included an attack on Melancthon.

In 1520, Rome recognised his efforts in defending the faith; upon the presentation of his latest publication, *De primate Petri adversus Ludderum* (Ingolstadt, 1520), he was nominated to the office of papal protonotary, and later entrusted with the German publication of the bull pronouncing Luther's excommunication, *Exsurge Domine*. The publication of the bull in Germany led to widespread condemnation of the papal decree and also the messenger, a situation aggravated by Eck who transgressed his original commission and misused his unique position of authority to attack other leaders of the Reformation and his humanist critics. Indignant with the negative reception of this bull, Eck resorted to calling upon the highest secular authority by appealing to Emperor Charles V in his *Epistola ad Carolum V* (February 18, 1521) to take active measures to oppose Luther, a demand which precipitated the edict of Worms (1521). In 1521 and 1522, Eck journeyed to Rome to report on the results of his nunciature. Returning from his second visit, he became one of the foremost disseminators of the Bavarian religious edict (1522) that effectively established the senate at the university of Ingolstadt as a tribunal of the Inquisition, leading to further years of persecution directly opposing the leaders of the Reformation. He was also present at the Augsburg Diet (1530), the colloquy of Worms (1540) and at the diet of Regensburg (Ratisbon) in 1541. A zealous champion of Catholicism to the end, he died at the age of fifty-seven in Ingolstadt.

Upon our analysis of Eck's influence, we begin to comprehend more accurately Faustus' efforts to camouflage his past reputation in the close proximity of Rebdorf — he was evidently manipulating those he encountered in this locality to ensure a favourable, or less hostile reception for his visit to the ultra-conservative city of Ingolstadt. Eck, a declared enemy of heretics, would have undoubtedly reacted negatively to Faustus' presence in Ingolstadt due to his occupation as a diviner. The refusal of unhindered freedom of the city or permission to remain in the area would be the least of the punishments that could befall him if arrested and tried as a necromancer or sorcerer. His one documented influential patron in the Church, the Bishop of Bamberg, had died six years previously in 1522, leaving him no option but to reinitiate the process of fabricating a profile of respectability to insure his personal safety. Hence, in Rebdorf as in Bamberg, Faustus concentrated on the academic and less offensive form of prognostication, i.e. his knowledge of astrology. This attempt to appear conservative also accounts for his claim to be a member of the Hospitalers, he could not have devised a greater alibi when entering a stronghold of the Inquisition than to claim membership with an honourable religious order noted for defending Christian lands from the ravages of heathens.

However, his defence strategy failed; apparently, his past reputation preceded him to Ingolstadt. He was fortunate that the accusation did not extend to necromancy, for the city council recognised him simply as a soothsayer. It is also surprising the council did not detain and castigate him for his insolence when he "pledged himself not to take vengeance on or make fools of" them. Faustus had taken a considerable risk by pronouncing this threat. Was he implying he had other powerful patrons who would protect him, which to our knowledge are undocumented, or did he insinuate perhaps in an act of bravado, he had the preternatural power to curse them, but magnanimously refrained from carrying out his threat? Obviously, the council had concluded his remark signified the former, or he would not have escaped the city of Ingolstadt with the lenient sentence of banishment.

Subsequent to his experience at Ingolstadt, Faustus consequently adopted the practise of requesting safe passage before entering any locality. Three years and eleven months later, while residing in Fürth, we discover Faustus probed the current disposition of the authorities of Nürnburg (Nüremburg / Nuremberg) before attempting to proceed there:

[May 10, 1532]

Records of the City of Nüremburg:
"Safe conduct to Doctor fausto, the great sodomite and necromancer [Nigromantico], at Fürth refused. The Junior Burgomaster."

As discussed, his involvement with the occult, compounded by Trithemius' description of events at Kreuznach, incurred this serious accusation by the authorities. There is no evidence at this point that could convict Faustus of sodomy, merely speculation demonstrated by the order of exile pronounced upon him. Baron observes:

"The crime of sodomy was considered so serious at this time that it merited, if witnessed, capital punishment. In instances of suspicion, however, the general custom was exile from the city. [...] Thus, it seems that the decree in Nuremburg against him was based on the sincere belief on the part of the officials that Faustus was a reprehensible individual because of his morals and because he practised black magic."
[164]

Baron offers the theory that the authorities levelled accusations based on personal assumptions and distortions of the facts, deploying the judicial system to prevent Faustus from entering Nuremberg. Did the authorities harbour a concealed motive that incited them to brand Faustus an 'undesirable' before he had the opportunity to enter their city?

Baron observes Nuremberg became a noted centre of astrology and divination for many years. Melanchthon wrote a letter describing the favourable reception these arts received there and mentioned several humanists from past decades who were attracted to the city for this reason, including Willibald Pirckheimer.[165] Melanchthon then complimented the teachers of the current scholastic Gymnasium in Nuremberg, hailing them as the true successors of this academic tradition. Baron states:

"With apparent pride (Melanchthon had played a central role in the founding of this school) he stressed that no comparable school could

---

[164] H. Knapp, *Das alte Nürnberger Kriminalrecht* (Berlin, 1896), p. 223, in *Doctor Faust, from History to Legend*, pp. 49–50.
[165] *Doctor Faustus, from History to Legend*, p. 50.

claim as great a number of learned men in this field. [mathematics, i.e. astrology]. Though he mentioned no names, he was clearly referring specifically to his good friends Johannes Schöner, professor of mathematics, and Joachim Camerarius, professor of history as well as director of the school. Both Schöner and Camerarius had been employed by the city since 1526."[166]

Baron then speculates these two scholars may be directly responsible for the denial of Faustus' request with the ulterior motive to remove the threat of competition — a theory that may be substantiated with the following evidence:

"[…] Nuremberg, already so well-endowed in astrology, could expect to gain little by the presence of an outsider of questionable reputation. Just three years before Faustus' arrival, a controversial figure, Paracelsus [*] had been in Nuremburg, and unpleasant disputes had arisen between the local doctors and the outsider. Was it in the interest of the city, and especially of the academic astrologers Schöner and Camerarius, who were in its services, to allow such competition? Was there any need for a nonscholarly astrologer in a city with so many illustrious and presumably reliable men of its own?" (Baron)[167]

There is evidence Camerarius scrutinised Faustus' reputation and the skills he professed, for quite some time.[168] According to Camerarius' letter to Daniel Stibar (dated August 13, 1536),

---

[166] Melanchthon, *Mathematicarum encomia*, fol. B8. On Schöner, see the article *in Allgemeine Deutsche Biographie*, Vol. 32, pp. 295–97, in ibid. pp. 50–51.

[*] Philippus Aureolus Paracelsus (1493? –1541) was born in Einsiedeln, located in present day Switzerland. He obtained a degree in medicine, but chose a wandering career in search of knowledge, his interests extended to the fields of alchemy and mineralogy. He was a quarrelsome character, and defied the medical theories of his time, i.e. challenging the theory that internal 'bodily humors' (fluids) were the source of disease, maintaining that ailments were caused by external sources, which could be cured by chemical remedies. His treatments resulted from his belief "like cures like", and are the ancient precursors to modern homeopathic treatments. Although his writings contain elements of magic, his unorthodox theories liberated medical ideology.

[167] *Doctor Faustus, from History to Legend*, p. 51.

[168] Baron ventures the theory Camerarius may have first encountered Faustus at Nuremberg in 1529 according to a letter he wrote to Stibar in August of that year, however, there is no mention of Faustus' name. Therefore, this theory is merely speculative. Baron writes: "In August of 1529 Camerarius wrote to his friend Daniel Stibar about a doctor who was visiting Nuremberg and was a friend of Stibar. Since Stibar was known to have been a friend of [Doctor] Faustus it is conceivable that this letter is actually about Faustus: "Non fui apud doctorem amicum tuum. Nam cum ille mihi literas ante coenam misisset, credo quod cuperet me apud se esse ego qui non possem venire statim significavi ei, adventurum me post coenam. Retinebar autem domi cum illo inveterate malo pedis, tum cuiusdam amici praesebtia. Post coenam in multam sane noctem veni in cauponam, sed ille adhuc coenabat, et occurrit mihi quidam tum metus, ut non exspectarim finam coenae. De illo metu narrabo tibi cum adveneris," Joachim Camerarius,

and Philipp von Hutten's letter to his brother Moritz von Hutten (dated January 16, 1540), we learn that during the 1530s, Camerarius was acquainted with a family connected with Faustus, the von Huttens, and a man who considered Faustus a close friend, Daniel Stibar.

Joachim Camerarius (1500–1574) became famous for his work as a philologist, historian and biographer. Born in Bamberg, Camerarius left the city at the age of thirteen to enrol at the University of Leipzig. From there, he continued his studies at the University of Erfurt. During his university days at Erfurt, Camerarius maintained a close friendship with Stibar, who became canon of Würzburg in 1530.[169] In 1527, Stibar attended the University of Basel and encountered Moritz von Hutten, the future Catholic Bishop of Eichstätt.[170] Consequently, Camerarius made the acquaintance of Moritz and Phillip von Hutten through his friendship with Stibar.[171] Obviously, Ulrich von Hutten introduced Faustus to his cousins Moritz and Philip von Hutten, who in turn introduced Faustus to their close friend, Stibar, and indirectly to Camerarius. Baron observes:

> "During the 1530s Camerarius, Stibar, and [Moritz von] Hutten remained close through a very diligent correspondence and numerous reunions. [...] There was a genuine interest in exchanges of views on scholarly questions. Camerarius had encouraged Moritz von Hutten, for example, to take an interest in the literary remains of his famous cousin, Ulrich von Hutten. Ulrich's dialogue *Arminius* was in fact published by Moritz in Nuremberg in 1529. Camerarius frequently consulted with Stibar in his publications, asking him to examine the accuracy of his texts or interpretations.[172] The three men also shared an interest in astrology and this interest was closely tied to their common scholarly and political interests.[173] When Moritz's brother set off for the New World, a question of personal pride and concern intensified their contacts with each other, and they turned to astrology as a matter of natural course. After Hutten's departure the correspondence and meetings of the friends reflects their concern about the fate of the venture.[174]

Epistolarum libri quinque posteriors (Frankfurt: P. Fischer, 1595), p. 119." In *Doctor Faustus, from History to Legend*, n. 10, p 102.

[169] Ibid. pp. 54–55.

[170] Ibid. p. 55.

[171] Ibid.

[172] Baron's footnote, n. 29, ibid: "Mayer, pp. 487–87."

[173] Baron's footnote, n. 30, ibid: "The interest of Moritz von Hutten in these matters is reflected in a book dedicated to him by Jacob Kubel. Besides being very favourable and flattering to Charles V it contains a poem about prophecy. Jacob Kubel, *Elegia in fine continens vaticinium* (s.l., 1547.) In locating this rare book I had the kind help of Dr. Schneiders of the Bayerische Staatsbibliothek."

[174] Baron's footnote, n. 31, ibid: "Camerarius to Stibar on March 5, 1536: "Fuit apud nos Mauricius Huttenus, attulitque iucundissimum nuncium adventus tui. Utinam modo nihil interveniat, quo ille impediatur. Collacuti (ut solemus) de variss sumus, et praebebatur locuples occasio sermonum de literis Philippi fratis illius proficientis cum Velseriana classe Indiam. Ab eo accepi hunc fasciculum literarum curandum tibi." Joachim Camerarius, *Epistolarum familiarum libri V*, (Frankfurt: pud haeredes Adreae

Camerarius had been acquainted with Philip von Hutten as early as 1529. In the fall of that year Hutten had passed through Nuremburg and stopped at Camerarius' house to report on the health of his brother Moritz.[175][176]

In contrast to his friends, the von Huttens and Stibar, Camerarius obviously did not approve of Faustus' astrological methods, as we later discover in his letter of August 13, 1536. The fact Camerarius was an acquaintance of the Junior Burgomaster, Hieronymus Holzschuher, who refused Faustus safe passage, Baron notes it is possible Camerarius was aware of Faustus' petition,[177] suggesting he may have influenced Holzschuher to deny Faustus' request. When Faustus requested safe passage (1532), Camerarius was occupied with several major tracts on the subject of astrology. In 1531, the discovery of a rare astrological phenomenon created a sensation, recognised today as Halley's comet, many predicted this event heralded a period of pestilence. Camerarius had completed a book featuring his observations of the comet entitled *Norica sive de ostentis* and anticipated its publication in the near future, which incidentally did not occur until the autumn of the following year (1532).[178] In 1532, Camerarius, occupied with the translation of several Greek works encompassing astrology and the occult sciences, published them under the title *Astrologia*.[179] It is possible, Camerarius attempted to prevent Faustus' arrival, a competitor, at this critical time when he was publishing major astrological accounts.

Continuing with Johannes Schöner, there is evidence he harboured an intense animosity towards Faustus, greater than that of his friend Camerarius. As we previously discovered, the Bishop of Bamburg employed Schöner as his personal bookbinder, notwithstanding his significant skills as an astrologer and geographer. He was educated at the university of Erfurt, and later studied astronomy and astrology, on his own initiative, at Nuremberg.[180] He fashioned globes illustrating the discoveries made in the New World, and printed his own books.[181] Perchance Schöner regarded this limited occupation at the Bishop's court degrading as it did not reflect his unique talents and qualifications in other fields. It is conceivable Schöner was incensed that he was overlooked in favour of the infamous charlatan, Faustus, on that one, rare occasion when the bishop commissioned a horoscope. Consequently, Schöner may have attempted to inform the bishop concerning the suspect reputation attributed to this notorious diviner. Hence, we may speculate Faustus made an enemy in Schöner while he was at Bamberg when we recall the Bishop's generous reward of ten gulden presented "as a testimonial" signifying a public declaration of his approval. This supports our previous observation that the

Wecheli, 1583), pp. 144–45"
[175] Baron's footnote, n. 32, ibid: "Camerarius wrote to Stibar: ' Iam transiens hac et praeteriens meas aedes, salutavit me de equo Philippus Huttenus cum fratre, narravitque mihi Mauricium convalescere, quo sum valde delectatus.' Ep. V, p. 119"
[176] *Doctor Faustus, from History to Legend*, pp. 55–56
[177] Ibid, p. 51.
[178] Ibid. p. 53.
[179] Ibid. p. 52.
[180] Ibid. p. 43.
[181] Ibid.

Bishop was settling a dispute regarding the authenticity of Faustus' claims, and in so doing, endeavoured to silence the 'philosopher's' detractors.

Hypothetically, Schöner fostered antipathy from his previous experience in Bamberg, providing him with a personal motive to prevent Faustus from infiltrating and competing with him in his new centre of patronage at Nuremberg. As with Camerarius, he was also engaged in the publication of various astrological texts at that time. Baron observes, "In gratitude to the city for the position he held as mathematician, Schöner resolved to draw up an astrological prediction for Nuremberg for the years 1531 and 1532."[182] He also collaborated with his friend Camerarius regarding the predictions resulting from the discovery of the comet.[183] Coincidentally, Camerarius came from a respected family affiliated with the Bishop's court in Bamberg, he may have received information of Faustus obtaining the horoscope commission through his connections at court, and disapproved of the Bishop's decision in this matter. In addition, Lazarus Spengler (1479–1534), a town clerk of Nuremberg, was familiar with the Bishop of Bamberg's activities, for as we previously discovered, Spengler reported to Pirckheimer events that occurred at the Bishop's court. It is possible Spengler sympathised with Schöner at Bamberg, and used his position at Nuremberg to influence the negative decision Faustus received from the council. Therefore, Schöner may have had supporters in the Nuremberg town council upon whom he could exert his influence. In summary, we may deduce the threat of competition to the leading astrologers of Nuremberg was the determining factor that caused the authorities to refuse Faustus the freedom to enter their city.

This was only the beginning of the competition between Camerarius and Faustus. Two years later, both astrologers crossed paths through their association with Stibar and the von Huttens when they offered conflicting predictions concerning Philip von Hutten's expedition to Venezuela as leader of the Welser troops in 1534.

Focusing on Camerarius, we discover first hand his optimism for Philip's new adventure expressed in his book entitled *Erratum* (1535). Baron observes this particular work resulted from a quarrel with Erasmus, who accused him of formulating errors in his astrological judgements.[184] In *Erratum*, Camerarius defended his methodology, and included three extensive poems depicting certain methods of divination and their practise from times of antiquity. Baron states:

> "The dedications are noteworthy: the first poem was dedicated to Moritz von Hutten, and the other two were written for Daniel Stibar. The introductory section of the first poem treats the future of the Hutten expedition.
>
> Unfortunately, the information provided is not very specific and does not shed much light on the nature or circumstances of the original expedition. Lines 5 and 6 appear to indicate that Camerarius had examined the question whether the time was propitious for the undertakings of Hutten.[185] This distich suggests that he had made the prediction before Hutten set off for America on October 19, 1534. The

---

[182] Ibid. p. 51.
[183] Ibid. p. 53.
[184] Ibid. p. 56.

poem dwells at length on the glory that Philipp will bring to his nation and family. Camerarius alludes to his audience with Charles V, which is known to have taken place before his departure on August 22, 1534. [186] Finally, the poet stresses his ardent desire for a good outcome of the expedition.[187,188]

In contrast to Camerarius, Faustus, who may be sojourning at Würzburg[*] at this time, predicted the expedition would encounter misfortune. Philip would admit that Faustus "[...] hit the nail on the head, for we struck a bad year", i.e. 1534, yet the accuracy of this prediction remained undisclosed until Philip actually wrote his letter in 1540. Therefore, there would be a considerable waiting period before they could prove the accuracy of their horoscopes. Apparently, this feud between the astrologers concerning the expedition had reached Peter Seuter who by then was practising law[189] in Kempten. Perhaps the intrigue surrounding the heated debates prompted him to send Helmstetter's horoscope chart of 1490 to Ellenbog for a second

---

[185] Baron's footnote, ibid, n. 35, p. 103: "The poem is entitled 'Joachimi Camerarii Aeolia, ad clarissimum virum Mauricium Huttenum.'
      Sic liquido coepta auspicio quemcunque habiture
      Sunt finem, finis non erit malus.

Joachim Camerarius, *Erratum,* [2nd ed.] (Basel: B. Lasius and T. Platter, 1536), fol. 17v. Subsequent excerpts from the poem are also from this edition. On the Hutten expedition see Konrad Haebler, *Die überseeischen Unternehmungen der Welser und iher Gesellschaftler* (Leipzig, 1903), p. 228."

[186] Baron's footnote, n. 36, ibid.: "Lines 17–18 refer to this event: Frater in augusta Caroli celeberrimus aula / Gentis honor patriae, gentis honorque suae. *Erratum,* fol. 18. For Hutten's own reference to the audience with Charles V see Fernando Cortes, *Von dem Newen Hispanien* (Augsburg: B. Ulhart, 1550), fol. 51."

[187] Baron's footnote, n. 37, ibid.: "Cf. lines 35–38: Omnia sint terraque marique secunda, / Virtuti iuvenis nate Philippe, tuis: / Ut quondam incolumi patriaeque tuisque reverso, / Nemo sit in terra par tibi Teutonide. Friedrich Kluge presents lines 5–6 and 35–38 together as one continuous poem. Since he does not indicate his source at all, it is impossible to say with certainty whether there is any justifiable basis for his arrangement of the lines. It is reasonable to assume that line 5–6 do, in fact, refer to the Hutten expedition. Friedrich Kluge, "Vom geschichtlichen Dr. Faust", in *Bunte Blätter. Kulturgeschichtliche Vorträge und Aufsätze* (Freiburg, 1908), p 7."

[188] *Doctor Faustus, from History to Legend*, p. 56.

[*] Baron writes: "There are strong indications that Würzburg was the place where Faustus had been consulted. The same letter from Hutten that confirms the accuracy of the prognostication by Faustus refers to this city a number of times. Hutten asked his brother to give special greetings to Daniel Stibar and, similarly, to all his good comrades at the Würzburg Court. [...] Philipp von Hutten himself had been born in Arnstein, about twenty kilometres north of Würzburg. Würzburg was, consequently, a place that Hutten had visited on numerous occasions, and Daniel Stibar was a mediator to his acquaintances there. Since it is known from a letter of Camerarius that Faustus was a good friend of Stibar's, it is reasonable to conclude that the latter was responsible for soliciting the help of Faustus in this matter." *Doctor Faustus, from History to Legend*, pp. 59, 60.

[189] 'Faustus: His Life and Legend'.

opinion. We noted earlier Ellenbog was not appreciative of Magister Georgius Helmstetter's practise of conflating various forms of divination with astrology.

While Camerarius was occupied with his future hopes of success for von Hutten and his publication of *Erratum* (1535), there is no evidence to suggest Faustus was overly concerned at that time with this venture — alternatively, he decided to direct his prophetic energies towards other important events shaking the political spheres.

Discovering the locations Faustus journeyed to during the remainder of his life following his rejection at Nuremberg is a difficult process, for the letters of Camerarius and Philip von Hutten do not disclose this information. In addition, later sources become increasingly suspect due to the juxtaposition of facts with sensational fiction drawn from legends of previous magicians, including imaginative embellishments invented for entertainment or errors that resulted from misquotation. However, one final document exists, the Waldeck Chronicle, that provides us with a definite location Faustus travelled to in 1535:

From the *Waldeck Chronicle*

"Francis I. By the grace of God, son of Philip II [Count of Waldeck], by his second marriage, Bishop of Münster, on June 25, 1535, invested and captured the city of Münster, which had been occupied by the Anabaptists, and with the aid of princes of the Empire, under the leadership of Hensel Hochstraten, expunged the farcical [*farcinatore*] John of Leyden, who called himself King of Israel and Zion, together with his leading supporters Knipperdollinck and Krechting, their bodies being lacerated with white-hot (glistening) pincers [*forcipibus*], enclosed in iron cages and suspended from the tower of St. Lambert's Church on the 23rd of January, 1536. It was at this time that the distinguished necromancer D. Faustus, diverted [*divertens*] early that day from Corbach, prophesied, before it was taken, that the city of Münster would be expunged by the bishop on that very night."[190]

According to this document, Faustus delivered a prophecy that pivoted upon the overthrow of the Anabaptists, a religious sect first established in Zurich during the 1520s by Konrad Grebel, Hans Denck, and Balthasar Hubmaier. Originally referred to as the Swiss Brethren, they believed in the supreme authority of the Bible, declaring that there was no basis laid down in scripture for infant baptism and therefore advocated adult baptism as the legitimate

---

[190] Text from *Sources of the Faust Tradition*, p. 91:
"Franciscvs I. Dei gratia, filius Philippi II. Ex secundo matrimonio natus, Episcopus Monasteriensis, qui anno 1535· 25 Jun. urbem Münster ab Anabaptistis occupatam, obsidione cinxit, & auxilio procerum imperii, ductore Henselino Hochstraten expugnauit, de Johanne de Leiden farcinatore, qui se Regem Israelis & Sionis nominabat, Knipperdillingio & Krechtio supplicia sumsit, quorum corpora candentibus igne forcipibus lacerata, & ferries inclusa caueis e turris St. Lamberti suspense sunt, 23 Han. An. 1536. quo tempore insignis ille Nigromanticus D. Faustus eo ipso dis Corbachii diuertens, praedixit, fore nimirum, vt eadem nocte vrbs Münster ab Episcopo expugnetur."

form of the sacrament. They also believed in re-administering this sacrament to adults previously baptised in their infancy, hence the origin of 'Anabaptist', signifying 'one who baptises again'. The Anabaptists did not recognise the Holy Mass as a re-enactment of Christ's sacrifice on Calvary, but worshiped at a memorial of the Lord's Supper. The sect also rejected the hierarchy of the Church and the authority of civil government in religious matters. They refused to take oaths, and many chose to renounce the world, advocating the abolition of the right to own private property. However, the most controversial practise adopted was polygamy. Denounced and persecuted as heretics by both Catholic and Protestant leaders, the Anabaptists were banished from Zurich, and the movement dispersed to the Netherlands, Germany, and Central Europe. In 1529, the council of Speyer declared the practise of anabaptism a capital offence throughout the Empire.

Upon the expulsion of the Dutch Anabaptists and their leader Jan Matthijs from Amsterdam in 1534, the sect relocated to northern Germany. This particular branch, supporters of chiliasm, believed the time was fast approaching when Christ would establish His Kingdom on earth for one thousand years. In preparation for His coming, the Anabaptists preached on the destruction of the godless and conducted an armed procession through the streets of Amsterdam. Following their expulsion, they fled to Westphalia and were welcomed in the city of Münster, and consequently perceived this city to be the divinely chosen site for the establishment of Christ's kingdom. The Mayor, Knipperdolling, and his chancellor, Krechting, converted to this sect and were re-baptised. In addition, Jan van Leyden (Leiden), the Anabaptist 'prophet' also known as Jan Beuckelzoon, was elected 'King of Zion' by the collective, and they entrusted him with the task of establishing the "New Jerusalem" at Münster. He was enthroned with great ostentation in contrast to the prescribed lifestyle of humble simplicity dictated by their beliefs. They drafted a new constitution, established laws legalising polygamy, and abolished a monetary economy and the right to own private property. However, their kingdom heralding the New Millennium did not survive one year—the city fell to the Bishop and his Imperial allies, and consequently, the three self-proclaimed religiocrats of Münster were tortured and executed as heretics.

Surprisingly, this chronicle received little attention in the early research conducted on the historical aspect of the Faust legend. Baron did not include it in his selection of consistent Faustus documents, nor did he explain its omission from his important study. Therefore, the question remains, should we regard this extract as suspect, or possibly a reliable piece of evidence?

Philip Palmer and Robert More do not supply detailed information on the nature of this account, their source for the text is the *Jahrbuch der Sammlung Kippenberg*, I (1921), a document with a chronological difference of nearly four centuries from the date Münster was recaptured. However, there is no evidence in the context of the account to suggest it had been fabricated. According to the text, Francis I von Waldeck (1491–1553), Bishop of Münster and son of Count Philip II of Waldeck, was either the author of the original document or personally responsible for its commission. When the event was actually transcribed remains an enigma; however, a single word within the narrative, *farcinatore,* displays it was composed circa the middle to the latter half of the sixteenth century.[+] *Farcinatore,* obviously an attempt to fashion a

---

[+] According to the New Oxford Dictionary of English, (Oxford University Press, 2001 edition).

Latin derivative from the early sixteenth-century French *farce,* i.e. a comic dramatisation featuring slapstick buffoonery. This French word was adapted from the Latin *farcire* "to stuff", a metaphor to denote the vulgar integration of comic interludes with religious dramas. In addition, the tone of the text is factual and Spartan in its description, including the barbaric demise of the Anabaptist leaders, with the exception of the two descriptive words "farcinatore" (farcical) and "insignis" (distinguished), the account is undeniably objective in its narration, and therefore, let us assume this particular document originated as a historical account.

Commencing with the premise it originated as an official record, it contains one peculiar anomaly for it is evident the concluding section recounting the activities of Faustus is a later addition. The genealogy and title of Francis I is announced formally in the first sentence; "[…] *filius Philippi II* […] *Episcopus Monasteriensis,*" a tone that continues throughout the narrative, yet the final sentence reads as an unofficial, parenthetical observation, "[…] Faustus predicted […] the city of Münster would be expunged by the bishop on that very night". If Francis had completed or endorsed this document personally, it is logical to assume the tense would have remained constant. The last sentence reads as a later observation appended by a second party relating information that they considered relevant to the original account sanctioned by the bishop. However, this does not detract from the historical value of the chronicle — one could assume the anonymous editor would not alter a valuable document unless they felt secure in their conviction this new information was factual. There are also several consistencies with previous documents considered reliable: although his first name "George" is not recorded, Faustus is referred to as "Doctor", he is recognised particularly as a practitioner of necromancy, and his surname is spelled in its Latin form.

According to this source, Faustus departed Corbach° early on June 25, 1535, and arrived in Waldeck on the same day. Did Faustus attempt to formulate a prophecy that would attract a patron from the court of Waldeck? Obviously, the court would pay attention to an auspication proclaiming the recapture of Münster by Bishop Francis I. On this occasion his prophecy impressed an official in Waldeck, for we may presume only employees entrusted with the record-keeping or notary duties of the principality would have access to the chronicle commissioned by Francis I and the opportunity to make additions. Here we observe the reputation of the soothsayer as a "Nigromanticus" did not deter the editor from recognising him as a "distinguished" individual. In addition, this document once again demonstrates Faustus was not ignorant of the political events and current affairs that shaped his world, and may have used this information to his advantage. This prediction, which forecasted the overthrow of a sect considered dangerous to Christian faith, morals and civil authority, could falsely infer his support of the established political order and a belief in traditional values. We have discussed the previous difficulties he encountered with the constant accusations that questioned his morality and occupation. In the past, Faustus would either portray the academic side of his character, or allude to a religious association to suit the current political climate or the conservative mentality of an area to escape persecution. On this occasion at Waldeck, the siege of Münster presented Faustus with a further opportunity to render past accusations suspect and fortify his façade as a respectable subject of the Empire by supporting the conservatives.

° A town circa 80 miles / 128 km. southeast of Münster.

Notwithstanding this excursion to Corbach and Waldeck, Faustus could not escape the competitive scrutiny of Camerarius, who by that time had moved to the town of Tübingen in 1535 when he was requested to aid in the reformation of the local university.[191] Still obsessed with the predictions that ensued from the von Hutten expedition in 1534, Camerarius warned his friend Stibar in a letter dated May 18, 1536, not to become embroiled with charlatans who claimed to wield prophetic powers. While Camerarius did not name any individual whom he considered culpable of this deceit, it is possible he intended to insinuate his suspicion of Stibar's close acquaintance — Faustus:

> "Don't think that one should accept any divinations of astrologers or soothsayers with greater faith than those of men who discovered the essence of prophecy, not steeped in some kind of superstition, but endowed with a certain instinct and divine power."[192]

In this same letter, he brought to Stibar's attention the forms of divination he considered more acceptable, i.e. *sorts,* or passages drawn from the texts of Homer and Virgil at pages opened at random, and gave examples of his own predictions regarding Emperor Charles V. Finally, in his conclusion to Stibar, Camerarus' writes:

> "These things, my Daniel, you will hopefully share with our [Moritz von] Hutten, whose brother Philip, a youth destined for fame, having returned from the Indian expedition, we perceive to be leading a number of troops to the Emperor. For his most praiseworthy undertakings we prayed to insure a favourable turn of fortune. This he had indeed achieved with such brave and great spirit beyond his age that in this matter the very inconstant goddess appears to be steadfast. For whatever happens, I desire and prophesy an entirely propitious outcome."[193]

We can appreciate Camerarius' concern regarding his predictions of von Hutton's new venture in Venezuela when we take into account his great devotion to the Emperor. Baron states:

> "This enthusiastic dedication to the cause of Charles V comes to light in many writings of Camerarius during this decade, and his letter to Stibar [May 18, 1536] treats this theme at length. The devotion to the Emperor went hand in hand with a great interest in interpreting the astrological signs that had bearing on his future. [...] A prediction about the success of the Hutten expedition, which was to add to the glory of the Emperor, follows directly upon the discussion of prophecies concerning

---

[191] *Sources of the Faust Tradition,* n. 32, p. 92.
[192] Joachim Camerarius, *Commentarius captae urbis ductore Carlo Borbonio* (Basel: J. Herwagen, 1536), p. 4, in *Doctor Faustus, from History to Legend, p. 57.*
[193] Camerarius, *Commentarius,* p. 5, in *Doctor Faustus, from History to Legend,* pp. 58–59.

Charles V. In Camerarius' eyes the stars and fortunes of Hutten and Charles V were closely linked."[194]

Hence, we deduce this competition was a matter of personal pride to Camerarius, rising to the challenge, he became obsessed with his mission to ultimately prove Faustus a mountebank, particularly for the benefit of his friend Stibar captivated by this hoaxer, thus explaining Camerarius' growing anxiety to promote his own predictions.

While Camerarius and his associates were compelled to await the arrival of news from the New World, an important event became the focus of attention, the outbreak of war between Charles V and Francis I, King of France. In July of 1536, Charles V invaded Provence, and eventually laid siege to the city of Marseilles. Baron observed that Camerarius' "[...] involvement [with the Emperor's political future] became particularly intense in 1536 when another great confrontation between Charles V and Francis I appeared imminent [...]".[195] Maintaining his staunch support of Charles V, three months later on August 13, 1536, Camerarius expounded upon his letter of May to Stibar. In this new correspondence, Camerarius announced he intended to dedicate his new book to him, *Commentarius captae urbis ductore Carlo Borbonio* (1536) that included his previous letter of May in the preface, three poems extolling the past military glories achieved by the Emperor, and his prognostication of von Hutten's expedition.[196] In his letter of August, Camerarus also declared:

> "When the moon stood in Pisces in opposition to Mars, on August 4, I endured a very difficult night. Your Faustus is responsible for the fact I discuss these matters with you. I wish he had taught you something more about this art, rather than inflating you with the wind of most fruitless superstition or holding you in suspense with I don't know what kind of tricks. But pray, what does he tell us at last? And what new things? I know you have diligently inquired about everything. Is the Emperor not going to be victorious? That is, in fact, what will have to happen. Tübingen, the 13th August, 1536."[197]

According to his letter to Stibar (August 13), Camerarius was concerned with the conjunction of the moon, a sphere associated with matters of health, and Mars, the planet named for the Roman mythical god of war and therefore a messenger of ill omen. Obviously, this astrological phenomenon signified that an event of momentous proportion was about to occur. In

---

[194] *Doctor Faustus, from History to Legend*, p. 57.

[195] Ibid. p. 61.

[196] Ibid. pp. 56, 60.

[197] Baron's footnote, n. 54, p. 105: "Prid. Non. noctem moestissimam sustinui cum Luna Marti objiceretur in Piscibus. Faustus enim tuus facit, ut tecum lubeat ista disserere, qui utinam docuerit te potius aliquid ex hac arte, quam inflaverit ventulo vanissimae superstitionis, aut nescio quibus praestigiss suspensum tenuerit. Sed quid ille ait nobis tandam? Quid etiam? Scio enim te diligenter de omnibus percontatum. Caesar ne vincit? Ita quidem fieri necesse est." Camerarius, *Libellus novus* (Leipzig: H. Rambau, 1568), fol. X"
See also Palmer and More's translation in *Sources of the Faust Tradition*, p. 92.

the concluding sentences, we promptly discover the main topic that truly preoccupied Camerarius —the tumult of the battle: "Is the Emperor not going to be victorious?" This preoccupation also influenced his other correspondences, for on the same day he wrote to Stibar, August 13, he penned the following letter to his friend, Eoban Hesse:

> "The news about the French war holds everyone in suspense. It will undoubtedly cause a great and unforeseen revolutionary change. But this 'I do not say in prophecy, but judging from the state of things,' as the Tiresias of Euripides says, so that you won't ridicule me as an astrologer, as you are accustomed to doing."[198]

While Camerarius was reluctant to disclose his opinions to Eoban Hesse, formed from any astrological observations, in his letter to Stibar he revealed that he was confident with his prediction of a victorious outcome.

However, his over-confidence did not deter him from the temptation to coerce his friend Stibar into divulging any details he obtained concerning Faustus' latest predictions, for Camerarius was anxious to learn what Faustus would finally proclaim. Baron therefore suggested Camerarius was prepared to match a second prognostication with one drawn by his rival concerning the threat of war with the King of France.[199] From this confident prediction, we detect Camerarius suspected Faustus would contradict his calculations, and he endeavoured to convince Stibar not to rely on the pronouncements made by Faustus. Obviously, Camerarius' words demonstrate that he did not change his negative opinion of Faustus; in fact, this letter emphasises the cynicism in which he held his rival. He conveys that Faustus was not completely ignorant in the skills of prognostication, e.g. "I wish he had taught you something *more* about *this art*", yet infers Faustus often obscured his knowledge with an entertaining smokescreen e.g. "[…] rather than inflating you with the wind of most fruitless superstition or holding you in suspense with I don't know what kind of tricks". Hence, Camerarius recognised, in the illusive Faustus, a magician with the talent to charm his patrons with small and almost insignificant plums of information gilded with vague promises and preternatural intrigue.

We suspect Camerarius did not reveal the full extent of his apprehensions in his letters concerning Stibar's close association with the diviner. To avoid incurring Stibar's indignation by directly opposing a man he admired, Camerarius resolved not to openly address more serious issues occurring at that time and hoped to dissuade Stibar from associating with Faustus by concentrating diplomatically on his rival's horoscopes. In the 1530s, the notorious reputation Faustus originally spawned with the launching of his professional career received new impetus through two sources: the conversations of Martin Luther with his close circle of acquaintances, and the posthumous publication of Trithemius' letter of 1507 in *Epistolarum familiarum libri duo* (Hagenau 1536). Through Luther's discussions we glean more information concerning his theological struggles and spiritual confrontations with the devil, and we also discover his

---

[198] Camerarius, *Epistolarum libri quinque posteriors* (Frankfurt: P. Fischer, 1595) VI. p. 394, in ibid., p. 62.

[199] *Doctor Faustus, from History to Legend*, p. 61.

opposition to magicians. Nicolaus Medler recorded one conversation held sometime between October 24, 1533 and September 14, 1535:

> "When one evening at the table a certain magician named Faustus was mentioned Doctor (Luther) said seriously: 'The devil does not make use of the services of magicians against me, but if he had been able to harm me, he would have done it long ago. To be sure, he had me by the head, but he had to let me go. Yes, I have dealt with him, and at times, when he came with the Bible, he fixed it so that I hardly knew whether I was dead or alive; he made me despair so that I didn't know whether there was a God, and he almost made me lose hope in God. In sum, there is no true refuge except directly in God himself; he can help you; for this just a single word is needed ...'."[200]

Evidently, Faustus implied a diabolical association with his calling cards as early as 1507, (which Trithemius immediately recognised), yet it is here for the first time we see his alliance with the devil discussed openly and not obscured by theological inference. In his mission to proclaim the 'new-found' Gospel in preparation for the Last Days, it would not be characteristic for Luther to side-step an opportunity to reveal the snares of the devil and those whom he believed were directly under his influence and subject to him as his disciples. Following this particular dialogue, the letter that Trithemius wrote condemning Faustus was published in the aforementioned *Epistolarum* (1536). Henry Jones relates: "The collection would have been widely read, especially in Würzburg, Trithemius' last domicile, and there was no possible redress."[201] Hence, the vague rumours circulating for several years regarding Faustus' allegiance with the devil are confirmed in print! His reputation remained as black as ever. Subsequently, Antonius Lauterbach recorded the following conversation with Luther that occurred sometime between June 18, and July 28, 1537:

> "Mention was made of conjurers and the art of magic and how Satan blinded men. Much was said about Faustus, who called the devil his brother in law, and the remark was made: 'If I, Martin Luther, had given him even my hand, he would have destroyed me, but I would not have been afraid of him; I would have given him my hand in the name of the Lord, with God as my protector. For I believe many magic tricks have been attempted against me.'"[202]

---

[200] Martin Luther, *Tischreden* #1059 (Weimar: Böhlau, 1912–21), in *Doctor Faustus, from History to Legend*, p. 78. This extract was first printed in the 1566 Aurifaber edition of the *Tischreden*.
[201] William Empson, John Henry Jones (ed.), *Faustus and the Censor: The English Faust-book and Marlowe's* Doctor Faustus, (Oxford: Basil Blackwell Ltd., 1987), p. 7.
[202] Luther Tischreden #3601, in *Doctor Faustus, from History to Legend*, p. 78. This extract first published in 1903 by E. Kroker *in Luthers Tischreden in der Mathesischen Sammlung*, (Leipzig).

In this extract, we discover one particular rumour that would seal Faustus and his reputation as one of Satan's minions forever — his alleged claim to be the devil's brother-in-law. We do not know with absolute certainty at this point if this is factual. However, as this report originated during his lifetime, we cannot dismiss the possibility he actually initiated this anecdote declaring his unholy union with the Prince of Darkness. We also observe that if Faustus had openly declared he was the brother-in-law of the devil *at this point in time*, this would infer he was not refuting Trithemius' letter in the least, he was confirming the contents without a moment's hesitation! Was he finally revealing his true colours? The term 'brother-in-law', an expression of endearment between close acquaintances often used in Medieval Germany, becomes perverted as Faustus allegedly employed this phrase to declare his friendship with Hell. However, if this rumour was interpreted literally, this expression contained further sinister implications that would inflate his notoriety, if Faustus was the devil's brother-in-law, what diabolical marriage ceremony took place? Did this indicate a union with a *succubus*, the female counterpart of the male *incubus*, demons that according to legend seduced mankind, or did this signify his whole-hearted devotion to witchcraft and sorcery? What manner of 'marital certificate' was signed as proof of this union? Hence, we may also conclude this is the first document alluding to a signed contract with the devil. Trithemius believed that a signed compact was necessary before the powers of necromancy would be granted, but he did not explicitly declare a connection in this regard with Faustus as he left this possibility open, allowing the recipient of his letter to draw his own conclusion. This extract from Luther's *Tishreden* is the first document that infers this contract with Hell. Similar to Trithemius, Luther also believed that the acquisition of extra-ordinary powers from evil sources required the forfeiture of the immortal soul, the *Tischreden* and his other writings contain several accounts of magicians whom he believed received preternatural gifts from the devil upon an agreement to relinquish their soul and abandon their Christian beliefs.

Obviously, these rumours and Trithemius' letter were major topics discussed by Luther's contemporaries. For example, we discover that Melanchthon, Luther's closest acquaintance, was not immune to the gossip Faustus was in league with the devil as his lecture notes display. It is possible the Protestant Camerarius was aware of these events and rumours, for Melanchthon was also his close friend. Hence, we comprehend his anxiety to warn his friend Stibar not to place his faith in astrologers who became steeped in occult mysticism, as stated in his earlier letter of May 1536. He advised his friend to consider those who were divinely gifted, thus explaining his impatience to prove his 'legitimate' forms of prognostication.

Camerarius, however, would be humbled by the accuracy of the predictions calculated by his notorious rival when the siege of Marseilles failed. Charles V retreated and finally abandoned the effort, in 1538, the war came to an end with the signing of the Treaty of Nice. There still remained the outcome of the von Hutten expedition to look forward to, their competition persisted!

At last, Philip von Hutten sent his report to his brother two years later in 1540. Describing his fruitless adventure in detail, Philip also wrote:

> "Here you have a little about all the provinces so that you may
> see that we are not the only ones who have been unfortunate in Venezuela
> up to this time; that all the abovementioned expeditions which left Sevilla

before and after us perished within three months. Therefore I must confess that the philosopher Faustus hit the nail on the head, for we struck a very bad year. But God be praised, things went better for us than for any of the others. God willing I shall write you again before we leave here. Take good care of our dear old mother. Give my greetings to all our neighbours and friends, especially Balthasar Rabensteiner and George von Libra, William von Hessberg and all my good comrades. Pay my respects to Herr N. of Thüngen, my master's brother. Done in Coro in the Province of Venezuela on January 16th, 1540."[203]

Philip's misfortune would not end there. In 1541, he would leave Coro and spend six more years exploring as far as the Omagua region until 1546 seeking the fabled golden city of El Dorado without success. He finally met his demise at the hands of a Spaniard when he became embroiled in a pugilistic conflict that erupted between competing explorers.

Faustus, Death and the Devil

The "philosopher" Faustus proved once more he was the undisputed master of astrological prognostication when news arrived regarding the von Hutten expedition. Fate decreed, however, he would not live to see this new success. As early as 1539, the historical / legendary documents of Faustus begin to appear in the past tense. The first of these documents is the *Index Sanitatis* (1539) by Philipp Begardi, a physician who practised in the city of Worms. Having acquired twenty years of experience in the medical field, he wrote the *Index* in an effort to expose the abuses practised by his contemporaries in the profession.[204] In one particular chapter, where we discover his description of Faustus, Begardi also denounced those whom he considered "undesirable doctors":[205]

> "There is another well-known and important man whom I would not have mentioned were it not for the fact that he himself had no desire to remain in obscurity and unknown. For some years ago he travelled through almost all countries, principalities and kingdoms, and himself made his name known to everybody and bragged much about his great skill not only in medicine but also in chiromancy, nigromancy, physiognomy, crystal gazing, and similar arts. And he not only bragged but confessed and signed himself as a famous experienced master. He himself avowed and did not deny that he was called Faustus and in addition signed himself "The philosopher of philosophers." The number of those who complained to me they were cheated by him was very great.

---

[203] *Sources of the Faust Tradition*, pp. 95–96.
[204] *Doctor Faustus, from History to Legend*, p. 68.
[205] Ibid.

Now his promises were great, like those of Thessalus; likewise his fame as that of Theophrastus. But his deeds, as I hear, were very petty and fraudulent. But in taking or—to speak more accurately—in receiving money he was not slow. And afterwards also, on his departure, as I have been informed, he left many to whistle for their money. But what is to be done about it? What's gone is gone. I will drop the subject here. Anything further is your affair."[206]

Baron observes Begardi did not encounter Faustus personally and only received second-hand reports of his activities,[207] yet his information appears convincing. For example, his description of Faustus relating his conceits and wandering lifestyle is consistent with early historical documents. Of particular interest is the attention Begardi pays to the custom Faustus adopted in "signing himself" an experienced practitioner in the occult arts and a philosopher. As discussed, Faustus printed personal calling cards he may have used solely for his debut in the Heidelberg area that featured a detailed list of these skills. The city of Worms, where Begardi resided, is located close to Heidelberg and Kreuznach, the vicinity in which Faustus first embarked upon his career. It is possible the infamy of these cards survived in the area for many years after Faustus had distributed them.

We also discover new information revealing that Faustus claimed to be a skilled physician, this is the first document alluding to this additional occupation. According to the reports Begardi received, he judged Faustus to be an impostor in the profession, criticising him as a counterpart of Thessalus and Paracelsus. Thessalus, a Greek physician who lived during the reign of Nero, considered himself superior to his predecessors with the exception of Galen. Paracelsus was a contemporary of Faustus whose controversial theories regarding the origin and treatment of disease, in addition to his tendency to dabble in magic, earned him the reputation of a charlatan. It is difficult to determine from this criticism if Faustus presented himself sensationally as a 'spiritual / occult' healer, or if he experienced additional difficulties during his later years due to the opposition unleashed by Luther and his close acquaintances. The latter would imply Faustus conveniently assumed the aspect of a respectable career that publicly distanced him from the ominous realm of occultism. Begardi, however, maintained the opinion Faustus was simply interested in filling his coffer box.

Begardi's extract refers to Faustus in the past tense, and may be regarded as an important guideline in determining the year of his death. As stated, the *Index Sanitatis,* was printed in 1539, Begardi dedicated this work to the mayor of Worms on January 8, of that year.[208] We may presume the overall compilation of this book entailed a greater duration of time than eight days, therefore Faustus may have died sometime in 1538. The translator of the 1592 Dutch version of the famous German 'Spies' *Faustbook* ventures to provide the specific month and date of his death, October 23, 1538,[209] although there is no evidence from surviving historical documents to support these details. From Begardi's document, we therefore have the year 1538 as a possibility

---

[206] *Sources of the Faust Tradition*, pp. 94–95.
[207] *Doctor Faustus, from History to Legend*, p. 69.
[208] Ibid.
[209] Alfred E. Richards, 'Some Faustus Notes,' *Modern Language Notes* 22 (February, 1907), p. 39.

in determining the time of Faustus' death, although the circumstances of his death are not mentioned.

The first document we encounter describing Faustus' death subsequent to Begardi's work is an extract from the second volume of Johannes Gast's *Sermones Convivales* (1548):

Concerning the Necromancer Fausto

He puts up at night at a certain very rich monastery, intending to spend the night there. A brother places before him some ordinary wine of indifferent quality and without flavor. Faustus requests that he draw from another cask a better wine which it was the custom to give to nobles. Then the brother said: "I do not have the keys, the prior is sleeping, and it is a sin to awaken him." Faustus said: "The keys are lying in that corner. Take them and open that cask on the left and give me a drink." The brother objected that he had no orders from the prior to place any other wine before guests. When Faustus heard this he became very angry and said: "In a short time you shall see marvels, you inhospitable brother." Burning with rage he left early in the morning without saying farewell and sent a certain raging devil who made a great stir in the monastery by day and by night and moved things about both in the church and in the cells of the monks, so that they could not get any rest, no matter what they did. Finally they deliberated whether they should leave the monastery or destroy it altogether. And so they wrote to the Count Palatine concerning the misfortune in which they were involved. He took the monastery under his own protection and ejected the monks to whom he furnishes supplies from year to year and uses what is left for himself. It is said that to this very day, if monks enter the monastery, such great disturbances arise that those who live there can have no peace. This the devil was able to bring to pass.

Another story about Fausto

At Basle I dined with him in the great college and he gave to the cook various kinds of birds to roast. I do not know where he bought them or who gave them to him, since there were none on sale at that time. Moreover I never saw any like them in our regions. He had with him a dog and a horse which I believe to have been demons and which were ready for any service. I was told that the dog at times assumed the form of a servant and served the food. However, the wretch was destined to come to a deplorable end, for he was strangled by the devil and his body on its bier kept turning face downwards eventhough it was five times turned on its back. God preserve us lest we become slaves of the devil.[210]

---

[210] Ibid. pp. 96–98.

Unfortunately, Gast's anecdotes are highly suspect as historical documents for his credibility is undermined by the humorous and diverting nature of this collection, and also his alarming editorial practises. Baron explains:

> "As the title indicates, it is a compilation of convivial discourses and stories, including jokes and witty sayings. [...] On the whole, Gast's expressed purpose was to entertain as well as to be useful raises the question whether historical truth was an important consideration in reporting particular incidents.
>
> Several passages in the *Sermones* correspond to material in Gast's diary. A comparison shows that Gast tended to expand and refine the original material for the sake of effect.[211] Often Gast's anecdotes can be shown to be based on third-hand information. Most critical, however, is Gast's questionable practise of telling anecdotes that he obviously derived from other sources in the first person.[212]"[213]

We also note a lack of *historical* detail concerning the place and time of death, although he describes the cause as strangulation by the devil. Hence, in the ten-year period following the presumed year of Faustus' death extracted from Begardi's account, (1538), we observe the onset of the legend formation process with the addition of didactic overtones. However, it is possible to extract information from these latter sources, and hopefully reconstruct the historical account of his death.

Ten of the latter documents in our timeline chart in Appendix One mention the death of Faustus, which we shall refer to as the 'Mortis Documents'. As we have observed, Gast, a Protestant clergyman at Basel, was the first to claim Faustus was strangled by the devil and his body returned to its grotesque position on its bier five times. Physically, this would be impossible with the onset of rigor mortis. This facet of the legend, without doubt, is drawn from sources influenced by Martin Luther who believed that the devil strangled his victims. In fact, Luther alluded to this personal belief in one of his comments referring to Faustus — a juxtaposition that may be more than a mere coincidence. Earlier we discovered Luther calmly declared that the devil did not resort to using sorcerers to oppose him and his mission to preach the 'rediscovered' Gospel: "To be sure he [the devil] has often had me by the head but he had to let me go again." Yet from a theological viewpoint, if the devil preternaturally twisted Faustus' remains, it is difficult to credit this occurring five times in succession — if charitable bystanders,

---

[211] Baron's footnote, n. 2, p. 108,: "Paul Burckhardt writes: 'Gewisse Stücke der Sermonen, die aus dem Tagebuch stamen, hat Gast für Buchausgabe zu epischer Breite erweitert und rhetorisch stilisiert.' Paul Burckhardt, "Die schriftstellerische Tätigkeit des Johannes Gast," *Basler Zeitschrift für Geschichte und Altertumskunde*, 42 (1943), 185. Cf. Paul Burckhardt, *Das Tagebuch des Johannes Gast* (Basel: Schwabe, 1945), p. 16."

[212] Baron's footnote, n. 3, ibid.: "Burckhardt, "Die schriftstellerische Tätigkeit," pp. 176–8; & Burckhardt, *Das Tagebuch*, pp. 50 & 94."

[213] *Doctor Faustus, from History to Legend*, pp. 71–72.

disregarding his sinful reputation, attempted to place his body in a position of respect twice or three times, it is unlikely they would have made a further fourth or fifth attempt. The first three occasions would clearly signify to the religious / conscientious person, or the superstitious, that he was a lost soul. It is probable they would be loathe to repeat this act of mercy a further fourth or fifth time, being compelled to dispose of him as quickly as possible in the customary manner reserved for a suicide, generally deemed a lost soul during those days, i.e. without a Church service nor a grave provided in consecrated ground.

We may therefore conclude that Gast's detail of Faustus turning five times on his bier was included for dramatic effect. Of the ten 'Mortis Documents' in our time-line, four other texts also record Faustus' head was turned, yet there is no indication of multiple occurrences. These four documents are Johannes Manlius' publication of quotes attributed to Melanchthon in the *Locorum Communium Collectanea* (1563), the fourth edition of Johannes Wier's *De Praestigiis Daemonum* (1568), the *Promptuarium Exemplorum* (1568) by Andreas Hondorff, and *the Operae Horarum Subcisivarum* (1591) by Philipp Camerarius.

Manlius' *Collectanea* is the second of these ten sources:

> "I knew a certain man by the name of Faustum from Kundling, [Knittlingen], which is a small town near my birthplace. When he was a student in Cracow he studied magic, for there was formerly much practise of the art in that city and in that place too there were public lectures on this art. He wandered about everywhere and talked of many mysterious things. When he wished to provide a spectacle at Venice he said he would fly to heaven. So the devil raised him up and them cast him down so that he was dashed to the ground and almost killed. However he did not die.
>
> A few years ago this same Johannes Faustus, on the day before his end, sat very downcast in a certain village in the Duchy of Württemburg. The host asked him why, contrary to his custom and habit, he was so downcast (he was otherwise a most shameful scoundrel who led a very wicked life, so that he was again and again nigh to being killed because of his dissolute habits). Then he said to the host in the village: "Don't be frightened tonight." In the middle of the night the house was shaken. When Faustus did not get up in the morning and when it was almost noon, the host and several others went into his bedroom and found him lying near the bed with his face turned toward his back. Thus the devil had killed him. While he was alive he had with him a dog which was the devil, just as the scoundrel who wrote "De vanitate atrium" likewise had a dog that ran about with him and was the devil. This same Faustus escaped in this town of Wittenberg when the good prince Duke John had given orders to arrest him. Likewise in Nuremberg he escaped. He was just beginning to dine when he became restless and immediately rose and paid the host what he owed. He has hardly got outside the gate when the bailiffs came and inquired about him.

The same magician Faustus, a vile beast and a sink of many devils, falsely boasted that all the victories which the emperor's armies have won in Italy had been gained by him through his magic. I mention this for the sake of the young that they may not readily give ear to such lying men."[214]

As previously discussed, Manlius' rendition of Melanchthon's lectures is also highly suspect as a historical text, for Manlius changed his source material to create an intriguing subject for his readers. In contrast to the early historical documents, this is the first account that called Faustus "Johannes", i.e. Johann or John, and changes the city of Helmstadt to Knittlingen as Faustus' place of origin. This is also the first document to claim Faustus studied at the University of Cracow where, verily, a degree in black magic was offered.

Nevertheless, we may glean some information from this version of Faustus' death. Manlius claims Faustus died in a village in the Duchy of Württemberg, although he fails to state the year of this event. According to the text, Faustus had a premonition of misfortune approaching and ambiguously forewarned his host not to be fearful that night. The house shook during the night, and approximately at noon the following day, Faustus is found close to his bed in a contorted position with his head turned backwards. Manlius marks the twisted head, an omen of a lost soul, and declares, "Thus the devil had killed him." However, this statement is semi-ambiguous, it could signify his conviction Satan personally came to claim Faustus in a physical form, or, his belief Faustus was eternally damned judging from the unnatural position of the corpse after death.

In the third of our ten 'Mortis Documents', the *Zimmerische Chronik* (1564–66) maintains this latter interpretation of Manlius' description. Written by Count Froben Christoph von Zimmern (d. 1566 or 1567) and his secretary, Hans Müller (d. circa 1600), this work relates the history of the Swabian noblemen, who became the counts of Zimmern.[215] This work presents a record of local folklore and popular legend. Of particular interest, the *Chronik* is the first detailed description of Faustus' death that approximately corresponds with the presumed year (1538):

> "That the practise of such art [soothsaying] is not only godless but in the highest degree dangerous is undeniable, for experience proves it and we know what happened to the notorious sorcerer Fausto. After he had practiced during his lifetime many marvels about which a special treatise could be written, he was finally killed at a ripe old age by the evil one in the seigniory of Staufen in Breisgau.
>
> (After 1539).† About this time also Faustus died in or not far from the town of Staufen in Breisgau. In his day he was as remarkable a sorcerer as could be found in German lands in our times. He had so many

---

[214] *Sources of the Faust Tradition,* pp. 101–103.

[215] Ibid. p. 103.

† According to Baron's source for this text, i.e. Palmer and More's *The Sources of the Faust Tradition* (1936), this date is recorded as "After 1541". However, the second printing of Palmer and More's work (1966) cites "After 1539". We may conclude this is a correction in the original print.

strange experiences at various times that he will not easily be forgotten for many years. He became an old man and, as it is said, died miserably. From all sorts of reports and conjectures many have thought that the evil one, whom in his lifetime he used to call his brother-in-law, had killed him. The books which he left behind fell into the hands of the Count of Staufen in whose territory he died. Afterwards many people tried to get these books and in doing so in my opinion were seeking a dangerous and unlucky treasure and gift. He sent a spirit into the monastery of the monks at Luxheim in the Vosges mountains which they could not get rid of for years and which bothered them tremendously, — and this for no other reason than that once upon a time they did not wish to put him up over night. For this reason he sent them the restless guest. In like manner, it is said, a similar spirit was summoned and attached to the former abbot of St. Diesenberg by an envious wandering scholar."[216]

Although the *Zimmerische Chronik* was completed nearly thirty years after the presumed year of Faustus' death, it portrays a unique quality of objectivity in its narration and contains significant details, particularly in the second paragraph of the extract, not generally observed in the preceding and subsequent historical documents. Apparently, one author wrote the first paragraph, while the second author appended additional information comprising the second, as these two paragraphs contrast in style and description. The first obviously contains didactic elements present in other Faustus documents, as with the typical warning to prospective readers regarding the diabolical art of soothsaying, and the horrific consequences one might expect when choosing this path as a vocation, i.e. a woeful death ordained by the devil. Alternatively, the second paragraph is more objective and records the correct spelling of 'Faustus'. The author of this particular section did not condemn Faustus, in fact he regarded him as a "remarkable" individual, denoting a certain degree of interest in him as an infamous celebrity. Significantly, this author observes that many *rumours* and *conjectures* declared Faustus was snatched away by the Evil One, a consequence of his habitual reference to the devil as his brother-in-law. Hence, we may consider the author of the second paragraph did not completely agree with the popular view that Faustus met his death by the claws of the devil *in person*, his death is described objectively as "miserable". The author also reports new information; certain books Faustus held in his possession, undoubtedly rumoured to contain the secrets to acquire occult power, became the property of the Count of Staufen. The author declared he knew of many individuals who were aware of this transfer of property and endeavoured to obtain these books for their own use.

Baron observes that "[…] it has not been possible to verify the death of Faustus in Staufen, nor has anyone succeeded in proving that Faustus had left behind a legacy of books,".[217] There are, nevertheless, a few theories that we may propose. If these two paragraphs in the *Chronik* were not written by a single author, but compiled as a joint effort by two collaborators, then there are *two* confirmations of Staufen as the place of death. Staufen is a village in the locality of Baden-Württemberg, hence, this corresponds with Manlius' account of "a Duchy in

---

[216] *Sources of the Faust Tradition*, pp. 103–105.
[217] *Doctor Faustus, from History to Legend*, p. 68.

Württemberg". In addition, there is a well-known local oral-account that survives today in the town of Staufen, (now employed as a promotional tool for tourism), explaining the lack of certain details in these documents, and also offers new information not recorded in sources that originated during and shortly after the time of Faustus.

A certain Dr. Lawrence F. Glatz published an English transcript of a film entitled "Staufen in Breisgau: the historical city of Faust" (c. 1999) that offers intriguing information on Faustus:

"[…] The tour guide Dieter Rainer tells of the founding of Staufen: 'We are now on the castle hill of Staufen. This castle, which we see here as a ruin, was built about 850. It was then given in the year 1111 as a gift to the Lords of Staufen by the Zähringer Dynasty. It is a very large castle complex. About 1000 people can be sheltered inside the courtyard. The castle itself was destroyed roughly about the middle of the Thirty Year's War, in 1634, because the Schwedes could not fill up their war chest, as no money was left in Staufen. So they simply put the castle to flames out of disappointment.'

One discovers here the medieval world, Staufen's earliest history. Staufen is located in the southwest corner of the Federal Republic, in the vicinity of the university city of Freiburg. This region is called Breisgau, and Staufen is its most beautiful jewel. The most famous of all of Staufen's inhabitants was however Dr. Johann Georg Faust, whose life became the basis for many works of literature and art. Because of his supposed magic powers and the legend of his pact with the devil, this figure of Faust — the scholar who died so horribly in Staufen — remains continually fascinating. The truth behind the legend of Faust was his unfulfilled promise to provide the impoverished Lord of Staufen with gold through alchemy. It was religion and not magic powers, however, which determined life in medieval times. Staufen was a catholic small town, which also had an important monastery for a long time. Unfortunately, almost all documents concerning Faust's time in Staufen burned in the flames of the Thirty Year's War. The history of the magician Dr. Faust was portrayed in popular folktales, published later as the famous chapbook 'History of Dr. Johann Faust' in 1587. Shortly before the Thirty Year's War, the male line of the Lords of Staufen was extinguished. […] The citizens of the town have made substantial efforts to renovate and preserve the buildings of their city. Good examples are the Lower Castle or City Castle, the residence of the Lord of Staufen in the city, the small hotel "The Crown," one of the oldest of Staufen's businesses, the "Hotel of the Lion," the building in which Staufen [Faustus?] allegedly met his demise, and the Town Hall, with the heraldic

crests of those noble families, cities and monarchies connected to Staufen.
[...]"[218]

Local tradition records the last activity of Faustus, peddling his skills as an alchemist to the Count of Staufen, who hoped to quickly regain his wealth by unorthodox methods. Tradition also maintains the location where Faustus supposedly died, the Hotel of the Lion, and explains why no written record of his sojourn in Staufen survives, i.e. due to the extensive damage caused by arson inflicted on the town during the Thirty Years War — this accounts for the lack of evidence regarding Faustus' legacy of occult books.

A second article written by Steenie Harvey (2002) also supports this local tradition:

"Devilish Deeds in Staufen"

Staufen, a Black Forest village famous for its connections with the real Dr. Faust. Full of perfectly maintained houses, it is set amongst vineyards and Faust performances are held in summertime up in its ruined castle.

I'd always thought that Faust, the doctor who sells his soul to Mephistopheles, was entirely a literary creation. Not so. Goethe was inspired by a real Dr. Faust who came to a nasty end in 1540 in the Black Forest village of Staufen.

This Faust was an alchemist, employed by the local Count to turn base metal into gold. He took up residence in Staufen's Gasthaus Lowen (Lion Inn) and it was there that he blew himself up in an experiment that went very badly wrong. Soon after that the rumor mill started.

A Franciscan monk testified that he'd seen Faust consorting with the devil in the form of a dog (obviously it can't have been a good idea in those days to say hello to a friendly hound in the street.) But long before Goethe published his story, a German chapbook from 1587 was doing the rounds. It was 'compiled and prepared as a horrible example and severe warning for all conceited, clever and godless people.' The title page proclaimed that this was the true 'Historia of Doktor Johann Faust, the widely acclaimed magician and black artist, how he pledged himself to the Devil...what strange adventures he saw...until he finally received his well deserved wages...' [...]"[219]

This source, with elements based on the local tradition of Staufen, also affirms Faustus resided at the Lion Inn and claims he died from an alchemy experiment that tragically went awry,

---

[218] Dr. Lawrence F. Glatz, Metropolitan State College. Website: http://www.lawrenceglatz.com/staufeneng.htm
[219] Steenie Harvey, "Devilish Deeds in Staufen" (2002). Website: http://www.internationalliving.com/postcards.cfm?pcard=2379

which is possible as many alchemists often became the victims of their own experiments, inhaling toxic mercurial fumes, not to mention their dabbling with various forms of hazardous nitrates. For example, potassium nitrate, or saltpetre, an ingredient in many alchemic experiments, was used to make gunpowder. A great explosion would account for the house shaking vigorously as Manlius reports and explains the contorted position of Faustus' body when it was discovered. This also corresponds with the second paragraph in the *Zimmerische Chronik* that states Faustus "died miserably". We are not surprised, therefore, that many of Faustus' contemporaries believed his unnatural death signified his eternal damnation, with the possibility the devil came and claimed him personally. To die suddenly without receiving the last rites of the Church, Catholic or Reformational, was recognised as a sinister omen for the deceased would have lost their final opportunity to repent and obtain salvation. Hence, we observe the origin of prayers asking for a happy and peaceful death. Oberman states physicians believed they could determine from the circumstances of a person's death those unfortunates who fell to the Inferno:

> "While simple believers imagined the Devil literally seizing his prey, the enlightened academic world was convinced that a descent into Hell could be diagnosed medically — as apoplexy and sudden cardiac arrest. Abruptly and without warning, the Devil would snip the thread of a life that had fallen to him, leaving the Church unable to render its last assistance."[220]

Undoubtedly, Gast and Manlius' reports contributed to the popular belief Faustus had sold his soul to the devil. Manlius in particular specified Faustus was aware of some tragic event with his downcast demeanour and his remark to the innkeeper, "Don't be frightened tonight", we may presume this element of Manlius' narration was responsible for generating the infamous deadline regarding Faustus' contract with the devil, i.e. twenty-four years, present in later literature. However, we may extract one further observation from these sources — could this remark indicate Faustus was preparing to commit suicide? In the *Zimmerische Chronik*, the two paragraphs state Faustus lived to be an old man, and one version of local tradition states Faustus was unable to fulfil his promise to produce gold through his skill as an alchemist. Having finally entered the twilight years after living the life of a charlatan for the most part, with no permanent abode or known family members surviving, faced with failure and his inability to fulfil his promise to the Count of Staufen, Manlius' account ultimately suggests Faustus had succumbed to a state of depression and was prepared to end his wretched existence by his own hand. An act of suicide, as stated earlier, also signified in those times, a soul already damned to Hell.

The five remaining 'Mortis Documents' that recount Faustus' death are a reiteration of those we have already examined. The following extract taken from the fourth edition (1568) of Johannes Wier's *De Praestigiis Daemonum* was obviously based on Manlius' account:

> "Johannes Faustus was born in a little town in Kundling and studied magic in Cracow, where it was formerly taught openly; and for a few years pervious to 1540 he practiced his art in various places in

---

[220] *Luther, Man between God and the Devil*, p. 3.

Germany with many lies and much fraud, to the marvel of many. There was nothing he could not do with his inane boasting and his promises. I will give one example of his art on the condition that the reader will first promise not to imitate him. This wretch, taken prisoner at Batenburg on the Maas, near the border of Geldern, while the Baron Hermann was away, was treated rather leniently by his chaplain, Dr. Johannes Dorstenius, because he promised the man, who was good but not shrewd, knowledge of many things and various arts. Hence he kept drawing him wine, by which Faustus was very much exhilarated, until the vessel was empty. When Faustus learned this, and the chaplain told him that he was going to Grave, that he might have his beard shaved, Faustus promised him another unusual art by which his beard might be removed without the use of a razor, if he would provide more wine. When this condition was accepted, he told him to rub his beard vigorously with arsenic, but without any mention of its preparation. When the salve had been applied, there followed such an inflammation that not only the hair but also the skin and the flesh were burned off. The chaplain himself told me of this piece of villainy more than once with much indignation. When another acquaintance of mine, whose beard was black and whose face was rather dark and showed signs of melancholy (for he was splenetic), approached Faustum, the latter exclaimed: 'I surely thought you were my brother-in-law and therefore I looked at your feet to see whether long curved claws projected from them": thus comparing him to the devil whom he thought to be entering and whom he used to call his brother-in-law. He was finally found dead near his bed in a certain town in the Duchy of Württemberg, with his face turned towards his back; and it is reported that during the middle of the night preceding, the house was shaken."[221]

In this account, Wier claimed to be acquainted with at least two people who personally encountered Faustus, therefore, it is curious that his information concerning Faustus' place of origin does not resemble the early historical documents, but rather the account inscribed by Manlius. In addition, the final sentence corresponds with Manlius' narration. This is not an indication, however, that the two anecdotes Wier recorded were fictitious, we shall examine this point later.

Wier (1515–1588), a Dutch physician, strongly opposed the prosecution of witches; his work, *De Praestigiis Daemonum* (1563) was intended to curb the spread of superstition.[222] The extract relating to Faustus was not included until the fourth edition. We may deduce from Wier's lenient attitude regarding those accused of practising witchcraft, he attempted to write a clear and objective account of Faustus from the information he acquired. Of particular interest is the sentence "For a few years previous to the year 1540", indicating he was personally aware Faustus had lived before this time. It is possible he did not know Faustus' origin nor the location of his

---

[221] *Sources of the Faust Tradition*, pp. 105–107.
[222] Ibid. p. 105.

death, researched the information to provide details for his readers, and unfortunately accepted Manlius' account in the *Collectanea* as a credible source.

Andreas Hondorff went further and paraphrased Manlius' narrative in his *Promptuarium Exmplorum* (1568) and included his own minor addition to the last words uttered by Faustus:

> "Such a necromancer was Johann Faustus, who practised many tricks through his black art. He had with him always a black dog, which was a devil. When he came to Wittenberg he would have been arrested by order of the Prince Elector, if he had not escaped. The same would have happened to him in Nuremberg also, where he likewise escaped. But this was his reward. When his time was up, he was in a tavern in a village of Württemberg. Upon the host asking him why he was so downcast, he replied, 'Do not be afraid to-night, if you hear a great banging and shaking of the house.' In the morning he was found lying dead in his room, with his neck twisted round."[223]

Presently we arrive at one of four rediscovered narratives of the Faust-legend penned by a Nuremberg teacher, Christoph Rosshirt (circa 1575). The fourth narrative corresponds with Manlius' rendition of Faustus' demise to a certain degree, yet it is apparent the legend-making process had further distorted historical accuracy:

> "[...] 4. On the evening before he is due to fulfil his pact with the devil, Faust [i.e. Faustus] arrives at a village inn and asks for a room for the night. In the tap-room there is a crowd of drunken, noisy peasants, who refuse to be quiet when Faust asks them. The magician bewitches them so that they remain sitting with their mouths wide open, and he is able to have his last meal in peace. He pays the bill, tips all the servants, and goes to bed, but is persuaded by the host to disenchant the drunken clowns. On the next morning, Faust is found dead in his bed."[224]

In contrast, the extract from the third edition of the *Christlich bedencken und erinnerung von Zauberey* (Speyer; 1597) by Augustin Lercheimer von Steinfelden (1522–1603), is a refreshing account in contrast to the previous documents as it was published as an *erratum* intended to rectify the contemporary misconceptions regarding the historical figure of Faustus following the publication of the *Spies Faustbook* (1587). At present, we shall examine the quotations that pertain to Faustus' place of origin and manner of death:

> "He was born in a little place called Knittlingen, situated in Württemberg near the border of the Palatinate. For a time he was

---

[223] Rose, *Damnable Life and Deserved Death of [...] Faustus*, p. 12.

[224] Synopsis by Rose in ibid. p. 33. Unfortunately, Rose did not mention if this manuscript described Faustus' manner of death, nor the details concerning the condition of his body. The manuscript was rediscovered by Wilhelm Meyer and edited by him in *Nürnberger Faustgeschichten* [Munich, 1895].

schoolmaster in Kreuznach under Franz von Sickingen: he had to flee from there because he was guilty of sodomy. After that he travelled about the country with his devil; studied the black art at the University of Cracow; [...] He was choked to death by the devil in a village in Württemberg, not Kimlich near Wittenberg, since there is no village by that name. For he was never allowed to return to Wittenberg after he had fled from there to avoid arrest. [...]"[225]

John A. Walz observes Lercheimer mentioned in the third edition of the *Christlich Bedencken* that Faustus had departed this earth sixty years prior to its publication. As this third edition was published in 1597, the date may be approximated to 1537–1538, supporting our previous deductions.[226] It is remarkable that Lercheimer, employed at the University of Heidelberg as professor of Greek from 1563 to 1579 and professor of mathematics from 1584 until his death,[227] was not familiar with Faustus' place of origin, Helmstadt — particularly when he had knowledge of the scandal that had occurred in Kreuznach. In this instance, it is obvious Manlius' account had considerably altered the perception of the historical Faustus by this time.

Wier's account also became a source for other documents. The subsequent 'Mortis Document' that relates the demise of Faustus in our list of historical sources is the *Operae Horarum Subcisivarum* (1591) written by Joachim Camerarius' son, Philipp Camerarius (1537–1624). In this work, Philipp unreservedly states his information originates from Wier's account:

> "[...] The same conjurer's tricks are ascribed to him as we have just related of the Bohemian magician.[+] Just as the lives of these magicians were similar, so each ended his life in a horrible manner. For Faustus, it is said, and this is told by Wier, was found in a village in the Duchy of Württemberg lying dead alongside his bed with his head twisted round. And in the middle of the preceding night the house was shaken. The other, as we mentioned a little while ago, was carried off by his master while he was still alive. These are the fitting rewards of an impious and criminal curiosity. [...]"[228]

As stated previously, Wier's account was influenced by Manlius' rendition to a certain degree although he refrains from stating Faustus' death was the result of diabolical intervention. However, Philip Camerarius ventures to draw attention to this association.

The penultimate source, an excerpt from *The Second Report of Doctor John Faustus* (anon. author, London: 1594), is curious as it refers to a local tradition relating Faustus' death occurred in the town of *Wittenberg*, a location far removed from Staufen:

---

[225] *Sources of the Faust Tradition*, pp. 119, 121.

[226] I have not been able to discover a direct quotation from the *Christlich Bedencken*. See n. 18 in John A. Walz, 'An English Faustsplitter,' *Modern Language Notes* XLII (June, 1927), p. 359.

[227] Ibid. p. 119.

[+] I.e Zyto.

[228] *Sources of the Faust Tradition*, pp. 123–124.

From *The Second Report of Doctor John Faustus*
(Quoted from Walz.)[229]

"*The Second Report* [...] even gives the Latin epitaph inscribed on the marble stone on Faust's grave 'at Mars Temple, as three miles beyond the Citty.' But the *Second Report* (p. 34) also quotes Wier's statement that Faust died in a village of the 'Duchy of Wittenberg,' [i.e. Württemberg][&] and Wier is to the author of the work a great authority."

Regrettably, Walz did not provide detailed information on this author nor his work. Apparently, the anonymous author declares Faustus was buried three miles beyond the city of Wittenberg at Mars Temple and printed in his *Second Report* the epitaph he saw on the alleged grave in that location. Yet, the anonymous author was seemingly unconvinced, for he also refers to Wier's account in his *Report*. We are fortunate that the final 'Mortis Document' may clarify this unresolved mystery: i.e., an excerpt from the *Itnerary* (1617) by Fynes Moryson:

"Besides, they shew a house wherein Doctor Faustus a famous conjurer dwelt. [I.e. in Wittenberg] They say that this Doctor lived there about the yeere 1500, and had a tree all blasted and burnt in the adjoyning Wood, where hee practised his Magick Art, and that he died, or rather was fetched by the Divell, in a Village neere the Towne. I did see the tree so burnt; but walking at leasure through all the Villages adjoining, I could never heare any memory of his end."[230]

Moryson matriculated at the University of Wittemberg in June 1591,[231] and resided there for several months. Apparently, during his free time he conducted his own research on this Faustian tradition, Moryson admits he was unsuccessful in establishing the truth of the Wittenberg claim that Faustus died in a village close to the town. Undoubtedly, the popularity of the *Faustbooks* caused this transfer of location from the Duchy of Württemberg to Wittenberg.[232]

---

[229] Walz, 'An English *Faustsplitter*,' *MLN*, pp. 355–356.

[&] According to *Sources of the Faust Tradition*, Wier describes the place as "Ducatus Vvirtenbergici". (*Sources*, p. 107). This was often mistaken for "Wittenberg" in early sources, but is identified today as "Württemberg". Also, Walz in 'An English *Faustsplitter*' may have misspelled "Wirtenberg" as he mentions Wier's information with the correct spelling of "Wirtenberg" on the following page of his article, (p. 356).

[230] Walz, 'An English *Faustsplitter*,' *MLN*, pp. 353–354.

[231] Ibid.

[232] This tradition continued to survive and was exploited in later years. Walz remarks:
"In recent years Bolte has discovered evidence of a local tradition about Faust's death in a village near Wittenberg. [...] The village referred to is Pratau on the Elbe. Neumann in his *Disquisitio historica de Fausto Praestigiatore*, Wittenberg, 1683, speaks of this tradition, but he believes that it originated during the Thirty Years War, [1618–1648] when the mayor of the town frightened off some marauding soldiers by showing them blood stains on the wall of a room and telling them that it was the room where

Our attention must therefore focus on the fact the author of the *Second Report* also considered Wier's document, (wherein Württemberg is named), a reliable authority on the subject of Faustus' demise. Hence, the credibility of Staufen / Württemburg as the true location of his death is not undermined.

In all, the majority of these texts recording the circumstances of Faustus' death can be traced to three in particular: Gast's *Sermones Convivales*, Manlius' *Collectanea*, and the *Zimmerische Chronik*. Combined with the date of publication / dedication of Begardi's *Index Sanitatis*, the approximation of sixty years subtracted from the publication date of Lercheimer's *Christlich Bedencken* (3rd. ed. 1597), and the local historical tradition perpetuated in the town of Staufen, there is substantial evidence to suggest Faustus had died there in 1538 purportedly by an explosion, which may have been set by Faustus in a suicide attempt. Whether his death was accidental or not, many of his contemporaries recognised the horrific circumstances as the definitive revelation of his allegiance with Satan. Today, it is possible for the daring visitor to stay where Faustus allegedly met his ghastly end in the medieval town of Staufen—room No. 5 at the Gasthaus zum Lowen.

Separating Historical Possibilities from Didactic Elements

As we discovered, the documents that originate after January 16, 1540, i.e. those succeeding Phillipp von Hutten's letter from Venezuela, become difficult to accept as historically accurate. Continuing our progress through these latter documents, we perceive the unavoidable influence Luther and his contemporaries exerted upon the burgeoning Faustian legend. The difficulty of analysing these records is compounded by the knowledge several of the authors adopted the practise of blending didactic or legendary material with additional information that may prove to be factual not previously disclosed in the early documents we have examined. For example, latter documents declare Faustus travelled to various countries, while records that originate during his lifetime demonstrate he resided in Germany for the greater part of his career, with the exception of one alleged journey through the region of Heilenstein, Styria. Is it possible to extract further information from these latter sources that may shed more light on Faustus and his life?

The most famous of these latter texts are the various *Faustbooks* that clearly demonstrate the legend rapidly eclipsed the historical Faustus. Henry Jones brought to our attention Helmut Häuser's discovery with respect to the mysterious "Dr. N. V. W." mentioned in the chapters that concentrate on Faust's dialogues describing the cosmos. (Spies [1587]: Chs. 29, 30, 31. English Orwin edition [1592]: Chs. 25, 26, 27.) Häuser identified the initials as that of Dr. Nicholas Winkler, city physician of Halberstadt, and posits Faustus may have visited this individual in 1521.[233] However, due to the mythical nature of the *Faustbooks* and the content of these

---

Faust came to his terrible end." ('An English *Faustsplitter*,' p. 356.)

[233] Helmut Häuser, ('Gibt es eine gemeinsame Quelle zum Faustbuch von 1587 und Goethe's Faust? Eine Studie über die Schriften des Arztes Dr. Nikolaus Winkler. 1973', cf. Gerd Wunder, *Nachwort* to

dialogues, we cannot assume these chapters are verbatim reports of their scientific discussions. For instance, these dialogues are first observed in the Wolfenbüttle manuscript (c. 1580–1587**), and contain material extracted from Schedel's *Elucidarius* while simultaneously promoting advanced scientific theories circa to the dating of the MS, namely a prototype of Tycho Brahe's hybrid Ptolemaic-Copernicus system (1588) of the cosmos.< Of note, the lost Latin precursor to the Wolfenbüttle MS circulated privately with the university elite, we may presume the original author of the Latin MS heard Faustus visited Dr. Winkler and embellished this information in his Latin text, and subsequently an anonymous author transcribed this narrative into the Wolfenbüttle MS.

We may surmise from this new discovery Faustus visited Halberstadt in 1521 as the guest of Dr. Nicholas Winkler. This event occurs approximately one year after his visit to Bamburg, and six to seven years before he travelled to Rebdorf in Bavaria. We could theorise Faustus was fraudulently practising medicine at this time, and perhaps it was through this field Dr. Nicholas made his acquaintance; however, the various *Faustbooks* also describe "Dr. N. V. W." as a competent astrologist, and his introduction to Faustus may have resulted from their common interest in this field. Hence, we may consider this theory inconclusive. Apart from discovering the identity of "Dr. N.V.W.", it is difficult to glean further information from the *Faustbooks*.

Returning to our analysis of the latter historical documents, in the second paragraph of the *Sermones Convivales* extract, the author Gast claims to have encountered Faustus on one occasion in the town of Basel Switzerland, where he resided. As we discovered, this may be a direct reproduction of an anecdote related by a third party, therefore, we cannot state with absolute certainty that Gast related the truth regarding Faustus' location. However, let us consider the first paragraph where Gast recounts an incident that occurred at a "rich monastery" when the brother refused to serve Faustus wine reserved for the nobles. This account parallels the *Zimmerische Chronik* where it is recorded the monks of "Luxheim" in the Vosges region refused Faustus quarters for the night. Could this be the famous monastery of Luxeuil (Luxeuil-les-Bains) established in the same locality by St. Columban? Founded in 585, Luxeuil was structured on St. Columban's Rule based upon Celtic monastic tradition that would be considered torturous by today's standards; however, by the end of the eighth century, the monastery was governed under the moderate Rule of St. Benedict. During the lifetime of Faustus, Luxeuil experienced a rapid decline in the strict application of this monastic rule with the institution of the commendatory abbots until 1634, hence we may deduce the rule of poverty was also relaxed, which would corroborate Gast's extract referring to a "rich monastery". In addition, Luxeuil is located circa 56 miles (90 km) from Basel, it is therefore conceivable Faustus may have travelled to Luxeuil and Basel in succession as these two locations are in close proximity. These two accounts, the *Sermones Convivales* and the more objective *Zimmerische Chronik*, substantiate this report to a certain degree.

---

facsimile ed. of Widman, 1978) in Henry Jones, The *English Faustbook*; A *Critical Edition based on the Text of 1592*, (Cambridge: Cambridge University Press, 1994), #1764, p. 227.
** The date of the Wolfenbüttle MS was previously estimated to be c. 1572–1587, however, recent research indicates the date could be within the 1580s, i.e. 1580–1587. See 'n. &' in Chapter 2 under 'The Faustian Texts and the Printing Press: The First Printed *Faustbook* (1587)'.
< See the relevant discussion in Chapter 2 under 'Faust, Astroseer and Cosmo Tourist'.

However, which is the most reliable account relating the details of his misadventure at the monastery? According to Gast, Faustus was refused the wine reserved for those of noble lineage. This anecdote has a basis in historical fact, many monasteries of Europe produced their own wine and other alcoholic beverages for their personal use and to provide additional income; often the best produce was reserved for members of the privileged classes. It is possible Faustus demanded the choicest wine and was furious when he was refused contrary to the common law of hospitality. Yet, the conclusion of Gast's account becomes less convincing, i.e. the course of action the monks take when Faustus vacates the premises. According to theological logic, if a locality was demonically besieged, particularly with the manifestation of physical objects moving inexplicably by themselves, the natural recourse for a Catholic religious would be to recite the rite of exorcism. The scenario of the monks considering the destruction of the monastery as a solution to their spectral infestation is ludicrous. In addition, the monks' decision to write, not to the superior general of their order, but to the Elector of the Palatinate resulting with their alleged expulsion by the same, appears equally absurd in retrospect. However, the detail that Faustus assumed an air of aristocratic arrogance in the monastery, and the rumour the monks corresponded their complaint to the Royal house of the *Palatinate,* does not escape our attention. We detect the monks may have had good cause to write to the Elector if Faustus was indeed an illegitimate member of this aristocratic family according to our previous speculations. The monks were possibly aware of Faustus' unacknowledged status, wrote to the Elector in an effort to compel the family to take responsibility for their relative's outrageous conduct, and thereby enforce upon him some form of discipline for his actions. The Elector, obviously, would not be pleased with this censure, and possibly used his secular authority to reprimand the monks for accusing him of neglecting his duties and daring to call him to task. Hence, Gast, or those who originally related this anecdote, may have altered this version of events to reflect the Protestant takeover of several monasteries during the Reformation.

Turning to the *Zimmerische Chronik,* this source states the monks refused Faustus lodgings for the night, an unusual course of action notwithstanding his evil reputation. From Medieval times, monasteries were noted locations of hospitality and merciful refuge — a thief or rogue whose crimes were as scarlet could cry out for sanctuary and would not be turned away. If he or she was pursued by officers appointed to arrest them, there was a clear understanding that when the culprit wished to leave, they would be permitted a head start before the pursuit could continue. However, this does not detract from the credibility of the *Chronik.* To be refused shelter in this manner would certainly justify an angry outburst from Faustus, thus precipitating his curse upon the monastery. It would also indicate how nefarious his reputation had become as the monks elected to break the sacrosanct custom of sanctuary, afraid to risk having him darken their threshold.

In summary, we may conclude the *Zimmerische Chronik* and Gast's narration contain elements of truth. Arriving at the monastery of Luxeuil, Faustus may have demanded the inhabitants to wait upon him according to the traditional manner of hospitality afforded the aristocracy that he believed he was entitled to, and perhaps brandished his connection with the royal family of the Palatinate in this regard. In the process, he may have ruined all possibility of a hospitable reception by his boorish behaviour. Additionally, his reputation as an ardent minion of Satan setting him beyond the pale of an average criminal would not make him a welcome guest. Upon the refusal of lodgings for the night, Faustus may have uttered a malevolent oath directed at the premises that entailed the summoning of a malfeasant spirit in a bombastic display of outrage. The monks thereby decided to correspond with the Elector and demanded that he deal with Faustus accordingly, yet, they incurred the Elector's displeasure and became the recipients of his reprimands. However, this does not indicate they were expelled from their monastery. The more objective author of the *Chronik* did not include this questionable detail, nor the scenario that the monks deliberated razing their monastery to the ground as observed in Gast's account, the *Chronik* simply states the monks were plagued by a poltergeist for many years. The author obviously did not see any reason to refute this element as historical fact, for demonic haunting was not considered unusual. In accordance with theological reason, if God could manifest His presence with miraculous occurrences to inspire the hearts of the faithful, so also the devil with his preternatural powers to foment fear and torment the flock. Martin Luther unreservedly admitted he too experienced unwelcome visitations from the Prince of Darkness, thus reaffirming the reality of these supernatural occurrences:

> "It is not a unique, unheard-of thing for the Devil to thump about and haunt houses. In our monastery in Wittenberg I heard him distinctly. For when I began to lecture on the Book of Psalms and I was sitting in the refectory after we had sung matins, studying and writing my notes, the Devil came and thudded three times in the storage chamber [the area behind the stove] as if dragging a bushel away. Finally, as it did not want to stop, I collected my books and went to bed. I still regret to this hour that I did not sit him out, to discover what else the Devil wanted to do. I also heard him once over my chamber in the monastery. But when I realized it was Satan, I rolled over and went back to sleep again."[234]

Resuming our study of Gast's document recording Faustus' sojourn in Basel as our subsequent topic, Gast states Faustus dined one evening at the "great college", obviously referring to the university. Beyond this point, however, the story assumes the aspect of a proto-gothic thriller. Faustus purportedly brought a rare variety of fowl for supper, the origin of which remained a mystery for his host did not recognise the poultry as from that locality. Clearly, Faustus brought fresh birds as he would not have offered cured or salted meat to be *roasted*. It was the cook's task in that era to prepare the carcasses *completely* from scratch, the fowl would be presented with full plumage that required plucking, which would explain why his host did not recognise them as from that region. If the meat was not salted, how could Faustus have procured fresh game from a distant region unless aided by unseen forces? Theologians would argue demons can transport anything they wish, hence Faustus' contemporaries, well versed in theology, would not refute the probability of this occurrence. Yet, this feature, due to its theological possibility, could be an appended detail to render this account credible.

Continuing with the tale, Gast reports Faustus owned a horse and a dog in keeping with fashionable men of the world, information which may be true, yet once again, this tale reverts to the sinister. Gast, (or the original author of the narrative), believed that these seemingly innocent

---

[234] *D. Martin Luthers Werke: Kritische Gesamtausgabe, Tischreden* [Table Talk], (Weimar, 1912–21), vol. 6 no. 6832; 219, 30–40, in *Luther, Between God and the Devil*, p. 105.

animals were in reality demons who served Faustus. We also discover this element in Manlius' account where he records Melancthon's alleged comparison of Faustus with the notorious Cornelius Agrippa von Nettesheim (1486–1535), a Doctor of Divinity and a scholar of the occult: "While he [Faustus] was alive he had with him a dog which was the devil, just as the scoundrel who wrote "De vanitate atrium" likewise had a dog that ran about with him and was the devil."[235] In addition, the feature of the 'demonic horse' is also present in latter Faustus documents, as in the extract from the *Von Gespänsten* (1569) written by Ludwig Lavater (1527–1586), a Protestant preacher:

> "To this very day there are sorcerers who boast that they can saddle a horse on which they can in a short time make great journeys. The devil will give them all their reward in the long run. What wonders is the notorious sorcerer Faustus said to have done in our own times."[236]

That the devil assumed the forms of various creatures or physically possessed animals is an ancient tradition. We discover numerous reports from the Medieval period recounting the belief a sorcerer was often accompanied by a *familiar* spirit, a demon, who could assume the shape of an animal. Hence the widely accepted association of wizards and witches with nocturnal animals, for example, cats, owls, dogs, bats, etc., with creatures who wallow in their own filth or were considered vermin such as swine, rats, and flies, and those associated with death, crows and ravens. Luther also believed demons were permitted to wield this power.[237] Theologians did not disagree with this belief, according to the Gospel, Christ had allowed the devils to possess a heard of swine that drowned in the Sea of Galilee:

---

[235] Cornelius Agrippa studied at the University of Cologne where he read the cabala and the work of Proclus. Later he became a professor at the University of Dole where he wrote his famous work on the occult, *De Occulta Philosophia* (1510, extended in 1533). Agrippa's paradoxical *De incertitudine et vanitate scientiarum et atrium atque excellentia verbi dei declamatio*, (*De Vanitate*), was written in 1526, and printed in 1530. In this work, he attacked every human science and upheld the authority of the Bible. Near the end of his life, Agrippa rejected the occult and devoted his time to the study of theology. Many strange accounts were associated with Agrippa, one in particular features a foolhardy student who stole one of his spell-books. The student unwittingly summoned a demon, which strangled him. Upon this gruesome discovery, Agrippa supposedly forced the demon to revive the student for the time it would take to escort him to the town market where a freak collapse would provide an alibi for his death, which did not succeed. "The origins of Dr. John Faustus: Cornelius Agrippa"; http://www.hants.org.uk/ssa/faustus/agrippa.htm   For an in-depth discussion on Agrippa, these two works, and his connection with the Faust legend, see Charles G. Nauert, Jr. 'Magic and Scepticism in Agrippa's Thought,' *Journal of the History of Ideas*, *vol. 18*, (April, 1957), pp.161–182, and Michael H. Keefer, 'Agrippa's Dilemma: Hermetic "Rebirth" and the Ambivalences of *De vanitate* and *De occulta philosophia*,' *Renaissance Quarterly* Vol. 41, 4 (Winter, 1988), pp. 614–653.
[236] *Sources of the Faust Tradition*, p. 107.
[237] Luther, *Tischreden*, nos. 5358b and 6830 (Weimar: Böhlau, 1912-21), in *Doctor Faustus, from History to Legend*, p. 72.

"And they came over the strait of the sea into the country of the Gerasens. And as He went out of the ship, immediately there met him out of the monuments a man with an unclean spirit, who had made his dwelling in the tombs, and no man now could bind him, not even with chains. […] And seeing Jesus afar off, he ran and adored him. And crying with a loud voice, he said: What have I to do with thee, Jesus the Son of the most high God? I adjure thee by God that thou torment me not. For He said unto him: Go out of the man unclean spirit. And He asked him: What is thy name? And he saith to him: My name is Legion, for we are many. And he besought him much, that he would not drive him away out of the country. And there was there near the mountain a great heard of swine, feeding. And the spirit besought him, saying: Send us into the swine, that we may enter into them. And Jesus immediately gave them leave. And the unclean spirits going out entered into the swine: and the heard with great violence was carried headlong into the sea, being about two thousand, and were stifled in the sea." (Matt. 5: 1–3, 6–13)

From a theological perspective, there is, nevertheless, one element of Gast's version regarding these *familiars* that display the legend formation process, Satan or one of his minions cannot perform one act of servitude, an act contrary to the sin of pride, the cause of their fall from grace — "I will not serve!" A demon may agree to impart knowledge beyond human understanding or grant wealth and power, yet this constitutes an *exchange*. For a demon to assume the role of a servant notwithstanding the great prize of Faustus' immortal soul, is theologically incredible. It is a dramatic detail that was obviously derived from Medieval lore, and undoubtedly influenced subsequent authors of the latter Faustus documents.

Continuing our analysis of these latter sources, we encounter two extracts in the *Explicationes Melanchtoniae* (1594), a collection of Melanchthon's commentaries on sacred Scripture dating from 1549 to 1560[*] published by a former pupil, Christopher Pezelius:

XV. Pars II.

There [in the presence of Nero] Simon Magus tried to fly to heaven, but Peter prayed that he might fall. I believe that the Apostles had great struggles although not all are recorded. Faustus also tried this at Venice. But he was sorely dashed to the ground.

XVI. Pars IV.

The devil is a marvellous craftsman, for he is able by some device to accomplish things which are natural but which we do not understand. For he can do more than man. Thus many strange feats of

---

[*] Baron states from 1554 to 1557. *Doctor Faustus, from History to Legend*, p. 76.

magic are recounted such as I have related elsewhere concerning the girl at Bologna. In like manner Faustus the magician devoured at Vienna another magician who was discovered a few days later in a certain cave. The devil can perform many miracles; nevertheless the church has its own miracles.[238]

According to the first extract, Melanchthon asserted Faustus had attempted to fly while he was visiting the city of Venice. In the second extract, Faustus reportedly journeyed through Vienna and swallowed another magician, presumably during a magic performance. The possibility that Faustus visited these two cities exists, particularly as the Styria region of Hospitaler fame, which we have discussed earlier, is situated between them. However, the remainder of these two extracts begin to lose their credibility as historical documents beyond this observation.

In the first anecdote, Melanchthon compares Faustus with the legendary aspect of the infamous magician, Simon Magus. The original account of Simon Magus is recorded in Acts (8: 9–24) from whence came the term *simony*:

> "There was therefore great joy in that city. Now there was a certain man named Simon, who before had been a magician in that city, seducing the people of Samaria, giving out that he was some great one: To whom they all gave ear, from the least to the greatest, saying: This man is the power of God, which is called great. And they were attentive to him, because, for a long time, he had bewitched them with his magical practises. But when they had believed Philip preaching the kingdom of God, in the name of Jesus Christ, they were baptised, both men and women. Then Simon himself believed also; and being baptised, he adhered to Philip. And being astonished, wondered to see the signs and exceeding great miracles which were done. Now when the apostles, who were in Jerusalem, had heard that Samaria had received the word of God, they sent unto them Peter and John. Who, when they were come, prayed for them, that they might receive the Holy Ghost. For he was not yet come upon any of them; but they were only baptised in the name of the Lord Jesus. Then they laid their hands upon them, and they received the Holy Ghost. And when Simon saw, that by the imposition of the hands of the apostles, the Holy Ghost was given, he offered them money, Saying: Give me also this power, that on whomsoever I shall lay my hands, he may receive the Holy Ghost. But Peter said to him: Keep thy money to thyself, to perish with thee, because thou hast thought that the gift of God may be purchased with money. Thou hast no part nor lot in this matter. For thy heart is not right in the sight of God. Do penance therefore for this thy wickedness; and pray to God, that perhaps this thought of thy heart may be forgiven thee. For I see thou art in the gall of bitterness, and

---

[238] *Sources of the Faust Tradition*, pp. 99–100.

in the bonds of iniquity. Then Simon answering, said, Pray you for me to the Lord, that none of these things which you have spoken may come upon me."

The figure of Simon Magus grew to legendary proportions in early Church literature, particularly in the *Clementine Recognitions* and the *Clementine Homilies*, a fourth-century collection of spurious origin not written by St. Clement I, but ascribed to him to increase their credibility.[239] In the *Recognitions* and the *Homilies*, the journeys of St. Peter and St. Clement were refashioned to present a suitable setting for the discussion of various theological and ethical disputations — Simon is the antagonist.

In the *Recognitions* for example, Simon is characterised as a precursor to the Antichrist and reported to have possessed a myriad of diabolical magic powers:

Book II.

Chapter 7. "This Simon's father was Antonius, and his mother Rachel. By nation he is a Samaritan, from a village of the Gettones; by profession a magician, yet exceedingly well trained in Greek literature; desirous of glory, and boasting above all the human race, so that he wishes himself to be believed to be an exalted power, which is above God the Creator, and to be thought to be the Christ, and to be called the *Standing One*. And he uses this name as implying that he can never be dissolved, asserting that his flesh is so compacted by the power of his divinity, that it can endure to eternity. Hence, therefore, he is called the *Standing One*, as though he cannot fall by any corruption."

Chapter 9. "But not long after he fell in love with that woman whom they call Luna; and he confided all things to us as his friends; how he was a magician, and how he loved Luna, and how, being desirous of glory, he was unwilling to enjoy her ingloriously, but that he would wait patiently till he could enjoy her honourably; yet so if we also would conspire with him towards the accomplishment of his desires. And he promised that, as a reward of this service, he would cause us to be invested with the highest honours, and we should be believed by men to be gods; 'Only, however, on condition,' says he, 'that you confer the chief place [of the sect] upon me, Simon, who by magic art am able to show many signs and prodigies, by means of which either my glory or our sect may be established. For I am able to render myself invisible to those who wish to lay hold of me, and again to be visible when I am willing to be seen. If I wish to flee, I can dig through the mountains, and pass through rocks as if they were clay. If I should throw myself headlong from a lofty mountain, I should

---

[239] *Sources of the Faust Tradition*, p. 10. For a more comprehensive account of the Simon Magus legend, see "The Forerunners of Faust" in Palmer and More.

be borne unhurt to the earth, as if I were held up; when bound, I can loose myself, and bind those who have bound me; being shut up in prison, I can make barriers open of their own accord; I can render statues animated, so that those who see suppose that they are men. I can make new trees suddenly spring up, and produce sprouts at once. I can throw myself into the fire, and not be burnt; I can change myself into a sheep or a goat; I shall make a beard to grow upon little boys; I shall ascend by flight into the air; I shall exhibit abundance of gold, and shall make and unmake kings. I shall be worshipped as God; I shall have divine honours publicly assigned to me, so that an image of me shall be set up, and I shall be worshipped and adored as God. And what need of more words? Whatever I wish, that I shall be able to do. For already I have achieved many things by way of experiment. In short,' says he, 'once when my mother Rachel ordered me to go to the field to reap, and I saw a sickle lying, I ordered it to go and reap; and it reaped ten times more than the others. Lately, I produced many new sprouts from the earth, and made them bear leaves and produce fruit in a moment; and the nearest mountain I successfully bored through.'"[240]

The popular element of this particular legend, i.e. Simon's conflict with St. Peter and St. Paul in Rome before the Emperor Nero, appeared in similar early literature, e.g. the *Acts of the Holy Apostles Peter and Paul* (circa fourth-century). The most pertinent narration to our current discussion on Faustus from this collection concerns Simon's attempt to fly before the Emperor:

> "Simon said: Listen, O Caesar Nero, that thou mayst know that these men [Peter and Paul] are liars, and I have been sent from the heavens: tomorrow I go up to the heavens, that I may make those who believe in me blessed, and show my wrath upon those who have denied me.

***

> Then Nero ordered a lofty tower to be made in the Campus Martius, and all the people and the dignities to be present at the spectacle. And on the following day, all the multitude having come together, Nero ordered Peter and Paul to be present, to whom also he said: Now the truth has to be made manifest. Peter and Paul said: We do not expose him, but our Lord Jesus Christ, the son of God, whom he has falsely declared himself to be. [...] Then Simon went up upon the tower in the face of all, and, crowned with laurels, he stretched forth his hands, and began to fly.

---

[240] Trans. Rev. Thomas Smith, the Ante-Nicene Christian Library, Vol. III, Edinburgh, 1871, in *Sources of the Faust Tradition*, pp. 12–14. In this narrative, Niceta and Aquila, Christian converts and former disciples of Simon are relating their account to St. Peter. Aquila is speaking.

And when Nero saw him flying, he said to Peter: This Simon is true; but thou and Paul are deceivers. To whom Peter said: Immediately shalt thou know that we are true disciples of Christ; but that he is not Christ, but a magician, and a malefactor. Nero said: Do you still persist? Behold, you see him going up to heaven. [...] And Peter, looking steadfastly against Simon, said: I adjure you, ye angels of Satan, who are carrying him into the air, to deceive the hearts of the unbelievers, by the God that created all things, and by Jesus Christ, whom on the third day He raised from the dead, no longer from this hour keep him up, but to let him go. And immediately, being let go, he fell into a place called Sacra Via, that is, Holy Way, and was divided into four parts, having perished by an evil fate."[241]

During the Medieval period, these legends retained their popularity and survived in the *Legenda Aurea*, a collection relating the legends of the saints written by the Archbishop of Genoa (c. 1230–c. 1298). The *Legenda Aurea* was one of the first books published on the newly invented printing press, by the year 1500, seventy-four Latin editions had been published, and translations in other languages soon followed.

Considering the boastful claims of Faustus, it is not surprising he should be associated with the Simon Magus legend. According to the letters of Trithemius and Mutianus Rufus, it is conceivable Faustus was familiar with these tales and adopted a 'Simon Magus approach' as a crucial element of his public debut where he claimed he possessed the ability to accomplish the same miracles as Christ. Faustus therefore may have actively initiated the formation of his own legend during his lifetime! It is not surprising that these learned theologians would instantly ridicule and condemn him. With regard to the latter documents, it is difficult to separate fact from fiction. Baron admits that Faustus' alleged attempts to fly...

"[...] might seem credible if we did not have the story of Faustus eating up another magician. In this second anecdote it becomes clear that, like Johannes Gast and Martin Luther, Melanchthon assumed Faustus had associated with the devil. Since the lectures in question were delivered between 1554 and 1557, Melanchthon was undoubtedly influenced by Luther's tendency to see in Faustus a magician and a representative of the devil. Melanchthon had access to information about the historical Faustus because of his friendship with Joachim Camerarius and Johannes Virdung, but apparently his strongly superstitious nature and his interest in using the example of Faustus to make statements of theological significance made the historical figure unrecognisable."[242]

---

[241] Trans. Walker in the Ante-Nicene Christian Library, Vol. XVI, Edinburgh, 1873, in *Sources of the Faust Tradition*, pp. 32–34.
[242] *Doctor Faustus, from History to Legend*, p. 76.

In addition, Manlius' quotation of Melanchthon deviates from these two extracts compiled by Pezelius, which question the credibility of these documents. For example, Manlius recounts the tale where Faustus attempts to fly in Venice, but drawing his inspiration from the Simon Magus reference, included the detail it was the devil who raised Faustus up and then dashed him to the ground. Manlius also records the incident where a magician reportedly ate another in Vienna, but he fails to mention the name of Faustus, unlike Pezelius' narration, hence the name of Faustus may have been appended to add credibility to this account.[243]

As the years progressed, scholars continually injected new elements to Faustus' affiliation with the devil in accordance with the growing trend to expand his biography. For example, we have discussed Manlius' supposed quotation of Melanchthon where he asserts Faustus was born in Kimlich and studied black magic at the University of Cracow. In a separate document, a letter from the Swiss physician Conrad Gesner to Johannes Crato, we find a conflicting opinion as to the origin of the occult skills Faustus acquired:

From the *Epistolae Medicinales* of Conrad Gesner.

A letter by Gesner dated August 16, 1561 to Johannes Crato, Physician in Ordinary to the Emperor, Ferdinand I.

"Oporinus of Basle,[244] formerly a disciple and companion of Theophrastus [i.e. Paracelsus], narrates some wonderful things concerning the latter's dealings with demons. Such men practise vain astrology, geomancy, necromancy, and similar prohibited arts. I suspect indeed that they derive from the Druids who among the ancient Celts were for some years taught by demons in underground places. This has been practised at Salamanca in Spain down to our own day. From that school came those commonly called 'wandering scholars' among whom a certain Faustus, who died not long since, is very celebrated."[245]

Similar to the physician Begardi, Gesner associates Faustus with the infamous Paracelsus. However, Gesner offered the new speculation that Oporinus, Paracelsus, Faustus, and the numerous "wandering scholars" of their era, were all products of an ancient demonic tradition originating with the Celtic culture, (which he believed had survived in the Province of Salamanca). This theory represents a departure from Renaissance 'natural', cabalistic and 'black' magic by which the historical Faustus was heavily influenced, nevertheless, we can appreciate Gesner's attempt to offer a new academic theory.

Other latter documents continue to delve into the legendary aspect of Faustus, particularly the lengthy rendition of his escapades in Erfurt based upon the lost sixteenth-century

---

[243] Ibid.
[244] Footnote in the *Sources*, p. 100: "Johannes Oporinus (1507–1568), a Swiss teacher, physician, and in later years publisher and bookseller. The name Oporinus is a translation of Herbst or Herbster."
[245] *Sources of the Faust Tradition*, pp. 100–101.

Reichmann–Wambach chronicle, which survives in the *Chronica von Thüringen und der Statdt Erffurth* written by Zacharias Hogel sometime in the seventeenth century:

From the *Chronica Thüringen und der Stadt Erffurth*

a)   It was also probably about this time [1550] that those strange things happened which are said to have taken place at Erfurt in the case of the notorious sorcerer and desperate brand of hell, Dr. Fausten. Although he lived in Wittenberg, yet, just as his restless spirit in other instances drove him about in the world, so he also came to the university at Erfurt, rented quarters near the large Collegium, and through his boasting brought it to pass that he was allowed to lecture publicly and to explain the Greek poet Homer to the students. When, in this connection, he had occasion to mention the king of Troy, Priam, and the heroes of the Trojan war, Hector, Ajax, Ulysses, Agamemnon, and others, he described them each as they had appeared. He was asked (for there are always inquisitive fellows and there was no question as to what he was) to bring it to pass through his art, that these heroes should appear and show themselves as he had just described them. He consented to this and appointed the time when they should next come to the auditorium. And when the hour had come and more students than before appeared before him, he said in the midst of his lecture that they should now get to see the ancient Greek heroes. And immediately he called in one after the other and as soon as one was gone another came in to them, looked at them and shook his head as though he were still in action on the field before Troy. The last of them all was the giant Polyphemus, who had only a single terrible big eye in the middle of the forehead. He wore a fiery red beard and was devouring a fellow, one of whose legs was dangling out of his mouth. The sight of him scared them so that their hair stood on end and when Dr. Faust motioned him to go out, he acted as though he did not understand but wanted to grasp a couple of them too with his teeth. And he hammered on the floor with his great iron spear so that that the whole Collegium shook, and then he went away.

Not long afterward the commencement for masters was held and [at the banquet given in connection therewith], in the presence of the members of the theological faculty and of delegates from the council, the comedies of the ancient poets Plautus and Terence were discussed and regret was expressed that so many of them had been lost in times gone by, for if they were available, they could be used to good advantage in the schools. Dr. Faust listened to this and he also began to speak about the two poets and cited several quotations which were supposed to be in their lost comedies. And he offered, if it would not be held against him, and if the theologians had no objections, to bring to light again all the lost comedies and to put them at their disposal for several hours, during which time they would have to be copied quickly by a goodly number of students or clerks, if they wanted to have them. After that they would be able to use them as they pleased. The theologians and councilmen, however, did not take kindly to the proposal: for they said the devil might interpolate all sorts of offensive things into such newly found comedies. And after all, one could, even without them, learn enough good Latin from those which existed. The conjurer accordingly could not exhibit one of his masterpieces in this connection.

He was accustomed to spend a good deal of his time while he was in Erfurt at the Anchor House of Squire N. in the Schlössergasse, entertaining him and his guests with his adventures. Once, when he had gone to Prague in Bohemia, a group of such guests gathered at the inn and, because they desired to have him present, begged mine host to tell them where he was. And one of the guests jokingly called him by name and begged him not to desert them. At that instant someone in the street knocks at the door. The servant runs to the window, looks out and asks who is there. And behold, there, before the door, stands Dr. Faust, holding his horse as though he had just dismounted, and says: "Don't you know me? I am he whom they have just called." The servant runs into the room and reports. The host refuses to believe it, saying that Dr. Faust was in Prague. In the meantime he knocks at the door and master and servant run again to the window, see him, and open the door, and he is given a cordial welcome and immediately led in to the guests. The host's son takes his horse, saying that he will give it plenty of feed, and leads it to the stable. The squire immediately asks Dr. Fausten how he returned so quickly. "That's what my horse is for," says Dr. Faust. "Because the guests desired me so much and called me, I wanted to oblige them and to appear, although I have to be back in Prague before morning." Thereupon they drink to his health in copious draughts, and when he asks them whether they would also like to drink a foreign wine, they answer: "Yes." He asks whether it shall be Rheinfall, Malmsey, Spanish, or French wine. And when one of them says: "They are all good," he asks for an auger and with it makes four holes in the table and closes them with plugs. Then he takes fresh glasses and taps from the table that kind of wine which he names and continues to drink merrily with them. In the meantime the son runs into the room and says: "Doctor, your horse eats as though he were mad; he has already devoured several bushels of oats and continually stands and looks for more. But I will give him some more until he has enough." "Have done," says the Doctor, "he has had enough; he would eat all the feed in your loft before he was full." But at midnight the horse utters a shrill neigh so that it is heard throughout the entire house. "I must go," says the doctor, but tarries a little until the horse neighs a second and finally a third time. Thereupon he goes, takes leave of them outside, mounts his horse and rides up the Schlössergasse. But the horse in plain sight rises quickly into the air and takes him back through the air to Prague. After several weeks he comes again from Prague to Erfurt with splendid gifts which had been given him there, and invites the same company to be his guests at St. Michael's. They come and stand there in the rooms but there is no sign of any preparation. But he knocks with a knife on the table. Soon someone enters and says: "Sir, what do you wish?" He asks, "How quick are you?" The other answers: "As an arrow." "No," says Dr. Faust, "you shall not serve me. Go back to where you came from." Then he knocks again and when another servant enters and asks the same question, he says: "How quick are you?" "As the wind," says he. "That is something," says Dr. Faust, but sent him out again too. But when he knocked a third time, another entered and, when he was asked the same question, said he was as quick as the thought of man. "Good," says Dr. Faust, "you'll do." And he went out with him, told him what he should do, and returned again to his guests and had them wash their hands and sit down. Soon the servant with two others brought in three covered dishes each, and this happened four times. Thirty six courses or dishes were served, therefore, with game, fowl, vegetables, meat pies and other meat, not to mention the fruit, confection, cakes, etc. All the beakers, glasses, and mugs were put on the table empty. Soon Dr. Faust asked each one what he wished to drink in the way of beer and wine and then put the cups outside of the window and soon took them back again, full of just that fresh drink which each one wanted to have. The music which one of his servants played was so charming that his guests had never heard the like, and so wonderful as if several were playing in harmony on harmoniums, fifes, cornets, lutes, harps, trumpets, etc. So they made merry until broad daylight. What was to be the outcome? The man played so many tricks that the city and country began to talk about him and many of the nobility of the country came to Erfurt to him. People began to worry lest the devil might lead the tender youth and other simpletons astray, so that they also might show a leaning towards the black art and might regard it as only a clever thing to do. Since the sorcerer attached himself to the squire in the Anchor House, who was a papist, therefore the suggestion was made that the neighbouring monk Dr. Klinge, should make an effort to tear him from the devil and convert him. The Franciscan did so, visited him and spoke to him, at first kindly, then sternly; explained to him God's wrath and the eternal damnation which must follow on such doings; said that he was a well educated man and could support himself without this in a godly and honorable way: therefore he should stop such frivolity, to which he had perhaps been persuaded by the devil in his youth, and should beg God for forgiveness of his sins, and should hope in this way to obtain that forgiveness of his sins which God had never yet denied anyone. Dr. Faust said: "My dear sir, I realize that you wish me well; I know all that, too, which you have just told me. But I have ventured so far, and with my own blood have contracted with the devil to be forever his, with body and soul: how can I now retract? Or how can I be helped?" Dr. Klinge said: "That is quite possible, if you earnestly call on God for grace and mercy, show true repentance and do penance, refrain from sorcery and community with devils, and neither harm nor seduce anyone. We will hold a mass for you in our cloister so that you will without doubt get rid of the devil." "Mass here, mass there," said Dr. Faust, "My pledge binds me too absolutely. I have wantonly despised God and become perjured and faithless towards Him, and believed and trusted more in the devil than in Him. Therefore I can neither come to Him again nor obtain any comfort from His grace which I have forfeited. Besides, it would not be honest nor would it redound to my honor to have it said that I had violated my bond and seal, which I had made with my own blood. The devil has honestly kept the promise that he made to me, therefore I will honestly keep the pledge that I made and contracted with him." "Well," says the monk, "Then go to, you cursed child of the devil, if you will not be helped, and will not have it otherwise." Thereupon he went to his Magnificence, the Rector, and reported it to him. The council was also informed and took steps so that Dr. Faust had to leave. So Erfurt got rid of the wicked man. However, this affair with the aforesaid sorcerer probably took place in this year or shortly before or afterwards, during the lifetime of Dr. Klinge.

b) Also the Lord God afflicted Dr. Klinge, the above mentioned obdurate monk and abbot in the Franciscan cloister in Erfurt, so that he despaired of his life. But he recovered again and because, it was reported to him that they said of him in the city that he had become Lutheran, he wrote and published his book called *Catechismus Catholicus*, printed in 1570 in Cologne. And in the introduction he bore witness that he would remain in the doctrine which he had preached in Erfurt for thirty-six years. And this was the monk who wanted to turn and convert the notorious Dr. Fausten from his evil life. Dr. Klinge however died in the year 1556 on the Tuesday after Oculi [i.e. the fourth Sunday before Easter], on which Sunday he had still preached in the church of Our Lady. And he lies buried in that church opposite the chancel, where his epitaph may be seen.[246]

As the original document, the *Reichmann-Wambach Chronicle*, is lost, it is impossible to state with certainty that Hogel's rendition remains faithful to this early chronicle.

In the first paragraph, Hogel mentions Faustus was granted an appointment to lecture in Greek at the University of Erfurt. Although we know from Mutianus Rufus' correspondence that Faustus was at Erfurt in 1513, and perhaps may have rented lodgings "near the large Collegium" as this present text states, we are unaware of current research that evinces he was offered a

---

[246] *Sources of the Faust Tradition*, pp. 108–119.

position at the University. Hogel records an incident that became a classic in the legend formation process, the summoning of the ancient heroes for his contemporaries to gaze upon. We discover a similar entry in the *Epitome Historiarum* (1576) by Wolffgang Bütner, however the location is set in Wittenberg, a detail we will discuss shortly. It is possible the *Reichmann-Wambach Chronicle* of the mid-sixteenth century was influenced by the *Epitome* account, and was later altered by Hogel during the transcription process. On the initial reading of this tale, as with many facets of the Faust legend, it may be construed as a fable embellished upon for dramatic effect, or as an imaginative example of the power the devil bestows on those who follow him in accordance with their advancement in evil. We may also perceive the basis from which this account was derived. It is a possibility that Faustus *boasted* he could call the spirits with his powers of necromancy in a bombastic display, which by hearsay had been altered in these latter documents to state he *actually* summoned these spirits. We have observed similar alterations and embellishments in other documents, e.g. the last words of Faustus described by Manlius, "Don't be frightened tonight," as opposed to that of Andreas Hondorff, "Do not be afraid tonight, if you hear a great banging and shaking of the house".

The second tale from the *Chronica von Thüringen*, i.e. Faustus' offer to restore the lost comedies of Plautus and Terence, is an obvious product of the legend formation process. Immediately, a link to Faustus' early claim that he could restore the complete philosophical works of Aristotle and Plato as recorded in Trithemius' letter is apparent. Once again we notice chroniclers of the day were eager to rewrite certain information to reflect the various current events. The fact Hogel, or perhaps the authors of the *Reichmann-Wambach Chronicle,* substituted the philosophers Aristotle and Plato for the dramatists Plautus and Terence displays an interest in methods used to teach ancient languages at the local university of Erfurt — more than a simple narration of a single exploit of Faustus, this particular account also reveals a definite academic trend. During the Renaissance period, ancient dramas were employed to instruct students in the art of Latin and Greek rhetoric in lieu of teaching the appreciation of dramatic arts. In addition, it was generally believed virtue could be acquired through ancient drama due to popular credence in the humanistic ideal that all human beings as rational creatures, whether pagan or Christian, possessed the ability to express truth and righteousness. This perception of ancient drama elucidates the regret of the theological faculty expressed in the *Chronica* concerning the loss of many ancient classics and their apprehension that "[…] the devil might interpolate all sorts of offensive things into such newly found comedies," should they accept Faustus' offer.

Obviously, the author(s) were avid admirers of the works of Plautus (254? –184 BC) and Terence (190?–159 BC), the undisputed geniuses of ancient Latin comedy. Academically, the fact new examples of Latin rhetoric could be studied was not the sole purpose of rediscovering these plays in the first instance. These two playwrights modelled their comedies on the Greek 'New Comedy' form developed by Menander (342?–291? BC), a lighter style that focused on the Athenian middle classes rather than the political and social elements as displayed in the 'Old Comedy'. Only fragments of Menander's works survived until 1957, when one comedy *Dyskolos* (*The Curmudgeon,* 317 BC) was rediscovered in Egypt, currently the sole example of the New style that exists intact. Faustus' contemporaries would be interested in Plautus and Terence for a myriad of reasons, these playwrights adapted Menander's comedies as they translated them into Latin, and in the process preserved a general concept of Menander's original work. If the lost works of Plautus and Terence were uncovered, this would also have signified a partial rediscovery of Menander's classics, recognised as milestones in the development of Greek comedy. Possibly, the flat refusal of the theological faculty portrayed in the *Chronica* was intended to reflect a cynical attitude on behalf of the author(s) towards the academic elite of their time, who in their opinion were simply satisfied to dream of accomplishing something of note but could not follow through with their grandiose plans, and despite their professed learning, could not recognise a rare cultural treasure when presented to them on a platter. Simultaneously, this particular tale was intended as didactic praise for those who would resist the temptation of resorting to any artifice the devil would proffer, regardless of the benefit or prize one might hope to achieve by these means.

The following accounts in this *Chronica* feature the familiar Medieval perception of the devil in his ability to appear as an animal prepared to assist those who have contracted their soul to him in return for great power, and also the story Faustus prepared a banquet and ordered a devil to serve his guests, insinuating an elaborate adaptation of Gast's account. Theologically, all devils are "fast as the thoughts of man" as they are spirit in nature; hence, we detect a measure of artistic license employed for effect when Faustus interviews each prospective "servant" on the basis of their agility. We may consider the circulation of the *Faustbook* manuscripts and chapbooks influenced Hogel's rendition of the *Reichmann-Wambach Chronicle*. Due to these mythical and artistic associations, we cannot deduce with absolute certainty the verity or fictitiousness of other possible historical facets of these *Chronica* tales, for instance, his alleged journey to Prague or that he stayed at a location called St. Michael's at Erfurt.

There is, however, a possible element of truth to the tale Faustus frequented, at one time, an inn named the "Anchor House" and was approached by a Franciscan, Dr. Klinge, who attempted to convert him. There are details that evince a certain familiarity with the locality, i.e. information that the landlord of the inn was Catholic, and a specific awareness of the biography of Dr. Klinge. Konrad Klinge (also spelled Conrad Clinge) was born in Nordhausen c. 1483–84 and became a Franciscan in 1518. He was stationed in Erfurt where he obtained his PhD in theology in 1520, and held a prominent position within the order as guardian of the cloister and as sexton of Thüringen. From 1530 until his death in 1556 he preached in Erfurt, defending the Catholic faith. The book mentioned in the *Chronica*, i.e. Klinge's *Catechismus Catholicus,* was first published in Cologne in 1562 and reprinted in 1570, the author of the *Chronica* is referring to the second edition.

It is possible many individuals attempted to convert Faustus, but it is difficult to determine the veracity of Dr. Klinge's alleged effort. Unfortunately, the fact the author(s) state this attempt to convert Faustus "took place in this year [i.e. 1550] or shortly before or afterwards" — a timeframe which considerably postdates our proposed year of Faustus' death, 1538 — coveys a degree of uncertainty and ambiguity regarding this event despite the accurate information about Dr. Klinge. We further note Klinge was not stationed in Erfurt at the time Faustus was known to have visited in 1513 according to Rufus' letter to Urbanus. It is possible Faustus may have revisited the town during the time Klinge became a prominent preacher during the 1530s, unfortunately there are no credible historical documents to support this suggestion.

In addition, the remainder of the *Chronica von Thüringen* bears the hallmark of Lutheran didacticism, particularly displayed in the author(s)' criticism of Dr. Klinge's beliefs as the reason for his unsuccessful attempt to convert Faustus, which in turn clouds the reliability of the public affirmation allegedly pronounced by the reprobate that he had actually written a contract to Satan in his own blood. Faustus demonstrates he agrees with the initial argument presented by Dr. Klinge, but lacks the Lutheran "justification by faith" and the hope of forgiveness for his sins, venturing so far as to state that he had "trusted more in the devil" and therefore entertained no hope to obtain salvation. To add insult to injury, in an act of absolute pride, Faustus claims he has no intention of breaking his bond for the devil, the Father of Lies, "honestly kept" the pledge he made to him! This detail, we may therefore conclude, was an inventive piece of narrative embroidery. In fact, this account may have been intended as an antithesis of the famous anecdote Luther recounted concerning the conversion of a fortuneteller who had sold his soul:

> "In Erfurt they burned a soothsayer and a practitioner of black magic. For a number of years he had been very sad because of his great poverty. Then he came upon the devil himself, who promised him great things, that he would be rich if he were to reject baptism and salvation through Christ and to deny the will ever to do penance. The poor man accepted these conditions, and the devil then gave him a crystal ball from which he could tell the future and thereby receive fame and riches. Finally, the devil really deceived him and showed his true character by having him accuse innocent people of theft on the basis of his crystal ball. Because of this he was thrown into prison. He revealed then that he broke the pact he had made with the devil, and asked for a pastor. He performed penance, and his example put the fear of God into many people. He died with a joyful heart, in spite of his punishment. Thus, the devil was beaten at his own game, and his evil intentions were made evident."[247]

Hence, we observe Faustus in the *Chronica* has assumed the role of a legendary demonic miscreant employed to foster a salutary fear of the devil's artifices among the Reformed faithful.

The *Chronicle* (1575) by Christoph Rosshirt, as we have previously discussed, focuses on the mythical element of his character in four separate accounts that had already been in circulation regarding other soothsayers:

> When Dr. Georgius Faustus is lecturing to the students at the University of Ingolstadt on philosophy and necromancy, he invites some friends to dinner, and tells them that the food and drink they are enjoying come from the wedding-feast of the King of England. He instructs them to hold on to the edge of the towel when water is brought for them to wash their hands, and he will take them to the dance at the King's wedding. When they are discovered in the ball-room, they are taken for spies and arrested. They are condemned to be hanged, but Faust rescues them in the same way that he had brought them there. They wash their hands in England and dry them in Germany.

---

[247] Luther, *Tishreden*, no. 3618B, in *Doctor Faustus, from History to Legend*, p. 81.

Faust asks a Jewish merchant at Frankfort Fair to change him some French money into good talers. The merchant promises to call on Faust at his inn and bring him the money, but when he arrives, Faust is laying on a couch, apparently asleep. The Jew puts his bag of talers on the table and shakes Faust by the arm, but cannot rouse him; he becomes annoyed and shakes him violently by the leg, which comes off in his hand. He rushes in terror from the house, leaving behind him cloak and money-bag which are shared by Faust and his servant.

Faust sells a swineherd in Bamberg some fat pigs, but warns him against driving them into flowing water. On the next day the swineherd neglects the warning and the pigs are turned into bundles of straw. By this time Faust is well on the way to Nuremberg.

[Previously quoted.] On the evening before he is due to fulfil his pact with the devil, Faust [i.e. Faustus] arrives at a village inn and asks for a room for the night. In the tap-room there is a crowd of drunken, noisy peasants, who refuse to be quiet when Faust asks them. The magician bewitches them so that they remain sitting with their mouths wide open, and he is able to have his last meal in peace. He pays the bill, tips all the servants, and goes to bed, but is persuaded by the host to disenchant the drunken clowns. On the next morning, Faust is found dead in his bed.[248]

Evidently, Rosshirt modernised these popular tales of previous ages to reflect historical authenticity, for we discover several localities are mentioned with well-noted associations to the notorious magician, e.g. Ingolstadt, Bamberg and Nuremberg.

As time progressed, impetus to use Faustus' biography for edification or entertainment expanded, generating monumental confusion between fact and fiction, for example, the excerpt from the *Operae Horarum Subcisivarum* (1591) written by Philipp Camerarius, the son of Joachim Camerarius. It is disappointing when we realise that his information with regard to Faustus, i.e. his university education and place of birth, was based upon semi-credible sources, particularly when we would expect that his father provided him with solid facts on these points at one time. Philip confirms the incident concerning the magical grapes was an anecdote told by those who knew Faustus well, yet we may perceive that these personages read the earlier 1587 Spies *Faustbook* wherein a similar Faust tale is recorded, which they accepted as historical fact. Hence, this information was obviously misinterpreted when Philipp wrote his *Subcisivarum*:

From the *Operae Horarum Subcisivarum* (1591)
[Full extract.]

"We know, moreover, (not to mention Scymus of Tarentum,
Philistes of Syracuse, Heraclitus of Mytilene, who as we read were very

---

[248] Synopsis of Rosshirt's *Chronicle* by William Rose in *The Historie of the Damnable Life and Deserved Death of Doctor John Faustus: 1592*, pp. 32–33.

distinguished and accomplished sorcerers in the time of Alexander the Great) that among the jugglers and magicians who became famous within the memory of our own fathers, John Faustum of Kundling, who studied magic at Cracow where it was formerly taught, acquired through his wonderful tricks and diabolical enchantments such a celebrated name that among the common people there can hardly be found anyone who is not able to recount some instance of his art. The same conjurer's tricks are ascribed to him as we have just related of the Bohemian magician. [i.e. Zyto] Just as the lives of these magicians were similar, so each ended his life in a horrible manner. For Faustus, it is said, and this is told by Wier, was found in a village in the Duchy of Württemberg lying dead alongside his bed with his head twisted round. And in the middle of the preceding night the house was shaken. The other, [Zyto] as we mentioned a little while ago, was carried off by his master while he was still alive. These are the fitting rewards of an impious and criminal curiosity. But to come back to Faustum. From those in truth, who knew this impostor well, I have heard many things which show him to have been a master of the magic art (if indeed it is an art and not the jugglery of a fool.) Among other deeds which he performed there is told one in particular which may seem ridiculous but which is truly diabolical. For from it may be seen how subtly and yet seriously, even in things which seem to us ridiculous, that arch conjurer, the devil, undermines the well being and safety of mankind. ... It is reported that Faustus' deception was of this kind. Once upon a time when he was staying with some friends who had heard much about his magician's tricks, they besought him that he should show them some example of his magic. He refused for a long time, but finally, yielding to the importunity of the company, which was by no means sober, he promised to show them whatever they might wish. With one accord therefore they besought him that he should show them a full grown vine with ripe grapes. For they thought that on account of the unsuitable time of year (for it was toward the end of December) he would by no means be able to accomplish this. Faustus assented and promised that they should immediately see on the table what they wished but with this one condition: they should all wait without moving and in absolute silence until he should order them to cut the grapes. If they should do otherwise they would be in danger of their lives. When they had promised to do this, then by his tricks he so befuddled the eyes and the senses of this drunken crowd that there appeared to them on a beautiful vine as many bunches of grapes of marvellous size and plumpness as there were people present. Made greedy by the novelty of the thing and a thirst from too much wine, they took their knives and awaited his orders to cut off the grapes. Finally, when Faustus had held these triflers in suspense for some time in their silly error, suddenly the vine with its grapes disappeared in smoke and they were seen, each holding, not the grapes which each thought he had seized, but his own nose with his knife suspended over it so that if anyone had been unmindful of the directions given and had wished to cut the grapes without orders, he would have cut off his own nose. And it would have served them right and they would have deserved other mutilation, since, with intolerable curiosity, they occupied themselves as spectators and participants in the illusions of the devil, which no Christian may be interested in without danger or rather sin."[249]

Notwithstanding these past errors in historical transcription, other documents offer valuable plums of information, for example, the excerpt from Johannes Wier's *De Prastigiis Daemonium* (1568). Although his information concerning Faustus' name, birthplace, and the locality of his *alma mater* is questionable, in the previously quoted extract of *De Praestigiis* we discover two separate incidents that Wier's personal acquaintances experienced upon their encounter with Faustus. The first anecdote relates Faustus was apprehended as a criminal, undoubtedly as a result of his heretical career, near the border of Geldern, (Gelderland) at Batenburg on the Maas; a small village near Demen that was once a ferry crossing site on the Maas River. There is little reason to doubt the authenticity of this first narrative as Wier discloses the source of his information, Dr. Johannes Dorstenius, who as Wier states, "[...] told me of this piece of villainy more than once with much indignation". We therefore learn Faustus travelled to the Netherlands at one point; curiously, the region that is described in this source is approximately one-hundred miles (c. 160 km) from the town of Münster. Could it be possible Faustus had visited the Netherlands circa 1535 when he prophesised that the Anabaptists who occupied Münster would be overthrown? This remains an inconclusive, yet tantalising speculation.

A detail of particular interest is Faustus' dangerous advice to Dorstenius, i.e. advising him to use arsenic to remove his beard. Today we may view Faustus' blunder as a misfortunate case of cosmetic malpractice; however, in those times a general or minor surgeon, who was entrusted with medicinal tasks that included stitching wounds, pulling teeth, removing tumours and bloodletting, also performed the duties of a barber. Of note, using arsenic to treat skin diseases is an ancient Chinese remedy, and arsenic sulphides, such as realgar and orpiment, were used for depilating and tanning hides. Orpiment in particular was used by alchemists in their various experiments, the compound is still used today in rural India as a depilatory. Therefore using arsenic for medicinal purposes may have been a common experiment that Faustus inexpertly botched. Hence, this information from Wier's document supports Begardi's *Index Sanitatis* stating Faustus attempted to include certain medical skills to his list of 'accomplishments' later in his career. This account also concurs with Begardi's opinion that Faustus was incompetent in this field as Wier remarks Faustus did not disclose, or was unfamiliar with the correct method of mixing the depilatory salve for Dorstenius that resulted in an excruciating facial injury. In summary, there is convincing evidence Faustus became a charlatan in the practise of medicine. Obviously, one of Faustus' main objectives was to earn a fast thaler rather than care for the sick as Begardi indicated; "[...] his deeds [...] were very petty and fraudulent. But [...] in receiving

---

[249] *Sources of the Faust Tradition*, pp. 123–126.

money he was not slow. And afterwards also, on his departure, as I have been informed, he left many to whistle for their money."

Of importance, historical knowledge concerning the barber-surgeon trade in Europe allows us to speculate how Faustus would have lived in his later years. During the 1500s, a barber-surgeon was not held in the same high esteem as a regular physician, the latter being dignified by a rule issued by the Church declaring that it was unlawful for a physician to shed blood, therefore the barber-surgeons were required to carry out the 'dirty work' of the medical profession.[250] Considering Faustus' very mobile lifestyle, he may have followed the armies of Germany on occasion to earn a living. The soldiers of those days were not provided with a regular medical service; the nobles had their own private physicians, while the soldiers either tended to their own wounds, relied on the assistance of the self-employed barber-surgeons, or became the victims of the many profiteering quacks and charlatans, who like the barber-surgeons, also followed the armies.[251] Perhaps this may explain why Faustus travelled to Münster, he hoped to make a tidy income by tending to the wounded soldiers, but realised a successful prognostication would prove more lucrative. We can comprehend his change of tactics, according to Ambroise Paré (c. 1510–1590), the earnings of a travelling barber-surgeon were not regular. However, it was possible to receive costly presents if you were fortunate to attend the nobles and had succeeded in healing their wounds or curing their illnesses. Paré had received on odd occasions a cask of wine, a diamond or two, a horse and fifty double ducats, a bag of crowns and half-crowns collected from the ranks of the soldiers, to name just a few presents.[252] Faustus had become notorious as a charlatan and provided many patrons with nothing but empty promises of a cure according to the information we have, he obviously could not remain within the camps on a long-term basis during a war without being apprehended and punished. One hazard the surgeons faced according to Paré was to be captured by the enemy, and obliged to heal important captives that could be held for ransom. If surgeons failed to cooperate, their lives could be forfeit. On one occasion, Paré writes he had been taken prisoner and was ordered to tend to another valuable captive, Lord de Martigues; "[…] I feared, if I did not show I was a surgeon and had dressed M. de Martigues skilfully, they would cut my throat."[253]

However, if Faustus risked dabbling with men's lives, he must have caused untold pain. When we examine the skills of the trained 'professionals', we find the medical procedures of those times were horrific, the successful remedies they prepared were discovered by mere guesswork at the best of times. Paré writes that one treatment for gunshot wounds, according to John de Vigo's book *Of Wounds in General*, consisted of pouring scalding oil of elder mixed with treacle directly on the wounds.[254] Having run out of elder oil on one occasion, he was forced to mix an impromptu dressing of his own, a 'digestive' made from egg yolks, rose oil and turpentine. To his surprise, this new mixture did not poison their wounds, and it also prevented

---

[250] Introductory Note, Ambroise Paré, 'Journeys in Diverse Places (1537–1569)', in Charles W. Eliot, ed., *Scientific Papers: Physiology, Medicine, Surgery, Geology. The Harvard Classics vol. 38* (New York: P.F. Collier and Son Corp., 1963), p. 8.

[251] Ibid.

[252] Ibid.

[253] Ibid. p. 38.

[254] Ibid. p. 11.

them from becoming inflamed. Moreover, it was naturally less painful than the trusted boiling-oil method! Paré used this new medicine from that point on for gunshot wounds, and later was given the recipe of a similar concoction used by a surgeon from Turin that also proved successful: new-born puppies, and earthworms prepared with Venetian turpentine, boiled in oil of lilies.[255] And these were medicines devised by the trained surgeons and doctors! What could we expect from Faustus? We find Paré records an incident with a Spanish quack-surgeon, who made an emphatic promise to the Lord de Martigues' captors that he could cure him. The impostors' 'remedy' appears nothing short of an occult spell—taking one of the injured man's shirts and tearing it into little strips, he laid them cross-wise over the patient, "muttering and murmuring certain words over the wounds", concluding his treatment with the announcement that the patient need not follow the usual restricted diet for his wounds, but that he would take this diet upon himself, apparently he believed he could mystically transfer the benefits of the diet onto the dying man! Paré concludes, "Nevertheless, two days later, M. de Martigues died: and my friend the Spaniard, seeing him at the point of death, eclipsed himself, and got away without goodbye to any man. And I believe if he had been caught he would have been hanged and strangled for the false promise he made […]."[256] A rapid exit ala Faustus!

Continuing with the second anecdote, Wier transcribes an incident where a colleague was insulted by Faustus who mocked his choleric countenance and disposition; "I surely thought you were my brother-in-law and therefore I looked at your feet to see whether long curved claws projected from them." Wier did not mention the name of this splenetic individual, perhaps in an effort to remain discreet; however, as he actually knew the man in question, we may deem this a credible historical event. Also, Wier was not a supporter of the witch trials and he condemned superstitious prejudices, his attempt to display that Faustus was not a sorcerer but a man who had used boasting and commonplace charlatanism to defraud the populace evinces this document is an objective rendition of fact. In this instance, Wier was obviously demonstrating Faustus' habit of creating a sensation by 'taboo shock treatment', we would not consider having the devil for a relative or a close acquaintance a topic worthy of public praise! Thus, there is evidence confirming the report offered by Luther's associates that Faustus called the devil his "brother-in-law" to promote his own evil reputation.

Latter documents in our timeline contain similar interesting details that correlate previous documents, for example, several extracts from the *Christlich bedencken und erinnerung von Zauberey* (Heidelberg, 1585; 3rd Ed., Speyer, 1597) by Augustin Lercheimer:

Extracts from the *Christlich Bedencken*
[Full quotations as printed in *Sources of the Faust Tradition*.]

"He was born in a little place called Knittlingen, situated in Württemberg near the border of the Palatinate. For a time he was schoolmaster in Kreuznach under Franz von Sickingen: he had to flee from there because he was guilty of sodomy. After that he travelled about the country with his devil; studied the black art at the university of

---

[255] Ibid.
[256] Ibid. p. 40.

Cracow; came to Wittenberg and was allowed to stay there for a time, until he carried things so far that they were on the point of arresting him, when he fled. He had neither house nor home in Wittenberg or elsewhere; in fact he had no permanent abode anywhere, but lived like a vagabond, was a parasite, drunkard, and gourmand, and supported himself by his quackery. How could he have a property at the outer gate in the Scheergasse in Wittenberg, when there never was any suburb there, and therefore also no outer gate? Nor was there any Scheergasse there."

***

"He was choked to death by the devil in a village in Württemberg, not at Kimlich near Wittenberg, since there is no village by that name. For he was never allowed to return to Wittenberg after he had fled from there to avoid arrest."

***

"I do not touch upon other trivial, false, and nasty things in the book [I.e the Spies *Faustbook*]. I have pointed out these particular things because it has vexed and grieved me greatly, as it has many other honest people, to see the honorable and famous institution together with Luther, Melanchthon, and others of sainted memory so libelled. I myself was a student there, once upon a time. At that time the doings of this magician were still remembered by many there."

***

"The lewd, devilish fellow Faust stayed for a time in Wittenberg, as I stated before. He came at times to the house of Melanchthon, who gave him a good lecture, rebuked and warned him that he should reform in time, lest he come to an evil end, as finally happened. But he paid no attention to it. Now one day about ten o'clock Melanchthon left his study to go down to eat. With him was Faust, whom he had vigorously rebuked. Faust replied: Sir, you continually rebuke me with your abusive words. One of these days, when you go to table, I will bring it about that all the pots in your kitchen will fly out of the chimney, so that you and your guests will have nothing to eat. To this Melanchthon replied: you had better not. Hang you and your tricks. Nor did Faust carry out his threat: the devil could not rob the kitchen of the saintly man, as he had done to the wedding guests of whom mention was made before."[257]

---

[257] *Sources of the Faust Tradition*, pp. 119–122.

113

Previously discussed, Lercheimer intended his comments on Faustus to correct information published in the *Spies Faustbook*, (although he also believed the conflicting reports Faustus was born in Knittlingen and studied in Cracow). Of historical note in this document, however, is the detail Faustus frequented the town of Wittenberg. Seven other sources in our timeline also refer to this location as one of his regular haunts — we shall refer to these as the 'Wittenberg Documents'. The first and most important of these seven sources is Manlius' quotation of Melanchthon's lectures in the *Locorum Communium Collectanea* (1563), here it is recorded that...

> "[...] Faustus escaped in this town of Wittenberg when the good prince Duke John had given orders to arrest him. Likewise in Nuremberg he escaped. He was beginning to dine when he became restless and immediately rose and paid the host what he owed. He had hardly got outside the gate when the bailiffs came and inquired about him."

Although Manlius' document is slightly suspect, Lercheimer, also a former student and friend of Melanchthon, supports this information in his third edition of the *Christlich Bedencken*, (the fifth of our 'Wittenberg Documents'). Lercheimer discloses additional data, (see the footnote below), which Manlius did not include or had no knowledge of, i.e. Luther and Melanchthon tolerating Faustus' presence in Wittemberg in the hope he would be converted.[258] Apparently, the fathers of the Reformation were unsuccessful in influencing the notorious sorcerer, as his confrontation with Melanchthon evinces. Faustus attempted his 'taboo shock treatment' on Melanchthon by threatening to use his black arts to sabotage the kitchen. However, true to his character, Faustus was merely boasting. Undoubtedly, Faustus became increasingly brazen and attempted to sway the public with his theatrics and impress or intimidate them with his occult practises, thus precipitating the decision of the Elector Prince to arrest him.

According to Walz, the Elector who ordered Faustus' arrest was Johann der Beständige, (John the Steadfast), a defender of the Reformation who reigned from 1525–1532.[259] By comparing the years that John the Steadfast reigned with the information we already discovered, we may determine when Faustus was forced to flee Wittenberg. This period of the Elector's reign coincides with the exact year Faustus was refused safe conduct to Nuremberg (1532) — it may be more than a coincidence that Manlius mentions Faustus' escape from Wittenberg with an additional detail that he had also escaped arrest in Nuremberg. We note Andreas Hondorff also

---

[258] "Zur zeit D. Luthers und Philippi hielt sich der schwartzkünstler Faust, wie obgemeld, ein weile zy Wittnberg: das ließ man so geschehen, der Hoffnung er würde sich auß der lehr, die da im schwang gieng, bekehren und bessern. Da aber das nicht geschahe, sondern er auch andere verführte ... hieß jn, den Faust, der Fürst eynziehen in gefengnuß. Abersein geist warnete jn, daß er davon kam. Von dem er nicht lang darnach grewlich getödtet ward, alß er jm vier und zwentzig jar gedienet hatte.", Lercheimer, *Christlich Bedencken* (3rd Ed. 1597 – Ed. Binz, Strassburg, 1888), in John A. Walz, 'An English Faustsplitter', MLN, p. 359.

[259] Walz, 'An English *Faustsplitter*', MLN, p. 359.

juxtaposes these two incidents in his *Promptuariam Exemplorum* (1568), the second of our 'Wittenberg Documents':

> "[...] When he [Faustus] came to Wittenberg he would have been arrested by order of the Prince Elector, if he had not escaped. The same would have happened to him in Nuremberg also, where he likewise escaped. [...]"[260]

Did Faustus ignore the refusal of safe conduct issued to him at Fürth and proceeded to Nuremberg in 1532? In the same time-period, we notice separate evidence supporting this observation. Manlius records Faustus claimed that the Emperor's (Charles V) victories during the Italian campaigns (1525–1530) were *due* to his occult intervention, i.e. his skills in the black arts (!), which was refuted by Melanchthon. This remark would certainly explain the animosity displayed by Camerarius towards Faustus in Nuremberg, his fervent attempts in later years to convert his friend Stibar to the "honourable" field of classical divination, and the initiation of his competition with Faustus that focused on the future success of Charles V. Luther's associates suddenly become interested in the infamous magician following this year, as established by the conversation recorded in the *Tischreden* by Nicolaus Medler (1533). Hence, we may conclude that 1532 was the year Faustus fled Wittenberg and Nuremberg, although we cannot determine in which order he was obliged to flee these two cities.

The third record in our 'Wittenberg Documents' is the *Chronica von Thüringen* by Hogel, however, this is a minor document where the Wittenberg tradition is concerned. This city receives only a brief mention regarding Faustus before his escapades of Erfurt are recounted: "Although he [Faustus] lived in Wittenberg, yet, just as his restless spirit in other instances drove him about in the world, so he also came to the university of Erfurt, [...]." Apparently, this account shares information drawn from one famous Faustian tale with an extract from our fourth 'Wittenberg' source, Wolffgang Bütner's *Epitmoe Historiarum* (1576), i.e. the claim that Faustus could summon the spirits of past heroes from the netherworld:

From the *Epitome Historiarum* (1576) by Wolffgang Bütner

> "I have heard that Faustus, at Wittenberg, showed to the students and to an exalted man N —, Hector, Ulysses, Hercules, Æneas, Samson, David and others, who came forth with fierce bearing and earnest countenance and disappeared again, and princely personages are also said to have been present at the time and to have looked on, [which Luther did not praise.*]"[261]

As mentioned, the fact Hogel records Wittenberg in the first instance, it is possible this city was the original setting for this tale with Faustus as the antagonist. Conceivably, the authors

---

[260] Rose, *Damnable Life and Deserved Death of [...] Faustus*, p. 12.
* Bracket section quoted from the *Epitome* in John A. Walz, 'An English *Faustsplitter*', *MLN*, p. 361.
[261] Rose, *Damnable Life and Deserved Death of [...] Faustus*, p. 16.

of the lost *Reichmann-Wambach Chronicle* (c. mid sixteenth century) were familiar with this account, as reflected upon by Bütner in his *Epitome,* and included it in their chronicle, which Hogel subsequently altered, taking artistic license, to reflect the city of Erfurt.

However, is Bütner's *Epitome* a credible historical source? In the 1569 edition of the *Tischreden* (Aurifaber) we discover the possible origin of this Faust legend. On one occasion, Luther was questioned whether the woman with the python spirit in the Book of Kings had summoned the prophet Samuel, or if a demon had appeared in his shape. In contrast to Catholic theology, Luther believed that a demon actually appeared as God had prohibited necromancy. Continuing with his response, Luther offers one further example of a similar incident that allegedly occurred, that Trithemius of Sponheim once summoned the ancient heroes to entertain Emperor Maximilian I (1459–1519):

Tishreden (Aurifaber, 1569) DLXXII.

> The doctor answered: "[…] In like manner, [i.e. in the same manner as the woman with the python spirit] the abbot of Spanheim, [sic. Sponheim] a sorcerer, exhibited to the emperor Maximilian all the emperors his predecessors, and all the most celebrated heroes of past times, who defiled before him each in the costume of his time. Among them were Alexander the Great and Julius Caesar. There was also the emperor's betrothed, whom Charles of France stole from him. But these apparitions were all the work of the demon."

We detect Bütner rewrote the original *Tischreden* story for his Faust rendition in the *Epitome,* but retained certain details. For example, the anonymous reference to a specific individual, an "exalted man N", and the mention of "princely personages" in the *Epitome* indicate a possible link with the emperor Maximilian and his court described in the *Tischreden.* Also, the report Luther was displeased with the attendance of the "princely personages" at Faustus' exhibition as told in the *Epitome* parallels his negative reactions to Trithemius found in the *Tischreden,* further revealing the *Tischreden* as the true origin of this particular Faust tale.

Our penultimate 'Wittenberg Document' features two of the three extracts of *The Second Report of Doctor John Faustus* (London: 1594) from Walz's article 'An English Faustsplitter':

> "In the introductory statements (p. 33) we read: 'Secondly, there is yet to be seene [in Wittenberg] his (i.e. Faust's) tree, a great hollow Trunke, wherein he used to reade Nigromancy to his schollers, not farre from the towne in a very remote place, which I thinke is sufficient testimony to any reasonable eare. And enquire of them which have been there, see if they will not affirme it.'

***

'First there is yet remaining the ruins of his (i.e. Faust's) house, not farre from Melanchtons house as they call at the townes end of Wittenberg, right opposite to the Schooles.'

Remarkably, *The Second Report* mirrors the seventh and final source in our 'Wittenberg Documents', the extract from Moryson's *Itinerary* (1617):

"Besides, they shew a house wherein Doctor Faustus a famous conjurer dwelt. [i.e. in Wittenberg] They say that this Doctor lived there about the yeere 1500, and had a tree all blasted and burnt in the adjoyning Wood, where hee practised his Magick Art, and that he died, or rather was fetched by the Divell, in a Village neere the Towne. I did see the tree so burnt; but walking at leasure through all the Villages adjoining, I could never heare any memory of his end."

We therefore have two accounts by separate authors who had visited the vicinity, and each account substantiates the other in considerable detail. As stated, Moryson remained in Wittenberg for several months in 1591 with the opportunity to learn the history of Faustus pertaining to that particular area directly from the inhabitants. Although we do not know the author of *The Second Report*, the descriptive passages suggest that he also explored the town and its environs.

Before we continue, however, there is conflicting data in Moryson's narrative that should be addressed. First, the locals claimed Faustus frequented their town sometime close to the year 1500, leading Walz to conclude Faustus had visited the town before it achieved fame as the cradle land of the Reformation frequented by Luther and Melanchthon.[262] It is possible Faustus visited the town on several occasions circa 1500, yet this speculation predates our theory Faustus had commenced his career in the black arts c.1506–1507 in the Heidelberg region, and fails to correspond with our analysis of Manlius and Lercheimer's documents, sources obviously based on data obtained from Melanchthon (notwithstanding some discrepancies). There is stronger evidence to substantiate the theory Faustus' connection with Wittenberg originated in the 1530s, thus we have certain reservations with Walz's suggestion. It is quite possible that by this late date (1591) when Moryson temporarily resided in Wittenberg, the detail regarding the year Faustus actually lived there became a vague generalisation.

Resuming our study of this Wittenberg Period, two items remain for our consideration: the particulars of Faustus' house and the tree where he practised his occult arts. According to the early Wolfenbüttel Manuscript (c.1580–1587), which prefigures the printed *Spies Faustbook*, Faustus' house was "[...] located on the Ring-Wall in Scherr Alley, not far from the Iron Gate and indeed right beside the houses of Ganser and of Veitt Röttinger [...]."[263] In the *Spies Faustbook* (1587), the site of this house is located "[...] neben dess Gansers und Veit Rodingers Hauss gelegen, bey dem Eysern Thor, in der Schergassen an der Ringmawren (cap. 60)."[264] Yet,

---

[262] Walz, 'An English Faustsplitter', MLN, p. 364.
[263] H.G. Haile, *The History of Doctor Johann Faustus*, (Urbana, University of Illinois, 1965), p. 120.
[264] Walz. p. 357.

Lercheimer, a former student of the university familiar with the city, emphatically declared that a 'Scheergasse' did not exist, nor an outer gate (eusser thor) in Witternberg, and Faustus maintained no permanent abode. Possibly, this particular in the Wolfenbüttel MS and the *Spies Faustbook* is a misquoted description from an early rendition of the <u>Erfurt</u> adventures, (the lost *Reichmann-Wambach Chronicle* ?) where it is alleged Faustus resided at the Anchor House of "Squire N." in the <u>*Schlössergasse*</u>.[265] Notwithstanding Lercheimer's refutation, Walz argues Faustus became associated with the residence he temporarily occupied during his sojourn in the city:

> "It is equally clear, however, that Moryson found a local tradition in Wittenberg designating a certain house as Faust's residence and this house was pointed out to him by the people of the town. There is no necessary contradiction between the statement of Lercheimer and that of Moryson. While Faust was staying in Wittenberg, he must have lived in some house of the town. He doubtless did not own it, but his name became attached to it in the minds of the townspeople."[266]

We propose Faustus stayed at an inn. Manlius records that Faustus was about to dine when he suddenly became restless and "paid the host what he owed" before the bailiffs arrived on the scene to arrest him. This confirms Lercheimer's statement that Faustus did not have a permanent abode anywhere but "lived like a vagabond". This inn or guesthouse was in close proximity to Melanchthon's place of residence. Lercheimer records Faustus visited Melanchthon at home on several occasions. This account configures neatly with the information the anonymous author of the *Second Report* presents, i.e. Faustus' house was not far from that of Melanchthon and the colleges. This explains Melanchthon's numerous opportunities to rebuke Faustus as he resided a short distance away!

Finally, we arrive at one fascinating tale, the Wittenberg tree, information Walz observed is not recorded in any surviving German source. The *Spies Faustbook,* one of the primary

---

[265] Walz also offers a quotation from Carl Kiesewetter's *Faust in der Geschichte und Tradition* (Leipzig, 1893, p. 241) which discredits the information in the *Spies Faustbook* regarding the location of Faustus' house in Wittenberg:
"Herr Oberbürgermeister Dr. Schild zu Wittenberg hatte die Güte, auf meine Bitte hin Nachforschungen über Fausts Haus anzustellen. Die Scharrn nicht Scheergasse liegt weder an einem Thor, noch an einer Mauer; auch ist in ihr kein Haus Fausts, Gansers oder Rödingers aufzufinden. Wohl aber wohnte 1595 ein George Rödinger in der Klostergasse und ein Hanns Faust besaß 1571 in der Bürgermeistergasse ein Haus neben dem Hans Lufts, des Luther'schen Bibeldruckers." (in 'An English *Faustsplitter*', p. 357)
Apparently, Kiesewetter discovered a certain George Rödinger who lived in the Klostergasse in 1595, and a Hanns Faust who lived in the Bürgermeistergasse in 1571. However, the date of this Rödinger extends far beyond the date of the *Spies Faustbook*, and this Hanns Faust may not be the same person. It is possible Kiesewetter restricted his inquires to the *German* name Faust, and did not consider the Latin *Faustus*. Also, new information may be obtained upon further research of the name *Röttinger* as found in the Wolfenbüttel MS, instead of *Rödinger*.
[266] 'An English *Faustsplitter*', p. 358.

literary sources that associated the infamous conjurer with the famous town, did not refer to any particular tree where Faustus practised his devilish arts. Moryson was impressed by the condition of the tree, describing it as blasted and burnt. According to *The Second Report*, the tree was a large "hollow Trunke" in a remote location where Faustus performed his black magic, and imparted this art to others, additional proof to his contemporaries that Faustus was a serious practitioner of the black arts. This report confirms Lercheimer's statement that Faustus did not intend to profit from his visit to the home of the Reformation, spiritually that is, or repent of his evil ways. Alternatively, he proceeded to initiate curious followers into the occult, compelling the authorities to issue orders for his arrest. We are not aware of existing information that refutes this detail regarding the 'Creepy Hollow' of Wittenberg, we may, for the present, assume this local tradition has a basis in fact.

In summary, these seven 'Wittenberg Documents' provide vital clues to events that occurred c.1532 not found in sources preceding the assumed year of Faustus' death (1538). Reconstructing all our information, we have discovered Faustus, at his own peril, ignored the official order issued at Fürth refusing him safe conduct and proceeded to the city of Nuremberg where he narrowly escaped arrest. In the same year, he claimed the Emperor's victories in Italy were a direct result of his diabolical intervention, an exaggerated boast that may have infuriated Camerarius and fuelled the competition between them in later years. Faustus also visited the town of Wittenberg that year, although we cannot state if he arrived here or at Nuremberg first. In the hope he would repent, the founding fathers of the Reformation permitted him to stay in Wittenberg despite his evil reputation. Melanchthon obviously had many opportunities for this evangelisation plan as Faustus lodged at an inn or guesthouse not far from where he resided. Faustus also visited Melanchthon at home on various occasions. However, the conjuror continued to promote his black arts, encouraged aspiring students to follow in his footsteps, and imparted his occult knowledge to them at a secluded location marked by a burnt hollow tree. Melanchthon may have changed 'conversion tactics' at this point and resorted to aggressive reprimands, thus precipitating an ominous warning from Faustus, who threatened to use his black arts in payment for these puritanical admonitions. This blatant threat displays a remarkable change in Faustus' attitude towards the founders of the Reformation. Three years following the posting of the *Ninety-Five Theses* that initiated the Reformation, Faustus anxiously sought and acquired a 'conservative façade' in Bamberg (1520). By 1532, Faustus, his confidence bolstered by his successive escapes from arrest, trials and the Inquisition, no longer feared incurring the wrath of Luther and Melanchthon — the devil's latest adversaries. Faustus finally realised he had overstayed his tolerated period of sanctuary in Wittenberg when Prince John the Steadfast ordered his arrest, but, once again he escaped to swindle another day. Faustus had unleashed strong opposition with his conduct in Wittenberg, explaining his attempt to repair his camouflage of respectability in 1535 by predicting the forthcoming victory of the Bishop of Münster and the downfall of the heretical Anabaptist sect.

In retrospect, we discovered the latter historical documents originating after the time of Faustus' death c. 1538 offer substantial information, and in many instances supply details not recorded in the earlier sources, enabling us to piece together significant biographical events with a certain degree of confidence. (See the Table below.) Faustus, familiar with the Simon Magus legends, apparently fabricated his Antichrist image based on this infamous figure in Biblical history to initiate his scandalous career. In keeping with the fashionable trends of the elite, he may have acquired a horse and a dog that his contemporaries regarded as his *familiars*, or demon companions. Faustus apparently was once the guest of Dr. Nicholas Winkler in Halberstadt, may have visited the town of Basel, Switzerland, and also the famous Luxeuil Monastery in the Vosges Mountains that he reportedly cursed when the monks refused him hospitality. Allegedly, he was arrested in a little village in the Netherlands named Batenberg on the Maas. Faustus' fraudulent practise as a barber-surgeon in later life is most certainly a disturbing report, one can only imagine the extent of the suffering he caused when we consider the medical standards of that era! By wilfully engaging in medical malpractice, Faustus could be accused of indulging in sadistic pleasure.

His contemporaries, who witnessed first hand his nefarious lifestyle, considered they had sufficient proof to determine he was a man willingly heading down the wide path to perdition. However, the most startling information concerns Faustus' ominous revelation that the devil was his 'brother-in-law', stated in Luther's *Tischreden* and supported by Wier's document based on information gleaned from the reports of personal acquaintances. Hence, Faustus, undaunted by the publication of Trithemius' letter (1507) in 1536, dared to confirm he had advanced beyond the level of a scarlet sinner — he was a conscious follower of the Prince of Darkness. The fact he could publicly project an Antichrist image with pride, having no fear of reprisal, and his seeming diabolical art of escaping all punishment when others who were considered heretics had burned at the stake for less, would certainly signal that an unnatural individual walked in their midst. It is true in many respects he assumed the role of the charlatan, yet how apropos, considering his willingness to follow his 'brother-in-law' known as the Father of Lies and deception. Notwithstanding the vogue for astrological prognostications that many academics practised, the fact *his* recorded prophecies proved to be correct, when legitimate and accredited professionals such as Camerarius had failed, may have caused many to recognise his constant accuracy to be preternatural, particularly when the results of his last prediction beckoned from beyond the grave. Equally incredible was Faustus' ability to sway and ingratiate himself with those in high Church positions to acquire a respectable front for his sinister career, particularly the Bishop of Bamberg. How did he manipulate these circumstances for so many years? That Faustus would candidly affirm kinship with Satan, even as a *coup de carrière*, had provided sufficient evidence to affirm to his contemporaries the true source of his abnormal protection —there is no diabolical smoke without an infernal fire! When Faustus met his sudden and gruesome demise in Staufen, all suspicions alluding to his allegiance with the forces of Darkness were finally accepted as undisputed fact.

Therefore, it is not difficult to comprehend the upsurge in legendary and didactic material following his death. Faustus, who embraced evil and shunned righteousness, became the foremost symbol of the misuse of free will, that sublime gift from God with its inherit opportunity to choose virtue and reject iniquity. "What shall a man gain if he has the whole world and lose his soul," (Matt. 16: v. 26) — but for a notorious name, the ethereal shadow of a career, and a brief life of fleeting pleasure with no true peace? This was the blackest and most captivating tragedy of all, few could have remained indifferent to the growing intrigue of this individual who apparently shook hands with the devil and freely chose to descend to the molten, sulphuric chasm of Hell for all eternity for so little in exchange. It is a drama that continues to fascinate today as powerfully as when Faustus first disseminated his infamous card in the Heidelberg locale to the scandal of his generation. *In fine*, a life of good or evil, the hope of

Heaven or the despair of Hell, Faustus stands as a reminder that the choice between these two absolutes also falls to us.

Year	Known Major Events or Places Visited According to Historical Documents as Discussed in this Work
1466 or 1467 (?)	Possible year of (Georgius "Sabellicus") Faustus' birth; evidently in Helmstadt near Heidelberg.
January 9, 1483	Enrols at Heidelberg University using the name 'Helmstetter'.
July 12, 1484	Graduates with a Bachelor's degree ranking sixteen of his class out of seventeen students.
March 1, 1487	Graduates with a Master's degree ranking second of his class out of ten candidates.
1490	Heidelberg. May have remained a further two years to fulfil teaching requirement. (i.e. until c. 1489-1490). Drafts a horoscope for a student, Peter Seuter, using a unique combination of astrology, chiromancy and physiognomy.
May, 1506	Gelnhausen, a town between Fulda and Frankfurt. Boasts at an inn, but refuses to meet with Trithemius. (May have embarked on his career as a wandering scholar / diviner during this time, c.1506–1507)
Sometime after June 2, 1506	Würzburg. Boasts he could accomplish the same miracles as Christ. (Compares himself to Simon Magus?)
Towards end of Lent, 1507	Kreuznach, (or Bad-Kreuznach), c. 30 km / 18.6 miles southwest of Mainz. Appointed as schoolteacher. Flees due to accusations of "nefarious fornication."
c. August, 1507	Virdung in Heidelberg awaits the arrival of Faustus.

October 1, 1513	Erfurt. Boasts at an inn.
February 10, 1520	Bamberg. Faustus paid 10 gulden for preparing a horoscope for the Bishop of Bamberg. Recognised as a 'philosopher'.
1521 (?)	Halberstadt.(?) Guest of Dr. Nicholas Winkler, city physician.
June 5, 1528	Near the vicinity of Rebdorf in Bavaria. Claims to have been a "commander or preceptor" of the Knights of St. John (The Hospitalers, later known as the Knights of Malta) in Heilenstein, Styria: a province in southeastern Austria, or in the northeast of present day Slovenia. (Evidence Faustus had travelled through Heilenstein, Styria? c. 1522–1528) Possibly made a prediction based on the conjuction of Mercury, Mars and Jupiter in the sign of Cancer that summer when the sun entered the constellation. (With his reference to the Hospitalers, did he insinuate war with the Ottomans was at hand?)
June 15, 1528	Ingolstadt: Faustus is banished from the city, an order possibly influenced by Johann Eck. Faustus pledged not to take vengeance on the authorities.
May 10, 1532	Fürth: Faustus refused safe passage to Nuremberg at Fürth. (Due to the fear of competition by local astrologers?) Recognised as a sodomite and necromancer, perchance by the circulation of Trithemius' letter. Apparently, ignored the warning, proceeded to Nuremberg and was nearly arrested.
Same year (1532)	Wittenberg: apparently stayed at an inn not far from Melachthon's home. His presence in the city tolerated by Luther and Melanchthon with the hope of his conversion. Apparently, Faustus threatened Melanchthon because of the latter's rebukes to change his evil ways. Faustus was not influenced, and he promoted his black

	arts. (Local tradition states he taught these arts under a burnt hollow tree in a remote place near the town.) Prince John the Steadfast ordered the arrest of Faustus, but he escaped. (Unknown whether this incident occurred before or after his journey to Fürth / Nuremberg). (Apparently, Faustus boasted c. 1532 that Charles V's victories in Italy were due to his magic. Melanchthon declared Faustus a liar. May have precipitated / aggravated the competition with Camerarius in later years.)
c. 1534	(Würzburg?): Faustus predicted an unfavourable outcome of the von Hutten Expedition to Venezuela. (Result unknown until 1540). The competition between the astrologers in Nuremberg piques Peter Seuter's curiosity. He sends the horoscope he received in 1490 from 'Helmstetter' to his friend, Nicolaus Ellenbog. Ellenbog is confused by the unorothodox combination of astrology with chiromancy.
June 25, 1535	Corbach → Waldeck: Faustus predicted the successful capture of Münster by Bishop Francis I. Faustus recognised as a "distinguished Necromancer".
August 13, 1536	Camerarius asks Stibar to approach Faustus concerning Charles V, obviously about the war in France. Camerarius' own predictions prove inaccurate. (1536: A collection of Trithemius' letters is published, which includes the correspondence condemning Faustus dated August 1507.)
1537	Martin Luther's acquaintances report Faustus called the devil his "brother-in-law": Wier's account written years later supports this claim.
1538 (?)	Staufen, (near present day Stuttgart): Death of Faustus. Apparently was alchemist to the

	Count of Staufen at this time. Current local tradition records he died by an explosion in room No. 5 at the Gasthaus zum Lowen (Lion Inn). Was this an accident, or suicide? According to rumour, Faustus' legacy of books fell into the possession of the Count. Local tradition also states these books and all written records of Faustus in the town were destroyed by arson during the Thirty-Years War.
෨ඣ❖෨ඣ	෨ඣ❖෨ඣ
	Addtional Details from Historical Documents (Dates of Occurrence Unknown)
(?)	Visited the town of Basel, Switzerland. May have visited the university. Possibly owned a horse and a dog.
(?)	Luxeuil, in the Vosges Mountains: Faustus was refused lodging at the famous monastery. Monks had therefore broken the ancient custom of sanctuary. He may have uttered a curse upon the monastery in revenge.
(?)	Visited the Netherlands: was arrested in Batenburg on the Maas near the border of Gelderland.
(?)	According to Begardi's *Index Sanitatis*, Faustus added the profession of medicine to his list of 'accomplishments'. Begardi regards him as a charlatan. Weir's document, *De Praestigiis Daemonium*, suggests Faustus was a barber-surgeon: skills of this career included teeth-pulling, bloodletting, removal of tumours, wound-stitching. Wier records one indident of malpractice: Faustus prescribes a depilatory salve made from arsenic for a Dr. Johannes Dorstenius without mentioning how it should be properly prepared, which causes severe facial injuries. The salve was possibly made from realgar, or an alchemical concoction using orpiment.

	(From this information, we may speculate Faustus followed the armies as customary with barber-surgeons and quacks of the time in order to earn a living. Perhaps he followed the armies planning to lay seige to Münster, which allowed him to make an educated guess as to the outcome of the battle.)

ଛଓଔ❖ଛଓଔ

Chapter 2

The Dawn of Faustian Literature

Subsequent to Faustus' death, the evolution of his story from biographical fact and oral legend to polished literary genres was a gradual process. With the exception of a few publications featuring passing references to the magician until the year 1587, the first Faustian literature in Germany generally circulated as unsophisticated compilations of folklore in manuscript form. The earliest of these collections may be the *Reichmann-Wambach Chronical* of the mid-sixteenth century, unfortunately, this record survives through a secondary source, therefore Chistoph Rosshirt's *Chronicle* (c. 1570–1575) examined in Chapter One is generally recognised by scholars as the first official attempt in assembling the popular Faust tales.[267] Of greater importance, the emergence of the Faust legend as a structurally unified work centres on the Wolfenbüttel Manuscript (c.1580–1587*), the earliest extant example of the handwritten texts that prefigured and set the foundation in both content and pseudo-biographical style for the original printed Spies *Faustbook* of 1587.

The Wolfenbüttel Manuscript

In view of the rapid dissemination of humanist ideology heralded by the revolutionary Gutenberg press (c. 1450), the considerable delay of the first publication of the *Faustbooks* (Spies 1587), circa one-hundred and thirty seven years following the debut of this momentous invention, is perplexing. However, H. G. Haile presents one reasonable possibility for this time-lapse in his new 1965 edition of the Wolfenbüttel Manuscript when recalling:

> "Four centuries back, you would have read the Faust Book on
> folio parchment, handwritten by a professional scribe. […] Your Faust
> Book was not in print because the people regarded it as a horrible,
> blasphemous account which endangered the soul of its reader."[268]

According to the preface of the Wolfenbüttle text, an 'official' Latin compilation of Faust's 'biographical' adventures was already in existence and circulated privately within certain privileged circles. It was the opinion of the translator that the Latin version was not written nor

---

[267] Palmer and More, *Sources of the Faust Tradition*, p. 129.

* The date of the Wolfenbüttle MS was previously thought to be c. 1572–1587, however, recent research indicates the date could be within the 1580s, i.e. (1580–1587). See 'n. &' below at 'The Faustian Texts and the Printing Press: The First Printed *Faustbook* (1587)'.

[268] *Haile, History of Doctor Johann Faustus*, p. 16.

printed in German prior to that time due to certain apprehensions, namely that the uneducated would be inclined to follow the reprobate's example and summon demons to their utter destruction:

> "My very dear friend and brother, this translation of Doctor Faustus and his wicked design is the result of your repeated request that I should put the Latin into German, which, so far as I am aware, has not been done. The reason it has not been printed or written in German is clear: so that no wicked and uneducated persons will use it as a model on which to build their fantasies and attempt to do as he did. [...] I could not forbear from adding this preamble and the anecdotes within the work itself, both as an apology and a caution. I am quite confident that you will find the deeds of Doctor Faustus a pleasant diversion, especially since these events are true and consequently you will enjoy them more than other, fictitious stories. Dear friend and brother, take it and read it to enliven your garden walk."[269]

Today, we who are accustomed to the graphic nature of modern horror films, may be amused at the intensity of the discretion with which the seemingly unrefined Faustian manuscripts were regarded. Similar to the earlier Faust anthologies, the Wolfenbüttel text features a diverse collection of popular Faust myths with legends initially attributed to other magicians, thus precipitating the comment from Palmer and More: "It is a crude piece of compilation of no literary value."[270] In that religiously conscious era, however, when the concept of a distinct separation between Church and State was unheard of, the welfare of the immortal soul was of paramount importance in the clerical and secular spheres collectively. Similar to scholars trained in the hermetic tradition who preferred not to divulge their interest in the occult fearing reprisals, enterprising publishers refrained from printing a definitive book of Faustus or Faustian folklore, discouraged by the possible threat of punishment from the authorities for seducing gullible readers with tales purportedly glorifying an evil individual. The Renaissance era, a time of insatiable scientific enquiry and exploration, was nevertheless restrained by the spiritual prudence of the Medieval age.

Unfortunately, the original Latin manuscript was lost; however, its extant successor, the Wolfenbüttle text, displays the first attempts to inscribe a serious literary representation of Faustus for study within private academic circles, a development that ultimately prepared the legend for general publication in future years. We may presume it was the author of the Latin text who ingeniously discovered a licit method of recording these myths, rather than simply gather a 'perilous' collection of Faustian folklore, he refashioned the history of Faustus by creating a fictitious biography of a noted Epicurean to serve as an admonition to those of discernment. Evidently, the translator of the Wolfenbüttle text recognised the efficacy of this idea and embellished the text with his personal admonishing "anecdotes" as mentioned in his preface. In the Introduction of the Wolfenbüttle text it is announced:

---

269 Empson, Henry Jones (ed.), *Faustus and the Censor*, pp. 31–32.
270 *Sources of the Faust Tradition*, p. 129.

The sorcerer, wherein is described specifically and veraciously:
His entire life and death,
How he did oblige himself for a certain time unto the Devil,
And what happened to him,
And how he at last got his well-deserved reward.

Rare revelations are also included, for these examples are most useful and efficacious as a highly essential Christian warning and admonition, that the laity, in order to protect themselves from similar maculations of the most shameful sort, have especial cause to heed and to avoid such a desperate fate.[271]

Contemporary readers already familiar with the profusion of semi-credible Faustian myths through oral tradition, obviously did not challenge what appeared in ink and parchment, it would be inconceivable that a text intended for moral edification would have an element of falsehood contained within! The author of the original Latin text, probably aware that this work would be credibly received, used this knowledge to his utmost advantage when transcribing his version — the translator of the Wolfenbüttle manuscript, in the transcription intended for his friend, also declared the veracity of the 'biographical' information, notwithstanding his own additions. Faustus was thereby transformed into *the* emblematic antithesis to Protestant morality for those who supported the new theology of the Reformation.

Certainly, the Wolfenbüttel text may indeed be perceived as a primitive, "crude compilation" of famous Faust[*] tales upon first inspection; however, we observe that the majority of these popular myths were not introduced immediately in the narration and were deliberately reserved for the latter sections. In fact, the first half of the manuscript features distinctive, carefully constructed material pertaining to Faust's experiences with the demons of Hell that are not included in surviving documents or works of fiction dating from the era the text was compiled. Obviously, it was not the author's objective[§] to produce a mere anthology — his primary concern was to fashion an original and structured, coherent rendition of the legend in an

---

[271] *History of Doctor Johann Faustus*, p. 17
[*] As the Wolfenbüttel manuscript features the various forms and spellings of Faustus' name, e.g. Faustus, Fauste, Faust, for our discussion of the text the names "Faust" and "Faustus" are used respectively in this Chapter to distinguish between the legendary character of literature and the historical figure, with the exception of direct quotations.
[§] There is a certain difficulty in discussing the *author's* intentions as the original Latin MS upon which the Wolfenbüttle text was based is now lost. We must also acknowledge this Latin text may be previously embellished by other scribes. Additionally, the "author" of the Wolfenbüttle text is actually the *translator* of this lost MS, but he also added to the material. For the remainder of our analysis of the Wolfenbüttle text, we have used the term "author" to reflect what appears to be the original material retained from the lost text, and consider the 'translator' one of the scribes. (Hence, the use of the term "Wolfenbüttle" in our study also takes into account the lost Latin document.)

effort to present an academic text for moral edification and philosophical interest, albeit for a select readership and not for the general public.[272]

The work is divided into four[**] sections: the first pertains to Faust's university education in the field of theology and his seduction by the black arts leading to the twenty-four year contract for his soul. The second part in general narrates his exploits in the realm of astronomy and astrology, while the third section displays his digression into pandering to the great princes and potentates of the day with his magic powers. Finally, in the fourth section, Faust continues to assist and entertain his associates and students with his skills and indulges in a variety of vices. When his last day on earth draws to a close, he laments his horrid fate, bids farewell to his acquaintances, and is torn limb from limb by demons when the appointed hour of his death befalls him. Notably, this four-part structure of the text parallels one of Luther's deductions regarding the devil's subtle plan to attack the faith of Christians. Oberman relates:

> "The Devil himself appears on the scene and will not content himself with simple 'temptations,' as Luther termed the seducer's arts. The Devil drives a person to doubt his election, and seduces the doubter into wanting to penetrate God's hidden will to find out whether or not he is really among those chosen by God. This undertaking must fail and the ensuing uncertainty leads to fear, blasphemy, and hatred for God, and finally to doubts about the existence of God altogether. What the Devil would most like to do is to push all Christians to the brink of revelation, tempt them to try to penetrate God's nature, and then let them fall where he fell himself: into the void."[273]

In the Wolfenbüttel Text, Faust rejects his university education in the field of theology, and embraces occult mysticism to which he devotes all his energies, attempting to penetrate the mystery of creation by demonic intervention and trusting in their sundry 'revelations'. Yet in the second half of the text, when the devil has succeeded in numbing Faust's conscience to God's justice and replaces it with despair marring his hope to receive Divine mercy, Faust grows

---

[272] The text we used for our analysis of the Wolfenbüttel manuscript is from H. G. Haile's translation in *The History of Doctor Johann Faustus* (University of Illinois Press, 1965). Haile reorganised the layout of the text, and deleted several chapters due to repetitions that occurred when scribes began to add their own folklore to the MS, and claims this version "[…] is probably just as close as we shall ever get to how the Faust Book [i.e. the manuscript] looked when it was first written." (Haile, p. 16) It is clear he intended to present a text that is an approximate *of the original Latin edition*. Unfortunately, this poses two difficulties: the edition as an example of the Latin original is merely speculative, and second, this edited version impairs a detailed study of the actual Wolfenbüttle MS. Hence, any discovered omissions from the Wolfenbüttle MS or other editing by Haile will be indicated in the course of our study. For the original German reprint of the Wolfenbüttle MS, see Gustac Milchsack, *Historia D. Johannis Fausti des Zauberers nach der Wolfenbütteler Handschrift* (Wolfenbüttel, 1892).

[**] That is, in Haile's edited edition. John Henry Jones relates the Wolfenbüttle MS is very close to the first printed book by Spies, which actually has three sections with the last subdivided into two parts. *Faustus and the Censor,* p. 30.

[273] Oberman, *Luther, Man Between God and the Devil,* p. 179.

indifferent to the philosophical and scientific realm altogether, abandoning himself to all manner of iniquity in a life of habitual sin. Finally, his spiritual paralysis is complete as he relinquishes all hope of salvation — compelled to submit to his fate, he plummets into the Abyss.

Faust: The Speculative Theologian

When we delve deeper into the text, we uncover further clues that may indicate to what extent the author was influenced by Luther's life and theology, an influence that also inspired the scribes who embellished the legend as they recopied the manuscript. Beginning with Part One of the text, the first particulars introduced in the narration are Faust's social background and place of birth; described as hailing from a farming family, he is reported to be a native of Roda[√] in the Province of Weimar. However, Faust's parents are not without certain connections as we are informed they had many associates in the town of Wittenberg; in particular, a wealthy relative without children of his own who adopted Faust, educated him, and legally declared him his heir. This section of the manuscript parallels Martin Luther's background and early life. Luther was born in the town of Eisleben about seventy miles southwest of Wittenberg and circa seventy miles northeast of Weimar. Luther's family on his paternal side came from a farming background, however, as it was traditional for the youngest son to inherit the farm property, Luther's father, Hans Luder, was obliged to earn his living by some other trade and therefore worked in the copper mining industry. Luther also had privileged and influential relatives on the maternal side of his family, the Lindemanns. Oberman writes:

> "In Luther's time we encounter two cousins, the sons of his [Luther's] mother's eldest brother, whose name we do not know. The elder cousin is Johann Lindemann from Eisleben († 1519), doctor of law and electoral councillor in Saxony; his younger brother Kaspar (†1536) received his degree of doctor of medicine after studying in Leipzig, Frankfurt on the Oder, and Bologna. He became personal physician to Elector Frederick and to his successor John and treated Luther occasionally. During the last four years of his life Kaspar Lindemann was professor of medicine in Wittenberg."[274]

Obermann also relates the decision to send Luther to Eisenach for the remainder of his secondary education was due to his family connections in that particular town:

> "The decision to give Martin [Luther] an education was a well-established Lindemann family tradition. The abrupt move from Magdeburg […] to Eisenach probably had family reasons as well. No,

---

[√] Now called Stadtroda.
[274] *Luther, Man Between God and the Devil*, p. 90.

Martin was not a poor lonely boy being pushed from one strange town to another; he was Margaret [Lindemann's] son, who had uncles and aunts in Eisenach to look after him and who in fact went to stay there with Heinrich Schalbe, a friend of the family. Luther owed a great deal to Schalbe, himself a town councillor and ultimately mayor of Eisenach."[275]

Hence, there is evidence to suggest this fictitious biography of Faust was fashioned to reflect Luther's youth. However, there is one major disparity that the author makes explicitly clear; Faust, in contrast to Luther, did not live according to his training in theology, but "[...] strayed from his godly purpose and used God's Word vainly."[276] We may observe one possibility, the author of the Wolfenbüttel text intended to portray Faust as the antithesis of Luther who pivoted all his theological studies and beliefs on the importance of adhering to the word of God as recorded in sacred Scripture. A vast portion of the text appears to be influenced by the reformer's doctrines and writings, as we shall discover.

Subsequent to this initial introduction of the reprobate, the narrative is interrupted by a short moral admonition[♦] exhorting readers not to place any blame on Faust's parents for the evil life he chose to lead stating, "Therefore pious parents do sometimes have godless, naughty children, and I point this out because there have been many who imputed great guilt and calumny to these parents whom I would herewith pardon."[277] We therefore may acquire a greater insight on how the general populace regarded, or speculated upon, the upbringing of the historical Faustus. This section of the manuscript evinces many contemporaries blamed a liberal, godless childhood for the heretical lifestyle of the real Faustus and therefore had slandered his parents by malicious gossip. According to the text, they and their relations were accused of teaching him his black arts, permitting "wantonness in his youth", of not supervising the progress of his studies in theology, or had neglected their duty to suppress any interest he displayed towards the occult. However, the author defends Faust's relatives stating that they were worried when they discovered his cleverness as he could misuse his natural talent and "[...] sin against the Lord". Also, the author clearly states they were unaware he did not intend to choose a career in theology for he was a ...

"... most percipient and adroit fellow [who ...] performed so well at his examination that the rectors also examined him for the *Magister* Degree. There were sixteen other candidates, to whom he proved in address, composition, and competence so superior that it was immediately concluded he had studied sufficiently, and he became *Doctor Theologiæ*."[278]

---

[275] Ibid.
[276] *History of Doctor Johann Faustus*, p. 21.
[♦] This may have been included by the Wolfenbüttle translator.
[277] *History of Doctor Johann Faustus*. p. 22.
[278] Ibid. p. 22.

This admonitory addition to the Faust-text exhorting readers to refrain from committing detraction and bearing false witness may also have originated with similar experiences Luther endured when his parents were slandered by his adversaries. A rumour spread that Luther's father was the very devil, his mother an adulteress and a bathhouse attendant.[279] Thus, Luther, the heretic, was regarded as the progeny of an infernal relationship to account for his evident inclination towards apostasy and his attacks upon the papacy. It is possible the author of the Wolfenbüttel Text attempted to display a similar scenario with his version of Faust's life to reveal how despicable it is to slander and defame parents for the decisions made by their children. Luther's adversaries deemed they were justified in regarding him as an evil individual, nevertheless, to extend these opinions and accusations to his parents was inexcusable. The same applies to Faust in the manuscript, it was his decision to study the occult, a career option that had no direct relation with his family's aspirations for him and his future. In summary, the author demonstrates malicious gossipers will root out a subject from any situation worthy of their tongues, a vice one would do well to avoid.

Continuing with his narrative in Chapter One, the author declares that notwithstanding Faust's competence at the university, "[…] he was also a stupid, unreasonable and vain fellow, whom, after all, his companions always called the *speculator*. He came into the worst company, for a time laid the Holy Scriptures behindst the door and under the bench, did not revere God's Word but lived crassly and godlessly […]."[280] He then consorts with those who studied the languages associated with the occult, i.e. "Chaldean, Persian, Arabian, and Greek" and delves into their books with great interest, learning all the various characters, figures and enchantments associated with the black arts. Faust eventually elects to concentrate his studies in these nefarious subjects, becomes an astrologer and mathematician, and declares himself a Doctor of Medicine, which may be one of the few references to Faustus that is historically accurate.

Chapter Two of the Wolfenbüttel text reveals how Faust's obsession with the occult overpowered him to such an extent that he wished to seek out the "[…] very foundations of Heaven and Earth." Finally, the temptation to experiment with the various magical formulae he discovered spurs him into action to satisfy his academic curiosity. Venturing into a wood called the "Spesser Wald" near Wittenberg, Faust inscribes various circles at a crossroads with which he summons the devil "[…] between nine and ten o'clock",[281] undoubtedly a detail inspired by the infamous Faust Tree of Wittenberg where Faustus taught his arts to his pupils. The author of the text may have been familiar with incantation books; Henry Jones observes "[…] the *grimoires* mention crossroads as among the very best places for conjuring — they were always dangerous, and prime sites for gibbets."[282] It was believed that magic circles could force a demon to appear and simultaneously protect the magician from the spirits they summoned.[283]

---

[279] *Luther, Man Between God and the Devil*, p. **88**.

[280] *History of Doctor Johann Faustus*, pp. 22–23.

[281] Ibid. p. **24**.

[282] *Faustus and the Censor*, p. **15**.

[283] David Bevington and Eric Rasmussen, eds., *Doctor Faustus, A- and B- texts (1604,1616): Christopher Marlowe and his Collaborator and Revisers* (Manchester: Manchester University Press, 1993), n. 8, p. 126.

The devil feigns his unwillingness to appear when called and initiates a series of dramatic theatrics when Faust commences his spell:

> "[The Devil] caused such a tumult in the forest that everything seemed about to be destroyed. He blew up such a wind that the trees were bent to the very ground. Then it seemed as were the wood with devils filled, who rode along past Doctor Faustus' circle; now only their coaches were to be seen; then from the four corners of the forest something like lightening bolts converged on Doctor Faustus' circle, and a loud explosion ensued. When all this was past, it became light in the midst of the forest, and many sweet instruments, music and song could be heard. There were various dances, too, and tourneys with spears and swords. Faustus, who thought he might have tarried long enough now, considered fleeing from his circle, but finally he regained his godless and reckless resolve and persisted in his former intention, come whatever God might send.
>
> He continued to conjure the Devil as before, and the Devil did mystify him with the following hoax. He appeared like a griffen or a dragon hovering and flattering above the circle, and when Doctor Faustus then applied his spell the beast shrieked piteously. Soon thereafter a fiery star fell right down from three or four fathoms above his head and was transformed into a glowing ball. This greatly alarmed Faustus, too. But his purpose liked him so well, and he so admired having the Devil subservient to him that he took courage and did conjure the star once, twice, and a third time, whereupon a gush of fire from the sphere shot up as high as a man, settled again, and six little lights became visible upon it. Now one little light would leap upward, now a second downward until the form of a burning man finally emerged. He walked round about the circle for a full seven or eight minutes. The entire spectacle, however, had lasted until twelve o'clock in the night. Now a devil, or a spirit, appeared in the figure of a gray friar, greeted Doctor Faustus, and asked what his desire might be. Hereupon Doctor Faustus commanded that he should appear at his house and lodging at a certain hour the next morning, the which the devil for a while refused to do. Doctor Faustus conjured him by his master, however, compelling him to fulfil his desire, so that the spirit at last consented and agreed."[284]

The next morning, i.e. Chapter Three, Faust summons the spirit to his chambers with his various conjurations and demands obedience from him, specifying three terms in particular:

---

[284] *History of Doctor Johann Faustus*, pp. 24-26

"Firstly, that the spirit should be subservient and obedient to him in all that he might request, inquire, or expect of him, throughout Faustus' life and death.

Secondly, that the spirit would withhold no information which Faustus, in his studies, might require.

Thirdly, that the spirit would respond nothing untruthful to any of his *interrogationes*."[285]

The spirit immediately refuses the terms offered with the explanation that as a lesser demon he could not fulfil these desires unless permitted by "[…] the Hellish god", Satan. Faust is surprised to learn the demon is not his own master and is bound by the hierarchal authority of the Abyss. Faust requests the spirit to explain this matter in more detail, whereupon the spirit replies:

"Now shalt thou know, Fauste, said the spirit, that among us there is a government and sovereignty, just as on earth, for we have our rulers and governors and servants — of whom I am one — and we call our kingdom Legion. For although the banished devil Lucifer brought about his own fall through vanity and insolence, he raised up a Legion, nevertheless, and a government of devils, and we call him the Oriental Prince, for he had his sovereignty in Ascension. It is thus a sovereignty in *Meridie*, *Septentrione* and *Occidente* as well. Well, inasmuch as Lucifer the fallen angel now hath his sovereignty and principality beneath the Heavens, we must, on account of this transformation, betake ourselves unto mankind and serve them. But with all his power and arts man could not make Lucifer subservient, except that a spirit be sent, as I am sent. Certainly we have never revealed to men the real fundament of our dwelling place, nor our rule and sovereignty. No one knoweth what doth occur after the death of the damned human — who learneth and experienceth it."[286]

The origin of this fascinating narration is discerned from basic theology. When Christ was accused of casting out devils by Beelzebub, the Prince of devils, He highlighted the error of His accusers' judgement replying "[…] Every kingdom divided against itself, shall be brought to desolation, and house upon house shall fall. And if Satan also be divided against himself, how shall his kingdom stand? Because you say, that through Beelzebub I cast out devils. […] But if I by the finger of God cast out devils; doubtless the kingdom of God is come upon you." (Luke 11: 17–18, 20) Therefore, the devil's kingdom, like all kingdoms with "house upon house", must be ruled by a hierarchal system. The name "Legion" points to the passages of the Gospels where Christ dispels the demons from a possessed man and permits them to enter the heard of swine, e.g. "For he said unto him: Go out of the man, thou unclean spirit. And he asked him: What is

---

285 Ibid. p. 27.
286 Ibid. pp. 28–29.

thy name? And he saith to him: My name is Legion, for we are many." (Mark 5:8–9) The title of *Oriental Prince,* i.e. 'Eastern Prince' for Satan is particularly resourceful. The first reference to this title is recorded in the Old Testament in the book of Zacharias. God reveals to the prophet Zacharias a vision in which Satan accuses Josue, the son of the high priest Josedec, of sin. Josue is also referred to as *Jesus*:

> "And the Lord shewed me Jesus the high priest standing before the angel of the Lord: and Satan stood on his right hand to be his adversary. And the Lord said to Satan: The Lord rebuke thee, O Satan: and the Lord that chose Jerusalem rebuke thee: Is not this a brand plucked out of the fire? […] And the angel of the Lord protested to Jesus saying: Thus saith the Lord of hosts: If thou wilt walk in my ways, and keep my charge, thou also shalt judge my house, and shalt keep my courts, and I will give thee some of them that are now present here to walk with thee. Hear, O Jesus thou high priest, thou and thy friends that dwell before thee, for they are portending men: for behold I WILL BRING MY SERVANT THE ORIENT." (Zacharias 3: 1–2, 6–8)

> "And thou shalt take gold and silver: and shalt make crowns, and thou shalt set them on the head of Jesus the son of Josedec, the high priest. And thou shalt speak to him, saying: Thus saith the Lord of hosts, saying: BEHOLD A MAN, THE ORIENT IS HIS NAME: and under him shall he spring up, and shall build a temple to the Lord. Yea, he shall build a temple to the Lord: and he shall bear the glory, and shall sit, and rule upon his throne: and he shall be a priest upon his throne, and the counsel of peace shall be between them both." (Zacharias 6: 11–13)

This vision in the Book of Zacharias foretells the coming of Christ, "My servant the Orient", a servant because according to His humanity He is the servant of God, and the title 'Orient' foretells His rising like the sun from the east to enlighten the world. This luminous title, 'the Orient', is also found in the New Testament when Zachary's tongue is loosened to confirm Elizabeth's pronouncement of John as the name of their newborn son and to herald him as the prophet of the Messiah:

> "And thou, child, [i.e. John], shalt be called the prophet of the Highest: for thou shalt go before the face of the Lord to prepare his ways: To give knowledge of salvation to his people, unto the remission of their sins: Through the bowels of the mercy of our God, in which the Orient from on high hath visited us: to enlighten them that sit in darkness, and in the shadow of death: to direct our feet into the way of peace." (Luke 1: 76–79)

In summary, the prophesy declares as Saviour and eternal High Priest, Christ will be given authority over the kingdom of God in heaven and on earth and will rule as King of Kings.

In the Book of Isaiah we discover this is the position Lucifer, i.e. Satan, the "morning star" of the east, attempted to usurp when through pride he declared himself "like unto God":

> "How art thou fallen from heaven, O Lucifer, who didst rise in the morning? How art thou fallen to earth, that thou didst wound the nations? And thou saidst in thy heart: I will ascend to heaven, I will exalt my throne above the stars of God, I will sit in the mountain of the covenant, in the sides of the north. I will ascend above the height of the clouds, I will be like the most High. But yet thou shalt be brought down to hell, into the depth of the pit." (Isaiah 14: 12–15)

Returning to the Wolfenbüttel text, the spirit 'reveals' to Faust that Satan continues to lay claim to the title "Oriental Prince". However, as Satan has fallen from Heaven to the earth, his kingdom has been established in the air "beneath the heavens" in the Orient (east), the Occident (west), Meridian (south) and Septentrio (north); a detail that refers to Ephesians (6:12): "For our wrestling is not against flesh and blood; but against principalities and powers, against the rulers of this world of darkness, against the spirits of wickedness *in the high places*. [i.e. the celestial regions beneath Heaven]."

An unexpected admission disclosed to Faust by the spirit concerns the task of the lesser demons to "[…] betake ourselves unto mankind and serve them. But with all his power and arts man could not make Lucifer subservient, except that a spirit be sent, as I am sent." The second half of this statement in theological terms is true; Lucifer, a spirit who by the sin of pride refused to serve God, certainly cannot be forced into servitude by any human! However, the spirit continues with a partial deception in saying the lesser devils "serve" man or minister unto him — a task they also denounced when they refused to serve God as ministering angels — yet this phrase could imply they are apparently forced to "serve" man through diabolical pacts, as with the agreement Faust is currently negotiating. However, the deception lies in that the demon is in reality providing a 'disservice' under the guise of benevolence for his ultimate intention is evil, that Faust should suffer the loss of his soul. The demon thus announces Faust had no power over Satan during his conjuring in the "Spesser Wald", explaining the author's description of the devilish antics in the forest as a "hoax". Obviously, the author intended to emphasise that one cannot control Satan or his legions with arts of their own invention, i.e. black magic and necromancy — on the contrary — the temptation to experiment with these arts and the delusion of receiving complete superhuman power from them are lures by which Satan draws in curious victims.

Faust, blinded to this observation, prefers to believe he may still control the lesser demons and have a spirit subservient to him. He is more concerned with the disclosure that the demons have never revealed the nature of their kingdom to any human, only those mortals who are damned may attain this knowledge from them and experience this hellish kingdom for themselves first hand. Faust exclaims he will not allow himself to be eternally lost for the spirit's service, but the spirit retorts with another lie: Faust is already damned because of his "insolent heart" that wished to search out every celestial secret hidden from mankind with their demonic assistance. The demon purposely obscures the theological truth that the damnation of a soul does not commence until the moment of death, hope of salvation lives as long as the life of the individual, provided they do not live in habitual sin with the presumption of receiving forgiveness on their terms. In addition, the demon attempts to forge the 'logical' conclusion within Faust's mind that if a lesser demon must receive permission from Lucifer before submitting to a human, the same would apply before they may reveal their knowledge to a human. Hence, the demon would have Faust believe that the information already disclosed regarding their kingdom would not be permitted at this point in time if what he said concerning Faust's damnation was not true. Once more, Faust is misled, for as we proved in our discussion above, the details 'revealed' by the spirit pertaining to Lucifer's kingdom are not previously undisclosed secrets for they are recorded in Scripture. The devil successfully confounds the supposed theologian, sinking his hook into Faust's wavering conscience and faulty reasoning. Faust demands the spirit to depart, but his resolve to bridle his curiosity and reject evil crumbles, he instantly changes his mind, conjuring the spirit to return once more at vespers. Apparently, Faust has abandoned his will to the devil's artful delusions, believing the deception that his particular predestined fate was eternal damnation.

The spirit returns at vespers, the Fourth Chapter, and having completely misled Faust, it is his turn to make the demands. In return for his subservience, the demon stipulates three articles that must be fulfilled:

> "Firstly, that he, Faustus, would agree to a certain number of years, at the expiration of which he would promise and swear to be his, the spirit's own property.
> Secondly, that he would, to the further confirmation thereof, give himself over with a writ to this effect authenticated in his own blood.
> Thirdly, that he would renounce the Christian Faith and defy all believers."[287]

Craftily, the demon has manipulated Faust's three demands. First, Faust had audaciously commanded the spirit to be subservient to him in life *and* after death, but the demon mitigates this service to continue only for the duration of Faust's lifetime and states Faust must also agree to a time limit. In death, Faust must ultimately become the demon's own property. Second, Faust demanded that the spirit not withhold any information he would request. In response to this, the demon states he requires a written contract in Faust's own blood. Hence, as Faust wishes to obtain "all knowledge" he must sign over his inheritance of Eternal Life, that is his soul, with the *physical* symbol of life, which according to the Book of Leviticus is blood: "For the life of all flesh is in the blood: [...]" (Lev. 17:14). Third, Faust demanded that the devil never utter an untruth to him when questioned; a paradoxical request, as all devils are liars — we already discovered the demon blinded Faust with lies and distortions of the truth. In return for this third request, the spirit demands that Faust deny his Christian faith, and thereby renounce Eternal Truth for the 'seeming' truth that he supposedly will reveal to him. However, the demon throws in a bonus to the deal, that Faust would be granted a "spirit's form and powers". This declaration may signify the power of bilocation, the ability to travel in spirit while simultaneously remaining physically present elsewhere. Hence, the familiar belief is displayed in the text that

---

[287] Ibid. p. 30.

Satan attempts to parody God in all things, including the granting of supernatural abilities to a certain number of His specially chosen souls on earth. This phenomenal offer that the cunning spirit dangles before Faust immediately tantalises the scholar's pride and his voracious desire to seek out the "foundations of Heaven and Earth", causing him to cast aside all concern for the welfare of his eternal soul.

The details relevant to the signing of the pact are dispersed between the fifth and sixth chapters. In Chapter Five, Faust requests the spirit to appear the next morning in the form of a Franciscan monk complete with alms bell to sound an advance warning when he approaches, a form already assumed at the first apparition. Faust subsequently chooses this form as the permanent profile for his *familiar* spirit. One origin of this anti-Catholic barb may be traced to a particular cynicism Cornelius Agrippa inscribed in his *De vanitate* when he stated that the Devil "[…] invented the monkish cowl,"[288] a sarcastic comment obviously believed by contemporary readers to be a serious presentation of historical fact. Yet, it is probable that Luther's anti-monastic sentiment was the main inspiration for this element in the Wolfenbüttel text. Luther believed the monastic orders had misled the 'true' Church of Christ with their 'idolatrous worship', i.e. promoting an over exaggerated ideal of poverty, enforced penance, perpetual spiritual devotion and chastity as the perfect path to achieve sanctification, which in his estimation, demeaned the secular life that God also sanctified and ordained as an important element of His Creation:

> "[…] All manner of religion, where people serve God without his Word and command, is simply idolatry, and the more holy and spiritual such a religion seems, the more hurtful and venomous it is; for it leads people away from the faith of Christ, and makes them rely and depend upon their own strength, works, and righteousness. […]"
>
> "In like manner, all kinds of orders of monks, fasts, prayers, hairy shirts, the austerities of the Capuchins, [i.e. of the Franciscan order] who in popedome are held to be the most holy of all, are mere works of the flesh; for the monks hold they are holy, and shall be saved, not through Christ, whom they view as a severe and angry judge, but through the rules of their order."[289]

Continuing with the Wolfenbüttel narration, we observe Faust finally learns the name of his *familiar*: Mephostophiles. This is the first time in the history of literature, both spiritual and secular, that the name of this particular demon is recorded, indicating an ingenious nomenclature invented to include a dynamic dimension to the Faustian texts. H. B. Cotterill remarks the meaning of the name "[…] is probably 'not loving the light' — μή φώςφιλών — a compound which […] must have been concocted by a rather second-rate Greek scholar."[290] There is a further possibility, the name could also be a derivative from the Hebrew "mephistoph" signifying

---

[288] Charles G. Nauert, Jr., 'Magic and Scepticism in Agrippa's Thought', *JHI* (April, 1957), p. 162.

[289] Luther, 'Of Idolatry', # CLXXI *Tischreden* (Aurifaber: 1569).

[290] H. B. Cotterill, *The Faust-Legend and Goethe's 'Faust'* (London: George G. Harrap & Company, 1912), p. 37.

"the destroyer of good". Butler argues it could be a dual reference to "Me-photo-philes" = "No friend to the light" *and* "Me-Fausto-philes" = "No friend to Faust."[291] Henry Jones favours the interpretation of Ernst Zitelmann: "Me-to-phos-philes", which in Greek means "The light is not a friend".[292] Henry Jones relates, "This seems far-fetched until it is remembered that nouns in a Greek lexicon are always followed by their article: *phos, to,* and at once the interpretation becomes acceptable."[293] Yet, there is one other interpretation that apparently has not been considered, although it is less accurate, the name may be a combination of a corrupted version of the Latin word "mephiticus" = "noxious exhalation" and the Greek "phile" = "loving", which would mean in general the "lover of stench". It is believed that sin not only befouls the soul, but it also creates a spiritual reek, hence the expression "the stench of sin". In this instance, Mephostophiles would be a demon that revels in the putrefaction of souls.

Undaunted in his purpose, Faust performs a phlebotomy on his left hand and proceeds to drain enough of his blood into a crucible to write the diabolical compact. Immediately, the Latin words "*o homo fuge — id est*: o mortal fly from him and do what is right"[294] appears graven precisely where the incision was made. Hence, Faust has broken one of the commandments of the Old Testament: "You shall not make cuttings in your flesh, for the dead, neither shall you make in yourselves any figures or marks: I am the Lord." (Lev. 19: 28). We learn from 3 Kings this was the common practise of Baal worshipers to attract the attention of their god: "So they cried with a loud voice, and cut themselves after their manner with knives and lancets, till they were all covered with blood." (3 Kings 18:28) In Deuteronomy, we also discover that worshipers of false gods sacrifice to devils. Hence, the priests of Baal were offering their blood to a devil: "They sacrificed to devils and not to God: to gods whom they knew not: [...]." (Deut. 32: 17). In a similar manner, Faust also offered his blood, the symbol of life, to a devil. But the graven words that appear on his hand, "o, mortal fly!", serve as a merciful reminder of Deuteronomy (6: 5–6, 8) to Faust; "Thou shalt love the Lord thy God with thy whole heart, and with thy whole strength. And these words which I command you thee this day, shall be in thy heart: [...] *And thou shalt bind them as a sign on thy hand*, and they shall be and shall move between thy eyes." Hence, Faust is not yet damned as Mephostophiles would have him believe — he may still turn away from evil.

Once more, Faust remains ignorant of the warning that appears on his own flesh in blood-streaked, graven letters and continues to inscribe the contract in Chapter Six:

> "I JOHANN FAUSTUS, Dr.,
>   Do publicly declare with mine own hand in covenant & by power of these presents:

---

[291] Butler, *The Myth of the Magus* (Cambridge 1948), in *Faustus and the Censor*, p. 203.

[292] Ernst Zitelmann, Germanisch-Romanisch Monatsschrift, XIV, 1926, pp. 65f, in *Faustus and the Censor*, ibid.

[293] *Faustus and the Censor*, p. 203.

[294] *History of Doctor Johann Faustus*, p. 32. Of interest, we note that the parenthetical translation is an obvious elaboration. The translation from the Latin actually reads: "O man, fly—that is." We suspect the original scribe was not an expert in Latin and recorded a segment from the following sentence as part of the gruesome inscription.

Whereas, mine own spiritual faculties having been exhaustively explored (including the gifts dispensed from above and graciously imparted to me), I still cannot comprehend;

And whereas, it being my wish to probe further into the matter, I do propose to speculate upon the *Elementa*;

And whereas mankind doth not teach such things;

Now therefore have I summoned the spirit who calleth himself Mephostophiles, a servant of the Hellish Prince in Orient, charged with informing and instructing me, and agreeing against a promissory instrument hereby transferred unto him to be subservient and obedient to me in all things.

I do promise him in return that, when I be fully sated of that which I desire of him, twenty-four years also being past, ended and expired, he may at such a time and in whatever manner or wise pleaseth him order, ordain, reign, rule and possess all that may be mine: body, property, flesh, blood, etc., herewith duly bound over in eternity and surrendered by covenant in mine own hand by authority and power of these presents, as well as of my mind, brain, intent, blood and will.

I do now defy all living beings, all the Heavenly Host and all mankind, and this must be.

In confirmation and contract whereof I have drawn out mine own blood for certification in lieu of a seal.

Doctor Faustus, the Adept
In the *Elementa* and in Church Doctrine"[295]

Ironically, Faust, who has signed himself "the adept in the Elementa and Church Doctrine" believes as a Doctor of theology he is learned in these matters, yet he knows nothing of the meaning in relation to the theological subjects he studied. He is a master of books and practised in university examinations, but his erudition is far removed from the heart of the Scriptures, their message, and the Supreme Author who inspired them. In a sardonic twist of circumstances, it is Mephostophiles who revealed himself to be the true Master in this situation by ensnaring the Doctor in the same academic *modus operandi* employed by universities at that time for the attainment of a degree, which Faust excelled in — i.e. the completion of three disputations, via Chapters Three, Four and Five.[ø] While Faust assumed he had gained control of

---

[295] Ibid. pp. 33–34.

[ø] We acknowledge this tripartite plan may be the result of Haile's selective editing, however, his aim was to present a text that closely resembled the Latin original before latter scholars and scribes included new material: the possibility remains that there were initially three major disputations in the text. Henry Jones presumes the original Latin text circulated within a select university readership, (*Faustus and the Censor*, p. 31), a logical hypothesis as this readership would be thoroughly familiar with this language. We argue the theory that the tripartite chapter structure was inspired by contemporary university policies regarding academic disputations is still valid.

Mephostophiles with his magic, "compelling" the spirit to answer certain questions, in reality it was the demon with his half-truths and theological distortions who succeeded in confounding Faust into submission. In addition, the evil spirit is rewarded with a grisly degree certificate for his labours, the contract written by Faust with his "own blood [...] in lieu of a seal."

We also perceive, at one stage during the compilation of the Wolfenbüttel manuscript, the drawing up of this pact was influenced by a separate source of popular moral literature, namely Sir Thomas Malory's rendition of the Grail Legends in his famous *Morte D'Arthur* (1485). Two points of interest direct us to this observation. The first pertains to the information that Faust uses a crucible placed over hot coals to prevent the extracted blood from congealing while he writes. This would appear to be an explicit description of how Faust proceeded with his pact when a simple mention that the contract was signed in blood would fulfil the required suspense for the narration. Could the crucible of the Wolfenbüttel text be an intended antithetical allegory of the Holy Grail, the chalice that held the Blood of Christ as depicted in Sir Malory's work? The second detail concerns Faust's own decision to limit the duration of his pact to twenty-four years, this particular number is unique to the Faustian myth.[○] As mentioned previously in

---

° Henry Jones postulates that as the first edition of Lercheimer's *Christlich Bedencken* (1585) actually contains the earliest published mention of Faust's pact with a number of twenty-four years, he theorises Lercheimer's work was the source of inspiration for the original Latin manuscript, which was subsequently used for the German translation of the Wolfenbüttle MS. He thereby dates the lost Latin text and the Wolfenbüttle text as "post 1585." (*Faustus and the Censor*, pp. 12, 31.) However, other evidence suggests the Latin text was handed down from an earlier date. The Preface to the Wolfenbüttle MS clearly states it was not translated into German before that time due to certain apprehensions the story of Faust would be misused for evil purposes, demonstrating the Latin text had circulated for a considerable period. Additionally, we do not know for how long the translator's colleague made his "repeated requests" before he obliged him with his German translation. This evidence therefore displays that the Latin text existed before Lercheimer's publication of 1585. Possibly, Lercheimer's publication initially spurred Spies into searching for a written history of the Faust legend for Spies declared, "[...] Indeed, a *number of modern writers* have touched here and there upon the subject of the magician, [...] but I have often wondered that, as yet, no one has presented this terrible tale in an orderly fashion and published it as a warning to the whole of Christendom. [...]"

We postulate an alternative theory Lercheimer heard of this particular detail of the twenty-four year pact by word of mouth from a colleague who read the Latin document. By the time the 1585 *Christlich Bedencken* was published, this detail may not be considered 'new'. For instance, Lercheimer appears considerably out of touch with the 'Faustian Phenomena' with regard to his opposition to Spies' work. Notice Lercheimer only printed his objections to the biographical errors in Spies' *Faustbook* of 1587 *ten years later* in the third edition of his *Christlich Bedencken* (1597), describes Spies work as "recently published", and is unfamiliar with Spies' name as though someone else had mentioned the details to him:

"I am obliged to give him [Faustus] some considerable attention by reason of a book recently published by some toady, whoever he may be, in which the school and church of Wittenberg are particularly abused and slandered. [...]" (Excerpt in *Faustus and the Censor*, p. 13.)

Hence, we posit that Lercheimer's *Christlich Bedencken* (1585) may be the earliest *extant* publication that specifically mentions a pact of twenty-four years, but the possibility remains this detail

141

Chapter One, this element may be attributed to Manlius' document where it appears the historical Faustus was aware of his approaching end. Yet, it was common knowledge if a sorcerer desired to bind a spirit, an exact term of servitude was agreed upon. Henry Jones relates that a term of twenty or fifty years was the norm, but he was unable to discover any example of other historical or mythical magicians that specifically mentioned the number twenty-four.[296] However, we notice this stipulation of a twenty-four year limit to the Faust legend bears a striking correlation with the adventures of Sir Lancelot. In Sir Malory's version of the Arthurian Legend, Lancelot is not worthy to complete the Quest for the Grail due to his numerous transgressions; in particular, sins of the flesh and his prideful thirst to accomplish chivalrous deeds for personal fame rather than offering all his achievements for the honour and glory of God. As the adventures unfold, we are informed Lancelot's sinful life continued for a considerable period, and he is described as being "[…] the devil's servant four and twenty years."[297]

However, Lancelot is not beyond the power of Redemption. Confessing his transgressions and performing works of penance, Lancelot is permitted to gaze upon the Grail, but as a punishment for his sin, is not allowed to enter the chamber wherein it is kept, similar to Moses who was not allowed to enter the Promised Land because he struck the rock twice in the desert. As he stands without, Lancelot witnesses a mystical representation of the Transubstantiation at Mass, i.e. when the bread and wine become the Flesh and Blood of Christ. Lancelot did not see the Host or the chalice, but three figures representing the Trinity; "And it seemed to Lancelot that above the priest's hands were three men, whereof the two put the youngest by likeness between the priest's hands; and so he lift it up right high, and it seemed to show so to the people."[298] Hence, the two figures placing the youngest figure in the hands of the priest represent the Father and the Holy Spirit ordaining the Incarnation of Christ and His willingness to descend from Heaven to Earth for the salvation of mankind. The priest raising the youngest figure represents the Elevation, i.e. when the Host and the chalice are raised to symbolise Christ raised on the cross, the perfect offering to the Father in atonement for the sins of mankind. As this occurs in the vision, the priest appears overpowered with the immensity of the offering and Lancelot rushes into the chamber in an attempt to help him, but he is struck down as

---

was first included in the original Latin text.

Of interest, Henry Jones observed the specific number of twenty-four years that Faust settles upon within the contract could have a particular Lutheran connection. If the author of the text assumed the historical Faustus had died in 1541, the year Faust signed his pact would be 1517 — the same year Luther nailed his *Ninety-Five Theses* to the door of the Castle Church in Wittenberg. (*Faustus and the Censor*, p. 11.) Henry Jones believes this to be previously unnoticed anti-Lutheran propaganda, however, when we argue that Faust is portrayed as the *antithesis* of Luther, the reverse is the case. Luther believed he had signed his name to parchment for Christ and His Church. Alternatively, Faust signs his name to a Hellish document. Additionally, the actual date of their signing would be apropos as Luther nailed the document up on the 31st of October: to Luther, this would signify an important holy vigil, 'All Saint's Eve', while to Faust, this is 'November Eve', a time of the year also associated with the dark side of the occult.

[296] *Faustus and the Censor*, p. 11.
[297] Sir Thomas Malory, 'The Holy Grail,' *Morte D'Arthur*, (Caxton: 1485), reprint in Charles W. Eliot, ed. *Chronicle and Romance: Froissart, Malory, Holinshed. The Harvard Classics vol. 35* (New York: P.F. Collier and Son Corp., 1963), p. 161.
[298] Ibid. p. 201.

if dead for twenty-four days to atone for the years he lived as the devil's servant; an admonishment not to approach the Altar and the Blessed Sacrament in a state of grievous sin. Following his comatose punishment of twenty-four days, Lancelot awakes and is informed by those around him that as the Quest for the Grail is now ended where he is concerned, he cannot expect to see the Grail again. Humbly accepting his lot, Lancelot declares "Now I thank God [...] of His great mercy of that I have seen, for it sufficeth me; for as I suppose no man in this world hath lived better than I have done to achieve that I have done."[299] In contrast, an unrepentant Faust wholeheartedly signs his soul over to the devil for twenty-four years with his own blood in an 'unholy' cup, which is then suspended over hot coals as a figure of Hell — a devilish sacrifice for the vainglory of the world.

Reviewing the first six chapters, we detect that Faust's gradual descent to the dark kingdom, as previously stated, was predominantly inspired by the theology and philosophy of Luther. Many of these associations are not immediately apparent, however, one unique key to unravelling the Luther-links encrypted within the narration is the description of Faust as "the *speculator*". Luther remarked in 1532:

> "I did not learn my theology at once, but had to seek ever deeper and deeper after it. That is where my spiritual distress led me; for one can never understand the Holy Scriptures without experience and tribulations. [...] If we do not have such a Devil, then we are nothing but speculativi Theologi, who handle their thoughts badly and speculate about everything with their reason, that it must be like this and like that: [...]."
> [300]

Once more, we discover Faust theologically portrayed as the antithesis of Luther. In contrast to the Reformer who agonised over Scripture throughout his life, Faust is declared "adept" in theology at Bachelor level, advancing from Master to Doctor in one progressive leap without a third examination. Apparently, Faust's fellow students recognised that his 'experience' with theology was exclusively on an academic level, for his preoccupation with the occult and his wanton lifestyle evinced he existed without any fear of God and thereby lacked the "experience and tribulations" Luther described. Hence, Faust had no "spiritual distress" that could direct him to meditate efficaciously upon the scriptures, at least at this point in the narration.

It may be argued that Faust's yearning to seek out "the foundations of Heaven and Earth" may be a form of "tribulation". Solomon states in the Book of Ecclesiastes (1:13) that this quest to "[...] seek out [...] all things that are done under the sun [...]" is a "[...] painful occupation hath God given to the children of men, to be exercised therein." After much contemplation, Solomon observes that everything of this temporal world is nothing but "vexation of spirit". We cannot add anything to this world that is not already created by God, nor can we take away anything from this world when we die. Every work we have accomplished on this earth will either crumble away, or be left to incompetent and unappreciative mankind, the 'eternal child'

---

[299] Ibid. p. 202.

[300] Luther, D. Martin Luther Werke: Kritische Gesamtausgabe, *Tischreden*, (Weimar, 1912–21), no. 352; 147, 3–14, autumn 1532, in Oberman, *Luther, Man Between God and the Devil*, p. 185.

that never learns until it is too late when each generation that has grown wise with experience passes away. We can only find contentment in the present with the work of our hands that is wrought without sin and blessed by God. Hence, Solomon ultimately declares; "Vanity of vanities, and all is vanity." (Eccles. 1:2) Notwithstanding the seeming bleakness of his conclusion, there is a certain joy in the realisation that he has discovered the aim of this "painful occupation" set before mankind:

> "I have seen the trouble, which God hath given the sons of men to be *exercised* in it. He hath made all things good in their time, and hath delivered the world to their consideration, *so that man cannot find out the work which God hath made from the beginning to the end.* And I have known that there was no better thing to rejoice, and to do well in this life. For every man that eateth and drinketh, and seeth good of his labour, this is the gift of God. I have learned that all the works which God hath made, continue forever: we cannot add any thing, nor take away from those things which God hath made *that he may be feared.*" (Eccles. 3:10–14)

In fine, Solomon has truly searched all these matters "wisely" (Eccles. 1:13), i.e. with spiritual profit, as he proclaimed. He realised that Creation, although finite and temporal, is nevertheless immeasurable, incomprehensible and beyond the control of mortal man — an intrinsic design intended by God to display His eternal, unfathomable power with the ultimate aim of directing and encouraging mankind to acknowledge Him as Creator and Lord, with love and filial fear.

However, Faust's desire for knowledge is not the same as Solomon's quest for wisdom; in contrast, he "used God's word vainly." Like all gifts and tools that can be misused, Faust did not use this inner compulsion as God intended, for turning to the Book of Ecclesiasticus we discover Faust allowed his yearning to fester into an illicit curiosity rather than truly meditate on the "things God hath commanded" him:

> "Seek not the things that are too high for thee, and search not into things above thy ability: but the things that God hath commanded thee, think on them always, and in many of his works be not curious. For it is not necessary for thee to see with thy eyes those things that are hid. In unnecessary matters be not over curious, and in many of his works thou shalt not be inquisitive. For many things are shewn to thee above the understanding of men. *And the suspicion of them hath deceived many, and hath detained their minds in vanity.* A hard heart shall fear evil at the last: and he that loveth danger shall perish in it." (Ecclus. 3: 22–27)

The words that appear on Faust's arm, "O homo fuge," are intended as a stark reminder of this theological truth. They originate from St. Paul's first letter to Timothy, Ch. 6, v. 11; "Tu autem, O homo Dei, haec fuge," i.e.; "But thou, O man of God, fly these things". In the preceding and concluding verses of this passage, we discover the "things" Faust should flee from:

"*If any man teach otherwise*, and consent not to the sound words of our Lord Jesus Christ, and to that doctrine which is according to godliness, *he is proud, knowing nothing, but sick about questions and strifes of words; from which arise envies, contentions, blasphemies, evil suspicions, conflicts of men corrupted in mind, and who are destitute of the truth, supposing gain to be godliness.* But godliness with contentment is great gain. For we have brought nothing into this world: and certainly we can carry nothing out. But having food, and wherewith to be covered, with these are we content. [...] O Timothy, keep that which is committed to thy trust, avoiding the *profane novelties of words, and oppositions of knowledge falsely so called. Which some promising, have erred concerning the faith.* Grace be with thee. Amen." (1 Tim. 3–8, 20–21)

Hence, through his misguided curiosity, Faust's great incompetence in interpreting sacred Scripture in everyday practise is manifest. Faust admits in his contract to Mephostophiles that he has exhausted all the spiritual gifts "dispensed from above" and still cannot comprehend everything of Creation. Faust pays no heed to Solomon, who acknowledged God's plan regarding man's limitations, and conveniently ignores St. Paul who reiterated this wisdom, but wishes to "probe further into the matter" beyond lawful contemplation and to "speculate on the *Elementa*," as written in his pact. He also ignores the warning in Ecclesiasticus that confirms Solomon's observation we may ponder on God's works for our own enlightenment, yet discourages an over-extensive study of them as our meagre, mortal efforts to theorise upon and understand their very incompressibility will foster sentiments of dissatisfaction, futility, and "detain our minds in vanity". Faust finally commits a heinous sin by relying on a fallen spirit for advice and inspiration rather than relying upon God by whom they were both created. We may therefore conclude that Faust was not concerned with living his theology and did not suffer the "tribulations" Luther mentions in the earlier quotation. Ironically, when Faust debates with Mephostophiles he is actually afforded an opportunity to save his soul, as he now has "a Devil" to cause "tribulations" whereby he may gain spiritual "experience" as Luther described. Yet, as Faust never intended to progress in Scripture beyond an academic level and is motivated by mere scientific inquisitiveness, he is easily blinded by the demon's false teachings, falls prey to his snares, and subsequently remains one of the "speculativi Theologi".

Returning to the manuscript, Chapter Seven discloses the new lifestyle Faust enjoys following the signing of his contract. We are informed Faust continued to live in the house bequeathed to him by his wealthy relative in Wittenberg. Lodging with Faust is his famulus, a schoolboy named Christoph Wagner. Apparently, Wagner is a "reckless lout" intrigued with his master's newfound powers and flattered by Faust's promise to "[...] make a learned and worthy man of him".[301] At this point the reader is reminded that "[...] youth is always more inclined towards wickedness,"[302] hence, admonishing the readers on the importance in setting a good example for youth as they are easily led astray. This is the first time the character Wagner is

---

[301] *History of Doctor Johann Faustus*, p. 35.
[302] Ibid.

introduced to Faustian literature that we are aware of, a character undoubtedly inspired by the legendary tradition of sorcerers maintaining an apprentice to whom they entrust their secrets for posterity. Mephostophiles, we discover, is occupied most of the time filling the house with all manner of provisions such as wine, food and clothes pilfered from the very best estates and merchants. Faust's magic also provides for the table as the author declares; "[…] he was so cunning in sorcery that when he opened a window and named the fowl he desired, it came flying right in through the window",[303] a detail obviously derived from earlier lore. In addition, Mephostophiles grants Faust twenty-five Crowns (gulden?) a week, or thirteen hundred Crowns a year, a sum three times the highest wage, four-hundred gulden, a professor at Wittenberg could expect to earn circa 1540.[304] If we consider the scenario of a professor maintaining an expensive household during that era, or encountered unforeseen debt problems, it appears he would not usually spend more than one or two hundred gulden over budget. For example, Luther, by 1540 earned four hundred gulden, yet due to his numerous guests and the continual aid he afforded to new Protestant converts who left the monasteries, he once calculated his household expenditure at the Black Monastery extended to five hundred gulden.[305] Therefore, when we reflect that Faust lives on stolen property and does not pay for the provisions of his house, he has a small fortune at his disposal for sheer 'pleasure' spending, no doubt part of the devil's plan to lead Faust into a deeper life of vice.

Chapter Eight features a unique catechetical addition to the Faustian legend regarding erroneous beliefs concerning the afterlife and the motives for entering into the state of matrimony. Now enjoying a luxurious, Epicurean lifestyle "[…] day in and day out […] with faith neither in God, Hell nor the Devil, Doctor Faustus' *aphrodisia* did day and night so prick him that he desired to enter matrimony and take a wife."[306] Subtlety, it has been intimated that a rich lifestyle, particularly gluttony and intoxication, is an occasion for spiritual danger as it leads to pampering the body and provoking *aphrodisia*, i.e. lustful desires.

Henry Jones observes the various terms associated with "Epicurean" may be intentionally conflated in this section of the *Faustbooks*.[307] In ancient Greek philosophy, the Cyrenaics proposed that human knowledge is unreliable and therefore useless, that the human race should control the circumstances by which it is surrounded rather than be controlled by them, and that the pursuit of sensual gratification above intellectual pleasures is the sole purpose of life, although pleasure should not be sought beyond the dictates of law and custom. This branch of philosophy was the forerunner of, (and became associated with) Epicurus' doctrine, which maintains that pleasure is the supreme goal one should aim for in life, particularly intellectual pleasures above those of sensual ones. Epicurus taught that one could only acquire true happiness and serenity by conquering one's fear of the gods, death, and the afterlife. He also believed that humans ceased to exist after death, declaring the soul died with the body. Yet, he also taught the importance of justice, honesty and prudence, stressing that happiness and serenity could only be attained by self-restraint and moderation. Today, the term "epicure" is used to

---

[303] Ibid. p. 36.
[304] *Luther, Man Between God and the Devil*, p. 280.
[305] Ibid.
[306] *History of Doctor Johann Faustus*, p. 37.
[307] *Faustus and the Censor*, p. 18.

describe a person who enjoys food and drink in particular. Possibly, the author was reminding readers of the spiritual dangers in studying ancient pagan philosophy without first having a firm foundation in Christian theology as those not strong in their faith could be tempted to practise or experiment with these pagan ideologies.

Returning to Faust's 'aphrodisia' dilemma, his solution is to consider the sacrament of matrimony, a peculiar decision for one who has just sold his soul to the devil. Faust questions Mephostophiles about this new decision, but he is immediately rebuked by the demon:

> "What is the purpose with thyself? […] Had Faustus forgot his commitment, and would he not hold to the promise wherein he had vowed enmity to God and mankind? If so, then neither by chance nor by intent dare he enter matrimony. For a man cannot serve two masters (spake the devil), God and us, too. Matrimony is a work of the Lord God. We, who take our profit from all that pertains to and derives from adultery and fornication, are opposed to it."[308]

Mephostophiles warns Faust that should he ignore his pact in this regard he would be torn to pieces. Then, the demon proceeds to dissuade Faust by remarking that marriage is often the harbinger of "unquiet, antipathy, anger and strife […]."[309] Faust ponders this matter, and decides to defy the devil in this instance notwithstanding the consequences. Suddenly, a great wind engulfs Faust's house and threatens to destroy it, while simultaneously the atmosphere inside becomes stifling. Faust attempts to flee, but is thrown back inside by a demon who assumed the shape of a man. Terrified he is to be burned alive, Faust shouts out to Mephostophiles for help, and renews his pledge promising to live by all their demonic precepts. Immediately, Satan appears and demands that Faust account for his disloyalty. Faust attempts to excuse his transgression contrary to the terms of the contract stating he did not consider his pledge also included abstinence from marriage whereupon he begs for leniency, which Satan grants after curtly warning Faust to remain steadfast. Mephostophiles returns and informs Faust if he remains faithful to their pact he would satisfy his lust by other means:

> "[…] if thou canst not live chastely, then will I lead to thy bed any day or night whatever woman thou seest in this city or elsewhere. Whoever might please thy lust, and whomever thou might desire in lechery, she shall abide with thee in such a figure and form."[310]

The chapter concludes with the disclosure that the women Mephostophiles brings are not mortal as Faust spends his time "[…] today with one devil and having another on his mind tomorrow."[311] Hence, Faust entered into an unholy union with the Prince of Darkness through

---

[308] *History of Doctor Johann Faustus*, p. 37.
[309] Ibid. p. 38.
[310] Ibid. p. 39.
[311] Ibid.

various succubae, an idea obviously drawn from the historical Faustus who declared the devil was his brother-in-law.

There is sound theological reasoning why Mephostophiles should be furious with Faust's decision to marry. Matrimony is a sanctified, lawful vocation for one who is not called to the heroic life of perpetual chastity. Christ emphasises not all receive the gift to live in perpetual chastity, and those who choose this path should pray for God's grace to strengthen them; "All men take not this word, [i.e. chastity] but they to whom it is given." (Matt. 19: 11) St. Paul emphasises that "It is good for a man not to touch a woman. But for fear of fornication, let every man have his own wife, and let every woman have her own husband." (1 Cor. 7: 1–2) However, there is one peculiarity in the Wolfenbüttel text that displays a Lutheran view of marriage: i.e. that Mephostophiles would refer to chastity as a demonically acceptable custom to avoid the holy sacrament of matrimony. Apparently, in his eagerness to address Luther's ideology, the author partly misrepresented Luther's objections concerning the overemphasis of chastity. Luther acknowledged there are those who are called to celibacy for God's sake, but stressed it was an exception to the norm as he declared, "[…] these [callings] are rare; not one in a thousand can do it: it is one of God's special miracles."[312] Hence, chastity as "God's miracle" cannot be the work of a demon. According to Catholic belief, those that remain chaste, either choosing not to marry or to refrain from a second marriage after the decease of their spouse, are in a better position to achieve a higher state of holiness:

> "He that is without a wife, is solicitous for the things that belong to the Lord, how he may please God. But he that is with a wife, is solicitous for the things of this world, how he may please his wife; and he is divided. And the unmarried woman and the virgin thinketh on the things of the Lord, that she may by holy both in body and in spirit. But she that is married thinketh on the things of the world, how she may please her husband. […] Therefore, both he [i.e. a father] that giveth his virgin in marriage, doth well; and he that giveth her not, doth better. A woman is bound by the law as long as her husband liveth; but if her husband die, she is at liberty; let her marry to whom she will; only in the Lord. But more blessed shall she be, if she so remain, [… i.e. a widow]. " (1 Cor. 7: 32–34, 38–40)

However, notwithstanding his belief that a life of chastity was a God-given gift, Luther was not of the opinion that celibacy elevated a person to a higher level of holiness as marriage was also a divinely inspired vocation.[313] Luther objected to the over-emphasis placed on chastity as the perfect path to God for it not only separated faith from human love, but also demonised human desires God ordained thus simultaneously debasing the sacrament of matrimony through which they may be lawfully expressed. Ultimately, Luther concluded the Church was forcing

---

[312] Luther, D. Martin Luthers Werke: Kritische Gesamtausgabe, Abteilung Werke, vols. I (Weimar, 1883), 10 II. 279, 19–21; 1522, in Oberman, *Luther, Man Between God and the Devil*, p. 272.
[313] *Luther, Man Between God and the Devil*, p. 271.

individuals into a monastic life they were not called to by fostering spiritual guilt and humiliation. Luther declared:

> "Whoever is ashamed of marriage is also ashamed of being and being called human, tries to improve on what God has made. Adam's children are and will remain human; that is why they should and must beget more men. Dear God, we see daily the effort it costs to live in a marriage, and to keep the marital vows. And we try to promise chastity as if we were not human, had neither flesh nor blood.
>
> But it is the god of the world, the Devil, who so slanders the marital state and has made it shameful — and yet allows adulterers, whores, and dissolute knaves to survive in high esteem all the same — that it would be fair to marry in order to spite him and his world and to accept his ignominy and bear it for God's sake."[314]

Hence, in his effort to represent Luther's reasoning that the Church was enforcing a misguided, zealous promotion of chastity, the author of the Wolfenbüttel manuscript inadvertently distorted the virtue of chastity in his narration to be a work of the demon. Trusting Haile's translation, it would be a less inaccurate statement if the original author had written; "*As thou canst not live chastely*" rather than "*If thou canst not*".

We also observe in his concentrated effort to portray Luther's ideology on the divinely ordained sacrament of marriage, the author transcribed a theological paradox. True, the hellish kingdom takes their "profit from all that pertains to and derives from all adultery and fornication," but in dissuading Faust from entering the sacrament of marriage in favour of fornication outside of wedlock, Mephostophiles prevented his protégé from committing the more grievous sin of adultery. It may be argued that the demons would not risk Faust finding a virtuous wife who would attempt to redeem him, for in Scripture it is written: "For the unbelieving husband is sanctified by the believing wife; and the unbelieving wife is sanctified by the believing husband: [...]. For how knoweth thou, O wife, whether thou shalt save thy husband? Or how knowest thou, O man, whether thou shalt save thy wife?" (1 Cor. 7:14,16) Yet, we observe the women who are brought to Faust are actual demons and not human; consequently, Faust is not tempted to destroy the marriage of another and commit adultery in this fashion. Surely, the demons would have Faust, although a signed and sealed reprobate at this point, sink as deep as possible? The inconsistencies do not end here. For instance, the author accurately portrayed Luther's opinion that the devil was responsible for debasing the concept of marriage through Mephostophiles' slander of the sacrament, i.e. his claim that it is a primary source of strife in the world. Yet, the author does not take advantage of the opportunity to display the absolute evil that the devil is capable of hurling against matrimony. Turning to the Book of Tobias in the Old Testament, the archangel Raphael reveals that the devil has power over those who use matrimony as a medium for lust rather than for God's purpose of procreation:

---

[314] Luther, *D. Martin Luthers Werke: Kritische Gesamtausgabe, Abteilung Werke*, vols. I (Weimar, 1883), 18.277, 26–36; 27 March 1525, in ibid., p. 273.

"Hear me, and I will shew thee who they are, over whom the devil can prevail. For they who in such manner receive matrimony, as to shut out God from themselves, and from their mind, and to give themselves to lust, as the horse and mule [in a sterile union], which have not understanding, over them the devil hath power." (Tobias 6:16–17)

St. Paul also addressed the importance of temperance in the married state: "Defraud not one another [i.e. regarding conjugal rights], except, perhaps, by consent, for a time, that you may give yourselves to prayer; and return together again, lest Satan tempt you for your incontinency." (1 Cor.7:5) Hence, in his singular desire to enter matrimony to satisfy his lust Faust displays his attraction to the demonic, however, Faust is not used to degrade the sacrament further in the text. *In fine*, the author concentrated on portraying the Lutheran motives for *entering* into matrimony to the extent that he transcribed certain errors and excluded more sinful actions that according to theological logic a demon would prefer to see executed as a greater abomination against God.

In addition, a new characteristic of Faust is revealed in this chapter, his spiritual cowardice. Ironically, the tables are now turned from that time he went conjuring in the Spesser Wald, when allowed to believe he had power over Satan, Faust remained confident and steadfast, refusing to retreat from the preternatural terrors until he obtains an audience with a spirit. However, when Faust attempts to exert this defiant control again in his decision to marry, the devil finally reveals in public who is truly the master and who is the slave. Now terrified into submission by the fury of the Abyss, Faust refuses to profit from this frightening spectacle and the realisation he was witnessing a minor version of Hell, a thought that would as a rule inspire a soul to repent. In his cowardice, Faust begs leniency from the demons rather than imploring God for help. Also, it is only when Faust becomes frightened by the fiendish paranormal activity and the actual appearance of Satan that Mephostophiles reminds Faust he can satisfy his lust out of wedlock and thereby keep their agreement intact. This is a curious chain of events as Mephostophiles could have avoided this whole confrontation by informing Faust of this diabolical loophole before his charge ever thought of marriage. We therefore suspect the demons *purposely withheld this information* and awaited this confrontational day to arrive; as mentioned, Faust's rebellious decision to marry allows the demons to terrorise him further into submission, yet of greater importance, the terror they artfully provoke in Faust ultimately dissuades him from having recourse to *a sacrament*. This observation also eludes Faust who is now trapped in fear, and therefore fails to realise that if the demons abhor the sacraments to this extent, they truly are the God-given weapons to withstand the powers of Hell, which he may rely on for spiritual help if he had the inclination to convert. In all, he is bereft of faith in God and the courage to stand firm and marry "to spite the devil" as Luther urged.

Now having introduced libidinousness to Faust's list of demonic leisure activities, in Chapter Nine Mephostophiles presents him with a new book featuring "[...] all manner of sorcery and *nigromantia*."[315] The tome incites Faust's previous curiosity in magic and the mystical nature of the supernatural world, and he desires to learn more about his *familiar* spirit: "Tell me, my servant, what manner of spirit art thou?"[316] Mephostophiles feigns uneasiness with

---

[315] *History of Doctor Johann Faustus*, p. 40.
[316] Ibid.

this question, stating that his answer will move Faust towards discontentment and meditation, with the addition that he should not have asked this question as it pertains to the devils' "arcana". Mephostophiles nevertheless condescends to his request: "— But I must obey thee."[317] However, he feigns obedience to Faust and circumvents his question by focusing on Lucifer instead; as the demon immediately replies to the question in both the Spies and English *Faustbooks* we sense Haile's radical editing may be responsible for this inconsistency. The deletion of the text in Haile's edition, however, serves another purpose. Mephostophiles' hesitant acknowledgment of his obedience to Faust in giving these answers refreshes the doubt he placed in Faust's mind by alluding he is allowed to learn more of their occult secrets as his soul has supposedly been forfeited beyond all redemption. Mephostophiles' evasion of Faust's initial question also portrays the rebellious spirit's inability to honourably comply with his side of their contract.

True to fiendish form, Mephostophiles begins by telling Faust a partial theological fallacy that Satan after his fall from Heaven was "[...] graciously and kindly disposed toward man, who had just been created."[318] Continuing with his account, Mephostophiles then states Satan immediately changed his attitude and declared war on mankind — he proceeds to describe all manner of horrific occurrences, particularly suicide, as an example of their handiwork:

> "Lucifer [...] did presume to work all manner of tyranny upon men — as is every day manifest when one falleth to his death; another hangeth, drowneth or stabbeth himself; a third is stabbed, driven mad, and the like other cases which thou might have observed."[319]

In summary, the first statement is a lie, as, from the very moment of his rebellion Satan became the archenemy of God's creation without exception. However, the information that Satan and his minions cannot harbour any feelings of compassion is true; demons are only capable of displaying great pride, rage and malevolence, particularly towards the human race made in God's image and likeness predestined to fill the angelic thrones in Heaven left vacant after their fall with Lucifer. Mephostophiles masks the falsehood of his first statement with a camouflage of accurate information — a process he continues throughout the remainder of the chapter by vacillating between truth and error when quoting from Scripture the activities of the demons in their mission to harass and destroy the human race.

Beginning with the temptation of Adam and Eve in the Garden of Paradise and Original Sin, Mephostophiles remarks Satan was also responsible for the fall of Cain who slew his brother Abel in a fit of anger and jealousy, the first murder perpetrated on earth. According to Scripture, Cain subsequently lied to God when he said he knew not where his brother was, and proceeded to sin against the virtue of charity when he replied he was not responsible for the welfare of his brother: "Am I my brother's keeper?" (Gen. 4:9) Cain then committed the most grievous sin of despair, the unpardonable transgression of doubting God's mercy and His desire to forgive; "My iniquity is greater than that I may deserve pardon." (Gen. 4:13) Notwithstanding the merciful

---

[317] Ibid.
[318] Ibid.
[319] Ibid. p. 41.

judgement God placed upon him *after* his transgressions by promising him Divine protection, Cain persisted in his despair, convinced he could not be forgiven.

Mephostophiles states Satan caused Israel to worship him by tempting the nation into idolatry, and then enticed them with the sin of lust whereby they resorted to pagan women contrary to God's commandments as stated in Deuteronomy (7:1–5). The demon proceeds to relate their part in the ruin of King Saul who refused to destroy King Agag of Amalec and all his possessions as God commanded, the prophet Samuel compared this sin of disobedience to witchcraft and idolatry (1 Kings 15:22). As Saul was unrepentant, Samuel announces the Kingdom of Israel shall be granted to another, (1 Kings 15:26, 28) and God permits an evil spirit to plague the disobedient king; "But the spirit of the Lord departed from Saul, and an evil spirit from the Lord troubled him." (1 Kings 16:14) To drive away Saul's moments of melancholy caused by the spirit, David is summoned to play the harp. Immediately, David finds favour with the king, and he is promoted to the rank of armour bearer. (1 Kings 16). As David becomes famous for his great deeds in battle, Saul realises he is the successor to his kingdom. This jealousy fostered by the evil spirit festers to the extent that Saul hurls his spear at David on several occasions intending to impale him. (1 Kings 18: 8–11; 19: 9–10). The king's transgressions do not cease, and he increases in his iniquities. Forsaken by God due to his wilful disobedience and refusing to repent, Saul did not receive help from God when preparing to do battle with the warring Philistines, and therefore he decides to seek a woman with the power of necromancy to aid him. (1 Kings 28) The diviner summons the spirit of Samuel who reiterates the punishment already foretold, adding that on the field of battle he and his sons will perish. This prophecy comes to pass; Saul's sons are felled by the Philistines, and to avoid capture, Saul commits suicide by falling on his sword.

Recounting the fall of the first king of Israel, Mephostophiles proceeds to name other infamous demons recorded in Scripture. Asmodeus receives a brief mention, the arch-demon of lechery that killed seven men when they attempted to marry for lust with no fear of God and His commandments as the archangel Raphael explained. (Tobias 3: 8; 6:16–22) Next, the pagan god of the Philistines, Dagon, is identified as an arch-demon; this is not a common identification in many theological works as with the arch-demon Beelzebub also referred to as the god of Accaron (4 Kings 1:2). However, this reference to Dagon in the Wolfenbüttel text is accurate for the Scriptures state all gods of the Gentiles are devils. How the author of the manuscript arrived at the conclusion the pagan god was an arch-demon rather than a devil of the lower minions is manifest by Mephostophiles' answer that this particular spirit aided the Philistines to overcome the Israelites with the result thirty thousand men perished and the Ark of the Covenant was captured. (1 Kings 4:10; 5:2–5) This defeat was a momentous calamity as the holiest object in Israel wherein the Presence of the Lord resided was placed within the pagan temple of the Philistines as a spoil of war. However, the Lord is not to be mocked: twice, the statue of Dagon falls face down before the Ark, and pestilence sweeps across the land of the Philistines until the Ark is returned with an offering from the thieving nation in atonement for their atrocities.

Subsequent to his account of Dagon, Mephostophiles arrives at an opportune moment to include a second fallacy in his narration to create confusion. Mephostophiles declares it was the arch-demon Belial who tempted King David with the sin of pride to number Israel and thereby test God's promise to Abraham that his seed would be numberless, whereupon sixty thousand men of Israel perished as a punishment. However, in the Bible it is recorded that Satan was responsible for David's temptation, and the number that perished was seventy thousand, not sixty thousand. (1 Par. 21: 1, 14) The demon proceeds with the statement another evil spirit was responsible for the fall of King Solomon. Although it is not specifically mentioned in the Bible that a devil participated in Solomon's demise as in the case of King Saul, it is not an illogical conclusion: Solomon forsook God's laws, built pagan temples in Jerusalem for his heathen wives, and following their example he committed idolatry (1 Kings 11) — a sin considered as heinous as witchcraft. Hence, by clouding his inaccuracy regarding Belial and King David with a considerable number of veracious references and rational theological conclusions mentioned in his narrative, Mephostophiles would have Faust believe the Scriptures feature several errors, which he 'graciously condescends' to 'correct' for him. However, it would appear Faust is spiritually numbed to the extent he will not challenge the sophistry used to blind him and assumes the demon is fulfilling his part of the contract, responding with what he believes to be absolute truth to his interrogations, for Faust makes no effort to contradict or question what his *familiar* 'discloses'.

Mephostophiles concludes his account with the information the demonic horde continues to insinuate its legions with the human race, their ultimate goal, to lead men into sin and away from the Faith, thus strengthening the forces of Hell against Christ. Mephostophiles reveals the evil spirits possess the hearts of the rulers of the world, hardening them against Christ and His followers. Faust finally poses a question to the spirit, asking whether he too was possessed. Mephostophiles responds in the affirmative, stating that as soon as he and his fellow demons perceived Faust's illicit curiosity and his conclusion that he could not speculate further upon mystical matters without the aid of the devil, the demons betook the opportunity to tempt him further with this thought and prodded him with the idea to experiment with sorcery. Mephostophiles finally reveals they were in full control during his conjuring in the Spesser Wald, and urged him onward in his diabolical quest for illicit knowledge until he ultimately forfeited body and soul to them. Faust truly believes he is irrevocably damned and begins to bewail his fate, lamenting "[…] there is no turning from my way now. I have ensnared myself. Had I kept god-fearing thoughts, and held to God in prayer, not allowing the Devil so to strike root within me, then had I not suffered such injury in body and soul. Ay what have I done, […]."[320] Faust is trapped in despair, the unforgivable sin committed by Cain. It is also the great sin of Judas, the apostle who betrayed Christ to the Pharisees and subsequently committed suicide because he believed his sin was unpardonable. In the midst of Faust's lamentations, Mephostophiles caustically concludes Chapter Nine with the response, "Look thou to it";[321] the identical, supercilious phrase used by the Pharisees when dismissing Judas, who repents his betrayal of Jesus, a remark that dissipates all his hope and seals his fate in despair:

> "Then Judas, who betrayed him, seeing that he [Jesus] was
> condemned, repenting himself, brought back the thirty pieces of silver to
> the chief priests and ancients saying I have sinned in betraying innocent
> blood. But they said: What is that to us? Look thou to it. And casting

---

[320] Ibid. p. 42.
[321] Ibid.

down the pieces of silver in the temple, he departed, and went and hanged himself with a halter." (Matt. 27:3–5)

Chapter Ten commences with Faust interrogating Mephostophiles a second time concerning the supernatural world; on this occasion Faust is curious to learn about the fall of Lucifer. After three days, the demon returns with his answer. He begins by explaining Lucifer was an angel of God, in fact, one of the cherubim.[322] This is not accurate for Lucifer was the most exalted of God's angels and therefore belonged to the choir of the seraphim, the highest of the nine choirs of angels. Perhaps this was a mistake by the author and not a reflection of Mephostophiles' deceit, for according to theological logic a demon would rather boast his leader once held the highest position. Mephostophiles continues his report, saying Lucifer "[...] outshone all other creatures and was an ornament beyond all other works of God, gold and precious stones, even the sun and stars,"[323] an accurate reflection as the angels are spirits that closely resemble God's spiritual nature and therefore are created superior to the human race. Mephostophiles also relates God placed Lucifer upon His Mount as a prince, where he beheld all the magnificence of Heaven and received great honour and dignity. This is another lie from Mephostophiles as he inflates Lucifer's former status as the most glorious angel of Heaven. According to Catholic belief today, the angels were created in the empyrean heaven, and were not allowed to enter the glorious Heaven of the Blessed Trinity until their fidelity was tested.[324] If the angels had fully experienced the Presence of God first, the test would be redundant as their free will would be instantly united to God's Holy Perfection without the necessity to reason. In effect, they would be slaves for their decision to serve God freely or to reject Him would be neutralised by the irresistible attraction to the Perfection of their Creator. Therefore, Lucifer could not have had received full honours as an angelic prince on the Mount of God as Mephostophiles relates since he had failed the test. We find that the demon has twisted Isaias (14: 12-14) out of context:

> "How art thou fallen from heaven, O Lucifer, who didst rise in the morning? how art thou fallen to the earth, that didst wound the nations? And thou saidst in thy heart: I will ascend into heaven, I will exalt my throne above the stars of God, I will sit in the mountain of the covenant, in the sides of the north. I will ascend above the height of the clouds, I will be like the most High."

Mephostophiles then correctly relates Lucifer rebelled against God, attempting to "exalt himself above Orient",[325] i.e. above God, and thus was cast down from Heaven into the fiery brimstone of Hell, which will never be extinguished and from whence he can never more rise up to Heaven. In summary, the partially accurate report Mephostophiles presents to Faust continues

---

[322] Ibid. p. 43.
[323] Ibid.
[324] Fr. Paul O'Sullivan, O. P., *All About the Angels* (Rockford: Tan Books and Publishers Inc., 1990), p. 50.
[325] *History of Doctor Johann Faustus*, p. 43.

to foment the scholar's sense of hopelessness. Contemplating on Lucifer, once the great Angel of Light, and his transmutation into Satan, the Prince of Darkness, Faust continues to bewail his comparable fate as in the previous chapter of the manuscript, but we are duly informed by the author that Faust …

> "[…] would not take faith, nor hope that he might be through penitence brought back to the Grace of God. For if he had thought: The Devil doth now take on such a color that I must look up to Heaven. Lo, I will turn about again and call upon God for Grace and Forgiveness, for to sin no more is a great penance. Then Faustus would have betaken himself to church and followed Holy Doctrine, thereby offering the Devil resistance. Even if he had been compelled to yield up his body here, his soul would nevertheless have been saved. But he became doubtful in all his tenets and opinions, having no faith and little hope."[326]

The author reiterates in Chapter Eleven the unprofitable contrition Faust experiences in forfeiting his soul to the devil for finite pleasures, stating that Faust's remorse did not advance beyond that of Judas or Cain as he despaired of receiving God's forgiveness and grace. The author informs us of Faust's recurring dreams of Hell and the devil, and relates he attempted on one specific occasion to meditate on his transgressions and excite true sorrow for his sins by engaging Mephostophiles in a debate upon the creation and torments of the Abyss. Again, we notice this is not a decision any adept theologian would make when we universally accept that demons cannot adhere to the truth.

Faust broaches the subject of Hell with the following four queries: (1) What exactly is Hell, (2) how was it created, (3) how the damned lament their fate, (4) if it is possible to return to God's favour and be released from Hell. Mephostophiles hesitates to answer these questions, fully aware Faust was not enquiring purely for academic elucidation. He angrily retorts, "I say to thee: what is thy purpose with thyself?"[327] Once more, Mephostophiles would have Faust believe the fallacy he cannot be saved as he now belongs to him body and soul, adding that meditating on Hell can hold no spiritual benefit for him: "If thou couldst ascend directly to Heaven, yet would I fling thee down into Hell again, for thou art mine, walking my path toward Hell even in thy many questions about Hell."[328] The demon then discourages Faust from pressing him with these queries in a display of false compassion, stating his account of Hell would make him so despondent he would utterly regret he asked. This is a further ruse employed by Mephostophiles to convince Faust he is already damned by intimating the uselessness of squandering what remains of his 'pleasure' years on earth with thoughts of the 'inevitable' torments he will face for eternity.

Faust pays no heed to this advice and insists he will not live unless he receives answers to his questions, an ignorant attempt to effect commiseration from Mephostophiles, who first of all would gain by Faust's death prior to the expiration of their contract, and second, is incapable of

---

[326] Ibid. p. 44.
[327] Ibid. p. 46.
[328] Ibid.

feeling sympathy for Faust. Mephostophiles nevertheless agrees to humour Faust, stating his reply to him "costeth me little grief", as mentioned, this is not a compromise offered from a sense of pity: for a demon to see Faust in a state of utter dejection would give him the utmost sadistic satisfaction.

The demon declares the soul of a mortal creature is incapable of comprehending the nature of Hell, for its origin and structure is God's own Wrath. This statement is theologically sound; after Lucifer and the rebellious angels defected, God's justified anger was kindled from which Hell was created for their eternal punishment. The author of the Wolfenbüttel manuscript may have embellished upon the familiar expression "the Wrath of God" to aptly portray His Divine Justice. Mephostophiles continues his description of the eternal prison, stating Hell is also recognised by diverse names: House of Shame, Abyss, Gullet, Pit, and *Dissensio*.[329] He explains Hell is called the House of Shame as "[...] the souls of the damned are also shamed, scorned and mocked by God and His Blessed Ones [...]".[330] Mephostophiles derives this rationalisation from Proverbs 1 (vs. 25–26): "You have despised all my counsel, and have neglected my reprehensions. I also will laugh in your destruction, and will mock when that shall come to you which you feared." Properly explained, all the contempt a habitual sinner hurls at God by his refusal to repent will return to haunt and mock him at his Judgement when his soul remembers its former wickedness, but then will be unable to obtain merciful forgiveness. However, Mephostophiles deliberately misinterprets the passage and presents a theological error, leading Faust to believe God literally taunts the damned. In fact, God desires not the eternal death of the sinner. (Ezech. 18: 23, 33) Hell was first "[...] prepared for the devil and his angels," (Matt. 25:41) and not primarily for the souls of mankind, however, if man chooses to serve Satan there is no other place for him to go but to Hell for eternity as God fashioned Hell from His omnipotent Justice. Heaven and the saints take no delight in the suffering of those who are lost, as mockery is a malicious pleasure contradicting the virtue of holy charity. Rather, it is the damned who torment and shame each other as all their hidden sins are revealed in that place of woe. Mephostophiles elucidates the titles Pit and Gullet, explaining that Hell "[...] ever gapeth after the souls which shall not be damned, desiring that they, too, might be seduced and damned."[331] Hence, we observe a popular Medieval and Renaissance allegory for the Mouth of Hell, it is not uncommon to see the Inferno or its gates depicted in various illustrated religious texts from this period as a hideous monster, or a Leviathan, with open maw swallowing lost souls. The demon continues, saying the moment Lucifer fell, Hell was instantly prepared for him:

"It is a Darkness where Lucifer is banished and bound with chains of darkness, here committed that he may be held for Judgement. Naught may be found there but fumes, fire and the stench of sulphur. But we devils really cannot know in what form and wise Hell is created,

---

[329] Ibid. p. 47.
[330] Ibid.
[331] Ibid.

156

either, nor how it be founded and constructed by God, for it hath neither end nor bottom."[332]

This account is theologically correct, Hell, not withstanding the flames therein, is described by Christ as a place of darkness (Matt. 22:13) because those who are damned will never be able to see God, who is the Eternal Light. Christ also uses the phrase "bound hand and foot" in certain parables to display that the damned are in a place of perpetual exile with no escape, having relinquished their freedom. It is also believed an intolerable stench permeates Hell, mainly sulphur, as all five senses will be punished, including the sense of smell. Hell is also known as the Bottomless Pit, it is quite possible God ordained this immeasurable dimension to humble the demons further who dared by their pride to proclaim they were greater than their Creator, forcing them to acknowledge their limitations as they cannot fathom the very construction of their own prison. We also recognise by Mephostophiles' admission to this limitation imposed upon the demons that Faust's claim to Doctor of Theology is pathetic and undeserved, having believed a fallen and limited creature like a devil could aid him in his quest for mystical knowledge rather than follow his Creator.

Before proceeding to answer Faust's third question on the lamentations heard in the abyss, Mephostophiles sarcastically proffers him the advice to consult the Scriptures on this topic with the addition of a parenthetical statement: "Perchance, my Lord Faust, thou shouldst consult the Scriptures (they being withheld from me)."[333] Mephostophiles has finally succeeded in confounding Faust to an alarming degree that he cannot resist mocking him in his ignorance, as the answer to his query is clearly recorded in the Bible: there will be "weeping and gnashing of teeth" (Matt. 8:12) to torment the sense of hearing. The damned are eternally doomed to hear each other wailing and cursing for eternity. Turning to Mephostophiles' parenthetical remark, we recognise it is theologically erroneous, demons can recite Scripture flawlessly, as when Satan tempted Christ in the desert, but they will present a perverted version of the truth and a distorted interpretation of the passages. This unusual remark voiced by Mephostophiles could not be a reference to any Lutheran belief, for Luther was convinced the devil was the principal enemy of his 'rediscovered Gospel' with its emphasis on 'justification by faith alone'. As Satan is knowledgeable in Scripture from the beginning, logically he recognised the distinction between the Traditional and Reformation schools of theology before declaring his infernal war upon Luther's 'Gospel of Justification'. We may then deduce this parenthetical comment is the author's own invention to illustrate the deception of the devils. Mephostophiles would have Faust believe *all* his infernal replies are veracious by emphasising his personal demonic experience of Hell, tempting Faust to question the accuracy of the Scriptures, as his semi-heretical descriptions have been surprisingly accurate for a spirit who stated the Scriptures were withheld from him. This is a clever tactic for it reiterates the error already introduced in Chapter Nine of the manuscript that the Scriptures require eyewitness correction, affording Mephostophiles further opportunities to introduce heretical statements as truth to Faust's eternal determent. Our observation is confirmed by Mephostophiles who continues, "Inasmuch as I have already given account of the former [i.e. the aspect of Hell], thy hellish speculations on the latter

---

[332] Ibid.
[333] Ibid.

157

[i.e. the agony of Hell] will I also satisfy with a report. The damned will encounter all the circumstances which I recounted afore, for what I say is true;"[334] thus intimating the 'inferior' nature of Faust's human speculative theories of Hell based on Scripture in contrast with his demonic 'veracious' first-hand knowledge.

Immediately, Mephostophiles takes advantage of the situation when answering the third question to include a derogatory reference to the fairer gender by declaring Hell, the insatiable pit, is "like womb of woman, and earth's belly,"[335] which is a borrowing from the book of Proverbs taken out of context; "There are three things that never are satisfied, and the fourth never saith: It is enough. Hell, and the mouth of the womb, and the earth which are not satisfied with water: and the fire never saith: It is enough." (Prov. 30:15–16) As this book of the Bible is attributed to King Solomon, his curious reference was obviously drawn from his experiences with his lascivious pagan wives who drew upon his weakness and tempted him to commit sin. However, Mephostophiles is attempting to re-establish the former chauvinistic preconceptions of women, painting them all seductresses, which according to Obermann, Luther attempted to eradicate during the Reformation:

> "[…] Luther disposed of two gross prejudices that had shaped the clerical image of women. The first, which the *Hammer against the Witches* (*Malleus Maleficarum*; circa 1487) had once again drummed into the Inquisitors, was that women were sexually insatiable hyenas and thus a constant danger to men and their society. The second prejudice reduced women to "bearing children," the procreation of the human race [… with emphasis on] the reproduction of the male. Luther was familiar with and disgusted by both of these contemptuous theses."[336]

In a few words, the author of the text has reminded his readers that Satan and his minions are also great enemies of women due to the prophecy a Woman would be their foremost adversary, as from her would spring the Redeemer: "I will put enmities between thee and the woman, and thy seed and her seed: she shall crush thy head, and thou shalt lie in wait for her heel." (Gen. 3:15)

Mephostophiles then continues by truthfully affirming Hell will never end, including the various torments inflicted there. The lost will forevermore bewail their wickedness and the "[…] hellish hideousness of the stench of their own afflictions."[337] They will also call out, scream, wail unto God, be filled with woe, tremble, whimper, yelp, howl and weep.[338] The demon also states that the souls in Hell will not experience equal torments as not all sins are the same, each soul will suffer for the particular sins they committed.

Once more, however, he diverges to partial fallacy by announcing the spirits hope to be saved and shall be freed at the end of time, (i.e. if we interpret the term "spirits" to indicate

---

[334] Ibid.
[335] Ibid.
[336] *Luther, Man Between God and the Devil*, p. 277.
[337] *History of Doctor Johann Faustus*, p. 47.
[338] Ibid.

"devils" for the present*), but truthfully maintains the damned from the human race will not. Mephostophiles retorts that this reply, and his responses to Faust's first two questions, already answers the fourth query whether God will receive the damned into His grace. However, the demon 'condescends' to elaborate further on this fourth issue, parenthetically reminding Faust "[…] that it will be in direct violation of thy contract and vow".[339] Mephostophiles resumes his semi-veracious narration of Hell, proclaiming damned human souls will never return to God's grace and are without hope, unlike the spirits. The devil adds that if the human soul in Hell could feel the same hope as the spirits, they would "take cheer and sigh in anticipation".[340] Yet, as there is no hope for them he says, "[…] neither their pleading, nor their prayer, their crying nor their sighing will be heard, and their conscience will not let them forget."[341] Mephostophiles proceeds to relate the various regrets each lost soul will bemoan with expressions such as "If only I had not done this," and "If only I had not blasphemed God […] But my sins are too great and cannot be forgiven me," etc.[342] *In fine*, Mephostophiles is prompting Faust to contrast the sensation of hope with his own feelings of desolation, and to compare his previous lamentations of having sold his soul with the regrets of those already damned. Mephostophiles subtly, yet masterfully, seals Faust in despair with this decisive conclusion placing emphasis on the word *soul:*

> "Let it be understood then, my Lord Fauste, that the damned man — or the soul, if you will — can no more attain Grace than can he hope for an end of his sufferings or a tide wherein he might be removed from such anguish. […] Their firm belief and faith in God — oh they will at last acquire it — will go unheeded, and no thought will be taken of them. […] It is possible to conceive of an elephant or a camel entering into a needle's eye, or of counting all the raindrops. But there is no conceiving of a time of hope in Hell"[343]

Mephostophiles pronounces he has presented the fourth and final answer, and warns Faust if he asks further questions on these mystical matters, he will not be attended to as the demon states "[…] I am not obligated to tell thee such things."[344]
According to the terms of their contract, this is true in one sense, as Faust agreed to abandon his Christian faith, this would include any meditation on Hell or Heaven with a view to conversion and thereby regain the grace of God. Yet, Faust, submerged in the depths of hopelessness, fails to recognise the fact Mephostophiles admitted he was posing questions in violation of their agreement, which the spirit nevertheless agreed to answer. In short, Faust is now released by Mephostophiles' own infringement of the third article. Mephostophiles is now utterly confident in his dominion over the despondent scholar, the written agreement is no longer necessary to bind

---

* See the section entitled 'Faust and the Realm of the Middle Spirits' below.
[339] *History of Doctor Johann Faustus*, p. 48.
[340] Ibid.
[341] Ibid. p. 49.
[342] Ibid.
[343] Ibid. pp. 49–50.
[344] Ibid. p. 50.

him, it has simply become another vindictive tool for his demonic taunting. Having mocked Faust the 'theologian' for his ignorance in the Scriptures, he is now questioning the calibre of his university education regarding the basic study of law taught in the *trivium*, and Faust's alarming lack of common sense.

Part One of the Wolfenbüttel Text concludes with Faust leaving Mephostophiles in a melancholic state, pondering upon all that he heard. He finally has received the spiritual / scriptural "tribulations" Luther described, but he does not profit from them. In contrast, "[…] there was no constancy in [Faust], for the Devil had hardened his heart and blinded him."[345] Furthermore, Faust allows himself to be distracted by the 'Tribulation Devil' rather than stand and oppose him, for "[…] when [Faust] did succeed in being alone to contemplate the Word of God, the Devil would dizen himself in the form of a beautiful woman, embrace him, […] so that he soon forgot the Divine Word and threw it to the wind."[346] Analysing Faust's ignorance by comparing it with Luther's beliefs and observations, we detect his predominant failure as a theologian originates from his inability to practise what he learned:

> "Divinity consists in use and practice, not in speculation and meditation. Every one that deals in speculations, either in household affairs or temporal government, without practice, is lost and nothing worth. When a tradesman makes his account, how much profit he shall reap in the year, but puts nothing in practice, he trades in vain speculations, and finds afterwards that his reckoning comes far too short. And thus it goes also with speculating divines, as is seen to this day, and as I know by experience."[347]

In summary, Faust is worthy of the title "Speculator". He lacks faith in the Word of God, or he would not have contented himself with a degree based on mere theory — his creed is nothing but a calligraphed title stamped with a university seal attained for the sole purpose of professional advancement in the world. If Faust had true faith, believing the contents of the Bible and the warnings contained therein, he would have rejected the dubious commentary on Hell presented by the demon and paid heed to St. Paul's prophesy: "Now the Spirit manifestly saith, that in the last times some shall depart from the faith, giving heed to spirits of error, and doctrines of devils, speaking lies in hypocrisy, *and having their conscience seared*, […] ." (1 Tim. 4:1–2) In addition, Luther warned: "The faith toward God in Christ must be sure and steadfast, that it may solace and make glad the conscience, and put it to rest. When a man has this certainty, he has overcome the serpent; but if he be doubtful of the doctrine, it is for him very dangerous to dispute with the devil."[348] Hence, Faust is goaded by the devil into a melancholic frenzy through his lack of faith, and in no condition to dispute with Mephostophiles on theological subjects. Furthermore, the idea that Faust required a second commentary on the Scriptures at all to prove

---

[345] Ibid.
[346] Ibid.
[347] Luther, 'Of Preachers and Preaching' # CCCLXXXIX, *Tischreden*.
[348] Ibid. 'Of God's Word', #XXXVII.

their certainty demonstrates his incompetence as a "master" of the Holy Writ. Luther observed that …

> "In all sciences, the ablest professors are they who have thoroughly mastered the texts. [...] but in our time, the attention is applied rather to glossaries and commentaries. When I was young, I read the Bible over and over and over again, and was so perfectly acquainted with it, that I could, in an instant, have pointed to any verse that might have been mentioned. I then read the commentators, but I soon threw them aside, for I found therein many things my conscience could not approve, as being contrary to the sacred text. `Tis always better to see with one's own eyes than with those of other people."[349]

Upon our reflection on this comment, Faust had no business entering the university in the first instance! In an ironic twist, the author re-enforces Mephostophiles as the true Master of Faust by reintroducing the familiar format of three disputations featured in Chapters Nine, Ten and Eleven: as stated previously, the examination for the degree of Master in general entailed the completion of three disputations. This is not the last time we will see a tripartite pattern.

Faust: Astroseer and Cosmotourist

Part Two of the Wolfenbüttle manuscript introduces Faust's interest in astrological science. Unable to probe further in mystical topics due to Mephostophiles' prohibition on the same, Faust turns his attention to the revolutions of the planets and stars. As previously noted in Chapter One of our study, astrology in that era was not always recognised in a strict sense as forbidden occultism or soothsaying, i.e. as a means of foretelling the future by objects that are not in themselves calculated to reveal them. Alternatively, many firmly believed the stars *influenced* rather than *foreshadowed* events that occurred on earth. The subtle difference may be explained by using our modern perception of weather forecasting as an example. We may watch the weather report on the news and discover that the day of an important job interview will be rainy, windy and heavily overcast. We would then mentally prepare ourselves for a dark, wet and chilly day based on a scientific and educated opinion, albeit the forecast may prove incorrect, rather than suddenly decide not to attend the interview at all on the superstitious assumption that the bleak prediction was an omen forewarning the job will prove to be an unhappy and depressing workplace. Although the validity of astrology was often questioned due to numerous false predictions and the gradual blurring between what was deemed a study of star-influence with divination, the skill of horoscope calculation in Faustus' time was nevertheless an acceptable, noble academic discipline placed in the same category as mathematics and geometry.

---

[349]   Ibid. #XXXIII.

We are informed in Chapter Twelve of the Wolfenbüttle text Faust soon excelled in this field with the aid of Mephostophiles, earning the admiration and praise of the aristocracy and the mathematicians of the day as his predictions always proved correct in explicit detail:

> "When he presaged fogs, wind, snow, precipitation, etc. these things were all quite certain. His almanacs were not as those of some unskilled *astrologi* who know of course that it gets cold in the winter, and hence forecast freezes, or that it will be hot in the summer, and predict thunderstorms. Doctor Faustus always calculated his tables [...] specifying the day and the hour and especially warning the particular districts — this one with famine, that one with war, another with pestilence, and so forth."[350]

This description of Faust's accuracy in horoscope calculations resembles the historical Faustus, another rare instance when legendary literature parallels historical documentation.

Two years elapse before Faust questions Mephostophiles in Chapter Thirteen upon the nature of astrology practised by the mathematicians of the day. Presumably, he noticed the superior calculations he provides through the demon's assistance in contrast with those drawn by his associates and desires to know why he is singularly precise in this skill. Mephostophiles immediately replies contemporary astrologers are hindered from making any accurate charts by the nature of their brief life expectancy. He explains the stars are great mysteries of God, which …

> "[...] mortals cannot plumb as we spirits can, who hover in the air beneath Heaven where we can see and mark what God hath predestined. Yes, we are ancient spirits, experienced in the Heavenly movements. [...] — Thou hast seen that I have never lied to thee."[351]

The demon relates this immortal knowledge allows him to predict exceptionally accurate horoscopes, almanacs and nativity predictions. Mephostophiles admits, however, the Patriarchs became adept at studying the movement of the stars due to their miraculous longevity. Because of their numerous years, they were able to observe when the "luni-solar" cycles repeated and passed on this knowledge to the younger generation until the art was lost with the passage of time as the life-span of the human race decreased. Mephostophiles concludes his account saying that apart from the Patriarchs, all astrologers "[...] set up their horoscopes arbitrarily according to conjecture."[352]

This appears a straightforward theological and scientific answer; however, Mephostophiles craftily concealed further examples of his diabolical values beneath his academic façade. First, there is his obvious attempt to mutate the Renaissance perception of astronomy cum astrology as a scholastic field with the occult astrology of soothsayers. For example,

---

[350] *History of Doctor Johann Faustus*, p. 53.
[351] Ibid. p. 54.
[352] Ibid.

Mephostophiles mentions scientific terms, astronomic almanacs and lunar-solar periods, and juxtaposes them to references emphasising the concept of preordained events and nativity prognostications. We may theorise once the perception of a certain discipline is altered, it is probable the practise in the field as a whole will also be affected. Mephostophiles' goal in this instance is to alter Faust's academic perception of astrology and have him focus on the divination aspect, thus forging him into an invaluable tool to lead people astray by manipulating them to place their hope on demonically influenced prophecies gleaned from created, powerless objects such as the stars rather than trust their future to God and His Divine Providence. This passage in the Wolfenbüttle Text corresponds with Luther's conclusion that the science of astronomy is a gift from God, while astrology is a tool of Satan:

> "[…] Astrology is framed by the devil, to the end people may be scared from entering into the state of matrimony, and from every divine and human office and calling; for the star-peepers presage nothing that is good out of the planets; they affright people's consciences, in regard of misfortunes to come, which all stand in God's hand, and through such mischievous and unprofitable cogitations vex and torment the whole life.
>
> Great wrong is done to God's creatures by the star-expounders. God has created and placed the stars in the firmament, to the end they might give light to the kingdoms of the earth, make people glad and joyful in the Lord, and be good signs of years and seasons. But the star-peepers feign that those creatures, of God created, darken and trouble the earth, and are hurtful; whereas all creatures of God are good, and by God created only for good, though mankind makes them evil, by abusing them. Eclipses, indeed, are monsters, and like to strange and untimely births. Lastly, to believe in the stars, or to trust thereon, or to be affrighted thereat, is idolatry, and against the first commandment."[353]

The author of the manuscript was illustrating the very fine line Luther observed between that which may be considered science and the godless art of soothsaying, warning his readers not to become embroiled with astrologers as it is too easy to cross that boundary and consult with those who receive their knowledge from devils.

Mephostophiles also has another ulterior motive for answering Faust's question on astrology in this manner. As the demon affirmed he never lied to Faust regarding his horoscope predictions, thus explaining their unrivalled success surpassing other astrologers, he leads Faust to believe his statement that the demons have the ability to see God's predestined plan is also veracious. According to theology, Mephostophiles lied for the demons are not knowledgeable about God's Eternal Plan in its entirety, as many details remain hidden from them. For example, the obedient angels of Heaven do not know when the Last Day will occur. However, the demons can predict the future to a certain point with a considerable degree of accuracy for they are

---

[353] Luther, 'Of Astronomy and Astrology' #DCCXCIX, *Tischreden*.

immortal spirits that have observed the idiosyncrasies of the human race and all that occurred on Earth since the time of Creation. Yet, if Mephostophiles can confound Faust into believing the devils are thoroughly and absolutely familiar with the plan God predestined, he is also intimating that the preceding answers to the theological disputations in Part One of the text were also true, particularly Faust's 'inescapable' fate of damnation.

We soon discover in Chapter Fourteen of the manuscript that Mephostophiles' sophistry succeeded in driving Faust into another fit of melancholy, a state of mind Luther identified as one of the devil's works. Mephostophiles, (feigning ignorance of the cause), wheedles Faust until he finally discloses the source of this depression: "Well, I have taken thee unto me as a servant, and thy service doth cost me dear enough. Yet I cannot have my will of thee, as would be proper of a servant."[354] Hence, Faust is mournful, believing his soul is already eternally lost for a half-loyal servant who fails to fulfil his promises. Mephostophiles replies that he served him faithfully in all things, except on one occasion when Faust desired theological answers on a specific subject that would breach the terms of their contract. The demon then asks what Faust desires of him; apparently, Faust was afraid to question Mephostophiles further on topics that remotely bordered on the theological. On this occasion, Faust confesses he was wondering how God created the world and the human race. However, Mephostophiles is not irritated by this new disputation, Faust already accepts his soul is lost, and therefore is simply broaching a theological subject from academic curiosity true to his old university habits without any thoughts of repentance. The demon proceeds to answer the question, yet true to *his* ancient custom, resorts to distorting the Scriptures:

> "The world, my Lord Fauste, hath never experienced birth and will never know death, and the human race has always existed. There is not any origin or beginning of things. The earth subsists, as always, of itself. The sea arose from the earth, and the two got along so very well that one would think they had carried on a conversation in which the land had required his realm from the sea, the fields, meadows, woods, grass and trees; and that the sea had likewise demanded his own realm of water with the fish and all else therein. Now they did concede to God the creation of mankind and of Heaven, and this is the way they finally became subservient to God. Thou wilt observe that I have explained how from one realm there finally arose four: air, fire, water, and earth. I know none other, nor briefer, way of instructing thee."[355]

Mephostophiles offered a paradoxical scenario in his version of Earth's primordial origins to confuse Faust further. He contradicts his own statements when proclaiming the land and sky conceded to God the creation of mankind, yet maintains the human race always existed and therefore was not "created". The same inconsistency he applies to the creation of Heaven: if the earth never had a beginning, heaven would also have to pre-exist with the earth for there to be a distinction between the firmaments of the stars, sky and the land. We note Mephostophiles

---

[354] *History of Doctor Johann Faustus*, p. 55.
[355] Ibid. p. 56.

164

placed God last in the order of the universe. The most obvious source for this version of creation is the pagan philosophy of Aristotle. Although the ancient philosopher believed there was a 'Prime Mover', or great divine being responsible for the ordering of nature, he proposed that the earth had always existed, i.e. the various elements of the physical world, which contrasts sharply with the Christian belief God created the elements of the earth from nothing. Aristotle theorised the landmass of the earth came into being as each of the four elements, earth, water, air and fire, separated according to their nature of gravity, each settling in their respective places in the cosmos.

A sobering point to observe, the author of the Wolfenbüttle text, in his endeavour to fabricate a blasphemous anti-Genesis perspective worthy for a devil to relate, had inadvertently devised topics predating modern speculations on the earth's origin and Darwin's controversial theory of evolution by several centuries. First, Mephostophiles remarks, contrary to the book of Genesis, the land existed before the oceans, and second, he intimates with the word "required" that the land 'acquired' living creatures for its kingdom directly from the sea, also contradicting Genesis that states all living creatures were created separately within and for their perspective habitats. Third, we may observe the devil's comment that the earth always existed refutes the traditional view the earth and all life contained therein was actually created by a Supreme being, and also implies the age of the earth is much greater than the biblical interpretation of approximately five to seven thousand years. In comparison with these observations, science today proposes that when the earth's crust was forming, volcanic eruptions emitted gaseous vapours that formed the atmosphere, followed by the condensation of water on the surface, suggesting the landmass appeared before the seas. Modern science also maintains the first living organisms on earth appeared in the oceans, slowly evolving into various life forms that were more complex until they finally adapted for survival on land and in the air. Furthermore, scientists theorise that the formation of the earth and the evolution of life was and is an ongoing process that began billions of years ago. Although this section of the Wolfenbüttle manuscript was intended to be an expression of demonic falsification and not a serious presentation of scientific conjecture, the foreshadowing of modern thinking to this extent in the text is startling; particularly, when we consider it was written when many contemporary academics were highly sceptical of Copernicus' basic heliocentric theory that the earth orbited the sun.

The chapter concludes with Faust pondering upon the matter; unable to comprehend the information Mephostophiles just related for his account bears no relation to the book of Genesis. Unfortunately, Faust remains silent and offers no objection to this devilish concoction opposing theological reason, refusing to recognise Mephostophiles for the liar that he is. Perhaps his silence displays sentiments of inferiority instilled in him by the demon in the previous chapter. Faust apparently presumes he, as an inferior mortal, could not dare to contradict a spirit who witnessed the Creation.

Arriving at Chapter Fifteen we learn eight years have elapsed since the signing of the contract, during which time Faust remained occupied with "inquiry, study, questioning and *disputations*."[356] That is, he redirected his focus on academic matters rather than engage in meditative contemplation. Once more, Faust dreams of Hell, causing him to summon Mephostophiles and ask if it would be possible to summon his demon-lord, Belial.

---

[356] Ibid. p. 57.

Mephostophiles responds in the affirmative, however, a more powerful demon appears: Beelzebub. Faust then inquires of this devil if it is possible "[…] for a spirit to conduct him into Hell and out again, so that he might see and mark the nature, fundament, quality and substance of Hell."[357] Beelzebub also answers in the affirmative and arranges a time when he will conduct this excursion. Apparently, Faust is now convinced that Mephostophiles' intimidations in Chapter Eleven are true, i.e. that his cogitations and various questions on Hell actually submerge him further into its depths. Hence, when his dreams of Hell return, Faust submits to the government of the Abyss, which declares permission must be granted for grave requests, as we discovered in Chapter Three of the manuscript. In conclusion, this petition placed with the rulers of Hell evinces Faust's continual acceptance of his supposed damnation. Definitely, Faust remembers his last encounter with Satan when he proposed plans for marriage, and on this occasion takes greater care to assure he will not break the rules of his agreement by placing his audacious request directly with the more powerful Princes of Hell to secure their approval. Yet, the arch demon displays no objection to Faust's desire to see Hell in this instance, for unlike the previous occasion when he disputed with Mephostophiles with the ulterior motive to seek spiritual amendment, Faust is simply curious regarding the construction of the Inferno and simply intends to study it as a modern scientist would scrutinise the Ebola virus under controlled laboratory conditions.

Now, for the first time we are presented with an opportunity to discover which choir of the demonic hierarchy[†] Mephostophiles hails from, before Faust's 'journey' to the Netherworld. As discussed earlier, it is believed Satan attempts to parody all of God's Creation, including the order of the angelic choirs of Heaven. Unfortunately, the author of the Wolfenbüttle text introduced the devils of Hell in random order throughout the manuscript and inventively included the pagan god Dagon as an official demon. It is possible he assumed his readers were already familiar with contemporary lists of the various infernal ranks and did not see the necessity to place them in the proper hierarchal order, or he intended his readers to decide which demonic choir Belial leads. We must therefore deduce from Scripture the choirs designated to these arch-demons. Belial, a name also used in reference to Satan, gradually became recognised as a separate demon as time progressed. In Part One, Chapter Nine of the Wolfenbüttle text, Belial was already mentioned separately from Satan / Lucifer, hence this distinction between the two devils must also extend to Chapter Fifteen. This particular demon could not be the prince of the first and highest demonic legion as this is a rank generally assigned to Beelzebub, who is described as the Prince of Devils (Luke 11), and may also be recognised as the antithesis of St. Michael, the Prince of the Angels and leader of the first Heavenly choir. Although "Beelzebub" was also used synonymously in reference to Satan, we have already encountered the Supreme Angel of Darkness in Part One of the text. It is evident from the context the author also intended Beelzebub to be introduced as a separate devil in his work; "[Mephostophiles] agreed to [summon Belial], but instead […] a devil was sent who called himself Beelzebub, a flying spirit reigning beneath Heaven."[358]

---

[357] Ibid.
[†] I.e. in Haile's version.
[358] *History of Doctor Johann Faustus*, p. 57.

It is a logical presumption Belial was perceived as the arch-demon in control of the second legion of Hell for several reasons. The name "Belial" appears numerous times in the Old Testament and is associated with the heinous sin of disobedience and idolatry, as observed earlier in Chapter One of our work the name Belial signifies "without yoke", i.e. without the law of God. Belial is also associated with impurity, slander and bearing false witness, the trademarks of his hellish king who is the Father of Lies. Hence, due to the prominence of his name in scripture and his numerous diabolical associations he is entitled to a high rank close to Satan, and may be rightly declared his 'Ambassador'. This indicates he is the antithesis of the second greatest archangel: St. Gabriel, the Ambassador of God and Herald of the Incarnation of Christ. Belial could not be in charge of the third legion of demons as Asmodeus, the arch-demon of lechery, is the enemy of St. Raphael, the third archangel of Heaven. In addition, it is not logical to conclude that Belial could be in charge of any of the lower hordes after the third hierarchy as he is associated with a greater number of evils than Asmodeus. However, this is our own observation for the present study and is open to further interpretation, other literature from the Renaissance period features diverse listings for the ranks of the arch demons. We may however state with a degree of certainty that Belial is a Prince close to Satan, perhaps one of the fallen cherubim, and ruler of one of the most powerful Infernal Legions. If Mephostophiles belongs to this choir, he is also a fallen cherub and may be recognised as an arch-demon. He therefore wields a considerable amount of authority in Hell and possibly more than we may have first perceived in the text.

Ultimately, we are forced to accept that if Satan deemed Faust worthy of having a mighty fallen cherub for his *familiar* spirit, the scholar had undoubtedly sunk to a grievous level of spiritual depravity by the time he decided to forfeit his soul. It is also more than mere coincidence that Faust should be granted a demon subservient to Belial. Turning to the book of 3 Kings (Chapter 21), we encounter the history of King Achab and Jezebel regarding their plot to steal the vineyard of Naboth by means of perjury. They seek out two false-witnesses, "sons of Belial" who swear an oath accusing Naboth of a grievous crime and thereby justify his execution as a traitor, allowing the evil rulers to 'legally' confiscate his vineyard. King Achab is also described in ominous terms: "Now there was not such another as Achab, *who was sold to do evil in the sight of the Lord: for his wife Jezabel set him on. And he became abominable. Insomuch that he followed the idols which the Amorrhites had made* […]". (vs. 25–26) Hence, Belial and his legion have the diabolical mission of gathering and commanding those souls who have purposely "sold themselves to do evil" like Faust.

Returning to the narration, eight years of the contract have elapsed, and Faust has now advanced in wickedness to the extent he is granted the dubious 'honour' of having the Prince of Devils, Beelzebub, as his guide through Hell in Chapter Fifteen rather than Lord Belial, Mephostophiles' commander. At midnight, Beelzebub arrives in the form of a great dragon[359] bearing upon his back a gruesome throne fashioned of bones whereon Faust embarks for his journey to the Bottomless Pit. Immediately, we realise that the devil tricked Faust with a deceptive vision of the Inferno: "Now hear how the Devil did mystify and gull him, so that he

---

[359] Although Haile's version of the Wolfenbüttle Manuscript did not feature this descriptive detail, it may be gleaned from the context of the third and fourth paragraphs of Chapter Fifteen, e.g. "Meanwhile, three more devilish dragons had flown up alongside Beelzebub. They were just like him and they went flying along ahead of him as he penetrated further into the abyss." Ibid. p. 58.

had no other notion that he really had been in Hell."[360] Faust is not permitted to question[Δ] his guide; therefore, we are aware the demons are weaving another web of deception by establishing this precondition. He cannot challenge what is shown to him for it could prove contrary to the traditional perception of Hell expounded by theologians.

They arrive "upon a mountain of a great island"[361] where sulphur, pitch and fire blow and crash together with great ferocity. Although everything surrounding Faust is ablaze, he feels no heat, "[…] but rather little spring breezes as in May." He hears extraordinary, beautiful music, yet the brightness of the flames prevents him from discovering the identities of the musicians, and as he cannot inquire about this phenomenon, he remains confused. In the interim, three more dragons appear and escort Beelzebub as they descend deeper. Suddenly, and without warning, a great flying stag with enormous antlers appears and charges at Faust; however, the dragons fight the stag and protect Faust from a near catastrophe. As they continue on their descent into the "spelunca",[362] a multitude of giant snakes and serpents encircle Faust. This time, flying lions battle with the reptiles and make secure the path for Faust and his entourage. The danger is not yet over, a flying bull charges from the opening of an old gate and succeeds in goring Faust from his *osteothronos* and sends him screaming into the Pit, however, an old ape catches Faust as he falls. Then, a black fog descends upon Hell obscuring Faust's view for a short time until two great dragons appear pulling a large coach, and the ape places him inside. Abruptly, a great storm breaks with a tremendous crash of thunder, fumes of sulphur, and the mountain quakes: Faust becomes filled with fear. The fog again descends for a quarter of an hour, becoming so thick, Faust can no longer see the dragons or the coach, and when the dark fog lifts once more, Faust witnesses great lightening bolts and flames shooting down into the abyss. Shortly thereafter, the coach arrives at a turbid body of water, and the reptilian steeds plunge into the hellish lake, Faust feels no water but a great radiance of heat. As the heat beats upon him in waves and swirls him around in currents, he is dislodged from the coach and becomes submerged in this lacustrine mirage. Suddenly and without warning, he discovers he is marooned upon a high, jagged, desolate crag, or what appears to be a volcanic vent surrounded by water, with no visible means of escape. In desperation, he lunges forward into the fiery fissure: he has now reached the very depths of Hell. Here he discovers thousands of lost souls that once hailed from the higher echelons of society — emperors, kings, princes, lords and knights — all tormented in a great fire. Faust encounters a cool stream flowing parallel to the flames where he observes a number of the souls are allowed a reprieve, while others are unable to bear the piercing cold of the water. Faust reaches out from the heat to catch one of the souls, but his quarry swiftly escapes his grasp, slipping through his fingers like a wispy shadow of smoke. Finally, he cannot withstand the heat, the cold, the choking fog, the reeking stench, the wailing of woe, and searches for a way to escape this hellish nightmare. As though on cue, Beelzebub appears and bears the now sleeping Faust back to his home, hurling him onto his bed.

---

[360] *History of Doctor Johann Faustus*, p. 57.

[Δ] This detail that Faust must remain silent confirms the illusory nature of their journey as silence was essential for certain conjurations. Cornelius Agrippa once explained a magical experiment could be ruined by a talkative bystander. (*Doctor Faustus; A- and B- Texts*, n. 25, p. 186.)

[361] *History of Doctor Johann Faustus*, p. 58.

[362] Ibid.

While this vision occurred, the text states Faust actually disappeared: "Now Doctor Faustus had not been at home for a long while. His famulus [Wagner] felt sure that, if he had achieved his desire of seeing Hell, he must have seen more than he bargained for and would never come back."[363] Faust awakes at dawn the next morning and reflects upon the events he witnessed; his initial impression is an interior sense of prolonged confinement in a dark tower, and at first is convinced he actually visited the Inferno. Later, he begins to doubt the scenes of horror he witnessed and finally concludes it was just a vision. Parenthetically the author writes: "And this is true, for he had not seen Hell, else he would not have spent the rest of his life trying to get there."[364]

We may question why Beelzebub would bother to transport Faust from his place of residence if he was not prepared to guide him through the genuine Inferno. The answer may lie in that through Faust's disappearance, Beelzebub would have the opportunity, as observed with Wagner, to encourage other characters in the narration to conclude Faust had actually visited Hell and therefore would be more inclined to believe this less terrifying account and be tempted to regard Hell with complacency. Indeed, this narration is a fabrication very loosely based on the traditional Christian view of Hell. The author retains some recognisable elements as with the different levels or sections of the Pit, the torments of fire, darkness, the unbearable stench of sulphur, lightning, thunder, and wailings of woe. However, it is obvious from the beginning Beelzebub elected to withhold the true nature of the Abyss in all its hideousness. Faust hears extraordinary music of incomparable beauty, a paradox to the traditional concept that the Inferno is a place of absolute torment. This vision portrays a Hell that is unexpectedly sparse in population, and despite the bizarre attacks of the spectral animals upon Faust, we do not encounter many demons nor any damned souls until we reach the final level. This allows for the false impression very few souls are lost, and those that are damned to the lower level experience a certain measure of peace as they have their own private quarters in Hell where they are not tormented by the demons. A number of these lost souls may also refresh themselves in a cool river if they find the flames too hot for their comfort! Certainly, this fails to portray a true, terrifying image of the Inferno. By diligently confirming that Beelzebub revealed a false vision to Faust, the author intimates to readers they should not minimise the fury contained within that place of woe for the salutary fear of Hell is also diminished and a powerful tool for inspiring repentance and the spirit of amendment is blunted and thereby rendered inconsequential.

This unconventional vision of Hell leads to further significant observations. Two details in the narration, namely, the description of Hell as a "mountain of a great island", and the ravaging phantasmal beasts appearing during the first stages of Faust's journey, suggests the author of the Wolfenbüttle Manuscript was inspired by 'The Inferno' in Dante Alighieri's immortal classic, *The Divine Comedy* (c. 1321).[365]

The *Divine Comedy* is a monumental allegorical narration of Dante's interior journey through the pits of Hell and up the purifying mountain of Purgatory, ultimately reaching the eternal bliss of Heaven. In Canto I of the *Inferno*, Dante allegorically declares he reached middle

---

[363] Ibid. p. 60.

[364] Ibid. p. 61.

[365] Dante Alighieri, *The Divine Comedy*, in Charles W. Eliot, ed., *The Divine Comedy of Dante Alighieri, The Harvard Classics vol. 20* (New York: P.F. Collier and Son, 1963).

age and had strayed from the 'true path' in life whereupon he becomes lost in a gloomy wood that fills him with dread. After a gruelling struggle through the overgrown forest, he approaches a mountain and is convinced he must conquer the obstacle and reach the top if he is to attain his heavenly goal. As he begins his arduous ascent to Heaven, three animals advance towards him, a panther, a lion, and a she-wolf, the sight of which fills him with fear and utterly discourages him from continuing. The panther is a symbol of pleasure and luxury,[366] but unfortunately, the significance of the other two predators remains a mystery. Possibly, they represent the cares of the world and Dante's political enemies. We note the source for this allegorical symbolism may be found in the book of Jeremias (5:6) where the prophet comments on the punishment that will befall the unrepentant sinners of Jerusalem: "Wherefore a lion out of the wood hath slain them, a wolf in the evening hath spoiled them, a leopard watcheth for their cities: every one that shall go out thence shall be taken, because their transgressions are multiplied, their rebellions are strengthened." The poet Virgil, who represents human reason, rescues Dante and declares he is sent to conduct him on another path that passes through Hell and Purgatory before he may attain the glory of Heaven. It is important to observe the allegories Dante uses to symbolise the ascent to Heaven in his initial introduction; Purgatory is not only depicted as a mountain where purification is achieved through suffering, but Dante's personal struggle in life to attain salvation is also compared to a mountain, difficult to climb and beset with tribulations represented by ferocious animals.

Apparently, the author of the Wolfenbüttle text borrowed this latter element of Dante's work, but wrote a contrasting symbolic representation of Faust's real spiritual descent into the actual Inferno. Faust espies the "great mountain" that seemingly represents his life, but is not confronted with a frightening and discouraging forest like Dante — he is captivated by beautiful music: possibly a symbol of Satan's willingness to make life easy and carefree for those who choose to follow him. We note that in Book Two of Milton's *Paradise Lost*, one group of devils amuse themselves by singing beautiful music for this art can also be misused as a seductive charm, or dull the senses and reason: "Their song was partial; but the harmony / [...] suspended Hell, and took with ravishment / The thronging audience, ([...] Song charms the Sense)."[367] Three animals then attack Faust; the allegory of which is open to many interpretations. As the text is mainly based on theological subjects to this point, it is logical to presume these animals are also theological representations. Of particular interest, not all of these creatures are those commonly recognised as *demonic* symbols, i.e. the stag and the bull, for example. In fact, there appears to be a battle between Hell and Heaven for the eternal possession of Faust's soul.

Initially in this first attack upon Faust, the dragons are triumphant as they succeed in driving off the hart. The flying hart or stag may be a reference to Psalm 41; "As the hart panteth after the fountains of water; so my soul panteth after thee, O God. My soul hath thirsted after the strong living God; when shall I come and appear before the face of God?" Hence, Faust's own soul, symbolised by the stag, attacks Faust for having sold it for the vanities of the world. We may also observe the stag could be related to the symbol of a particular saint, possibly St. Hubert (d. 727) of the Ardenne region who according to tradition was hunting in the forest on a Good

---

[366] Ibid. p. 6.

[367] John Milton, *Paradise Lost*, Book II, in *The Complete Poems of John Milton, The Harvard Classics, vol. 4* (New York: P. F. Collier and Son Corp., 1963), p. 122.

Friday and was converted to Christianity when a stag approached bearing a crucifix between its antlers. Perhaps this signifies a reproach to Faust, for unlike St. Hubert who was converted from an unchristian life while in a forest, Faust first publicly turned to Satan when conjuring in the Spesser Wald. There is also a possible reference to the allegorical symbols depicted in Sir Mallory's Grail Legends. In Book Seventeen, Chapter Nine of *The Holy Grail*, Sir Galahad and two of his companions see a vision where Christ appears as a hart. A hermit-priest interprets their vision saying: "And well ought Our Lord be signified to an hart, for the hart when he is old he waxeth young again in his white skin. Right so cometh Our Lord from death to Life [...]."[368] If this reference was intended in the Faust manuscript, this could signify Christ's sacrifice on the cross was in vain for Faust, who of his own free will, elected to follow Satan.

Next, various serpents and snakes surround Faust, but flying lions save him; on this occasion, it appears benevolent creatures save Faust from those that are demonic. The lions could represent St. Mark the Evangelist, whose symbol is a lion with wings. St. Mark's Gospel was written particularly for the benefit of the Christians in Rome and pronounces Christ to be the Son of God: hence, this may symbolise a reminder to Faust that he may be saved if he places his faith in Christ, the Son of God. Another reference to Sir Malory's Grail Legends may also be intended here.[369] In the Fourteenth Book, Chapter Six of *The Holy Grail*, Sir Percivale espies a lion fighting a great serpent with a lion cub in its mouth. The knight joins the lion and succeeds in killing the snake; thereafter, the lion befriends him and becomes his travelling companion. That night, Sir Percivale dreams of two women, one is young and rides upon a lion, the other is older and sits upon a serpent. The young woman warns him that he must prepare for a battle that may end badly if he is overcome. The dream continues into the following chapter whereupon the older woman rebukes the knight for killing her serpentine companion that day, and demands that he become her paramour to make restitution for this deed, a demand Sir Percivale flatly rejects as he declares his allegiance to Christ alone. When Sir Percivale awakes, a priest explains the significance of this dream. The young lady on the lion symbolises the law of the New Testament and holy Church, i.e. "faith, good hope, belief, and baptism",[370] who out of love came to warm him of a great battle that would befall him. The older woman symbolised the old law, and the serpent he had slain was a devil. The priest explains: "And when she asked thee amends and to become her man, and thou saidst thou wouldst not, that was to make thee believe on her and leave thy baptism."[371] In sum, the flying lions may represent the possibility of redemption for Faust if he returns to the holy faith he received at his baptism.

Finally in the third attack, a flying bull rages straight at Faust, but an old ape rescues him. The bull could indicate a reference to the Evangelist and physician St. Luke, who is represented by an ox with wings. His Gospel was written for the instruction of a Roman citizen named Theophilus, and it contains many details not included in the other Gospels. The ape is a medieval symbol of Satan, for in his various attempts to be like unto God, Satan parodies or imitates all of God's actions. Luther once remarked, "Thus is the devil ever God's ape."[372] The third attack in

---

[368] Malory, 'The Holy Grail', p. 193.
[369] Ibid. pp. 140–143.
[370] Ibid. p. 143.
[371] Ibid.
[372] Luther, 'Of God's Works,' # LXVII, *Tischreden*.

this vision of Hell could represent the spiritual physician St. Luke reproaching Faust for his refusal to place his faith in the Gospel whereby he would be healed: finally, Faust is caught in the arms of Satan.

The full significance of this triple attack is gradually clarified when we continue our analysis and include the second level of the allegorical Hell Faust witnesses. When the ape places Faust on the coach, they drive through a dark, obscure region where thick fog descends twice: does this signify Faust had lost true enlightenment twice? Notice in Part One of Haile's Wolfenbüttle manuscript, Faust enters into a disputation with Mephostophiles in Chapters Three, Four, and Five. During this three-part disputation, Faust makes at least one attempt to extract himself from the demon's snares by declaring in Chapter Four his refusal to be damned for the spirit's service. This attempt to withdraw from negotiating with Mephostophiles may be symbolised by the flying lions that rescue Faust from the serpents. However, Mephostophiles dominates the two remaining debates and Faust believes the theological deceits presented to him; this scenario may be symbolised in the vision by the two demonic animals that triumph twice over Faust in contrast to the lions that rescue him only once. As we have previously observed, this pattern repeats once more; Faust ventures to dispute with Mephostophiles on a separate occasion in chapters Nine, Ten, and Eleven. During one of these disputes, Faust attempts to excite true sorrow for his sins by meditating on Hell, i.e. in Chapter Eleven, yet Mephostophiles maintains his command during these disputations and succeeds in utterly confounding Faust. Hence, these three attacks by the animals possibly represent Faust's triple theological disputations with the arch-demon, and the two regions of darkness in the allegorical Hell signify the result of both occasions when Faust was plunged ever deeper into the realm of spiritual ignorance, particularly following the second round of disputations. Notice the second section of fog he passed through was "deep" and lasted for "about a quarter of an hour" in contrast to his journey through the former section, which appears to last for a shorter duration.

To this point, this illustration of Hell reflected Faust's past theological dealings with the demon: now in the remaining phases of his journey through the third, fourth, and fifth levels of the Pit, it appears the author incorporated allegorical representations of Faust's new life when he signed the contract relinquishing his soul, and possibly future predictions. This element in the narration may also be inspired by Dante, who integrated allegorical symbols representing contemporary historical events, i.e. past, present and his forecasts for the future, in the *Divine Comedy*.

The third level of Faust's figurative Inferno, the turbid body of 'water' where he became submerged and tossed about like a piece of driftwood, may symbolise his aimless life of vice, and the new occupations into which Faust 'submerged' his energies, as with his horoscope prognostications, and his new godless academic speculations on the Creation and Hell conducted solely to satisfy his intellectual curiosity. As Faust sinks for a considerable time "deeper and deeper into the terror of the water"[373] we may presume this signifies he will continue these occupations. Hence, we have entered the section of the allegorical Hell that passes from the present time towards that realm of future predictions. In the fourth level, Faust finds he is mysteriously abandoned upon a high crag surrounded by water. He concludes that he can either

---

[373] *History of Doctor Johann Faustus*, p. 59.

hurl himself "[…] into the water or into the abyss",[374] thus the crag must be a volcanic crevice of some form. It is possible this indicates Faust will be afforded one last opportunity to repent. The volcanic vent obviously represents the option to go to Hell by his own free will. The body of water could signify the choice to 'brave the elements' of conversion and to amend one's life. The personal, lifelong struggle for salvation is oftentimes symbolically compared by Christians to a ship that crosses a perilous ocean before it reaches the safe harbour of Heaven. However, Faust is driven to extreme rage and despair at the prospect of choosing between Hell and the deep blue sea, his reason gives way to madness and he leaps into "[…] the fiery hole, calling out as he cast himself in: "Now spirits, accept my offering. I have earned it. My soul hath caused it."[375] Finally, he falls to his doom in the fifth level; here he encounters many souls who in the land of the living held positions of importance and enjoyed worldly acclaim and ceremonious pomp, i.e. kings, lords, knights — a prediction that he too may earn a great reputation on earth by his diabolical powers, but will not escape falling to the lowest level of the Insatiable Pit. To his credit, Faust eventually realises he did not experience the Hell created by God and finally concludes it was only a vision, but he fails to reflect further upon this image to discover its significance, and therefore another warning is ignored and passed over, a situation that we have come to expect when considering his previous myopic comprehension of theological subjects.

Having ventured through Hades, albeit allegorically, Faust soon refocuses his attention on the planetary orbs and their motions in the heavens. In Chapter Sixteen, Faust reveals in a 'letter' to a close acquaintance in the medical profession at Leipzig, Jonas Victor, that the rumours regarding his "Ascension into Heaven" are all true. Faust acknowledges Victor's suspicions on whether this impossible feat was accomplished by sorcery or not, with the nonchalant reply, "Well, whatever means might have been used, it hath finally been accomplished, and of this *figura*, *actus* and event I can make the following report".[376] Faust implies in certain terms that personally for him, notwithstanding the consequences, knowledge attained by scientific enquiry in the name of progress is far more important than the means by which he achieves this advancement: he admits his complete disregard for ethics in the academic workplace.

Faust's 'letter' continues with the report of his visit to the Heavens. He relates that he suffered one night from insomnia caused by his overactive mind pondering upon his almanacs and horoscopes, whereby he began to question how mankind could interpret the portents of the sky when it was impossible to study and measure them closely. This observation lead him to consider that as academics of his day could not research nor visualise these objects properly, they were forced to rely on equivocal information recorded in books, hence the imprecision associated with astronomy and astrology. While contemplating this scholastic predicament, a great desire stirred within him to see and study the portents of the heavens directly and correct previous miscalculations. Immediately, a great wind blasted his house, followed by a thunderous voice: "Get thee up! Thy heart's desire, intent and lust thou shalt see."[377] Looking out his window, he saw descending from the sky two dragons drawing a coach illuminated by the flames of the Abyss. Before embarking, he had the presence of mind to set a condition whereby he would

---

[374]   Ibid. p. 60.
[375]   Ibid.
[376]   Ibid. p. 63.
[377]   Ibid.

enter the coach provided he could ask questions concerning all that he may witness. The bodiless voice granted permission and he jumped out of his window into the carriage. The coach suddenly soared into the sky and Faust relates Mephostophiles then joined him and told him not to be confused by the spectacle he was about to witness.

Faust continues his report to Victor in Chapter Seventeen. He declares he set out on his mysterious journey on a Tuesday, returning one week later on the same day during which time he remained completely invisible and did not experience any sleep, nor found he required it. In addition, he felt neither hunger nor thirst. On the morning of the first day, Faust enquired of Mephostophiles how far they had travelled that night, and received the answer they had travelled forty-seven miles into the sky. [*] Faust relates from that height he could look down upon the world and survey the various kingdoms and seas on the earth, i.e. the regions of Asia, Africa and Europe. He then asked Mephostophiles to point out and instruct him on the names of the regions he was observing:

> "This he did, saying: This over here on the left is Hungary. Lo, there is Prussia. Across there is Sicily — Poland — Denmark — Italy — Germany. Now tomorrow shalt thou inspect Asia and Africa and canst see Persia, Tartary, India and Arabia. — But just look, right now the wind is changing and we can observe Pommerania, Muscovy and Prussia. See, there is Poland — and Germany again — Hungary — and Austria."[378]

Faust states that on the third day he inspected Turkey, Persia, India and Africa, and viewed the city of Constantinople (Istanbul). He also witnessed hundreds of warships commuting in the Persian and "Constantinopolitan" seas.

Next, he reports he observed the weather patterns on earth, explaining that his journey commenced sometime in July when the weather was hot. Looking towards the east, south and north, he noticed that while it rained in one place, it thundered in another. In addition, while hail fell in one area, the weather remained fair and tranquil elsewhere. "In fine, I saw all things in the world as they do usually come to pass,"[379] he writes to his friend.

Finally, he recounted his observations of the sky overhead as the week ended. He writes that the heavens moved and rolled around at such a great speed that they "[...] seemed to fly asunder into many thousand pieces, the cloud sphere cracking so violently as if it were about to burst and break the world open."[380] He describes the Heavens as a region of intense light, the brightness obscuring a detailed study of the upper spheres, and the heat so intense that he would have burned to a cinder if Mephostophiles had not protected him with his spells. He describes the "cloud sphere" as a single, thick solid mass like a stonework wall that remained translucent as

---

[*] A German mile was equivalent to 3 or 4 English miles. The 'great league of Germany' was considered 5 English miles. (Henry Jones, *The English Faust Book; A Critical Edition*, n. 1128, p. 212.) Faust and Mephostophiles have travelled either 141, 188, or 235 English miles.

[378] *History of Doctor Johann Faustus*, pp. 65–66.

[379] Ibid. p. 66.

[380] Ibid.

crystal, stating the rain, originating in that sphere and falling upon the earth, was so clear he could see his and Mephostophiles' reflection in it. Faust also explains that the powerful motions of the "cloud sphere", running from east to west, are responsible for the motions of the sun, moon and stars as these bodies cannot withstand the force of that region. He also describes the sun, that he previously thought to be no bigger than "the head of a barrel",[381] was in fact larger than the whole world, and he continues with the explanation that the moon receives its light from the sun. Faust also declares that directly beneath Heaven there exists so much light it remains perpetually daytime in that region, even when night falls upon the earth. He discovered that certain stars are larger than the earth, and that one of the planets was in fact as large as the world. Faust also reveals "[…] in the aery sphere, there I beheld the spirits which dwell beneath Heaven."[382] As he descended to the earth, the world seemed no larger than an egg yolk: as they drew closer, the mass of earth appeared to be barely a span, or nine inches, long, "[…] but the oceans looked to be twice that size."[383] Faust concludes his letter to Victor, relating he arrived home on the seventh day, and slept for a further three days. Now in the process of updating his almanacs and horoscopes, he advises his friend to examine his own books to "[…] see whether the matter is not in accordance with my vision. And accept my cordial greetings, Dr. Faustus, The astroseer."[384]

The inspiration for this lengthy account in the Wolfenbüttle manuscript may be traced by the phrase "Ascension to Heaven" back to the documents of Melanchthon and Manlius from which spread the rumour that the historical Faustus allegedly attempted to fly by the powers of sorcery. An interesting quote in Cicero's (106–43 B.C.) treatise *On Friendship* may also have inspired this chapter:

> "[…] this is the point of the observation of, I think, Archytas of Tarentum. […] It was this; 'If man could ascend to heaven and get a clear view of the natural order of the universe, and the beauty of the heavenly bodies, that wonderful spectacle would give him small pleasure, though nothing could be more delightful if he had but had some one to whom to tell what he had seen.'."[385]

In the Wolfenbüttle text, Faust relates the details of his adventure to a friend, a certain Dr. Jonas Victor of Leipzig. There is no evidence presented to date suggesting Victor was a historical person, we may assume the author of the manuscript included this specific name to fabricate a tone of veracity for his pseudo-biography of Faust. The addition of this 'friend', when compared with Cicero's quotation, also emphasises the emptiness of the satisfaction Faust derives from viewing the heavens by demonic intervention, he may enjoy the pleasure of recounting

---

[381] Ibid. p. 67.
[382] Ibid.
[383] Ibid.
[384] Ibid.
[385] Marcus Tullius Cicero, 'On Friendship'. Reprint, Charles W. Eliot, ed., E. S. Shuckburg, trans., in *Letters and Treatises of Cicero and Pliny: The Harvard Classics, vol. 9* (New York: P. F. Collier and Son Corp., 1963), p. 38.

these experiences to a close acquaintance, but at the expense of his immortal soul? Are the joys of earthly friendship worth this loss?

In the course of the narration, we discover Faust begins to question the journeys the demons permit him to undertake. Obviously, he was dissatisfied with his voyage to Hell, which he ultimately deduced was only an enchanted vision. Finally, he realised he allowed the demons to lead him blindly in the past with the condition of silence forced upon him, a situation that suited Beezlebub who could then steer Faust away from notions of efficacious contemplation on the true terrors of Hell. Now in Chapter Sixteen, Faust is probing whether or not the demons are planning to mystify him with another illusion, or are they earnestly prepared to guide him through the cosmos. If he is permitted to make various enquiries, the probability of the latter scenario occurring is greater. Unfortunately, his attempt to challenge the demons is not a reflection of a true endeavour to rise from his spiritual despondency, but rather demonstrates his striving to obtain accurate worldly knowledge.

Apparently, Faust did indeed travel to the upper stratosphere, confirmed by the silence maintained for the most part by Mephostophiles during the journey, as he refrains from interjecting any deceitful comments. The arch-demon simply indicates and identifies the regions of the earth as requested, knowledge that Faust could verify later from contemporary maps. There is no need to charm a false vision, for as we observed, Faust is merely interested in academic elucidation and is focusing his attention on the finite world, not on philosophical ponderings. In addition, we may argue the demons profit by Faust's increased sin of pride in boasting of being the first to have accomplished the impossible and observe the true dimensions of the universe. Already, Faust is triumphantly proclaiming the success of his "Ascension to Heaven" — a phrase Christians only attribute to Christ — without any fear or shame that, in contrast to Christ, the forces of evil had accommodated his voyage to the stars.

To the modern world, now grown accustomed to the recent discoveries in outer space, this account of our planet and the solar system is beset with several inaccuracies. Readers today might be excused for concluding that Mephostophiles duped Faust with another hallucination! However, when considering the limited means scientists had at their disposal over five hundred years ago, this antiquated view of the universe is accurate according to the established 'facts' of those times.

For nearly fourteen hundred years, Claudius Ptolemaeus' (i.e. Ptolemy, AD 100?–170?) geocentric theory whereby the moon, sun, and planets revolved around a stationary earth remained the accepted explanation of the cosmos. According to charts drawn from the Ptolemaic system, three concentric circles represent the earth: the landmass of the earth at the centre, followed by what we would describe today as the atmosphere, subdivided into two. The first circle around the landmass represents the visible atmosphere of the clouds, or "the firmament that divides the waters from the waters" (Gen. 1:6). The second sphere consists of a band of flames surrounding the 'cloud sphere' which represents the element of fire. Hence, all four elements found in Creation are included: earth, water, air and fire. This band of fire could also mystically depict the sphere of air where the devils of the 'high places' reside immediately preceding the orbits of the planets, as Divine Justice decrees they are required to suffer the pains of Hell wherever they roam. Following the three circles of the earth, the concentric circles of the planets commence. The heavenly bodies orbit the earth in the subsequent order: the Moon, Mercury, Venus, the Sun, Mars, Jupiter, Saturn, (the other planets had not yet been discovered), followed by the region of the "fixed stars". Astronomers in the sixteenth century included two more spheres,[386] a ninth sphere beyond the region of the fixed stars, i.e. the constellation sphere, also called *coelum cristallinum* or crystalline sphere, to explain the occurrences of the equinoxes, and a tenth sphere, or the *primum mobil*, a region that scholars believed was responsible for the movements and orbits of the heavenly bodies. Finally, one last circle was included in later Ptolemaic charts to represent the Empyrean Heaven of God. For decades, however, scholars continued to debate whether these two new outer spheres, i.e. the ninth and the tenth, actually existed in the region before the Empyrean Heaven.

This system, naturally, was woefully inaccurate. For example, the medieval theories explaining the unusual movements of certain planets, as with the retrograde phenomena when these spheres appear to travel in reverse and then resume their natural orbit, were incorrect.[**] To account for this brief planetary retro-orbit, astronomers maintained that each planet revolved on the edge of a circle called the *epicycle*, and the centre of each epicycle revolved around the earth on the *deferent*. Faust's view of the planets corresponds with the Ptolemaic system, i.e. with his phrase concerning the different "spheres". However, Faust contradicts the traditional Ptolemaic view of the cosmos in two instances. First, he maintained that the "cloud sphere" is similar to a singular piece of thick crystal, a description we might traditionally associate with the ninth sphere, or *coelum cristallinum*. Second, he declared that the "cloud sphere" was responsible for the movement of the planets, and not the *primum mobil*.[+] Interestingly, Faust stated the Heavenly bodies "strive against" the cloud sphere, but are then forced to continue on their path from east to west; therefore, he presents a new explanation for the retrograde motion of the planets rather than the conventional theory of *epicycles* and *deferents*. We know from the context of the narration Mephostophiles did not charm a second vision, and Faust observed this phenomenon first hand without any demonic interference, thus Faust could not relate any faulty information, nor did a reason exist for him to utter an outright lie. Obviously, these inconsistencies were intended to reflect an educated guess. Was the author deliberately presenting a new scientific theory according to the Ptolemaic System through his *Faust* manuscript in order to keep his anonymity intact?

Today, we may question why the author was apprehensive to formally publish a new theory to be considered by the scholastic community, yet when we consider the historic introduction of the heliocentric Copernican System and the subsequent controversies that ensued following its presentation to the academic world, this decision to remain anonymous is clarified.

The Ptolemaic System remained the unquestioned academic explanation of the ordering of the universe for several centuries, particularly as it corresponded neatly with the Judeo-Christian

---

[386] Francis R. Johnson, 'Marlowe's Astronomy and Renaissance Skepticism,' *Modern Language Notes* 35 (January, 1920): pp. 244-245.

[**] Today we know that the 'retrograde phenomena' is an optical illusion caused by the various orbits of the planets around the sun. The closer a planet is to the sun, the faster it completes an orbit. Hence, the earth overtakes the slower planets with the result they appear to travel backwards for a certain period.

[+] That is, if we continue to presume Haile's translation is accurate. In Spies' text, this area in space is called "Gewülcke", and if this is the same term used in the MS, this description of a "cloud sphere" appears correct. Compare with the German "Gebeit" = "sphere" (as in spatial area) and "Wolke" = "cloud". (Henry Jones has translated this as "firmament".) *The English Faust Book; A Critical Edition*, n. 1156–8, p. 213.

belief of Creation. According to the first sentence of Genesis, the two polar realms of existence, Heaven, the centre of the spiritual world, and Earth, the centre of physical creation, were fashioned by God before the celestial bodies. "In the beginning God created heaven and the earth." (Gen. 1:1). Apparently, many Medieval and Renaissance scholars misinterpreted the following verses pertaining to the creation of the "lights", or planetary spheres, in a manner indicating God intended a *linear* connection between the *spiritual* Heaven and the *physical* earth: "Let there be lights made in the firmament of heaven, [...] To shine in the firmament of heaven, and to give light upon the earth." (Gen. 1:14–15). The term "Firmament" indicates the sky or physical heavens, but scholars also associated this expression with the spiritual Heaven. This interpretation of a celestial "bridge" between the spiritual and physical Heavens with the physical Earth is upheld in the Ptolemaic System, that placed the earth at the centre, with the moon, sun and the planets arranged in a linear fashion to the firmament of the fixed stars and onto the Empyrean Heaven of God. Hence, for anyone to challenge this astronomical system that had been revered for over a millennia, notwithstanding its numerous mathematical flaws, also signified for many individuals an attack on a sacrosanct article of faith pertaining to the Creation as recorded in Genesis. In that zealous atmosphere, great philosophical ideas and scientific discoveries remained in obscurity due to a fear of persecution.

We recognise today the heliocentric idea was not an entirely new concept: the ancient Pythagoreans believed the earth was globular in shape and orbited a celestial fire, and the Greek philosopher Aristarchus of Sámos (310?–250? B.C.) maintained that the earth rotated on its axis and revolved in conjunction with the planets around the sun, yet these theories were not formerly upheld as academic fact and were set aside until certain scholars of the Renaissance began to bravely question geocentrism. For instance, the German cardinal Nicholas of Cusa (1401–1464) and Leonardo da Vinci (1452–1519) challenged the validity of the geocentric theory.

However, when the Polish astronomer Nicolaus Copernicus (1473–1543) eventually published his groundbreaking work *De Revolutionibus Orbium Coelestium* (*The Revolutions of the Heavenly Bodies*) in 1543, he thereby became the first modern scholar to promulgate the heliocentric theory for serious consideration as the logical explanation of the cosmos. Copernicus was reluctant for many years to reveal his theories to the world, fully aware of the heated controversies his work would foment. In his dedication to Pope Paul III, he declares it was not his intention to avoid any judgement of his work by those who were either educated or not: hence his decision to proceed directly to his Holiness for consideration.[387] He defends his work, declaring that his studies are in accordance with the ordinances of God pertaining to human reason that allows a philosopher to seek the truth in all things, adding that it is his sincere belief one should avoid theories contrary to orthodox teachings.[388] Nevertheless, Copernicus confesses his anxiety regarding the reception of *De Revolutionibus*:

> "I can easily conceive, most Holy Father, that as soon as some
> people learn that in this book which I have written concerning the

[387] Nicolaus Copernicus, 'Dedication of the Revolutions of the Heavenly Bodies to Pope Paul III' (1543), in Charles W. Eliot, ed., *Prefaces and Prologues: The Harvard Classics vol. 39* (New York: P. F. Collier and Son Corp., 1963), p. 56.
[388] Ibid. p. 52.

revolutions of the heavenly bodies, I ascribe certain motions to the Earth, they will cry out at once that I and my theory should be rejected. [...] Accordingly, when I considered in my own mind how absurd a performance it must seem to those who know that the judgment of many centuries has approved the view that the Earth remains fixed as center in the midst of the heavens, if I should, on the contrary, assert that the Earth moves; I was for a long time at a loss to know whether I should publish the commentaries which I have written in proof of its motion, or whether it were not better to follow the example of the Pythagoreans and of some others, who were accustomed to transmit the secrets of Philosophy not in writing but orally, and only to their relatives and friends, [....] Therefore, when I considered this carefully, the contempt which I had to fear because of the novelty and apparent absurdity of my view, nearly induced me to abandon utterly the work I had begun."[389]

Copernicus continues, stating he actually commenced his research many years previously, thirty-six years to be exact (1507*), and the resulting work remained dormant in his study until persuaded by his friends, the Cardinal of Capua and the Bishop of Culm, to publish it.[390] In fact, Copernicus finished De *Revolutionibus* in 1530, yet his prudent apprehension was the reason he withheld it from the world.

The reluctant astronomer then relates in his dedication the motivation for persisting with this theory of heliocentrism notwithstanding his numerous reservations. Copernicus declares: "[...] the only thing which induced me to look for another way of reckoning the movements of the heavenly bodies was that I knew that mathematicians by no means agree in their investigations thereof."[391] He explains they were unable to calculate the most basic occurrences, such as the duration of a complete year, resulting from their inability to comprehend the movements of the sun and moon. Mathematicians had also been unable to adequately explain the movements of the planets. His conclusion: these failures originated with faulty methods as academics continued to work from mere conjecture and did not "[...] employ consistently one set of first principles and hypotheses."[392] Alternatively, they developed two diverse speculations that failed to offer definite answers upon which future study could be firmly grounded. Several mathematicians promoted a Ptolemaic system based primarily upon concentric circles, while others included a more elaborate system of eccentric circles and epicycles. Copernicus states that a system based only on concentric circles may explain various motions of the planets to a certain degree, "[...] yet [they] have not succeeded thereby in laying down any sure principle,

---

[389] Ibid. p. 53.
* We may therefore conclude Copernicus was constantly at work developing previous theories first posited in his astronomical treatise De Hypothesibus Motuum Coelestium a se Constitutis Commentariolus completed sometime between 1507 and 1515, yet remained unpublished until the nineteenth century.
[390] Copernicus, 'Dedication of the Revolutions', p. 53.
[391] Ibid. p. 54.
[392] Ibid.

corresponding indisputably with the phenomena,"[393] i.e. the retrograde motion of the planets. The second more elaborate system may account for most of the revolutions of the planets with "[...] calculations by which these [eccentric circles] are made to fit, [but] have nevertheless introduced many things which seem to contradict the first principles of the uniformity of motion."[394] In addition, he argues that in using these systems, mathematicians were unsuccessful in establishing, as scientific law, the true shape of the world or its dimensions. Copernicus declares their motley speculations ...

> "[... have] been as if someone were to collect hands, feet, a head, and other members from various places, all very fine in themselves, but not proportionate to one body, and no single one corresponding in its turn to the others, so that a monster rather than a man would be formed from them. Thus in their process of demonstration which they term a 'method,' they are found to have omitted something essential, or have included something foreign and not pertaining to the matter in hand."[395]

Dismayed by the lack of a "consistent scheme", Copernicus searched for evidence of other theories not considered by his contemporaries that could provide an alternative answer. He found inspiration in the writings of Cicero and Plutarch wherein he discovered that several of the ancients, particularly the Pythagoreans, believed the earth moved. He admits that at first he also thought the idea absurd, but decided that as he had the same freedom as his contemporaries to develop his ideas, he declares:

> "[...] I thought I also might easily be permitted to try whether by postulating some motion of the Earth, more reliable conclusions could be reached regarding the revolution of the heavenly bodies, than those of my predecessors."[396]

In the text proper of *De Revolutionibus,* Copernicus described the motions of the earth: that it rotates daily on its axis and revolves once a year around the sun. His theory described the motions of the planets and explained the retrograde phenomena, and the yearly movements of the sun and stars. This new system also allowed for alternative measurements of the planetary orbits, i.e. the greater the radius of an orbit, the greater the time a planet requires to complete one revolution around the sun. He also discovered that Mercury and Venus do not move beyond a certain distance from the sun. Although Copernicus retained several Ptolemaic conventions, such as the sphere of fixed stars, and his calculations proved as cumbersome as those of his contemporaries, his theories had forever altered the study of astronomy by offering, for the first time, a more coherent explanation for the movements of the solar system.

---

[393] Ibid.
[394] Ibid.
[395] Ibid.
[396] Ibid. p. 55.

Unfortunately, these theories failed to earn immediate acclaim and were regarded as contentious topics for they dared to question a time-honoured system generally believed to be indivisible with an article of Christian faith. From the year 1543 to the early 1600s, a small number of academics who had private patrons and worked independent of the universities championed Copernicus' ideas.

One of the most famous of these pioneering intellectuals is the Italian physicist and astronomer Galileo Galilei (1564–1642). In 1595, he commenced his studies of astronomy, championing the Copernican system as it supported his own theories regarding tidal movements based upon the premise of a moving earth. Fourteen years later, Galileo discovered that a new device, namely, the spyglass, was invented in Holland. He recognised its invaluable application for maritime use and immediately that autumn presented one of these instruments to the Doge of Venice, (claiming it to be his own invention), and then focused on the possibilities it held for other disciplines. In December of that year (1609), he constructed a powerful telescope, becoming one of the first astronomers to gaze upon the stars with the aid of this device that magnified distant objects. He realised that numerous individual stars constituted the optical light-band of the Milky Way, observed the various craters and mountains on the moon's surface, and discovered the four largest moons of Jupiter. In 1610, he published these findings in *The Starry Messenger* and continued with his observations, by December, he discovered the phases of Venus, which proved the Ptolemaic System was erroneous and confirmed the validity of the Copernican System.

However, the fame that Galileo achieved following the publication of *The Starry Messenger* soon dissipated. He amassed many adversaries among professors who championed the philosophy of Aristotle, for according to this branch of reasoning it was believed only perfect spherical bodies could exist in the heavens and that nothing new could ever appear in space as nothing new could be created; hence, Galileo's new discoveries of Jupiter's four moons and the phases of Venus was misinterpreted as a direct challenge to this respected branch of philosophy. His work in physics, i.e. his theories on hydrostatics and his 1612 publication on the subject of floating objects, also became a target for hostile academics. Continuing amidst these obstacles, he published a work on sunspots in 1613 in which he also predicted the eventual success of the Copernican System. This was too much for his opponents to tolerate; a professor from Pisa attempted to discredit Galileo and his theories by declaring to Galileo's employers, the Medici's of Florence, the theory of a moving earth was heretical. Apparently, this rancorous comment spread as a vicious rumour accusing Galileo of promoting heresy; in 1614, a priest in Florence denounced the followers of Galileo from the pulpit.

St. Robert Bellarmine (1542–1621), a Roman cardinal who was on affable terms with Galileo, advised him to prudently treat his work hypothetically for the purpose of science without attempting to reconcile his ideas with the Bible. However, by 1616 all Copernican based works were subject to censorship by edict, hence St. Bellarmine instructed Galileo he could no longer hold nor publicly defend the concept of a moving earth. We may presume this 'instruction' was intended to be precautionary advice, as St. Bellarmine provided Galileo with a certificate stating he was not subject to further restriction, no more than any other Roman Catholic under the 1616 edict allowing a text to be published following censorship by the proper Catholic authorities. Galileo followed St. Bellarmine's advice for several years and worked on various scientific endeavours, that is, until 1624. In that year, he commenced a work entitled *Dialogue on the*

Tides in which he discussed tidal movements with reference to both the Copernican and Ptolemaic systems: this he accomplished, albeit by a thinly veiled disguise, stealthily presenting his scientific arguments in the course of a philosophical disputation between allegorical characters representing the 'Aristotelian / Ptolemaic' and 'Progressive / Copernican' factions. The work was reviewed and approved by the Roman Catholic censors in 1630; however, they altered the title to *Dialogue on the Two Chief World Systems*. The *Dialogue* was finally published in Florence. However, after its publication in 1632, Galileo was summoned to Rome by the Inquisition, charged with 'grave suspicion of heresy' on a false accusation he was ordered in 1616 not to discuss orally or in writing the work of Copernicus. Obviously, enemies of Galileo attempted to manipulate St. Bellermine's cautionary instruction to resemble a direct order issued by the Church, which he was required to obey under pain of mortal sin. In addition, these adversaries succeeded in convincing Pope Urban VIII that Galileo purposely intended to mock his Holiness in his Ptolemaic beliefs, pointing out that the astronomer spared no effort in presenting this system in his *Dialogues* as the most senseless and backward of the current schools of thought. In 1633, Galileo was threatened with torture and forced to abjure, notwithstanding the two official licenses he was granted for the publication of the *Dialogue,* and the certificate issued by the then deceased St. Bellarmine that had only restricted him to the condition of censorship. His initial sentence was life imprisonment, although his sentence was speedily commuted to permanent house arrest, nevertheless the *Dialogue* was ordered to be burnt. The blame for Galileo's unjust condemnation was habitually placed solely with the Catholic Church, however history now recognises the initial role that Galileo's adversaries in the field of Aristotelian philosophy played in convincing theologians of his alleged heresy. In a belated, albeit profound gesture of amendment, an investigation of Galileo's condemnation was instigated in 1979 by Pope John Paul II; in 1992, a papal commission acknowledged the Vatican's mistake.

In summary, we can appreciate the motives of the author of the original *Faust* manuscript in presenting a new scientific theory hidden behind the safeguard of anonymity when we consider this significant threat of envy and persecution that existed! We also notice that the Wolfenbüttle manuscript was compiled sometime c. 1580–1587, precisely when the Copernican-Ptolemaic controversy was gaining considerable momentum.

Continuing our study, the context of Faust's musings in Chapter Sixteen of the manuscript implies the author was inspired to develop a new hypothesis due to the fact contemporary mathematicians failed to explain the movements of the heavenly orbs as their work consisted of mere speculation based on inaccurate information promulgated in books. This is not dissimilar to Copernicus' reasons for developing his heliocentric theory, which may suggest the author had read *De Revolutionibus* and was determined to present new theories to these same questions. As we discovered, the new theory presented by the author, i.e. that the "cloud sphere" moved the planets, still adhered to the accepted geocentric Ptolemaic system. Is it possible the author intended to make a deliberate reference to Copernicus' dedication in the Wolfenbüttle manuscript, challenging his controversial heliocentric theory? We may question why the author would choose to present his theory anonymously if he was defending the ecclesiastically approved Ptolemaic system in this instance, however, we must also observe his proposal would be viewed with suspicion of heresy for his 'cloud sphere momentum theory' still contained serious implications regarding Biblical interpretation. His new theory implies that the planets were primarily moved by a force originating from a region associated with the earth rather than directly from the *primum mobile* below the Empyrean Heaven, which is contrary to the 'linear' understanding of "Let there be lights [...] to shine [first] in the firmament of heaven, and [then] to give light upon the earth." (Gen. 1:14–15) Hence, this new 'cloud sphere momentum theory' could also be subject to professional ridicule if presented in an official scientific publication.

The theories continue, in the latter half of Chapter Seventeen, Faust makes several declarations: he describes the sun as being much bigger than the earth, that a planet was as large as the world, and relates that the stars were larger than previously believed. Obviously, the author had arrived at these conclusions by applying to the celestial orbs the common fact that large objects appear smaller when seen from great distances. Although these observations transcribed in the manuscript are now recognised as fact, they precede Galileo's historic use of the telescope (1609) by approximately two decades. Either the author was presenting his new hypothesis or supporting controversial contemporary speculations with regard to the dimension of the Heavens in addition to his 'cloud sphere theory', and therefore had sufficient justification to remain anonymous. One could wonder why he did not simply write a serious anonymous treatise for publication rather than associate his ideas with a manuscript portraying a demonic individual, however, we must remember that despite the author's additions and his refashioning of the legendary material, the manuscript was presented as a veracious biography. Possibly, the author also recognised the opportunities associated with infamous publicity and realised his ideas would circulate more rapidly under the notorious banner of Faust.

In addition to the scientific study of the cosmos, the author did not completely neglect the mystical and literary aspects of this subject. Returning to the first half of Chapter Seventeen we discover an unusual chronological anomaly pertaining to Faust's inspection of the earth — there is no mention whatsoever of the recent discoveries made in the New World. Columbus had undertaken several return voyages after the initial sailing of 1492, Cortéz conquered the Aztecs in 1521, and Magellan's expedition was the first to circumnavigate the globe in 1522. This is indeed a peculiar omission from the text, particularly when the historical Faustus was embroiled with predictions concerning the von Hutten expedition to Venezuela in the mid 1530s. In contrast, Faust in the manuscript hovers over the westernmost point of the Old World with his back turned to what is now North and South America, and observes only the east, south and north, i.e. Asia, Africa and Europe.

This initial, deliberate omission of the New World evinces a second reference to Dante's *Divine Comedy* (c. 1321). According to Dante's symbolic ideology of the earth, the fall of Lucifer caused untold changes on our planet.[397] First, a great section of landmass was gouged out in a conical shape as he fell into the centre of the globe thereby creating the Pit of Hell. Second, the land that he displaced was forced up to the surface, forming the high mountain of Purgatory directly at the antipodes to Jerusalem. Thirdly, the remaining land from the southern hemisphere was pushed into the northern hemisphere, forming the Pangaea portion of the earth populated by the human race, i.e. Europe, Africa, and the East. Needless to mention, the New World had not yet been discovered, and therefore it did not enter into Dante's equation.

Following Dante's journey through Hell and Purgatory, he is guided through the various levels of Heaven represented by the planets, until he passes through the Empyrean Heaven, and enters the presence of the Holy Trinity. Before he progresses beyond the region of the "fixed

---

[397] Malcolm Bradbury, ed., *The Atlas of Literature* (London: Greenwich Editions: 2001), p. 14.

stars" or the Eighth Heaven (*Paradise*, Canto XXII), Dante pauses to gaze down upon the "petty area" of the earth.[398] Faust's journey is similar, but with one significant difference, he eventually returns to *terra firma*. He is permitted to penetrate beyond the 'cloud sphere' barrier, and may view certain planets from a distance, but the brightness emanating from the Empyrean Heaven impedes any further progress. Possibly the author of the Wolfenbüttle Text intended to contrast Dante's advancement towards spiritual perfection with Faust's gravitation towards evil.

This second journey now accomplished, Faust decides to undertake a third journey to explore the earth during the sixteenth year following the signing of his contract (Chapter Eighteen). Immediately we encounter blatant anti-Catholic and anti-Islamic material emanating from a pro-Lutheran perspective.[#]

On the first stage of his tour, Faust decides to pay a visit to the Vatican and travels invisibly on a 'pilgrimage' accompanied by Mephostophiles. He marvels at the wealth and splendour enjoyed by the pope, and also the vast array of vices committed at the papal court, and exclaims: "Methought I were the Devil's own swine, but he will let me fatten for a long while yet. These swine in Rome are already fatted and ready to roast and boil."[399] Faust remains for three days and plays all manner of mischievous pranks during mealtimes in the papal palace. Whenever the pope made the sign of the cross before saying grace, Faust would blow directly into his face. Or, he would play the poltergeist by laughing aloud or moaning thereby frightening the servants. The pope concludes, "[…] it was a dammed soul of which he had exacted penance and which was now begging for absolution."[400] Finally, Faust (who is still invisible) raises his arms whereupon all the dishes levitate from the table and soar into his outstretched hands. He then flies away to enjoy his stolen repast at the Capitoline Hill, one of the Seven Hills of Rome. It was here the mythical founder of Rome, Romulus, established an asylum for runaway slaves and homicides. Faust also sends Mephostophiles to steal the best wines, goblets and flagons from the pope's table. When the pope learns that vast quantities of store has inexplicably disappeared from the palace "[…] he caused all the bells to be rung throughout the entire night and had mass and petition held for the departed souls. In anger towards one soul, however, [i.e. the soul who begged for absolution, which was really Faustus] he formally condemned it to purgatory with bell, book, and candle."[401] Faust is not bothered by this 'curse', (he believes he is already damned), and continues to enjoy the pilfered delicacies as an "[…] especial dispensation."[402]

In these first paragraphs of Chapter Eighteen, we observe references to Luther's views on the contemporary state of the papal court and on the practise of making pilgrimages to Rome. In his *Address to the Christian Nobility of the German Nation* (1520) Luther wrote:

---

[398] Dante, *The Divine Comedy*, p. 382.
[#] Haile omitted considerable material from this chapter, and concentrates on Faust's journey to Rome and Constantinople; consequently, we have concentrated on this aspect for the present. However, for more details on Faust's travels, see the subsequent discussion regarding the London *Faustbook* (1592).
[399] The *History of Doctor Johann Faustus*, p. 68.
[400] Ibid. p. 69.
[401] Ibid.
[402] Ibid.

"It is a distressing and terrible thing to see that the head of Christendom, who boasts of being the vicar of Christ and the successor of St. Peter, lives in worldly pomp that no king or emperor can equal, so that in him that calls himself most holy and most spiritual there is more worldliness than in the world itself. [...] If this resembles the poverty of Christ and St. Peter, it is a new sort of resemblance. [...] His office should be nothing else than to weep and pray constantly for Christendom and to be an example of all humility."[403]

"Pilgrimages to Rome must be abolished, or at least no one must be allowed to go from his own wish or his own piety, unless his priest, his town magistrate, or his lord has found that there is sufficient reason for his pilgrimage. This I say, not because pilgrimages are bad in themselves, but because at the present time they lead to mischief; for at Rome a pilgrim sees no good examples, but only offence. They themselves have made a proverb, 'The nearer to Rome, the farther from Christ,' and accordingly men bring home contempt of God and of God's commandments."[404]

According to this perspective, Faust has made a 'pilgrimage' that culminated in mischief for he experienced the immorality of the papal court and failed to find the good example one might expect to encounter there. Faust regrets the devil did not make him the pope!

There are also several Lutheran barbs in the text directed at certain articles of Catholic faith and devotional practises. For instance, the disconcerting presumption of the pope that the "spirit" who was causing all the paranormal activity was "[...] a damned soul of which he had exacted penance and which was now begging for absolution".[405] This statement is an obvious attack on the Catholic Sacrament of Penance by which all sins are forgiven. In order to understand the misinterpreted context of this statement in the manuscript it is necessary to first examine the fundamentals of the sacraments of Baptism and Penance: the Catholic dogma on the forgiveness of sin.

The sacraments are the visible, outward signs instituted by Christ to signify the transferral of grace to the immortal soul. The sacrament of Baptism is of paramount importance as it removes the stain of Original sin from the soul and confers sanctifying grace for the first time, the supernatural gift from God that makes the soul holy and pleasing to Him, allowing it to ultimately share in His Divine Nature. Those who are in sanctifying grace are the adopted children of God and the temples of the Holy Ghost. In sum, this grace is necessary for salvation. However, this grace is lost by *mortal* sin: an act that is committed contrary to the law of God in grave matters by any wilful thought, word, deed, or omission with *clear knowledge and with full consent.* For

---

[403] Luther, *Address to the Christian Nobility of the German Nation (1520)*, in Charles W. Eliot, ed., 'Machiavelli, More, Luther' *The Harvard Classics vol. 36*, (New York, P.F. Collier and Son Corp., 1963), pp. 275–276.

[404] Ibid. p. 298.

[405] Haile, *History of Doctor Johann Faustus*, p. 69.

instance, if someone were to purposely slander the reputation of another by wilfully disregarding or ignoring the fact that they were breaking the Eighth Commandment. (This is not the case with venial sins, i.e. acts committed without full knowledge or consent, although they obstruct the path towards perfection. Also, human imperfections do not deprive the soul of sanctifying grace.)

If a person commits a mortal sin, sanctifying grace is restored through the Sacrament of Penance whereby sins are forgiven by the power of God, which Christ granted to his apostles when He said; "Receive ye the Holy Ghost, whose sins you shall forgive, they are forgiven them, and whose sins you shall retain, they are retained." (John 20: 22–23) This power is passed down through the ages to the priests of the Church by Apostolic succession. Hence, a priest may grant absolution from sin, or may refuse absolution if the penitent is not rightly disposed to receive the sacrament. In order to be rightly disposed, a penitent must have either perfect or imperfect contrition, and the purpose of amendment or firm resolution to avoid sin in the future. Contrition is perfect when the sinner is repentant for having offended God who is infinitely good; imperfect contrition is when sorrow for sin originates from a supernatural motive less than the pure love of God, such as fear of His punishments. The procedure for receiving the Sacrament of Penance is as follows:

First, the penitent must examine their conscience according to the laws of God, the precepts of the Church, and one's daily duties to discern the sins committed by thought, word, deed, or omission. The penitent must then have either perfect or imperfect contrition for their sins, for without sorrow and purpose of amendment the penitent simply goes to the sacrament out of habit and thereby derives no spiritual benefit from it. Sorrow for sin must originate from the heart, spring from a supernatural motive, extend to all mortal sins committed, and regard sin as the greatest of all evils.

Second, the penitent must confess their sins to an authorised priest: this is obligatory with mortal sins, which have not yet been confessed and forgiven. General absolutions without a confession are not valid in the case of mortal sin. Until these sins are confessed, the penitent may not partake of the Eucharist worthily: mortal sin makes the soul an enemy of Christ and therefore to receive the Eucharist in the state of mortal sin constitutes a sacrilege. The number of times a mortal sin is committed, or an approximate number, and their kind must also be confessed. Any circumstances that may determine the grievousness of the sin must also be explained, for example simple theft, although mortal, is not as grievous as robbery committed by violence. A mortal sin must not be wilfully concealed either through fear or shame — this is also sacrilege, and the sins that are confessed are not forgiven. If mortal sins have been concealed from a previous confession(s), the penitent is required to confess those sins, including the sacrilege of which they are guilty of, i.e. a bad previous confession(s), and all other mortal sins committed since their last good confession. If a mortal sin is honestly omitted through forgetfulness, it is forgiven with the understanding it must be confessed as soon as one remembers and returns to the Sacrament of Penance. Venial sins and imperfections do not need to be confessed before one approaches the Eucharist, although it is a spiritually healthy practise even though the penitent may have no mortal sins on their conscience. The priest will usually give advice and counselling on how to avoid certain sins in the future, the penitent will then be asked to say an Act of Contrition to express their sorrow and purpose of amendment.

Third, the priest may grant absolution with the blessing, "I absolve thee from thy sins, in the name of the Father, and of the Son, and of the Holy Spirit. Amen." Hence, this sacrament is intended by God to impart great peace to a soul as the forgiveness of sin is thereby visibly assured. The priest will give the penitent a penance to perform. The Sacrament remits the *eternal* punishment due to mortal sin, i.e. the sentence of Hell, but it does not always remit the *temporal* punishment that God requires as satisfaction for all sins committed, venial as well as mortal. God requires temporal punishment in order to repair the offence against His Divine Majesty and to instil a horror of sin. Hence, the priest imposes a penance on the penitent to begin the task of paying the temporal punishment due. The penance will not always fully satisfy the whole debt due to God, but what is wanting may be supplied by other good works, e.g. prayer, fasting, almsgiving, works of mercy, enduring suffering, the gaining of indulgences etc., when they are all performed in the state of sanctifying grace. However, the priest may in certain, rare instances withhold absolution if he has reason to believe the penitent has neither sorrow for the sins committed nor the intention to amend their life and endeavour to avoid sin. He may advise the penitent to change their life in earnest before they approach the Sacrament of Penance in the future. Although this may appear harsh, it reminds the penitent not to take the Sacrament for granted, or to commit the sin of presumption, i.e. to expect salvation without making any earnest effort to obtain it.

It is on this last point that the author of the Wolfenbüttle Manuscript directed his first dart at the "damned soul". The context of the pope's declaration could be interpreted in two ways. First, this sentence may infer that the pope advised a certain individual to change their life through performing penance and withheld absolution until there was evidence of a firm purpose of amendment, but then believed that the individual had died in the interim and did not receive absolution in time. Hence, this sentence could indicate an attack on a dogma perceived to be an unjust practise promoting spiritual tyranny, i.e. commanding complete obedience with the *threat* of withholding the assurance of salvation, in contrast to the Catholic belief that the *possibility* of absolution being withheld is an effective means to inspire a horror of sin by preventing an individual from unilaterally declaring their own conditions for forgiveness. Luther did not believe in the Sacrament of Penance or the need to discern between perfect and imperfect contrition: his belief in the forgiveness of sin was based on his creed of 'Justification by Faith' i.e. faith that Christ came to save repentant sinners and that through His sacrifice on the cross this promise of forgiveness is assured. A Christian must confess he is a sinner, but it is a private affair between the sinner and God without the need of a formal absolution given by a priest — he must simply believe by faith that he is forgiven:

> "God forgives sins merely out of grace for Christ's sake; but we must not abuse the grace of God. God has given signs and tokens enough, that our sins shall be forgiven; namely, the preaching of the gospel, baptism, the Lord's Supper, and the Holy Ghost in our hearts. […] The forgiveness of sins is declared only in God's Word, and there we must seek it; for it is grounded on God's promises. God forgives thee thy sins, not because thou feelest them and art sorry, for this sin itself produces, without deserving, but he forgives thy sins because he is

merciful, and because he has promised to forgive for Christ's sake." (Luther)[406]

The second interpretation of the pope's statement in the Faust text may also be read to infer he had exacted an individual to approach the *sacrament* of Penance, but this individual refused and was now in Hell begging for absolution because of his obstinacy. Possibly, the author was insinuating it was a heretic who did not believe in sacramental confession, (understood to be a supporter of Luther's theology), who was ordered to return to the Church by confessing his apostasy but who had refused to submit. The pope therefore declares he is in Hell, a 'presumptuous' remark that the promoters of the Reformation would find rather droll, as they believed they were in possession of the 'Rediscovered Gospel' and members of Christ's 'true' church. Therefore, they could not be among the damned! Apparently, Faust is a product of the Reformation as he is also amused at the reactions his tricks have caused; "[... he] enjoyed this very much, for such mystifications well pleased him, too."[407]

The barbs directed at the Catholic faith continue with the sentences, "When the Pope had found out how many things had been stolen from him, he caused all the bells to be rung throughout the entire night and had mass and petition held for the departed souls. In anger towards one departed soul, [i.e. the "damned" soul] however, he formerly condemned it to purgatory with bell, book and candle."[408] To commence our analysis, we must focus our attention on the phrase "bell, book, and candle" — this is a direct reference to the ceremonies of the severest form of excommunication in the Roman Catholic Church: the anathema. Individuals who publicly refused the faith and / or make themselves an enemy of the Church were branded with the anathema, and this involved the declaration of a formal sentence pronounced upon the offender. Similar to the minor forms of excommunication, those on whom anathema is pronounced are excluded from the sacraments of the Church, however, the anathema is not as easily revoked. Consequently, those who are excommunicated, having made themselves an enemy of God by spurning His gift of faith, they are deprived of the spiritual benefits of the Church and the necessary means to obtain His graces, particularly the Sacraments of Penance and the Eucharist, until they reconvert. The anathema featured a solemn ceremony whereupon the bishop reads the sentence of condemnation from the Bible (the book) and closes it, twelve priests throw down or extinguish a lighted candle to represent the quenching of God's grace within the offending soul. The church bell tolled during the ceremony as for one who is dead. This strict punishment was obviously derived from Christ's instructions to the Apostles regarding those who maliciously adhere to their sins and obstinately reject the teachings of the Church:

> "But if thy brother shall offend against thee, go, rebuke him between thee and him alone. If he shall hear thee, thou shall gain thy brother. And if he will not hear thee, take with thee one or two more: that in the mouth of two or three witnesses every word may stand. And if he will not hear them: tell the church. And if he will not hear the church, let

---

[406] Luther, 'Of Sins' #CCLI, *Tishreden.*
[407] *History of Doctor Johann Faustus*, p. 69.
[408] Ibid.

him be to thee as the heathen and the publican. Amen I say to you, whatsoever you shall bind upon earth, shall be bound also in heaven; and whatsoever you shall loose upon earth, shall be loosed also in heaven." (Matt. 18:15–18)

Hence, this sentence "bell, book and candle" in the Faust text confirms our theory above that the "damned soul" begging for absolution was a satirical representation of a Reformation apostate who refused to recant and was thereby anathematised and doomed to Hell, a point intended to portray the 'folly' of the Catholic faith. The author therefore had a definite agenda for his text and did not necessarily confuse the anathema ceremony with that of exorcism. This point enables us to continue with our observations. We note the "damned / departed soul" is condemned in this ceremony to *purgatory*, not Hell, which is an unusual development. This is an obvious attack against the Catholic belief of Purgatory and the practise of praying for the dead. We have examined the Catholic doctrine of the nature of mortal and venial sin: as mentioned, the Sacrament of Penance removes all the eternal punishment due to sin — but not the temporal punishment, this may or may not be fully atoned for in a lifetime. If the temporal punishment is not fulfilled, that soul must suffer in Purgatory after death. Apart from the fact that Purgatory is not everlasting, souls confined there also suffer a purging fire and other torments, which vary in duration and intensity according to the gravity of the sins committed. However, these sufferings are alleviated, or even remitted, by the prayers and good works of the faithful who are living. Of all the spiritual help that could benefit the souls in Purgatory, the sacrifice of the Mass offered for the dead grants the most relief. This belief in praying for the dead has a basis in scripture in 2 Machabees (12:39–46):

"And the day following Judas came with his company, to take away the bodies of them that were slain, and to bury them with their kinsmen, in the sepulchres of their fathers. And they found under the coats of the slain some of the donaries of the idols of Jamnia; which the law forbiddeth to the Jews: so that all plainly saw, that for this cause they were slain. Then they all blessed the just judgement of the Lord, who had discovered the things that were hidden. And so betaking themselves to prayers, they besought him, that the sin which had been committed might be forgotten. But the valiant Judas exhorted the people to keep themselves from sin, forasmuch as they saw before their eyes what had happened, because of the sins of those that were slain. And making a gathering, he sent twelve thousand drachms of silver to Jerusalem for sacrifice for the dead, thinking well and religiously concerning the resurrection, (For if he had not hoped that they that were slain should rise again, it would have seemed superfluous and vain to pray for the dead,) And because he considered that they who had fallen asleep with godliness, had great grace laid up for them. It is therefore a holy and wholesome thought to pray for the dead, that they may be loosed from their sins."

Luther, however, discarded 2 Machabees declaring, "I am so great an enemy to the second book of the Maccabees, and to Esther, that I wish they had not come to us at all, for they have too many heathen unnaturalities."[409] He therefore refused to believe in the existence of Purgatory. Rather than viewing Purgatory as a further proof of God's mercy, Luther maintained that belief in Purgatory undermined Christ's grace and merits, for him, there was either Heaven or Hell:

> "[…] God has, in his Word, laid before us two ways; one which by faith leads to salvation, — the other, by unbelief, to damnation. As for purgatory, no place in Scripture makes mention thereof, neither must we any way allow it; for it darkens and undervalues the grace, benefits, and merits of our blessed, sweet Saviour Christ Jesus. The bounds of purgatory extend not beyond this world; for here in this life the upright, good, and godly Christians are well and soundly scoured and purged."[410]

In addition, Luther believed that prayers for the dead were idolatrous practises. According to his doctrine, only Hell and Heaven exists in the afterlife, the damned cannot receive any benefit from prayers whatsoever. Therefore, any Masses and other prayers for the dead were being offered for saints who likewise did not need spiritual assistance:

> "[…] The pope's greatest profit arises from the dead; for the calling on dead saints brings him infinite sums of money and riches, far more than he gets from the living. But thus goes the world; superstition, unbelief, false doctrine, idolatry, obtain more credit and profit than the upright, true, and pure religion."[411]

Hence, if the Catholic Church was offering pointless, 'idolatrous' Masses for the saints, this could also be twisted into an accusation of 'sacrificing' to the reprobates of Hell. The fact that the perturbed soul, (i.e. Faust) is described as 'damned' or *in Hell*, yet is also "condemned to *purgatory* with bell, book and candle", we may conclude this phrase in the manuscript reflects this latter interpretation of the Lutheran doctrine of 'Only Hell and Heaven'. *In fine*, we deduce the 'damned' soul had dared to reject certain canons as laid down by the Church in the Council of Trent condemning Luther's doctrine dismissing the Sacrament of Confession and the existence of Purgatory:

<u>Session VI. January 13, 1547</u>

Canon 30. If anyone says that after the reception of the grace of justification the guilt is so remitted and the debt of eternal punishment so blotted out to every repentant sinner, that no debt of temporal punishment

---

[409] Luther, 'On God's Word' #XXIX, *Tischreden*.
[410] Ibid. 'Purgatory'. #DXV.
[411] Ibid. 'Of Idolatry', #CLXXVIII.

remains to be discharged, either in this world or in Purgatory, before the gates of Heaven can be opened, let him be anathema.

Session XIV. November 25, 1551

Canon 12. If anyone says that God always pardons the whole penalty together with the guilt and the satisfaction of penitents is nothing else than faith by which they perceive that Christ has satisfied for them, let him be anathema.

Canon 13. If anyone says that satisfaction for sins, as to their temporal punishment, is in no way made to God through the merits of Christ by the punishments inflicted by Him and patiently borne, or those imposed by the priest, or even those voluntarily undertaken, as by fasts, prayers, almsgiving or other works of piety, and that therefore the best penance is merely a new life, let him be anathema.

Canon 14. If anyone says that the satisfactions by which penitents atone for their sins through Christ are not a worship of God but traditions of men, which obscure the doctrine of grace and the true worship of God and the beneficence itself of the death of Christ, let him be anathema.

Canon 15. If anyone says that the keys have been given to the Church only to loose and not also to bind, and therefore priests, when imposing penalties on those who confess, act contrary to the purpose of the keys and to the institution of Christ, and that it is a fiction that there remains often a temporal punishment to be discharged after the eternal punishment has by the virtue of the keys been removed, let him be anathema.[412]

Upon the completion of his 'pilgrimage' to Rome where he is duly anathematised, Faust travels to Constantinople to experience the pomp of the Sultan's court for a few days. Similar to his escapades in Rome, Faust and Mephostophiles decide to make their trip memorable by creating their fair share of salacious havoc. One evening as the Sultan commences his feast, Mephostophiles conjures up great blazing tongues of fire in the banquet hall, making it as bright as the sun, and simultaneously paralyses the Sultan so that he can neither stand nor be carried. The arch-demon then appears "[…] in the figure, ornaments and trappings of a Pope," and pronounces, "Hail Emperor, so full of grace that I, thy Mahomet do appear unto thee!"[413] after which he disappears into thin air. The next day Faust shrouds the palace in a great mist with his magic powers, while in the interim the Sultan admonishes his subjects to perform many rites in honour of their 'holy' visitor. Donning the same raiment that Mephostophiles wore the previous

---

[412] Fr. F. X. Schouppe, S. J., *Purgatory: Explained by the Lives and Legends of the Saints* (Reprint; Rockford Illinois: Tan Books and Publishers, 1986), pp. vi–viii.
[413] *History of Doctor Johann Faustus*, p. 70.

night, Faust makes an extended appearance in the Sultan's harem posing as Mohammed before ascending into the sky. Upon Faust's departure, the fog lifts and the Sultan inquires of his wives who had visited them. They reply "[…] it was the god Mahomet who at night had called this one and that one to him, […] and said that from his seed would rise up a great nation and valiant heroes,"[414] this, the Sultan deems "a great benefit". The "priests" declare the visitor to be a ghost, but the royal wives assure them he was like any mortal man, and was "[…] well fitted out."

This degenerate, perverse adult humour in the manuscript is prime evidence of European propaganda directed at the Turkish Empire. For years, the constant threat of invasion lurked dangerously close to the south-eastern borders from the time the Byzantine capital city of Constantinople fell to the Ottomans in 1453. In 1516 Sultan Selim I captured Syria, a victory that was followed by the fall of Egypt in 1517. However it was Selim's son, Suleiman I "The Magnificent", who brought the Ottoman Empire to its greatest heights of glory. Upon ascending the throne in 1520, Suleiman I rapidly aggrandized his kingdom with a series of crushing conquests. In 1521, he captured Belgrade, and succeeded in driving off the Knights of St. John of Jerusalem (the Knights of Malta) from the island of Rhodes in 1522. The Hungarians were defeated in the Battle of the Mohács in 1526, and Vienna was besieged in 1529. Suleiman I then expanded his campaign eastwards into Persia. During the 1540s, he once again concentrated his efforts on Europe by extending his territory along the Danube and succeeded in capturing Budapest in 1541. Two years later, his fleet ravaged the coasts of Italy and ransacked the city of Nice. In 1566, he died while on a campaign in Hungary. By this time, the Ottoman Empire had reached its zenith and commanded the most powerful fleet in the Mediterranean; the borders of the realm stretched from Tripoli, Libya, to Yemen, and from Poland to Persia. Although the Ottoman Empire gradually declined following Suleiman's death, the Ottomans succeeded in maintaining their navel presence in the Mediterranean by capturing Cyprus (1570–1571). However, European rulers realised that the Empire was indeed in decline and decided it was time to take action. In 1571, John of Austria led the Holy League to victory by destroying the Turkish fleet during the Battle of Lepanto in the Gulf of Corinth, this was the first major success the Christians achieved in defying the Ottoman Empire. Unfortunately, the Ottomans quickly rebuilt their fleet thus nullifying this victory.

We have previously encountered in the manuscript, a passing reference to the Ottoman fleet during Faust's inspection of the earth from the heavens: "I saw Constantinople before me and, in the Persian and Constantinopolitan Sea, many ships with war troops shuttling busily back and forth."[415] Now in the second half of Chapter Eighteen, the author concentrated on disseminating propaganda ridiculing the Sultan and the religion of Islam. It is not a coincidence that Mephostophiles is the first to appear as the prophet Mohammed, a direct reference to the devil as the founder of Islam was the intention. We must also note the author had not yet finished his criticism of Catholicism as 'Mohammed's' attire resembles the "trappings of a pope"! Faust's intrusion into the royal harem "[…] where the Turk has his wives or whores,"[416] highlights the contemporary European disapproval with the Islamic custom where a husband is permitted to have more than one wife. According to Christian belief, these polygamous unions

---

[414] Ibid.
[415] Ibid. p. 66.
[416] Ibid. p. 70.

are adulterous for a binding marriage before God consists of the union between one man and one woman only. Luther once remarked, "'Tis horrible to see their [the Turks'] contempt of marriage. 'Twas not so with the Romans."[417] Hence, true to our earlier observations concerning Faust and the sacrament of marriage, he did not actually destroy the Sultan's marital union by his acts of adultery for the 'wives' he visits are not considered legally married by Christian standards, but are regarded as "whores". European readers would be amused with the irony of the Sultan believing that he and his empire would be blessed with Mohammed's progeny, which would in fact be the illegitimate offspring of an infernal degenerate. We also discover a number of deliberate inaccuracies regarding the perception of Islam, e.g. that Muslims consider Mohammed a 'god' while in fact, he is recognised as a prophet, and that the Islamic religion features a hierarchy of priests, which is not true. The author made full use of the opportunity to ridicule "[…] the people of the wrath of God,"[418] as Luther described the Turks.

At this stage in the manuscript, Faust has completed three journeys, and in the process, a new tripartite sequence. We immediately observe that while the first two journeys parallel the structure of Dante's *Divine Comedy* to a certain degree, this third adventure on earth appears incongruous, i.e. Dante's 'Hell-Purgatory-Heaven' sequence is at variance with that of Faust's 'Hell-Heaven-Earth' cycle. However, if the author was intending to contrast Faust's adventures with Dante's inner journey from a Lutheran perspective, the sequence is comprehensible. As discussed, Dante first experiences the torments of Hell, no doubt to rouse him from his spiritual lethargy, and then discovers he must tread the purifying paths of Purgatory to cleanse his soul of imperfections before he may pass through the various levels of Heaven and onto the presence of the Blessed Trinity. Faust, on the other hand, experiences a selection of the torments of Hell, but did not pay heed to the allegorical warnings presented to him, which portends an ominous future. He is permitted to tour the physical cosmos, but is impeded by the brightness of the Heavens and cannot enter the Presence of God. He then returns to Earth, which Luther describes as the true 'Purgatory' for Christians. Here, Faust receives a period of grace to choose between Heaven or Hell, but rather than amend his ways and assume the hardships of life as his penance, he has already decided to resume his debauched lifestyle, therefore the causeway to Hell looms ever before him. Once again, the triple chapter pattern symbolises the stranglehold Mephostophiles succeeds in maintaining over Faust.

Finally, we arrive at the last segment of Part Two in the manuscript, returning us to the subject of Faust's superior study in astronomy.* Chapter Nineteen commences with Faust's invitation to dinner with a prominent scholar in Halberstadt, an anonymous "Doctor N. V. W.", who in all eagerness desires to learn more about the cosmos from his guest. This one detail may be based on historical fact. Helmut Häuser identified the initials as belonging to a certain Dr. Nicholas Winkler, who was the city physician of Halberstadt.[419] It is proposed that the historical

---

Luther, 'Of the Turks', #DCCCXXXI, *Tischreden*.

[418] Ibid.

✿ According to Rose, Faust's discourse on the cosmos can be traced to the *Elucidarius*, a collection of scientific dialogues. *Damnable Life and deserved Death of [...] Faustus*, p. 30.

[419] Helmut Häuser, ('Gibt es eine gemeinsame Quelle zum Faustbuch von 1587 und Goethe's Faust? Eine Studie über die Schriften des Arztes Dr. Nikolaus Winkler. 1973', cf. Gerd Wunder, *Nachwort* to facsimile ed. of Widman, 1978) in Henry Jones, *The English Faust Book*; *Critical ed.*, n. 1764, p. 227.

Faustus may have visited this physician in 1521;[420] this is possible, for the Wolfenbüttle MS first circulated privately with the university elite, a number of which perchance were acquainted with, or, remembered stories told by the few noted scholars who encountered Faustus. However, we can be certain these cosmic discussions recounted in the MS are not authentic dialogues with the historical Faustus, as the scientific knowledge debated is either transcribed from the *Elucidarius*, suggesting hackwork by a scribe, or in other instances can be dated closer to the time of the Wolfenbüttle MS (c.1580–1587) evincing fresh material was injected into the Faust legend.

Gazing from a window, they contemplate the harvest night whereupon Dr. N. requests Faust to explain the nature of shooting stars. Faust agrees to enlighten him on the subject, but explains he must elucidate other facts as this question "[…] doth presuppose certain other matters which ye must understand first."[421] Faust then commences to describe the dimension of the Heavens, i.e. that the planets and stars are in reality much bigger than man can comprehend: "— See over there is one as large as the dominion of the Roman Empire. This one right up here is a large as Turkey. And up higher there, where the planets are, ye may find one as big as the world."[422] In fact, we are now reintroduced to a subject first encountered in Chapter Seventeen, which the author uses to serve as a prologue for the following tripartite sequence, chapters Twenty, Twenty-one and Twenty-two.

In Chapter Twenty, Dr. N. asks Faust why the demonic spirits are allowed to thwart the works of man at night as well as day. Faust first begins his tutorial by explaining their daytime activities. The demons are forced to ascend during the day when the sun rises into the cloud sphere where they are committed to by God "[…] that they may discover all His portents."[423] As the demons are creatures of darkness and have "[…] no affinity with the sun,"[424] they strive to climb higher in the heavens as the sun shines brighter. Hence, they hunger for the light that is now denied them for all eternity. We may deduce the author of the text concluded if the demons can discover the portents of God, they also observe mankind from their places in the cloud sphere and thereby devise plans during the day to destroy it. Faust continues by stating that at night, the demons may walk amongst men:

> "[…] for the brightness of the sun — even though it is not shining here — is in the first Heaven so intense that it is as daylight there, [….] It followeth therefore that the spirits, not being able to endure or to suffer the aspect of the sun, which hath now ascended upwards, must come near to us on earth and dwell with men, frightening them with nightmares, howling and spooks."[425]

This explanation may appear contradictory on first inspection — if the demons seek the light of the sun during the day, why are they unable to tolerate the sun at night? Moreover, how

---

[420] Ibid.
[421] *History of Doctor Johann Faustus*, p. 72.
[422] Ibid.
[423] Ibid. p. 73.
[424] Ibid.
[425] Ibid. pp. 73–74.

is it possible the sun can be so intense in the first Heaven that according to the traditional Ptolemaic System is the path of the moon?

We find the answers in the following chapter when Faust proceeds to respond to a further query put forward by Dr. N.; namely, why the stars are so bright and why they appear only at night. Faust explains that the sun actually ascends in the Third Heaven, adding parenthetically that the sun does not, in reality, travel in the First Heaven, as it would destroy the earth, a phenomenon which will not occur until the Day of Judgement. He then states that when the sun "[…] so far withdraws itself,"[426] (i.e. travels the same distance in the Third Heaven under the world), then the stars begin to shine as they are in the First and Second Heavens, and are as luminous as two summer days. He concludes by stating, "Night, therefore, observed from Heaven, is nothing else than day, or, as one might also aver, the day is half the night. For ye must understand that when the sun ascends, leaving us here in night, the day is just beginning in places such as India and Africa."[427] However, this explanation remains paradoxical; according to the traditional Ptolemaic System, the moon is in the First Heaven, Mercury, Venus, and the Sun are in the Second, Third and Fourth respectively, and the fixed stars and constellations are set in the Ninth and Tenth Heavens. We have concluded in our analysis of Chapter Seventeen that Faust did not have a motive to report a falsehood regarding his knowledge of the cosmos, hence, the author may actually be presenting a whole new concept of the solar System for academic consideration.

Faust's account to N.V.W. implies the immobile earth is at the centre, the "fixed stars" are in the First Heaven, the constellations are in the Second Heaven, the Sun is in the Third, and the moon must then be in the Fourth. Let us return briefly to certain points Faust introduced in Chapter Seventeen: "At night, when the sun goeth down, the moon must take on the sun's light, this being why the moon shineth so bright at night. And directly beneath Heaven there is so much light that even at night it is daytime in Heaven — this even though the earth remainth quite dark."[428] Hence, if Faust states that when the sun is obscured by the earth when it travels under the world in the Third Heaven, the stars in the first two Heavens actually reflect the sun's light similar to the moon, which explains why they are so bright like two summer days and shine at night. At that time, it was believed the earth's shadow caused the night.[429] Although this information is not scientifically correct according to our contemporary knowledge, from this perspective, we can decipher Faust's explanation regarding the demons. "But at night, when it is pitch dark, then they are among us, for the *brightness of the sun* — even though it is not shining here — [i.e. the sun's *rays* shining from up under the earth] is in the first Heaven so intense [where the stars are] that it is as daylight there [i.e. for the stars shine as bright as "two summer days", a light which the demons would finally be unable to bear]. It followeth therefore that the spirits, not being able to endure or to suffer the *aspect* of the sun, [i.e. the bright rays,] which hath

---

[426] Ibid. p. 75.

[427] Ibid.

[428] Ibid. p. 67.

[429] Bevington and Rasmussen write; "The *locus classicus* for this pre-Copernican belief may be Macrobius's *Commentum*, I.xx.18: 'the shadow of the earth which the sun, after setting and progressing into the lower hemisphere, sends out upwards, creating on earth the darkness which is called night' (John Norton-Smith, N&Q, n.s. xxv (1978), 436–7)." In *Doctor Faustus; A- and B- Texts*, n.1, p. 125.

now *ascended upwards*, [i.e. from under the planet and onto the stars thus giving them their light] must come near to us on earth and dwell with men. [...] [i.e. for at night the earth is dark; the rays of the sun project upwards to the Heavens and not downwards as in daytime.]"

We now realise the author was preparing the way in Chapter Seventeen to present more groundbreaking theories (albeit now inaccurate and outdated) in the final chapters of Part Two. He may actually be presenting a prototype of the 'Brahe Hybrid System', featuring a combination of the Ptolemaic *and* Copernican formats. The Danish astronomer Tycho Brahe (1546–1601), with the aid of a simple globe and a compass, made great progress in correcting grave errors recorded in astronomical charts with the result his work featured the most accurate mathematical calculations, that is, until the invention of the telescope. However, he did not accept the Copernican System in its entirety and developed his own chart of the cosmos, (1588). According to Brahe, the sun revolves around an immobile earth each year. In turn, the five planets orbit the sun. Thus, we conclude the moon circles the earth in the First Heaven. In addition, Brahe maintained that the regions of fixed stars revolved around the earth once a day. The 'fixed stars' and the constellations could then be considered the Second and Third Heavens, with the sun in the Fourth. Hence, Faust's (that is, the author's) conception of the solar system, although he interchanges the stars, moon and the sun, is not completely at variance with Brahe's idea. Possibly, the author was influenced by Brahe's new mathematical calculations thus accounting for his amazing proximity to Brahe's theory previous to 1588.

Finally, Faust concludes the tri-chapter pattern by answering in Chapter Twenty-two Dr. N.'s original question, i.e. what causes the stars to fall. Faust explains that while the elements and the firmament of the Heavens are immutable, they do undergo various changes whereby they shoot off sparks and are like "[...] bits of match," that are "[...] hard, black and greenish,"[430] and appear as shooting stars. Faust explains a real star never falls, unless sent "[...] as a scourge of God. Then such falling stars bring a murkiness of the Heavens with them and cause great floods and devastation of lives and land."[431]

Similar to Chapter Seventeen, the theological world is not completely neglected in these three chapters. Faust admits that the order of the Heavens is set according to the ordinance of God, and refers to God's decree when stating that the demons are committed to the cloud sphere during the day. The stars also shine as long as He ordains, and only fall at His command when His Divine Justice demands it. Notwithstanding the evidence that Faust observed concerning God's power and might with regard to the Universe, he remains spiritually unchanged, and broaches the subject of God's Presence as a simple matter of fact before explaining the scientific aspect of the cosmos, which is his main focus of interest. Of significance is the observation that the familiar tripartite chapter pattern now serves a different purpose; this time, it is Faust who is the Master among his fellow men, while the academics remain in awe of his knowledge. We therefore see Mephostophiles' tactics continuing with his protégé in a pernicious attempt to ensnare other members of the human race with the allurement of knowledge caused by their vain curiosity. This may be a warning intended for academics to be wary of those who influence them.

---

[430] Ibid. p. 76.
[431] Ibid.

Faust: The Sought-after Courtier

Now, having concentrated all his energies to absorb everything pertaining to theology, (if and when permitted by Mephostophiles), and also the various sciences, including the occult, Faust in Part Three of the manuscript officially begins to put his newfound knowledge to work to establish a reputation and earn a daily living among the elite. It is also at this point in the manuscript that we begin to encounter the popular Faustian legends, or rather, the author's / scribe's inventive versions of these tales.

In Chapter Twenty-three, we learn Faust has temporarily taken up residence in the town of Innsbruck, Austria, at an opportune time, for the Emperor Charles V and his court arrive in this same vicinity. Faust already attracted attention among the aristocracy, in particular, those whom he healed through his skill in medicine. As a result, his newfound friends invite him to attend court sometime after the Feast day of St. Philip and St. James, i.e. after May 1. The Emperor notices the stranger and enquires about him, whereupon the courtiers inform his Imperial Majesty that it is "Dr. Faustus". When the banquet concludes, the Emperor invites Faust to his private council chamber where he admits that he considers him "[...] adept at *nigromantia*,"[432] and asks him to perform a favour with the Imperial promise that no ill shall befall him for fulfilling this special request. Faust agrees to oblige the Emperor, whereupon his Imperial Majesty confesses his great desire to see his ancestor Alexander the Great and his consort exactly as they appeared during their prime of life. Faust admits he cannot raise the dead, but that he may summon spirits who will then appear in their shapes. The Emperor agrees, and lo, 'Alexander' walks into the council chamber and bows to the Emperor. His 'consort' follows him, and also makes a polite curtsey of respect to the Emperor. In the interim, the Emperor ponders the matter and realises this is exactly what occurred when the woman with the python spirit raised the prophet Samuel for King Saul. However, to be certain that the spirits are not deceiving him, the Emperor muses: "I have often heard tell that she had a great wen on her back. If it is to be found upon this image also, then I would believe it all the better."[433] And so, the Emperor lifts her skirts to discover the legendary cyst on her posterior!

As we first observed in our study of the historical Faustus, the tradition that he allegedly summoned the great heroes of the past originates from hearsay Luther once related concerning Emperor Maximilian I (1459–1519):

> "Dr. Luther was asked, whether the Samuel who appeared to
> king Saul, upon the invocation of the pythoness, as is related in the first
> Book of Kings, was really the prophet Samuel. The doctor answered: 'No,
> 'twas a spectre, an evil spirit, assuming his form. What proves this is, that
> God, by the laws of Moses, had forbidden man to question the dead;
> consequently, it must have been a demon which presented itself under the

---

[432] Ibid. p. 79.
[433] Ibid. p. 81.

form of the man of God. In like manner, abbot of Spanheim, [Trithemius] a sorcerer, exhibited to the emperor Maximilian all the emperors his predecessors, and all the most celebrated heroes of past times, who defiled before him each in the costume of his time. Among them were Alexander the Great and Julius Caesar. There was also the emperor's betrothed, whom Charles of France stole from him. But these apparitions were all the work of the demon."[434]

When this legend was later attributed to Faustus, the locale changed from the Imperial court to the universities of Wittenberg and Erfurt. However, the author of the Wolfenbüttle Manuscript manipulated this legend to reflect the current political and religious issues of the times. On this occasion, it is the Holy Roman Emperor Charles V, the defender of Catholicism, who takes the brunt of the author's quill. The Emperor is portrayed in a sardonic light from a Lutheran prospective. Despite his prestigious religious titles, in private the Emperor consorts with a known necromancer, seeks aid through his black arts, and provides him with royal protection. This is a stark contrast to documents relating his conduct in connection with Martin Luther; when Luther was excommunicated in January 1521, the Emperor convened the famous Diet of Worms in April of that year to afford him one last opportunity to recant his heretical teachings. Luther refused with his legendary answer, "[…] I cannot and will not recant, because acting against one's conscience is neither safe nor sound. Here I stand, I cannot do otherwise. God help me. Amen." In response the Emperor declared, "I have decided to mobilise everything against Luther: my kingdoms and dominions, my friends, my body, my blood, my soul."[435] Hence, Luther was condemned to death by the Emperor, but was granted a place of refuge by his protector, Prince Frederick the Wise of Saxony. It is probable that the author was attempting to lampoon the Diet of Worms and display the Emperor's 'true colours', i.e. that the 'Holy' Roman Emperor will consort with reprobates and the sons of devils, yet persecute and sentence a man to death who only desired to seek what he believed was the truth in the 'rediscovered Gospel'.

The author also takes the opportunity to inject an element of lewd humour at the Emperor's expense when the monarch lifts the skirts of Alexander's spouse under the pretext of discovering the authenticity of the image before him. Certain additional theological articles are addressed in this chapter, i.e. that Faust cannot raise the dead, (a theological truth as this is one power God did not grant to devils), and also the Lutheran belief that a demon appeared at the command of the python woman, in contrast to the Catholic belief, that Samuel was permitted to appear.

Of historical interest, it was not a mere whim of the author to decide to pare down the original legend featuring numerous Greek heroes to include only Alexander the Great and his consort in this version of mythical events. We immediately notice that the Emperor's musings, which encouraged him to make this audacious request of Faust in the manuscript, actually reflects the contemporary political events affecting the German nation. In the text the Emperor remarks:

---

[434] Luther, 'Of the Devil and his Works,' #DLXXII, *Tischreden*.

[435] Deutsche Reichstagsakten, Jüngere Reihe. Deutsche Reichstagsakten unter Kaiser Karl V., vols. I–, ed. Historische Kommission bei der Bayerischen Akademie der Wissenschaften (Gotha, 1893–'2nd ed. [reprint] Göttingen, 1962–), 2·595, 23-25, 34f, in Oberman, *Luther, Man Between God and the Devil*.

"In my camp I once did stand athinking, how my ancestors before me did rise to such high degree and sovereignty as would scarcely be attainable for me and my successors, especially how Alexander the Great, of all monarchs the most mighty, was a light and an ornament among all Emperors. Ah, it is well known what great riches, how many kingdoms and territories he did possess and acquire, the which to conquer and organize again will fall most difficult for me and my succession, such territories being now divided into many separate kingdoms."[436]

Charles V (1500–1558) was the son of Philip I of Castile and Joanna 'the Mad', the maternal grandson of Ferdinand V of Castile and Isabella I, the paternal grandson of the Holy Roman Emperor Maximilian I, and the great-grandson of Charles 'the Bold', Duke of Burgundy. When his father died in 1506, Charles V inherited the realm of Burgundy, and later Spain when Ferdinand died in 1516. In 1519, he gained the Hapsburg lands upon the death of Maximilian I, and was elected Holy Roman Emperor that same year. Finally, he was crowned King of Germany in 1520. His empire therefore included the Kingdoms of Castile and Aragón, (including the Spanish conquests in Africa and the New World), the Netherlands, Naples, Sicily and Sardinia, and the Hapsburg lands in central Europe. However, the realm did not enjoy a period of peace and stability as controlling this scattered empire was a geographical and political challenge. The borders were often threatened by external forces, namely the Turks and the French, and the realm also suffered internal turmoil from the various revolts between Catholic and Protestant factions. Surviving years of constant war and strife, a weary Charles conferred the Netherlands in 1555 to his son Philip II, followed by Spain the next year. In 1558, he abdicated the Imperial throne in favour of his brother Ferdinand I and retired to a quiet monastery in Spain where he died a short time later. The contemporary yearning for a successful united empire equalling that of Alexander the Great, and the gradual dissipation of this dream, is thereby evident in the Wolfenbüttle Manuscript.

In the following chapter, Twenty-four, Faust continues to amuse the Emperor and decides to play a joke on one of the courtiers. Before supper, Faust spies a knight who succumbed to the summer heat and has fallen asleep with his head leaning from a window. Faust charms a pair of deer antlers onto the unfortunate knight's head so that when he awakes he discovers, to his great embarrassment, he cannot move in nor out of the casement. We are informed: "The Emperor, observing his plight, laughed and was well pleased withal until Doctor Faustus at last released the poor knight from the spell again."[437] The original source of this legend is obviously from the *Tischreden* of Martin Luther:

"The emperor Frederick, father of Maximilian, [i.e. Holy Roman Emperor Frederick III (1440–1493)] invited a necromancer to dine with him, and, by his knowledge of magic, turned his guest's hands

---

[436] *History of Doctor Johann Faustus*, pp. 79–80.
[437] Ibid. p. 82.

into griffins claws. He then wanted him to eat, but the man, ashamed, hid his claws under the table.

He took his revenge, however, for the jest played upon him. He caused it to seem that a loud altercation was going on in the court yard, and when the emperor put his head out of a window to see what was the matter, he, by his art, clapped on him a pair of huge stag's horns, so that the emperor could not get his head into the room again until he had cured the necromancer of his disfigurement. I am delighted, said Luther, when one devil plagues another. They are not all, however, of equal power."[438]

In Chapter Twenty-five,[#] Faust returns to Wittenberg where three young noblemen approach him with a particular request. They desire to attend the wedding of the Duke of Bavaria's son and offer to pay Faust handsomely for his services in this matter. Faust agrees to lend them aid and requests they arrive at his house in their best apparel on the day of the wedding. They arrive at the appointed time, and he spreads his cloak out in the garden, ordering them to sit on it with strict instructions not to speak to anyone they meet. In addition, he advises them to be ever ready for his command "Up and away!" whereupon they are to immediately grab hold of his cloak to ensure their safe return. Faust then conjures a great wind that lifts them up and carries them on their journey to Munich. However, one of the young noblemen forgets Faust's instructions and speaks to one of the Bavarian courtiers. Immediately Faust cries "Up and away!", but one of the noblemen did not grab the edge of Faust's cloak in time and therefore is left behind while the others vanish into thin air. The alarmed Bavarians mistake the intruder to be a spy and demanded he state the reasons for his intrusion, particularly in light of the perplexing disappearing act performed by his companions. The nobleman refuses to betray his friends and is subsequently imprisoned; to add fuel to the fire, he will be tortured on the morrow until they extract his confession explaining his uninvited attendance. However, Faust rescues the nobleman the next day with his magic tricks and brings him speedily back to Wittenberg, whereupon Faust is handsomely rewarded.

Christopher Rosshirt's *Chronicle* (c. 1575) is the first document that mentions Faust transporting guests to a wedding. In the original tale, Faust is a lecturer of philosophy at the university of Ingolstadt. He invites guests to dinner where he serves several dishes allegedly stolen from the wedding feast of the King of England. Then, he transports his guests by magic to view the actual banquet where they are mistaken for spies, but Faust returns them home safely. We may assume the King in the first tale was Henry VIII (1509–47) as this is the only male English monarch with dates that configure with the approximated date of Rosshirt's *Chronicle*. However, the author of the Wolfenbüttle Manuscript inferred a different wedding; obviously, the nuptials of Wilhelm V[*], son of Albrecht V of Bavaria. Albrecht is famous for patronising important musicians, Orlande de Lassus (1532–94) and Andrea Gabrieli (1510?–1586), uncle of Giovanni Gabrieli (1553–1612). Hence, the Duke's appreciation of music evinces a certain aptitude for planning celebrations. This wedding was most certainly an important social event at

---

[438] Luther, 'Of the Devil and His Works,' #DLXXV, *Tischreden*.
[#] Ch. 37 in Spies' edition. (*Faustus and the Censor*, p. 25)
[*] Wilhelm V succeeded his father in 1579.

that time, awaited with much anticipation, and remained a blissful memory for many, not readily forgotten. Apparently, as Bavaria remained a staunch Roman Catholic state, the author could not resist overshadowing this happy reminiscence with a little literary mischievousness by arranging for Faust and his sycophants to arrive uninvited at the wedding reception.

In Chapter Twenty-six, we read a popular Faust legend, i.e. Faust decides to fill his empty pockets with a little conning-conjuring. The author states, "Much had been promised by his spirit, but much had been lies, for the Devil is the spirit of lies."[439] Clearly, Mephostophiles refused to pay Faust his salary: "With the skill where with I have endowed thee thou shouldst acquire thine own wealth. Such arts as mine and thine can scarcely lose thee money."[440] Of course, the arch-demon knows full well that Faust has now grown accustomed to his generous income of 25 Gulden a week, or 1,300 Gulden per year with no effort or work on his part. Hence, if Faust is to maintain the lifestyle he enjoyed up to now, he may be obliged to resort to drastic measures as we presume an honest career would hardly cover his extravagances. In effect, he intends to lead Faust into a deeper life of vice. We discover this is the exact scenario that ensues; taking out a loan of sixty thalers, or silver coins, from a Jewish money lender, (a sum he does not intend to repay), Faust tricks the Jew by offering his leg as collateral, which is readily accepted as a sound surety of repayment. Of course, Faust did not amputate his actual leg, but duped poor old 'Shylock' with a magical carbon copy. However, the moneylender soon regrets this business arrangement, realising the leg is of no value to him:

> "What good to me is a knave's leg? If I carry it home it will begin to stink. I doubt that he will be able to put it on again whole, and besides, this pledge is a parlous thing for me, for no higher pawn can a man give than his own limb. But what profit will I have of it?"[441]

With this resolution, he discards the leg, throwing it into the river. Three days later, Faust returns to 'pay' his lawful debts, only to 'find' that the Jew is no longer in possession of his leg, (a dilemma Faust was anticipating). He immediately demands his leg to be returned, or that another settlement be made. Eager to be rid of Faust, the Jew offers him an additional sixty Guilders (Gulden); hence, the magician by his deceit made a considerable profit in less than three days when compared with the former weekly salary of twenty-five Gulden Mephostophiles previously bestowed upon him!

---

[439] *History of Doctor Johann Faustus*, p. 86.

[440] Ibid. Mephostophiles continues, saying, "Thy years are not yet over. Only four years are past since my promise to thee that thou wouldst want neither for gold nor for goods. Why, thy meat and drink hath been brought thee from the courts of all the great potentates, all by mine art (what the spirit here states, we did already report above)." We posit this legend was originally intended to be included after Chapter Seven in the manuscript and was reinserted in this section at a later date. Alternatively, Henry Jones remarks this unusual limitation was a later addition originally intended to be a shrewd codicil Faust failed to notice: "[...] apparently, by a clause not even in the small print, the Devil's promise that he would never lack for money or goods was only valid for four years from the date of the contract. (It sounds like a publisher's invention.)" *Faustus and the Censor*, p. 25.

[441] *History of Doctor Johann Faustus*, p. 88.

The first surviving record of Faust's name associated with familiar medieval legends of magicians deceitfully defrauding Jewish moneylenders is found in Christopher Rosshirt's *Chronicle*. In that tale, Faust arranges for a Jewish moneylender to meet him at his house for the purpose of exchanging French currency, yet upon his arrival, the Jew finds him asleep. In an attempt to wake Faust, the Jew pulls on his leg, which appears to fall off with the result the Jew runs out of the house in sheer terror leaving behind the thalers he brought for the exchange. However, the author of the Wolfenbüttle Manuscript altered his Faustian rendition to cast a darker anti-Semitic shadow in contrast to his predecessor. When considering Faust's drastic collateral we are told; "The Jew (for Jews are enemies to us Christians, anyhow) pondered the matter and concluded that it must be a right reckless man who would place his limbs in pawn. But still he accepted it."[442] In other words, the moneylender had no compassion on a man, who from his point of view, appeared to be in a desperate need for money, yet because he was a Jew and "an enemy to us Christians" he agreed to the grisly surety. Alternatively, he could be merciful and waiver the necessary pawn, trusting he would be repaid rather than see a man cut off his leg in desperation. (Although we, the readers, know it was a magical hoax, the Jew did not!) In addition, the Jew decides to throw the leg away for it offered no *profit or benefit to him*, he does not care that a man amputated his limb and only considers it had no resale value should the deal fall through. At least he could show a sense of decency to keep his side of the gruesome bargain and preserve or bury the leg with a view to return it, no matter what condition the owner would find it in. The Jew is portrayed, albeit in a bizarre manner, a man without honour and an enemy of Christians consumed with greed and who eventually receives his just deserts.

This narration reflects the anti-Semitic sentiments of the time, particularly Luther's harsh criticism of 'stubborn' Jews.[443] Luther believed in tolerance and did not desire to see the Jews expelled from Germany: he was the first to recognise Christ was a Jew, that Christians were God's adopted 'heathens', and believed the Jews should be protected as 'guest citizens' provided they follow the laws of the land and were willing to 'improve', i.e. convert to Christianity. However, if they refused to improve and convert, the only recourse would be expulsion, particularly for those 'stubborn' Jews who misrepresented his views on tolerance as a pretext to remain entrenched in their faith and their unchristian customs. These 'stubborn' Jews were perceived to be a particular menace. Luther considered them professed enemies of Christ who were not only blasphemers, but also a faction that would willingly rob the common man of everything he owned through usury, or exterminate every Christian if given a further opportunity. Slanderous reports that these Jews were necromancers became commonplace. In his pamphlet *Of the Jews and Their Lies* (1543) Luther described these obstinate Jews as "children of the Devil" and laid down a ground plan that he believed would hasten their 'improvement', which he described as "harsh mercy". He proposed that their homes, schools and synagogues be burned or razed to the ground and that the buildings permitted for their use be nothing better than stables. Their rabbis forbidden under pain of "life and limb" from teaching, and their prayer books "filled with curses" to be taken from them. That all roads and escorts be forbidden them, their usury outlawed, and all their wealth confiscated. Finally, that all able-bodied Jews, men and women alike, be forced into manual labour and earn their bread by the sweat of their brows. It is no

---

[442] Ibid. p. 87.
[443] See Obermann, *Luther, Man Between God and the Devil*, pp. 289–297.

surprise that this portrayal of Jews as "enemies to Christians" and notorious extortionists is propagated in the Wolfenbüttle Manuscript.

The next chapter appears to be less sinister. In Chapter Twenty-seven,[↔] Faust is invited to the Count of Anhalt's castle for a banquet and with his magic contributes dainties for the table. Observing that the Countess is with child, Faust asks her to name any food that she desires, whereupon she replies that she wishes for fresh fruit as it is now wintertime and out of season. Faust declares this task is easy for him to accomplish, and immediately sets two silver bowels on the window ledge. One hour later, he retrieves the bowls, now filled to the brim with a variety of exotic fruits. Faust explains that his spirit (Mephostophiles) travelled to a part of the world that was now approaching mid-summer while their country was just beginning the New Year, which explains how he could procure these delicacies:

> "Gracious Lord, may it please your Grace to know that the year is divided into two circles in the world, so that it is summer in Orient and Occident when it is winter here, for the Heavens are round. Now, from where we dwell the sun hath now withdrawn to the highest point, so that we are having short days and winter here, but at the same time it is descending upon Orient and Occident — as in Sheba, India and the East proper. The meaning of this is that they are having summer now. They enjoy vegetables and fruit twice a year there. Furthermore, gracious Lord, when it is night here, day is just dawning there. The sun hath even now betaken himself beneath the earth, and it is night; but in this same instant the sun doth run above the earth there, and they shall have day. [...]"[444]

Obviously, the author altered the legends concerning Mephostophiles' spiriting away strange and exotic food to suit his own scientific purpose. Notice that in his explanation above Faust mentions that the Heavens are round, i.e. spherical, the short days of winter are caused by the sun moving farther away from the earth (thus explaining the equinoxes), and there are two separate zones to the earth (similar to hemispheres). These details are Copernican, yet he also states that the sun moves, a Ptolemaic ideal. This description confirms our observations of Chapters Twenty and Twenty-one that the author was promoting a combination of the Copernican-Ptolemaic systems, i.e. possibly a prototype of the 'Brahe Hybrid System' featuring a stationary earth and an orbiting sun, which in turn is orbited by the planets.

Chapter Twenty-eight continues with Faust's exploits at the Count's residence stating the magician entertained his host by conjuring all manner of exotic and fantastic creatures for him to admire. Faust then returns to Wittenberg where he plans to celebrate Shrovetide *ala Dionysus*. Inviting a number of students to his feast, they crown him as Bacchus, and spend the night in revelry. "Bacchus" then invites his guests to join him in his clandestine adventure to sample the Bishop of Salzburg's cellar. Laying down a ladder in his garden, he tells each student to sit on a rung, and immediately they fly off to Salzburg. However, as they are blithely swilling the Bishop's wine, the butler discovers them in the cellar and attempts to raise the alarm, but Faust

---

[↔] In Spies' edition, Ch. 43. (*Faustus and the Censor*, p. 25)
[444] *History of Doctor Johann Faustus*, p. 90.

orders the students back onto their rickety steed. As they fly past, he seizes the poor butler by the hair and sets him atop a great fir tree.[√] The band of merry wine marauders thereby return to Wittenberg and polish off another bottle that Faust had managed to swipe during their speedy escape.

This chapter in general narrates Faust's continuing lifestyle of debauchery and his unashamed disregard for the opportunities presented for conversion. Just at Shrovetide, the three days before Ash Wednesday that begin the Christian penitential season of Lent, Faust is crowned as Bacchus, the Greek god of revelry and wine. The origin of the word 'shrove' is derived from the medieval 'shrive', i.e. to attend the Sacrament of Confession. In previous eras, Shrovetide was the traditional time for a penitent to approach Confession and begin preparations for the liturgical season of Lent. However, as time progressed, the revelry and licentiousness of the Carnival season begins to dominate these days once devoted to spiritual conversion. For instance, Shrove Tuesday is now more readily recognised as Mardi Gras. Although Lutherans do not believe in sacramental confession, the notion that Carnival customs encouraging depravity and presumption of God's mercy were overshadowing the sanctity of Shrovetide would prove just as abhorrent. Faust is therefore portrayed as one of the devilish facilitators of this sensual violation in opposition to the Christian tradition, and in the process, coerced others to partake in the same vice-filled customs of the Carnival.

The students now enjoy following Faust's example and his Bohemian lifestyle, for this disrespect for holydays continues in the following chapter. On Whitsunday, or the feast of Pentecost, the students arrive unannounced at Faust's house, yet are readily welcomed as they have brought all their own fare for supper. During the meal, the students begin to converse about beautiful women; they express their desire to see Helen of Troy whose legendary beauty caused her to be abducted from her husband that fomented the famous ten-year war that destroyed a nation. Faust states as he had accomplished a similar feat in bringing Alexander the Great before the Emperor, he was ever ready to grant their desire to see the renowned queen. He then presents to them a spirit in Helen's flawless shape who looks at them with a "right wanton mien", and immediately the students are inflamed with passion. When she disappears, they beg Faust to allow them send artists to his house to paint a portrait of her, and Faust agrees after explaining their painters will have to copy from a mere picture when he is able to procure one, for he cannot summon her spirit to appear at will. That night, the students are unable to sleep as the image of Helen burns in their minds. The author concludes the chapter with the admonishment, "[...] and from this we may learn how the Devil doth blind men with love [i.e. lust] — oh it doth often happen that a man goeth awhoring for so long that at last he can no longer be saved from it."[445] Hence, on a feast day that commemorates the descent of the Holy Spirit upon the Apostles, which fired them with holy zeal, the students in contrast are swayed by the devil, allow the evil spirit of

---

[√] When writing the butler's punishment it is clear the author / scribe borrowed from the myth of King Pentheus of Thebes. The ancient king dared to mock the existence of the wine god, Bacchus (Dionysus). He planned to spy on the Bacchantes who worshipped this deity, but Bacchus, in disguise, lured the king out of hiding and placed him in a pine tree, telling him he would have a better view of the sacred mysteries, yet this position exposed his presence to the Bacchantes who tore him to pieces in their ecstatic devotion.

[445] *History of Doctor Johann Faustus*, p. 95.

lewdness to enter them, and sin mortally by wilful impure thoughts: "But I say to you, that whosoever shall look on a woman to lust after her, hath already committed adultery with her in his heart." (Matt. 5: 28) They have desecrated the sanctity of the day as they had previously during Shrovetide with their Carnival revelry.

Continuing with Chapter Thirty,± we discover the author inserted a popular myth in his text with the purpose to include a moral admonishment and a prejudicial viewpoint, yet in the process appended material that is anomalous with Faust's character. Faust is summoned to the town of Brunswick to cure a marshal who is suffering from consumption. We are told Faust preferred to walk to his appointments, but on that particular occasion asked a passing cart-driver for a ride. Faust, however, was not tired and was testing the peasant to see if he would offer him charitable assistance. The cart-driver refuses and he is duly rewarded for his lack of charity. Faust angrily rebukes the peasant, and puts a hex on his wagon so that the four wheels fly off and settle at each of the four gates of the town. In addition, the team of horses fall down as though dead and refuse to stir. The peasant begs Faust for forgiveness, promising never to behave towards others in this same manner. Faust takes "[...] pity on the clown's humility," scolds him again for his churlish pride and restores the horses, but informs the peasant that he must still pay for his rudeness, and thereby refuses to retrieve the four wheels. The author concludes, "The peasant went along and found them as Doctor Faustus had said, but with great effort, travail and neglect of the trade and business which he had intended to accomplish. And thus will churlishness ever punish its owner."[446]

In his efforts to display the importance of performing a kindness towards others, the author paradoxically used Faust to promote Christian virtue. True, Faust may have vindictively enjoyed tormenting the peasant, but we would not expect to see a reprobate who formerly renounced his faith to teach others to behave in a Christian-like manner. In addition, Faust "[...] took pity upon the clown's humility,"[447] and corrects him regarding the sin of pride, a display of heart that we would not associate with one of Satan's minions. This is not unlike the theological inconsistencies the author transcribed when concentrating in Chapter Eight on Luther's reasons for entering the sacrament of matrimony.

This chapter also serves a further purpose, i.e. to prejudice the peasant class. The author writes that churlishness "[...] such as is, after all, commonly found among peasants."[448] This taunt in the text may be derived from Luther's involvement in the controversies of the Peasants' War (1524–1526). The discontented peasants, in an attempt to improve their situation, drew up a series of demands to present to the nobles supported by arguments drawn from Luther's writings. Although the peasants had misrepresented his theological teachings to their own advantage, Luther advocated their political demands in his pamphlet *An Admonition to Peace: A Reply to the Twelve Articles of the Peasants in Swabia* (April 1525). Nevertheless, when the peasants became violent, he withdrew his support and joined forces with the princes in order to restore peace, and appended the following to his pamphlet; *Against the Robbing and Murdering Hordes of Peasants* (May). Luther would later disapprove of the harsh methods employed by the nobles.

±   Ch. 50 in Spies' edition.
[446]   *History of Doctor Johann Faustus*, p. 98.
[447]   Ibid. p. 97.
[448]   Ibid. p. 96.

Once more, the text delves into anti-Semitic propaganda in Chapter Thirty-one.[≠] Arriving in time for the Carnival in Frankfurt, Faust receives a report from Mephostophiles informing him that four sorcerers in Jews Alley were creating a sensation by cutting off their heads, sending them to the barber to be trimmed, and then reattaching them without any personal injury. Thus the medieval prejudice that 'obstinate' Jews were involved in black magic is reinforced. This news piques Faust's jealousy for he "[…] liked to think that he were the only cock in the Devil's basket."[449] Faust decides to witness a performance of this spectacle, and observes how they accomplished this magic feat: before each head was cut off, the chief sorcerer would simultaneously place his hands on the 'condemned' and charm into a cruse of distilled water a lily, which he called the "Root of Life". Through this medium, the life force of each sorcerer was preserved until the decapitated heads were re-attached. However, Faust decides to teach his competitors a lesson, when the chief sorcerer's turn arrives, he slices the lily stem so that he dies "[…] with his sins upon his severed head."[450] Faust has now added murder to the list of his accomplishments. The sorcerers are alarmed, for they cannot discover who interfered with their magic, (presumably Faust remained invisible during the proceedings). The author declares, "This is the way the Devil at last rewards all his servants, absolving them thus, the manner in which Doctor Faustus dealt with this man being entirely consonant with the shameful absolution which he did himself receive when he was repaid for his own sins."[451] The moral of the tale — the devil and his cohorts will always betray their own. As observed earlier, Luther once remarked, "I am delighted, when one devil plagues another. They are not all, however, of equal power."[452]

In Chapter Thirty-two,[†] the text abruptly reverts to the subject of Lutheran salvation theology, with an additional attack opposing 'stubborn' Jews. An old pious neighbour becomes concerned at the number of young students who frequent Faust's residence for …

> "[…] he considered such a den as bad as a brothel, for he did compare Faustus to all Jews, who, so soon as they fell away from God also became His declared enemies, dedicating themselves unto sorcery for the sake of prophecy and deceit, seeking not only the bodily harm of many a pious child whose parents have devoted much effort to his Christian rearing, but also causing him to forget the Lord's prayer."[453]

And so, the old man decides to invite Faust to his house with the purpose of converting him, a detail that may be inspired by Hogel's *Chronica von Thüringen* where it is alleged a Franciscan monk attempted to convert Faustus in the town of Erfurt.

[≠]   Ch. 51 in Spies' edition.
[449]   *History of Doctor Johann Faustus*, p. 99.
[450]   Ibid. p. 100.
[451]   Ibid.
[452]   Luther, 'Of the Devil and His Works,' #DLXXV, *Tischreden*.
[†]   Ch. 52 in Spies.
[453]   *History of Doctor Johann Faustus*, p. 101.

Faust politely listens to the old man's argument: he must consider the eternal welfare of his soul and regard not the body, for it is not yet too late to change his ways and return to God. The old man presents as an example Simon Magus from the Acts of the Apostles, a man who deceived others with his black arts, yet who was saved by accepting faith and baptism from St. Philip. Continuing, the old man relates one need only turn away from sin to seek grace and pardon from God through Christ, to sin no more is the penance God seeks for He does not desire the death of the sinner. (The old man did not mention confession, as this is a Catholic sacrament.) Faust's neighbour then pleads with him to forsake his evil sorcery as God expressly forbids such practises in the Old and the New Testaments.

Faust ponders upon this carefully, thanks the old man for his advice, and promises to comply with his sage counsel. However, upon arriving home, Mephostophiles perceives Faust's desire for conversion and attempts to twist off his head, uttering the familiar rebuke: "What is thy purpose with thyself?"[454] The arch-demon reminds him of his pledge vowing enmity towards God and all mankind, and instils fear into Faust with the lie that it was too late for him to convert for he was already the devil's property. Furthermore, Mephostophiles imperiously announces:

> "The Devil hath the power to fetch thee away. I am in fact now
> come with the command to dispose of thee — or to obtain thy promise
> that thou wilt never more allow thyself to be seduced, and that thou wilt
> consign thyself anew with thy blood. Thou must declare immediately
> what thou wouldst do, or I am to slay thee."[455]

We know this to be a fallacy, there is always an opportunity for conversion. In addition, Mephostophiles already reneged on his side of the pact by revealing to Faust theological information on Hell, which he admitted was "[…] in direct violation of thy contract and vow," thus, a binding agreement had not existed between them for years! Mephostophiles now realises Faust may slip through his claws unless he can somehow swindle a renewed blood contract from him by brandishing the familiar line that it is already too late to be saved as he is the "Devil's own property". Unfortunately, Faust is unaware his pact had been previously nullified for years by Mephostophiles' overconfidence in his ability to manipulate him, and he is terrified by the arch-demon's threats into writing the second contract. According to popular folklore, a second contract[456] with the devil ultimately sealed an irrevocable agreement.

Chapter Thirty-three◻ commences with Faust's new contract:

"I, Doctor Johann Faustus,
    Do declare in this mine own hand and blood:

---

[454] Ibid. p. 103.
[455] Ibid. p. 104.
[456] Ibid. p. 11.
◻ Ch. 53 in Spies.

Whereas I have truly and strictly observed my first *instrumentum* and pact for these nineteen years, in defiance of God and all mankind;

And whereas, pledging body and soul, I therein did empower the mighty God Lucifer with full authority over me so soon as five more years be past;

And whereas he hath further promised me to increase my days in death, thereby shortening my days in Hell, also not to allow me to suffer any pain;

Now therefore do I further promise him that I will never more heed the admonitions, teachings, scoldings, instructions or threats of mankind, neither as concerneth the Word of God nor in any temporal or spiritual matters whatsoever; but particularly do I promise to heed no man of the cloth not to follow his teachings.

In good faith and resolve contracted by these presents and in mine own blood, etc."[457]

From this second contract, we learn Faust has renewed the former agreement, i.e. the twenty-four years with reference to the past nineteen years and the remaining five years, and his promise to utterly denounce his faith, including all admonition directed towards the salvation of his soul. Satan bribed him with additional concessions that we know will not be honoured. The devil promised to "increase Faust's days in death", namely, that his days will be shortened in Hell. Does this indicate that Satan agreed Faust's soul will not be taken directly by the demons nor judged by God immediately, but will wander temporarily in a Limbo-like state between both worlds? Christian tradition states Limbo is a place where the just souls awaited the coming of Christ, and where unbaptised, yet innocent souls, reside in a state of tranquil happiness. Satan has no authority in this realm of just souls, and therefore cannot send Faust there. We also presume the devil will not wait a moment longer than he initially agreed upon to take possession of Faust's soul, and therefore did not intend to grant Faust any reprieve whatsoever. Satan also promised Faust that he will not experience pain in Hell, an offer the devil cannot comply with as he cannot lessen his own infernal sufferings one iota. We detect the author was demonstrating the theological absurdity of the Mortalist heresy, i.e. that until the body is resurrected on the Last Day, the soul is held in a state of abeyance between this world and the next and will not enter into the *eternal* afterlife until the day of Judgement when body and soul will be reunited.[458]

Now that Faust has signed and sealed his fate, he turns his venom upon the old man who tried to convert him and conspires to take his life with the aid of Mephostophiles. At first, the devil haunts the man's house, creating all manner of noises and rumblings, but the old man shows no sign of fear, he mocks the arch-demon and drives him away. Mephostophiles returns to Faust and reports he is unable to approach the old man as his faith and prayers protect him. The author concludes; "Now the spirits and devils cannot suffer a good humor, particularly when they are reminded of their fall. Thus doth God protect all good Christians who seek in Him succor against

---

[457] *History of Doctor Johann Faustus*, pp. 105–106.
[458] *Faustus and the Censor*, p. 106.

the Evil One."[459]   This comment parallels Luther's belief one need not fear the devil's preternatural activity, it is a mere diversion. When convinced a devil was haunting him, Luther would either rebuke the demon, or simply go back to sleep or to work, whatever the case might be. One need only fear Satan's attacks that attempt to undermine faith in the Word of God, for this is where the fiend accomplishes utter destruction and leads souls to perdition. Hence, according to Luther, strong faith in the Word of God is the only requirement necessary to drive the devil away. He also believed faith should make the conscience glad for depression was the work of Satan.

This chapter concludes the third section of the Wolfenbüttle Manuscript, the prophecy that Faust would eventually dismiss his last chance of conversion and choose the Inferno has come to pass as depicted in his vision of Hell when he threw himself into the volcanic fissure rather than brave the sea of repentance. Faust has now only five years remaining — and time is running out fast.

Faust: The Twilight Years

Convinced he had forfeited all hope of salvation, Faust returns to his customary bad habits of amusing himself and others with his devilish arts. In this final section, the chapters are shorter in length and not as theologically absorbing, thereby requiring less meditative concentration. Possibly, the author constructed these chapters to resemble the diminishing sand of an hourglass, which appears to fall more rapidly near the completion of its allotted time notwithstanding the quantity of sand is sifting at the same rate—we are watching Faust's last years swiftly fade away.

In Chapter Thirty-four,[ⓞ] Faust learns one of his noblemen friends, a man named Reuckauer, is pining away with a mysterious illness. Mephostophiles informs him that his friend is wasting away from unrequited love as the lady he wished to marry rejected him. Faust immediately visits his friend and encourages him not to despair, he has a magic plan to ensure his lady will love him and no other. Faust instructs him to dress in his best apparel as she will be hosting a dance at her house. He places a magic ring on Reuckauer's finger and explains he must touch her with this ring finger when they dance, and she will forsake all others. However, Faust forbids his friend to propose to her until she entreats him first for reacceptance. Everything comes to pass as Faust predicted; she entreats Reuckauer to accept her as his wife and declares she cannot love another, consequently the nobleman weds his ladylove, and of course, Faust receives a rich reward for his services.

At first, this chapter may lend the impression the author fabricated an additional theological paradox, for as Faust renounced the sacraments, it is logical to assume that Mephostophiles would expect him to discourage others from entertaining any plans for marriage. Nevertheless, as the lady is compelled by the influence of demonic arts to accept a man she previously rejected, the marriage is not valid as it was accomplished without her free will. There

---

[459]   *History of Doctor Johann Faustus*, p. 106.
[ⓞ]   Ch. 54 in Spies.

was obviously a sound reason for her not to accept him, which she now sets aside. Her affections are bewitched, she is no longer capable of judging whether or not Reuckauer is a *suitable* partner for marriage or reflect upon the duties of marriage. Does he believe in the Faith? Does he wish to raise children with the love and fear of God, or, is he pursuing her only to satisfy his lust? Will their marriage be a true partnership in Christ where a man is bound to *protect* his wife with the authority given to him over her, or is it simply a legal agreement that the 'possessor' may now legally take her as his 'possession'? Faust's sympathies obviously rest with his friend, therefore he is simply interested in forming a union, valid or not, for Reuckauer's benefit, the lady is now 'charmed' into the role of a submissive slave. Although Reuckauer was possibly sworn to silence to ensure the charm would not be broken, (a condition essential to guarantee the successful performance of magic), notice how she is to first humiliate herself in recompense for her initial rejection of Reuckauer before he may reaccept her. Hence, this union may prove to be a source of antipathy and strife in later years, as it is not a marriage ordained by Heaven from the beginning. The detail of the magic ring is also of interest, this may be inspired by popular legends attributed to King Solomon who is reported to have possessed such an artefact that enabled him to control spirits and the forces of nature, including living creatures.[460] Faust is therefore portrayed as the antithesis of the wise King for he did not acquire the heavenly wisdom granted by God, but rather a prodigious level of diabolical cunning.

The following chapter, Thirty-five, appears more incongruous when considered with the text as a whole, for there is no visible theological or moral admonition included, nor a prejudicial dart aimed at current events, but rather we read an entertaining tale displaying Faust's skills of thaumaturgy. During the Christmas season, several gentlewomen arrive in Wittenberg to visit their brothers and cousins, i.e. the students acquainted with Faust. Desiring to repay his social debts, for the students had invited him to supper on various occasions, he decides to invite them and their relations to his home for an evening. The streets are covered with snow and it is bitterly cold, but on arriving at Faust's house, the guests discover that his residence and garden are experiencing the full effects of high summer — the sun is warm, the grass is fresh and green, and

---

[460] *Doctor Faustus; A- and B- Texts*, p. 7. This legend is also displayed in the *Thousand and One Arabian Nights* where it is related King Solomon imprisoned devils, or evil Jinn, in bottles sealed with his mystical ring. According to a footnote in the Harvard Classics edition of the *Arabian Nights*:

"No man ever obtained such absolute power over the Jinn as Suleymann Ibn-Da'ud (Solomon, the Son of David). This he did by virtue of a most wonderful talisman, which is said to have come down to him from heaven. It was a seal-ring, upon which was engraved 'the most great name' of God; and partly composed of brass, and partly of iron. With the brass he stamped his written commands to the good Jinn; with iron [which they greatly dread], those to the evil Jinn, or Devils. Over both orders he had unlimited power; as well as over birds and the winds, and, as is generally said, the wild beasts. His Wezir, Asaf the son of Barkhiya, is also said to have been acquainted with 'the most great name,' by uttering which the greatest miracles may be performed; even that of raising the dead. By virtue of this name, engraved on the ring, Suleyman compelled the Jinn to assist in building the Temple of Jerusalem, and in various other works. Many evil Jinn he converted to the true faith; and many others of this class, who remained obstinate in infidelity, he confined in prisons." — Charles W. Eliot, ed., Edward William Lane, trans., revised by Stanley Lane-Poole, *Stories from the Thousand and One Nights: The Harvard Classics*, vol 16 (New York: P. F. Collier and Son Corp., 1963), p. 26.

all manner of flowers and plants are blooming, an unexpected surprise that thoroughly delights the company. Not wishing to write a conspicuous moral, perhaps the author intended his readers to reflect upon the travesty of the situation, for in the season commemorating the event of Christ's birth in a stable at midnight in the piercing winter cold, ordained by God for love of mankind, Faust and his guests are glorying in a summer mirage wrought by the work of Satan, who in contrast despises them and yearns for their eternal ruin. Rose writes this tale was drawn from a separate legend concerning Albertus Magnus who allegedly conjured a magic garden for the Emperor in the midst of the winter season.[461]

The subsequent tale also lacks an apparent moral or propagandist interjection, however, we notice it serves to form structural cohesion as it continues with the events initiated within the Emperor's court in previous chapters. In Chapter Thirty-six, Faust rides to the town of Eisleben, (Luther's birthplace), and happens to encounter the knight upon whom he had charmed deer antlers. The knight immediately recognises Faust and attempts to arrest him with the aid of his personal guards. Faust pretends to flee, and rides over a hill and out of sight. As his enemies ride up the hill and search for him in the copse below, they are suddenly surrounded by a second army: Faust's phantom troop conjured by his sorcery. Faust's assailants are forced to surrender, and their muskets and horses are confiscated. However, Faust arrives in disguise dressed in knight's armour and announces; "[…] the commander of this army hath bid me let you go this time — but upon condition and probation. Will ye confess that ye did pursue a man who hath sought and received, and is henceforth shielded by, our commander's protection?"[462] They confess to their 'crime', are granted probation, and are handed back what they believe to be their own horses and muskets, but in fact, they are charmed bundles of straw. When the men ride their mounts into water, the steeds revert to their original form. Faust then sells the real horses and weapons and his pockets are bulging once again. This element of the charmed straw bundles is not new, but are also attributed to other magicians and their celebrated schemes to defraud the populace. In conclusion, the knight gave his word, receives probation, and is therefore compelled to forgo any further thoughts of vengeance upon the reprobate: twice Faust has made a fool of him.

With the exception of Faust's 'letter' to his friend in Chapter Seventeen, the title of this chapter in the manuscript was written in the first person: "Concerning an Army Raised Against My Lord of Hardeck". Unless the original author changed his mind, this particular tale is obviously a later addition by a scribe, for the knight in question remained anonymous in Chapter Twenty-four, "I would not name the person, for it was a knight and a gentleman by birth."[463] Possibly, "Hardeck" is a variation of "Hradec", or the town of Hradec Králové in the northern Czech Republic, and this may be one indication of how far the earliest Faustian manuscripts circulated. Of course, the original source of the deer antler tale has been traced back to Luther and his anecdotes of earlier emperors, thus we may conclude this scribe simply included the title "My Lord Of Hardeck" to this sequel to place his personal stamp on the Faustian literature for his private satisfaction.

---

[461] *Damnable Life and Deserved Death of […] Faustus*, p. 29.
[462] *History of Doctor Johann Faustus*, p. 115.
[463] Ibid. p. 82.

Chapter Thirty-seven[#] returns to theological matters, however, this tale addresses an ominous topic familiar to those who believed, like Luther, that the Last Days were already upon them. One midnight coming to the conclusion of his twenty-second year, Faust's thoughts turn to Helen of Troy, and the next morning, he commands Mephostophiles to present her to him for he intends to make her his mistress. Mephostophiles obeys, and Faust falls so deeply in love (or lust!) that he cannot bear to be parted from her. As time passes she bears him a son, and they name him "Justus Faustus" — a chilling thought, for we know that devils cannot procreate or resurrect the dead, they send a demon in their place. Apparently, this devilish progeny could speak as soon as he was born, for "[…] This child told him many things out of the future history of numerous lands."[464] We are duly informed that upon Faust's death, Helen and the 'child' vanished without a trace, no doubt the author intended his readers to conclude this child was destined to reappear at the appointed time as the Antichrist, who according to prophecy, will have powers that appear miraculous, but will actually be diabolical in origin. Rose theorises that the embroidered form of the Simon Magus legends influenced this chapter as Simon was reported to have a consort named Helen or Helena-Luna.[465]

The following tale breaks the foreboding atmosphere of the previous chapter by resorting once more to lewd humour. In Chapter Thirty-eight, a nobleman named Johann Werner of Reuttpueffel from Bennlingen is introduced as one of Faust's acquaintances. (This name, like several others, may be fabricated to instil 'authenticity' into the text.) The nobleman is blessed with a beautiful wife named Sabina of Kettheim with whom he was happily married for six years, however, consuming too much drink one night, he is persuaded to swear an oath to visit Turkey and the Holy Land, and he decides to fulfil his pledge. (We suspect this was an oath to join a Crusade, or, to complete a pilgrimage.) When five years had elapsed, a report arrives informing Sabina that her husband is dead, thus she mourns for him a further three years, while all the time, suitors constantly surround her similar to Penelope, the wife of Ulysses. Finally, she accepts a young nobleman whom the author dares not mention. On the day of the nuptial celebrations, Faust hears of this misadventure and asks Mephostophiles if his friend Werner is still alive. Mephostophiles reports that "[…] he be alive and in Egypt in the city of Lylopolts where he lay captive, having attempted to visit the city of Al-Cairo."[466] Faust is displeased with Sabina for remarrying as "[…] He knew her husband loved her well,"[467] and decides to intervene. Using his magic, he informs his friend that his wife is about to take a new husband, and reassures him that 'nothing' will be allowed to take place. That night, Mephostophiles places a hex on Sabina's new husband, consequently, he loses his potency and the marriage cannot be consummated. Faust transports her lawful husband back to their castle and she begs him to forgive her and receive her back as his wife, for the other "[…] had been able to accomplish naught."[468] Finding all had come to pass as Faust predicted, Werner accepts her back, yet continually torments her

---

[#] Ch. 59 in Spies edition.
[464] *History of Doctor Johann Faustus*, p. 117.
[465] *Damnable Life and Deserved Death of […] Faustus*, p. 30.
[466] *History of Doctor Johann Faustus*. p. 119.
[467] Ibid.
[468] Ibid.

with accusations of 'infidelity', she had deserted him for another, notwithstanding she was innocent of intentional adultery.

Faust has once again become the catalyst for introducing disorder and strife to a marriage. Although drawn to reunite the couple by the sympathy he feels for his friend, Faust forever holds his peace and refrains from halting Sabina's marriage celebration. Of course he would not stop the ceremony, this would entail accomplishing the Christian duty of informing Sabina that Werner was still living and an impediment existed to this second marriage. We must not forget Faust renounced all compliance with any and every Christian duty. Alternatively, he deliberately allows events to proceed to the point where Sabina and her new husband become complete fools on the night of their nuptials. Werner, who is tormented by jealousy, now possesses an emotional whip with which he may lash Sabina; "[...] and the good lady must hear from him, [...] how she did after all lie with another [...] and, had he been able to cover her, would have done that too."[469] In addition, this acrimonious conclusion corresponds with Luther's sentiments on the matter of pilgrimages, he believed that one should not make any rash oath to undertake a pilgrimage, for often the fulfilment of this promise would be undertaken at the expense of the duties set before them by God, and was not a holy or a pleasing act to the Almighty. For instance, the first duty for those in the married state centred on the care of their family and to attend to matters at home, not spending vast amounts of money and years of their life on what he believed were excessive devotional practises, which could lead to poverty and strife in the union. In this chapter, we have witnessed the spiritual destruction of the happy marriage of Werner and Sabina.

Finally, Faust enters the twenty-fourth year of his pact, and he begins to settle his affairs.[*] In Chapter Thirty-nine, he calls for a notary and several magistrates to draft his will in which he declares Wagner to be his sole beneficiary. Wagner is bequeathed Faust's house, and the remainder of all their ill-gotten gains:

> "He also left him 1,600 guilders lent out on usury, a farm worth 800 guilders, 600 guilders in ready money, a gold chain worth 300 crowns, some silver plate given him by a man named Kraffter, as well as such other things as he had taken from various courts — those of the Pope and of the Turk, for example."[470]

The chapter concludes with the observation Faust's domicile obviously lacked the comforts of a regulated Christian lifestyle: "There was not really much household stuff on hand, for he had not lived much at home, but at inns and with students, in gluttony and drunkenness."[471]

The settlement of Faust's estate continues in the following chapter. Having drawn up his last will and testament, Faust calls for Wagner and informs him that he made him the sole

---

[469] Ibid.

[*] According to Rose, Faust makes several predictions in his last year concerning the papacy, and the Huguenot Massacre, (which occurred in Paris on St. Bartholomew's Day, August 24, 1572), however, Haile omitted this from his translation of the Wolfenbüttle MS. Rose, *Damnable Life and Deserved Death of [...] Faustus*, p. 26.

[470] *History of Doctor Johann Faustus*, pp. 120–121.

[471] Ibid. p. 121.

beneficiary, and states that he would now like to grant any additional request for he was a faithful servant who never disclosed his secrets. Wagner asks Faust if he may be the recipient of his knowledge, and Faust answers he will acquire it if he diligently studies the various books on sorcery he intends to bequeath him. Faust then inquires if there be any other request, and Wagner states he wishes Mephostophiles to become his *familiar* spirit. Faust replies this demand is impossible to grant as "[...] Mephostophiles oweth me no further debt, nor doth he bear affinity to any other man,"[472] a phrase intended to reiterate the common belief that the devil assigns a particular destroying demon to every person on earth to thwart the protection of their guardian angel and thus tempt them to perdition. However, Faust relates it is possible to receive a different spirit, and asks Wagner what shape he would like his *familiar* to assume. Wagner replies he would like him to appear as an ape, and immediately an ape leaps into the room. Faust reminds Wagner if he wishes to take command of the spirit, he must fulfil the usual requirement, (although it is not stated in the text, we understand this condition is the forfeiting of his immortal soul with a contract written in his blood). Faust then reveals the name of the simian-like spirit, Urian, and requests as a personal favour, that Wagner write his biography with the aid of his *familiar* should he forget any details, and publish the work after his death, as "[...] men will expect these things of thee."[473] The author was clearly inspired by the rumours the historical Faustus left behind a legacy of books on sorcery and necromancy, and included this element in his manuscript.♦ Additionally, the author incorporated an effective tactic to create suspense within the narration by insinuating to the readers they may be holding in their hands the very *Historia* written by Wagner under the guidance of a devil.

Of interest, the demon Urian,□ assigned to Wagner, was derived from the familiar term 'Herr Urian', initially a form of 'Ur-jan', or 'Ur-Hans', a slapstick name for the devil similar to 'Old Nick'.[474] However, for the theology enthusiast, 'Urian' also provides fascinating comparisons, it may be viewed as the demonic counterpart of the archangel Uriel, one of the Seven Archangels who stand before the throne of God. According to the apocryphal Book of Enoch (although not included in the Vulgate), the name 'Uriel' signifies "the light of God", and this angel is assigned as the guardian over all the luminaries in the heavens. In this capacity, Uriel would be the guardian of order, as the planetary bodies divide time on earth. He could also be considered one of the angels of enlightenment. In the same Apocrypha Book, he is reported to

---

[472] Ibid. p. 122.

[473] Ibid. p. 123.

♦ Booksellers were eager to capitalise on this facet of Faustian history as Rose relates there was a roaring trade in black magic manuscripts attributed to Faust. The most famous of these manuscripts was the *Conquest of Hell* (*Höllenzwang*). Rose writes: "They were usually disposed of secretly by disreputable people at exorbitant prices, (it is reported one of these manuscripts sold in Holland for eight thousand gilders!) but later the publishers brought out volumes which they ascribed to the authorship of Faust, and some of these were even supplied with false dates to give them an appearance of antiquity." *Damnable Life and Deserved Death of [...] Faustus*, p. 20. A *Conquest of Hell* published in 1607 was attributed to a certain "Johann de Luna", the apprentice of Christoph Wagner. Ibid. p. 22.

□ In Spies' *Faustbook*, Wagner's demon is named "Auerhahn" = "Heathcock". *Faustus and the Censor*, p. 28. It is a popularised form of Urian derived from Urhahn. David Luke, trans. *Goethe: Faust, Part One. Oxford World's Classics* (Oxford: Oxford University Press, 1998), n. 97, p. 169.

[474] Luke, *Faust, Part One*, Ibid.

guard the world, and the lower region of Tartarus. According to one tradition, Uriel is the archangel of music and literature. Thus, through Uriel's counterpart, Urian, Wagner is granted an arch-demon who wields the power of darkness, chaos, and the occult knowledge of astrology. We also observe the name Urian is compatible with that of Urania, the *pagan* muse of astronomy. As the pagans did not differentiate between astronomy and astrology, the demon Urian desires this pagan ideal to continue, creating diabolical confusion to God's plan for the planets. Urian may also be the arch-demon that is assigned to destroy or corrupt the humanities; hence, it is apropos he should aid Wagner in his literary endeavours to publish Faust's demonic 'biography'.

Faust, having distributed all his worldly, ill-gotten gains, enters the final month of his contract, and falls into a deep state of melancholic depression in Chapter Forty-one. He moans and weeps, and cannot endure the company of Mephostophiles. In Chapters Forty-two and Forty-three, we are permitted to read a sample of his various sighs and self-reproaches as it is duly reported Faust wrote them down that he may not forget them:

> "Alas, thou reckless, worthless heart! Thou hast seduced the flesh round about thee, and my fate is fire. The blessedness which once thou didst know is lost.
>
> Alas, Reason and Free Will! What a heavy charge ye do level at these limbs, which may expect naught else than rape of their life!
>
> Alas ye limbs, and thou yet whole body! It was ye let Reason indict Soul, for I might have chosen succor for my soul by sacrificing thee, my body. [...] Alas, of what help is this complaint? [...] Who will release me? Where am I to hide? Whither must I creep? Whither flee? Wherever I may be, there am I a prisoner."[475]

We thereby have completed the last tripartite chapter cycle in the manuscript. It is unquestionably clear who finally earned that Master's degree in the manipulation of theology. Mephostophiles has successfully trapped Faust in black despair, stripping him of his ability to hope for any deliverance — desolate in spirit, he awaits his damnation.

In the final chapter, Mephostophiles appears to Faust, announcing that he has twenty-four hours remaining on earth and advises him to prepare for death. Faust's lamentations begin anew and Mephostophiles 'consoles' him, while giving one last prejudicial kick to the Jews and the Turks:

> "My Fauste, be not so faint of heart. Thou dost indeed lose thy body, but thy time of judgement is yet far distant. Why surely thou must die — even shouldst thou live for many hundreds of years. The Jews and the Turks must also die expecting the same perdition as thou — even emperors die thus, if they be not Christian. After all, thou knowest not yet what it be that awaiteth thee. Take courage, and despair not so utterly.

---

[475] *History of Doctor Johann Faustus*, pp. 125–126.

Dost not remember how the devil did promise thee a body and soul all of steel, insensitive to the pain which the others will feel in Hell?"[476]

The arch-demon thereby reiterates the new 'concessions' Satan promised to grant Faust as he wrote his second contract, promises we know will not be honoured, but are now employed to ultimately dissuade Faust from final thoughts of repentance.

Resigned to his fate, Faust invites his various friends to spend the day with him at an inn in the village of Rimlich where he entertains them with a costly brunch and then later that evening with a grand supper. When they have eaten, Faust announces why he called them together:

> "For many years now, ye have known what manner of man I be, the arts and the sorcery I have used. All these things come from none other than the Devil. I fell into such devilish desires through none other cause than these: bad company, mine own worthless flesh and blood, my stiff-necked, godless will, and all the soaring, devilish thoughts I allowed in my head. I gave myself up unto the Devil and contracted with him for a term of twenty-four years, setting my body and soul in forfeit. Now are these twenty-four years run out. I have only this night left. An hourglass standeth before mine eyes, and I watch for it to finish."[477]

Faust continues, requesting them to convey his greetings to other friends, entreating them to forgive any wrong he committed against them in the past, and explains that his *Historia* is written as an example for them that they may avoid the same drastic fate. He advises them to love God and pray for His Divine protection against the Devil, to avoid all bad company, attend church regularly, and to withstand the Devil with renewed faith in Christ. Finally, Faust warns them when they go to bed, let nothing disturb or trouble them, "[…] even if a crashing and tumult be heard in the house. Be not afraid. No injury shall befall you," [478] a remark obviously drawn from documents stating the historical Faustus advised the innkeeper on the night of his death not to be terrified by any disturbances he might hear. Faust remarks he dies as a "bad" and a "good" Christian: bad, because he dared to sell his soul, good, because contrition is in his heart and his mind begs for grace and salvation, but nevertheless he believes this grace will not be granted.

His friends are alarmed at this drastic speech, and they implore him to explain why he did not disclose this information earlier, exclaiming, "Why, we should have brought learned *Theologi* who would have torn you out of the Devil's nets and saved you. But now it is too late and surely injurious to body and soul,"[479] a statement that configures with Luther's belief in the efficacious power of intercession within the church of Christ. Faust admits this help would not be permitted as the Devil often threatened to take his life the minute he thought of repentance. His friends make one last entreaty that he pray at least for the salvation of his soul, although he

---

[476] Ibid. p. 127.
[477] Ibid. p. 129.
[478] Ibid. p. 130.
[479] Ibid.

may be forced to forfeit his body to the devil, advice Faust attempts to comply with, but finds he cannot pray for he believes his sins are too great to receive pardon, particularly as he signed that second contract.

Finally, Faust and his friends bid goodnight and they retire to their rooms. Between twelve and one o'clock in the morning, a great blast of wind rocks the building and the hissing of serpents fill the air, a detail drawn from Isaiah (13:21): "[…] their houses shall be filled with serpents […]". The following morning, a horrific sight in Faust's apartments confronts the inhabitants of the inn:

> "The parlor was full of blood. Brain clave unto the walls where the Fiend had dashed him from one to the other. Here lay his eyes, here a few teeth. O it was a hideous *spectaculum*. Then began the students to bewail and beweep him, seeking him in many places. When they came out to the dung heap, here they found his corpse. It was monstrous to behold, for head and limbs were still twitching."[480]

As with other sections of the manuscript, we may trace the original inspiration for this detailed narrative in Luther's *Tischreden*:

> "At Mohlburg, in Thuringia, not far from Erfurt, there was a musician, who gained his living by playing at merry makings. This man came to the minister of his parish, and complained that he was every day assailed by the devil, who threatened to carry him off, because he had played at an unlawful marriage. The minister consoled him, prayed for him, recited to him numerous passages of Scripture, directed against the devil; and, with some other pious men, watched over the unfortunate man, day and night, fastening the doors and windows, so that he might not be carried off. At length the musician said: 'I feel that Satan cannot harm my soul, but he will assuredly remove my body;' and that very night, at eight o'clock, though the watch was doubled, the devil came in the shape of a furious wind, broke the windows, and carried off the musician, whose body was found next morning, stiff and black, stuck on a nut tree. 'Tis a most sure and certain story, added Luther."[481]

Faust's friends receive permission to inter the body, and returning to his house, they find Wagner mourning the loss of his beloved master. We also discover that we have not seen the last of Faust's misadventures, for the author states, "This little book, *Doctor Faustus His Historia* was already well written out. Now as to what [Wagner] wrote, that will be a different, new book." [482] The author obviously recognised the possibilities for a sequel when concluding the manuscript and apparently regretted inserting the detail in Chapter Forty-one that Faust requested

---

480   Ibid. p. 131.
481   Luther, 'Of the Devil and His Works' #DCXXIV, *Tischreden*.
482   *History of Doctor Johann Faustus*, p. 131.

Wagner to write the original *Historia*. However, another aspiring author may have inserted this information. Henry Jones relates these references to an additional *Faustbook* were included to allow for its publication:

> "Certainly there was more than one Faust book. [...] This 'pseudo-Wagner' work (which is not the later, [post-Spies] 'Wagner book' of 1593), is lost but its one-time existence is corroborated in yet another life of Faustus which was being written in 1587, the 'Authentic Life' by the Halberstadt lawyer Georg Rudolf Widman. This was not published until 1599, well after the author's death, but Widman began his work before Spies published his Faust book (he probably knew [Spies' edition] in a manuscript version.) His extended 'biography' relies heavily on this source but includes much extra material he claims to have collected from the students and much from the account of 'Johannes Wäiger', as he names the house-boy."[483]

Returning to our analysis, we are informed that following Faust's death, his house became uninhabitable due to the "uncanny" happenings that continued to occur there. Faust's ghost haunts the premises and appears frequently to Wagner, to whom he reveals many secrets. In addition, "[...] passers-by reported seeing [Faust's] face peering out at the windows."[484]

Finally, the author concludes the manuscript with one final word of caution to all readers of his work:

> "Now this is the end of his quite veritable deeds, tale, *Historia* and sorcery. From it the students and clerks in particular should learn to fear God, to flee sorcery, conjuration of spirits, and other works of the Devil, not to invite the Devil into their houses, nor yield unto him in any other way, as Doctor Faustus did, for we have before us here the frightful and horrible example of his pact and death to help us shun such acts and pray to God alone in all matters, love Him with all our heart and with all our soul and with all our strength, defying the Devil with all his following, that we may through Christ be eternally blessed. These things we ask in the name of Christ Jesus our only Lord and Saviour. Amen. Amen."[485]

---

[483] John Henry Jones, ed., *The English Faustbook: A Critical Edition Based on the Text of 1592*, (Cambridge: Cambridge University Press, 1994), p. 7.
[484] *History of Doctor Johann Faustus*, p. 132.
[485] Ibid. pp. 132–133.

The Faustian Texts and the Printing Press

The First Printed Faustbook (1587)

Little did the anonymous authors / scribes realise when tediously compiling and recopying these early texts by hand that they had prepared the foundations for the first great Faustian *zeitgeist*. Primarily intended for edification, and at one point to further scientific conjecture regarding the solar system, this collection of myths was destined to become a popular classic, that is, when it attracted the interest of a man named Johann Spies.

According to Spies' dedication of his *Faustbook* dated Monday 4 September, the story of Faust had long intrigued him, particularly as the legends captured the imagination of the populace for years and yet remained unpublished as a warning to the faithful. Spies continues:

> "[…] I have also not hesitated to enquire from scholars and wise people whether this history has perhaps already been written down by anyone, but I have never been able to discover anything certain, until recently it was communicated and sent to me by a good friend in Speyer, with the request that I should publish and present it as a fearful example of devilish deceit, murder of body and soul, as a warning to all Christians."[486]

Hence, Spies received one of the privately circulated handwritten manuscripts,[&] which he duly published in 1587 with the following title:

---

[486] *Damnable Life and Deserved Death of […] Faustus*, p. 24.

[&] Henry Jones presents a theory that the Wolfenbüttle MS could actually be a copy of the manuscript that Spies' received from his acquaintance in Speyer. Henry Jones states the man in Speyer could be informed of the Latin edition by a colleague who possessed a copy, and remembering Spies' request for a German translation, he repeatedly begged this colleague to translate the Latin version for his own use without mentioning his intention of sending a copy of it to Spies for publication. (Henry Jones highlights the repeated requests for translation in the Preface of the Wolfenbüttle MS as evidence.) Henry Jones proposes: "[…] that the man at Speyer then removed the preface [of the Wolfenbüttle MS to hide the translator's identity from Spies] and sent the truncated MS on to Spies at Frankfurt who, after making his own editorial amendments, rushed it into print." (*Faust and the Censor*, pp. 31–32.) Henry Jones presents further evidence in *The English Faust Book; A Critical Edition* (n.25, pp. 5, 75.) supporting this theory based on previous research from Haile. In 1961, Haile discovered that the Wolfenbüttle MS remained in pristine condition and was still heavily covered in blotting sand, indicating it was not often read as it was just superseded by Spies' publication. Henry Jones also remarks the MS is "clearly a dictated copy." (*The English Faust Book,* ibid.) Hence, it is possible the man in Speyer had a second MS of the German translation rapidly transcribed for his own use in the event Spies never published the copy sent to him. If accepted, this theory could date the Wolfenbüttle MS closer to the year 1587. For our study, we have settled on the 1580s as the most probable period: (c. 1580–1587). Furthermore, this theory evinces a lost German language precursor. We do not know how long the man at Speyer made repeated

"History of D. Johann Faust, the notorious Magician and Necromancer, how he sold himself for a stipulated Time to the Devil, What strange Things he saw, performed and practised during this Time, until at last he received his well-merited Reward. For the most Part extracted and herewith printed from his own posthumous Writings as an awful and abominable Example and sincere Warning to all presumptuous, inquisitive and godless Persons. "Submit yourselves to God. Resist the Devil, and he will flee from you" (James iv). Cum Gratia et Privilegio. Printed at Frankfort-on-the-Main by Johann Spies. M.D.LXXXVII."[487]

We notice Spies honestly believed the artistic deception worked into the handwritten text by an anonymous author, i.e. the document was originally written by Faustus! Spies also included a "Preface to the Christian Reader", a section that Rose observes, "[...] contains much quoting of the Bible."[488]

The book was speedily printed for the Frankfurt book fair held in September 1587[489] and proved to be one of the bestsellers of those times: four reprints and a new original edition were printed that same year.[490] An extended version featuring eight new chapters■ also appeared in 1587, but Rose suggests this was an unofficial edition of Spies' work as his printer's monogram is missing.[491] The Spies book also attracted the artistic, (or enterprising) imagination of a few aspiring Faustian authors, students at the University of Tübingen. In the winter of 1587–1588, these students published a rhymed edition;◊ however, when the ducal commissioners sent a complaint to the senate of the University, the authors and the publisher, Hock, were punished for their efforts with several days of incarceration and a severe reprimand.[492] Presumably, the authorities were concerned that these youths were leading their fellow students astray by introducing them to the occult through their interest in Faust. The Spies book was also fair game for the book pirates as with Balhorn, the "blundering book pirate of Lübeck", who published a

---

requests for a German translation: his colleague was possibly reluctant to translate it for several years prior to this. Hence, the dates for the lost German precursor could still be considered c. 1572–1587.

[487] *Damnable Life and Deserved Death of [...] Faustus*, pp. 23–24.

[488] Ibid. p. 25.

[489] *Faustus and the Censor*, p. 12.

[490] *Damnable Life and Deserved Death of [...] Faustus*, p. 25.

■ Rose writes the sequence of chapters was altered, and the eight new chapters were drawn from Wier's *De Praestigiis Daemonum* and Lercheimer's *Christliche Bedenken*. See *Damnable Life and Deserved Death of [...] Faustus*, pp. 34–36 for a synopsis of the new chapters.

[491] Ibid. p. 34.

◊ A facsimile of this edition is available: *Der Tübinger Reim-Faust von 1587/8*, ed. Günther Mahal, Tübingen (Schweier) 1977.

[492] *Damnable Life and Deserved Death of [...] Faustus*, p. 40. See also *Sources of the Faust Tradition*, p. 130.

Low German edition in 1588.[493] The following year, 1589, a new edition of the Spies *Faustbook* was printed, which Rose observes is an important version as it contains six additions known as the "Erfurt Chapters" drawn from the local tradition of that same town.[494] It is possible the *Reichmann-Wamback Chronicle* was the source of these stories before the manuscript was lost.⸱ In 1590, a hybrid edition featuring the Spies and also the enlarged 1589 'Erfurt Addendum' versions was published in Berlin, and in 1598, the last of the known Spies *Faustbooks* appeared in Germany, which is thought to be the eighteenth edition.[495]

We observe the popularity of the *Faustbook,* printed as a warning to Christians, may be credited to the socio-religious paranoia of the times. Empson writes:

> "[…] this period was the height of witch-burnings. A French traveller reported in 1590: 'Germany is almost entirely occupied in building fires for witches. Switzerland has been compelled to wipe out many of her villages on their account. Travellers in Lorraine may see thousands and thousands of the stakes to which witches are bound.'"[496]

However, a select few did not receive Spies' *Faustbook* with enthusiasm. Augustin Lercheimer denounced the book in the third edition of his *Christliche Bedencken und Erinnerung von Zauberei* (1597):

> "I am obliged to give him [Faustus] some considerable attention by reason of a book recently published by some toady, whoever he may be, in which the school and church of Wittenberg are particularly abused and slandered. It says that Faustus was born in the vicinity of Weimar and Jena, that he matriculated at Wittenberg and was there made Master of Arts and Doctor of Divinity … This is all badly and childishly told and he lied …"[497]

> "It is all malicious lies. … [Faust] had neither house nor yard at Wittenberg or elsewhere, was never at home, lived like a vagabond, was a

---

[493] *Sources of the Faust Tradition*, p. 130.
[494] *Damnable Life and Deserved Death of [...] Faustus*, p. 36.
▸ The new chapters are the same tales as found in Hogel's *Chronica von Thüringen*. The sixth chapter features the myth where Faust and some University students visit the Leipzig fair. They see several draymen unable to lift a giant wine cask out of a cellar, and in desperation the owner of the wine cask offers to give the barrel to anyone who can accomplish the task. Faust sits on the barrel and rides it up the stairs like a horse. He receives the wine as a present and shares it with the students. Concerning this myth, Rose writes: "The story […] is recorded in two paintings on the wall of Auerbach's wine-cellar in Leipzig, which bear the date 1525, but are in reality no earlier than the seventeenth century. The wine-cellar itself was not built till 1530." Ibid. pp. 36, 39.
[495] *Sources of the Faust Tradition*, p. 130.
[496] Henry Boguet: *An Examen of Witches* (translation of *Discours des Sourciers*, 1590), tr. and ed. Montague Summers, London (John Rodker) 1929, p. xxxiii, in *Faustus and the Censor*, p. 49.
[497] *In Faustus and the Censor*, p. 13.

parasite, guzzled, swilled and lived by his conjuring. How could he have a house and yard by the outer gate of the town in the Scheergasse, since there never was a suburb and therefore no outer gate? Neither was there ever a Scheergase there. That in such a University, a man whom Melanchthon used to call a cesspool of many devils should have been made Master, to say nothing of Doctor of Theology, which would be an eternal disgrace to the degree and a honourable title, who believes that? … About all the other vanity, lies and *Teufelsdreck* in the book, I will say nothing. … It is, to be sure, nothing new and no cause for surprise that such calumnies are issued by the enemies of our religion, but it is unwarrantable and lamentable that our printers also should publish such books without shame, whereby honest people are slandered and inquisitive youths led to attempt similar magic feats; to say nothing of the abuse of the beautiful and noble art of printing, which has been conferred on us by God."[498]

Lercheimer obviously misread the intentions of the anonymous author of the first Faustian manuscripts upon which the Spies Books were based and did not discern that this Faust 'biography' was a new fabrication primarily intended to portray Luther's life and teachings antithetically as a warning for the faithful and articles to avoid when following the 'Rediscovered Gospel'. We have discovered in our analysis, that in contrast to Luther, Faust "used God's Word vainly" thus explaining his gradual descent to despair and the Dark side. The message — follow Luther's example by living the Word of God, and you will escape the vortex to Hell and the devil's snares. However, Lercheimer assumed these publications were intended to libel the father of the Reformation due to their false, pseudo-biographical presentation, and was indignant that the historical Faustus should be associated with the town of Wittenberg and its university. In fact, this debate continues to the present day within academic circles, if indeed, this paralleling of Luther's biography in the texts, both handwritten and printed, was intended as an approbation of Luther by supporters of the Reformation, or an outright attack initiated by Catholic scholars to undermine his theology.

ഇരു ❖ ഇരു

At this juncture, when attempting to discuss the content of the Spies *Faustbook*, we encounter a particular academic setback pertaining to Faustian research that needs to be addressed, where English speaking scholars are concerned; namely, the difficulty of acquiring a modern, unabridged translation of the Wolfenbüttle text and the Spies *Faustbook* for those with little or no knowledge of sixteenth-century German. Haile includes only forty-four chapters in his edition of the Wolfenbüttle manuscript by omitting or condensing material, hence twenty-seven chapters are missing as the original contains seventy-one.[499] Palmer and More assert that

---

[498] *Damnable Life and Deserved Death of [...] Faustus*, pp. 31–32.
[499] Ibid. p. 25.

the actual Wolfenbüttle text and the first printed Spies book are almost identical, however, this will not solve the language barrier as they decided to refrain from reprinting the Spies version, electing to refer scholars to the 1592 English translation / adaptation by the anonymous Mr. P.F. for various reasons:

> "[…] it has seemed best not include a reprint of the Spies book in this collection of source material. [i.e. *Sources of the Faust Tradition*] In the first place the Spies text is readily available in the excellent Brauner Petsch reprint No. 7. 8. 8a/b of the Haller Neudrucke. Then again the 16th century German is an effective stumbling-block to all those who are not experts in the field. And in the third place, the English version is the source of Marlowe's *Dr. Faustus*, which opens the series of Faust dramas. The English version, which is more an adaptation than a translation, is still close enough to the Spies text to give the student an adequate notion of the content." [500]

Hence, for scholars who elect to study the gradual development of the Faustian texts, yet are hindered by the German language, we observe new translations would be particularly useful. We will shortly examine the 1592 English adaptation. Henry Jones announced his forthcoming translation of Spies' work,[**] which he planned to entitle *The German and English Faust-books: Parallel Texts,* however, published *The English Faust Book: A Critical Edition [...]* (1994) in its place.[√] We have selected this work to continue our analysis.

The Faustian Legend in England and the First English *Faustbooks*

The earliest surviving reference to Faustian lore in the British Isles is an excerpt in the 1572 English edition of Ludwig Lavater's *Von Gespänsten* (1569) translated by an anonymous 'R. H.':

> "There are also conjurers founde even at this day, who bragge of themselves that they can so by inchauntments saddle an horse, that in a

---

[500] *Sources of the Faust Tradition*, p. 132.

[**] i.e. in *Faustus and the Censor*.

[√] Henry Jones explains: "In my edition of William Empson's *Faustus and the Censor*, [...] I promised as forthcoming a parallel-text edition of the German and English Faust books in which the EFB would have been printed in parallel with an exact translation of the German Faust Book of 1587. In the event, this proved too ambitious a publication project. However, its main aims are met by the present edition which clearly indicates which parts of the EFB text deviate substantially from the German and supplies exact translations of the German passages excluded, thus managing to convey the contents of both works." (*The English Faust Book; A Critical Edition*, p. ix.)

fewe houres they will dispatch a very long journey. God at the last will chasten these men with deserved punishment. What straunge things are reported of one Faustus a German, which he did in these our dayes by inchauntments?"[501]

In 1588–1589, an entry was recorded in the Stationers' Registers dated February 28, with the following description: "A ballad of the life and deathe of Doctor Ffaustus the great Cunngerer. Allowed under the hand of the Bishop of London."[502] Unfortunately, the original ballad did not survive into posterity.

The English scholar and poet, Gabriel Harvey (1550?–1631), later used the name Faustus in his sarcastic, unpublished[503] reply to John Lyly's article *Pappe With An Hatchet*:

An Aduertisement for Papp-hatchett (Harvey, November 5, 1589)

"As for that new-created Spirite, [i.e. Harvey] whom double U. [i.e. Lyly] like an other Doctour Faustus, threateneth to coniure-upp at leisure, (for I must returne to the terrible creature, that subcribeth himself Martins Double U. and will needs also by my Tittle-tittle) were that Spirite disposed to appear in his former likenesse, and to put the Necromancer to his purgation, he could peraduenture make the coniuring wizard forsake the center of his Circle."[504]

In 1590, a passing reference to Faustian literature was published in Henry Holland's *A Treatise Against Witchcraft* (Cambridge). In one particular discussion, two narrators, Theophilus and Mysodaemon, discuss the alleged power granted to witches:

"[…] I will not deny, Mysodaemon, but the devil may delude his witches many ways in these transportations, & that many fabulous pamphlets* are published, which give little light and less proof unto this point in controversy. […]

* Faustus. Druken Dunstan. art. & in p. 156."[505]

Although this brief footnote appears insignificant, it has become a vital clue in determining when English translations of the Spies *Faustbooks* first appeared. Paul Kocher argues this reference to Faustus "pamphlets" in Holland's *Treatise Against Witchcraft* actually

---

[501] *Damnable Life and Deserved Death of [...] Faustus*, p. 42.
[502] Ibid.
[503] Paul H. Kocher, 'The English *Faust Book* and the Date of Marlowe's *Faustus*,' *Modern Language Notes* 55 (February, 1940): p. 100.
[504] Paul H. Kocher, 'The Early Date for Marlowe's Faustus,' *Modern Language Notes* 58 (November, 1943): p. 540.
[505] Kocher, 'The English *Faust Book* [...] Marlowe's *Faustus*' *ML N,* p. 96.

evinces the existence of another early English *Faustbook* for several reasons.[506] First, the term "pamphlets" in the Elizabethan era was often used in conjuction with sizeable prose narratives. Kocher explains this term "[...] was probably inapplicable to mere ballads, most of which were single sheet affairs. NED cites no instance of its being used to describe a ballad, nor does independent research uncover any such usage."[507] Therefore, this footnote is not a reference to the lost Faust ballad mentioned in the Stationer's registers, but indicates an extensive text. In addition, the pamphlets are described as 'published' works, which suggests this lost Faust text was not an early handwritten manuscript. Second, if Holland was referring to the German Spies editions, it is very probable he would have used a form of the German title, *Historia Von D. Johann Fausten [...]*, as "Faustus" is the name employed in all the English adaptations. Supporting this observation is the subsequent footnote with the title of "Drunken Dunstan" demonstrating that Holland was referring to English publications. Kocher also observes few educated Englishmen of this period could read German, hence it is likely Holland referred to an English edition. Kocher finally concludes: "We do not arrive at certainty through it, but it does make probable in my judgement, the existence of an edition of the English *Faust Book* at least as early as 1590."[508]

Kocher presents a theory that this lost early edition of the English *Faustbook* may be a publication from Cambridge circa 1589.[•] In the record of the Court of the Stationer's Company in London, Kocher discovered the following entry dated December 6, 1591:

> Cambridge /
> Alsoe at this Courte it was motioned/ that for quietnes to be established between the Uniu'sitie of Cambridge and theire Printers and this Companie for matters of pryntinge, and for the avoidinge of divers disorders and troubles alredie arisen and hereafter like to arise between the said Partyes about printinge / Yt might be Lawfull for the saide Uniu'sitye and printers of Cambridge for the space of one monnethe after the Retorne of everie ffrankford mart, to haue the choise of anie forayne Bookes cominge from the said marte, The same to be allowed to the saide Printers of Cambridge and by them to be printed /...[509]

Kocher initially observes from this excerpt that the printers in Cambridge obtained books from Frankfurt in Germany a considerable period before 1591, adding that it is possible they

---

− The earliest extant copy of an English translation is by the anonymous P.F. (London, 1592). However, the title page reads: "Newly imprinted, and in convenient places imperfect matter amended: [...]". Therefore, other English translations existed before this time.

[506] See Kocher, 'The English *Faust Book* [...] Marlowe's *Faustus*' MLN, for his full argument.

[507] 'The English *Faust Book* [...] Marlowe's *Faustus*' ML N, p. 97.

[508] Ibid. p. 98.

• Kocher first suggests in 'The English *Faust Book* [...] Marlowe's *Faustus*' MLN, p. 95 that the date could be 1590, but later changes his opinion to 1589 in 'The Early Date' MLN, p. 542.

[509] *Records of the Court of the Stationers' Company*, ed. W. W. Greg and E. Boswell (London, 1930), p. 39, in Kocher, 'The English *Faust Book* [...] Marlowe's *Faustus*' MLN, p. 99.

could have acquired one of the first German Spies *Faustbooks,* published in the same town. Kocher then refocuses his attention on Holland, the author of *A Treatise Against Witchcraft,* due to Holland's association with Cambridge:

> "Holland [...] was at this time in touch, probably quite close touch, with the Cambridge publishing trade: after taking his M.A. at the university in 1583 he was until 1592 vicar at Orwell, scarcely a dozen miles from Cambridge, and in 1590 he secured John Legatt, printer to the university, as a publisher of *A Treatise Against Witchcraft.* Holland could be expected to be well acquainted with Cambridge publications between 1587 and 1590; on the other hand, there is no indication that he went to London at this time or had special access to books brought out there."[510]

When considering Holland's reference to a certain Faustus publication in his *Treatise Against Witchcraft* and the above information, it is possible Holland encountered an English *Faustbook* during this period (1587–1590) at Cambridge. Kocher then continues to support this argument by examining Gabriel Harvey's brief allusions to Faustus. Kocher observes that Harvey "[...] lived and read there [Cambridge] during the period which interests us."[511] Of importance is his unpublished *Advertisement for Papp-hatchett* (November 5, 1589) that was written at Trinity Hall. This "advertisement" could refer to the lost Faust ballad of 1589, but Kocher dismisses this theory in favour of a lost English *Faustbook,* a conclusion he formed when considering other evidence. Harvey was accustomed to writing considerable annotations in his books; Hale Moore discovered that in one of these annotated volumes, (a 1539 translation of Frontinus' *Strategematicon*), Harvey wrote the following marginalia sometime between 1589–1591:

> "[...] If Doctor Faustus could rear Castles, & arm Devils at pleasure: what wonderful, & monstrous exploits, might be achieved by such terrible means."[512]

Similar magic feats are also mentioned in the Wolfenbüttle MS and the German Spies *Faustbook*, however, Kocher emphasises that Harvey could not read German, thus there is a strong possibility he was referring to an earlier English *Faustbook*.[513] Kocher adds that this detail of Faust's various powers is also included in chapters XL and LII in the extant 1592 English *Faustbook* translated by P.F..[514]

Of interest, the famous Elizabethan playwright, Christopher Marlowe (1564-1593), author of *The Tragical History of Doctor Faustus* (1588?–1589?) also attended Cambridge where he

[510] 'The English *Faust Book* [...] Marlowe's *Faustus' MLN,* p. 99.
[511] Ibid. p. 100.
[512] Hale Moore, 'Gabriel Harvey's References to Marlowe,' *SP.,* XXIII (1926), 337–57, in 'The English *Faust Book* [...] Marlowe's *Faustus' MLN,* p. 99.
[513] 'The Early Date [...] *MLN,* p. 541.
[514] 'The English *Faust Book* [...] Marlowe's *Faustus' MLN,* p. 100.

received his M.A. in 1587. Scholars have argued that these allusions to Faustus by Holland and Harvey are actually references to Marlowe's tragedy, and not to an early English *Faustbook*. However, there are strong contra-arguments to this theory, primarily, that Holland mentions published "pamphlets", i.e. a sizable prose publication, and not a play. Although Kocher explains that it is not known if Harvey attended a production of Marlowe's work, he states "[...] no such visit [made by Harvey to a London playhouse to view it] is recorded and on the whole Harvey does not seem to have been much of a playgoer."[515] In addition, Harvey's marginalia referring to magical castles and devil warriors points to two details existing in the extant English *Faustbook*, while this facet may have been appended to Marlowe's play after his death.[516] Kocher concludes Marlowe probably maintained certain ties with Cambridge after the year 1587, and either his friends there introduced him to this lost *Faustbook*, or he encountered a copy during an occasional visit to the town of his *alma mater*.[517] This is not an illogical theory as we may presume a printed source of some description would have first inspired Marlowe. Hence, there is strong evidence suggesting this lost English *Faustbook* was published circa 1589 at Cambridge.

Kocher then posits that this lost Cambridge *Faustbook* may be an earlier edition of the text translated by the anonymous P.F. *Gent.* (i.e. Gentleman) and "newly imprinted" in London (1592). We notice on the title page of the London edition the words "[...] according to the true Copie printed at Franckfort, and translated into English by P.F. Gent." The "and" is of significance and indicates a conflation of both the Spies edition and P.F.'s lost work: if the translation was completed specifically for the 1592 printing, it is probable the imprint concerning the translator would have commenced as a separate statement without this conjunction. Turning to the extant 1592 London *Faustbook*, we discover that P.F. actually translated the text within the same timeframe that the lost *Faustbook* is thought to have appeared in public. This information is gleaned from the sentence referring to the 'Julius Cæsar' obelisk at the Vatican, which Faust admires during his visit to Rome:

> "[...] he visited the Church yard of S. Peter's, where he saw the Pyramid that Julius Cæsar brought out of Africa: it stood in Faustus his time leaning against the Church wall of Saint Peter's, but now Papa Sixtus hath erected it in the middle of S. Peter's Church yard; [...]"[518]

This was the only ancient obelisk in Rome that was not razed to the ground by the ravages of war and pillaging; however, on April 30, 1586 it was removed by order of Pope Sixtus V from its former site near the sacristy of St. Peter's basilica, and resettled in a new position in Rome on September 10th.[519] As the sentence referring to the pope is in the present tense, (Pope Sixtus died

[515] 'The Early Date [...]' *MLN*, p. 541.
[516] F. S. Boas edition of Marlowe's *Fasutus* (London, 1932), pp. 9–10, in 'The English *Faust Book* [...] Marlowe's *Faustus' MLN*, p. 100.
[517] 'The English *Faust Book* [...] Marlowe's *Faustus' MLN*, p. 100.
[518] *Damnable Life and Deserved Death of [...] Faustus*, p. 124.
[519] Sarah Morehouse Beach, 'The "Julius Cæsar Obelisk" in the *English Faust Book* and Elsewhere,' *Modern Language Notes* 35 (January, 1920): pp. 27–28.

on August 27, 1590), the precursor text of the London *Faustbook* was translated sometime between 1587 and August 1590.

Next, it must be established if P.F. was possibly a temporary resident of Cambridge. It is possible he may have received his degrees there, Empson has brought to our attention that the title "Gent." implies Mr. P.F. had at least attained his B.A. by the time he completed his translation.[520] Second, few Elizabethans were familiar with German, however, it would appear this was not the case with the scholastic circles of Cambridge as books from the Frankfurt mart were in great demand by both the University and the printers of that locality. Kocher discovered a certain individual by the name Peter Frenche who received his B.A. (1582) and M.A. (1585) degrees from Magdalene College, Cambridge.[521] Of interest, Holland received his B.A. from the same college in 1580 two years before Mr. Frenche, and it is a possibility that they became acquainted. Is this the mysterious P.F. *Gent.*? Kocher concludes:

> "One may remark that P.F.'s being a Cambridge man, quite possibly acquainted with Marlowe, Holland and Harvey, would help to explain why the attention of these three was attracted by the English *Faust Book*."[522]

The Continuing Quest for Mr. P. F., *Gentleman*

We have presented Kocher's theory as one of the more convincing arguments for our study to this point,[□] however, scholars continue to speculate upon the identity of P.F.. Concentrating on other possibilities for discovering the identity of "P.F.", Henry Jones lists several students with the same initials who enrolled at Oxford University and Cambridge, any one of these individuals could also be the mysterious translator.[523]

However, in other studies it is argued that the initials P.F. remain suspect as later editions of the English *Faustbook* contain contradicting information: the 1608 printing reads "P.R. Gent.", and the 1648 edition states "P.K. Gent." [524] Although assumed to be misprints, Henry Jones first reminds us these variants "[...] undermine the security of our knowledge."[525] Jones then continues:

---

[520] *Faustus and the Censor*, p. 73.

[521] 'The English *Faust Book* [...] Marlowe's *Faustus' MLN*, p. 101.

[522] Ibid.

[□] Henry Jones observes there were numerous students with initials that configure with 'P.F.' who matriculated at Cambridge, (see *The English Faust Book; A Critical Edition*, pp.79-80), yet their dates of matriculation and graduation do not align as neatly with Kocher's observation concerning Harvey, Holland and Peter Frenche.

[523] *The English Faust Book; A Critical Edition*, pp. 79–80.

[524] *Faustus and the Censor*, p. 200.

[525] Ibid.

"Neil Brough^Φ has drawn attention to an 'R.F. Gent.' who appears as translator of Friedrich Dedekind's *Grobianus*, and has aired his possible identity with 'P.F.'. Latin and German editions of this work, [*Grobianus*], originally published in 1549, were printed in Frankfurt in 1584 and 1586 respectively and certainly the place and dates are suggestive."

In his subsequent research, Henry Jones amends this information, when he discovered that *all early editions* of the English Faust book contain the initials "P.F.", and were changed to "P.P." in the 1622 edition, and finally to "P.R." in 1636, an alteration that was retained through all the seventeenth-century reprinting and was originally mistaken as "P.K.".[526] In light of this research, Henry Jones concludes the translator of the *Grobianus* seems an unlikely candidate as the mysterious P.F..[527]

Empson, however, composed a highly speculative profile of Mr. P.F.. He writes P.F. could be the son of a London business man who entertained aspirations for him to enter the family firm and learn German in an effort to expand the business. On graduating from college, P.F. was promptly employed in their trading business and dispatched to Germany, but proved not to be too successful and accomplished his duties grudgingly. Empson then speculated Mr. P.F. found employment in the English spy network as a translator, but this too was an unsuccessful endeavour. Finally, he returned home and settled to work for the family firm after 1588, occasionally accepting work as a translator for printers despite the dire wage.[528]

Whether he attended the university at Cambridge, or Oxford, this scenario might be remarkably accurate, at least where acrimonious family relations are concerned. In the text, we notice an alteration from the original Spies' book pertaining to Faust's upbringing where P.F. 'translated' the following ...

> "[…] his father a poor husbandman, and not able well to bring him up: but having an uncle at Wittenberg, a rich man, and without issue, took this Faustus **from his father** and made him his heir, **insomuch that his father was no more troubled with him,** for he remained with his uncle at Wittenberg, where he was kept at the university in the same city to study divinity. But Faustus **being of naughty mind and otherwise addicted,** applied not his studies, but took himself to other exercises: **the which his uncle oftentimes hearing, rebuked him for it, as Eli ofttimes rebuked his children for sinning against the Lord; even so this good man laboured to have Faustus apply his study of divinity that he might come to the knowledge of God and his laws.**"[529] (P.F. omits the passage exonerating Faust's parents from any

Φ ('Doctor Faustus and "P. F."', *Notes & Queries*, NS.32 (1985), no. 1 pp. 15f)
526 *The English Faust Book; A Critical Edition*, p. 30.
527 Ibid. n. 111, p. 79.
528 *Faustus and the Censor*, pp. 74, 200.
529 *The English Faust Book; A Critical Edition*, pp. 91–92.

blame for his evil inclinations, which is included in Spies. The bold font indicates P.F.'s additions.)

We detect from P.F.'s alterations he may not have enjoyed a close relationship with his father, perhaps they had a serious altercation that caused P.F. to leave his father's house and take up residence with a kinsman. We note a particular bitter tone in the phrase, "insomuch that his father was no more troubled with him". In addition, by omitting the section exonerating Faust's parents, P.F. may be displaying his resentment towards his own parents. Similar to Faust, it would seem P.F. was not content with the career mapped out for him by his kinsman, yearning to set a completely different course for his future, he became rebellious, accounting for the abovementioned rebukes that Faust receives from his uncle for not following the laws of God. It is probable P.F. observed a parallel between his life and the character of Faust, namely, his desire for independence to study subjects that were of interest to him, i.e. the occult. Apparently, P.F. studied magic clandestinely for we discover these additions a few sentences later: "Faustus […] gave himself **secretly** to study necromancy and conjuration, **insomuch that few or none could perceive his profession**."[530] P.F. replaced the following material from Spies with the word "secretly": "[…] it was common knowledge that he [Faust] was dabbling in magic", while the remainder of the sentence is P.F.'s own addition.[531] This profound interest in the magic arts is plainly manifest with his radical alteration of Faust's disputation on astronomy in Chapter Eighteen. P.F. included an ecstatic speech for Mephostophiles wherein the devil exhorts Faust to "learn of me" regarding the motions of the planets and the hidden properties of nature, promising he would also reveal where to find hidden treasure, and to accomplish magic feats the like of which the world has never previously witnessed. Perhaps the most radical alteration is P.F.'s adamant support of the Copernican system during Faust's journey to the heavens, suggesting that he was not the dutiful conformist he was expected to be, particularly with regards to his studies in divinity as this new theory challenged the theologically accepted Ptolemaic system. This continual paralleling with Faust is also evident in his journey through Europe. P.F. inserted considerable material to this section that insinuates this new data was acquired from personal experience. More than likely, he was required to take a cultural proto-Grand Tour of the continent to augment his education, hence his kinsman was obviously affluent similar to Faust's relative as mentioned in the text. In sum, Empson's scenario may be partially correct. P.F. was possibly a member of a wealthy, influential family from the upper-middle classes, and unfortunately did not have a close relationship with his father, whereby he was eventually fostered by a relative. The fact P.F. learned German is unusual for the Elizabethan period, and as Empson proposes, P.F. was obliged to learn this language to benefit the family firm. Apparently, this relative spared no expense to have him educated, sending him on a tour of Europe to enhance his education and refinement; however, P.F. may have proved to be a rebellious youth, and as the text suggests, secretly studied the occult subjects that commanded his interest, yearning to achieve a measure of importance in the world and carve out his own niche. This scenario would not be out of place if the anonymous translator was a student from Cambridge.

---

[530] Ibid. p. 92.
[531] Ibid. nn. 36, 37, p. 187.

Henry Jones, in contrast, recently presented a new candidate for our consideration, a certain Paul Fairfax who claimed to be a gentleman and a physician. Reportedly, he developed certain questionable cures, however he was decried as a dangerous unlicensed practitioner of medicine by the Royal College of Physicians. According to the Annals of the Royal College, the governing council discussed his case on September 30, 1588 as recorded:

> "Paul Fairfax of London, a travelled man, gave out in the market places pamphlets full of arrogance and ostentation describing the admirable properties of a water which he called his 'Aqua Coelestis', with which he had cheated the people of their money. He confessed that he had practised medicine in London for four months: and that he had cured the son of Mr Treen of Southwark, suffering from dropsy, also the daughter of Mr Spagman, afflicted with a pain in the head and many more others by this distilled water and other divers potions and pills.
>
> It was decided that for his previous practise he should pay five pounds to the College as a fine: and give his bond that he would not practise medicine in the future. If he refused or did otherwise, he would be imprisoned."[532]

Sir Francis Walsingham wrote to the College on behalf of Mr. Fairfax requesting they reconsider their decision in light of the cures he performed, however, he received the following reply, his lordship was duly misinformed and Fairfax was a public menace due to his ignorance in the practise of medicine.[533] Having arrived at one impasse, it would seem Mr. Fairfax subsequently appealed to Sir Henry Carey, the Lord Chamberlain, to write on his behalf, however the following answer was prepared and approved by the College at a Council meeting (December 23, 1588):

> "Right honourable and our very good Lord, having received a letter from your Lord in the behalf of one Paul Fairfax for the liberty of his practise in physic here in London: and understanding by the contents of the same that your honour hath been misinformed as well of the quality of the man as also of our dealings towards him: we most humbly beseech your good Lord to accept of our answer which we here present in most dutiful wise. Touching the man, albeit by some travel he seemeth to have gotten some kinds of language and therewithal hath boldly put himself into some empirical practise, most dangerous in truth to the patient than in any wise commendable to the practitioner: yet, upon just examination, we find the man very weak in the substance of all kinds of good learning and rather to be pitied for his fantastical conceits, and well weening of his own ignorance, than in any wise to deserve toleration in so dangerous a function: a man never trained up in any good school of learning, ignorant

---

[532] 'Annals of the Royal College of Physicians', London (MS: II. Fol. 69a), in ibid. p. 31.
[533] *The English Faust Book; A Critical Edition*, p. 32.

in the very principals of the art; and for lack of other good matter, furnished with certain ridiculous terms and childish phrases, invented only to entertain the simple hearer and to delude the unlearned multitude withal.

And whereas he layeth some challenge to a doctorship, he hath indeed showed unto us his letters testimonial for the same. Yet we, being better acquainted with the course of universities better than he, have a better opinion of Frankfurt than to think that, wittingly and willingly, they would commit so foul an error as to admit either him or the like. And having made good survey of the letters, find by evident proof that they are vehemently to be suspected, to have been rather by sinister means devised, than by any ordinary course obtained. [...]

For being a gentleman, as he himself sayeth, and having so good acquaintance, as he protested: being offered to be set at liberty if he would have put in but any one sufficient surety (a matter of great ease for him to us, if the rest of his talk had been to be credited), he, as one rather contemning us and our friendly dealing, more upon stomach than discretion, made choice of imprisonment. [...]"[534]

Henry Jones thus concludes his findings with the following analysis: we have a candidate who used the initials 'P.F.' and claimed to be a 'gentleman', who was present in London during 1588. He had influential friends, was a 'travelled man' and boasted of having some skill in languages, further claiming he attained a doctoral degree at Frankfurt, which indicated he could understand German. Jones notes the only university that possessed a medical faculty in the two Frankfurts was the city on the Oder, however, Jones did not discover any record of a 'Paul Fairfax' in the matriculation files of that particular university, which supports the Royal College's suspicions he had not obtained a valid medical degree. Jones further writes:

"[...] But what is impressive about Fairfax in relation to PF is his arrogant self-assurance and self esteem, his 'fantastical conceits' and his 'well-weening of his ignorance', i.e. thinking highly of his (superficial) knowledge. The letter reads much like the early, contemptuous reports of the historical Faustus by Humanists such as Trithemius and Mutianus; here was Fairfax behaving just like Faustus, advertising his 'waters' and cures and wandering from one locality to another. Such persons were anathema to the RCP [...]; the qualities grudgingly admitted in the (exceptionally long) letter must therefore be granted extra weight: this is no illiterate, common peddler, but a proud man capable of putting a good case to Sir Henry Carey. Until, hopefully, more is discovered,[#] the case for identifying Paul Fairfax with PF remains slender, but what is revealed by Fairfax's single emergence into

---

[534] *Annals of the Royal College of Physicians, London*, transcript II., pp. 55f (MS: II. Fol. 70b–71a), in ibid, p. 32.

the spot-light is highly suggestive and he must be considered the most promising candidate to date for the authorship of the English Faust Book. [...].[535]

This analysis of Paul Fairfax is not at variance with our proposed hypothesis concerning P.F.'s upbringing. If P.F. was a rebellious, arrogant youth who elected to secretly study the subjects that were of paramount interest to him, Henry Jones' observations concerning Fairfax as a conceited, self-proclaimed man of learning is remarkably accurate. We observe in the text P.F. omitted that Faust publicly claimed the title "Doctor of Medicine", and inserted the information Faust referred to his accomplishments in the following terms: "for a shadow [i.e. as a front], **sometimes a physician, and did great cures**, namely, with herbs, roots, waters, drinks, receipts and clysters."[536] This also bears a striking resemblance to Fairfax's career and his claim to having cured several people with his alchemical Aqua Vitae, or "Water from Heaven". Hence, Henry Jones proposes that if Paul Fairfax was travelling through Eastern Europe prior to 1588, he had the opportunity to acquire a copy of Spies' *Faustbook*, which he subsequently translated and printed. We therefore have a promising second candidate, Paul Fairfax, who autocratically declared he was a man of breeding who practised medicine illicitly.

The 1592 Orwin Edition of the English Faustbook

The earliest extant English *Faustbook* was printed in London by Thomas Orwin, and is the most popular edition with Faust scholars.[*] This edition is fascinating for its exceptional design, setting it apart from all subsequent publications of that era. It contains unique page breaks, is the only paginated English text, and the sole publication that features a table of contents.[537] Henry Jones notes the Orwin text is "well set and cleanly printed" with extra spacing in the chapter headings that significantly enhances the overall appearance of the layout.[538] The

---

[≠] Henry Jones states in a footnote all attempts to uncover more information concerning Paul Fairfax have proved unsuccessful, and proceeds to list the archives and sources searched. Additionally, he identifies the various patients Fairfax claimed to have cured. See *The English Faust Book; A Critical Edition*, n. 120, pp. 80–81.

[535] *The English Faust Book; A Critical Edition*, pp. 33–34.

[536] Ibid. pp. 93, 187.

[*] Early in the last century, a signature English *Faustbook* sheet, the Shrewsbury Fragment, was discovered during rebinding work in the Shrewsbury school library. It had been mistakenly collated with Orwin's edition in *A Short-Title Catalogue*, however, Henry Jones presents evidence it was printed c. 1592 by Edward Allde judging from the printer's device. However, it is unknown whether this version was ever competed or published. See *The English Faust Book; A Critical Edition* for Henry Jones' full analysis of this text.

[537] *The English Faust Book; A Critical Edition*, p. 35. Scholars argued that Orwin's edition was based on a paginated precursor. See Appendix Six; 'Evidence of a Paginated Precursor to Orwin's 1592 *Faustbook*' for more details.

[538] Ibid. pp. 35, 38.

measurement format is slightly different as the lines are 103 mm in length, compared with that of the Windet 1608 printing, which are 102 mm. Orwin also used considerably fewer contractions, unlike Windet and the Allde 1610 edition. One feature that may disclose Orwins' fortunes had changed for the better, the astrological symbols are correctly printed in the sections narrating Faust's discussions of the cosmos. Henry Jones states these font omissions in the latter texts "[…] appear to be due to an inadequate fount for astrological signs,"[539] or, perhaps the latter books were printed on older presses that were missing a few pieces of movable type. Orwin's press had been seized[540] by the Stationers' Company the previous year (1591), and he obviously acquired a new press by 1592 judging from the complete astrological type present in his text. Moreover, this edition does not contain the three major line omissions, one of which is a double line error, that are present in the 1608 Windet and 1610 Allde texts.[541] In all, we suspect this particular book, according to modern terms, was designed as a special collector's edition considering the time and effort Orwin expended on its presentation.[542] The title page reads as follows:

The
Historie
of the damnable
life, and deserved death of
Doctor Iohn Faustus,

Newly imprinted, and in convenient places imperfect matter amended:
according to the true Copie printed
at Franckfort, and translated into
English by P. F. Gent.

Seene and allowed.

Imprinted at London by Thomis Orwin, and are to be
solde by Edward White, dwelling at the little North
doore of Paules, at the signe of the Gun. 1592.

---

[539] Ibid. p. 38. Windet printed, "Jupiter Jupiter, Mars, Sun, Venus, Mercury & Moon" — we surmise he was missing the type for Saturn, had planned to compensate by printing the first "Jupiter" upside-down, yet actually printed it right side up thus negating his improvisation. This error was transcribed into the 1610 Allde edition. Ibid. p. 39.

[540] *Faustus and the Censor*, p. 203.

[541] Henry Jones argues these omissions suggest there were at least two precursors to the 1608 and 1610 editions that are now lost. For his complete analysis, see *The English Faust Book; A Critical Edition*, pp. 34–52.

[542] Did Jeffes and Orwin prepare this book for the new release of Marlowe's drama (the B Text) for May / June of 1592? See Chapter 3: 'Christopher Marlowe and Faustus: "That Which Nourishes Me Destroys Me"', and also Appendix Eight: 'The Earliest English *Faustbook* Editions: Lost and Extant.'

Immediately, scholars recognise this work is an inaccurate version of the German original. Palmer and More state that:

> "As a translation it is no better and no worse than other contemporary work, true to the cavalier custom of the Elizabethan translator in using his original. [...] the translator [...] omitted some of the uninteresting matter in Spies, elaborated or condensed at will, and added a number of descriptions and anecdotes, particularly in that part of the text which deals with Faust's travels."[543]

Henry Jones, however, asserts that P.F.'s translation is far from careless, bringing to our attention that his imprecise translation did not detract from the work, but actually enhanced it:

> "PF's translation is by no means exact. Like other Elizabethan translators, he felt free, even impelled, to improve on the original and tailor it to his own design in a manner which would be unthinkable today. But his handling is rarely cavalier; his paraphrasings show a concern for the intention of the source text and, apart from a few clear mistranslations, all his amendments are deliberate. [...] PF possessed three qualities notably lacking in the German author: a flair for pungent expression, a vivid visual imagination and a taste for ironic humour; in combination they served to exalt the humble Faust book to a work of considerable art."[544]

For the most part, the content of the London *Faustbook* retains the basic structure and plot development of the Wolfenbüttle Manuscript, a factor not entirely unexpected as the original German Spies *Faustbook* was adapted from a similar handwritten source. However, P.F.'s numerous alterations to Spies' original, as Henry Jones relates, transformed the book into a significantly polished piece of literature. Reiterating every minute editing completed by P.F. is not our intention, as this would press beyond the scope of this work, however, we can compare the significant changes in the text with our previous study.[∞]

---

[543] *Sources of the Faust Tradition*, p. 132.
[544] *The English Faust Book; A Critical Edition*, p. 12.
[∞] Henry Jones' new critical edition of the English *Faustbook* has been used for this study. Henry Jones edition highlights the innumerable additions and alterations P.F. made to Spies' work, and includes references and comparisons with the Wolfenbüttle text and also the latter English *Faustbooks* where appropriate. For our analysis of the London publication, the term "manuscript" refers to the Wolfenbüttle text, unless stated otherwise. **Bold text** indicates significant alterations / additions by P.F., brackets, [ ], indicate our own clarifications within the text.

Part One

Faust's early life and university education, as mentioned above, are slightly modified in the London book, in particular, the detail that his wealthy uncle who adopted him discovers his interest in the occult and reprimands him for his unchristian obsession, a new facet intended to display Faust's rebellious nature and his unwillingness from an early age to be led on the path of righteousness. The passage relating his growing interest in the occult is generally unchanged, except for the section where he publicly declared he was a "Doctor of Medicine", and the "devilish nature" of his newfound interests is accentuated:

> "For he accompanied himself with divers **that were seen** [i.e. those that were accomplished] **in those devilish arts, and** that had the Chaldean, Persian, Hebrew,[^] Arabian, and Greek tongues, using figures, characters, sooth-saying, witchcraft, enchantment, being delighted with their books, words, and names so well, that he studied day and night therein: insomuch that he could not abide to be called doctor of divinity, but waxed a worldly man, and named himself an astrologian, and a mathematician: and **for a shadow** [i.e. as a front to his occult practises] **sometimes a physician, and did great cures,** namely, with herbs, roots, waters, drinks, receipts, & clysters. [i.e. enemas]."[545]

Faust's conjuring in the Spessar Wald is almost identical to the manuscript, except the proceedings are not described as a "hoax", and Faust specifically calls for the spirit Mephostophiles in the name of Beelzebub; hence, there is a change of perception regarding the summoning of spirits.[a] In our study above, we observed the devil played a "hoax" in the Spessar Wald by feigning his unwillingness to appear, thus allowing Faust to believe, he could at will, control the devils and bid them to come and go at his command with his magic conjurations. Later, Mephostophiles reveals Faust never exerted control over them and was in fact snared by the devils through his interest in this alleged magic power. In the London version, when summoned, Mephostophiles appears to be held bound by Faust's conjurations that evinces particular emphasis is placed on the belief that special seals, i.e. magic circles, could actually control demons. Of importance, this passage is indicative of reverse borrowing from Marlowe's tragedy. In that play, Faust specifically calls for Mephostophiles in the name of Beelzebub. However, if P.F. added this detail, then Marlowe could not have used P.F.'s translation as his source, suggesting the existence of a separate, lost early English *Faustbook*.[546] However, it is possible a later publisher who attended Marlowe's tragedy added this unusual phrase. We also

---

[^] "Hebrew" included in Spies.

[545] *The English Faust Book; A Critical Edition*, pp. 92–93.

[a] Spies: same material; Faust did not call for any specific spirit.

[546] In Chapter 3 of this study, 'Christopher Marlowe and Faustus: "That Which Nourishes Me Destroys Me"', we propose that Marlowe first performed the A Text format of his drama in 1589, later revising it in 1592, which we recognise today as the B Text. As the lost early English translation is dated c. 1589, this corresponds with the drafting of the A Text.

observe P.F. restricts the shapes that the devil assumes, i.e. he discreetly excludes the griffin, which coincidentally is the symbol for the city of London. P.F. retains one parenthetical detail featured in Spies' book — Faust's boast that Satan became subject to him and that he could command him at his pleasure:

> **"Oftentimes** after to his companions he would boast, that he had the stoutest head (under the cope of heaven) [i.e. the greatest authority under heaven] at commandment: whereat they answered, they knew none stouter than the pope or emperor: but Doctor Faustus said: 'The head that is my servant is above all on earth,' and repeated certain words out of St. Paul to the Ephesians to make his argument good: The prince of this world [i.e. Satan] is upon earth and under heaven."[547]

Faust commands the spirit to return to his house the following day, and the scenario is almost identical to the early manuscript. However, one of the three demands[β] Faust presents to Mephostophiles is changed, the second demand, i.e. that any information Faust requires for his studies should not be withheld, has been changed to whatever object Faust desires it should be brought to him. There is now additional emphasis placed on the acquisition of worldly possessions in the London *Faustbook*, thus depicting Faust as ultimately deluded by the temporal luxuries of the world rather than noble aspirations to attain mystical enlightenment as first presented in the manuscript. Mephostophiles' initial refusal of these terms and his explanation that he must follow the government of the Abyss remains intact, although all the devils are now described as "Oriental princes" hence this title is not solely reserved for Lucifer here, which Henry Jones therefore concludes to be a mistranslation. Faustus is disconcerted he must sell his soul, but in the London edition he was nevertheless "[...] **resolved in himself, rather than to want his pleasure, to do whatsoever the spirit and his lord should condition upon.**"[548] He waits for the appointed time when Mephostophiles is expected to reappear without stirring from his position due to his "[...] **fervent love to the devil.**"[549]

Finally, Mephostophiles returns in the evening, and we encounter an unusual variance from Haile's edition. The spirit returns with his answer stating that his demands would be granted if he agreed to sign body and soul directly over to him. However, Mephostophiles utters a bizarre statement: "[...] this answer I bring thee, and an answer must thou make by me again, yet will I hear what is thy desire, because thou hast sworn me to be here at this time." This identical statement is featured in Spies' edition. Henry Jones observes this could be a conflation with an additional Faust text as the spirit already knew Faust's demands.[550] Obviously, Mephostophiles' remark is a separate addition made by a scribe who held the opinion Faust should reconsider his requests while he still had the opportunity! Faust declares he desires

---

[547] *The English Faust Book; A Critical Edition*, p. 94.
[β] Spies, Ch. 3 lists the same three conditions as in Haile's Wolfenbüttle edition.
[548] *The English Faust Book; A Critical Edition*, p. 96.
[549] Ibid.
[550] *Faustus and the Censor*, p. 16.

nothing more than to become a devil, or at least one of his limbs, and presents his revised demands to the spirit, which now number five˜ in all:

1. That he might be a Spirit in shape and quality.
2. That Mephostophiles should be his servant, and at his commandment.
3. That Mephostophiles should bring him any thing, and do for him whatsoever.
4. That at all times he should be in his house, invisible to all men, except only to himself, and at his commandment show himself.
5. Lastly, that Mephostophiles should at all times appear at his command, in what form or shape soever he would.

When we consider that Haile's edition of the Wolfenbüttle MS is a hypothetical reconstruction of the original Latin text,ˣ we discover this alteration featuring Faust's revised demands present in the Spies and the London *Faustbooks* depicts him as an overtly demonic individual, rather than the previous foolish, speculative theologian in the manuscript who allowed the evil one to snare him. Notice that in the manuscript, Mephostophiles originally offers the powers of bilocation, i.e. a "spirit's form and powers", as an additional bonus to persuade Faust and finalise the contract, while Faust now burns with eagerness to become a demon, or a demonic human, and initially demands to be granted these powers. We also observe Faust now places more importance on the conditions of Mephostophiles' service to him, and has entirely forgotten his request that the spirit answer truthfully to all his disputations and interrogations. The craving for worldly pleasures that the devil can procure now overshadows the desire for mystical and philosophical knowledge. We notice this slight change in the texts regarding Faust's character and his motives for engaging the devil's service has eliminated many of the subtle, yet engrossing, theological and philosophical inferences contained within the early manuscript.

Mephostophiles now stipulates five conditions in response to Faust's demands:

First, that Doctor Faustus should give himself to his Lord Lucifer, body and soul.∞

Secondly, for confirmation of the same, he should make him a writing, written with his own blood.

Thirdly, that he would be an enemy to all Christian people.

Fourthly, that he would deny his Christian belief.

˜ Spies has six articles: Henry Jones states P.F. combined the 4th and 5th articles for his version of the 4th article, and that P.F.'s 5th article corresponds with the 6th in Spies. (*The English Faust Book*, nn. 185, 187, p. 191.)

ˣ Haile obviously recognised this section as a later addition due to Mephostophiles' odd, repetitive statement, and decided to cut Faust and Mephostophiles' new agreement.

∞ In Haile and Spies' editions, Faust would become the spirit's, i.e. Mephostophiles', property, not Lucifer's. (*Faustus and the Censor*, p. 17.)

> Fifthly, that he let not any man change his opinion, if so be any
> man should go about to dissuade, or withdraw him from it.[551]

Consequently, the demon has demanded two major conditions before granting Faust the powers of a spirit and condescending to become his servant, i.e. the forfeiting of his soul, and a contract in blood binding him to this agreement. The last three stipulations Mephostophiles' exacts, i.e. that Faust deny his Christian faith and become an enemy of Christendom, is an equal exchange for Faust's demands. If the spirit must become a human's servant, so then must Faust become a loyal servant of Satan in his hellish warfare opposing the kingdom of Heaven. Henry Jones notes the fifth article is a necessary inclusion as Faust actually allows himself to be persuaded by the Old Man to convert in Chapter Forty-eight, hence this provides a dramatic motive to introduce the necessity of the second pact.[552] This scenario varies from Haile's edition in which Mephostophiles repeatedly breaks the contract, now the emphasis of 'blame' is placed on Faust — he later realises he has broken his pact, yet rather than seize the opportunity to ultimately rescind their agreement, he proceeds to rewrite the contract, thus placing the responsibility of damnation solely upon his own head. Returning to the first contract, the demon did not declare Faust must choose a time-limit as part of his demands, but promises Faust that he would grant him a certain number of years where he would live in health and pleasure until the time came to claim him. This promise of health is unique to the London Book, Christopher Rick theorised that this element was included as an enticement for Faust, offering him a 'health policy' in an age that was constantly besieged by plague and pestilence.[553]

The following day, Faust calls the demon and states his desire to have his *familiar* spirit appear as a friar from that moment on, a detail that is also in the manuscript. We observe an alteration in the London version, that is, Faust requests the name of the spirit, and receives the reply "[…] my name is **as thou sayest**, Mephostophiles […]"; now a necessary adjustment to the text as Faust actually summoned the spirit by name during his conjuring in the forest. Faust also wishes to learn what manner of devil the spirit is, and Mephostophiles replies he is a flying prince that rules the entire circuit of the heavens from Septentrio (north) to the meridian (i.e. the south, not the Prime Meridian), but is subservient to Lucifer, information that feeds Faust's pride for he now marvels at his "good fortune" in commanding so great a spirit.[554] This addition by P.F. to Mephostophiles' status suggests he is now an arch-demon promoted from his position in the early manuscript as a lost cherub under the command of Belial; as Faust summoned him by the power of Beelzebub, he is now a lost seraph-prince of the first choir commanded by the Lord of Flies.

The drafting of the contract has changed little from the manuscript, except Faust adds a new conclusion: "And to the more strengthening of this writing, I have written it with mine own hand and blood, being in perfect memory, and hereupon I subscribe to it with my name and title, **calling all the infernal, middle, and supreme powers to witness of this my Letter and subscription.**" This dramatic touch includes the realm of the nature spirits, i.e. goblins, nymphs,

---

[551] *The English Faust Book; A Critical Edition*, p. 97.
[552] Ibid. n. 198f , p. 191.
[553] Christopher Ricks, 'Doctor Faustus and Hell on Earth', *Essays in Criticism* 35 (1985), pp.101–20, in ibid. n. 200f , p. 191.
[554] *The English Faust Book; A Critical Edition*, p. 97.

salamanders, together with the demons of Hell, to stand as witnesses to the compact. There is also an additional chapter, i.e. Chapter Seven, featuring Mephostophiles' arrival to claim a second written copy.[Φ] Until he can grasp his personal copy in his claw, the deal is not closed, and Faust takes advantage of this grace period to contemplate all the marvels Mephostophiles is prepared to offer as further proof of the powers of Hell before making the pact official. The demon amuses him with a series of preternatural allegories; Faust hears the sound of a great hunt approaching and suddenly a giant hart is chased into the hall, which is then killed by the phantom huntsmen. He witnesses a great battle between a lion and a dragon, but the lion is overcome, and the scene vanishes. Next, a large peacock enters the room fanning his majestic tail at a peahen, the peacock beats his mate unmercifully with its tail and they disappear. Faust is alarmed to discover a fierce bull rampaging straight for him, but he too vanishes. A great ape approaches next and offers him his paw, but Faust refuses to stretch forth his hand and the creature runs away. A great mist descends, and when it lifts, Faust discovers two giant sacks, one filled with silver, the other with gold. Finally, he is spellbound by the most beautiful music he ever heard played on all manner of instruments.[**] Faust at last exclaims: "[…] thou hast done me a wonderful pleasure in showing me this pastime, if thou continue as thou hast begin, **thou shalt win my heart and my soul, yea and have it**."[555] Mephostophiles promises this vision was nothing compared to the wonders he could show him if he agreed to hand over his copy of the contract. Faust agrees, the transaction is completed.

Immediately we notice this section configures with Faust's alleged journey to Hell in Part Two of the manuscript where we first observed various animals that symbolically represented the mystical battle waged between Good and Evil for Faust's immortal soul. Haile possibly eliminated this preternatural demonstration preceding the completion of the contract due to the recurrence of this material later in the MS during Faust's journey to Hell. At this point in the London edition, we discover how the devil displays his subjective, false view of eternity, that evil will prevail over good, to finally convince Faust he is making the correct choice in becoming a willing subject of Satan. The entrance of the various creatures and their significance are changed, and those representing the theological Absolute of 'good' are actually slain. Faust sees a hart, the symbol of Christ, but it is killed by demon huntsmen, contrasting with the vision of Hell in the early manuscript where the hart actually survives and flees; evidently, this adaptation represents Satan's delusional conviction that he will eventually triumph over Christ. Next, the dragon conquers the lion; Faust is shown the fallacy that a life of vice is more profitable than a life of virtue. This is not the case in Haile's manuscript where the flying lions representing virtue and faith overcome the giant serpents symbolising lust and infidelity.

[Φ] Ch. 8 in Spies' edition.

[**] Organs, clarigolds [i.e. clavichords], lutes, citterns, waits, [i.e. wind instruments such as hautboys, or shawms], "anomes", harps, and "[…] all manner of other instruments." The "anomes" were not identified; Palmer and More believe this could be a misprint in the London *Faustbook*. However, we notice the 'anomes' are inserted between the flutes, a wind instrument section, and the harps, which are string instruments. It is possible the "anomes" are Aeolian harps, ancient string instruments that produced musical sounds by wind power. Compare "anomes" with the Greek word for wind, *anemos*.

[555] *The English Faust Book; A Critical Edition*, p. 100.

There are two new creatures introduced, a peacock and its mate, the symbolism of which requires further investigation. These animals may allude to the Greek myth of Io and Argus. Io, daughter of the river god Inachus, became the mistress of Zeus, Olympian monarch of all the gods. To protect Io from his jealous wife, Hera, the goddess of marriage, Zeus transformed Io into a white heifer to conceal her identity. Hera discovered the deceit and dispatched the giant Argus to guard the heifer, a plan that appeared foolproof for this giant possessed one hundred eyes that did not all close at one time, even when asleep. However, Zeus sent the messenger god, Hermes, to rescue Io. Hermes succeeded in lulling the giant into a deep sleep with enchanting music and he finally closed all his eyes, Hermes subsequently slew him. In other versions, Hermes bores Argus into a deep sleep by recounting monotonous tales. Hera transferred the eyes of Argus to the tail of the peacock, and it became her sacred animal. The story symbolises lustful infidelity, jealousy and strife within marriage. It is possible, the male peacock beating its mate into submission represents the violent authoritarian power the devil tempts men to exert over their spouses to destroy the sanctity of matrimony.

The concept of the old ape is reintroduced, one of the symbols of Satan, but he simply offers Faust his paw, and runs away when it is refused — a detail suggesting Faust, as yet, remains indecisive. Faust's hesitation at this point is interesting, until then, he had witnessed all the promises of power the devil would afford him, but as he did not accept the ape's paw, it would appear Faust was not attracted by this particular lure.

Continuing with the allegory in the London *Faustbook*, we learn what exactly appeals to him. A dark mist surrounds Faust, but as it clears, he discovers sacks of silver and gold, and is enthralled by beautiful music. Hence, Faust is persuaded not to fear the loss of the Eternal Light, for the Kingdom of Hell will provide for his every sensual passion well beyond the bounds of licit pleasures. With this last vision and the promise of more wondrous marvels to come, Mephostophiles finally wins Faust and he officially concludes the deal without further ado. The misguided theologian of the Wolfenbüttle manuscript, who believed he would acquire a spirit that would aid him in attaining the heights of mystical knowledge, but was unwittingly steered towards the pleasures of the world by the demonic trap of despair, has vanished. We now discover a man who ultimately sold his soul cheap for lucre, unrestrained luxury and the temporal vanities of the world.

The account of Faust's Epicurean lifestyle in the following chapters is almost identical to the manuscript. Mephostophiles steals all manner of costly provisions for the house to keep Faust and Wagner in luxury. However, there is no mention of Faust's annual allowance of several thousand Crowns.[=] The subsequent chapter[≤] where Faust announces he must have a wife is also virtually unchanged, except for three particular details. First, there is an extended description of Faust's disbelief in "God, Hell and the Devil" — he also "thought that the body and soul died together **and had quite forgotten divinity of the immortality of his soul but stood in his damnable heresy day and night**", a statement that is also in Spies' book, and embellished upon by P.F. Second, there is a sentence missing in the London edition, which Spies had included in his version. Rose writes; "The Devil endeavours to dissuade [Faust from marriage] by declaring that marriage is a divine institution, but Faust retorts that the monks and

---

[=] Faust's allowance is retained in Spies' edition, Ch. 9. (*Faustus and the Censor*, p. 18)
[≤] Ch. 10 in Spies.

nuns do not marry. This passage is lacking in the Wolfenbüttle MS."[556] Spies was a staunch supporter of Luther and his theology, and this may account for his decision to include this anti-religious remark, perhaps he was convinced Luther's contempt for the monastic orders, with their 'idolatrous worship' and their 'exaggerated' ideals of chastity, was not demonstrated sufficiently to his satisfaction in the original manuscript. However, P.F., or the printers, discreetly omitted this sentence. The next variation we discover in the London version is Mephostophiles' statement, Faust need not marry and break his compact as any woman he desires, *either living* or dead, can be brought to him. Hence, Faust is now presented with the opportunity to destroy the marriages of others if the devil is willing to bring him live conquests in addition to the demonic succubae.[▲]

From this section onwards, we encounter the various theological disputations Faust engages in with Mephostophiles. It is here we are faced with numerous variances in the arrangement of the text due to previous editorial endeavours. As mentioned, Haile condensed and eliminated several chapters in his new translation of the Wolfenbüttle text thus making a comparison of the manuscript with the printed books for English scholars particularly difficult. However, much of the content remains constant, the following table features the arrangement / content of Haile's edition compared with the London *Faustbook*:

London 1592 Faustbook: Chapters X–XVI. (Corresponding Chapters in Spies are XI–XVII.)	Wolfenbüttle Manuscript: Corresponding Chapters
X. Questions put forth by Doctor Faustus unto his Spirit Mephostophiles	IX. Doctor Faustus' Quæstio of His Spirit Mephostophiles (First paragraph only: this initial description of Lucifer's former glory not in Haile's edition.)
XI. How Doctor Faustus dreamed he had seen hell in his sleep, and how he questioned his Spirit of matters concerning hell, with the Spirit's answer	(This initial description of Lucifer's fall, and the substance of Hell condensed in Haile's edition in Ch. XI.)
XII. The second question put forth by Doctor Faustus to his spirit, what Kingdoms there were in hell, how many,	(Not in Haile's edition.)

---

[556] *Damnable Life and Deserved Death of [...] Faustus*, p. 28.
[▲] Mephostophiles promises to bring only succubae in Spies' edition, Ch. 10. (*Faustus and the Censor*, p. 19.)

and what were their rulers' names	
XIII. Another question put forth by Doctor Faustus to his Spirit concerning his Lord Lucifer, with the sorrow that Faustus afterwards fell into	X. A Disputatio Concerning the Prior State of the Banished Angels
XIV. Another disputation betwixt Doctor Faustus and his Spirit, of the power of the Devil, and of his envy to mankind	IX. (Remainder of chapter)
XV. How Doctor Faustus desired again of his spirit to know the secrets of and pains of Hell; and whether those damned Devils and their company might ever come into the favour of God again or not?	XI. A Disputatio Concerning Hell, How It Was Created and Fashioned; Concerning Also the Torments in Hell.
XVI. Another question put forth by Doctor Faustus to his Spirit Mephostophiles of his own estate	(Not in Haile's edition.)

As we have extensively studied the disputations presented by Haile, we need only examine those sections that differ or have been excluded.

In Chapter Ten of the London *Faustbook*, Faust is presented with a magic book by the demon, (here P.F. eliminates Spies' reference to the demon-concubine who has taken up residence with Faust and is also "entertained" by the book). Faust then enquires about the skills Mephostophiles possesses as he would like to know in what manner the spirit may serve him. The demon explains to his new master that he is a flying spirit and can move at the speed of thought.[√]　Faust then asks Mephostophiles the cause of Lucifer's fall from Heaven.[†]

[√]　Henry Jones states that in the Spies edition, Ch. 11, Mephostophiles relates he is a flying spirit, but also declares his realm is beneath the heavens, i.e. beneath the Ptolemaic sphere of the moon. (*Faustus and the Censor*, p. 19)

[†]　The original source used for this discourse on the angelic hierarchy was taken from Schedel's *Weltchronik*. Henry Jones writes, "There is evidence that the disputations as they are given in the Spies Faust-book have undergone considerable transposition in their transference from an earlier source. This would account for many of the non sequiturs: [...]" (*Faustus and the Censor*, p. 19.) P.F. has re-written this whole section; in Spies, this passage originally reads: "Such angels are called *Hierarchiae*, and they were three: the seraph, the cherub and the throne angel. The first prince ruled the office of the angels; the duty of the second is to govern, preserve and protect mankind; those of the third rank keep our devilish power in check. These are therefore called princes and powers. They are also called the angel of great

Mephostophiles answers that Lucifer was one of the seraphim and held the most superior position of all the angels, yet dared to aspire to the Throne of God and depose his Creator. As a consequence for this sin of pride, Lucifer was cast headlong down from Heaven into Hell. Now, when called by God to appear before the Heavenly Court, he may not approach the Throne as the archangel Raphael is permitted, nor the second degree of Heaven ruled by Michael and Gabriel, the "Angels of God's wonders", but must have his audience in the lowest choir. The demon concludes, "**And thus far Faustus, because thou art one of the beloved children of my Lord Lucifer, following and feeding thy mind in manner as he did his, I have shortly resolved thy request, and more I will do for thee at thy pleasure.**"[557]

In this version, the character of Mephostophiles is enhanced to reflect the powerful demon that he is, i.e. a flying spirit that reigns under the heavens. Lucifer's rank in Heaven is amended, in the manuscript, he was erroneously described as one of the cherubim, not a seraph. Of interest, Mr. P.F. decided to correct a theological error in the Spies *Faustbook* by accurately declaring Raphael a 'separate' angel who may approach the Throne, for Spies had erroneously stated that Lucifer was actually called 'Raphael' before the Fall.[558] Spies either made an honest blunder, as his source for this particular information on Lucifer remains unknown, or he intentionally included an error to highlight the demon's ingrained trait of mendacity. However, P.F.'s correction still deviates from the traditional order of the Heavenly hierarchy after the Fall, as St. Michael is recognised as the first Prince of the Angelic Hosts, St. Gabriel second, and St. Raphael third. We detect this confusion originates with Spies' decision to mention Raphael first, and Michael and Gabriel collectively at the conclusion of his statement on the angelic hierarchies *before the Fall*, which P.F. may have misinterpreted as stating there are two major angelic choirs, not three. (See the footnote below.) Finally, Mephostophiles declares he is willing to disclose to Faust this information as the scholar is one of Lucifer's beloved children, who of his own free will, is following the same path to perdition. At first, Faust conveniently ignores this revelation on his character, he simply thanks the spirit and retires for the night, thus displaying his innate evil inclinations to serve the powers of Darkness.

In Chapter Eleven, Faust dreams of Hell, but the experience leaves him uncertain with regards to its substance and location. He questions Mephostophiles on this subject who informs him Hell did not exist before the fall of Lucifer, "[…] but even then hell was ordained." It has no 'substance' but is a "**confused thing**": Mephostophiles relates it is a place without perceivable borders, yet, has a 'foundation' notwithstanding his ignorance of its whereabouts. Hell is recognised as a physical place, but simultaneously as a state of existence in perpetual darkness. Mephostophiles reveals:

> "[…] **for I tell thee, that before all elements were made, and the earth seen, the Spirit of God moved on the waters, and darkness was over all: but when God said let it be light, it was so at his word,**

---

works of wonder, the angel of the annunciation and the angel who cares for human expectations. So, Lucifer was one of these beautiful archangels and was called Raphael, the other two, Gabriel and Michael." (*The English Faust Book; A Critical Edition*, n. 415–31, p. 197.)

[557] *The English Faust Book; A Critical Edition*, pp. 103– 104.
[558] Ibid. n. 415–31, p. 197.

and the light was on God's right hand, and God praised the light. Judge thou further: God stood in the middle, the darkness was on his left hand, in the which my Lord was bound in chains until the day of Judgement: in this confused hell is nought to find but a filthy, sulphurish, fiery, stinking mist or fog. Further we devils know not what substance it is of, **but a confused thing. For as a bubble of water flieth before the wind, so doth hell before the breath of God."**[559]

Theologically, this description of hell is not entirely accurate. God made the spiritual heaven and the physical elements necessary for the Creation, also referred to as "earth", before Lucifer and his rebellious legions of angels fell into everlasting Darkness. The first two verses of Genesis read: "In the beginning God created heaven and earth, and the earth was void and empty, and darkness was upon the face of the deep; and the spirit of God moved over the waters." As water is mentioned, the four elements were already created at this point, although the world as we understand it was not yet fashioned. However, the remainder of Mephostophiles' speech is credible. When the rebellious legions fell, Hell was then prepared for them, a place of punishment God did not intend to exist in His Creation, but nevertheless was preordained or existed in the Eternal Thought as God knew what would come to pass. However, the remainder of Mephostophiles' dialogue regarding the separation of light and darkness with reference to Hell is accurate according to Scripture. When God created the earth, a particular darkness hovered over the primordial earth, however, when God created light, he *separated this darkness* from the light (Gen. 1:2–4), He did not *create* this darkness. Hence, in addition to the physical creation of daylight that was separated from the night, a more profound significance to this passage of Scripture is evident — the Angelic Fall from Heaven and their perpetual banishment from the Eternal Light. When the rebellious angels fell, they not only fell into darkness, but hovered over the earth, hence their title, the "principalities and powers in the high places". As Hell is also a state of being, the demons still suffer its torments even when wandering the physical earth. Compare Mephostophiles' description with Isaiah (30:33): "For Topheth [i.e. Gehenna / Hell] is prepared from yesterday, prepared by the king, deep, and wide. The nourishment thereof is fire and much wood: the breath of the Lord as a torrent of brimstone kindling it." The idea that Hell is also a "confused thing" is exact, as a place of total suffering and punishment, completely devoid of that sense of order and harmony that only peace and serenity can bestow, it is a location that perpetually confounds its denizens.

Chapter Twelve continues with Faust's academic probing. Intrigued by Mephostophiles' description of their abode, Faust desires to learn more. His *familiar* does not object to this question and explains that Hell not only exists under the earth, but above it and onto the physical Heavens — thus in the lower and upper regions that encompasses the physical earth there are ten kingdoms in all:

1. Lacus mortis [The Lake of Death]
2. Stagnum ignis [The Pool of Fire]
3. Terra tenebrosa [Land of Darkness]

---

[559] Ibid. p. 104.

4. Tartarus
5. Terra oblivionis [Forgotten Land, or Land of Oblivion]
6. Gehenna
7. Herebus [Erebus?]
8. Barathrum
9. Styx
10. Acheron

Mephostophiles relates these ten kingdoms are governed by five Infernal kings: "Lucifer in the orient, Beelzebub in *septentrio*, Belial in *meridie*, Astaroth in *occidente*, and Phlegeton in the middest of them all: whose rule and dominions have none end until the day of doom. And thus far Faustus, hast thou heard of our rule and kingdoms."[560]

Haile omitted this chapter in his edition of the Wolfenbüttle manuscript as there is evidence to suggest it was a clumsy addition inserted by a scribe.[561] Faustus scholars also recognise that for several chapters of the manuscript, an individual simply referred to separate reference texts and copied verbatim whole passages and definitions as parchment fillers.[562] According to Haile, this chapter is one of these mechanical concoctions; "At the point where Faust asks Mephosto what Hell is, the copyist took down an old Latin-German, German-Latin dictionary and copied out several pages of names for Hell together with their derivations."[563] To be precise, the *Elucidarius* was the actual source used.[564]

While this liberal borrowing detracts from the original author's inventiveness, we can at least appreciate the efforts of the scribe to aptly illustrate the government of Hell and its various kingdoms. The first three kingdoms and the fifth are traditional titles for Hell. The sixth, Gehenna, is also a conventional title derived from the Hebrew *ge' hinnóm*, which literally means the "valley of Hinnom" where children were sacrificed to Baal outside the walls of Jerusalem. In a later period, this area became a refuse dump and its name subsequently used as a synonym for "Hell" due to the continuous fires burning there to prevent pestilence. We recognise at least four of the ten kingdoms are derived from Greek mythology: Tartarus, Herebus, Styx, and Acheron. Tartarus was considered the lowest region of the underworld where the damned were consigned, but often referred to as a synonym for Hades. Herebus is an obvious misspelling for Erebus, the upper region of the underworld where the virtuous and damned souls of the dead entered when they passed from the land of the living. The Styx, one of the five rivers of Hades, was the entrance to this underworld, and Acheron, one of the tributaries that separated Hades from the earth. The eighth title, 'Barathrum', is derived from the ancient Athenian 'prison-pits' where criminals were thrown, although it is not certain if these pits were intended to serve as mass

---

[560] *The English Faust Book; A Critical Edition*, p. 105.
[561] *History of Doctor Johann Faustus*, pp. 12, 15.
[562] For instance, the German-Latin dictionary by the Swiss humanist, Peter Dasypodius, was used to alphabetically describe the various fish, wine and game for the chapters relating Faust's feasts with the Count of Anhalt: another detail not in Haile's edition. (*Damnable Life and Deserved Death of [...] Faustus*, p. 30.)
[563] Ibid.
[564] *The English Faust Book; A Critical Edition*, n. 466–70, p. 198.

graves for convicts, or used to incarcerate prisoners.[565] Compare this title with the loose derivative of the Greek 'bathos' = 'depth', or 'bathus' = 'deep', combined with the Latin word 'rumen' = 'throat'. The anonymous author / scribe noted the similarity with the traditional Medieval titles of Hell, 'Pit' and 'Gullet', and accordingly employed 'barathrum' as an apt title for one of the ten Hellish kingdoms. We note these pit-prisons may have spawned the infamous secret *oubliette* dungeons of the Middle Ages. These cells, devoid of all light, were usually situated in the lowest, dankest parts of the foundations of a prison or castle and entered from above by a trapdoor in the ceiling. Normally used for life-sentences or for purposes of revenge, prisoners would be hidden by vindictive captors in these cells and conveniently 'forgotten', hence the name *oubliette*, which originates from the French 'oublier', 'to forget'.

However, as these are titles transcribed from a secondary source and incorporate terms from Greek and Roman myth, we must remember this is not an accurate theological rendition of Hell but rather a piece of entertaining theofiction. Additionally, the idea that Satan would govern his kingdom equally with Beelzebub, Belial and Astaroth[◊] who rule the remaining locations of north, south and west respectively is theologically erroneous. Satan, who takes pride as once occupying the highest angelic throne in Heaven, would not consider the other demons his equal. To confuse matters, P.F. completely mistranslated Spies' rendition of the diverse monarchies, further corroding the theological credibility of the narrative. Spies originally printed that these ten kingdoms are ruled by "[…] the devils called Phlegeton. There are four monarchies among them."[566] I.e. Spies' source employed the name of the mythical fire-river of Hades as the official title for the system of government by which the four arch-princes rule their kingdoms. However, P.F.'s mistranslation and transposition of the text alters the reader's perception of Phlegeton, now introduced as a demon that apparently holds a superior rank to Satan! P.F. inadvertently allocated the "fire-river demon" a place in the midst of the "Five Kingdoms", this allocation essentially denotes a position more important than that of Lucifer, which of course Satan would never permit as the Supreme Prince of Hell.

Continuing with Chapter Fifteen, the material we read is equivalent to the information we encountered in the manuscript, although there are new theological and theofictional embellishments on the various torments of Hell. Mephostophiles declares:

> "[…] Hell hath also a place within it called Chasma, **out of the which issueth all manner of thunders, lightnings, with such horrible shriekings and wailings, that ofttimes the very devils themselves stand in fear thereof: for one while it sendeth forth winds with exceeding snow, hail, and rain congealing the water into ice; with**

[565] According to a footnote in the Dryden translation of *Plutarch's Lives: Aristides*, corrected and revised by Arthur Hugh Clough (1859). Reprint: Charles W. Eliot, ed., *Plutarch's Lives: The Harvard Classics*, vol 12, (New York: P.F. Collier and Son Corp., 1963), p. 80.

[◊] *Astaroth*, or *Ashtaroth, Astarte, Astoreth*, etc.: the corresponding female deity to Baal. It was in her temple that the Philistines hung King Saul's armour after his death. (1 Kings 31: 9–10) As a pagan goddess, she was also recognised as a devil in other Renaissance literature, such as Milton's *Paradise Lost*.

[566] *The English Faust Book; A Critical Edition*, n. 471, p. 198.

which the damned are frozen, gnash their teeth, howl and cry, and yet cannot die. Otherwhiles, it sendeth forth flames of fire and brimstone, wherein the sorrowful souls of the damned lie broiling in their reiterated torments: yea Faustus, hell is called a prison wherein the damned lie continually bound; it is also called *Pernicies*, and *Exitium*, **death, destruction, hurtfulness, mischief, a mischance, a pitiful and an evil thing**■ world without end. **We have also with us in hell a ladder, reaching of an exceeding height, as though it would touch the heavens, on which the damned ascend to seek the blessing of God; but through their infidelity, when they are at the very highest degree, they fall down again into their former miseries, complaining of the heat and of that unquenchable fire**: yea sweet *Faustus*, so must thou understand of hell, the while thou art so desirous to know the secrets of our kingdom. And mark *Faustus*, hell is the nurse of death, the heat of all fire, the shadow of heaven and earth, the oblivion of all goodness, the pains unspeakable, the grief unremovable, the dwelling of Devils, Dragons, Serpents, **Adders, Toads, Crocodiles**, and all manner of venomous creatures, **the puddle of sin, the stinking fog ascending from the Stygian lake,**⁺ Brimstone, Pitch, and all manner of unclear metals, the perpetual and unquenchable fire, the end of whose miseries was never purposed by God: yea, yea *Faustus*, thou sayest, I shall, I must, **nay I will** tell thee **the secrets of our kingdom, for thou buyest it dearly [...].**"[567]

The description of a specific location called "Chasma", the Latin word for "chasm", originates from medieval concepts of Hell. The tortures of cold and ice are unfamiliar aspects of the Inferno for us today — the expression "when Hell freezes over," attests to this — however, in earlier times it was assumed Hell contained every torment that could be imagined.↓ For the bottommost region of the Inferno where Satan resides, Dante envisioned in his *Divine Comedy* a place of desolation comprised of ice and frozen lakes that excluded the element of fire — the six colossal bat-like wings of the fallen seraph stir up the bitter winds that blast the last circle of Hell

---

■ P.F. has elaborated on the names of Hell, and has omitted "Confutatio" = confusion, "Damnatio" = damnation, "Condemnatio" = condemnation. (*The English Faust Book; A Critical Edition,* n. 627f, p. 201.)

⁺ P.F.'s embellishment for Spies' "a stench of water".

[567] *Sources of the Faust Tradition*, pp. 155–156.

↓ This detail of a frozen Hell is P.F.'s unique addition to the *Faustbook*. This text replaces Spies' description of the infernal chasms: "[...] like the bottomless rift produced by an earthquake when bedrock is cleaved and shaken apart; the depths of the chasms are very windy. The passages of hell are regular, now broad, now narrow, then broad again, and so forth. Hell is also called Petra, a rock or cliff, for indeed, there are rocks of several kinds, as *saxum, scopulus, rupes* and *cautes*. There are no loose stones or earth among the fields of hell, for God laid the foundations like the firmament of heaven, quite hard, pointed and rough, like a mountain top." (*The English Faust Book; A Critical Edition,* n. 618–22, p. 201.) Possibly, the "windy chasms" and "firm foundations" suggested to P.F. Dante's version of the bowels of Hell.

and freeze the river Cocytus.[568] No doubt this freezing element is attributed to the demons' complete lack of charity, as Christ explained, in the Later Days, iniquity and chaos would increase as the charity of men grows cold. (Matt. 24:12) An additional popular belief of Hell dating from medieval times is the concept it contains many loathsome creatures, snakes, flies, worms, dragons and other similar animals, that increase the pains and terror for those imprisoned there. P.F. could not resist adding a few more adders, toads, and reptiles. We may once more turn to Dante's *Divine Comedy;* for example, those who did not live for God but lived to serve their own existence, yet did not purposely choose evil, they are consigned by Dante to a less terrifying section inside the Gates of the Inferno where they are tormented by hornets, wasps and worms.[569] The titles in the *Faustbook* of "Pernicies" and "Exitium" (Exilium?), the Latin words for "destruction" and "banishment" respectively, are congruous with fundamental theology and are apt descriptions of Hell. One curious element included in Mephostophiles' speech is P.F.'s additional description of a ladder that nearly reaches the heavens whereby the lost souls climb with the desire to attain once again God's mercy and blessing, but are hurled back into the Abyss. We detect this is not a conventional aspect of Hell, it is understood a lost soul cannot hope for, nor, receive the blessing of God once it is consigned to that place of perpetual banishment. The lost souls also exist in a state of perpetual hatred, and have no desire for Heaven as they now yearn to hide within the bowels of Hell where they feel at liberty to blaspheme God's Holy name. This bogus detail is another fallacy of Mephostophiles as he is now manipulating Faust's question of whether or not the damned may receive forgiveness, fostering the scholar's increasing despair. The idea may have originated from Jacob's dream wherein he saw a myriad of angels ascending and descending a great ladder that stretched from the earth to Heaven. (Gen. 28:12) In the *Faustbook*, the ladder in Hell symbolically displays the damned have eternally forfeited their true inheritance to the Kingdom of Heaven. Henry Jones alternatively suggests this figure of the ladder is an attack on Giordano Bruno's neoplatonic magic. Bruno wrote the following in *Lo Spaccio della bestia trionfante* (*Expulsion of the Triumphant Beast*, London, 1584): "wise men … with magic and divine rites rose to the height of Divinity by means of that same ladder of Nature by which Divinity descends to the lowest of things in order to communicate herself."[570]

Chapter Sixteen of the London *Faustbook*, which concludes the First Part, features an interesting theological disputation. Faust desires to know if God had made Mephostophiles a man and not a spirit, would he live his life to please his Creator and mankind. Although the demon is now vexed by Faust's incessant questioning, he decides to humour Faust on this last occasion, albeit proffering him a series of lies:

> "[…] Faustus said: 'I would gladly know of thee, if thou wert a man in manner and form as I am; what wouldst thou do to please both God and man?' Whereat the spirit smiled saying: 'My Faustus, if I were a man as thou art, **and that God had adorned me with those gifts of nature as thou once haddest**; even so long as the breath of God were by,

---

[568] *Divine Comedy*, 'Inferno', Canto XXXIV.
[569] Ibid. Canto III.
[570] Quoted in translation by Roy T. Eriksen: *The Forme of Faustus' Fortune*, (1987), p. 64, in *The English Faust Book; A Critical Edition*, n. 628–33, p. 201.

and within me, would I humble my self unto His Majesty, endeavouring all that I could to keep his commandments, praise him, glorify him, that I might continue in his favour, so were I sure to enjoy the eternal joy and felicity of his kingdom.' Faustus said: 'But that have not I done.' 'No, thou sayest true,' quoth Mephostophiles, 'thou hast not done it, but thou hast denied thy Lord and maker, which gave thee the breath of life, speech, hearing, sight, and all other thy reasonable senses that thou mightest understand his will and pleasure, to live in glory and honour his name, and to the advancement of thy body and soul, him I say being thy maker hast thou denied and defied, yea wickedly thou hast applied that excellent gift of thine understanding, and given thy soul to the devil: therefore give none the blame but thine own self-will, thy proud and aspiring mind, which hath brought thee into the wrath of God and utter damnation.' 'This is most true,' quoth Faustus, 'but tell me Mephostophiles, wouldst thou be in my case as I am now?' 'Yea,' saith the spirit (and with that fetch a great sigh), 'for yet would I so humble my self, that I would win the favour of God.' 'Then,' said Doctor Faustus, 'it were time enough for me if I amended.' 'True,' said Mephostophiles, 'if it were not for the great sins, which are so odious and detestable in the sight of God, that it is too late for thee, for the wrath of God resteth upon thee.' 'Leave off,' quoth Faustus, 'and tell me my question to my greater comfort.'"[571]

Mephostophiles lies when he 'admits' he would have served God if he were made a man and had all the gifts that were bestowed upon mankind. This is a fallacy as the angels possess a more noble spiritual nature than mankind, and have greater knowledge and power. If Mephostophiles could not avoid the sin of pride at the height of his angelic glory with all his superior intellect and reasoning before he fell, he certainly would not humble himself as a man. We recognise that the first two perfect humans on earth, Adam and Eve, did not survive the first day in the garden without falling to Satan's temptation! Furthermore, as with all the fallen angels, he has no intention nor the wish to repent, therefore, this remark that he would serve God if he were human cannot be considered a regretful yearning from hindsight for circumstances to be different— the demon eventually admits that he would be in the exact same position as the scholar. We see that Mephostophiles is pointing out Faust's wicked life to implant the notion he is beyond redemption. Faust observes if Mephostophiles would still repent if he was a man in the same predicament and receive grace (another lie as Mephostophiles has no desire to be forgiven), he could also do likewise, but the demon says this is impossible as his sins are too great. This is a paradoxical answer: why would he alone receive forgiveness, and not Faust? Yet, the supposed theologian did not detect the deceit in the demon's answers and is engulfed in spiritual desolation. Henry Jones observes Mephostophiles obliterates Faust's last vestige of hope with

---

[571] *The English Faust Book; A Critical Edition*, pp. 112–113.

fallacious compassion for his plight. He sighs and (unexpectedly!) smiles; "Mephostophiles' one smile is his cruellest weapon and it is used to kill."[572]

Part Two

Discouraged from attempting any further theological queries, Faust turns his attentions to his almanacs and horoscopes. The description of Faust's uncanny accuracy with regards to predictions remains the same as in the manuscript; however, when Faust questions the application of the science, he receives a different answer from the explanation we first encountered. In the Wolfenbüttle and Spies texts, Faust asks why his charts are more accurate than those of other astrologers and Mephostophiles replies that the ancients were once skilled in the art of predictions, as by their longevity, they could accurately observe and learn the art of astronomy / astrology, a skill the demons still possess due to their immortal nature, but which mankind lost as the life-span of the human race decreased. Comparing this with Chapter Eighteen[X] of the London *Faustbook*, we are presented with a completely different tableau.

Faust attempts to study astronomy and astrology on his own initiative, but becomes utterly confused and turns to Mephostophiles to elucidate certain points: "[…] I find the ground of this science very difficult to attain unto: for that when I confer [compare] a*stronomia* and a*strologia*, as the mathematicians and ancient writers have left in memory, **I find them to vary and very much to disagree**: wherefore I pray thee to teach me the truth in this matter."[573] Evidently, the diverse polemical tracts attempting to explain the various Ptolemaic-based theories of the universe bewildered him. Mephostophiles explains why so many contrasting theories exist. Inventors of this art had accomplished little, if anything of worth, by their individual efforts regarding planetary prognostication, yet if they happened upon a discovery by chance, they did not clearly record their findings but obscured them with enigmatic esoteric language and symbols, making it impossible for others to learn the art without the aid of a spirit or the grace of God.■ Promptly, Mephostophiles encourages Faust to have recourse to him rather than God to learn this skill as he states:

"[…] yet do we spirits that fly and fleet in all elements, know
such, and there is nothing to be done, or by the heavens pretended, but we

---

[572] *Faustus and the Censor*, p. 22.
[X] This chapter is a conflation of Chs. 19–21 in Spies.
[573] *The English Faust Book; A Critical Edition*, p. 114.
■ Henry Jones relates this significant deviation in the text may be attributed to Agrippa's *De Vanitate*. Agrippa writes; "very skillfull mathematicians … confess that it is impossible to find out any certain thing concerning the knowledge of judgements … they … write so divers and contrary opinions upon one thing, that is impossible for an Astrologian to pronounce any certain thing upon so variable and disagreeing opinions, except there be in him some inward perceiving of things to come and hidden, and inspiration of foreknowledge, or rather a secret and privy inspiration of the devil … .' *Henry Cornelius Agrippa, of the Vanitie and Uncertaintie of Arts and Sciences*, Englished by Ja. Sa[nford]. Gent, (London 1575), pp. 45–46, in *The English Faust Book*, pp.203–204.

know it, except only the day of doom. **Wherefore, Faustus, learn of me: I will teach thee** the course and recourse of [Saturn, Jupiter, Mars, Sun, Venus, Mercury, and the Moon°], the cause of winter and summer, **the exaltation and declination of the sun, the eclipse of the moon, the distance and height of the poles, and every fixed star, the nature and operation of the elements, fire, air, water, and earth, and all that is contained in them, yea, herein there is nothing hidden from me, but only the fifth essence, which once thou hadst Faustus at liberty, but now Faustus thou hast lost it past recovery: wherefore leaving that which will not again be had, learn of me to make thunder, lightening, hail, snow, and rain: the clouds to rent, the earth and craggy rocks to shake and split in sunder, the seas to swell, and roar, and overrun their marks. [...]"**[574]

Hence, the demon promises to educate Faust in all matters pertaining to astronomy and correct the previously held misconceptions of the earth and the cosmos. The only information withheld from the spirit is knowledge of the "fifth essence", this term is a direct translation of the Latin word "quintessence", or the 'fifth element' that Aristotle believed the heavenly spheres were comprised of and was invisibly inherent in all creation. This belief continued into medieval times. Here, the term also implies the invisible Essence of God and His grace that unceasingly binds Creation and keeps it in existence. Once more, the demon falsely insinuates to Faust that he has forever lost the grace of God and will never obtain it again.

Mephostophiles then announces the various arts he can teach him, including the ability to fly through the air, swim like a fish, change into wild beasts, walk through walls, doors and gates, tread on knives and not be harmed, etc. He also declares he will reveal to Faust all the secrets of nature and the significance of the planetary motions. (Here Mephostophiles provides one academic answer to prove the scope of his knowledge, explaining the cloud sphere and the "sphere of waters" protect the earth from the scorching heat put forth by the stars of the Zodiac and the sphere of fixed stars beyond the circuit of Saturn.) The demon also promises to escort him to undiscovered mines from which he may draw a dragon's hoard of wealth for his own use, and promises to show him how he may sit at the banquets of kings and enjoy all the proceedings at their expense — invited or not. ←↑→

° In the text, the planets are referred to by their astrological symbols.
[574] *The English Faust Book; A Critical Edition*, p. 114.
←↑→ Mephostophiles' "Learn of me" soliloquy replaces the following passages from Chapters 20 and 21 in Spies' edition, (bold text highlights sentences / material retained by P.F.);

"Concerning Winter and Summer. [Ch. 20] Faustus thought it very strange that God should have created winter and summer upon earth, so he asked his spirit the origin of the seasons. The spirit replied very briefly: 'My lord Faustus, surely you, as a physicist, can deduce this for yourself from the movement of the sun! Know then, that from the moon to the fixed stars is the region of fire, **but the earth is cold and frigid. For the deeper the sun shines the hotter it is**, and that is the cause of summer. When the sun stands high, then it is cold resulting in winter. *Concerning the Course of the Heavens, its Lights and Origin*. [Ch. 21] As mentioned before, Doctor Faustus had been forbidden to ask any more questions on

In the course of his dialogue, Mephostophiles makes one unusual statement that has perplexed Faustian scholars: "**I will learn thee [...why] Lady Saturnia [Pieces]** in *occulto*, **[is] more hotter than the sun in** *manifesto*." Presumably the demon was presenting an example of how human scholars had confused the science of astrology / astronomy with their vague phrases and symbols. When speaking in terms of astronomy, the Latin word "Occulto" means "eclipsed": notice the Latin word "occult" = "covered over". "Manifesto" is a derivative of the Latin "manifestus" = "obvious"; in this instance, the term refers to the sun being "manifest" or in full view. We could interpret the sentence as: "I will teach thee why Saturn when eclipsed in the sign of Pisces, notwithstanding it is the outermost of the planets, is hotter than the sun in full view." (As mentioned, the other planets Uranus, Neptune, and the dwarf-planet Pluto were as yet undiscovered.) This may refer to the contemporary belief that certain planetary alignments in the sign of Pisces were particularly bad omens that foretold disastrous events. For instance, Baron observes that in 1524 the sun, moon and all the great planets were aligned in the sign of Pisces and the astrologers deemed this phenomenon to be the astrological event of the century; many academics predicted a great flood would occur.[575] Of interest, Camerarius, a contemporary and a rival of the historical Faustus, observed another unusual alignment with the sign of Pisces in 1536. A disturbed Camerarius wrote to his friend Stibar; "When the moon stood in Pisces in opposition to Mars, on August 4, I endured a very difficult night. Your Faustus is responsible for

---

divine or celestial matters. This troubled him sorely; day and night he plotted how he might camouflage his interest in the divine creation. So he no longer asked about the joys of the blessed, or about the angels or the pains of hell, for he knew his spirit would not entertain such questions. Instead he had to feign an interest where he might receive an answer, so he decided to frame his questions under the pretext that the information was serviceable and necessary to the philosopher for the study of astronomy or astrology. Accordingly he asked his spirit to expound the course of the heavens, its lights and origins.

'My Lord Faustus,' said the spirit, 'it was God, your Maker, who created the world and all the elements beneath the heavens, for in the beginning, God created the heavens out of the midst of the waters and separated the waters from the waters and called the firmament heaven. It is a mobile, spherical disc created from water congealed and solidified like a crystal, **and up in the sky it looks like a crystal, wherein are fixed the stars.** Through the revolution of the heavens **the world is divided in four parts: East, West, North and South.** The heavens rotate so fast that the world would break in pieces were it not prevented by the motion of the planets. **Heaven is also furnished with fire so hot, that were it not for the clouds with their cooling waters the elements beneath would ignite.** Within the firmament of the fixed stars are **the seven planets: Saturn, Jupiter, Mars, Sol, Venus, Mercury and Luna** and all the heavens move except the fiery heaven. The world is divided in four parts, namely **fire**, air, earth and water and so are the spheres and their creatures, each taking their matter and characteristics from one of these. Thus the uppermost heaven is fiery and shining, the middle and lower are clear and airy. The uppermost is heated and illuminated directly owing to the nearness of the sun, but the lowest is lit by reflection of earth-shine and is cold and dark in those places which the reflected rays cannot reach. Here in this gloomy air we spirits dwell, cast out into the darkness, amidst violent storms, thunder, hail, snow and the like, so that we may tell the seasons of the year and what the weather should be. Heaven has also twelve spheres encompassing the earth and the water, if they may also be called heavens.' The Spirit also told him the ruling of the planets and the grade of each with respect to the rest." (*The English Faust Book; A Critical Edition,* pp. 204–205.)

 ↔ The sign of Pisces is also referred to in the text by its astrological symbol.
[575] Baron, *Doctor Faustus, from History to Legend,* p. 45.

the fact that I discuss these matters with you."[576] Hence, Mephostophiles may be referring to the 'heat' of controversy regarding the astrological alignment of Saturn in Pisces rather than to physical heat.

Following this section, we discover that P.F.'s decision to combine material from Chapters Twenty and Twenty-one from the Spies book caused a serious context anomaly. In Chapter Nineteen, Faust is overcome with self-pity and voices his grievance to the spirit, i.e. complaining it had cost him much to acquire his services, yet he refuses to be obedient to him in all things according to their contract. This scenario appears bizarre, as one would expect Faust to be rather enthusiastic with the promises Mephostophiles proposed in his "Learn of Me" speech. In Spies Chapter Twenty-one, Faust's plan to covertly interrogate the demon on theological matters is fully explained, and Mephostophiles, perceiving the true nature of these disputations on the cosmos, supplies the standard text-book answers and side-steps revealing any significant secret regarding divine matters. Similar to Faust, P.F. apparently was dissatisfied with Mephostophiles' rudimentary replies and decided to exclude them. (See note ←↑→.) Returning to Chapter Nineteen of the London text, Mephostophiles cajoles Faust until he explains the reason for his melancholy. The demon explains he is not required to provide information on certain matters to "the hurt of their kingdom", nevertheless he grudgingly agreed to answer, and asks Faust what he now desired of him. Faust replies he is curious to learn more on the creation of the world and why man was made after the image of God. This first section corresponds with the early text we have studied, however, Faust in Haile's edition of the MS only requests academic knowledge of the Creation, and the demon willingly answers his question, albeit he lies to Faust and gives an Aristotelian, anti-Genesis fabrication to confuse him.[♦] Now in the London *Faustbook*, the narration changes direction at this point, as the demon perceives this question was asked with a spiritual purpose. Deciding he had humoured Faust sufficiently, Mephostophiles retorts: "**'Faustus thou knowest that all this is in vain for thee to ask, I know thou art sorry for that thou hast done, but it availeth thee not, for I will tear thee in thousands of pieces, if thou change not thy opinions,'** and hereat he vanished away."[577] Faust is overcome with sorrow and weeps bitterly, not for his own misdeeds, but that he should have asked a question that roused the spirit's anger suddenly leaving him in a rage. At once, Lucifer and his troop of hideous demons enter Faust's chamber to reaffirm his loyalty:

> "[...] Lucifer spake in this sort: 'Faustus, I have seen thy thoughts, **which are not as thou hast vowed unto me, by virtue of this letter, and showed him the obligation that he had written with his own blood,** wherefore I am come to visit thee **and to show thee some of our hellish pastimes, in hope that will draw and confirm thy mind a little more steadfast unto us.' 'Content,' quoth Faustus, 'Go to, let me see what pastime you can make.' At which words, the great devil in his likeness sat him down by Faustus,** commanding the rest of the devils

---

[576] Ibid. p. 60.

[♦] This anti-Genesis account is retained in Spies, Ch. 22. P.F. eliminates this chapter, and concentrates on the episode featuring the Seven Demons.

[577] *The English Faust Book; A Critical Edition*, p. 116.

to appear in their form, as if they were in hell: first entered Belial in form of a bear, with curled black hair to the ground, his ears standing upright: within the ear was as red as blood, out of which issued flames of fire, his teeth were a foot as least long, as white as snow, with a tail three ells long * (at the least) having two wings, one behind each arm, and thus one after another they appeared to Faustus in form as they were in hell. Lucifer himself sat in a manner of a man, all hairy, but of a brown colour like a squirrel, curled, and his tail turning upwards on his back as the squirrels use, **I think he could crack nuts too like a squirrel.** After him came Beelzebub in curled hairs of horse flesh colour, his head like the head of a bull, with **a mighty pair of horns**, and two long ears down to the ground, and two wings on his back, with pricking stings like thorns: out of his wings issued flames of fire, his tail was like a cow. Then came Astaroth in form of a worm, going upright on his tail; he had no feet, but a tail like a slow-worm: under his chaps [jaws] grew two short hands, and his back was coal black, his belly thick in the middle, and yellow like gold, having many bristles on his back like a hedgehog. After him came Chamagosta, being white and gray mixed, exceedingly curly and hairy: he had a head like the head of an ass, the tail like a cat, and claws like an ox, lacking nothing of an ell broad. Then came Anobis; this devil had a head like a dog, white and black hair **in shape of a hog, saving that he had but two feet, one under his throat, the other at his tail:** he was four ells long, with hanging ears like a blood-hound. After him came Dythycan, he was a short thief in form of a pheasant, with shining feathers, and four feet: his neck was green, his body red, and his feet black. The last was [Brachus→], with four short feet like a hedgehog, yellow and green: the upper side of his body was brown, and the belly like blue flames of fire; the tail red, like the tail of a monkey. [...]"[578]

This motley procession continues as hordes of devils arrive in various forms of wild beasts and pay homage to Lucifer. As the hall shakes with thunder, the demons turn their pitchforks towards Faust to display how they amuse themselves in Hell by tossing lost souls back and forth with these implements, (a unique detail of P.F.'s). Lucifer asks Faust what he thinks of this phantasmal exhibition, but the scholar asks why they could not appear in shapes other than the forms before him. The Fiend replies that they have all appeared as they are in Hell and cannot change their true form, but that they possess the power to befuddle the senses of humans so they can appear as angels although they dwell in darkness. Faust is uncomfortable with the crowd of demons surrounding him, and Lucifer commands them to depart. The scholar then asks if Mephostophiles may appear in his true shape, and lo, in flies a fire-breathing dragon that subsequently turns into the familiar shape of a friar, which is also P.F.'s addition. Now, Faust

---

* One ell equals forty-five inches.
→ Henry Jones has amended this name: it is "Drachus" in Spies.
[578] *The English Faust Book; A Critical Edition*, pp. 116–117.

desires to know if he too may learn how to change his appearance, and Lucifer presents him with a tome of magic spells whereupon Faust immediately begins to experiment, turning into a hog, a worm and then a dragon. Faust asks Lucifer why all the filthy forms of wild beasts that he had just seen were allowed by God to roam the world, and the Fiend replies they are permitted as plagues upon the earth, (no doubt as punishment for sin), wherewith Faust is immediately tormented by scorpions, wasps, and bees, until he cries to Mephostophiles for help. Lucifer retorts laughing, "[…] **how likest thou the creation of the world** […]," and suddenly everything vanishes. Faust is now left alone in his chamber, enchanted by beautiful music, causing him to forget the horror of the scenes he has witnessed and repents "[…] **that he had seen no more of their pastime.**"[579]

This diabolical demonstration introduces us to the seven principal demons that stand before the throne of Satan; however, we note a section of the narrative is a complete invention appended to certain traditional concepts of Hell. We recognise several traditional names among the horde of demons, but there are some unique additions, for example, the demon "Chamagosta" seems to be P.F.'s innovation. Empson writes, "[Chamagosta] clearly derives from the Greek *chamai* and *agostos*, and a likely meaning is 'bowed (or cursed) to the earth', presumably referring to the serpent of Genesis 4."[580] We also recognise this name parallels "Chemos", or as seen in older translations of the Bible, Chamos, the god of the Moabites and Ammonites. (Judges 11:24 and 3 Kings 11:5) Henry Jones observes a parallel with "Cham": Reginald Scot in *The Discoverie of Witchcraft* (London 1584) reported this iniquitous son of Noah was credited with the invention of sorcery and necromancy.[581] This belief was perpetuated in Holinshed's *Chronicle* (1587, p. 21 col. b); "[… other nations than the Egyptians] abhorred him for his wickedness, calling him Chemesencia, that is, the impudent, infamous and wicked Cham."[582] Henry Jones concludes: "Chamagosta presumably means 'seducer of Cham'."[583] Focusing on the remaining demons, "Anobis" is an obvious borrowing from Egyptian mythology, Anubis, the god of the dead, mummification and the guardian of tombs, was believed to possess the head of a jackal. "Dythycan" is an unfamiliar name, it may be a refashioning of the word "dithyramb", i.e. an ancient Greek choral hymn sung to honour the god Dionysus, (Bacchus), the pagan deity of wine whose rites of worship included licentious revelry. The name of the last demon, "Brachus", is a misprint for "Drachus" in Spies' work. The original 'Drachus' may be a derivative from the Greek "drakōn" = "serpent" and / or "dragon". Yet we observe the misprint "Brachus" could be intentional; the word is not unlike "Bacchus" and thus in the London version the last two demons

---

[579] Ibid. p. 118. In the Spies book, Belial, and not Lucifer, appears to Faust to announce he has read his thoughts and would like to grant his desire to see the principal demons of Hell. Although Faust is still horrified when the demons plague him as insects, Henry Jones remarks; "[…] the tone is generally merry and the plaguing is short lived." (*Faustus and the Censor*, p. 23.) Hence, the demons are entertaining Faust in Spies' version and do not appear with the ultimate aim of terrifying him into submission. Empson discusses these variants between the two books in more detail. See *Faustus and the Censor*, pp. 67–71.

[580] *Faustus and the Censor*, p. 69.

[581] *The English Faust Book; A Critical Edition*, n.902, p. 207.

[582] Ibid. p. 208.

[583] Ibid.

share a common denominator. In all, we see a blending of accepted tradition with a dash of imaginative material.

The vision where the demons appear as grotesque animals[+] is also a traditional concept of Hell, however, the particular mutant shapes prescribed to each of the principal seven we may deduce to be an invention of the author / scribe. We notice that P.F. included his own personal comment with the squirrel-like description of Lucifer; "**I think he could crack nuts too like a squirrel**." Henry Jones writes, "[...] this may [...] be a reference to Luther's experience in Wartburg of a strange nocturnal intruder (presumed to be a devil) which took hazel nuts, one by one, from a sack on the table and cracked them on the roof beam."[584] Empson alternatively muses that if P.F. intended a grim description rather than a jovial sketch, he may be referring to some unidentified method of torture.[585] He may be correct: P.F.'s possible source could be Dante's concept of the fallen seraph in the *Inferno* — Satan is portrayed as a three-headed monster that perpetually gnaws the damned souls of Judas, Brutus and Cassius in its massive jaws.[586] The London text then reverts to accurate theology when Lucifer states the demons may befuddle the eyes of men and appear as angels of light, which is P.F.'s enlightened improvement to the text. St. Paul admonished the Galatians who were straying from the path of Christ by stating:

> "I wonder that you are so soon removed from him that called you into the grace of Christ, unto another Gospel. Which is not another, only there are some that trouble you, and would pervert the gospel of Christ. But though we, or an angel from heaven, preach a gospel to you besides that which we have preached to you, let him be an anathema. [...] For I give you to understand, brethren, that the gospel which was preached by me is not according to man. For neither did I receive it of

---

[+] Of interest, this interpretation of Hell with demons assuming the shape of horrific beasts is not a mere vestige of Medieval and Renaissance belief: this detail was confirmed during one of the six apparitions of Our Lady to three shepherd children at Fatima, Portugal (1917), which were later approved by the Roman Catholic Church. One of the three seers, Lucia, who was ten at the time, writes that during the apparition of July 13, they were permitted to see the torments of Hell:

"[...] Our Lady showed us a great sea of fire which seemed to be under the earth. Plunged in this fire were demons and souls in human form, like transparent burning embers, all blackened or burnished bronze, floating about in the conflagration, now raised into the air by the flames that issued from within themselves together with great clouds of smoke, now falling back on every side like sparks in a huge fire, without weight or equilibrium, and amid shrieks and groans of pain and despair, which horrified us and made us tremble with fear. The demons could be distinguished by their terrifying and repellent likeness to frightful and unknown animals, all black and transparent. This vision lasted but an instant. [...]" (Ed. Fr. Louis Kondor, SVD, *Fatima: In Lucia's Own Words. Sister Lucia's Memoirs, vol. I*, Fatima, Portugal: Secretariado Dos Pastorinhos, 2004), p. 123.

[584] Tischreden Vol. 6, No, 6816, in *The English Faust Book; A Critical Edition*, n. 893f , p. 207.
[585] *Faustus and the Censor*, p. 70.
[586] Dante, *Inferno*, Canto XXXIV.

man, nor did I learn it; but by revelation of Jesus Christ." (Gal. 1: 6–8,11–12.)

St. Paul was therefore reminding the Christians in Galatia to beware of false prophets and apparitions that would distort heavenly truth — it is understood a genuine angel would not attempt to corrupt the teachings of Christ. St. Paul also reminds the Corinthians to be watchful of false apostles by using the same example: "For such false apostles are deceitful workmen, transforming themselves into the apostles of Christ. And no wonder: for Satan himself transformeth himself into an angel of light". (2 Cor. 11: 13–14.)

One unusual detail that resurfaces in all the *Faustbooks* is the devil's use of beautiful music to sway Faust during his 'fits' of repentance.# We most often consider exquisite music to be associated with the heavenly choirs and not with demons. We notice Luther acknowledged music was a special gift of consolation created by God to lift melancholy hearts and souls in times of distress. However, philosophers and theologians of that era would also recognise that music could be used for the wrong purpose. The *Confessions* of St. Augustine is one obvious source for this dual aesthetic. He writes that music was one source of his temptation before he returned to the Catholic faith; "The delights of the ear had more firmly entangled and subdued me; but Thou [God] didst loosen and free me."[587] St. Augustine admits his concern regarding the allure of music as a temptation also extended to Church music, stating this was a further source of trepidation for him. He struggled with that fine line between the pleasurable and the noble characteristics of the art, being at times raised to the noble heights of devotion, yet on other occasions convinced he had sinned by taking pleasure in it:

> "At other times, [...] I err in too great strictness; and sometimes to that degree, as to wish the whole melody of sweet music which is used to David's Psalter, banished from my ears, and the Church's too; and that mode seems to me safer, which I remember to have been often told me of Athanasius, Bishop of Alexandria, who made the reader of the psalm utter it with so slight inflection of voice, that it was nearer speaking than singing. Yet again, when I remember the tears I shed at the Psalmody of Thy Church, in the beginning of my revered faith; and how at this time I am moved not with the singing, but with the things sung, when they are sung with a clear voice and modulation most suitable, I acknowledge the great use of this institution. Thus I fluctuate between peril of pleasure and approved wholesomeness; inclined the rather (though not as pronouncing an irrevocable opinion) to approve of the usage of singing; that so by the delight of the ears the weaker minds may rise to the feeding of devotion. Yet when it befalls me to be more moved with the voice

---

Henry Jones posits P.F. actually intensifies the Calvinist inference in Spies that secular music is dangerously alluring. (*The English Faust Book; A Critical Edition*, n. 296f, p. 194.)

[587] St. Augustine, *Confessions*, in Charles W. Eliot, ed., *The Harvard Classics, vol. 7* (New York: P.F. Collier and Son Corp., 1963), p, 186.

than the words sung, I confess to have sinned penally, and then had rather not hear music."[588]

Summarising St. Augustine's philosophy on music, Bowman writes:

> "Augustine's personal record of his love-hate relationship with the 'delights of the ear' wielded considerable impact. Music continued in its inexorable ascent as a science serving reason, and its simultaneous descent as experience: take music in, Augustine cautioned, but do not be taken in by the perils of pleasure that threaten to usurp mind's rightful supremacy. Unthinking enjoyment and performance of music is characteristic of animals, but is beneath human dignity. Knowing music is thus more important and valuable than performing it or hearing it, however seductive its sensual charms. Per corporalia ad incorporalia."[589]

In the Faustian manuscript and books, we witness this misuse of music by the demons who succeed in obliterating from Faust's memory the horrendous spectacle of their true shapes and the torment he endured from the plaguing vermin. Repressing the memories of these occurrences, Faust loses a precious means by which he may excite true contrition for his misspent life, i.e. the fear of Satan, hell, and the punishment for sin.

In Chapter Twenty[√] of the London *Faustbook*, we return to the familiar tale of Faust's journey to Hell. Beelzebub appears as a great bear, not a dragon, and he carries with him a chair made of beaten gold, not the sinister throne constructed of bones. Henry Jones notes; "It is uncharacteristic of P.F. to delete the curious, but here he applies moral allegory: the road to hell is paved with gold, etc."[590] They are greeted in Hell by three other devils, not dragons. In addition, storks battle with the serpents that attack Faust, not flying lions. Henry Jones remarks P.F. was including a more appropriate combatant for the snakes,[591] although it is possible P.F. had intended to use a different Christian allegory, but confused theological symbols, and included storks, not pelicans. Pelicans became a symbol for Christ and the Blessed Sacrament due to their extreme parenting instincts, in times of drought or famine, they will feed their young with the flesh from their breast. P.F. also 'corrects' a detail that may have appeared to him to be an unintentional theological inaccuracy in Spies, i.e. that the dammed may refresh themselves in a cool stream: "[…] **and thus** [the damned souls] **wearied themselves and spent their endless torments out of one labyrinth into another, one while in heat, another while in cold**: […]"[592] Once more, we see P.F. expanding the descriptive element of freezing cold as one of the torments of Hell. He obviously did not consider the demon was taking Faust on a tour through a false vision to convince him that Satan could fulfil his promise in suspending the punishment of

---

[588] Ibid. pp. 186–187.
[589] Bowman, *Philosophical Perspectives on Music*, p. 66.
[√] Ch. 24 in Spies.
[590] *The English Faust Book; A Critical Edition*, n. 980, p. 209,.
[591] Ibid. n. 1001, p. 210.
[592] Ibid. p. 121.

physical suffering for his chosen damned with a refreshing stream, confounding him into believing Hell was "not as hot as people say." P.F. also removed the parenthetical comment "[…] for had he really seen hell he would have never wished to go there,"[593] and altered Faust's conviction he had seen only a vision: "[…] **but he rather persuaded himself that he had been there than otherwise, because he had seen such wonderful things;**".[594] Unfortunately, this variance unravels the theological inferences of the demon's illusions displayed in the original text. Save for these few points, the narrative of Faust's journey, i.e. his vision of Hell, is almost identical to the earlier manuscript.

This is not the case with the subsequent Chapter[≤] as Faust's description of his voyage to the stars contains elements not in the Wolfenbüttle text. P.F. rearranged the various countries Faust gazes down upon, and the fourth direction of "West" is now included when he casts his eyes upon the world, however, the New World remains unmentioned for the present, thus the possible Dante-links observed in the early manuscript are not completely eradicated. Spies obviously did not understand the reason for the exclusion of "west" and decided to amend a seemingly clumsy omission. We also note Faust espies many battleships, but in geographical terms, he refers to the Ocean and not the seas that surround Constantinople.

Overall, these are minor changes, however, we observe one significant alteration in Faust's explanation of the cosmos. In the Wolfenbüttle manuscript and the Spies *Faustbook*, the description of the heavens is based on the geocentric Ptolemaic system, i.e. that the sun, moon and planets revolve around an immobile earth.[•] In the London *Faustbook*, the opposite is the case as Faust describes the cosmos as heliocentric, or revolving according to the theories of Copernicus! "[…] **and we think that the Sun runneth his course, and that the heavens stand still: no, it is the heavens that move his course, and the Sun abideth perpetually in his place, he is permanent, and fixed in his place, […].**"[595] Apparently, Mr. P.F. was a supporter of the Copernican System,[◊] explaining why he cut the chapters featuring Faust's questions on the origin of the planets with their fundamental Ptolemaic explanations earlier in the text in favour of inserting Mephostophiles' "Learn of Me" speech. This drastic insertion demonstrates that various scholars and scribes of the period recognised the potential of the Faustian texts to promote scientific thought and re-edited them in support of their academic preferences.

Continuing with P.F.'s description of the cosmos, the heavens are placed in a state of erratic flux, or "Chaos", moved by the Spirit of God at His pleasure, or 'wind'. P.F. explains this phenomenon with the depiction of a bubble blown in an air stream, a description we saw previously in Chapter Eleven of the London text when Mephostophiles attempted to explain the

---

[593] Ibid. n. 1061, p. 211.

[594] Ibid. p. 122.

[≤] Ch. 25 in Spies.

[◄] Spies retains the word "das Gewülcke" as the force that moves the planets. (Haile = "cloud sphere". Henry Jones assumes this was to indicate the word "firmament", and translated thus in his edition.)

[595] *The English Faust Book; A Critical Edition*, p. 125.

[◊] Empson theories P.F. was possibly influenced by Thomas Hariot, author of *A Brief and True Report of the New Found Land of Virginia (1588),* who believed that "[…] hushing up Copernicus was a great wrong." (*Faustus and the Censor*, p. 78.) We also recognise P.F. may have received his introduction to the Copernicus Theory through his university education.

creation and existence of Hell. This concept of a state of "chaos" existing collectively between Hell, earth, and the physical heavens may be drawn from the parable of Lazarus and Dives (Luke 16:26). Dives, a rich man who refused to help Lazarus, a poor beggar, is damned for his lack of charity and the selfish misuse of his wealth. Lazarus, in contrast to Dives, is saved and taken up to the bosom of Abraham. Amidst unspeakable torments, Dives begs Abraham to send Lazarus to relieve him, but Abraham replies each has received their just reward, and he informs Dives "[…] between us and you, there *is fixed a great chaos*: so that they who would pass from hence to you, cannot, nor from thence come hither." Focusing on the motion of the spheres, it is clear that the theory of the "cloud sphere" as the point of origin of this cosmic movement is redeveloped. The notion of wind-power is retained, although the sun is now described as 'fixed' in place. While we recognise that air does not exist in outer space and that gravity controls the orbits of the planets, it is fascinating that this theory is not far removed from the actual phenomenon of magnetic solar wind that influences the motions of objects in the solar system. In addition, this description of "wind" is not without a theological foundation; the Third Person in the Holy Trinity, the Holy Spirit, is also recognised as the "Breath of God", for the literal translation of "Holy Spirit" from the Latin, *Sanctus Spiritus*, is also "Holy Breath". According to Genesis (2:7), man did not receive his soul or become a living being until God in the Person of the Holy Spirit breathed life into him: "And the Lord God formed man of the slime of the earth: and breathed into his face the breath of life, and man became a living soul." In early Christian art, the Holy Spirit was occasionally depicted as the breath of the Father and the Son converging onto the Third Person. Hence, Mephostophiles' remark in Chapter Eleven that "[…] **as a bubble of water flieth before the wind, so doth hell before the breath of God**," is not incorrect as the Spirit of God indeed controls Hell and keeps it in existence. This same concept applies to the motions of the heavens.

The new additions to Chapter Twenty of the London *Faustbook* do not conclude here. Someone was obviously abhorred by this theo-heliocentric explanation. (See Appendix Five.) We notice an intrusive insertion to Faust's letter, beginning with "*Yea Christian reader […]* "*I will open to thee the divine opinion touching the ruling of this confused Chaos, far more than any rude German Author, being possessed with the devil, was able to utter […]*", and ending before "And farther my good schoolfellow […]". As this section can be entirely omitted from the chapter without distorting what appears to be P.F.'s original editing, we suspect this to be the work of a third party, perhaps a censor. It is obvious that the pious editor did not realise this theory of the planets blown around a stationary sun was not part of the original German edition! (E.g. "rude German Author".) Although Henry Jones assumes this entire passage to be P.F.'s invention, he remarks, "[…] PF's […] exact translation is fluently commingled with paraphrasings, inventions and asides and no distinction would be apparent to a reader who did not know the [German] original."[596] Furthermore, observe that the last paragraph of this sequence is mere repetition, suggesting the new editor attempted to seamlessly merge his latest text by recalling the original commentary and thereby return to the subject at hand.

This new addition to the original insertion by P.F. bears the stamp of an over-zealous champion of Christian morals. First, the Copernican theory was strictly censored in the

---

[596] *The English Faust Book; A Critical Edition*, p. 15.

Elizabethan era, and this element in the translation may have posed a theological dilemma.[597] Second, the editor(s) were possibly scandalised by the proposal that the confused mass or "chaos" of the heavens was controlled by wind, or concluded the theological concept of "the breath of God" was not adequately explained, and decided to include an extended Christian elucidation of this theory at this point by differentiating between God's "words" and "works". The editor requests the reader to refer to Genesis and observe that during the process of Creation physical wind was not mentioned until God breathed life into man; "*But all this while where was wind?*" In contrast, he maintains it is the "word" of God that created and continues to move the Heavens, the physical and spiritual. At first, this point seems logical: God made the Heavens and the Earth before mankind, and if there was allegedly no physical wind until man received his first breath, (for it is not mentioned in scripture until then), another physical source must control the cosmos. However, we discover a number of errors that display our editor lacked the competence to theologically interpret the process of Creation. God created the animals before humans, and although He did not physically breathe immortal souls into them as with mankind made in His image, they obviously did not exist in a vacuum — animals also need air! They are also animate beings, therefore the concept that the animals were God's "words" that did not move until God created Man as His ultimate "work" is asinine. The editor additionally states that the Spirit of God moved on the deep of the waters *before* heaven and earth were made, this is not true when we observe the importance of sequential order; 1) God made heaven and earth, 2) the *earth was void and empty* and the spirit of God moved over the waters. These first sentences in Genesis relate the creation of the spiritual Heaven and the physical world. The editor obviously confused this first act of Creation with the following sentences in Genesis that refer to the formation of the physical cosmos, also called "Heaven," and the appearance of the dry land, which God also called "Earth". The correct sequence continues as; 3) light was made, 4) night was separated from day, 5) the *firmament* of Heaven was made, 6) the waters were gathered into one place, 7) dry land appeared, and was called Earth. Hence, there is reason to believe this editor may also have inserted in Chapter Eleven the section of God's "words" to prepare for this intrusive explanation in Chapter Twenty-one, and the few sections which include any passage addressing the "Christian Reader".

If this is exactly what occurred, we may question why the editor did not simply remove P.F.'s Copernican based rendition of this passage; however, if he believed this unorthodox theory was part of the German narration, it is possible he wanted to preserve the integrity of the original. As his solution, he provided an obvious warning to the "Christian Reader" that this particular section should be read with reservation as the 'German author' was clearly "possessed by the devil" to have blatantly written this heretical gibberish. From this point onwards, however, the narrative of Faust's visit to the stars parallels the early manuscript, with the minor exception P.F. omitted the detail explaining how the moon receives its light from the sun.

The following Chapter, i.e. Twenty-two,[∞] features Faust's journey through "the most famous lands of the world." Haile condensed this chapter in his edition of the Wolfenbüttle manuscript and concentrated exclusively on Faust's visit to Rome and Constantinople as the majority of the original text appears to be a perfunctory insertion by a scribe. Gustave Milchsack

---

[597] *Faustus and the Censor*, p.77.
[∞] Ch. 26 in Spies.

observed that the geographical descriptions of each region were heavily plagiarised from Hartmann Schedel's *Nürnberger Chronik* (1493).[598] Rose remarks the peculiar 'zig-zag' nature of Faust's journey was actually caused by Schedel's procedure of naming towns in his *Chronik* chronologically according to the assumed year they were founded, which the author, i.e. the scribe, then listed mechanically in his text.[599] Haile also notes the characteristic rambling of the cities Faust visited as proof of this copious copying method conducted by a separate scribe.[600] Spies retained this element in his edition of the *Faustbook*, however, as previously stated, the English translator Mr. P.F. also stamped his personal perceptions into the English edition, making this chapter particularly interesting.

The chapter commences with Faust entering the fifteenth year of his contract and his travel plans to distant countries.[ɸ] Mephostophiles transforms into the legendary flying horse[ɸ] upon which Faust rides to view the entire world in twenty-five days — we may observe the unimaginative list actually benefits the text as it portrays to our senses the speed in which they travelled. By adding several new locations, P.F. also indulged his enthusiasm for express travel:

> "[...] Faustus came through many a land & Province; as *Pannonia*,[601] *Austria, Germania, Bohemia, Slesia*,[602] *Saxony, Missene*,[603] *During*,[604] *Fracklandt*,[605] *Shawblandt*,[606] *Beyerlandt*,[607] **Stiria**,[608] **Carinthia**,[609] *Poland, Litaw*,[610] *Liefland*,[611] *Prussia*, **Denmarke**,

---

[598] *Sources of the Faust Tradition*, p. 129.

[599] *Damnable Life and Deserved Death of [...] Faustus*, p. 30.

[600] *History of Doctor Johann Faustus*, pp. 12–13.

[ɸ] Henry Jones presents E. M. Butler's findings that wanderings to distant lands is one of the ten stock features of fully developed magus legends, therefore these journeys are consequential to the Faust legend. (*Faustus and the Censor*, p. 23.)

[ɸ] In Spies, it is stated Mephostophiles changes into a horse "winged like a dromedary". Cotterill remarks; "It is I believe, not generally supposed that a dromedary has wings; but I suppose the old chronicler must have confused a camel and an ostrich, thinking of the name which some Greek authors give to the ostrich, namely *stroutho-camelos* or 'sparrow-camel.' " (*The Faust Legend and Goethe's Faust*, p. 40.)

[601] (Palmer and More's footnotes for this excerpt are in brackets.) [The Region of Hungary.] Originally, it was the ancient country of Illyria and it received its name from the Pannonians, people who lived there since ancient times.

[602] Silesia, historic region of central Europe, which is now southwestern Poland.

[603] [Meissen.] A city in Saxony.

[604] [Thuringia.]

[605] [Franconia.]

[606] [Suabia.] Swabia.

[607] [Bavaria.]

[608] Styria; an alpine province in south-eastern Austria near Slovenia.

[609] Carinthia; a province in southern Austria. After WWI, the province lost some of its territory to Yugoslavia and Italy.

[610] [Lithuania.]

[611] [Livonia.] Part of Latvia and Estonia.

Muscovia,[612]   *Tartaria,*[613]   *Turkie, Persia, Cathai,*[614] *Alexandria,* **Barbaria,**[615] **Ginnie,**[616] **Peru, the strayghts of *Magelanes,*[617] India, all about the frozen *Zone,* and *Terra Incognita,*[618] *Nova Hispaniola,*[619] the Isles of *Terzera,*[620] *Mederi,*[621] *S. Michaels,*[622] the *Canaries,* and the *Tenorrifocie,*[623]** into *Spaine,* the *Mayne Land,*[624] *Portugall, Italie,* **Campania, the Kingdom of *Naples,* the Isles of *Sicilia, Malta, Maioria,*[625] *Minoria,*[626] to the Knights of the *Rhodes,*[627] Candie, or Creete,*[628] Ciprus,*[629] Corinth,*[630] Switzerland,*** France, *Freesland,*[631] *Westphalia,*[632] *Zeland,*[633] *Holland, Brabant,*[634] **and all the 17• Provinces in *Netherland, England, Scotland, Ireland,* all *America,* and *Island,*[635] the out Isles of *Scotland,* the *Orchades, Norway,* the Bishoprick of *Breame,*[636] and so home agayne: [...]"**[637]

---

[612]   Muscovy, Moscow.

[613]   Tartary. In medieval times, the region stretching from Dnieper River to the Sea of Japan. Later, a distinction was made between European and Asian Tartary; gradually, Asian Tartary became recognised as Turkistan.

[614]   China.

[615]   Barbary Coast, the northern coast of Africa from Egypt to the Atlantic Ocean.

[616]   "Ginnie" could be Guinea.

[617]   The Straights of Magellan near the tip of South America.

[618]   [Probably the unknown regions near the poles.] Early maps indicate the unexplored regions of Canada just above the Great Lakes as "Terra Incognita".

[619]   [Mexico.]

[620]   [One of the Azores.] I.e. Terceira, second largest of the islands.

[621]   [Probably Madeira.]

[622]   [One of the Azores.] I.e. São Miguel, largest of the islands.

[623]   [Probably Teneriffe.]

[624]   [Perhaps the old province of Maine in France.] Today, Maine is bordered by Normandy in the north, Poitou in the south, Orléanais in the east, and Brittany in the west.

[625]   [Majorca.]

[626]   [Minorca.]

[627]   I.e. the island of Rhodes. The Knights of St. John of Jerusalem (Knights of Malta) held the island until defeated by the Muslims in 1522; in 1530, Emperor Charles V bestowed to them the island of Malta as their new headquarters.

[628]   Candia, now Iráklion, is the largest seaport on the island of Crete.

[629]   Cyprus.

[630]   City of Corinth.

[631]   Frisia, Friesland / Frisian Islands in the Netherlands.

[632]   Former Prussian province now part of the German state of North Rhine-Westphalia.

[633]   Zealand / Sjaelland, the largest island of Denmark.

[634]   Brabant, once a duchy comprising the present day provinces of the North Brabant in the Netherlands, and of Antwerp and Brabant in Belgium.

[635]   [Iceland.]

[636]   [Bremen.]

[637]   *Sources of the Faust Tradition,* pp. 174–175. (Original spelling retained in this excerpt.) Bold text, *The English Faust Book; A Critical Edition,* pp. 127–128.

This preoccupation with the ability to travel the world in a matter of days seems inconsequential to modern generations accustomed to jet planes and the instantaneous velocity of electronic communication technology; however, the novelty of achieving great speeds through superhuman mediums was a fantasy that captured the popular imagination of that era. Transport, trade, and the dissemination of news was a slow and painstaking process. Denys Hays writes:

> "How slow was commercial traffic? On land an unencumbered man on a tolerable horse, following a regular road without obstacles on it, could average something like fifteen miles in an hour and, with regular changes of horses, some remarkable performances were achieved: the 400-odd miles between Paris and Avignon were covered in four days in 1349 by a courier sent by Charles VI to anticipate the conclave. [...] Edward IV in 1482 arranged relays of riders to cover the 200 miles between Newcastle and London in two days. But these were emergency journeys. The usual messenger did not ride by night; papal couriers in the fourteenth century covered in a day about sixty miles in good terrain and only half that in mountain areas. Merchants' letters were normally slower still. And all schedules were liable to be put out by illness, lack of horses, or the suspicion of the authorities through whose territories the messenger passed. Consequently even for urgent despatches the margin between prompt delivery and later delivery was enormous.[...]* And the moment sea routes were also involved the uncertainty was even greater: Venice–London could take only nine days, or it could take over fifty.
>
> If this was the speed of news, and financial and other documents, the slowness of commodities in land transport can readily be imagined. A convoy with horses and mules might cover between fifteen and twenty miles a day. [...] even on a favourable network of canals and rivers the speed was no better. [...] At sea, while ships could make seventy-five miles to eighty miles in a day, they were usually able to steer straight for their destination only for very short periods and consequently even a fast boat seldom averaged as much. The voyage from Venice to Candia (Crete), which could be done in eighteen days in favourable conditions, normally took between twenty-three and thirty in summer, between forty-five and sixty in winter. [...] A record voyage (1509) from Southampton to Otranto brought the Venetian Flemish galleys over the 2,500 miles in thirty-one days."[638]

---

* Hay lists some examples of these margins from late fifteenth-century Venetian documents. Venice to Augsburg Max. 21 days, Min. 5 days; Venice to Florence Max. 13 days, Min. 1 day; Venice to Genoa Max. 15 days, Min. 2 days; Venice to Paris Max. 34 days, Min. 7 days; Venice to Vienna Max 32 days, Min. 8 days.

[638] Denys Hay, *Europe in the Fourteenth and Fifteenth Centuries*, (New York: Longman Group Ltd. 1989), pp.391–392.

This fascination with the ability to travel at great speeds or the possibility of receiving news in record time is not an exclusive element of the Faust legends. Tales of nobles willing to resort to *familiar* spirits for their abilities to travel at the speed of human thought abound in medieval anecdotes. We distinguish two examples in Book Three (1386–88) of Jean Froissart's *Chronicles*.[639] During his stay at the court of the Count of Foix, Froissart learned from a squire that the Count had an uncanny ability to discover all that occurred in the castle, and also in far away lands before the arrival of messengers, with the result the courtiers were convinced the Count was a practitioner of necromancy. The squire relates one instance where the Count was already aware of the disastrous outcome of the Battle at Aljubarrota in Portugal on the very day it was fought, while the official reports did not reach their region until the soldiers returned ten days later. Froissart's informant also relates a separate anecdote concerning the Lord of Corresse, a noble believed to have a familiar spirit named Orton that brought him all the news from every kingdom at prodigious speed.

Faust, however, is not entirely satisfied with his breakneck journey and desires to spend additional time as a sightseer discovering the secrets and pleasures of each city for a further year and a half.[640] It is here we encounter the detailed descriptions of towns and places, which Henry Jones describes as "a 'Blue Guide' nearly a century out of date [... by 1587]".[641] Some of these accounts are borrowings from Schedel's *Nürnberger Chronik* (1493), which were transcribed into Spies' book. Other descriptive passages are new additions by P.F. obviously inspired by his own travel experiences — his major embellishments to the text are as follows:

- The reference to Virgil's tomb in the "Kingdom of Naples" and the road he allegedly built in one night: "[...] **there saw he the Tomb of** *Virgil*; **and the highway that he cut through that mighty hill of stone in one night, the whole length of an English mile.** [...]"[642] Faust them observes the ships in the port, also the "windmill"♪ and the castle in

---

[639] Jean Froissart, Geoffrey Brereton, trans., *Chronicles*, (Penguin Classics: 1978), pp. 295–302.
[640] The places Faust visits on this second journey are: Trier, Paris, Mentz (Mainz, or Mayence) on the Main river, Campania / Naples, Venice, Padua, Rome, Milan, Bologna, Florence, Lyon, Cologne, Aix-la-Chapelle, Genf (Geneva), Strasbourg, Basil, Costuitz [Constance, Konstanz], Ulm, Würzburg, Nuremberg, Augsburg, Ravensburg, returned to Mentz in Bavaria (Palmer and More state this second 'Mentz' is actually 'Munich' due to the combined reference with Bavaria. There must have been a confusion in the translation as Faust "returns" to Mentz, which is now a totally different city!) Salzburg, Vienna, Prague, Breslaw (now Wroclaw), Cracow, Buchnia (Bucharest?) Sandetz (in Eastern European Galicia), an unknown "new town" near Sandetz with an order of "St. Dioclesian" nuns, Hungary, Transylvania, Shede (Schedia of Egypt?), Ingratz (Ingush / Ingushetia?), Sardinia, Constantinople, Alkar (i.e. Chairam, or Memphis: Palmer and More state this confusion in names originated with Schedel's *Chronik*, where "[...] there is a picture labelled Memphis vel Chayrum. The descriptive paragraph identifies the two places." *Sources of the Faust Tradition*, n. 85 p. 188.) Ofen (Budapest), Sabatz (Šabac in Yugoslavia?), Austria, through Slesia (Silesia?) to Saxony, Magdeburg, Leipzig, Lubeck, Hamburg, Erfurt, back home to Wittenberg.
[641] *Faustus and the Censor*, p. 24.
[642] *The English Faust Book; A Critical Edition*, p. 129.

the water. Virgil was also recognised as a magician, thus explaining the apropos reference to him in the *Faust Book*.

- The additional description of the waterways in Venice, including the plaza of St. Mark's and the cathedral of the same.[643]
- In the town of Padua, Faust signs himself "**Doctor Faustus, the insatiable Speculator**" in the guest book of the "**University of the German Nation**": (a detail that has no substantive proof as a factual event).[644]
- The comparison of the travel time in which the boats travel between Venice and Padua with those of London: "[…] **as they do here betwixt *London* and *Gravesend*.**"
- The description of the four stone bridges over the river Tiber in Rome; "[…] over the river Tiber, the which devideth the City in two parts: **over the river are four great stone bridges, and upon the one bridge called Ponte S. Angelo is the castle of S. *Angelo*, wherein are so many great cast pieces as there are days in a year, […] to this castle cometh a privy vault from the church and palace of St. Peter, through which the Pope (if any danger be) passeth from his palace to the castle for safeguard.**"[645]
- The description of the Campo Santo in Rome, the sentence referring to the 'Julius Cæsar' obelisk at the Vatican: "[…] **it stood in *Faustus* his time leaning against the Church wall of Saint Peters, but now Papa Sixtus hath erected it […].**", and a list of the seven churches.[646]

---

* Henry Jones writes P.F.'s source for the "windmill" in the sea was the *Civitas Orbis Terrarum* (first Latin Editions, 5 vol: 1572–1598). The *COT* I fol. 47, displays what seems to be a windmill (or windlass) on the *molo grande*; "[…] if PF was not at Naples, he may have confused *moles* (piers) and *molae* (mills)." (*The English Faust Book; A Critical Edition*, n. 1275, p. 215.)

[643] *The English Faust Book; A Critical Edition*, p. 129.

[644] Ibid.

[645] Ibid. p. 130.

[646] Ibid. Henry Jones writes that P.F.'s measurements for the obelisk are ludicrously wrong, suggesting P.F. had never seen the monument, and therefore had never visited Rome. P.F. writes: "[…] it is 24 fathom long and at the lower end is six fathom four square, and so forth smaller upwards; […]". (One fathom = 6 feet.) Henry Jones states that a measurement of 24 *yards* (i.e. height = 72 feet) with a base measurement of 8 feet, four inches would be correct, as calculated from Fulvius. (*The English Faust Book; A Critical Edition*, n. 1321, p. 217) Apparently, Henry Jones misread P.F.'s measurements as 24 fathoms in height (144 feet) + the width the base as 6 fathoms 4 'squared' multiplication style. (Perhaps 6.4 fathoms squared: 38.4 x 38.4 = 1474.56 feet wide, or, 6 fathoms + 4 squared: 36 + 16 = 52 feet wide.) Naturally, these measurements would not correspond with the slender demensions of an obelisk.

However, P.F.'s phrase "and so forth smaller upwards" is curious, and obviously reflects the tapering dimensions of the monument. It is possible the word 'square' was intended as a *separate* description, not only in reference to its geometircal shape, but also its *height*, not its width. For instance, Sarah Beach writes that the total height of the obelisk is 132 feet, but the shaft alone without the plinth is 83 feet. (See 'The Julius Cæsar Obelisk' *MLN*, n. 6, p. 28) Therefore, if we subtract the shaft height (83) from 132, the plinth alone is 49 feet. P.F. was accurate to a point if he was simply averaging by a quick glance the *total height* of the obelisk as 144 feet, and then mentioned separately the *vertical measurements of its plinth* as 6 fathom, 4 feet (perhaps 36 + 4 = 40). Therefore, the possibility remains P.F. visited Rome.

- Faust smotes the Pope a 'blow' on his face rather than *blowing* into his face, and prattles a ribald speech mocking the religious as being violators of the vow of celibacy.[647] There is a confusion between the Capitoline Hill with Monte Cavallo, or Monte Quirinal, upon which Pope Sixtus V built his palace. Faust also drops his stolen silverware over a religious procession.[648]
- The city of Sienna is included.[649]
- P.F. inserts further mockery against the tradition that the relics of the Three Kings lie in Cologne.[650]
- The description of the steeple of Strasbourg, the legend pertaining to the founding of Basel, and the naming of the city of Constance. P.F. edited the description of Würzburg.[651] He also added to or modified the descriptions of Prague, Breslau (i.e. Wroclaw), Cracow, and Leipzig.[652]

Several of these details listed above are interesting due to the additional information gleaned from local traditions resulting in an entertaining narrative. However, we discover a considerable number of these alterations evince that this is not a typical travelogue concentrating exclusively on descriptions for their sight-seeing interest. Many of P.F.'s more intriguing insertions contain enigmatic, sarcastic barbs intended to make a point regarding topics related to the Reformation and other contemporary issues.

In his narrative on Rome, we read several anti-Catholic references: the misspelling for the Vatican Hill, i.e. "Vaticinium", instead of *Vaticanum* is the first of these sarcastic innuendos. Henry Jones observes this is an anti-papal pun as the word "vaticinium" is indicative of prophesy, or soothsaying.[653] Notice the comparison with the rare word "vaticinate", which means, "to foretell the future".

P.F.'s next blatant criticism focuses on the perceived abuses of the Confessional, i.e. that confessions are not heard in the Vatican unless the pilgrim has money ready in his hand — hence, the indulgence controversy is alluded to. To undertake a pilgrimage in that era was an arduous task, the journey was often expensive, time consuming and fatiguing due to the nature of travel back then. However, pilgrims often went a step further; in a spirit of penance, many travelled on foot and relied on the charity of those whom they would meet for shelter and provisions in imitation of the poverty of Christ and thereby exercise their trust in Divine Providence. Thus, the fathers of the Reformation were scandalised at the perceived opportunism of corrupt clerics that preyed upon souls searching for God. A cryptic statement in the text concerning the "Campo Santo" adjoining St. Peter's then follows: **"Adjoining to this Church, is the *Campo Santo*, the which *Carolus Magnus* [Charlemagne] built, where every day thirteen Pilgrims have their dinners served of the best: that is to say, Christ and his twelve Apostles."** Palmer and More

---

[647] *The English Faust Book; A Critical Edition*, p. 130.
[648] Ibid. p. 132.
[649] Ibid. p. 133.
[650] Ibid.
[651] Ibid. pp. 134–135.
[652] Ibid. pp. 134–142.
[653] Ibid. p. 216, n. 1312.

surmise this reference to the 'thirteen Pilgrims' may allude to the *mandatum* ceremonies of Maundy Thursday[654] when the priest washes the feet of twelve participants to symbolise Christ washing the feet of His Apostles as an example of the humility they were to attain. If this observation is correct, P.F. in this instance would be mocking the seeming hypocrisy of the Church at that time, i.e. while pardon and forgiveness would be withheld from weary, impoverished pilgrims until they bought an indulgence, there were other 'pilgrims' who played the poor servant only once a year and afterwards feasted sumptuously everyday on the indulgence money they were receiving. This interpretation, however, only explains one part of the enigmatic phrase, there are also the unusual references to "Campo Santo" and to Charlemagne. Palmer and More state that 'Campo Santo' or 'Holy Ground' is the Italian expression for a cemetery, this is not far removed from historical fact as the basilica of the Vatican is built upon the ancient Roman cemetery where St. Peter was buried. At first, this observation fails to explain the reference to Charlemagne as he did not construct the cemetery. The term 'Campo Santo' therefore has a dual inference and may collectively refer to the "Holy Ground" of the Papal States that were greatly enlarged with Charlemagne's conquests and donations, and also to the Holy Roman Empire, first founded by Charlemagne — P.F. is continuing his sarcastic observations by alluding to the great land-wealth the Church was amassing in addition to the granting of indulgences. We note he could also be reinforcing this concept with the numerical connection between the Pope and Charlemagne by his reference to the twelve apostles; this may also intimate the legendary "Twelve Peers" of Charlemagne's rearguard that were massacred in the Pyrenees as recounted in the legendary epic, *The Song of Roland* (1100?).

The anti-Catholic annotations continue with Faust's visit to the Papal palace. We discover in addition to Faust's comment regarding the licentiousness of the papal court first seen in the manuscript, there is a rather explicit passage referring to the violation of the vow of celibacy between the friars and nuns.[655] Faust also invisibly drops his stolen wares from the palace over the heads of St. Bernard's "friars", or a group of Cistercian monks, taking part in a procession.

While visiting Cologne, Faust sarcastically plots the posthumous journey of the Three Kings to their final resting place in the city, a Reformational paragraph intended to question the validity of the traditional legends of the saints and the veneration of their relics. P.F. decided to embellish the voyage:

> "From thence he went to Cologne, which lies upon the river of
> Rhine, wherein he saw one of the ancientest monuments of the world, the
> which was the tomb of the three kings that came by the angel of God, and
> their knowledge they had in the star, to worship Christ: which when

---

[654] *Sources of the Faust Tradition*, n. 67, p. 177.

[655] "[…] the Devil might do well now to spit them all and have them to the fire, and let him summon the Nuns to turn the spits: for as none must confess the Nun but the Friar, so none should turn the roasting Friar but the Nun." Compare with the suggestive speech of Robin, the horse keeper, in Marlowe's *Doctor Faustus* (A text 1604) Act II, iii: Robin; "True, Rafe: and more, Rafe, if thou hast any mind to Nan Spit, our kitchen maid, then turn her and wind her to thy own use as often as thou wilt, and at midnight." *Doctor Faustus; A and B Texts*, n. 29–30, p. 149.

Faustus saw, he spake in this manner: 'Ah, alas good men how have you erred and lost your way, you should have gone to Palestine and Bethlehem in Judea, how came you hither? Or belike after your death you were thrown into **Mare Mediterraneum about Tripolis in Syria** [i.e. Tripoli, Lebanon]; **and so you fleeted, out of the Straights of Gibraltar into the Ocean Sea, and so into the bay of Portugal; and not finding any rest you were driven alongst the coast of Galicia, Biscay, and France, and into the Narrow Seas, then from thence into Mare Germanicum** [the North Sea], **and so I think taken up about the town of Dort in Holland,** you were brought to Cologne to be buried: **or else I think you came more easily with a whirl-wind over the Alps, and being thrown into the River of Rhine, it conveyed you to this place, where you are kept as a monument.**'."[656]

Departing from the town of Cologne, Faust proceeds to the town of Aachen, also called Aix-la-Chapelle. Here the text reads that Faust visited the "gorgeous Temple" that Charles IV ("*Carolus quartus*") built as a memorial to his Imperial personage where all his successors to the Imperial throne were to be crowned. Rose and Henry Jones maintain "Carolus quartus" is P.F.'s error in the text and that the information should refer to Charlemagne, i.e. "Carolus Magnus". This theory appears logical for Charlemagne, the first Holy Roman Emperor, built his palace and a cathedral there. Historians also believe Aachen was his birthplace. However, Henry Jones relates P.F. "[...] was possibly conditioned by knowledge learned at *Prague* where Charles IV founded St. Vitus's cathedral, and later, the Karlštejn castle where the imperial insignia where kept."[657] This may be true, but we continue to detect associations linked with the town of Aachen and Charles IV in this section of the text. During the reign of Charles IV (Holy Roman Emperor 1347–78), the town hall of Aachen was constructed on the remnants of Charlemagne's palace (1353), and the chancel of the cathedral containing the tomb and throne of Charlemagne was completed in the fourteenth century. The information in the *Faustbook* regarding a temple constructed of marble is therefore a possible reference to these structures. In addition, Charles IV was responsible for the drafting of the Golden Bull (1356), the imperial constitution in which the legal procedures relevant to the elections and coronations of successive emperors were specified, including who could participate in an election. The obligations and the various privileges bestowed upon the electors were also specified in the Bull. This constitution remained in effect until the dissolution of the Holy Roman Empire in 1806. We therefore note this data in the *Faustbook* may be a veritable acknowledgment of Charles IV's reign and the standards he established formalising the procedures for future coronation ceremonies.

In the *Faustbook* we find one interesting description of the folklore attributed to the Swiss city of Basel. Mephostophiles explains the city received its name from a huge serpent, or basilisk □ that once terrified the inhabitants of that area:

---

[656] *The English Faust Book; A Critical Edition*, p. 133.
[657] Ibid. n. 1427, p. 219.
□ A giant mythological serpent that could kill simply by looking at its victims.

"[...] this serpent killed as many men, women, and children, as it took sight of: but there was a knight that made himself a cover of crystal to come over his head, and so down to the ground, and being first covered with a black cloth, over that he put the crystal, and so boldly went to see the basiliscus, and finding the place where he haunted, [...] the basylike came forth, who, when she saw her own venomous shadow in the Crystal, she split in a thousand pieces; wherefore the knight was richly rewarded of the Emperor: after which the knight founded this Town upon the place where he had slain the Serpent, and gave it the name of Basel, in remembrance of his deed."[658]

According to recorded history, the town was founded in the year 374 A.D. by the Romans as a frontier post and was originally called Basilia. Henry Jones discovered one local tradition recorded by Felix Fabri (d. 1502) concerning the founding of Basel. Allegedly, there was a basilisk in that area, and was slain by a shepherd who was protected from the deadly serpent by a magical floral wreath.[659] Henry Jones suggests P.F. had also drawn inspiration from the myth of Perseus and Medusa for his unique rendition of this legend. However, there is one further possibility not yet considered; this may be a cryptic allusion to the Dutch humanist and scholar, Desiderius Erasmus (1466?–1536). Erasmus was born in Rotterdam and journeyed from city to city as a tutor and lecturer; he travelled to Basel where he lectured at the university. Upon his death, he was buried in the Münster Cathedral. Although he remained a staunch Catholic, Erasmus is regarded as one of the fathers of the Reformation resulting from the profound influence his literary works had affected those who championed reform in the Church. The story of the knight may allude to one of his books in particular, namely, *The Manual of the Christian Knight* (1503: trans.1533) in which he decried corrupt church practises and advocated a return to simplicity in the Christian faith. The knight defeating the basilisk in the *Faustbook* may therefore represent Erasmus and his work as a scholar eradicating a deadly foe in Basel, i.e. a corrupt church.

Faust subsequently visits the city of Konstanz, we are informed the name originated from "Costuitz", or "cost nothing" referring to an incident when the Emperor presented the city to a clown as a reward for correctly answering a riddle. Evidently this is a further enigmatic statement as the city was originally called Constantia by the Romans and existed since the third century A.D.. Palmer and More state the old name for the city was printed "kostnitz", (in the source text?), and that the "u", or inverted "n", is a printer's error in the London edition.[660] Henry Jones remarks this error in the London text unfortunately obscures the pun P.F. intended with "Cost**n**itz".[661] Obviously P.F. recognised the parallel with the German words "kosten" = "cost" plus "nichts" = "nothing" with the name "kostnitz", and discovered a double meaning could be implied. In 1192, Konstanz became an imperial free city, however this privilege was revoked in

[658] *The English Faust Book; A Critical Edition*, pp. 134–135.
[659] Ibid. n. 1449–61, p. 219.
[660] *Sources of the Faust Tradition*, n. 76, p. 182.
[661] *The English Faust Book; A Critical Edition*, n. 1462, p. 220.

1548 during the reign of Holy Roman Emperor Charles V when the city joined the Schmalkaldic League, an association founded by Protestant princes in 1531. Charles thereby presented the city to his brother, Archduke Ferdinand of Austria, who later became Holy Roman Emperor Ferdinand I. This reference to a "clown" receiving the city may refer to the suppression and the presentation of the city to Ferdinand.

Faust's visit to Nuremberg is interesting due to the excessive details recorded concerning this one town:

> "From thence he went to Nuremburg, whither as he went by the way, his Spirit informed him that the town was named of Claudius Tiberius the son of Nero the tyrant. In the Town are two famous Cathedral Churches, the one called Saint Sabolt, [Sebald] the other Saint Laurence [Lorenz]; in which Church hangeth all the relics of Carolus Magnus, that is his cloak, **his hose and doublet**, his sword and crowne, his sceptre, and his Apple. It hath a very gorgeous gilden conduit [fountain] in the market **of Saint Laurence**, in which conduit, is the spear that thrust our Saviour into the side, and a piece of the Holy Cross; **the wall is called the fair wall of Nuremberg, and** hath 528 streets, 160 wells, four great, and two small clocks, six great gates, and two small doors, eleven stone bridges, twelve small hills, ten appointed market places, thirteen common hothouses [i.e. public bathhouses], ten churches. Within the town are thirty wheels of water-mills; it hath 132 **tall ships**, two mighty town walls of hewn stone and earth, with very deep trenches. **The walls have** 180 towers **about them**, and four fair platform, ten apothecaries, ten doctors of the common law, fourteen doctors of physic." [662]

Needless to mention, the majority of this statistical information was plagiarised from Schedel's *Nürnberger Chronik*. However, one phrase in the text has puzzled scholars, P.F.'s reference to "132 tall ships" for a town that is approximately 350 miles (c. 563 km) from the ocean! Palmer and More mention that Spies had printed "132 Hauptmannschafft" in the German edition and P.F. simply mistranslated it. [663] This is a logical conclusion as he could have easily mistaken the German word "haupt" = "prime" or "main" for the French "haut" = "tall" and combined it with the German "schaft" = "shaft" to arrive at the English translation — "tall mast". P.F. simply did not crosscheck his translation with geographical reality! Henry Jones states "captaincies", (i.e. as in army rank), is the correct translation. [664] Notice this unusual phrase is combined with the description of the city's main structures of defence, namely, the walls, towers and trenches.

The intrigue continues with the supposed 'fact' of how the city "Norenberg" was named by Nero's son, Claudius Tiberius. First, Spies, (or Schedel!) was misinformed regarding ancient

---

[662] Ibid. pp. 135– 136.
[663] *Sources of the Faust Tradition*, n. 80, p. 183.
[664] *The English Faust Book; A Critical Edition*, n. 1499, p.221.

Roman history; the "Tyrant" Nero, presumably the emperor infamous for his persecution of the Christians, was the last of the Julio-Claudian line, and did not have a son named "Claudius Tiberius". He may have confused the infamous Nero with Claudius I, (Tiberius Claudius Drusus Nero Germanicus), whose father, Nero Claudius Drusus, was the younger brother of Tiberius Claudius Nero Caesar, who became the Emperor Tiberius. It is not difficult to see where the confusion arises, particularly as the "Tyrant" Nero's original name was Nero Claudius Caesar Drusus Germanicus. Second, the city of Nuremberg is not mentioned in historic documentation until the year 1050! We therefore suspect this reference to Nero the persecutor of Christians, notwithstanding the historical inaccuracy, is of cryptic significance. The second reference in the text to Charlemagne provides the vital clue to this mystery. We notice that the list of his various relics concludes with a sarcastic reference to his alleged preserved (Adam's ?) apple. In addition, P.F. contributed his peculiar addition to the list of relics by including the Emperor's hosiery! Hence, we observe further derogatory passages in the Faust text directed at the first Holy Roman Emperor and the religious practise of venerating relics. This brings to our attention that Nuremberg became the capital of the Holy Roman German Empire after 1356, with the falsification of the city's origins with Nero the "Tyrant" and the less than respectful reference to Charlemagne, we perceive further barbs directed at the current Holy Catholic Roman Emperor and the devotional practises of the Catholic Church.

Continuing with Faust's visit to the town of Salzburg, we find that on the hill overlooking the town he saw the form of "*Abel*", (which should read "a bell" according to later texts), that was fashioned from crystal:

> "[…] from Munich to Salzburg, where the bishop is always resident: **here saw he all the commodities that were possible to be seen, for at the hill he saw the form of *Abel* made in crystal, an huge thing to look upon, that every year groweth bigger and bigger, by reason of the freezing cold.**"[665]

If a monument of this description had indeed existed, evidence would have presented itself previously; hence, as with other sections relating Faust's travels, this may be an additional cryptic statement. We find in the First Book of Kings that during the days of Samuel the prophet when the Philistines returned the Ark of the Covenant, they set it down on a great stone called the 'Help of God' or 'Abel'. (1 Kings 6: 18) Beginning with the location of this giant bell in the *Faustbook*, the dominant hill that P.F. could be referring to is the Mönchsberg, or Monk's Mount, which rises above the town. We also observe the reference to the bishop's continual presence and the abundant supply of provisions the area enjoys. Could this reference to a "crystal bell" be yet again a derogatory barb directed at the 'rock' of the Catholic Church? We observe this unusual bell is similar to the crystal covering made by the 'Knight' of Basel who destroyed the 'basilisk'. The "freezing cold" could represent the increasing lack of charity and the growing vices of greed and jealousy, as Christ warned would occur when corruption abounds, especially near the end times. Perhaps P.F. presented a warning that a new "basilisk" could emerge in that

---

[665] Ibid. p. 137.

town due to its prosperity whereby its citizens would be in danger of losing their basic Christian simplicity as advocated by Erasmus.⁼

Later in the text, we encounter in the town of Breslau, i.e. Wroclaw, a disturbing account of a certain monument — a giant bronze statue of the Virgin Mary reportedly constructed for the execution of wayward youths:

> **"In this city he saw not many wonders, except the brazen virgin that standeth on a bridge over the water, and under the which standeth a mill like a powder mill, which virgin is made to do execution upon those disobedient town-born children that be so wild, yet their parents cannot bridle them; which when any are found with some heinous offence, turning to the shame of their parents and kindred, they are brought to kiss the virgin, which openeth her arms, the person then to be executed, kisseth her, then doth she close her arms together with such violence, that she crusheth out the breath of the person, breaketh his bulk, and so dieth: but being dead, she openeth her arms again, and letteth the party fall into the mill, where he is stamped in small morsels, which the water carrieth away, so that not any part is found of him again."**[666]

There is no historical evidence the city had this gruesome machine, although there are factual elements from which this tale was possibly inspired. Henry Jones relates:

> "There is no archival testimony to any such 'virgin' at Breslau, though there is a tale of an 'iron maiden' of Breslau in the Kaiserburg, formerly on the site of the Matthiasstift at the Oderthor.** An engine identical to the EFB 'virgin', but not associated with Breslau, is described by Arkon Darul (*Secret Societies*, 1961, p. 203) as a mode of execution employed by the Vehm courts, but no source is cited."[667]

We observe the town is described by P.F. as possessing few "wonders", yet this is not entirely true — the city can boast of four churches that are main points of interest: the cathedral of St. John the Baptist (started in 1158), the thirteenth-century Church of St. Elizabeth, the Church of the Holy Cross (13ᵗʰ –14ᵗʰ century), and the Church of Our Lady of the Sand (14ᵗʰ century). Considering that many churches are mentioned in the course of Faust's travels, it is atypical that for the city of Wroclaw these buildings are ignored and are not considered worthy of a brief mention. However, the title "Our Lady of the *Sand*" captures our attention in this

---

⁼ Henry Jones offers a different interpretation; " 'Abel', could be an attempted reminder of Faustus as Cain, but it is possibly a jibe at Abel Jeffes." (*The English Faust Book; A Critical Edition*, p. 221)

[666] *The English Faust Book; A Critical Edition*, p. 138.

** Henry Jones' source: 'Die eiserne Jungfrau von Breslau' in Hermann Goedsche (ed.): *Schlesischer Sagen-, Historien- und Legendenschatz*, Meissen 1840, pp. 39–42.

[667] *The English Faust Book; A Critical Edition*, n. 1559–71, p. 222.

instance, it is possible this name suggested to P.F.'s imagination the concept of a *powder* mill near the *river* in conjuction with the stories of the iron maiden and the torture mill described by Henry Jones above. It may be plausible the pro-Reformation Mr. P.F. derisively omitted the existence of these four ecclesiastical buildings in favour of fabricating a grotesque tale to depict the city as a stronghold of intense Catholic fanaticism. Alternatively, Empson proposes Mr. P.F. appended this fable as a general, "jovial insinuation against public sadism," having witnessed the "incessant witch-burnings" during his apparent sojourn in Germany.[668]

The noticeable anti-Catholic references conclude with the account of Faust's visit to Sandetz, i.e. Nowy Sącz, in the eastern European region of Galicia (Poland):

> "[…] **From thence, Faustus went to Sandetz: the captain thereof was called Don Spiket Jordan. In this town are many monuments as the tomb or sepulchre of Christ, in as ample manner as that is at Jerusalem, at the proper costs of a gentleman that went thrice to Jerusalem from that place, and returned again. Not far from that town is a new town, wherein is a nunnery of the order of Saint Dioclesian, into which order may none come, except they be gentlewomen, and well formed and fair to look upon, […].**"[669]

Faustian scholars previously paid little attention to P.F.'s inclusion of this township and its inhabitants, however, Henry Jones uncovered substantial new information that merits a full quotation:

> "The inclusion of Sandetz (Nowy Sącz), not exactly a tourist attraction, is decisive, although its significance has escaped previous commentators through their failure to identify 'Don Spiket Jordan,' 'the captain' of the town. Here, 'captain' is PF's word for the Polish *starost*, no mere platoon commander but a plenipotentiary regional governor of considerable military and political importance. Spytek Wawrzyniec Jordan (d. 1596),[#] a powerful Catholic nobleman, became *starost* of Nowy Sącz on the 20 July 1584 and held this office until 22 January 1590. In the power struggles following the death (12 December 1586) of King Stephen Batory, Jordan supported the Zborowski (pro-Austrian) faction against Jan Zamoyski; however, he took no part in the seige of Cracow (winter 1587–8), nor in the decisive battle of Byczyna (24 January 1588) in which Zamoyski defeated the imperial forces, but remained entrenched in his stronghold of Nowy Sącz. In the following year, at the cost of a huge fine, he made his peace with the new monarch

---

[668] *Faustus and the Censor*, p. 73.
[669] *The English Faust Book; A Critical Edition*, p. 139.
[#] Henry Jones' footnote: "*Polski Słownik Biograficzny*, xi (1964–5) pp. 284f: under Jordan, Spytek Wawrzynce. I am indebted to Prof. Jan Pirozyński of the Biblioteka Jagiellońska, Krakow, and to Dr Władysław Stępniak of the Archiwum Głowne Akt Dawynych, Warsaw, for this identification."

Sigismund, retaining his seat in the Diet (*Seym*) and continuing to oppose Zamoyski and promote Catholic interests. […]

The naming of Jordan and the inclusion of Sandetz suggests that PF was present in Cracow in 1587, perhaps shortly before the siege ('[the castle of Cracow] **is full of all manner of munition, and hath always victual for three years to serve 2000 men**') when the whole county was anxiously waiting to see how this powerful magnate would comport himself in the coming offensive. The actual description of Sandetz is full of confusions: the monastery of 'St. Dioclesian' (a nonsense), i.e. the convent of the Poor Clares (A retreat for aristocratic ladies as PF correctly observes), was located not in the 'new town' but in Old Sandetz (Stary Sącz); the tomb of 'Christ' cannot be substantiated.◆ I suspect PF gathered these details from his informant at Cracow rather than by direct experience, but they would never have been included if he had not been to Cracow."[670]

As far as we are aware, scholars have been unable up to this time to identify the location of the tomb; however, we propose if P.F. had travelled to Cracow, it is obvious that the "**sepulchre of Christ**" he refers to is the basilica of the Equestrian Order of the Holy Sepulchre in the town of Miechów forty kilometres from Cracow. The order was founded in Miechów in 1163 by Jaska of the Gryfici family and was the first to introduce devotion to the Holy Sepulchre in Poland and Europe. The basilica contains an exact replica of the Holy Sepulchre in Jerusalem. P.F. obviously confused Miechów with Nowy Sącz when trying to recall his experiences around Cracow. We see that the familiar reference to the extravagance of pilgrimages resurfaces, and we observe additional cynicism directed at religious orders. The Poor Clares P.F. mentions is no doubt the Franciscan order founded by St. Kinga of Hungary, daughter to King Bela IV, niece of St. Elizabeth of Hungary and great-niece of St. Hedwig. St. Kinga was the wife of King Bolesław the Chaste, after her husband's death in 1279, she became a Franciscan tertiary and went to live in the convent she founded in Stary Sącz. We suspect P.F. in his curious description of the Poor Clare congregation, singled out this order upon which to vent his anti-Catholic spleen. Apparently, there is no evidence of the existence of a "Saint Dioclesian", P.F. may have combined "Dio", from the Latin "Deo" = "God" with "Clare" and thereby concocted a name that resembles that of Diocletian (245–313), the Roman emperor infamous for renewing the persecution of the Christians. Hence, P.F.'s inspiration in associating the Church with the wealth of the aristocracy and Imperial tyrants is not yet exhausted in the text.

Subsequently, we come to Faust's visit to Constantinople where the Sultan and the religion of Islam receives its share of cynicism. With the exception of a few details, this section has changed little from the original version as seen in the Wolfenbüttle text. P.F. elaborates on the wealth of the Turkish court, declaring all the Christian monarchs could not equal the riches of the Sultan. Faust appears as Mohammed at all times, while in the manuscript Mephostophiles appears as the prophet first before Faust is allowed to join in the devilish prank played on the

---

◆ Henry Jones' Footnote: "I am grateful to Dr. Stepnik (see note above) for investigating these details."
[670] *The English Faust Book; A Critical Edition*, pp. 28–29.

Sultan's court. P.F. decided the salacious section of the narrative was not sufficiently described, and therefore embellished the text by including Faust's ritualistic selection of the fairest women in the harem during the length of his visit. P.F. also alters the detail of the Turkish subjects holding religious ceremonies in honour of their "holy guest", in the London book they "worship the image" of Mohammed. Henry Jones suggests this reflects P.F.'s ignorance of Islam as Muslims believe it is idolatrous to venerate any image, including that of Mohammed.[671] We may argue, however, this was intentional to portray the religion of Islam in a duplicitous light.

The remainder of Chapter Twenty-two lacks any further stimulating academic information. Faust makes a quick trip through Egypt, and then on to Hungary, where we find a misprint for the name of Budapest (Ofen in the text). P.F. translates Spies' work as follows: "[…] **we** Germans call this town Ofen, but in Hungarian speech it is Start."[672] Palmer and More explain this error regarding the word 'Start', "[…] goes back to Schedel's *Chronik* where 'start' is a misprint for 'statt,' city."[673] Henry Jones asserts that P.F.'s use of the word "we" is curious as Spies printed "the Germans".[674] P.F. may have obtained assistance from a native German speaker for certain passages and inadvertently included his aid's translation here; yet, Spies' use of the words "the Germans" is equally suspect.* Possibly, P.F. observed Spies' unusual error and literally corrected his text, without pausing to consider he included a fault in his English translation. In Ofen, Faust discovers a well named "Zipzar" that supposedly contains water capable of turning iron into copper; however, Palmer and More explain this factual spring actually contained copper which was precipitated by the introduction of iron.[675] They also observe Logeman's theory that the erroneous name "Zipzar" is the German adjective "Zipser" = "of Zips", an area north of Budapest.[676] In Leipzig, Faust visits a castle and marvels at the sight of a great wooden "vessel" bound with twenty-four iron hoops each weighing two-hundred pounds, (perhaps happily gauging all the wine it could contain), and then examines a new church yard and pulpit made of "white work and gold". The chapter closes with Faust's uneventful tours of Lübeck, Hamburg, Erfurt, and his return home to Wittenberg.

Upon completing this Grand Tour through Europe and the Middle East, Faust decides to undertake one final expedition around the world in Chapter Twenty-three.† This chapter offers less detail than the previous one, and features the familiar rambling itinerary characteristic of the additions inserted by scribes. Faust visits in rapid succession the countries of Spain, **Portugal**, France, England, **Scotland**, Denmark, Sweden, Poland, **Moscow**, India, **"Cataia"** (China), Africa, Persia, and the Barbary Coast. He then decides to visit the monuments on **Tenerife**, the "Isle of Brittany", (which obviously refers to Britain and not to Brittany in the North of France), and the "Orchades" behind Scotland, i.e. the Orkney Islands. P.F. also includes a reference to the

---

[671]   Ibid. n. 1651–4, p. 224,.
[672]   Ibid. p. 141.
[673]   *Sources of the Faust Tradition*, n. 89, p. 189.
[674]   *The English Faust Book; A Critical Edition*, n. 1683, p. 225.
◄   Could this strange error inserted by Spies indicate that his source text, and possibly the Latin original, was not compiled in Germany?
[675]   *Sources of the Faust Tradition*, n. 88.
[676]   Ibid.
†   Ch. 27 in Spies.

fabled "barnacle goose", a fruit that according to legend is transformed into a living fowl when it falls into water.[677] Cut from the London version is the reference to the "stone of God", which Faust is supposed to have brought back to Germany from Britain. Cotterill presumes this is the fabled "philosopher's stone" of the alchemists,[678] but we recognise this could be the 'Stone of Destiny', or the Stone of Scone. In 843, the first King of the Picts and the Scots, Kenneth I MacAlpin, brought the stone to Scone, upon which every Scottish king was crowned until 1296 when Edward I transported it to Westminster Abbey. Henceforth, all British monarchs were crowned seated on a throne containing the stone. It was returned to Scotland seven hundred years later in 1996 by an act of Parliament. We suspect P.F. or the printers omitted this reference complying with diplomatic discretion.

Faust's final and most significant adventure in this chapter is at the Caucasus Mountains[+] where he witnessed an unusual phenomenon away in the distance:

> "[...] and being on the hill of Caucasus, he saw the whole land of India and Scythia, and towards the East as he looked he saw a mighty clear strike [streak] of fire coming from heaven upon the earth, even as it had been one of the beams of the sun; he saw in the valley four mighty waters springing: one had his course towards India, the second towards Egypt, the third and fourth towards Armenia."[679]

Faust demands that Mephostophiles explain this spectacle and receives the reply he is beholding the Garden of Paradise set far off in the East; the fiery stream is the defence set around the garden, and the light he sees radiates from the guardian angel with the fiery sword. The devil then relates the four streams are the rivers that flow from the Garden; the first, Phison or the Ganges, the second "Gihon" (i.e. Gehon) is the Nile, the third is the Tigris, and the fourth is the Euphrates — a description that corresponds with Genesis (3:10–14). Mephostophiles further explains that the angel, St. Michael, stands under the constellations of Libra and Aries, i.e. on the equator, unto the Zenith of the sky and guards the tree of life. *In fine*, they are as close to the Garden as permitted by God.

Haile did not include this chapter in his edition of the Wolfenbüttle text apparently for the same reasons stated earlier, it was plagiarised from Schedel's *Chronik*, including the description of Paradise.[680] Although this chapter may originally be an uninventive borrowing, it nevertheless reminds the reader of Faust's spiritual condition. Turning to the book of Ecclesiasticus, the virtue of Wisdom is praised and compared with the four rivers of Paradise. This is first displayed in

---

[677] *The English Faust Book; A Critical Edition*, n. 1713–15, p. 225.

[678] *The Faust Legend and Goethe's Faust*, p. 41.

[+] We notice the author also included the Carpathian mountain range, for he writes that the Caucasus Mountains lie near the borders of Scythia — the *Carpathian* range is actually near Scythia. However, the author was not necessarily incorrect as the name Scythia was often applied by ancient geographers to the greater part of south-eastern Europe to central Asia, i.e. from the Danube region to the mountains of Turkistan.

[679] *The English Faust Book; A Critical Edition*, p. 143.

[680] *Damnable Life and Deserved Death of [...] Faustus*, p. 30.

(24:33–37) where the Messiah, foretold as the Eternal King descending from King David, is prophesied to have the fullness of this virtue:

> "He appointed to David his servant to raise up of him a most mighty king, and sitting on the throne of glory forever. Who filleth up wisdom as the Phison, and as the Tigris in the days of the new fruits. Who maketh understanding to abound as the Euphrates, who multiplieth it as the Jordan in the time of harvest. Who sendeth knowledge as the light, and riseth up as Gehon in the time of the vintage."

This comparison of wisdom with the rivers of Paradise continues with verses (40–45):

> "I, wisdom, have poured out rivers. I, like a brook out of a river of a mighty water; I like an aqueduct, came out of paradise. I said: I will water my garden of plants, and I will water abundantly the fruits of my meadow. And behold my brook became a great river, and my river came near to a sea: For I make doctrine to shine forth to all as the morning light, and I will declare it afar off. I will penetrate to all the lower parts of the earth, and will behold all that sleep, and will enlighten all that hope in the Lord."

While the edict of banishment from the garden also applies to Faust as with all mankind, Mephostophiles adds that "[…] **although thou thinkest thy self to be hard by,** thou hast yet farther hither from hence, then thou hast ever been. [...]"[681] In other words, "You may think yourself unfortunate that you are banished and cannot enter Paradise, but you in particular are destined to go much farther, that is, to Hell." It is directly after this biting remark the demon describes the four rivers; hence, discerning readers would recognise that Faust may claim fabulous powers, but for all that, has foolishly forfeited eternal wisdom by selling his soul. He certainly is not a philosopher — a 'lover of wisdom'.

The final chapters of Part Two$^{\surd}$ in the London *Faustbook* feature Faust's familiar explanation of the stars and other scientific matters to his colleagues. Chapters Twenty-five, Twenty-six, and Twenty-seven contain Faust's elucidation to Dr. "N.V.W." concerning the size of the stars, why demons plaque men at night, and why the stars appear to fall at times. However, there is one chapter missing in Spies, and therefore, the London edition; i.e. the chapter featuring Dr. N.V.W.'s question of why the stars appear at night, and why they are so brilliant with light. Perhaps Spies deemed Faust's answer was repetitious as the scholar already explains to a certain extent how the stars receive their light when he reveals why demons walk amongst men at night.

In addition, the London book features two chapters not contained in Haile's version, but are in Spies' book: Chapter Twenty-four, where Faust explains how comets are created, and Chapter Twenty-eight where the phenomenon of thunder is discussed. These scientific

---

[681] *The English Faust Book; A Critical Edition*, pp. 143, n. 1734, p. 226.
$^{\surd}$ Chs. 28–32 in Spies.

descriptions were originally borrowed from an older tract, the *Elucidarius*,[682] which may once again account for these omissions by Haile. Chapter Twenty-four is interesting as it refers to one major astronomical event that actually occurred during the lifetime of the historical Faustus, the appearance of a comet in August and September of 1531. Today it is recognised as Halley's comet. The event attracted the attention of the astronomers / astrologers of the day eager to discuss and write on its significance, particularly the Nuremberg set: i.e. Melanchthon, Joachim Camerarius and Johannes Schöner.[683] As seen previously in Chapter One of our study, it is possible Schöner and Camerarius may have caused Faustus to be barred from Nuremberg as they were currently working on various astrological tracts during this timeframe and did not desire additional competitors in their vicinity. This comet-chapter in the London *Faustbook* fails to mention this competition amongst the scholars, in fact, we are not aware if the real Faustus ever commented upon this particular astronomical event, yet we observe contemporaries dared to surmise the nature of his theories concerning this important topic of his time. Faust in the book explains that comets are created by a freak conjuction of the moon and the sun, and are an omen of pestilence, an interpretation that mirrors Camerarius' belief that the new comet was a bad portent and would bring pestilence upon the land.[684] It is possible Camerarius' writings influenced this chapter of the *Faustbook*.

In Chapter Twenty-eight, Faust describes the nature of thunder to his companions, declaring it is simply the converging of the four winds that beat the clouds against the crystalline firmament of the heavens. The clouds turn into ice and create a thundering echo when they strike the water of the firmament. This is P.F.'s own description, the original in Spies relates it is spirits who battle in the storm clouds that create this terrifying noise. Apparently, P.F. was not impressed with Spies' explanation and included a variation that was scientifically credible. Henry Jones writes that the example of colliding icebergs for the sound of crashing thunder suggests P.F.'s own experience in this matter.[685]

In principal, the character of Faust was used to illustrate the prevailing theories of the times. The second part of the London *Faustbook* concludes in a tedious, unspectacular style as Faust simply prattles the information he acquired through his experiences, yet this also serves a purpose in the text as this fairly uninspired attitude following his journey to the stars suggests the absolute emptiness he is now forced to contend with. He travelled the world and abounds with scientific information, but what once appeared so new and fascinating has lost its lustre — he discovered his earthly pleasures and achievements are in reality illusive shadows.

Part Three

We promptly commence the third part of the text where Faust resorts to employing his magic for amusement, to gain notoriety, and profit. The succeeding chapters are almost identical

---

[682] *Damnable Life and Deserved Death of [...] Faustus*, p. 30.
[683] *Doctor Faustus, from History to Legend*, p. 53.
[684] Ibid.
[685] *The English Faust Book; A Critical Edition*, n. 1828–31, p. 228.

to their counterparts that we studied in Haile's edition of the Wolfenbüttle text, however, there remains a few minor alterations by P.F., many of these changes include the rearrangement of certain details, or the embellishment of descriptive passages.

One example is evident in Chapter Twenty-nine♦ when the Emperor investigates the spirits conjured by Faust and looks for the wart on the neck of Alexander's spouse, rather than on her posterior, a detail also changed in Spies' rendition. Thus, we note discretionary editing in certain instances. In the Chapter of the money-lending Jew, i.e. Thirty-three,≤ it is not mentioned that the devil refused to provide Faust with pocket-money thus forcing him to become a thief. Now, Faust plots his roguish schemes simply because he enjoys the excitement. Hence, there is no added temptation devised by the devil for Faust to steal an annual allowance, for now this occupation stems from his own wicked desires. The second contract with the devil contains slight alterations, unlike Spies edition, there is no mention of extra promises made by the devil to Faust, i.e. that he would feel no pain in Hell, and, that his days there would be shortened by "lengthening his days in death". Spies' text features a distorted version of this statement, e.g. that the devil promises not to *shorten or lengthen* Faust's life "be it in death or Hell", consequently, P.F. amends this ambiguous statement by transcribing; "[… the devil] **shall have to do with me according as it pleaseth him, either to lengthen or shorten my life as liketh him.**"[686] P.F. also 'recorded' when the second pact was signed, "Wittenberg the 25. of July", and this is his unique detail. Henry Jones observed it is the feast of St. James the Great, although he fails to mention if a concealed symbolic significance for this feast day exists in the text, he simply states this may indicate the date P.F. completed his translation.[687] We observe P.F. included this date in Faust's *second* contract, but not the first — was P.F. compelled to amend his translation according to the dictates of the censors and sarcastically compared this imposed endeavour with Mephostophiles terrorising Faust into redrafting the pact? The prospect is amusing. The chapters concerning Faust's last will and testament are dissimilar in that (P.F.!) leaves Wagner less money, and the name of Wagner's familiar spirit is changed from "Urian" to "Akercocke". The alteration of this name is a conundrum, in Spies, the demon was called "Auerhahn" = "Heathcock". P.F. then translated the German "Auerhahn" to "Aker", an obsolete word for "acre", and combined it with "cock", i.e. 'Acre-cock' instead of 'heathcock'.[688] This name may not sound very impressive or intimidating, although when examined closely we still recognise this translation offers additional prospects as a fitting name for a demon. The first half "aker" resembles the Greek word "keras" for "horn" with the 'a' reversed, as "a" in Greek means "without". Thus "aker" could be reinterpreted as a word signifying "without horns". "Cocke" is a close parallel with the old English "cokeney" which signifies the expression a "cock's egg" denoting a small misshapen egg. We therefore observe a unique reference to the egg of a basilisk, as this mythological creature is also called a cockatrice. Hence, the name "Akercocke" could represent a hornless demon spawned by a basilisk. There is also a slight phonetic affinity with the word

---

♦ Spies, Ch. 33.
≤ Spies, Ch. 38.
▫ This concept of Faust's allowance is retained in Spies.
[686] *The English Faust Book; A Critical Edition*, n. 2516f, pp. 167, 238.
[687] Ibid. n. 2523, p. 238.
[688] *Faustus and the Censor*, p. 28. *The English Faust Book; A Critical Edition*, n. 2713, p. 241.

"acharnement" signifying "bloodthirsty ferocity" derived from the French "acharner" = "give a taste of flesh to (dogs, hunting falcons, etc.)".

We discover two major omissions in the London *Faust* Book. The first deletion comprises the salacious chapter pertaining to the reunion of Faust's friend Werner with his wife Sabina, i.e. Chapter Thirty-eight in Haile's work. Spies did not include this in his edition, either he used a manuscript that did not feature this chapter, or he removed it as discretionary censorship. Hence, it is not in the English *Faustbook*.[689] Second, P.F. eliminated chapter Thirty-six of the Spies Book altogether — "How Doctor Faustus ate a peasant's load of hay, together with wain and horses" — presumably as it is simply repeated material in Chapter Thirty-five, (Spies Ch. Forty), "How Doctor Faustus ate a load of hay".[690]

The most significant difference we encounter in this last section of the English book is the profusion of additional chapters for it was in this final section that Haile omitted substantial material in his edition of the Wolfenbüttle text. One primary example is the chapter of the knight in the Emperor's court who craved to wreak vengeance on Faust, a narrative that followed the story[#] of a pair of horns charmed on his head. (See Chapter Thirty-one of the London book. Here the knight chases Faust with an army, whereby Faust transforms the bushes into horsemen to protect him. Faust captures the knight's army, forcing them to pay a ransom, and permits them to depart, hexed with horns upon their heads and their horses.[◊]) Haile's argument for removing this chapter rests on his observation that it is a recurring story, he proposes a scribe heard of this Faust legend and included it, but in the process repeated a similar narrative already existing in the text. This may be correct, for the story is comparable to Chapter Thirty-six in the Wolfenbüttle MS entitled "Concerning an Army Raised against my Lord of Hardeck". We may, however, note that if any particular omission was truly necessary, the "Hardeck Chapter" would be the obvious choice due to the first person tense in the title suggesting this was the later insertion.

Haile also omitted chapters due to their connection with medieval popular folklore, assuming many of these were appended by a copyist who "[…] felt constrained to add some good Faust story which he thought the author had neglected."[691] It is possible the scribe was familiar with stories first recorded in Rosshirt's *Chronicles*. Although many of these chapters may be time-worn legends originally attributed to former scoundrel magicians, they have their function to portray the charlatan-nature of the historical Faustus well noted by his contemporaries for cheating people for lucre. In Chapter Thirty-four,[∞] Faust swindles a horse courser by selling him a horse that in reality is an enchanted bundle of straw, the horse resumes its original form when driven to water. The enraged horseman arrives at Faust's residence only to find him asleep, and tries to wake him by pulling on his leg. The leg magically falls off and the horse courser runs away in fright. Faust accomplishes a similar feat in Chapter Thirty-eight[₪] when he sells a heard of swine charmed from bundles of straw.

---

[689] *Damnable Life and Deserved Death of [...] Faustus*, p. 25.
[690] *The English Faust Book; A Critical Edition*, n. 1948, p. 230.
[#] Spies, Ch. 34.
[◊] In Spies, both 'revenge chapters' are included: Chs. 35, 56.
[691] *History of Doctor Johann Faustus*, p. 12.
[∞] Spies, Ch. 39.
[₪] Spies, Ch. 43.

Certain omitted chapters from Haile's edition, but present in the London book, display Faust's addiction to attract attention with his skills, a noted trait of the historical Faustus. These are effective folklore additions as they reflect the surviving reputation of the notorious conjuror in the popular imagination. In Chapter Thirty-five,[*] Faust amuses his friends by supposedly eating a load of hay to the horror of the cart owner who in jest sold the lot cheap to Faust thinking he could not possibly consume the entire load. Later, the cart owner discovers his hay has been mysteriously restored. A scribe obviously borrowed this tale from one of Luther's anecdotes:

> "[…] I have heard, too, of a seeming monk, who asked a wagoner, that was taking some hay to market, how much he would charge to let him eat his fill of hay? The man said, a kreutzer, whereupon the monk set to work, and had nearly devoured the whole load, when the wagoner drove him off."[692]

Chapter Thirty-six[°] relates a tale where Faust plays a prank upon a group of skirmishing students by blinding them and they continue to strike one another haphazardly to the amusement of the townsfolk. The citizens later lead each student to their homes where they immediately recover their sight. In the subsequent chapter,[□] Faust is vexed by a group of drunken revellers, and charms their mouths open so they are forced to remain quiet until they leave the inn. (According to Rosshirt's rendition, this happened on the night of Faust's death to allow him to enjoy his last meal in peace.) Chapter Forty[▶]relates the magical wonders Faust uses to entertain the Duke of Anholt, before their eyes he charms a great castle filled with exotic animals and sumptuous food for a banquet. As the day draws to a close, the castle disappears in a blaze of fire, and the Duke rewards Faust for this grandiose entertainment. As mentioned previously, the names for the animals and food were originally drawn from Dasypodius' Latin–German dictionary. Haile may not have deliberately omitted this chapter from his edition of the Wolfenbüttle text, there is a brief mention in chapter Twenty-eight of his work concerning these feats:

> "The greatest effort, skill and art produced by Doctor Faustus was that which he demonstrated to the Count of Anhalt, for with the aid of his spirit he accomplished not merely the things I have told about, but he created all sorts of four-footed beasts as well as winged and feathered fowl too."[693]

It is evident a scribe, (or Spies!), noted the possibilities these details presented, and therefore devised an elaborate chapter to describe the feats Faust performed for the Count.

---

[*]   Spies, Ch. 36.
[692]   Luther, 'Of the Devil and His Works,' # DLXXVI, *Tishreden.*
[☼]   Spies, Ch. 41.
[□]   Spies, Ch. 42.
[▶]   Spies, Ch. 44.
[693]   *History of Doctor Johann Faustus*, p. 89.

Other major differences between Haile's edition of the Wolfenbüttle text and the London *Faustbook* are observed in Faust's 'celebration' of Shrovetide and the first week of Lent. In the London book, this revelry is now an extensive five chapter narrative.[‡] Chapter Forty-two is a continuation of his feasting with the students and the vast variety of wines and foods he procured for them. In Chapter Forty-three the revelry is continued during the holy day of Ash Wednesday, disregarding the usual practise of prayer and penance, Faust and his rowdy group blasphemously decide to continue their Carnival carousing. Faust uses his magic to charm the pots, and they begin to dance to music played by invisible instruments. The students help themselves to wild game that comes through the window for their supper. Finally, they hold a Masque for their evening's entertainment by dressing in bewitched costumes. This detail was obviously drawn from the ancient custom of *mummings*, which later developed into the staged court masque of the Renaissance, i.e. the predecessor of classical opera featuring poetry, dance, and theatrical performances. These magical costumes, i.e. appearing headless, and later, sporting the head of an ass, also have their basis in occult practise. Reginald Scott in his *Discovery of Witchcraft* writes the "headless" trick is achieved by burning a candle prepared with a concoction of arsenic and sulphur, and he also mentions a special oil to make those anointed with it appear to have the head of an ass.[694]

The feasting and enchanting continues during the first Thursday of Lent in the subsequent chapter. On this occasion, the students prepare the banquet for Faust and he entertains them with thirteen apes dancing and frisking about. He jests with his hosts by enchanting their dinner of a calf's head to cry out when it is carved, and proceeds to conjure up a great chariot drawn by four dragons to their amazement. Henry Jones presents evidence this element of the dragon chariot was inspired by the carnival entertainments produced at Nuremberg only a few months before Spies printed his edition in 1587.[&] For the grand finale, Faust presents Helen of Troy that Sunday (not Whitsunday) in Chapter Forty-five.[√] Hence, several chapters portray the contemporary belief that the historical Faustus led many youths astray during his lifetime, and serve as a reminder that the young should watch the company they keep.

Chapter Fifty-three demonstrates Faust's continuous self-abandonment to his lust. Calling to mind that the time of his approaching end is closing in upon him, he decides to live his last days with seven of the fairest women he encountered during his travels, and the devil complies with his wish to bring them to him. We note the London text infers Mephostophiles brings him the actual women he had met, while Faust still consorts with succubae in Spies' rendition.[#] This is a recurring 'correction' in the London text, obviously the censors were discomfited by Faust's

---

[‡] In the London edition, these are Chs. 41–45. In Spies work, Chs. 45–49.

[694] *The English Faust Book; A Critical Edition*, p. 235, n. 2301.

[&] Henry Jones writes, "There is evidence for a carnival play of Faust (in which he seduces 'Grethle' with the aid of his devil 'Rabuntikus') [...]. A principal float in the carnival procession was a huge dragon: manned by the young citizens who were to perform the carnival plays later that day. One sat on the head, others in the belly and on the tail, all dressed in masquerade or character costume. But surely this is the dragon of the [Spies] Faust-book (chapter 48) in which Faustus and his student companions 'career around till midnight' on the fourth day of the carnival: [...]." *Faustus and the Censor*, p. 33.

[√] In Spies' version, Faust conjures Helen on the first Sunday after Easter, i.e. Quasimodo Sunday.

[#] In Spies, Ch. 57.

perverted relations with demons and elected to display the more common sin of adultery to highlight his life of debauchery. In the next chapter,‡ the devil finally fulfils one of his promises to Faust by showing him where he can unearth a great hoard of money. Faust digs under an old chapel wall, where he discovers a huge serpent sitting on fiery coals from which issues forth the screams and wailings of tormented souls — Faust now receives one final admonition to avoid sullying his hands with tokens proffered by the devil, but he ignores this warning, charms the serpent into submission and removes the coals. Upon his return home, the coals turn to silver and gold, a detail reminiscent of the bags filled with the same precious currency Mephostophiles presented to Faust in Part One as an enticement to complete the pact and sell his soul. Henry Jones relates this chapter corresponds with conventional *magus* traditions as portrayed in the ritualistic tomes circulating at the time; "The Solomonic literature, [i.e. the *Lemegeton* or *Lesser Key of Solomon*] usually assumes that the magician wants to discover buried treasure and his aim is to enslave a spirit (a diabolical minister) to lead him to it."[695]

Finally, we arrive at the chilling narration of Faust's demise in the London *Faustbook* and the admonishing conclusion. Apparently, Haile condensed material pertaining to Faust's various lamentations as this area is extended in the Spies and London versions. There is one interesting section where Faust finally bewails the torments he now knows he must face in Hell, which he blissfully ignored until then. We also observe that chapter Sixty-five of Spies' edition was not included wherein Mephostophiles mocks and torments Faust.[696] However, Faust's last farewell to his acquaintances and the horrendous finale in all its gory details is virtually unchanged in the London *Faustbook*, however P.F. highlights the sordid nature of black magic by embellishing Faust's despair and his conclusion that he was damned not only by signing the pact with the devil, but, going so far as to write it with his own blood: "[…] for all this thought was on his writing, he meant he had made it too **filthy** in writing it with his own blood." Emspon illustrates the ingeniousness of this translation:

> "Such a *smelly* thing to do; God might have loved [Faust] if he hadn't behaved in such a low-class way. It is a 'brilliant' addition to the German text, one that presumes the original needs polish. In [Spies], what matters so decisively is to have signed a contract with the Devil, but P.F. invents a point of etiquette which makes Faust seem almost infantile. The influence of Reginald Scot would be very strong, and he had insisted that magic was always 'slovenly', even when the classical Romans are messing about with the livers of chickens. It is not merely beneath a gentleman, it is beneath a grown man […]."[697]

The book concludes with the author's final warning to the readers, which has survived almost intact and features an additional aspiration that all may do God's work and so defy the

---

‡ In Spies, Ch. 58.
[695] *Faustus and the Censor*, p. 11.
[696] Ibid. pp. 28, 114.
[697] Ibid. p. 80.

devil to merit eternal joy with Christ: "Amen, Amen, that wish I unto every Christian heart, **and God's name to be glorified**. Amen."

Faust and the Realm of the Middle Spirits

The various *Faustbooks* are traditionally acknowledged as the typical 'devil-pact literature' admonishing Christian readers to avoid entering into disastrous contracts with the Evil One and to adhere to God and His precepts. As we have examined in detail above, this perception implies the conventional interpretation of Faust deliberately ignoring all truths of religion, shunning virtue, ultimately choosing Hell and rejecting the Eternal bliss of Heaven. There is, however, a second issue seldom addressed today with respect to these publications. During the time the *Faustbooks* were written and printed, the battle for the salvation of souls and snatching them from the Devil also included admonishments not to fall prey to one of Satan's popular snares, the belief in Middle Spirits. Empson raised this issue in *Faustus and the Censor*, and indeed, it is one topic worthy of our attention, as it appears the various *Faustbooks* were simultaneously used to address this theologically divisive subject.

What exactly are 'Middle Spirits'? This initial question was subject to considerable debate, and no definite answers were supplied that would define their existence as an indisputable dogma of faith. Many natural occult scholars believed the Middle Spirits were fallen angels who had not sinned as grievously as Lucifer and his staunch followers, who by their free will, had absolutely rejected God. This separate faction of spirits chose a neutral position and refused to follow God's Eternal Plan. Consequently, it was thought they did not merit eternal damnation in Hell as their free will had not mutated into absolute evil, yet, for their lukewarm neutrality they also were cast out of Heaven and doomed to roam the earth as a chastisement. Therefore, they were transformed into 'nature spirits', i.e. spirits of the air, earth, water and fire. A number of scholars considered they could be benevolent spirits, yet influenced by evil as they too were fallen creatures. It was also debated whether they retained their immortality, or if they were spirits who were granted a supernatural longevity as numerous legends recount they had assumed physical bodies, could live for thousands of years, produce offspring, and consequently would suffer death like any human. Many occultists postulated these spirits were not fallen angels, but, a separate invisible race made by God to populate every element of creation, yet, when Lucifer fell to earth, they were then conquered by the powerful demons and became subject to them. Scholars speculated if these spirits, as fallen angels or a spirit-race unto their own, were responsible for the invention of pagan deities as they too craved human worship, accounting for the prodigious learning and sciences of the heathens. Today, the concept of middle spirits survives in folklore, i.e. as fairies, leprechauns, sprites, gnomes, nymphs, mermaids, etc.. W. B. Yeats in his discussion on the origin of the Irish fairies writes:

"Who are they? 'Fallen angels who were not good enough to be saved, nor bad enough to be lost,' say the peasantry. 'The gods of the earth,' says the Book of Armagh. 'The gods of pagan Ireland,' say the Irish antiquarians, '[...] who, when no longer worshipped and fed with offerings, dwindled away in the popular imagination, and are now only a few spans high.' [...] Are they 'the gods of the earth?' Perhaps! Many poets, and all mystic and occult writers, in all ages and countries, have declared that behind the visible are chains on chains of conscious beings, who are not of heaven but of the earth, who have no inherent form but change according to their whim, or the mind that sees them. You cannot lift your hand without influencing and being influenced by hoards. The visible world is merely their skin. [...]

Occultists, from Paracelsus to Elephas Levi, divide the nature spirits into gnomes, sylphs, salamanders, undines: or earth, air, fire, and water spirits. Their emperors, according to Elephas, are named Cob, Paralda, Djin, Hicks respectively. The gnomes are covetous, and of the melancholic temperament. Their usual height is but two spans, though they can elongate themselves into giants. The sylphs are capricious, and of the bilious temperament. They are in size and strength much greater than men, as becomes the people of the winds. The salamanders are wrathful, and in temperament sanguine. In appearance they are long, lean and dry. The undines are soft, cold fickle, and phlegmatic. In appearance they are like man. The salamanders and sylphs have no fixed dwellings. [...]"[698]

However, the question remained, would these spirits be redeemed? Certain occult scholars postulated that they would be saved at the Last Judgement when their millennia of exile on earth were accomplished. Other speculators were of the opinion the Middle Spirits had forfeited their right to Eternal Life, and therefore would simply cease to exist after death similar to animals. In folklore, there often exists a conflation of both possibilities, i.e. that the spirits could regain their immortality if they succeeded in capturing human souls, or, if they could acquire a human body. In contrast, Scottish tales relate the fairies, as conquered spirits, were obliged to offer human souls in tribute to Satan.

Although these beliefs varied considerably, few occultists in the early 1400s to the 1500s doubted the existence of Middle Spirits. In fact, it was believed that by the power of magic, one could summon and control these spirits to acquire occult knowledge, or earthly wealth, etc.. Summoning these spirits was initially justified by the belief they were generally benevolent, and the possibility they would be saved, or at least, if they ceased to exist after death, were not part of the Satanical band. Alternatively, if they were subject to Satan when he established his kingdom on earth, they were not his willing subjects and could be 'safely controlled' by natural magic when executed by a professional in the field. Naturally, these convictions upheld by the occultists alarmed theologians, for Scripture clearly states all "pagan gods" are devils — there was no mention of *benign* "Middle Spirits", and a fallen angel by any description can have no association with God. If any spirit was willing to be summoned, it most undoubtedly was an evil

---

[698] W. B. Yeats, ed., *A Treasury of Irish Myth, Legend and Folklore: Fairy and Folk Tales of the Irish Peasantry* (Reprint, New Jersey: Gramercy Books, Crown Publishers, Inc., 1986), pp. 1–2, 319. (Fairy and Folk Tales of the Irish Peasantry first published in 1888.)

spirit that preyed on this belief in a Middle Realm and the fallacy that this Realm could be controlled by human or occult means. In addition, if there were spirits who claim a kingdom on earth within the four elements, it was veritably Satan as the "god of this world" stated in Scripture, (2 Cor. 4: 4 and Eph. 2:2), his minions described as "the princes and powers in high places", and all devils masquerading as pagan deities. Gradually, the belief in Middle Spirits became recognised as a form of idolatry, and the summoning of these spirits as an invocation of lesser demons, and therefore equivalent to the black art of necromancy.[+] Hence, in the various magical tomes, these 'Middle Spirits' were demons that magicians summoned and held bound by a pact, usually written in blood. Henry Jones writes of this change in perception of the 'Enlightened Renaissance magus' to that of the demonic necromancer:

> "A necessary consequence of this fierce belief in the Devil was the disrobing of the magus. Ficino and Pico della Mirandola had rehabilitated the magus in the late fifteenth century, turning him into a pious seeker of God's secret blessings. This view was extended by Trithemius and Agrippa in the early sixteenth-century Germany and taken to its limits by Dee and Bruno at the century's end, but it was not the

---

[+] This concept of the 'Middle Spirits' as demons in disguise continues in modern theology. The Catholic Church declared that the recorded biblical revelations of St. Anne Catherine Emmerich are not contrary to the Faith, i.e. they are granted the official *Nihil Obstat* and *Imprimatur*. These writings allude to these spirits: she relates she was shown visions of the Angelic Fall, how the 'Middle Spirits' came into being and how they were instrumental in instigating the earliest forms of idolatry and witchcraft:

"I saw the Fall of the angels in my childhood and ever after, day and night, I dreaded their influence. I thought they must do great harm to the earth, for they are always around it. It is well they have no bodies, else they would obscure the light of the sun. We should see them floating around us like shadows. [...] I have frequently seen that, when the angels fell, a certain number had a moment of repentance and did not in consequence fall as low as the others. [I.e. the 'Middle Spirits'?] Later on, these fallen spirits took up their abode on a high, desolate, and wholly inaccessible mountain whose site at the time of the Deluge became a sea, the Black Sea, I think. They were permitted to exercise their evil influence upon men in proportion as the latter strayed from God. After the Deluge they disappeared from that region, and were confined to the air. They will not be cast into Hell before the last day. I saw Cain's descendants becoming more and more godless and sensual. They settled further and further up that mountain ridge where were the fallen spirits. Those spirits took possession of many of the women, ruled them completely, and taught them all sorts of seductive arts. [...] They possessed a quickness, an aptitude for everything, and gave themselves up entirely to the wicked spirits as their instruments. [...] They could walk straight up trees and walls just as I have seen others possessed by the devil doing. They could effect the most wonderful things, they could do whatever they wished; but all was pure jugglery and delusion due to the agency of the demon. It is for this reason I have such a horror of every species of jugglery and fortune-telling. These people could form all kinds of images out of stone and metal; but of the knowledge of God they had no longer a trace. They sought their gods in the creatures around them. [...] They knew all things, they could see all things, they were skilled in preparing poisons, they practised sorcery and every species of wickedness." Rev. Carl E. Schmöger, ed., *The Life of Jesus Christ and Biblical Revelations: From the Visions of the Venerable Anne Catherine Emmerich as Recorded in the journals of Clemens Brentano, Vol. 1* (Illinois: Tan Books and Publishers Inc., 1986), pp. 3, 31–32.

popular view, nor that of the authorities, at the time of the witch-craze. The enlightened Lercheimer damns the magus more than the innocent women accused of witchcraft. The celestial demons of the Renaissance magus were the Devil in disguise: there was no magic but the magic of the Devil. [...] The more recondite accounts of magicians' pact with the Devil as they occur in the *Lemegeton* or *Lesser Key of Solomon* were also exposed around this time in Wier's *Pseudomonarchia Daemonum* (1577), and Scot translated some of the rituals from there in his *Discovery of Witchcraft* (1584; Book xv). The Solomonic literature usually assumes that the magician wants to discover buried treasure and his aim is to enslave a spirit (a diabolical minister) to lead him to it. An appropriate spirit to call on is Lucifuge Rofocale, who specializes in such work but of whom one must be wary as he will try to negotiate a bilateral pact in which the magician will have to pay the price. He is subjugated by smiting with a 'blasting rod' and threatening to send him to Hell."[699]

The practises employed by magicians to control the 'Middle Spirits', as described by Henry Jones, reveals that occultists were actually invoking *devils*. Notice that magicians could allegedly threaten spirits like 'Lucifuge Rofocale' with a premature imprisonment in Hell. This intimidation would frighten Middle Spirits, for according to certain traditions, they would not meet this fate until the Day of Judgement. However, this fear of premature imprisonment also extends to *demons* — according to Scripture, certain *devils* exorcised by Christ were terrified at the prospect of confinement in Hell before the Last Day: "And they [the demons named 'Legion'] besought Him that he would not command them to go into the abyss." (Luke 8:31) Subsequently, it was viewed, a misguided belief in 'benevolent' Middle Spirits posed a serious threat to scholars, and for this reason, the issue was addressed in the *Faustbooks*.

For instance, in Haile's manuscript, there are numerous parallels drawn with Satan, his devils, and the concept of Middle Spirits; the author obviously intended to discredit the alleged distinctions between the two spirit realms. Considering the numerous allusions to Luther's Reformation theology in the Faust texts, and taking into account Luther's firm conviction that Middle Spirits did not exist, this is not surprising. Luther once described certain devils with characteristics that could be associated with the Middle Spirits, but purposely did not differentiate them — 'nature spirits' are in fact devils:

> "The greatest punishment God can afflict on the wicked, is when the church, to chastise them, delivers them over to Satan, who, with God's permission, kills them, or makes them undergo great calamities. Many devils are in woods, in waters, in wildernesses, and in dark pooly places, ready to hurt and prejudice people; some are also in the thick black clouds, which cause hail, lightnings, and thunderings, and poison the air, the pastures and grounds. [...]"[700]

---

[699] *Faustus and the Censor*, pp. 10–11.
[700] Luther, 'Of the Devil and His Works', #DLXX, *Tishreden*.

The first indication in the manuscript of this Lutheran opposition to Middle Spirits is the term "hoax" when Faust conjures in the forest, indicating it is a sin of pride and presumption to believe a person could control or influence the world of spirits with natural magic or by their own efforts, for only God could control the spirits, and only by Faith may a Christian secure protection from demons. Of interest, the anonymous author states that Faust was summoning the Devil, however, another spirit appears. Here the author includes a curious phrase: "Now *a devil, or a spirit*, appeared in the figure of a gray friar".[701] It is therefore intimated that any 'Middle Spirit' summoned by conjuration is in fact the Arch-demon represented by his demonic servants, and the author continues to use both terms "devil" and "spirit" interchangeably throughout the text with his references to Mephostophiles to hone this point.[*] As a further example, Faust is first surprised that the 'spirit' is not his own master but subservient to Lucifer — this is true for the demons in Hell — however we suspect Faust erroneously assumed this to be a 'revelation' confirming the alternative view that the spirits are not benign fallen angels, but a separate spirit race conquered by Satan. Mephostophiles fosters this concept by disclosing to Faust that he has no power to command the devil, unless a spirit is sent in his place. We detect Mephostophiles is attempting to confirm the belief in the Middle Realm, but simultaneously alters Faust's perception to recognise them as servants of Satan. Of interest, in the pact the scholar initially promises to become the spirit's property after death, not Satan's,[702] thereby continuing the principle that these spirits hunger after human souls. However, by the associations with the devil already implied in the text, we understand this is not simply a Middle Spirit yearning for salvation, but a devil attempting to snatch Faust's soul, for this craving to capture human souls is also the work of Hell. This observation is confirmed in the text following Faust's attempts to convert, Mephostophiles responds, he must make a second pact because he was 'already' the property of the Devil. Significantly, the Spies and the London texts makes it clear in the second pact that Mephostophiles is a devil, and that through him, Faust actually forfeited his soul to Satan; "I Doctor John Faustus [...] give fully and wholly myself unto the devil [i.e. Mephostophiles] both body and soul, even unto the mighty god Lucifer," (P.F. inserted "great" for "mighty god").[703] In the Spies and the London texts, Faust's triumphant boasting in having the "Prince of the World" under his command", i.e. Satan as he is described in Ephesians, demonstrates the true demonic nature of these beings — the very connotation of the name 'Mephostophiles', as discussed in detail earlier, plainly demonstrates that this spirit is a demonic spirit.

---

[701] *History of Doctor Johann Faustus*, p. 26.

[*] The 'Authentic Life' of Faust by George Rudolf Widman is one exception to this pattern observed in the other texts. Mephostophiles in Widman's work is a friendly familiar spirit from the Middle Realm whose sole misery was to be overpowered and made subject to Lucifer. Faust actually draws up the pact with Lucifer, and is given Mephostophiles as his servant. Henry Jones remarks: "It is surprising that Widman should have accepted this characterization, for he was an ardent Lutheran, and to Luther all spirits were devils." *The English Faust Book; A Critical Edition*, p. 7.

[702] *History of Doctor Johann Faustus*, p. 30.

[703] *The English Faust Book; A Critical Edition*, n. 2514, pp. 167, 238.

Mephostophiles continues to entrap Faust with his belief in the Middle Spirits by promising him a "spirit's form and powers", i.e. a physical body capable of stupendous magic feats, namely transformation, but as stated earlier in our study, this could also be indicative of bilocation, which demons can grant to one who has sold their soul. The latter scenario seems most probable as throughout the text we perceive; first, that Faust cannot transform without the aid of a magic tome, and second, that he rarely travels by his own power. It is Mephostophiles who assumes the form of a black Pegasus and becomes his steed, or, Faust must be driven about in chariots provided by the demons. These points suggest, that in reality, he is not granted the powers of a 'Middle Spirit' as these beings may transform at will and fly swiftly in the heavens and around the earth without assistance. We suspect Faust's magic is therefore memorised by rote from books to accomplish his magic feats. Faust on occasion renders himself invisible, but this can be accomplished by spiritual bilocation. Eventually, Mephostophiles reveals the devils actually possessed him and spurred him into conjuring with their temptations, i.e. the ultimate snare the devils weave to capture the occultist. In fact, it is Faust's belief in the Middle Realm that actually snared him as evinced by the sentence; "While he lived thus day in and day out like an Epicure [...] with neither faith in God, Hell nor the Devil [...]."[704] If he had believed in Hell, or Heaven, he certainly would not have signed away his soul. As discussed this may be a veiled reference to the teachings of Epicurus who maintained true happiness could only be attained by conquering one's fear of the gods, death, and thoughts on the afterlife. He also taught that humans were not immortal, declaring the soul died with the body, this is similar to certain perceived traditions regarding the demise of the Middle Spirits.[†] Theologians would have perceived the devils' work in this particular doctrine and their demonic eagerness to promote it, for without the fear of death and the obligation to account to the Eternal Judge, a soul is quickly led to damnation.

In light of these observations, certain theological errors Mephostophiles introduces serve another purpose, i.e. to continually reinforce the ideology of the Middle Realm to Faust, consequently displaying to the reader its true diabolical origins. One important error to note is the statement that Lucifer was once amicable with the human race when it was first created, similar to the perceived 'benevolent' nature of the 'Middle Spirits'. As Faust is a believer of this Realm, he does not question this answer. This doctrine is theologically erroneous for Lucifer after his Fall was already a declared enemy of God and all His Creation, his rancour particularly directed towards mankind destined to fill their rejected angelic thrones in Heaven. Discerning readers would be conscious of how ludicrous this idea was according to Christian tradition, thus rendering suspect the theory of benign fallen angels "kindly disposed towards mankind". For a

---

[704] Ibid. p. 37.
[†] Of interest, W. B Yeats discovered one man in Ireland whose beliefs were not unlike Faust's epicurean convictions: "I had mentioned ghosts to this Sceptic. 'Ghosts,' said he; 'there are no such things at all, at all, but the gentry, [i.e. the fairies, or Middle Spirits] they stand to reason; for the devil, when he fell out of heaven, took the weak-minded ones with him, and they were put into the waste places. And that's what the gentry are. But they are getting scarce now, because their time's over, ye see, and they're going back. But ghosts, no! And I'll tell ye something more I don't believe in — the fire of hell;' then, in a low voice, 'that's only invented to give the priests and the parsons something to do.'." *A Treasury of Irish Myth, Legend and Folklore*, p.xxii.

further significant example we have Mephostophiles' statement that "we spirits sigh and hope" for salvation and that "we spirits" shall be saved, while continually stressing the alleged premature damnation of Faust's soul before his death. Here the demon is inferring he is a 'Middle Spirit' and may hope for Eternal Life, thus throwing Faust into a continual state of confusion and despair. This theme continues when Faust inquires of Mephostophiles how *he* would react in this same soul-binding predicament if *he* were a man: Mephostophiles sighs and declares "his wish" to earn salvation — a typical reaction we would expect of a Middle Spirit — but also a distinctive lie we would anticipate from a devil attempting to foment suicidal melancholy. Mephostophiles relates that he is a spirit of the air, (which P.F. elaborates upon by granting Mephostophiles an airy kingdom extending from the north to the south). Of course, devils are also spirits that reign in the atmospheric realm with the all-consuming passion to foster hopelessness, and tempt humans with luxury and wealth to entrap their souls, thus, the concept of benevolent Middle Spirits is immediately brought into question. However, a demon must reveal his true nature, and Mephostophiles eventually states in the course of their disputation on Hell: "But we *devils* really cannot know in what form and wise Hell is created [...]",[705] yet Faust is confounded, ignorant of the revelation Mephostophiles has unwittingly disclosed.

The succubae also illustrates the demonic nature of the Middle Spirits. As mentioned, according to several legends, the spirits could produce offspring and often abducted mortals to become their partners. However, with the Helena incident we understand it was *an illusion* she could bear children for Haile's text states "[...] she swelled up *as were she* with child."[706] An appropriate phrase if the aim was to illustrate a demon, incapable of reproducing, was attempting to fool Faust once more. P.F. further embellishes this demonic deception by writing "[...] **and to his seeming**, in time she was with child,".[707] Given that Helena's pregnancy was a fraud, so too must the child be a demon in disguise; nevertheless, as we now expect, Faust falls victim to the infernal illusion and is jubilant with the prospect of becoming a father. To the very end, the devil continues to lead Faust astray with his belief in the Middle Spirits and the Mortalist Heresy. In the second pact he is promised a body that will be insensible to pain, and assures him he will not be cast into Hell until the Last Day, which according to certain traditions is the Eternal pledge granted to spirits of the Middle Realm. Naturally, the conclusion where Faust's body is torn to pieces demonstrates the opposite has occurred.

In fine, the author of the early Latin manuscript positioned these fundamentals of the Middle Realm in conjunction with the conventional perceptions of Hell and its Kingdom to ultimately exemplify that they were one and the same. As the devils are liars, they have the ability to camouflage their true identity under the guise of Middle Spirits as easily as they can transform into illusionary angels of light. We note the fervent exhortation in the Wolfenbüttle MS to clerks and students in particular, i.e. those with less restricted access to Latin occult manuscripts and who were inexperienced in such theological complexities, not to fall prey to the glittering lures of power and wealth promised by the summoning of spirits that ensnared Faust.[708] P.F. advanced these observations in his translation, apparently he, or the censors, wished to

---

[705] *History of Doctor Johann Faustus*, p. 47.
[706] Ibid. p. 116–117.
[707] *The English Faust Book; A Critical Edition*, p. 172.
[708] *History of Doctor Johann Faustus*, p. 132.

remove the numerous ambiguities enveloping Mephostophiles' demonic nature by emphasising the wickedness of Faust and his "fervent love of the devil". In an age when considerable temptation existed to experiment in summoning nature spirits due to the popularity of natural magic, we can understand the author's and the subsequent editors' various attempts to denounce the nefarious nature of these practises.

ಐೞ ❖ ಐೞ

The first Faustian manuscripts and books, while they appear unpolished, were not works compiled solely for mediocre entertainment. First, the Wolfenbüttle manuscript displays a coherent structure combining substantial original material with popular folklore, fundamentally based upon Lutheran theology and the new ideology advanced by the Reformation. The character of Faust was carefully constructed to portray a veritable reprobate who did not live by the Word of God nor faith in Christ, and therefore an easy prey ensnared by the devil through his illicit yearning to penetrate the hidden mysteries of God and His Creation. One trap in particular features the delusion he could summon Middle Spirits and command their allegiance to gain this secret knowledge. While the emphasis placed upon Faust's motives for selling his soul were slightly altered when the manuscripts appeared in print, that is, his craving for mystical knowledge was gradually transformed into a perverted attraction for evil, material gain, pleasures of the flesh and world-renown, the original objective of the printed texts remains constant in the Spies and London editions — to present an example and warning to all Christians that they should lead God-fearing lives and avoid practising sorcery in all its forms. Second, there is considerable evidence suggesting the texts were also used as a means to promulgate controversial academic hypotheses, for instance, a new variation of the geocentric Ptolemaic ordering of the cosmos was advanced in the Wolfenbüttle manuscript, while on the opposite side of the spectrum, the Copernican System was championed in the London *Faustbook* — the Faustian legend had become a medium promoting scientific speculation! Although the texts do contain lighter elements, for example, the various travelogues and the fairy tale aspect of the popular myths included in the latter sections, they also display contemporary reflections on morality and the current events of the times. The first Faust texts are therefore worthy of consideration as they not only addressed many important issues of the day, but also captured the imagination of the populace and became a source of inspiration for the next generation of writers and artists. They represent the first significant step in the transformation of the historical Faustus to the classic character immortalised in drama and later in literature, and for this reason, have considerable academic value.

Chapter 3

Christopher Marlowe and Faustus:
"That Which Nourishes Me Destroys Me"

Fate, now preparing the way for the dramatisation of the Faustian legend, delivered the text into the hands of a determined young man equal to this task. The ink hardly dried on the first English translation of the Spies *Faustbook* when the tragic tale of this ambitious scholar-magician ensnared the unfathomable imagination of Christopher Marlowe. This Cambridge graduate had astounded London playgoers with his dramatic representations of Tamburlaine the conqueror, and eagerly searched for a unique subject for his next endeavour. Under Marlowe's poetic plume, the book-bound figure of Faust, caged within the homiletic framework of the early literature, became dynamically reinvigorated, his character redefined with three-dimensional intensity. This achievement is comprehensible when we consider the libertine lifestyle of the playwright bears an arresting resemblance to the historical Faustus.

A scholar of Divinity, Marlowe rejected the ecclesiastical expectations of his scholarship that stipulated he enter the Protestant ministry, and alternatively chose the exciting and morally objectionable career of the theatre. He covertly worked as a spy for the government in the reign of Queen Elizabeth I during his university years and therefore was easily enticed into the perilous cloak-and-dagger world of court espionage, counterfeiting and assassination plots. A quarrelsome young man by nature, he faced several criminal charges for duelling and disturbing the peace. On one occasion pending a court decision, he was incarcerated in the infamous Newgate prison as a murder suspect, but was released on bail, and eventually cleared of all wrongdoing. In the latter years of his brief life, Marlowe's contemporaries revealed he was a confirmed atheist who adamantly rejected the Scriptures and organised religion in general as the work of ambitious men, beginning with Moses and Christ, whom he believed endeavoured to control the masses with superstitious devotion and artful illusions. It was rumoured Marlowe drafted an academic tract on the subject and presented it at a private lecture attended by the Earl of Northumberland and his close circle of academic associates that included Sir Walter Raleigh. It was presumed, Marlowe wished to win many new proselytes to his Epicurean dogmas of religious scepticism. Contemporaries also 'disclosed' Marlowe's scandalous appreciation of pederasty with the allegation he declared: "That all they that love not Tobacco & Boies were fooles."[709] One night in Deptford, at the age of twenty-nine, Marlowe unexpectedly encountered the Grim Reaper when he was stabbed through the right eye during what was originally believed to be a skirmish over the reckoning of a dinner bill: a gruesome end interpreted by the religious-minded of his day as a omen revealing that a confirmed son of perdition had received Divine retribution. Re-examining the circumstances surrounding his death, modern scholars uncovered what may be considered a government assassination plot to silence their former agent. Due to his

---

[709] I.e. in the "Baines Note" (May 1593); see Appendix Seven.

unorthodox religious opinions, his loyalty to the Queen as the head of the Church in England and to the State was viewed with suspicion and held in question.

Marlowe, no doubt, recognised in the character of Faustus his personal cynicism in regard to the subject of religion and his ardent desire to accomplish great deeds in the world. As a result, he injected new life-blood into the Faustian tale using the syringe of his worldly experiences and education, his hopes, fears and ambitions. To understand and appreciate his representation of Faustus, we therefore in our study must also explore this tragic play against the backdrop of the playwright's biography. Marlowe was a product of his culture and times, and consequently so too were the personal creations that blossomed from his philosophy and imagination — his poetry, and in particular, his dramas.

Childhood Days and Education

Christopher Marlowe was born in the famous pilgrimage town of Canterbury in 1564 and was baptised on February 26, two months before his future rival, William Shakespeare (1564–1616), received the same sacrament in Stratford-upon-Avon. Christopher was the second child and the first son born to John and Katherine Marlowe. The couple were blessed with nine children in total, four boys and five girls although extant historical documentation and other sources indicate that at least three of their children did not survive into adulthood.

Christopher's parents hailed from the menial labouring class. In his early twenties, John Marlowe migrated from Ospring to Canterbury during the mid–1550s in search of work. During 1559 and 1560, he was apprenticed to a member of the local shoemakers guild and eventually moved to the parish of St. George the Martyr. One year had hardly elapsed in his apprenticeship when he married Katherine, a recent migrant from the city of Dover. The newly-weds did not live in a very pleasant area of the city as David Riggs illustrates:

> "This foul-smelling district [of St. George the Martyr parish] lay between the cattle market outside St. George's gate and the slaughterhouse within the city walls; it was an apt neighbourhood for the aspirant leatherworker. Carts bearing tubs of blood and offal trundled along St. George's Street. The town gallows stood just beyond the cattle market, on Oaten Hill, from 1575 onwards. [...] The bellows of cattle being driven to the butcher's shambles and the pervasive odour of blood were among [Christopher's] earliest sensations. In adolescence, he grew accustomed to the sight of condemned men being carted past his home to the gallows [...]."[710]

John Marlowe's fortunes unexpectedly took a turn for the better when his master died of the bubonic plague a few weeks after Christopher was born. St. George's parish had already

---

[710] David Riggs, *The World of Christopher Marlowe* (New York: Henry Holt and Co. LLC, 2005), pp. 12, 14.

experienced a shortage of artisans following an influenza epidemic that ravaged the city during the late 1550s, and thus having completed only four years of his apprenticeship, John Marlowe joined the Shoemakers' Guild (April 20, 1564) without completing the statutory seven years.[711] Membership to the guild opened up new opportunities and social liberties for his family and to some extent, raised their social standing within the community. Riggs writes:

> "As a freeman, John gained the right to open his own shop, sell his wares and enrol apprentices. He could now 'speak and be heard' at town meetings. He was entitled to sue for debt in the Borough Court. When his two-month-old son Christopher grew up, he could join his father's guild upon the payment of a nominal fee. The sons-in-law of freemen also enjoyed automatic access to this small group of privileged tradesmen. John Marlowe's daughter had gained a dowry. [... He] had secured a narrow foothold at the lower end of the 'middling classes' — a category that encompassed everyone who ranked a notch below the gentry, the clergy and the members of the professions, and a cut above day labourers and tenant farmers. Within this middle stratum shoemakers came [...] before only the most menial craftsmen (tillers, thatchers, miners.)" [712]

John Marlowe acquired additional skills that increased his prospects to further his fortunes — he could read and write. These accomplishments enabled him to find additional work as a freelance law clerk, and in later years, to become a parish clerk. He also found employment in many civil posts, e.g. he served as a sideman and churchwarden, and eventually exchanged his original trade of a shoemaker for that of a victualler before his death.[713]

The infant Christopher, as with all children born in that era, began life in a world of hardships fraught with daily hazards. Children would have to survive multiple diseases and illnesses prevalent in that age, and face a myriad of domestic and external dangers. During the first year, a child would most likely be wrapped in swaddling clothes and placed by the fire for warmth due to the inclement weather of England, placing the child in constant danger as the bedclothes could easily catch fire and required constant vigilance.[714] By toddler age, as with Christopher, mothers and older siblings needed to be ever watchful for as Riggs notes, "There was no way to childproof the home of an early modern artisan. [...] there was the ever present danger of playing with fire or his father's sharp tools."[715] Notwithstanding the dangers present within the home, the outdoors also presented particular hazards in that era. Marlowe's street contained an open sewage ditch that posed a constant threat to the health of the general public, or he faced the danger of stray herds of pigs, horses and cattle that roamed freely, in addition to the

---

[711] Ibid. 17.
[712] Ibid. pp. 17–18, 19.
[713] Constance Brown Kuriyama, *Christopher Marlowe: A Renaissance Life* (Cornwall University Press: 2002), p. 19.
[714] *World of Christopher Marlowe*, p. 21.
[715] Ibid.

constant traffic of wagons and horsemen, in particular, wagons loaded with the refuse of the slaughtered animals from the butchers' shambles.[716] Obviously, the early life of Christopher Marlowe was rugged and harsh in the extreme. However, by the time Marlowe reached his tenth year, his family had moved to the parish of St. Andrews, a marginal improvement.[717] Possibly, his father hoped to attract customers that were more affluent by choosing an area closer to the city centre.

School commenced for children generally at the age of six, and Marlowe's first lessons began in petty school where he was taught to read. However, these initial centres of learning were managed haphazardly in comparison with our modern standards and often lacked competent teachers. Riggs writes, "[...] Tudor elementary schools had no permanent buildings. Schoolmasters held classes wherever space became available; itinerant instructors came and went."[718] Marlowe's first teacher was possibly the Reverend William Sweeting, a poor and simpleminded tailor. Rev. Sweeting, and a motley group unqualified for these positions, had hastily received ordination as pastors in 1558 from Matthew Parker, the Archbishop of Canterbury. This decision was reached in a desperate effort to fill the ecclesiastical vacuum left by the mortal epidemics of influenza and bubonic plague, not to mention the vacancies resulting from the violence and altercations between the Catholic and Protestant factions that had decimated the numbers of the local clergy.[719] In point of fact, this shortage of ministers had reached a critical level forcing Church authorities to append the responsibilities of an additional parish to Rev. Sweeting's duties, notwithstanding he could not fulfil the simple task of preaching one sermon a year.[720]

This is a minor indication of the tremendous religious upheaval the city had experienced. The centre of Roman Catholic worship in England since the arrival of St. Augustine in 597, pilgrims flocked to Canterbury cathedral to visit the famous shrine where St. Thomas à Becket was martyred during his devotions in 1170 by four of King Henry II's men. Of all the pilgrimage sites in Europe, this shrine became the third most important, that is until 1538 when Henry VIII, as the newly appointed head of the Church of England, by royal command ordered this shrine to be dismantled and all its treasure and donations confiscated, his soldiers hauled away twenty-six cartloads of jewels and votive offerings to fill the royal coffers.[721] They sacrilegiously burned the relics of St. Thomas à Becket, and scattered his ashes to the four winds. Describing the destruction of other important monuments at that time, Riggs states, "Just outside the city walls, much of St. Augustine's Abbey lay in ruins, another victim of the reformers' iconoclasm and greed."[722] Protestantism continued during the reign of Henry's son, King Edward VI (b.1537— d.1553), and then radically suppressed with the succession of Catholic Queen Mary I (b.1516— d.1558). During her five-year reign, she earned the title 'Bloody Mary' for her persecution of

---

[716] Ibid.
[717] *A Renaissance Life*, p. 18.
[718] *World of Christopher Marlowe*, p. 25.
[719] Ibid. pp. 15, 25.
[720] Ibid. p. 15.
[721] Ibid. p. 17.
[722] Ibid.

Protestant supporters, she had approximately three hundred people executed as heretics. Riggs relates the terrible impact her reign inflicted upon the already distressed town:

> "[…] Mary I only aggravated the troubles that beset mid-century Canterbury. If [John] Marlowe had arrived by 1556, he could have joined the crowds that gathered at nearby Wincheap to watch forty-three Protestant martyrs burn at the stake. During the reign of 'Bloody' Mary, Canterbury saw more executions for heresy than any place in England, apart from London. John Marlowe came to a city in crisis."[723]

Finally, the kingdom experienced a period of stability during the reign of Elizabeth I (b.1533—1603) who re-established a moderate form of Protestantism, although the constant fear of a Catholic insurrection and civil war continued to linger. These cataclysmic changes from one regime to another wrenched the heart of the kingdom and shredded the fabric of society in England:

> "[…] Canterbury felt the full shock of these seismic alterations. Each time a new king [or queen] came to the throne, everyone in the ecclesiastical establishment had to adapt or be deprived. These vacillations left parish life badly demoralized. When the Crown lawyer and antiquarian William Lambarde visited Canterbury during the 1560s, the city was a shadow of its former self: 'And therefore no marvel,' he reckoned, 'if wealth withdrawn, and opinion of holiness removed, the places tumble headlong to ruin and decay.'[724]." (Riggs.)[725]

These religious broils fomented constant disruptions in local politics with factions supporting Catholic or Protestant creeds rising and falling according to each new succession to the throne. Hence migrants, as with Marlowe's family, who endeavoured to survive this period of civil strife had one safe option: drift with the tide and remain as 'invisible' and as neutral as possible, supporting those who currently held offices of power at any given time. John Marlowe prudently followed this policy:

> "John Marlowe kept a prudent distance from the ideological struggles that set long-time residents in ruinous conflict with one another.
> The father's wary detachment gives the first inkling of his son's ironic, uncommitted stance on questions of religious belief. Children discover their identities through exchanges with the world around them. […] Christopher Marlowe, the son of immigrants situated on the margins

---

[723] Ibid.
[724] Rigg's n.: 'William Lambarde, *A Perambulation of Kent* (London, 1576), p. 236.'
[725] Riggs, 'Marlowe's Life', in Patrick Cheney, ed., *The Cambridge Companion to Christopher Marlowe* (Cambridge University Press, 2004), p. 26.

of their community, spent most of his life in a place where elementary structures of religious belief were constantly being discredited." (Riggs)[726]

Returning to Christopher's initial school experiences, this early identity and character-shaping phase of his life started with a literacy-based indoctrination programme first established by Henry VIII. The king devised this basic course to instil a sense of duty in the new religious order of the realm rather than provide a service to develop practical skills.[727] Henry VIII declared the petty schools were, "for the better bringing up of youth in knowledge of their duty towards God, their prince and all other in their degree".[728] The original curriculum decreed for these schools by King Henry and reinstated by Queen Elizabeth I consisted of three very basic texts, *The ABC*, *The ABC and Catechism* and *A Primer or Book of Private Prayer*.[729] Young Marlowe learned his alphabet by rote, how to make the sign of the cross, and dutifully prattled off the Apostles' Creed, the Our Father and the Ten Commandments.[730] In memorising the Golden Rule, "To love my neighbour as myself", Marlow was obliged to append the following oath, "To honour and obey the king and his ministers. To submit myself to all my governors, teachers, spiritual pastors and masters. To order myself lowly and reverently to all my betters."[731] In sum, the petty school system did not encourage intellectual exchange or development, alternatively the course was a battering ram of dogma memorised by the students for the good of their souls and the future welfare of the state — pupils were regularly examined by Diocesan officials to ensure they were properly indoctrinated in the Royal catechism.[732] If parents failed to educate their children in their catechism by the age of eight, they were forced to pay a fine of 10s, unless the child was mentally incapable of learning.[733]

The main purpose of this 'catechetical' system was to promote steadfast loyalty to crown and country; however, it failed miserably in its religious objective. "Although the English Catechism and prayers were meant to instil belief," as Riggs states, "these foundational texts could also serve as objects of unbelief."[734] Without the benefit of adequate clarification of the King's religion other than a list of prayers, rules, and commandments, any child with intelligence would question the information drummed into them as their reasoning capabilities developed. For example, the oath appended to the Golden Rule intended to instil respect for elders and authority could also be reinterpreted and used to question the comportment of obedience that was expected: 'If I must love my neighbour as myself, are we then not equal? Why must the king, his ministers, and pastors expect me to conduct myself as a base inferior rather than respect them as an equal?' The inexplicable doctrine of the Trinity could hardly be grasped by simply teaching them the sign of the cross, "In the name of the Father, and of the Son, and the Holy Ghost". A

---

[726] *World of Christopher Marlowe*, p. 16.

[727] Ibid. pp. 25. 28.

[728] T. W. Baldwin, *William Shakespeare's Petty School* (Urbana: University Of Illinois Press, 1943) pp. 44-45, in ibid. p. 28.

[729] *World Of Christopher Marlowe*, p. 26.

[730] Ibid.

[731] Ibid. p. 28.

[732] Ibid.

[733] Ibid.

[734] Ibid. p. 29.

profound mystery of religious faith for adept theologians, this doctrine became a stumbling-block for those young minds bereft of any explanation of how, on the basis of faith alone, God could be three Divine persons, and yet simultaneously exist as One God. A principle that became "[…] the bedrock of moral order in Marlowe's England,"[735] as Riggs relates, was the 'fear of God'. However, it is clear that the *religious* inferences of instilling the 'fear of God' in young minds, i.e. the fear of God's wrath and the existence of Hell, could also be manipulated for secular purposes. As Church and State now had one supreme Head, disobedience to God's commandments simultaneously implied insubordination to the monarch or contempt of the commonwealth punishable by state laws, which in most cases, incurred the death penalty. Hence, Marlowe witnessed first-hand at a very early age how a secular government could usurp religion to wield power to control church and nation. This experience opened the doors for his future rejection of organised religion.

Marlowe, now eight years old, completed the petty school programme and progressed to the grammar school where he was taught the rudiments of Latin. Circumstantial evidence suggests for four years he attended the free school founded by Archbishop Parker in 1569 near the Eastbridge Hospital.[736] Here, Marlowe acquired one skill that is not often brought to our attention or commented upon — he was taught how to read music:

> "Since candidates for the Parker scholarship that sent Marlowe
> to Cambridge had to read music at sight, Christopher doubtless acquired
> this facility in the schoolhouse across the street from Eastbridge
> Hospital." (Riggs)[737]

He therefore acquired, at a young age, a skill and an appreciation of sound and rhythm that later contributed to the metrical construction of his poetry and dramas.

A daunting curriculum now loomed before him in this new school — he is presented with two texts purposely selected to reinforce his primary Protestant training and acquaint him with the weighty foundations of rudimentary Latin, i.e. *A Catechism or First Instruction of Christian Religion* by the Dean of St. Paul's Cathedral, Alexander Nowell, and William Lyly's *Short Introduction of Grammar*.[738]

On reviewing his prescribed religious text, we find Marlowe learned the fundamentals of Calvinist[739] doctrine — man lost the gift of free will after the Fall of Adam and Eve, therefore God had preordained certain men for Heaven while others He predestined to eternal damnation. A Christian could discover if they were destined for salvation only by practising the virtue of *obedience*, i.e. thoroughly observing God's Commandments, for according to the words of St. Paul, Christ the Saviour was *obedient unto death*. Riggs explains:

---

[735] Ibid. p. 30.
[736] Ibid. p. 35.
[737] Ibid.
[738] Ibid.
[739] Ibid. p. 38.

"True obedience depended on faith, the gift of God. [...] Nothing could secure forgiveness but a true and lively faith that one had already been forgiven. Even self-abasement, the sole remedy available to sinful humanity, could only produce despair 'unless God bring Comfort'. Comfort, when it came, brought a sense of ecstasy, a 'running of the spirit', that assured the fortunate [predestined] few of their place among the elect. [...]"[740]

Those unfortunate souls who did not experience this 'Comfort' were doomed to Hell. Riggs continues; "[...] Having been taught that many were called but few were chosen, the boys were prepared to remain unvisited by the Holy Ghost; that was part of God's plan."[741]

Similar to the methods employed in the petty schools, this Calvinist doctrine pertaining to obedience and faith were memorised without an opportunity for discussion or clarification — it is no marvel that many students encountered a spiritual crisis in later years, entertained serious doubts, and embraced atheism. This catechism contained many paradoxes that required elucidation! How could God, whom they were taught was infinitely good, *purposely* create souls destined for endless torment contrary to the evidence in Scripture that He does not desire the eternal death of a sinner? Either this theology of predestination was in error, or the Scriptures were! The one answer that was provided, i.e. *obedience* to God's Commandments as Christ was obedient unto death, was erroneous as this contradicted the Calvinist doctrine that corrupt mankind, which lost the gift of free will, is incapable of making one act of perfect obedience.[742] Yet, God would accept no other sacrifice *but* obedience![743] The teaching that not all 'obedient' souls would experience the 'Comfort of God' also undermined belief in the 'Obedience Guarantee'.

While this canon taught in the grammar schools posed several theological conundrums, it had other 'practical' uses. This catechism impressed upon young minds the importance of obeying God's laws *and* the precepts of the State Church for the welfare of society. For instance, this doctrine *compelled* Christians to live a life of compliance in the hope they would experience this 'Comfort' manifested in the 'running of the spirit'; therefore, those allegedly destined for Hell, although unaware of this 'reality', were 'prevented' from living a scandalous life and wreaking havoc on earth. Hence, Marlowe was taught many would appear righteous and publicly profess to be members of Christ's Church, but practised what was termed a 'general' faith for only God knew who He had granted this gift of 'true' faith. Nevertheless, these people of 'dead faith' were still considered members of the Church of God, and according to Nowell's *Catechism,* were required "[...] to retain a 'general' or 'dead faith' in the God who had doomed them to everlasting torment." (Riggs)[744] Ironically, as Riggs observes, this "[...] all embracing

---

740   Ibid. pp. 42–43.
741   Ibid.
742   Ibid. p. 42.
743   Ibid.
744   Ibid. p. 43.

criterion of outward submission made it easy for atheists to carry on as hypocrites within the Church of England."[745]

The Latin lessons proved equally taxing; Marlowe's reading material was considered important by his teachers mainly for the practical purpose of teaching correct grammar — God forbid the texts possibly contained a subject worthy of intellectual criticism and appreciation!

> "Users of Lyly's grammar had to internalise page after page of Latin verb forms and syntactical constructions with no overarching system to guide them through the maze. When the eleven-year-old student of grammar finally did begin to read literary texts, he was actively discouraged from thinking about what they meant. A standard school text of Terence's comedies published in 1574 advises teachers never to consider the work as a whole. 'For we do not present Terence to this end, that thence youth may learn to write comedies, but rather for seeing there the true and native nature and form of Latin speech'.[746]" (Riggs)[747]

Students literally absorbed the contents of tracts and silently formed their own conclusions without constructive supervision to assist the development of critical thinking skills, yet, in an ironic twist of circumstances, teachers diligently ensured that every letter their pupils read was etched deeply into the grey matter encased within their skulls. As part of their training in the art of handwriting, students learned how to correctly mix their inks, prepare their quills, and write without creating unsightly blots — they also had to copy every word of their textbooks, then considered the swiftest and most efficient method of learning and retaining as much information as possible:

> "The pupil's hands gathered in (the literal sense of 'apprehend') textual matter and inscribed it in the storehouse of memory. Under interrogation, he retrieved what he had recorded there and reproduced it in oral recitation. [...] Boys who balked at these mind-numbing routines were usually in for a beating. [...] The courses had less to do with learning Latin than with learning obedience, especially in the lower forms." (Riggs)[748]

Marlowe was about fourteen years old when he attended classes at the King's School within the grounds of the cathedral. The school accepted Commoners, i.e. paying students, and offered scholarships for fifty disadvantaged boys whose families lacked the financial means to ensure the completion of their grammar school education. Here, the adolescent encountered the

---

[745] Ibid.
[746] (Introduction to the 1574 school text): T. W. Baldwin, *William Shakespeare's Petty School*, pp. 570–571. in ibid. p. 39.
[747] *World of Christopher Marlowe*, p. 39.
[748] Ibid. p. 38–40.

harsh reality of the social hierarchal system and the divisions that existed between the sons of gentlemen and those of the labouring class.

According to Riggs' research, there appears to be a period unaccounted for when considering Marlowe was about twelve or thirteen when he left his former school that offered his first four years of grammar education, and was not awarded the King's school scholarship until 1578 when he was about to turn fifteen. Riggs proposes Marlowe entered the King's School as a Commoner when his father could raise the funds. Evidence suggests John Marlowe managed to procure the tuition fees when he won a settlement in a lawsuit. According to the records, the Headmaster of the King's School, Gresshop, failed to pay John Marlowe for shoes he ordered and also for the accommodation Marlowe provided for two Common students that were Gresshop's wards.[749]   Obviously, this was a one-time providential opportunity to send his son to school. Very often, artisans were forced to withdraw their children from the grammar school as the fees were expensive, or necessity required them to pull their weight in the family workplace. Educators of the day did not consider this a particular catastrophe as the rapid withdrawal rate facilitated the 'weeding out' process, and provided, other children with academic promise in the artisan class, an opportunity to compete for the few scholarship places that existed.   Any Commoner student in the King's School could win a scholarship between the ages of nine and fifteen, however, "To succeed in this contest," Riggs informs us, "the artisan's son had to be physically present in the classroom, and put himself forward with dispatch, before his father's assets ran dry."[750]   This competition between the students was a gruelling ordeal: only the most accomplished pupils received the King's School Scholarship when a place became available. Commoners were encouraged to surpass each other, and to expose their competitors' mistakes in class for this purpose.[751]   The system literally fostered intellectual rivalry and conflict.   In 1578, Marlowe was awarded a timely Scholarship, for he was a month away from reaching his fifteenth birthday, which would have disqualified him for the award.[752]

The Scholarship featured a maximum tenure of five years, but this did not ensure a student was secure as he could be forced to forfeit his place at any time for various infractions. Academic excellence remained the first prerequisite; if a student was found to be slothful in his studies or considered them distasteful he was immediately expelled, allowing a more worthy recipient to benefit from the scholarship funds.[753]   Maintaining this exceptional degree of academic excellence executed with unwavering enthusiasm was an almost impossible task considering the school schedule and rigorous policies provided little time for leisure. The school day commenced at six or seven in the morning and concluded at seven in the evening.[754] Saturday was considered a regular school day, and students received religious instructions on Sundays and holidays, but were also required to attend all religious services dressed in their school surplice.[755]   Students were expected to behave with all propriety becoming young

---

749 Ibid. pp. 35, 48.
750 Ibid. p. 47.
751 Ibid.
752 Ibid. p. 48.
753 Ibid. p. 46.
754 Ibid. p. 40.
755 Ibid. pp. 40, 28.

gentlemen by displaying a proper respect for their elders, (which is commendable), but were to accomplish this decorum by suppressing all feelings of superiority, bridling any characteristics that betrayed a forward nature, and to refrain from all demonstrations of prideful ambition.[756] They must display outwardly an attitude of modesty, humble refinement, and submissive obedience.[757] Kuriyama relates the students were allowed extended recess periods for meals and recreation,[758] on the other hand, Riggs reminds us their free hours were restricted to academic decorum: they were not to indulge in any games that did not befit a King's School Scholar, and were forbidden from speaking any language other than Latin or Greek.[759] Hence, the curriculum and policies of the school gradually whittled scholars into polished products of the academic elitist class in an effort to segregate them from their uncouth contemporaries, the artisan apprentices. The headmaster was obliged to examine each pupil at least three times in every seven days to verify they were dutifully complying with the rules of the establishment. "Scholars who did well had three chances a year to prove that they were ready for the next form; the drones were subject to expulsion at any time […]." (Riggs)[760]

However, Marlowe was forced to confront the stark reality that the sons of the privileged members of society were not subject to the full rigors of the school regime. *They,* these privileged students, would never be subjected to this indignity, to claw for survival in this system. In most instances the education of the elite was considered accomplished at the grammar school level, and therefore received noted positions without the prerequisite of a university degree, or the social standing of their family was sufficient to secure the same. These privileges were not afforded to the socially deprived Scholars, defined in the school statutes as "[…] fifty poor boys, […] destitute of the help of friends".[761] Marlowe, now educated far beyond his station as a lowly shoemaker's son, is encouraged to foster contempt for his former status, particularly when his fortune as a King's Scholar had vastly improved. The Scholars received a substantial annual stipend, enough to support an entire family, dined sumptuously on hearty meals of beef, mutton and beer, and participated in certain festive entertainments permitted during holydays.[762] Notwithstanding this improvement, without the benefit of influential connections, he had little opportunity to find a position that reflected his grammar school education and faced the prospect of returning to the lower stratum of society — unless he remained determined to achieve academic perfection and strive for a university scholarship. Although the sons of the gentry studied the same curriculum during their advanced grammar school years, they were only required to have a reading knowledge of their prescribed texts, and were exempt from partaking in the torturous oral examinations and extemporaneous verse work that prepared the less privileged Scholars for the university. Compounding this dichotomy, Marlowe and his classmates were constantly reminded of their status, for example, one prescribed text for their

---

[756] Ibid. p. 48.
[757] Ibid. pp.47, 48.
[758] *A Renaissance Life*, p. 32.
[759] *World of Christopher Marlowe*, p. 49.
[760] Ibid. p. 46.
[761] Ibid. p. 45.
[762] Ibid. p. 49.

coursework in rhetoric, the *Progymnasmata* by Aphthonious, highlighted the divisions between the rich and the less privileged, as Riggs illustrates:

> "Exercise Four, the pupil's first lesson on arguing a thesis, began with a nugget of proverbial wisdom: 'To flee poverty, O Cyrnus, one must fall down from the rocky heights into the sea.' [...] In the sections that followed, Christopher proved this thesis with arguments drawn from the 'places' [i.e. the 'figures of thought' and techniques of an orator] *of paraphrase* (the poor should be content to die), *cause and effect* (since the poor do not form good character when they are young, they will do bad things in adulthood), *contrast* (the rich do form a good character when they are young), *comparison* (just as chains obstruct actions, poverty hinders freedom of speech), *example* (when Odysseus pretended to be poor he was thrown out of his house), and the *testimony of the ancients* (Euripides says that it is evil to be in want since poverty is inconsistent with nobility of the soul). Once the pupil had mastered this system, he had essentially completed the grammar-school course on rhetoric."[763]

According to the Parker scholarship programme offered to select King's Scholars, a place at the university depended on their aptitude in the study and composition of classical Latin poetry. Convinced that Ovid and Virgil had composed their famous works by extemporaneous oral recitation, academics insisted students compose Latin verse using this method, making classical poetry the most toilsome course of the Scholars' syllabus:

> "In a well-made line of Latin verse, the quantity of every vowel in every word matches up with the set pattern of long and short vowel sounds that constitute the metrical line. The ability to make such lines spontaneously, with no recourse to dictionaries and reference works, presupposes an awesome mastery of Latin grammar."(Riggs)[764]

Due to its inherent descriptive nature, poetry became *the* esteemed discipline, an effective branch of rhetoric to aid students master the art of eloquent disputation.[765] Nevertheless, there existed diverse opinions separating the lofty status of the orator from that of the poet in Elizabethan society. An orator presented persuasive arguments and speeches on religion and matters of state: he must refrain from resorting to colloquialisms and figures of speech unless absolutely necessary.[766] A poet, in contrast, was a craftsman of syllables, words, metrical rhythm and figures of speech, and was at liberty to utilise all his skills of persuasion: his main objective

---

[763] Ibid. p. 52.
[764] Ibid. p. 53.
[765] Ibid. p. 57.
[766] Ibid. p. 58.

— to create descriptive and entertaining works.[767] *In fine*, the former was considered the superior skill, notwithstanding that through the art of poetry the humanists acquired the elegant Latin style they so highly esteemed.[768] Ironically, the lower middle classes were obliged to excel in both areas for their social improvement, yet the elite viewed them with disdain when the circumstances of their grammar school education compelled them to earn a living by these poetry skills they were taught.[769] In fact, the Parker Scholarship, which enabled Marlowe and other deserving poor boys to attend Cambridge, was awarded on the stipulation that the prospective recipients were "[…] well instructed in their grammar […]" and could "[…] make a verse."[770]

The Cambridge Scholar

In 1580, Marlowe completed his studies at the King's School and proceeded to Corpus Christi College, renamed at that time, Benet College, apparently to distance its association with its original founders referred to by William Harrison as "[…] the brethren of a Popish guild."[771] The new undergraduate discovered that students in the university were segregated according to a hierarchal system. First came the Fellow Commoners, privileged students from the gentry who stayed for a year or two with no ambition to pursue a degree, but attended simply for their own personal interest and refinement.[772] These students, when dining, sat in a position of honour with the Master at a table set upon a dais. The next in rank, the Pensioners, could afford to pay for commons and other tuition expenses, although they did not receive preferential seating arrangements in the dining Hall. Pensioners often did not complete their courses and attain degrees for as Riggs states, "[…] many of these young men were out to have a good time […] and acquire enough learning to qualify for the post of Justice of the Peace in their home counties."[773] The Scholars, next in the order of importance, were subdivided into their respective categories and sat in the Hall accordingly:

> "The four Bible Clerks held the most prestigious scholarships,
> received the most lucrative stipends and ate together in the group that sat
> next to the High Table. The six Nicholas Bacon Scholars […] came next.

---

[767] Ibid. pp. 58–59.

[768] Ibid. p. 60.

[769] Ibid.

[770] R. and J. Lamb Masters, *Master's History of the College of Corpus Christi and the Blessed Virgin Mary in the University of Cambridge* (London, John Murray, 1831), p. 98, in *World of Christopher Marlowe*, p. 54.

[771] William Harrison / Holinshed, "A Description of Elizabethan England", *Holinshed's Chronicles*, [1577, Book II., Chapter 6; 1587, Book II., Chapter 3.], reprint in Charles W. Eliot, ed., *The Harvard Classics; Chronicle and Romance: Froissart, Malory, Holinshed, vol. 35* (New York: P. F. Collier and Son Corp., 1963), p. 380.

[772] *World of Christopher Marlowe*, pp. 66–67.

[773] Ibid. pp. 66–69.

The adjacent table included all remaining Scholars who were on stipend. […] Pensioners […] occupied the rest of the tables in the Hall".[774]

Scholars, in contrast to the aforementioned privileged students, generally completed their degrees. The last group of students were the Sizars, young men who had scratched their way through the grammar schools with the Scholars, but who were "[…] unprepared for other employment, aside from waiting on tables," as Riggs writes, for these students worked in the Hall to pay for their food rations, or 'sizes'. [775] The majority of these students also succeeded in graduating with degrees.

This academic hierarchal regime did not conclude with the seating arrangements for mealtimes, a double standard existed in every sphere of the university system. Students from the aristocracy and affluent families were not subject to the strict regulations enforced upon the underprivileged Scholars. They could wear luxurious clothing, enjoyed extended periods of leisure time, and were at liberty to stroll freely on the campus grounds. Should they misbehave, they had recourse to their standing as 'gentlemen' and could benefit from the impunity their status afforded them. Scholars, in contrast, were permitted very little free time; a normal day started at four in the morning, and the work continued until ten at night.[776] They were not permitted to mix with boisterous company, or to leave the colleges in the evening unless escorted by Proctors,[777] although we may presume this regulation became a necessary precaution to protect the students. According to certain reports on football games that took place between the university students and the local town youths, rivalry became rampant and several students were injured in the scuffles that ensued.[778] A rigid dress code was obligatory — Scholars wore a plain black gown, while wealthy graduates with degrees were allowed to wear silk. Scholar graduates were forbidden to wear any external garment that was not made of "[…] woollen cloth of black, puke [i.e. puce (?): a dark red or purple brown], London brown, or other sad colour."[779] However, Scholars were consoled by the concession of a hood trimmed with white fur.[780] With the exception of this one privilege, they were prohibited from wearing barrelled hose, great ruffs, clocks (decorations woven in silk thread), and forbidden to wear their hair in long locks.[781] The graduate sons of nobles and the gentry were permitted to wear round caps of velvet, while graduate Scholars were obliged to wear square caps of cloth.[782] This marked difference in apparel publicly branded the poor Scholars as social inferiors.

Focusing on Marlowe's coursework, the BA years were relatively basic. He studied the art of dialectic disputation that taught him the rudiments to defend or argue a thesis or a theory on any subject. "The lectures on logic and rhetoric, together with daily exercises in debating

---

[774] Ibid. pp.66–67.
[775] Ibid. p. 68.
[776] Ibid. p. 69.
[777] Ibid.
[778] *A Renaissance Life*, p. 46.
[779] *World of Christopher Marlowe*, p. 69.
[780] *A Renaissance Life*, p. 53.
[781] *World of Christopher Marlowe*, p. 69.
[782] Ibid. p. 70.

techniques, taught him how to argue; the sermons and philosophy lectures taught him what to argue about." (Riggs)[783] As a first and second year student, Marlowe would learn that the academic skill of dialectic consisted exclusively in the ability to credibly argue any topic from either side of an issue. In other words, the objective of dialectic was to present a convincing or persuasive argument rather than defend or uphold philosophical truth.[784] Their disputations in general would be constructed of two-part syllogisms that rapidly accumulated to form a 'weighty' argument as they defended their position and deflected counter-arguments. Logic aided the student to find a subject for argument, while rhetoric enabled the student to express his arguments eloquently and with persuasive grace. "Moral goodness was superfluous to the orator's vocation. Persuasion was simply a means to an end — any end." (Riggs)[785]

During his third and fourth years, Marlowe studied moral and natural philosophy, but his previous courses did not adequately prepare him for the texts that were selected for these studies, in particular Professor John Case's extensive commentary edition of Aristotle's *Ethics* (1584).[786] Aristotle maintained the skill of dialectic was useful for the study of the philosophical sciences as it enabled the mind to analyse both sides of an argument to discover the disparity between truth and error.[787] However, it is apparent the method of dialectic Marlowe learned in Cambridge precluded this ideal in philosophy: "True and false were […] alien concepts in the Elizabethan arts course; […] philosophy *was* the puzzles on each side of a question," Riggs explains.[788] In Cambridge, aspiring divinity students were expected to competently argue, and in certain cases defend, topics that were often blasphemous:

> "A manuscript list of theses dating from around 1580 reveals that students disputed such propositions as: 'The style of sacred Scripture is not barbarous'; 'There is a place of hell'; 'The reprobate do not truly call on God'; 'God does not want everyone to be saved'; 'The will acts freely'; and 'Nothing is done without prior consent and volition by God'. Since dialectical disputation took up 'both parts of every question', one of the students had to argue that there is no place of hell, that the reprobate truly call upon God, that God wants everyone to be saved, that the will does not act freely, and that things are done without God's prior consent and volition. Any doctrine could be made credible; none could be proven." (Riggs)[789]

In fact, Marlowe's university education in the field of philosophy was an extraordinary programme of contradiction when considering many of the Scholarship places were awarded to students who hopefully would find positions in the Church, particularly the Parker Scholars. At

---

[783] Ibid. p. 79.
[784] Ibid. pp. 80–81.
[785] Ibid. p. 85.
[786] Ibid. p. 86.
[787] Ibid.
[788] Ibid.
[789] Ibid. p. 91.

that point in time, Scholastic theology with its emphasis on exploring the concept of Divine Truth, was banned in Oxford and Cambridge due to its Catholic origins.[790] To fill this theological vacuum, a humanities course was formulated with the core curriculum based on classical Latin (pagan!) authors.[791] Philosophy was imparted through the medium of classical poetry.[792] This training was completely irrelevant to the duties associated with a Christian Church and exposed students to the very subjects that were denounced as damnable. For instance, students studied the Creation through Ovid's version in the *Metamorphoses*, the objective was to display that ancient texts corroborated the Scriptures, however, this practise also had the reverse effect as the pagan texts could be used to argue that the Bible was not the sole source of divine truth.[793] The Judeo-Christian monopoly on divine revelation was compromised! Students inadvertently learned in the last book of the *Metamorphoses* that poets were responsible for creating all the 'myths' associated with religion: "O race of men, stunned with the chilling fear of death, why do you dread the Styx, the shades and empty names, the stuff that poets manufacture, and their fabled sufferings of a world that never was?"[794] Other ancient historians, i.e. Polybius, Plutarch and Livy, upheld the opinion that government officials had introduced the fear of the gods to control the Roman Empire.[795] Pythagoras preached the doctrines of Epicurus: hell is non-existent, belief in the same is mindless superstition, governments and poets fabricated the idea of divine punishment, the human body returns to the elements after death but there is no afterlife as the soul dissolves when it leaves the body.[796]

In addition to these classical texts, the university environment was not conducive to an orthodox Christian lifestyle. When Marlowe settled into his lodgings, he would find that …

> "[…] Like most college rooms, it held three or four students, or
> a Fellow and two students. […] The rooms reserved for Parker Scholars
> held little in the way of furniture […] two beds, two chairs, a table and
> three stools. Like other members of the college, Marlowe and his
> roommates would have slept with one another."[797]

Reviewing this situation with respect to Elizabethan conventions, this arrangement was not considered unusual as boys generally shared beds until they married; in many cases, bed-sharing was perceived an integral part of the male-bonding process that formed long-lasting friendships.[798] The students' philosophical texts actually included the topic of male friendship. As Riggs relates, "Love between men was intrinsic to the humanist educational programme."[799]

---

[790] Ibid. p. 72.

[791] Ibid.

[792] Ibid. p. 87.

[793] Ibid. p. 89.

[794] F. J. Miller, ed., *Ovid's Metamorphoses* (Massachusetts, Harvard University Press, 1976) II, p. 375, in *World of Christopher Marlowe*, p. 89.

[795] *World of Christopher Marlowe*, p. 89.

[796] Ibid.

[797] Ibid. p. 72.

[798] Ibid. p. 73.

[799] Ibid. p. 74.

However, these texts verily went one step further and broached the subject of homoerotic relationships. Chapter Twenty-six of Aristotle's' *Problems*, for instance, candidly raises this subject: homosexuality was not only a natural inclination, but a "[…] cultural practice that can be learned under the right conditions." (Riggs)[800] Ovid and Virgil, and especially Plato in his *Symposium*, also casually discussed these issues as matter of fact. It is probable that the students, when presented with this environment, would be tempted to experiment. Marlowe's contemporaries, for instance, the reformer Henry Barrow, noticed the young men of the universities could hardly be expected to remain chaste, "[…] especially being nose-led in such heathen vanity […]", and thereby ultimately commit sins "[…] contrary to nature […] and dishonour their own bodies amongst themselves."[801] However, in public, these subjects were considered a great scandal; homosexuality was punishable by death, nevertheless, a case of sodomy was rarely prosecuted.[802]

It is worthy to note that the divinity students were not completely bereft of Christian instruction. In preparation for the BA public disputation examinations, Marlowe and his fellow classmates read Musculus's handbook *Commonplaces of the Christian Religion*, which to all intents and purposes, was a reiteration of Calvin's doctrine of predestination learned in the grammar school.[803] Calvin's *Institutes of the Christian Religion* was also a standard textbook for divinity students at Oxford and Cambridge.[804] Students were now conducted through exercises of introspective conversion and repentance to acquaint them with the presence of the Holy Ghost in their souls to discover if God had preordained their salvation.[805] However, the reverse side of these exercises was spiritually catastrophic: "For the reprobate, who [was] predestined to sin and damnation, study and meditation only made things worse." (Riggs.)[806] Calvin maintained that God *purposely blinded* reprobates, either by withdrawing His grace that would have enabled those souls to understand His word, or (paradoxically we might add), by directing His Voice to them in such a manner to ensure they would remain deaf to His invocations.[807] In other words, a soul predestined for Hell and 'divinely blinded' to God's call read the Bible to their utter destruction. Ironically, the classic epics the students read, for one example, Virgil's *Æneid*, reinforced this concept of the gods 'conspiring to overthrow' civilisations by the inherent blindness of certain individuals contrary to common sense. In this epic, the civilisation doomed to destruction is Troy — Capys warns the Trojans to examine the equine colossus constructed by their enemies, the Greeks, to discover any hidden traps, and Laocoon throws his spear at the wooden monument and discovers it contains a hidden cargo, but the Trojans choose to ignore this revelation:

[800]   Ibid.

[801]   Henry Barrow, *Plain Refutation*, in *World of Christopher Marlowe*, p. 75.

[802]   *World Of Christopher Marlowe*, p. 75.

[803]   Ibid. p. 90.

[804]   Pauline Honderich, 'John Calvin and Doctor Faustus', *Modern Language Review* 68 (January, 1973): p. 4.

[805]   *World of Christopher Marlowe*, p. 95.

[806]   Ibid.

[807]   Ibid. pp. 95–96.

[…] His forceful spear, which hissing as it flew,
Pierc'd thro' the yielding planks of jointed wood,
And trembling in the hollow belly stood.
The sides transpierc'd, return a rattling sound,
And groans of Greeks inclos'd come issuing thro' the wound,
And, had not Heav'n the fall of Troy design'd,
Or had not men been fated to be blind,[*]
Enough was said and done t' inspire a better mind.
Then had our lances pierc'd the treach'rous wood,
And Illian tow'rs and Priam's empire stood. […][808]

 On Palm Sunday, 1584, Marlowe had completed all the requirements for his BA degree, i.e. his participation in four public disputations. According to the stipulation of his Parker Scholarship, he could continue his studies for a further three years and pursue his MA degree provided his studies culminated with his ordination in the Church of England. This restriction may have fomented a certain degree of resentment with Marlowe: he was now conferred, a BA graduate, with the Latin title 'Dominus',[809] (literal translation, 'Lord'), and could therefore be referred to as Sir Marlowe or Marlowe, *Gentleman*, only to realise this was a nominal honour, an empty title. The institutions of Cambridge University were designed to uphold the Elizabethan social hierarchy, and therefore students not from the nobility or the gentry were excluded from a career in law.[810] Hence, those from the less privileged classes of society were denied prominent positions associated with government. Lord Burghley, Chancellor of the University, recognised the need for a supply of pastors to fill Church and university positions, but this was reserved for the poor and less privileged scholars who were "[…] expected to remain in the lower echelons of the university and the Church." (Riggs)[811] Scholars were literally shepherded into certain careers, in this case, to tend the flocks of Her Majesty's Church, and in general had little option but to comply with the dictates of society. In addition, when Marlowe attained his BA degree, available parish positions were fast diminishing,[812] and the wages were paltry. Kuriyama observes, "[Marlowe] had earned almost half that much as a mere boy, a King's scholar, [i.e. £10 a year a clergyman might hope to earn] and his present scholarship was worth more than some ecclesiastical livings."[813] Considering his reported atheistic views disclosed in later years, Marlowe may not have entertained any inclination to join the ranks of the Church clergy and expressed his intention to fulfil the scholarship requirements with the ulterior motive of

---

[*] Italics added.
[808] John Dryden, trans., *Virgil's Æneid*. Reprint: Charles W. Eliot, ed., *The Harvard Classics, vol. 13* (New York, P. F. Collier and Son Corp. 1963), p. 102.
[809] *A Renaissance Life,* p. 53.
[810] *World of Christopher Marlowe*, p. 71.
[811] Ibid.
[812] Ibid. p. 97.
[813] *A Renaissance Life,* p. 51.

continuing his advanced studies. The BA degree he achieved would not procure for him many opportunities as this award was designed as a mere preparatory stepping-stone to the MA level.[814]

His MA years afforded him the opportunity to discover an alternative career that offered lucrative and intellectually stimulating prospects. As a graduate student, he was granted the freedom to leave the campus for extended periods, and he took full advantage of this new privilege:

> "He missed most of autumn 1584, came back early in December, but was gone for the last three weeks of January. He remained in residence from January to Easter, went away again and then returned for the first half of the summer term. All told, he missed about half the year. The absences persisted throughout his MA course. Marlowe remained at Corpus Christi for almost all of autumn and winter 1585–86, dropped out again during the spring and again returned for the summer term. He was at his college for most of the autumn and about half the winter of 1586–87, the term in which his scholarship expired. He last appeared at Corpus Christi in March 1587. Where did he go?"(Riggs)[815]

One absence can be accounted for: Marlowe decided to visit his family in Canterbury in 1585 during the second half of the summer term. While in Canterbury, he witnessed the signing of Katherine Benchkin's will, dated August 19, 1585. Apparently, the Marlowes were friends of the Benchkin family of Canterbury: we note that John Marlowe, his brother-in-law Thomas Arthur, and his son-in-law John Moore were also witnesses to this will.[816] In addition, the benefactor of the will, James Benchkin, had recently arrived at Corpus Christi in Cambridge on June 30, 1585[817] and it is possible he became closer acquainted with Marlowe at the college during his MA years.

A number of Marlowe's absences may be attributed to his interest in poetry and his attraction to the theatre. Marlovian scholars presume his English translations of Lucan's *Civil War* and Ovid's *Amores* were projects that date from his MA years.[818] Subsequently, he followed Dame Tragedy's advice to Ovid in the *Amores* by continuing with new works in a "grave, lofty style".[819] It is reported Marlowe translated Thomas Watson's Latin epic *Helenae Raptus* (*The Rape of Helen*) in 1587, however, a copy has not survived to support this claim.[820] Marlowe, ever inspired by the ancient classics, turned to Virgil's *Æneid* to produce his first drama, *Dido, Queen of Carthage*, which bears the following inscription on its original title page: "Written by Christopher Marlowe and Thomas Nashe Gent. [...] Played by the Children of Her Majesty's

[814] Ibid. p. 40.

[815] *World of Christopher Marlowe*, p. 98.

[816] See *A Renaissance Life*, pp. 194–198, for Katherine Benchkin's will, and the following depositions pertaining to the same.

[817] *A Renaissance Life*, p. 59.

[818] *World of Christopher Marlowe*, pp. 173, 188.

[819] Ibid. p. 111.

[820] *A Renaissance Life*, p. 87.

Chapel." Riggs observes this play may have premièred c. 1584–1585 prior to the time the Chapel Children company faded into obscurity for about sixteen years.[821] The children's companies offered an opportunity to budding playwrights from the universities to demonstrate their dramatic skills.[822] His second drama, *Tamburlaine the Great* (Part One), was performed in 1587, and commentators believe he composed this play while still at Cambridge. Hence, Marlowe possibly used these periods of absence from the university to work on his English translations, and may have visited London to oversee the premiere productions of his first two dramas.

In addition to his interests in the theatre, we know Marlowe considered one other possibility for employment: the Elizabethan secret service first established in 1581–1582[823] by the Queen's Principal Secretary, Sir Francis Walsingham. An age of intense political conspiracy, the government urgently needed to gather intelligence to protect their Queen, her life and her sovereignty as Riggs relates:

> "When Marlowe entered the queen's service in his early twenties a covert civil war between Protestants and Catholics had been underway for most of his life. The main Catholic figurehead in this struggle was Queen Elizabeth's cousin Mary Stuart, Queen of Scots, the widow of the King of France and the mother of the future King James VI of Scotland. Mary fled to England in 1568, under suspicion of conniving in the murder of her husband; she soon took a leading role in Catholic plots to dethrone Elizabeth. [...]
>
> The plots surrounding Mary, Queen of Scots, shared a common scenario. A Catholic prince would lead an army into the north of England. Native Catholics would rally around the invader, rising up in rebellion against the queen. The papists would liberate Mary, Queen of Scots, whom Elizabeth kept under house arrest. Mary, the rightful claimant to the English crown, would then depose Elizabeth and reinstate Catholicism throughout the land. Depending on the cast of characters, Queen Mary might wed her rescuer, or another suitable consort, resolving the bloody overthrow in a suitably romantic fashion."[824]

The universities became prime recruiting grounds for the various religio-political factions. The Jesuits of the English Catholic seminary in Rheims, a noted headquarters for Catholic agents, succeeded in planting priests at the universities of Oxford and Cambridge with the aim to recruit underground Catholic students and converts for the priesthood, returning as many as possible to England to assist and fortify the Catholic resistance.[825] Secretary Walsingham followed suit and searched for new operatives from the ranks of the students; "The industrious Parker Scholars — quick-witted, needy and beholden to the Church of England — were just the kind of men the

---

[821] *World of Christopher Marlowe*, p. 114.
[822] Ibid.
[823] Ibid. p. 140.
[824] Ibid. p. 128.
[825] Ibid. pp. 128, 140–141.

Secretary was looking for."(Riggs)[826] It was a period of extreme anti-Catholic mania and Marlowe's absences had aroused suspicion. A rumour spread he joined the English Catholic seminary at Rheims, and consequently the faculty considered withholding Marlowe's MA degree. Swiftly, the Privy Council came to Marlowe's aid and defended his reputation with a letter dated June 29, 1587 diplomatically explaining he had been involved in a covert operation, but that he loyally worked on behalf of Her Majesty's government:

> "Whereas it was reported that Christopher Morley [Marlowe] was determined to have gone beyond the sea to Rheims and there to remain, their Lordships thought good to certify that he had no such intent, but that in all his actions he had behaved himself orderly and discreetly whereby he had done her Majesty good service, and deserved to be rewarded for his faithful dealing: Their Lordships request was that the rumour thereof should be allayed by all possible means, and that he should be furthered in the degree he was to take this next commencement: Because it was not her Majesty's pleasure that anyone employed as he had been in matters touching the benefit of his country should be defamed by those that are ignorant in the affairs he went about;"[827]

Documents recording Marlowe's presence in the English seminary at Rheims are non-existent, thus it is not likely he matriculated as an English Catholic seminarian with the clandestine purpose to acquire information. It is logical to assume the government would not assign a mission of this sensitive nature to a young student with little experience in the turbulent world of the double agent. As Kuriyama observes, "[…] Rheims was a perilous place for an amateur to play spy."[828] A certain Richard Baines would discover this to his determent; apparently, this is the same Richard Baines who graduated with an MA degree from the Catholic-sympathetic Caius College, Cambridge in 1576. Baines enrolled to commence his studies for the priesthood at Rheims in 1578, and was ordained in 1581. However, he confided certain disturbing sentiments and his radical ideas for the future to a friend at the seminary. Baines remarked that the seminary was doomed to closure, and they should return to England where Her Majesty would handsomely reward them for any information they could offer.[829] He intimated the inhabitants of the seminary could be destroyed by poison, and therefore it was not a secure place.[830] Baines also disclosed to his friend he had many sacrilegious thoughts and mocked several Catholic articles of faith, including rituals associated with Catholic worship that he deemed misguided.[831] His anonymous friend became alarmed and informed the superiors of the seminary, with the result Baines was repeatedly tortured for three months by strappado until a satisfactory confession was rung from him admitting his intention was to overthrow the seminary,

---

[826] Ibid. p. 141.
[827] *A Renaissance Life*, pp. 202–203. [The spelling is modernised for this quotation.]
[828] Ibid. p. 70.
[829] Ibid. p. 67.
[830] Ibid.
[831] Ibid.

although he insisted he was not sent as a spy.[832]   Perhaps he entertained second thoughts concerning his ordination to the priesthood, and was tempted to seek a lucrative government position in England; "According to his first informal confession, Baines believed that such discoveries about the seminary would earn him fame and respect, a post in a noble household, and a reward of 3,000 crowns." (Kuriyama)[833]   We cannot state with certainty his denial in being a spy is the absolute truth for Baines was possibly one of Walsingham's agents from the beginning: "A lapsed Catholic who confessed and repented stood a better chance of leaving Rheims alive than a confirmed heretic and professional spy did." (Riggs)[834]

Returning to Marlowe, his first assignments in the secret service may have consisted of humble messenger duties, and perhaps he was simultaneously employed as a cryptographer. Poetry was recognised as an effective means of conveying secret messages due to its inherit quality of symbolic expression allowing for multiple interpretations of words. For instance, students already learned from an early age in the grammar schools that one could easily create puns in Latin by the nature of the language.[835]   Hence, messenger duties suited the poetical and linguistic skills the scholars acquired from their education, and prospective agents such as these were in demand as assassination plots thickened. These operatives were on the margins of the secret service and generally were not trusted as their job was of a mercenary nature, and their wages depended on the quality of the information they could provide.[836]   In addition, these marginal agents were rarely promoted to prominent positions in the civil service or other lucrative professions.[837]   Marlowe was possibly a courier sent to Rheims, however, Riggs alternatively demonstrates his missions dispatched him to the Low Countries:

"After the execution of his cousin Mary, Queen of Scots, on 8 February 1587, the Duke of Guise abruptly withdrew his patronage from the seminary at Rheims, which ceased to be a major centre for anti-Elizabethan conspiracies. Although the master spy Gilbert Gifford continued to operate out of Rheims, the focus of Catholic espionage and English intelligence shifted north to the Low Countries, where the Duke of Parma, who had conquered Antwerp in 1585, was poised to march on northern Holland and from there to invade England. On 29 June 1587, the Councillors' denial that they sent Marlowe to Rheims made perfectly good sense. The action had moved on to Brussels. [...] Many messengers, including Burghley's son Robert Cecil, shuttled back and forth between the English court and the Low Countries. Secretary Walsingham and his faction were kept in the dark about this venture, [i.e. a possible reconciliation with the Duke of Parma to avert war]

---

[832]   Ibid. p. 68.
[833]   Ibid. p. 67.
[834]   *World of Christopher Marlowe*, p. 131.
[835]   Georgia E. Brown, 'Marlowe's Poems and Classicism', in *Cambridge Companion to Marlowe*, pp. 107–108.
[836]   *World of Christopher Marlowe*, p. 183.
[837]   Ibid.

disapproved of it and refused to participate in any way. [...] When Marlowe appears in government archives he is dealing with Burghley or his agents, not with Walsingham."[838]

When we consider Marlowe's periods of absence from Cambridge and the extracurricular activities he became involved in, it is remarkable he managed to find time to prepare for his MA degree. The subjects he studied during these years, i.e. arithmetic, astronomy, geography and cosmography, helped to advance his career as a secret agent, and in particular, developed his creative skills as an aspiring playwright.[839] These subjects, based upon the medieval *quadrivium*, were believed to be a vital component for a divinity orientated curriculum as they directed students to contemplate the Eternal Creator through His Creation, yet simultaneously broadened the students' horizons and offered them additional skills that would be indispensable for diplomatic service or a career in the military.[840]

Marlowe studied optics, a multidisciplinary field encompassing math and geometry.[841] The subject of music, originally a feature of the early *quadrivium,* was replaced by cosmography, i.e. the subjects of geography and history.[842] Students learned to appreciate momentous historical events and the achievements of the great leaders of the world by reducing them to reference points on a map.[843] With a panoramic chart of the earth, students could plot the famous ancient and contemporary battles, and the rise and fall of the various empires. Of interest, ancient writers such as Pliny, whose work *Natural History* was one of Marlowe's set texts, equated the skill of cartography with martial and imperial conquest.[844] Astronomy was combined with cosmography as this subject enabled students to achieve proficiency in every mathematical science pertaining to spatial dimension.[845] Ptolemy's geocentric theory remained the standard astronomical system in the university curriculum at this point in time, although the Copernican theory was not unfamiliar. Giordano Bruno (1548?–1600) the famous Italian philosopher and poet, author of the controversial philosophical tract *The Expulsion of the Triumphant Beast* (1584), visited England from 1583 to 1585 and lectured in Oxford for a brief period where he championed the Copernican system. Students who attended Cambridge no doubt were informed of the important events that occurred in Oxford, and vice versa. Bruno would have been difficult to forget for his theories dared to challenge the philosophy of Aristotle upon which the theology and cosmology of the times were based. For instance, the Ptolemaic system of the Universe supported the current theological concept that the Earth and the planets were connected in a linear line directly to God in the Empyrean Heaven, supported by an interpretation of Aristotle's theories that suggested nothing new could be found in outer space. The Copernican System was not only 'new', but realigned the whole cosmos, where did God reside in this new order of the heavens?

---

[838] Ibid. pp. 182–183.
[839] Ibid. pp. 159–160.
[840] Ibid.
[841] Ibid. pp. 160–161.
[842] Ibid.
[843] Ibid.
[844] Ibid. p. 164.
[845] Ibid. p. 166.

Bruno proposed a radical solution in his *Triumphant Beast*: God does not simply reside in one predetermined place in heaven—He is pure spirit, and therefore is within the very fabric of Creation and is present in all that exists, from the smallest particle of dust, to the distant stars of the heavens. This complete Divine Integration also explains how God could be everywhere at one time, and control all the unceasing motions of the universe simultaneously and instantaneously. Thus, the cosmos need not be in a linear order as with the Ptolemaic system. However, Bruno dared to carry this idea further and suggested that as God is everywhere and also infinite in nature, then the Universe must correspond with these characteristics, proposing that there were not only nine planets, but an infinite number of worlds that had not yet been seen by the eyes of man, an idea that blatantly challenged contemporary interpretations of Aristotle. Eventually, Bruno was forced to leave Oxford for his radical views! In those times, anti-Aristotelian opinions would not be tolerated: Bachelors and Masters of Art at Oxford were fined five shillings for every theory that did not conform with the premises contained in Aristotle's *Organon*, a treatise on logic.[846] Bruno also attested that students were bound to take an oath to obey the following rule: "let no one be advanced to the degrees of Master and Doctor of Philosophy and Theology, unless he has drunk from the fountain of Aristotle."[847] Although Bruno did not mention Cambridge, it is reasonable to presume that anti-Aristotelian views were also frowned upon in that establishment.

Returning to Marlow's approved curriculum, astronomy was valued as an important component in the appreciation of classical poetry, for many ancient masters conveyed religious convictions and scientific theories in their works. For example, the song of the bard Silenus, as recorded in Virgil's pastorals, was recognised as a direct reference to the Aristotelian version of Creation with the self-ordering of the four elements.[848] In their poetry appreciation lectures, students simultaneously received instruction in the Epicurean concept that all forms of matter, organic and inanimate objects, will dissolve back into the elements from which they originated.[849]

Astronomy naturally prepared students for the study of astrology, although this was not a prescribed subject in their curriculum. MA students nevertheless "[...] routinely studied it and kept notebooks of occult learning," Riggs observes.[850] Scholars maintained the planets and stars embodied the qualities and properties of the four elements, and therefore influenced all matter in the natural world.[851] Thus, astrological prognostications became an important science determining how these cosmic influences would affect all aspects of life and the elements of the earth:

"The queen and her Councillors consulted great wizards like
John Dee and Thomas Allen about the timing of state occasions and

---

[846] Arthur D. Imerti, ed., trans., 'Editor's Introduction: The Making of a Heretic', in Giordano Bruno, *The Expulsion of the Triumphant Beast* (United States of America: Bison Books, University of Nebraska Press, 2004), p. 8.

[847] Ibid.

[848] *World of Christopher Marlowe*, p. 169.

[849] Ibid.

[850] Ibid. p. 174.

[851] Ibid.

military engagements. Doctors used astrological tables to determine when to apply the appropriate remedies. Families employed scholars to cast the horoscopes of their children." (Riggs)[852]

The science of astrology remained imprecise, for it was almost impossible to accurately predict results from these various influences wielded by the planets. One instance in England demonstrating the inaccuracy of astrology is Richard Harvey's attempt to predict the effects that would occur with the conjunction of the beneficial planet Jupiter with the malfeasant planet Saturn on the 28th of April 1583.[853] He speculated this conjunction would produce a great tempest, a theory that failed miserably, thus he became an object of derision in academic circles. However, this did not deter scholars from drafting and pondering upon astrology forecasts; a certain prediction by Regiomontanus of Nuremberg continued to intrigue scholars: *"Octogesimus octavus mirabilis annus."* ("The eighty-eighth, a year of wonders.")[854] As early as 1582, Cambridge scholars disputed whether or not this prediction was foretelling the final destruction of the world.[855] In retrospect of historical events, it would appear Judgement Day had almost arrived for the English; Thomas Bacon reflected years after the event contemporaries believed this prediction inferred a threat of invasion later confirmed with the arrival of the Spanish Armada in 1588.[856]

Astrology inevitably seduced students to experiment with magic and alchemical arts thought to contain all the secrets to comprehend the universe. Two leading natural philosophers, John Case and Everard Digby, taught students at Oxford and Cambridge respectively the basic principles of occult knowledge believed to control the natural world.[857] Riggs observes this was dangerous territory as, "The boundary [between 'natural' and 'black' magic] was imprecise, but somewhere along this spectrum the 'white' magician became an idolater practising a pagan religion."[858] Scholars had access to books that explained the various methods employed to summon spirits, such as John Dee's *Preparatory Teachings* and the *Hieroglyphical Monad*, and also the works of Giordano Bruno, including his *Expulsion of the Triumphant Beast* wherein the philosopher reiterated the hermetic teachings of Hermes Trismegistus who proposed the pagan Egyptians, through their wisdom and knowledge, had magically ascended the celestial heights to the realm of the divine.[859] Magic provided a window into the secret world of nature and the elements inherent in the Aristotelian and Epicurean versions of Creation that the poets eternised in their masterpieces. It comes as no surprise that graduates were fascinated by the occult arts following their initial introduction to classical poetry, astronomy and astrology, and as a 'natural progression', experimented with the various forms of conjuration. One Cambridge student,

---

[852] Ibid.

[853] Ibid. p. 175.

[854] Francis Bacon, 'Of Prophecies', *Essays or Counsels, Civil and Moral* (1625 edition), reprint in Charles W. Eliot, ed., *The Harvard Classics: Bacon, Milton's Prose, Thomas Browne*, vol. 3 (New York: P. F. Collier and Son, 1963), p. 92.

[855] *World of Christopher Marlowe*, p. 174.

[856] Bacon, *Essays or Counsels*, p. 174.

[857] *World of Christopher Marlowe*, p. 176.

[858] Ibid. p. 177.

[859] Ibid. pp. 177–178.

William Perkins, (MA 1584) confessed that having studied astrology, he was driven by an insatiable curiosity that he could not satisfy and was compelled to study all the secret subjects associated with that science. He admitted he eventually came to his senses by the grace of God, proclaiming the occult arts to be unadulterated idolatry.[860]

Marlowe, profoundly influenced by the world around him and the education he received, incorporated his experiences and opinions in all his dramas. In *Dido, Queen of Carthage* (c. 1584–1585), although written in collaboration with his friend Nashe, Marlowe's distinctive style as a revolutionary playwright is already emerging at this early stage in his career. For his first subject, Marlowe concentrates on the familiar legend of Dido and Aeneas drawn from Virgil's *Æneid* set after the fall of Troy. Aeneas, the son of Venus, the goddess of love, is forced to set sail when the city is taken, yet the heavens smile on the Trojan prince who is protected by Jupiter and destined to found a new empire in Italy and restore the former glories of Troy. However, Juno, the wife of Jupiter and the goddess of marriage is the sworn enemy of Aeneas provoked by her rivalry with Venus, and she attempts to destroy his fleet by causing a severe tempest. He is shipwrecked off the Carthaginian coast where he is graciously received by Queen Dido. Dido falls in love with Aeneas, and while out hunting one day, the couple are forced to find shelter in a cave when Juno unleashes another tempest with the consent of Venus, for the two goddesses have formed a temporary truce with ulterior motives and thereby have conveniently encouraged this love affair — Juno hopes Aeneas will settle in Carthage with Dido and thereby abandon his destiny, and Venus schemes to exploit Dido's love for Aeneas by having her restore his fleet. Juno's plans are unravelled when Jupiter sends a divine messenger to warn Aeneas, commanding him to continue his journey, and Dido is broken hearted when by this edict of the gods he prepares to leave her and fulfil his mission. He abandons her to establish his new empire and she takes her own life in despair.

Marlowe dramatised particular issues raised in the Trojan legend with his own unique acuity of life. According to the original legend, Juno has several reasons to harbour malice for the Trojans and confound Jupiter's plans for Aeneas. First, Juno suffered rejection when the Trojan prince, Paris, deceitfully resolved a dispute between her and the two goddesses, Minerva and Venus. The three goddesses asked Paris, who in his opinion was the most beautiful, and Venus cunningly bribed him by offering him Helen, the wife of King Menelaus of Sparta, should he name her the most beautiful. Thus, Paris not only rejected Juno, he defied the sanctity of marriage when he accepted the bribe and brought Helen to Troy, thus setting in motion the events that brought about the disastrous Trojan War and Juno's enmity with Venus and her children. Second, Jupiter cast Juno's love aside for the youthful attentions of Ganymede, a Trojan prince, favouring him with the honoured position of royal cupbearer that originally belonged to Hebe, the goddess of youth. In highlighting the polarities of the drama that contrast marriage and illicit love, Marlowe sidesteps the rivalry between the three goddesses and Paris' abduction of Helen and concentrates on Jupiter with Ganymede, blatantly casting him in a pederastic role. Act I opens with Jupiter "dandling" Ganymede on his knee, promising to shower him with delightful gifts.[861] He presents Ganymede with the same jewels he presented to Juno on their wedding day,

---

[860] Ibid.

[861] Source for play texts and references in this study unless otherwise stated are from J. B. Steane, ed., *Penguin Classics: Christopher Marlowe, The Complete Plays* (Great Britain: Penguin Book Ltd., 1986).

which alludes to scene four in Act III when Dido bestows to Aeneas the jewels from her previous marriage as they enter the cave to consummate their love under the guise of wedlock. Marlowe was obviously influenced by the homophile issues intrinsic in many of the Classical texts selected for the anti-Scholastic syllabus of Cambridge.

In the play, Marlowe also addressed issues related to the social status of monarchs and the privileged classes in contrast to the conditions endured by commoners as perceived from his personal experience. When Aeneas arrives in Carthage, he is homeless and dressed in tattered rags. Dido is appalled that a prince should suffer this base misfortune, orders him to be dressed in the royal robes her deceased husband once wore, and requests Aeneas to sit at her side. However, he entreats her not to insist on his company, but she dismisses his modesty:

> *Aeneas*: This is no seat for one's that's comfortless.
>   May it please your grace to let Aeneas wait;
>   For though my birth be great, my fortune's mean,
>   Too mean to be companion to a queen.
> *Dido*: Thy fortune may be greater than thy birth.
>   Sit down, Aeneas, sit in Dido's place;
>   [...]
> *Aeneas*: In all humility, I thank your grace.
> *Dido*: Remember who thou art; speak like thyself:
>   Humility belongs to common grooms.

[II. i. 88–93, 99–100]

Although Dido recognises Aeneas' status as a prince by lineage, Marlowe challenges this convention associated with the aristocracy when Aeneas sets aside all distinction between realm and title. His kingdom is razed to the ground and there is nothing left to govern — what significance has his lineage now? His fortunes are reduced to that of a poor beggar reliant upon Dido's charity and he assumes the role of the obedient servant, begging to serve the queen and her court. Marlowe may have drawn this observation from the preferential treatment lavished on students who were not dependant on scholarships donated by benefactors and therefore could afford to be proud and ambitious. However, Dido reinstates the 'Right of Lineage' on Aeneas and he ascends to his rightful place, the titles of the gentry still carry considerable weight and Aeneas is robed in royal garments, a token that symbolises social privilege. This concept obviously parallels the dress codes enforced at Cambridge University that distinguished the status of the different social classes.

Marlowe also presents a draconian view of state power. Dido as supreme monarch wields her power to control the fortunes of her subjects and dispenses with them at her pleasure:

> *Dido*: Those that dislike what Dido gives in charge,
>   Command my guard to slay for their offence.
>   Shall vulgar peasants storm at what I do?
>   The ground is mine that gives them sustenance,
>   The air wherein they breathe, the water, fire,

All that they have, their lands, their goods, their lives,
And I, the goddess of all these, command
Aeneas ride as Carthaginian king.

[IV. iv. 71–78]

Dido is portrayed as a goddess-queen who controls at will the four cosmic elements and thereby wields absolute power over her mortal subjects. Dido is also addressed as 'Elisa' or 'Eliza', and the association with 'Elizabeth' would not have passed unnoticed. Is Marlowe presenting a miniature portrait of Queen Elizabeth as head of the Church in England and her effective use of religion to control the state and her subjects? Marlowe also insinuates his sceptical view of religious belief via the motherly affection of Venus in Act I. Jupiter is distracted as he showers Ganymede with constant attention, and apparently ignores the plight of Aeneas who is tossed about on the sea due to Juno's wrath although Aeneas committed no offence to deserve this terrible trial. Venus reproaches Jupiter for his lack of consideration towards her son:

> *Venus*: Ay, this is it: you can sit toying there,
>   And playing with that female wanton boy,
>   While my Aeneas wanders on the seas,
>   And rests a prey to every billow's pride.
>   […]
>   False Jupiter, reward'st thou virtue so?
>   What, is not piety exempt from woe?
>   Then die, Aeneas, in thine innocence,
>   Since that religion hath no recompense.

[I. i. 50–53, 78–81]

Following the production of *Dido, Queen of Carthage*, Marlowe became absorbed with the history of the great rogue-conqueror of Asia, Tamburlaine (1336–1405), and produced his next two groundbreaking masterpieces based on the life of this intrepid emperor. Riggs suggests Marlowe's source text for the biography of Tamburlaine was Whetsone's *English Mirror: A Regard Wherein All Estates May behold the Conquests of Envy* (1586.)[862] Whetstone selected several histories dating from antiquity to Elizabethan times to demonstrate that atheists and followers of Machiavellian policy are all inevitably doomed to divine punishment. However, Tamburlaine was an exception among the godless leaders chosen by Whetstone as Riggs explains:

> "For Europeans, Tamburlaine's claim to fame lay in his defeat
> of Bajazeth, the event that lifted the Turkish siege of Constantinople.

---

[862] *World of Christopher Marlowe*, p. 203.

321

Since Tamburlaine had saved the eastern capital of Christendom, the usual rules did not apply in his case."[863]

According to Middle Eastern chronicles, Tamburlaine was the leader of a Scythian tribe whose wealth was acquired by amassing herds of sheep. He started out as a bandit-warrior and stole flocks from surrounding tribes with the assistance of a small group of men. Gradually, his band grew into an army and he surmounted his lowly origins by initiating momentous military conquests, thereby establishing a mighty empire that stretched from the Mediterranean to the subcontinent of India. Whetstone presented the conqueror as an ambitious man whose sole objective centred on the acquisition of power, and who strove to conquer an earthly kingdom and accomplished it as though it was a "work of virtue".[864] Tamburlaine's warfare stratagems and his methods in laying siege to cities were decried as cruel and barbaric, however, he allegedly justified his brutal tactics with the formidable reply; "Remember, I am the wrath of God."[865] This story attracted Marlowe for obvious reasons.

When Marlowe introduces Tamburlaine in Part I, [I. ii.], he and his marauders have just captured the caravan of Princess Zenocrate, daughter of the Egyptian Sultan. Immediately he confirms Zenocrate is correct to address him as 'lord', announces his plans to acquire an empire by deed rather than by the circumstances of his birth, and casts off his shepherd's pelts to don the majestic raiment of a warrior-emperor:

> *Tamburlaine*: I am a lord, for so my deeds shall prove,
> And yet a shepherd by my parentage.
> [...]
> And means to be a terror to the world,
> Measuring the limits of his empery
> By east and west, as Phoebus doth his course.
> Lie here, ye weeds that I disdain to wear!
> This complete armour and this curtle-axe
> Are adjuncts more beseeming Tamburlaine.

> [I. ii. 34–35, 38–43]

Hence, it is demonstrated in the drama that by sheer ambition and determination, Tamburlaine will forge his own destiny and prove it is the nobility of action by which one is proved worthy to govern a kingdom:

> *Tamburlaine*: [...]
> I hold the Fates bound fast in iron chains,
> And with my hand turn Fortune's wheel about;
> And sooner shall the sun fall from his sphere

---

[863] Ibid. p. 204.
[864] Ibid.
[865] Ibid.

Than Tamburlaine be slain or overcome.

[I. ii. 174–177]

Marlowe continues to develop the concept of equating royal government with divine power wielded by the gods when Tamburlaine and his friends contemplate the glory and authority associated with the kingship of Persia:

> *Tamburlaine*: And ride in triumph through Persepolis!
> Is it not brave to be a king, Techelles!
> Usumcasane and Theridamas,
> Is it not passing brave to be a king,
> And ride in triumph through Persepolis?
> *Techelles*: O, my lord, 'tis sweet and full of pomp!
> *Usumcasane*: To be a king, is half to be a god.
> *Theridamas*: A god is not so glorious as a king:
> I think the pleasure they enjoy in heaven,
> Cannot compare with kingly joys on earth; —
> To wear a crown enchas'd with pearls and gold,
> Whose virtues carry with it life and death;
> To ask and have, command and be obey'd;
> When looks breed love, with looks to gain the prize,
> Such power attractive shines in princes' eyes.

[II. v. 50–64]

In addition to his innate desire to achieve greatness in defiance to social convention, Marlowe finds expression for his atheistic and pessimistic views with regard to religion. When Tamburlaine conquers Cosroe, his former ally whom he once assisted to seize the Persian throne, Tamburlaine justifies his treachery by referring to Jupiter who overthrew his father, Saturn, and thereby became the leader of the gods. Can the actions of a god be questioned? Tamburlaine is presented as a classic case of ignominious deeds vindicated by pious expediency:

> *Tamburlaine*: The thirst of reign and sweetness of a crown,
> That caus'd the eldest son of heavenly Ops
> To thrust his doting father from his chair,
> And place himself in the imperial heaven,
> Mov'd me to manage arms against thy state.
> What better precedent than mighty Jove? […]

[II. vii. 12–17]

Tamburlaine concludes his speech with an explanation for the driving force of his ambition: a restless soul. Christian theologians and philosophers have acknowledged that this incessant yearning is the unrelenting search for eternal happiness and fulfilment that can only be granted in heaven by God Himself, the Source of all good. King Solomon recognised the *earthly* pursuit of happiness as "vanity of vanities" for we are to be consumed with the aspirations for that heavenly happiness that will never fade. St. Augustine capsulated this theological revelation in his famous sentence: "Our hearts are restless, O God, until they rest in Thee." However, Tamburlaine's sole ambition is to attain all that the world has to offer and he ignores the aspirations to attain a heavenly afterlife, his search for perfect fulfilment is founded upon the plinth of pagan Epicureanism:

> [...] Nature, that fram'd us of four elements
> Warring within our breasts for regiment,
> Doth teach us all to have aspiring minds.
> Our souls, whose faculties can comprehend
> The wondrous architecture of the world,
> And measure every wandering planet's course,
> Still climbing after knowledge infinite,
> And always moving as the restless spheres,
> Wills us to wear ourselves and never rest,
> Until we reach the ripest fruit of all,
> That perfect bliss and sole felicity,
> The sweet fruition of an earthly crown.

[II. vii. 18–29]

Tamburlaine's insatiable ambition to acquire kingdom upon kingdom knows no boundaries: he plans to obliterate the importance of Holy Jerusalem as the geographical focal point by making Damascus the centre of the world and redraft every map accordingly. He envisions the borders of his empire stretching from the Old World to the New and includes regions the "blind geographers" have not drawn in their charts. [IV. iv. 80–88.] He desires to gain the whole world, for as an Epicurean he did not believe he had a soul to lose. *In fine*, Marlowe presents Tamburlaine as a successful atheist King who rivals the Christian perception of Christ as Eternal King. The image of Tamburlaine wielding his sword to "scourge" the nations is symbolically used in the play to depict the conqueror subduing the world by his heroic martial actions in antithesis of Christ, who conquers the world as the Word of God with the Gospel of Truth. Notice in his physical description of Tamburlaine, Marlowe turned to the vision of Christ as depicted in the Book of the Apocalypse:

Menaphon: Of stature tall, and straightly fashioned Like his desire, lift upwards and divine. So large of limbs, his joints so strongly knit,	And in the midst of the seven golden candlesticks, one like to the Son of man, clothed with a garment down to the feet, and girt about the paps with a golden girdle. And his head and his hairs were

Such breadth of shoulders as might mainly bear
Old Atlas' burden. 'Twixt his manly pitch,
A pearl more worth than all the world is plac'd,
Wherein by curious sovereignty of art
Are fix'd his piercing instruments of sight,
Whose fiery circles bear encompassed
A heaven of heavenly bodies in their spheres,
That guides his steps and actions to the throne
Where honour sits invested royally.
Pale of complexion, wrought in him with passion,
Thirsting with sovereignty and love of arms,
His lofty brows in folds do figure death,
And in their smoothness amity and life.
[…]

[II. i. 7–22]

white, as white wool, and as snow, and his eyes were as a flame of fire. And his feet like unto fine brass, as in a burning furnace. And his voice as the sound of many waters. And he had in his right hand seven stars. And from his mouth came out a sharp two edged sword: and his face was as the sun shineth in his power. [Apoc. 1: 13–16]

And I saw heaven opened, and behold a white horse; and he that sat upon him was called faithful and true, and with justice doth he judge and fight. And his eyes were as a flame of fire, and on his head were many diadems, and he had a name written, which no man knoweth but himself. And he was clothed with a garment sprinkled with blood; and his name is called, THE WORD OF GOD. And the armies that are in heaven followed him on white horses, clothed in fine linen, white and clean. And out of his mouth proceedeth a sharp two edged sword; that with it he may strike the nations. And he shall rule them with a rod of iron; and he treadeth the winepress of the fierceness of the wrath of God the Almighty. And on his garment, and on his thigh written: KING OF KINGS, AND LORD OF LORDS. [Apoc. 19: 11–16.][866]

Tamburlaine's war strategies mirror the four horsemen of the Apocalypse. According to his customary 'chivalrous' terrorisation, when Tamburlaine besieges a city, he dons white apparel and pitches white tents to signify he will spare the lives of the inhabitants if they surrender peacefully. On the second day, he exchanges the magnanimity of white for bloodthirsty red, thereby announcing the time of mercy has passed: if he takes the city while arrayed in red, all

---

[866] Bible references for this chapter are taken from *The Holy Bible: Douay Rheims Version* (Old Testament translation, 1609, New Testament translation 1582: reprint Illinois: Tan Books and Publishers, Inc., 1989)

men capable of bearing arms will be destroyed. If this last warning goes unheeded, on the third day he changes his colours to black and will spare no one, including women and children. He is unconquerable, not losing a single battle. While the kings he vanquishes revile him, denouncing him as a thief of lowly birth and inferior to their noble lineage, he challenges them with his might, and confronts them with the stark reality he acquired their kingdoms by heroic deeds alone, which they were powerless to protect and secure despite all the royalty in their sapphire-blue blood.

In *Tamburlaine the Great, Part II* (c.1588), the one enemy that the great conqueror dreads to face is Death. Tamburlaine is struck with a mysterious terminal illness, and at first, rails against his appointed fate, bitterly observing that Death, which had been his servant, now arrives as the master. Christians traditionally interpret an attempt to evade the inevitability of death, the action of a soul that is unprepared for its eternal judgement. However, Marlowe defies this Christian concept: Tamburlaine's one lament — he cannot continue his great plan to conquer the earth, and this great disappointment is finally allayed when he passes this task on to his sons and completes his final arrangements, resting in the confidence they will accomplish his ambitious vision. He is undaunted by the abominations and cruelties committed during his campaigns, he is an Epicurean, and as he believes he will return to the four elements, there is no fear of Heaven or Hell, no remorse or regret. He dies peacefully without visible torment and therefore has 'vanquished' Death. Tamburlaine remains the optimistic self-made man of daring action with his roots planted firmly in the finite world.

Marlowe's obsession with the concept of advancing beyond the confines of the accepted social status by industry and self-accomplishment we may deduce burgeoned from his need to express his indignation at the duplicity of the world in which he lived. As a lowly scholar he was conditioned to view his status as a shoemaker's son with malcontent, he was expected to work harder in school and at the university, more than the privileged classes, and was falsely led to believe that he could rise in the world by progressing in academia, only to realise that it was the elite who ultimately received the positions of prestige and power. As Scholars allowed their expectations to soar beyond the boundless heights that knowledge proffered, they were simultaneously shackled with the cruel chains of reality. The illustrious world of the university with its mission to expand the minds of young men was a glorious illusion for the poor who would find themselves channelled into careers deemed undesirable by the gentry yet considered suitable for their station. The environment that fed Marlow's imagination and permitted it to thrive was also a place of bitter disappointment as observed from his alleged portrait in Corpus Christi College, which bears the following motto in the upper left-hand corner: "ANNO DNI, ÆTATIS SVÆ 21: 1585. QUOD ME NUTRIT, ME DESTRUIT" — Aged 21 in the year of Our Lord, 1585: That which nourishes me, destroys me.

Faustus Treads the London Boards

Marlowe graduated with his MA degree in 1587, and moved to the semi-rural liberty of Norton Folgate on the outskirts of London not far from the asylum, Bedlam. The liberties were suburbs free from the jurisdiction of the municipal authorities within the city walls, and therefore they became thriving centres for pleasure-establishments of all descriptions: alehouses, taverns, gambling dens, and brothels or 'stews'.[867] The location, notwithstanding its unsavoury aspect, suited the ambitious dramatist; the dubious and insalubrious liberties were also the home of the first English commercial playhouses:

> "In 1576, the carpenter and actor James Burbage erected the Theatre in the liberty of Shoreditch, by Finsbury Fields. It was the second customary built public playhouse in England, and the first to enjoy commercial success. Another playhouse, the Curtain, soon appeared a few hundred yards south of the Theatre. Around the same time, Jerome Savage and the Earl of Warwick's Men opened another theatre across the Thames at Newington Butts, a mile south of London Bridge. Savage's theatre stood alongside the sewage canal that ran east from Lamberth Marsh to Lock Hospital, the old leper house on Kentish Street, where it joined the Duffield sluice system. In 1587, the theatrical entrepreneur Philip Henslowe erected the Rose Theatre in the Liberty of the Clink on the south bank of the Thames. [...] Like Shoreditch, Bankside contained many dicing houses, brothels and inns that let rooms to prostitutes."[868]

Similar to the hedonistic 'pastimes' offered in the liberties, playhouses were considered equally disreputable. Puritan circles decried plays as blatant heathenish forms of entertainment that reinvigorated pagan ideology. While playwrights did not pass completely unrecognised by their contemporaries, (for instance, Marlowe's dramatisations of *Tamburlaine the Great* won him immediate recognition), admirers of the new dramas performed at the playhouses discreetly refrained from naming or acknowledging the authors in print. A number of dramatists eventually received due credit for their works in publications printed years after their initial performances.

Attempting to establish the premiere dates for many Elizabethan dramas is difficult to accomplish as the publications of these dramas often occurred many years after the event, and Marlowe's dramas are no exception. Determining when he poured his creative soul into *The Tragical History of Doctor Faustus,* the play that would be recognised in future ages as his magnum opus, has become a regular feature of academic debate. Two dates have been proposed for the first performances of *Doctor Faustus*: c. 1588–89 and c. 1592. As stated in Chapter 2 of this current study, there is convincing evidence Marlowe had access to an early English translation of Spies' 1587 *Faustbook* published (in Cambridge?) c. 1588–89, which is now lost.[*] Riggs observes that an Oxford student who passed away in 1589 had a copy of *The Damnable Life [...] of Doctor John Faustus* listed in his estate.[869] In addition, William Prynne wrote in 1633 that a performance of *Doctor Faustus* took place at the Belsavage playhouse during the reign of Queen Elizabeth, indicating the early date of 1588 or 1589 for Marlowe's drama.[870] Alternatively, the latter date of 1592 for Marlowe's *Doctor Faustus* rested on the observation that

---

[867] *World of Christopher Marlowe*, p. 190.
[868] Ibid. pp. 190, 192.
[*] See Chapter 2, 'The Faustian Legend in England and the First English *Faustbooks*'.
[869] *World of Christopher Marlowe*, p. 233.

the earliest surviving English translation of the *Faustbook*, i.e. Orwin's edition, was printed that same year. In modern research, many scholars have expressed their approbation of the former date as opposed to the latter.

Compounding this situation, however, is the reality that *two* versions of Marlowe's *Doctor Faustus* have survived: the A and B texts. In 1602, Philip Henslowe paid William Bride (or Borne) and Samuel Rowley £4 for what he described in his diary as 'adicyones in doctor fostes'.[871] Did they compile the additional material that constitutes the B text? The A text was first published in 1604 and was republished twice: A2 (1609) and A3 (1611).[872] The B text, first published in 1616, contains substantial material that is not in the A text. The B text was republished five times: B2 (1619), B3 (1620), B4 (1624), B5 (1628) and the B6 version (1631), originally known as B5 before the 1628 quarto was discovered.[873] To confuse matters further, printers made slight alterations to the texts that were conveyed in the subsequent publications. Which of the two texts is the definitive version, and when did the drama actually premiere?

Bevington and Rasmussen pose the important questions: "Did Marlowe write *Doctor Faustus* shortly after his great success with the two parts of *Tamburlaine*, [...] or is the play perhaps his last and greatest creation before his sudden death at a Deptford tavern in May of 1593?"[874] Perhaps, the answer may be 'yes' to both queries. In 1600–01, the Admiral's Men sold four plays in their repertoire to London publishers, which may have included a dramatist's manuscript of *Doctor Faustus* considered outdated at that point in time, particularly as the new additions were just commissioned by Henslowe.[875] This expendable quarto obviously became the A text that first went into circulation; however, was the A text deemed 'redundant' for other reasons? There is a possibility that the A text was Marlowe's original version of *Doctor Faustus*, c. 1588–89, which he revised in 1592 thus preparing a new version of *Faustus* that would later be recognised as the B text. Both texts could then be considered two distinct plays, the A text being the product of Marlowe's original inspiration after his initial reading of the *Faustbook*, while the B text features new additions influenced by current experiences in Marlowe's life in 1592, not to mention a myriad of new insights that motivated him following his first dramatisation of the Faustian legend. This scenario, as far as we are aware, is a new hypothesis; therefore, a detailed study of both texts in light of this argument is essential.

The A Text: (First printed 1604)

In the introductory Chorus, the poet-playwright promptly introduces the nature of the drama that he desires to present to the audience. *Doctor Faustus* is not a heroic or political play,

---

[870] Bevington and Rasmussen, *Doctor Faustus; A and B Texts*, p. 2. [All following references to Marlowe's *Doctor Faustus* are from this source unless otherwise stated.]
[871] Ibid. p. 62.
[872] Ibid.
[873] Ibid.
[874] Ibid. p. 1.
[875] Ibid. p. 71.

nor is it a play of courtly romance. Marlowe is now focusing on a novel theme distinct from his previous works of *Dido* and *Tamburlaine* — this is a drama portraying the life of an ordinary man, Faustus, whose fortunes are ambiguously described as "good or bad", the decision left to the "patient judgements" of the spectators. The Chorus speaks for Faustus "in his infancy", disclosing his origins and his progress in the world:

> Now is he born, his parents base of stock,
> In Germany, within a town called Rhode.
> Of riper years to Wertenburg he went,
> Whereas his kinsman chiefly brought him up.
> So soon he profits in divinity,
> The fruitful plot of scholarism graced,
> That shortly he was graced with doctor's name,
> Excelling all whose sweet delight disputes
> In heavenly matters of theology;
> Till, swoll'n with cunning of a self-conceit,
> His waxen wings did mount above his reach,
> And melting heavens conspired his overthrow.
> For, falling to a devilish exercise,
> And glutted more with learning's golden gifts,
> He surfeits upon cursed necromancy;
> Nothing so sweet as magic is to him,
> Which he prefers before his chiefest bliss.
> And this the man that in his study sits. [*Exit.*]

[Prol. 11–28]

Faustus, a lowly scholar, defies his humble origins by his prodigious advancement in the academic world, but, having reached the pinnacle of licit knowledge, turns to magic that promises to unlock the hidden secrets of nature and the universe. We are forewarned that in his new endeavour, he has ventured too far and is doomed like Icarus to be overthrown. Icarus, according to myth escaped with his father from the infamous labyrinth of King Minos on the island of Crete by flying out and away from the colossal trap with wings made from wax. Ecstatic with his ability to fly, Icarus ignored his father's warning not to ascend too high due to the intense heat of the sun, his wings dissolved, and he was cast headlong into the sea. Icarus became a symbol for excessive pride and reckless ambition — a pagan image of Lucifer's fall. The lack of a comma between "melting" and "heavens" in conjuction with "conspire his overthrow" is intriguing for there is a dual implication that Faustus' 'academic wings' have melted, and the heavens have metaphorically dissolved in an Apocalyptic description of brimstone descending upon the scholar 'predestined' for Hell. Of note, the first publication of the A text features the location of "Wertenberge" for Faustus' third-level education, i.e. the duchy of Württemburg, and not "Wittenburg", which editors later included in the subsequent reprints as a correction to conform with the *Faustbook*. Riggs informs us that the initial spelling of Württemburg is decidedly significant, "The duchy was well known to English Protestants as a stronghold of Calvinism."[876] Faustus' education in divinity has Calvinism as its pivotal influence, which echoes the instruction Marlowe received. In the Chorus, Marlowe skilfully concealed an allusion to the Garden of Eden and the various 'fruits' found there. Faustus' initial pursuit of theological matters is compared to a "fruitful plot" that "graces" him with a degree. The heavenly disputations are "sweet", thus suggesting the good fruit that may be lawfully eaten. The magic sciences are presented as delectable treats from the forbidden Tree of Knowledge. Faustus "falls to" this devilish science, a term synonymous with beginning a meal, and he "surfeits", or is "glutted" with the "golden-sweet" edibles. We must not overlook that the prohibited fruit mentioned in Genesis was pleasing to the senses — apparently, Faustus consumed more than one apple!

In general, Marlowe philosophically encapsulated the polemical 'Paradise' of the Cambridge divinity course, however, students encountered more Forbidden Trees in the university than that presented to Adam and Eve in Eden. Pagan philosophy with its anti-Genesis and amoral themes was one glaring error present in Elizabethan religious studies at Cambridge and Oxford, and magic taught in conjunction with natural philosophy studies was certainly another questionable practice. Is it logical to teach students, who are initially channelled towards Church positions, subjects that are contrary to Christian theology, and then expect their intellect to remain unscathed? Marlowe's reference to Icarus also alludes to the illusions the universities afforded to less privileged students. The waxen wings of education allowed them to escape the labyrinthine prison of their lowly status to which they were loath to return. However, if they failed to academically produce, they faced sinking into the sea with waterlogged plumes, or, they aspired to the great dazzling heights that were for the most part denied them and reserved for the privileged classes. They could dutifully follow the middle path between the ocean and the entrancing sky and arrive safely on land — a tiring church career that was badly paid. Under these circumstances, it is hardly surprising students opted for the less conventional paths offered to them. Thus, Marlowe posed the silent question: could aspiring Icarus be happy with a toilsome life on land managing a plough with plodding oxen having once tasted the weightless bliss of flight? Faustus, with fortunes "good or bad", is predestined for destruction via his 'Heavenly Calvinised' studies, a garden that contains both lawful and forbidden fruit.

Act I opens with Faustus alone in his study restlessly contemplating the subjects he studied, initially focusing his attention on Aristotle and logic:

> Settle thy studies, Faustus, and begin
> To sound the depth of that thou wilt profess.
> Having commenced, be a divine in show,
> Yet level at the end of every art,
> And live and die in Aristotle's works. [...]
>
> [I. i. 1–5]

Faustus has recently attained his MA degree. Although the Chorus relates Faustus earned the title of "Doctor", in Act I he is deciding which of the subjects he will "profess" to continue

---

[876] *World of Christopher Marlowe*, p. 238.

his advanced studies. According to Harrison in *Holinshed's Chronicles*, an English MA student could be referred to as "doctor" should they profess one or be generally skilled in all of the liberal sciences they previously studied during the BA and MA years.[877] From thence, they could elect to study divinity, law or medicine for their Doctorate.[878] Faustus sarcastically muses he may as well continue with the divinity studies he started, as a respectable front, while he decides to "level", or find the purpose of each subject, to discover which is worthy of his time and effort, and yield substantial rewards. We detect here Marlowe's resentment with the Parker Scholarship stipulation stating the prerequisite for recipients to express an interest in receiving Holy Orders before they could continue with their education.

Faustus declares he will "live" and "die" with Aristotle's works, and then amusingly exclaims: "Sweet *Analytics,*[†] 'tis thou hast ravished me!" [I. i. 6] — Marlowe in his BA years may have submissively "lived" for nothing else and figuratively "died" with his extensive disputation course grounded on logic and rhetoric. In this instance "ravished" could also signify being "seized" and academically molested. Taking up Aristotle's *Analytics*, a single sentence claims his attention and he ponders upon its significance:

> [*He reads*] *Bene disserere est finis logices.*[♦]
> Is to dispute well logic's chiefest end?
> Affords this art no greater miracle?
> Then read no more; thou hast attained that end.
> A greater subject fitteth Faustus' wit.
> Bid *Oncaymaeon* farewell. [...]
>
> [I. i. 7–12]

Faustus discovers that logic simply prepared him to dispute and argue a topic, that is all. He then dismisses logic, which he terms "being and not being" (*On kai me on*), considering he has already become a master in this art. We also detect a phonetic sound-game with '*Organon*', the logic treatise by Aristotle that Oxford students were not permitted to disagree with! Ironically, these two quotations are not from Aristotle. "Bene dissere" was Cicero's definition of logic, later assumed by the French dialectician Petrus Ramus (1515–1572) whose attempt to reform Aristotelian logic was received with hostility, his detractors considered he had reduced Aristotle's work to superficialities.[879] "On kai me on" is a diminutive synopsis[880] of Gorgias' (c. 485–380 B.C.) tripartite nihilistic philosophy — nothing exists. If anything exists, it cannot be known; if it exists and can be known, it cannot be explained. Marlovian commentators are generally puzzled why Faustus, an intellectual, should quote his sources incorrectly. We might

---

[877] *Holinshed's Chronicles*, pp. 376–377.
[878] Ibid.
[†] *Analytics* was the name applied to two of Aristotle's works on the nature of proof in argument. (Jump) In *Doctor Faustus; A and B Texts*, n. 6, p. 109.
[♦] 'To dispute well is the end of logic'. (Cicero / Ramus)
[879] *World of Christopher Marlowe*, p. 87.
[880] *Doctor Faustus; A and B Texts*, p. 16.

assume he is an inept scholar, but he is supposedly reading directly from university texts on the table in front of him. Is he actually comprehending the material he is reading? Marlowe may be stabbing at a paradox in the Elizabethan third-level course on logic. His lecturers failed to practise Aristotle's *reason for disputation*, i.e. to question an issue in order to discover what is true or false in philosophy, not to simply dispute well for the sake of argument whereby error can be persuasive and accepted as truth. Faustus 'fails' to "sound logic to its depths" for he should have immediately raised the question: if disputing well is the end of logic, then what is the purpose of argument but to find or to conclude upon an answer? Disputing well with no tangible result but to dispute, is similar to making the pointless query whether we truly exist or not, rather than asking *why* we exist and attempt to discover the answer. To be, or not to be: what a question! Marlowe highlights the illogical nature of his lessons in dialectic through Faustus' apparent ignorance. Having spent years mastering the art of incessant argument, Marlowe's mind was truly "ravished".

Defiantly rejecting 'Aristotle', the philosophical darling of the universities, Faustus embraces the work of Galen, the ancient physician:

> [...] Galen, come!
> Seeing *ubi desinit philosophus, ibi incipit medicus,*[§]
> Be a physician, Faustus. Heap up gold,
> And be eternised for some wondrous cure.
> [*He reads.*] *Summum bonum medicinae sanitas*:[‡]
> The end of physic is our body's health.
> Why Faustus, hast thou not attained that end?
> Is not thy common talk sound aphorisms?
> Are not thy bills hung up as monuments,
> Whereby whole cities have escaped the plague
> And thousand desp'rate maladies been eased?
> Yet art thou still but Faustus, and a man.
> Wouldst thou make man to live eternally?
> Or, being dead, raise them to life again?
> Then this profession were to be esteemed.
> Physic, farewell! [...]

[I. i. 12–27]

On this occasion, Faustus *is* quoting Aristotle: is Marlowe continuing his satirical observation that it is illogical to rely on commentaries written by others rather than refer to the experts, e.g. Galen, for a career in medicine? Faustus continues his one-to-self dialogue and decides to amass gold and become famous by wondrous remedies, but we detect a possible reference to Proverbs (22:1) "A good name is better than great riches: and good favour is above silver and gold." Faustus has already saved numerous cities while yet a student, his prescriptions

---

[§] 'Where the philosopher ends, there the doctor begins'. (Aristotle, *De Sensu et Sensibili*)
[‡] 'The greatest good of medicine is health'. (Aristotle, *Nicomachean Ethics*)

are regarded as "monuments", and entertains no desire for *material* wealth or he would not be freely disseminating his revolutionary medical precepts or "aphorisms" as casual conversation pieces with no apparent thought for remuneration. Apparently, there is a cryptic inference intended with the terms "gold" and "eternise". He has practised medicine for a considerable period if he performed great cures, and only abandons physic with his recent discovery it has its earthly limitations. Was Faustus actually attempting to discover the medical equivalent of the 'philosopher's stone'? He sadly ponders that notwithstanding all of his accomplishments in physic, he remains a mortal man. Faustus certainly has a point: he is considering the futility of spending years in combating diseases that are never entirely eradicated, and of curing people who will all inevitably die. Vanity of vanities! There must be a purpose for this ceaseless toil on earth! However, he blasphemously crosses the moral line when he alludes to Christ miraculously raising the dead, remarking that the medical profession would be worthy of esteem if the dead could be brought back to life. Faustus is searching for something that is beyond the reach of mortals, which he concludes cannot be obtained through medicine.

Casting Galen aside, Faustus scans the code of law established by Emperor Justinian (527–565 AD):

> [...] Where is Justinian?
> [*He reads.*] *Si una eademque res legatur duobus,*
> *Alter rem, alter valorem rei*, etc.
> A pretty case of paltry legacies!
> [*He reads.*] *Exhaereditare filium non potest pater nisi* —
> Such is the subject of the Institute
> And universal body of the Church.
> His study fits a mercenary drudge
> Who aims at nothing but external trash —
> Too servile and illiberal for me.
> When all is done, divinity is best. [...]

> [I. i. 27–37]

This time, Faustus is reading from Justinian's law as recorded in the *Institutes*, but it is Marlowe's free translation. The first quotation is: 'If one and the same thing is given as a legacy to two persons, one shall have the thing, the other the value of the thing.'[881] The actual passage from the *Institutes* reads: 'If the same thing is given as a legacy to two persons ... each is entitled to only a half.'[882] Bevington and Rasmussen argue that the differences in *Doctor Faustus* were caused by an approximation of memory, and that Marlowe did not consult the original *Institutes*. However, it is difficult to accuse Marlowe of slip-shod referencing when we consider he was taught the finer points in the arrangement and import of words including each individual letter and syllable in his grammar school years. As Marlowe's Ithamore would later disclose in *The Jew of Malta* (c. 1590) "The meaning has a meaning [...]" [IV. iv. 105], we suspect this

---

[881] *Doctor Faustus; A and B Texts*, nn. 28–9, p. 111.
[882] Ibid.

'mistranslation' in *Doctor Faustus* is significant. Marlowe may be *interpreting* Justinian's law in addition to translating it. However, we detect there are *two* avenues to explore in his interpretation of this law. A "case" may not only refer to a legal case, but also to a "brace" or "pair."[883]

First, Marlowe may be questioning the logic of a law that states a single article may be equally divided. Let us consider the scenario two siblings are bequeathed an item of sentimental value that cannot be divided or owned co-jointly without a certain degree of absurdity, e.g. a priceless vase that was originally given to the heirs' parents on a special anniversary. According to the *Institutes*, if they are entitled to half, will each get to keep it in their place of residence for six months of the year? Once it is in one heirs' possession, will they be willing to relinquish it after their six months of guardianship, or will that sibling become covetous and decide they will keep the Ming? The obvious solution would be to sell it and divide the proceeds, but then, what if one or both of the siblings do not desire to sell it as the sentimental value could never be replaced? The situation poses a continuous cycle of problems. Marlowe may be stating ironically that it is impossible to divide certain legacies in half — it is as impossible as it would be to extract the sentimentality and / or material value from the item for one heir and give the actual heirloom to the other than to divide it between two owners. We suspect from this viewpoint Marlowe was intimating the Decision of King Solomon in his construal. (3 Kings 3: 16–28) Two women approached the king both claiming to be the mother of the same child, and to settle the matter, he ordered the child to be cut in half. The mother begged him not to kill the child and give him to the other woman, but the other woman cried out to Solomon to have the child divided so that neither would have the whole. Immediately, he recognised the real mother and returned the child to her. Thus, according to Marlowe's seeming first reinterpretation, in an ideal world a legacy should be awarded to the heir who values the heirloom in its entirety and will take proper care of it rather than to see it divided for mercenary purposes.

The second example could refer to the *abuse* of a law when convenient. In this second scenario, the two siblings are entitled to half of the vase according to the *Institutes*, yet one manages to bribe the family lawyer to misinterpret the law so that the other sibling believes he is entitled only to the sentimental value of the vase: how can they collect a memory? This may also apply to the material value, for do the proceeds come from the remainder of the estate? By artful manoeuvring of an interpretation, one sibling may be entirely excluded from a legacy.

Faustus' second quotation from the *Institutes* is altered in a similar manner; "A father cannot disinherit his son unless —." The actual law reads; "male family heirs born after the making of a will, sons and other lineal descendants, are held not to be properly disinherited unless they are disinherited specially".[884] The law, as Faustus reads it, states the inheritance of a son is protected, however, there is strong emphasis on the word "unless" where he stops abruptly in mid-sentence, suggesting the law can also be used to exclude. In the end, the petty wrangling of superficial materialism and bureaucracy in the world revolts Faustus for the law is fit for "mercenary drudges", and therefore we might note, a step below the field of medicine that has already earned him notoriety and fame as a humanitarian-genius. Accordingly, Faustus (Marlowe?) rejects this subject as it leaves him without any "depths" for him to "sound"!

---

[883]   Ibid. n. 30, p. 112.
[884]   Ibid. n. 31.

Ironically, Faustus remarks this is a subject of the "Institute", a possible pun on Justinian's *Institutes* and the State government. Law is also described by Faustus as a subject specific to the Church, this could be a reference to Catholic canon law, which was influenced by Justinian's code.[885] Yet when considering the pun on "institute", this could indicate Marlowe's criticism pertaining to the Protestant monarchy's usurpation of religious authority in England as an effective governing policy for both ecclesiastical and secular affairs. *In fine*, Faustus recognises his career options in law may be limited to a 'clerical' job as a clerk, which is "too servile" and not befitting a scholar trained in the liberal arts.

He decides the study of divinity is the optimum choice of the sciences he examined, and begins to read the sacred Vulgate, yet once more, becomes disillusioned:

> Jerome's Bible, Faustus, view it well.
> [*He reads.*] *Stipendium peccati mors est.* Ha!
> *Stipendium,* etc.
> The reward of sin is death. That's hard.
> [*He reads.*] *Si peccasse negamus, fallimur*
> *Et nulla est in nobis veritas.*
> If we say that we have no sin,
> We deceive ourselves, and there's no truth in us.
> Why then belike we must sin,
> And so consequently die.
> Ay, we must die an everlasting death.
> What doctrine call you this, *Che serà, serà,*
> What will be, shall be? Divinity, adieu!
>
> [I. i. 38–50]

We observe Marlowe has not used a direct Latin quotation for his extracts. Riggs explains that the playwright actually included his own Latin rendering of the verses from an English Bible.[886] Marlowe reportedly declared that the New Testament was "filthily written"[#] (an ineloquent style?); therefore, these two verses in *Doctor Faustus* may be an early example of Marlowe's criticism and his endeavour to display in humanist fashion how the Bible may be more gracefully expressed in Latin.

Faustus first selects a passage from St. Paul to the Romans (6:23), which every Elizabethan was familiar with,[887] however, he stops in mid-sentence: "… for the wages of sin is death. But the grace of God, life everlasting, in Christ Jesus our Lord." He then skips several books in the Bible to select a reading from 1 John (1:8), but fails to continue with the following line (v. 9): "If we confess our sins, he is faithful and just, to forgive us our sins, and to cleanse us

---

[885] Ibid. n. 33.
[886] *World of Christopher Marlowe*, p. 239.
[#] See Appendix Seven.
[887] See Diane Elizabeth Dreher, "'Si Peccasse Negamus': Marlowe's *Faustus* and the *Book of Common Prayer*,' *Notes and Queries*, 30 (April, 1983): p. 144.

from all iniquity." Faustus concentrates on the punishment due to sin, and does not reflect upon the saving grace of God. Marlowe may be challenging a concept of Calvinistic theology promulgated within the Church of England that he considered ridiculous, i.e. that *God* supposedly blinds preordained reprobates when they read the Bible. Riggs writes:

> "The so-called 'devil's syllogism' based on Romans 6:23 and 1 John 1:8 held a special fascination for Marlowe's contemporaries because it so closely resembled the Calvinist dogma adopted in England and Württemburg. Calvin too isolates the first half of Romans 6:23 and insists that 'all sin is mortal'. Article 15 of the Church of England ended with the first half of 1 John 1:8 followed by a full stop. The Thirty-Nine Articles that constituted the Elizabethan Church nowhere suggests that all who confess their sins will be forgiven; on the contrary, God reserves the gift of grace for the elect [...]."[888]

An Elizabethan audience would realise that Faustus was not accurately quoting the Bible, particularly with his incomplete first quotation. How could he not complete a sentence? He is literate and a graduate scholar, after all! He is not 'blinded', but selecting what he wants to read and therefore is a 'heretic' in the literal sense of the word, which from the Greek means 'to choose'. If there are damned souls in Hell, it is because men blind themselves. Faustus' selective picking 'cafeteria style' from the legitimate delicacies of academic Eden also raised another paradox that apparently has not been examined. By omitting the second parts of the Bible passages that correctly explain how a sinner acknowledges truth and attains salvation, Faustus forms additional 'devil syllogisms': "belike we *must* [*commit*] sin" if we *desire to have* truth within us. Then, if we *must* commit sin to acquire truth, we *must* all be predestined to hellfire as no man is without sin in either case. "Ay, we *must* die an everlasting death." Ironically, Calvin and the Church of England have literally taught the *first verse of Romans Chapter 6*, i.e. 'What shall we say, then? Shall we continue in sin, that grace may abound?', omitting verse 2, 'God forbid. For we that are dead to sin how shall we live any longer therein?' Calvin and the Church of England are also 'blinded' to the scriptures and teach that damnation comes to all! "What doctrine call you this?" Faustus displays the illogical rationale of predestination according to Calvin's ideology, and in fact, portrays him as a hypocrite, for in the dedication to the *Institutes*, Calvin warns King Francis of France that many 'ungodly' shall accuse him of this misinterpretation, and pleads his innocence:

> "[...] The apostles were accused of stirring up popular commotions. Wherein does this differ from the conduct of those who, at the present day, impute to us all the disturbances, tumults, and contentions, that break out against us? But the proper answer to such accusations has been taught us by Elias, that the dissemination of errors and the raising of tumults is not chargeable on us, but on those who are resisting the power of God. There were 'unlearned and unstable' men,

---

[888] *World of Christopher Marlowe*, p. 241.

Peter says, who 'wrested the inspired writings of Paul 'to their own destruction.' (2 Pet. 3:16) [...] There were despisers of God, who, when they heard that 'where sin abounded grace did much more abound,' immediately concluded, Let us 'continue in sin, that grace may abound.' [...] But I return to you, Sire. Let not your Majesty be at all moved by those groundless accusations, with which our adversaries endeavour to terrify you [...]."[889]

Faustus' (or Marlow's!) syllogisms are a supreme example of the manipulation of religion and doctrinal truth with destructive results — by their bitter fruits, you shall know them:

"[...] Faustus is hideously mistaken about the Bible; but the Church he is rejecting has taught him to make precisely these mistakes. Marlowe, who had already been taxed with atheism, unveils in *Dr. Faustus* the ecclesiastical basis of his own unbelief. [...] Divine Justice was supposed to terrorize the reprobate into good behaviour; yet the godless had ample reason to disbelieve in a God who had already condemned them to sin and damnation regardless of their earthly conduct." (Riggs)[890]

Indignant with this threat of inescapable damnation, he hurls the subject of divinity back at God as though it were a rotten fig, "Divinity, *adieu!*" We note that the prefix 'a' in Greek also means 'without' suggesting the theology he studied is 'godless'. Why should he therefore believe in God?

Faustus finally chooses a subject that captures his imagination:

[*He picks up a book of magic.*]

These metaphysics of magicians
And necromantic books are heavenly,
Lines, circles, signs, letters, and characters —
Ay, these are those that Faustus most desires.
O, what a world of profit and delight,
Of power, of honour, of omnipotence,
Is promised to the studious artisan!
All things that move between the quiet poles
Shall be at my command. Emperors and kings
Are but obeyed in their several provinces,
Nor can they raise the wind or rend the clouds;

---

[889] John Calvin, 'Dedication of the Institutes of the Christian Religion' (Basil: 1536). Reprint: Charles W. Eliot, trans. *Prefaces and Prologues to Famous Books, The Harvard Classics, vol. 39* (New York: P. F. Collier and Son Corp., 1963), pp. 44–45.
[890] *World of Christopher Marlowe*, p. 241

But his dominion that exceeds in this
Stretcheth as far as doth the mind of man.
A sound magician is a mighty god.
Here, Faustus, try thy brains to gain a deity.

[I. i. 51–65.]

Here Faustus is voraciously eyeing the forbidden fruit contemplating how delightful it is to behold! Advanced now beyond the character of Tamburlaine whose ultimate ambition was to gain an earthly kingdom, Faustus desires to command the elements of the earth and be like unto God. He blasphemously remarks that his occult books are "heavenly", highlighting an ironic point: Marlowe was introduced to natural magic in his divinity course and the "heavenly" matters of natural philosophy, astronomy and astrology.

Faustus realises he has much material to learn in the occult, and he commands Wagner to summon his two friends, the "German Valdes" and Cornelius, to aid him in his studies; "Their conference will be a greater help to me / Than all my labours, plod I ne're so fast." [I. i. 70–71] As Faustus is pouring over his book and waiting for his guests, two new characters are introduced; the "Good" and "Evil" Angels, i.e. Faustus' Guardian and Destroyer Angels respectively. The Good Angel exhorts Faustus to lay his "damned book" aside and return to the Scriptures, while the Evil Angel tempts the scholar to continue in his new endeavour and learn nature's secrets. Having each delivered their advice they exit the stage. Apparently, Faustus does not 'see' the Angels, but he can hear (or ignore) their speeches. As he already rejected the concept of 'inescapable' divine punishment, he easily 'tunes out' the 'treble register' of the Good Angel who exhorts him not to "heap God's wrath on his head" [I. i. 74]. The 'bass' timbre of the Evil Angel holds a more melodious note: "Be thou on earth as Jove is in the sky, / Lord and commander of these elements." [I. i. 78–79] Faustus immediately responds to this tempting advice:

How am I glutted with conceit of this!
Shall I make spirits fetch me what I please,
Resolve me of all ambiguities,
Perform what desperate enterprise I will?
I'll have them fly to India for gold,
Ransack the ocean for orient pearl,
And search all corners of the new-found world
For pleasant fruits and princely delicates,
I'll have them read me strange philosophy
And tell the secrets of all foreign kings. […]

[I.i 80–89]

He fantasises on the powers the spirits will wield under his command and the various treasures that he can accumulate through the occult. Although it is a foregone conclusion that Faustus will gain materially from his pact and live a luxurious lifestyle as mentioned in the

Faustbook, we have already learned through his discourse on medicine that Faustus *in the drama* desires not *material* wealth. We deduce the treasure that Faustus seeks is of the philosophical, mystical form. He wishes to be "resolved of all ambiguities" i.e. understand all mysteries, and learn "strange philosophy" that he never encountered before. He desires to learn the "secrets" of foreign kings, which may not only be "secrets" of a bureaucratic nature, but also a reference to the Three Kings of the East and their mystical knowledge; notice the terms "orient pearl" and "India gold". The orient pearl is reminiscent of Christ's parable of the pearl of great price (Matt. 13: 45–46). A merchant discovers this pearl and sells everything he owns to acquire this one gem worth a priceless fortune. This parable is a figure of the Kingdom of Heaven and the wisdom of those who dispose of all earthly vanity and seek Eternal Truth. The "gold" may allude to the parable of the hidden treasure (Matt. 13: 44). A man discovers a treasure hidden in a field, and he sells everything to buy the field. The significance of the allegory is the equivalent to the parable of the pearl.

When we compare the references of "orient pearl", "India gold" and the allusion to Heavenly wisdom, we also discover a possible reference to King Solomon. On one occasion when Solomon offered a great sacrifice, God appeared to him in a dream and announced that He would grant whatever he asked. Solomon prayed for the gift of wisdom rather than for earthly rewards to aid him in governing the kingdom of Israel, and his request pleased God. Hence, by God's grace he became the wisest man to walk the earth, and in addition, God granted him all the wealth and glory he had not requested. (3 Kings 3:4–13) Of all the wealth in Solomon's kingdom, gold was readily abundant and is particularly associated with his reign: "Moreover all the vessels, out of which king Solomon drank, were of gold: and all the furniture of the house of the forest of Libanus was of the most pure gold: there was no silver, nor was any account made of it in the days of Solomon." (3 Kings 10:21) Solomon's source of gold was the land of Ophir, (3 Kings, 9: 28, & 10:11), also famous for its precious stones. Milton writes in Book Eleven of *Paradise Lost* that Ophir was believed to be Sofala, (now recognised as Mozambique), a land known for its rich gold deposits. Another theory proposes Solomon's ancient kingdom of gold was located in southeast Arabia. We suggest a further possibility, Ophir could be located in India according to Genesis (2: 10–12): "And a river went out of paradise, which from thence is divided into four heads. The name of the one is Phison: [the Ganges ?°], that is it which compasseth all the land of Hevilath, where gold groweth. And the gold of that land is very good: there is found

---

° Recognised in the *Faustbook* as the Ganges River. This was obviously based on an original theological interpretation, which Marlowe was certainly familiar with. Compare with the following lines:

° Aeneas: "From golden Indian Ganges will I fetch, / Whose wealthy streams may wait upon her towers," [*Dido*: V. i. 8–9]

° Cosroe: "{Men …} Have swarm'd in troops into the Eastern India, / Lading their ships with gold and precious stones," [*1 Tamburlaine*: I. i. 120–121] Tamburlaine: "Not all the gold in India's wealthy arms / Shall buy the meanest soldier in my train." [I. ii. 85–86] Tamburlaine: "What, think'st thou Tamburlaine esteems thy gold? / I'll make the kings of India, ere I die, / Offer their mines to sue for peace with me." [IV. i. 262–264]

° Tamburlaine: "[…] and this wound / As great a grace and majesty to me, / As if a chair of gold enamelled, / Enchas'd with diamonds, sapphires, rubies, / And fairest pearl of wealthy India, / Were mounted here under a canopy, / And I sat down […]" [*2 Tamburlaine*: III. iii. 117–123]

bdellium, and the onyx stone." Heavenly wisdom is compared with the four Rivers of Paradise (Ecclus. 24: 40–41), which would in this case symbolically include the Ganges river of India. Hence, Solomon's vast earthly wealth was symbolic of his great wisdom and knowledge. "And if riches be desired in life, what is richer than wisdom, which maketh all things?" (Wis. 8:5) The Book of Wisdom lists the gifts that Solomon received — we note this bears a strong resemblance to the riches of knowledge Faustus seeks:

> "Now all good things came to me together with her, [wisdom], and innumerable riches through her hands [...]. For in [God's] hand are both we, and our words, and all wisdom, and the knowledge and skill of works. For he hath given to me the true knowledge of the things that are: to know the disposition of the whole world, and the virtues of the elements, the beginning, and ending, and midst of the times, the alterations of their courses, and the changes of seasons, the revolutions of the year, and the dispositions of the stars, the natures of living creatures, and rage of wild beasts, the force of winds, and reasonings of men, the diversities of plants, and the virtues of roots, and all such things as are hid and not foreseen, I have learned: for wisdom, which is the worker of all things, taught me." (Wis. 7:11, 16–21)

Faustus desires wisdom, but he rejected God from Whom he may acquire true wisdom that ultimately leads to the attainment of this cosmic knowledge. Notice his desire to eat "pleasant fruits" and "princely delicates" — the allusions to the Forbidden Tree of Knowledge remain constant. We suspect this desire for "strange philosophy" and 'eastern knowledge of great price' stems from Marlowe's alleged interest in classical pagan texts contradicting the traditional Christian belief that the world existed approximately five to six thousand years.√

Faustus then contemplates the great deeds he may accomplish through spirits:

> I'll have them wall all Germany with brass
> And make swift Rhine circle fair Wertenberge.
> I'll have them fill the public schools with skill,
> Wherewith the students shall be bravely clad.
> I'll levy soldiers with the coin they bring
> And chase the Prince of Parma from our land,
> And reign sole king of all our provinces;
> Yea, stranger engines for the brunt of war
> Than was the fiery keel at Antwerp's bridge
> I'll make my servile spirits to invent.

°   Barabas: "Give me the merchants of the Indian mines, / that trade in metal of the purest mould; / The wealthy Moor, that in the eastern rocks / Without control can pick his riches up, / And in his house heap pearl like pebble stones, / [...] / And seld-seen costly stones of so great price," [*Jew of Malta*: I. i. 19-23, 28]

√   See Appendix Seven.

Faustus plans to fortify Germany with indestructible materials, and change the course of the Rhine to have it encircle the town of his *alma mater*, fortifying its natural defences and increase the commercial trade. He plans to fill the public schools, i.e. the university lecture halls, with "skill", which may insinuate his aspiration to reform the curriculum. Marlovian scholars noted that as he desires the students be "bravely clad" with the virtue of "skill", this could be an anagram for the word "silk", a sly reference that Marlowe (alias Faustus) entertained a fanciful scheme to alter the dowdy dress codes imposed upon poor Scholars. Editors subsequently replaced "skill" with "silk" in the A and B texts.[891]

He therefore contrives a stratagem to "levy" or raise an army with the "coin" (gold?) the spirits will bring, have his netherworld minions invent new weapons of war, and thereby zealously route out the Catholic Duke of Parma from the Low Countries. The "fiery keel" refers to a fireship[892] used on April 4, 1585 to destroy a bridge built by the Duke of Parma during his blockade of Antwerp; a detail inspired by the information Marlowe acquired during his covert work for the government. Ultimately, Faustus plans to reign as king of all the German provinces, yet, we detect this is not simply a martial or bureaucratic war he intends to engage in, but also a philosophical crusade. Faustus desires "mystical gold" of knowledge, not actual wealth, and hence we propose that he will conscript "soldiers", or *converts*, with the coin of his new belief in an atheistic-Epicurean movement raised upon the foundations of Protestantism. Notice his desire to strengthen and encourage the 'prosperity' of Württemburg, the seat of Calvinism in Germany, with the Rhine river — this could be a symbolic replacement for one of the four rivers of wisdom in Paradise. Despite Faustus' scepticism of Calvinist dogma, he is a product of its ideology and remains forever anchored to it, the root from which springs his desire for an alternative system that sets his mind free. Marlowe allegedly remarked in later years that he was capable of "writing a new religion" with a "more excellent and admirable method"[893] an opinion obviously formed from his belief that organised religion was the work of men to "keep men in awe". It was also reported Marlowe persuaded several of his contemporaries to accept his liberal ideology. Hence, Faustus wishes to convert men to a freethinking religion of his own invention with the knowledge he receives from the spirits. The term "to coin"[894] was also a colloquial expression for counterfeiting. There is a further ironic twist that Marlowe accentuates with regard to 'counterfeit religions'. Faustus muses that his dominion will not be subject to boundaries, for with magic he can surpass the authority held by every king and command the elements of the earth and the cosmos. However, when he introduces an *invented religion* for his Machiavellian policy to control mankind, he shackles himself with chains of his own forging and is encompassed within the "brass" borders of Protestant / Calvinist Germany. In other words, the lofty mind of man can be imprisoned by the artifices of its own making.

---

[891] *Doctor Faustus: A and B Texts*, n. 92, p. 116.

[892] Ibid. n. 98, p. 117.

[893] I.e, as reported in the "Baines Note" written c. three days before Marlowe's death in 1593. See Appendix Seven.

[894] *World of Christopher Marlowe*, p. 253.

Faustus is presently joined by his two friends:

> [...] Come, German Valdes and Cornelius,
> And make me blest with your sage conference!

Enter Valdes and Cornelius.

> Valdes, sweet Valdes, and Cornelius,
> Know that your words have won me at the last
> To practise magic and concealed arts.
> Yet not your words only, but mine own fantasy,
> That will receive no object, for my head
> But ruminates on necromantic skill.
> Philosophy is odious and obscure;
> Both law and physic are for petty wits;
> Divinity is basest of the three,
> Unpleasant, harsh, contemptible, and vile.
> 'Tis magic, magic that hath ravished me.
> Then, gentle friends, aid me in this attempt,
> And I, that have with concise syllogisms
> Gravelled the pastors of the German Church
> And made the flow'ring pride of Wertenberge
> Swarm to my problems as the infernal spirits
> On sweet Musaeus when he came to hell,
> Will be as cunning as Agrippa was,
> Whose shadows made all Europe honour him.

[I. i. 100–120]

Exactly who are these two friends of Faustus? They remain a scholastic mystery. They could be stage names with no special significance, except it is peculiar that Faustus, who is German, should refer to the nationality of Valdes as if he were a foreigner, i.e. the "*German Valdes*". We suspect these names were not selected without purpose. One name that configures with "Valdes" in the scholastic field is that of the famous Spanish theologian Juan de Valdés, greatly influenced by the works of Desiderius Erasmus. While not a German, Erasmus was born in the Netherlands, which, during the time of the historical Faustus was part of the Holy Roman Empire under Charles V, King of Germany and Spain. Erasmus, although a Catholic, is often recognised as the father of the Reformation; hence, Faustus may be metaphorically conversing with the "German Reformer" Erasmus via the name of his Spanish admirer, Juan Valdés. It would be a diplomatic disaster to associate Erasmus directly with a famous reprobate of history such as Faustus, and therefore Marlowe discreetly concealed his reference in a manner ensuring his philosophical idea would remain intact. We note this stress on "German" reinforces Faustus' ties to the 'Reformed' Protestant-based religions of Germany, i.e. Calvinism and Lutheranism.

"Cornelius" could be a symbolic reference to the famous scholar magician, Cornelius Agrippa; however, as Faustus mentions the same magician in line 119, it is evident he is speaking with another "Cornelius", or perhaps, to many recorded in history. Five famous names share an affiliation with the interests of Marlowe and his rendition of *Doctor Faustus*. The first is Lucius Cornelius Sulla (138–78 B.C.), a Roman general and statesman. In 86 B.C., Lucius Cornelius introduced the Egyptian tripartite cult of Isis, Horace and Serapis to the Roman rite of worship, becoming one of the most popular cults in ancient Rome until in due course it was superseded by Christianity. An allusion to Lucius Cornelius could therefore symbolise the effective manipulation of religion for secular purposes. The second name is Cornelius Nepos (100–25 B.C.), a Roman historian and biographer. He wrote many works on the lives of kings, generals, orators, and academics as with poets, historians, philosophers and scholars. A reference to Nepos may represent the historical knowledge imparted during Faustus' (Marlowe's!) tenure at the university. The third candidate is Gaius Cornelius Gallus (69?–26? B.C.), a Roman politician and poet who invented the love elegy later to be perfected by Ovid, a major influential force in Marlowe's poetry. In addition, Gaius was an intimate friend of the poet (and reputed magician), Virgil. The fourth person is Aulus Cornelius Celsus (1st century A.D.), a Roman writer who compiled an encyclopaedia featuring a number of subjects that included medicine, rhetoric, history, philosophy and warfare. Celsus, similar to Nepos, reinforces the academic training of Faustus. Finally, the Roman historian Cornelius Tacitus (55–c.117 A.D.) is a possibility for among his early works are the *Dialogue on Orators* and his encyclopaedic volume on Germany, *Germania*. These two works suggest links with Faustus' university skills as an orator and his Germanic background.

In sum, Faustus' two friends, the "German Valdes" and Cornelius, represent the complexities and polarities of his education. The ideals they represent, i.e. philosophy, law, physic, and Protestant / Calvinist divinity, he rejects; and yet, these subjects and the manner in which they have been taught are the driving force that compels him to seek after secret knowledge and to experiment with magic. This polarity is reflected in his remarks that now having "gravelled" the pastors of the German (i.e. Calvinist / Protestant) Church and surpassed their standards in "religious" education, he will proceed to magic whereby all Europe will honour him. Marlowe is demonstrating the 'hellish' path of magic is a natural step upon completing the "infernal" divinity course. Faustus compares his prodigious debating skills in Calvinist doctrine in Württemburg with the power of the semi-mythical poet, Musaeus, who guides Aeneas through the depths of Hell in Virgil's *Æneid*. Although we observe the "infernal spirits" refers to the spirits or "shadows" Faustus hopes to raise with magic similar to Agrippa, the reference to 'devilish' Calvinist theologians thronging Faustus, is also present. In a few lines, Marlowe is challenging the duplicity of his society that promotes an alleged moral divinity course for the 'good of souls', when in practise it utterly fosters disbelief in God and promulgates pagan ideology and Epicureanism, which is then hypocritically decried in public.

Valdes and Cornelius proceed to describe the benefits they would procure through magic. Valdes reassures Faustus that with his magic books, his "wit", and their experience will "make all nations to canonise" them. [I. i. 121–122] They will be venerated as saints! Valdes relates every spirit of the four elements will be subject to them, shall take whatever form they desire, e.g. appear as soldiers or lions to protect them, or as women more beautiful than Venus for their delight. The spirits will also bring them rich treasures, i.e. "Argosies" from Venice, and the

343

American "golden fleece / That yearly stuffs old Philip's treasury." [I. i. 132–134] Apparently, Valdes and Cornelius wish to be included in Faustus' venture as Valdes states the spirits shall always be subject "to us three". [I. i. 126] Cornelius describes the arts required for magic, (which Faustus already studied in his 'divinity' course), i.e. astrology, languages, and minerals learned from natural philosophy. He also reiterates the treasures they may gain, i.e. fortunes lost by shipwreck, and hordes hidden by past ancients "within the massy entrails of the earth". [I. i. 149]

We stress the possibility these 'treasures' are also 'intellectual gems' of hidden knowledge from the East. Valdes mentions the spirits shall go to Venice for "huge argosies", ships laden with riches of mythical proportions in reference to Jason's ship, the *Argo*, whereon he embarked to discover the Golden Fleece located in the kingdom of Colchis in the Black Sea region. Venice was a powerful maritime port with wealthy shipping lanes, particularly the routes to the Black Sea where goods from China where brought via the ancient Silk Road, whereby Venice became one of Europe's portals to the East. A famous resident of Venice, Marco Polo (1254–1324), played an important part in fashioning this international status. Members of a Venetian merchant family, Polo's father and uncle undertook a journey to the East (1260–1269), travelling as far as the Mongol Empire of Kublai Khan. The Emperor was delighted with the Polos and their tales of the West. Intrigued by Christianity, he asked them to return and requested that the Pope send him Christian scholars who could thoroughly explain to him the Western religion. In 1271, the Church appointed two missionaries to travel with the Polos, on this occasion, Marco journeyed with them. The missionaries, apprehensive of the hazards abandoned their mission, yet the Polos continued and remained in Asia for seventeen years. The Mongol Emperor was amused with Marco's talent for storytelling and he entrusted him with several diplomatic missions within the Mongol Empire. When he returned to Venice, Marco became famous for his numerous stories of the East, later recorded by Rusticello. His adventures are the epitome of the exchange of knowledge from one culture to another for the Polos almost succeeded in converting the Mongol Emperor to Christianity, and Marco provided medieval Europe with its first glimpse of the Far East and its exotic cultures. With the rise of the Ottoman Empire during the mid 1400s, the Republican-city of Venice fell into decline, yet retained its status as Europe's gateway to the East.

Concentrating on Valde's reference to the riches of the New World, he continues his allusion to the legend of Jason with the "golden fleece", also suggesting metaphorically the new 'flocks' received into the Church. Spain was certainly gaining vast riches from its American colonies, yet also acquiring a prodigious number of converts to Catholicism among the Aztecs following the apparitions of Our Lady of Guadalupe to Juan Diego, an Aztec convert, in 1531. An image of the vision appeared on Diego's *tilma*, a traditional Aztec cloak, thus authenticating the event. It is possible Marlowe was derisively referring to the famous cloak with the term "golden fleece", unaware that the *tilma* was not made from wool but cloth woven from maguey fibre.[895] Aztec conversions reached an unprecedented level subsequent to the miracle. A number of missionaries reported to have administered the Sacrament of Baptism to six thousand in a single day, another report stated two priests administered Baptism to fourteen thousand two

---

[895] Francis Johnston, *The Wonder of Guadalupe: The Origin and Cult of the Miraculous Image of the Blessed Virgin in Mexico* (Illinois: Tan Books and Publishers, Inc., 1981), p. 57.

hundred people in five days.[896] It was estimated that nine million Aztecs were admitted to the Church. This mass conversion was deemed a great miracle ordained by God to neutralize the loss of five million to the Protestant Reformation in Europe.[897]

It is probable that the 'venture' Valdes and Cornelius desired to share with Faustus also extended to his thirst for exotic knowledge from the Eastern world, and disseminating his new ideology in freethinking spiritualism thereby winning 'converts' from the East and the Newfound West. They predict Faustus will receive many devotees seeking his advice that will rival the number who flocked to the ancient augur of Delphi. Cornelius energetically remarks: "Then tell me, Faustus, what shall we three want?" [I. i. 150] Faustus replies they shall want for nothing, and entreats them to demonstrate how to conjure:

> *Faustus.* Nothing, Cornelius. O, this cheers my soul!
>   Come, show me some demonstrations magical,
>   That I may conjure in some lusty grove
>   And have these joys in full possession.
> *Valdes.* Then haste thee to some solitary grove,
>   And bear wise Bacon's and Albanus' works,
>   The Hebrew Psalter, and New Testament;
>   And whatsoever else is requisite
>   We will inform thee ere our conference cease.
> *Cornelius.* Valdes, first let him know the words of art,
>   And then, all other ceremonies learned,
>   Faustus may try his cunning by himself.
> *Valdes.* First, I'll instruct thee in the rudiments,
>   And then wilt thou be perfecter than I.
> *Faustus.* Then come and dine with me, and after meat
>   We'll canvass every quiddity thereof,
>   For ere I sleep I'll try what I can do.
>   This night I'll conjure, though I die therefore. *Exeunt.*

[I. i. 151–168]

His companions urge him to seek out a secret grove to conduct his magic experiments, and Valdes suggests he take the Psalms, the New Testament, and the books by Roger Bacon and Pietro d'Abano. As Ward observes, Reginald Scott's *The Discovery of Witchcraft* reports the abovementioned scriptures were considered integral to spirit conjuration.[898] Turning to the authors suggested to Faustus, Roger Bacon (1214?–1294) an English Scholastic, was educated at Oxford and Paris. In 1251, he returned to England, entered the Franciscan order and resettled at Oxford where he continued his various scientific experiments and scholastic studies. An

---

[896] Ibid. p. 72.
[897] Ibid. p. 56.
[898] *Doctor Faustus; A and B Texts*, n. 157, p. 121. Also, Paul H. Kocher, *Christopher Marlowe: A Study of his Thought, Learning, and Character* (New York: Russell and Russell, 1962), p. 153.

advanced academic in many fields, he studied several languages, alchemy, optics, astronomy, astrology, mathematics and mineral properties. His radical perception of science provoked condemnation from his order, which they proclaimed heretical, culminating with an edict from Pope Nicholas IV forbidding the reading of his works. Pietro d' Abano (1250?–1316?), an Italian philosopher and physician from Padua, became famous for attempting to reconcile the philosophical differences between medicine and theology, and also between the Arab philosophers and the works of Aristotle. He also maintained a thriving medical practise in his native city. His success as a physician, his writings, and his approbation of certain Arabic ideologies led his critics to condemn him as a practitioner of magic, resulting in two official summons by the Inquisition. He was acquitted on the first occasion, but died before the court deliberated upon the second accusation. Abano in his *Elementa magica* describes the rites of spirit summoning, and according to Kocher, "[…] make[s] the whole process of conjuring seem a rite of holiness."[899] Hence, the Renaissance magician is performing the functions of an *exorcist*, convinced he is using God's power to control spirits similar to a priest, which explains why the Scriptures were used for conjuration — demons are bound to obey the Word of God. If a spirit was reluctant to obey, the magician attempted to command it by the many titles attributed to God and the saints to do his bidding, similar to the rite of exorcism compelling a demon or spirit to depart by God's command.[900]

Despite this alleged 'holiness' in magic, we see that Faustus' friends are not prepared to divulge all their knowledge. Cornelius has already summoned spirits as seen in line 146, "The spirits *tell me they can* dry the sea," however, as the spirit only 'told' of the wondrous things he can perform we understand Cornelius hath not the courage to follow through with the ultimate sacrifice of his soul. When Faustus requests that they demonstrate their skill, Cornelius intimates to Valdes that Faustus should perform these experiments himself when he imparts the "words of art" and the "ceremonies" to him. Valdes receives the 'message' not to become involved, and reassures Faustus he will be "perfecter" than him when he has acquired the basics. They continually stress his superior aptitude in this art, and test Faustus' firm resolve to study the art of magic and all that it encompasses unlike they, who hypocritically "wish to live" and have not ventured to sign a pact:

> *Valdes*: So shall the subjects of every element
> Be always serviceable to us three.
> […]
> If learned Faustus will be resolute.
> [ll. 124–125, 135]
> *Faustus*: Valdes, as resolute am I in this
> as thou to live. Therefore object it not.
> [ll.136–137]

By praising Faustus and flattering him into believing he will quickly supersede them in magic, they hope to entice him to complete the act of conjuring, i.e. complying with any and all

---

[899] *Marlowe: Thought, Learning, and Character*, p. 156.
[900] Ibid.

demands the spirits set forth that they were unwilling to commit to, and thereby share in his discoveries without incurring any peril to themselves. Faustus is blinded by the flame of pride in his abilities fanned by his companions' persuasions, and fails to realise they are luring him to his death — "This night I'll conjure, though I die therefore"— while they "wish to live". A word of warning to beware of sycophants.

Scene Two features two Scholars enquiring of Wagner where they may locate Faustus. Wagner replies with waggish quips, and following a tedious war of words, they finally extract the information they are seeking, and are dismayed to learn he is dining with Valdes and Cornelius. Concerned he may be swayed by their dubious influence, the Scholars decide to meet with the Rector of the university in an attempt to "reclaim" him. What an ironic situation: the Scholars note that Cornelius and Valdes are "infamous" through the whole world with their "damnable art" although they never ventured to complete a pact with a spirit. Moreover, the irony continues with the Scholars' decision to visit the Rector in an attempt to save Faustus, when it is the subjects taught at the university symbolised by the names of "German Valdes" and "Cornelius" that lured Faustus to study the occult arts in the first instance. The result of the Scholars' visit to the Rector is not included in the play, an indication help was not forthcoming for Faustus there as the Rector is just as guilty by promulgating the pagan classics at the university. We also suspect Marlowe drew from his personal experience at the university concerning the underground factions covertly operating on campus, recruiting and informing upon students. Possibly, it was a well intentioned scholar who informed the authorities at Cambridge the 'reason' for Marlow's unusual absences from the college that almost resulted in his failure to obtain his MA degree.

In general, Scene Two with the Scholars provides a comic hiatus following the intensity of Scene One. Marlowe apparently worked with a collaborator on the comic scenes in *Doctor Faustus*, however, Scene Two in Act I with its strong sarcastic overtones in Wagner's discourse with the two Scholars, strongly suggests Marlowe may have composed this section without his collaborator. This scene therefore offers us a valuable insight into Marlowe's perception of the academic world. Wagner enters carrying a flask or flagon of wine for Faustus and his guests, and when the Scholars ask Wagner where his master is, Wagner replies, "God in heaven knows", (a significant remark considering Faustus has commenced his diabolical magic studies). Wagner banters in witticism with the Scholars for he simply stated a theological truth in that God knows where Faustus is, which does not preclude the possibility that he is also aware where Faustus is. However, Wagner suspects the Scholars will not pay strict attention to the construction of his sentence and will automatically assume he meant "God *alone* knows", and thereby erroneously imply he did *not* know where Faustus is either. Having assumed the wrong inference from Wagner, the second Scholar replies, "Why, does not thou know?" Wagner answers, "Yes, I know, but that follows not,". The expression 'that follows not' is a common form for academic disputation signifying to the second Scholar that his question did not follow the first answer, for Wagner did *not state* he had no knowledge of where Faustus was. It is a trifling argument, and the first Scholar believes Wagner is mocking them: "Go to, sirrah! Leave your jesting, and tell us where he is." Wagner continues his chip-chop logic lesson: "That follows not necessary by force of argument that you, being licentiate, should stand upon't. Therefore, acknowledge your error, and be attentive." This time, Wagner is saying it "follows not" that you as licentiate Scholars should "stand upon" this "force of argument" and ask me to tell you where Faustus is as you have not proven at this point if I actually know or not.' The second Scholar is befuddled: "Why, didst thou not say thou knew'st?" Translation: 'What error? You just said *you knew* where Faustus was! Then what is wrong with asking you to tell us where he is?' Wagner enquires if they have witnesses to support this claim. The first Scholar responds in the affirmative, stating he heard him say he knew where Faustus was. Wagner remarks, "Ask my fellow if I be a thief", an allusion to the proverb that the testimony of a thief cannot be trusted, i.e. that they have no proof his remark is true. We also note a possibility Wagner's "fellow" is the bottle of wine he is carrying as this was his 'fellow companion' when he entered the stage. In this sense he may be dropping the Scholars a comic hint by propping the decanter under their noses — 'Am I a thief? What am I doing with this?' The second Scholar is exasperated, "Well, you will not tell us," and Wagner finally concludes his annoying 'disputation':

> Yes, sir, I will tell you. Yet if you were not dunces, you would never ask me such a question. For is not he *corpus naturale*? And is not that *mobile*? Then, wherefore should you ask me such a question? But that I am by nature phlegmatic, slow to wrath, and prone to lechery — to love, I would say — it were not for you to come within forty foot of the place of execution, although I do not doubt to see you both hanged the next sessions. Thus, having triumphed over you, I will set my countenance like a precisian and begin to speak thus: Truly, my dear brethren, my master is within at dinner with Valdes and Cornelius, as this wine, if it could speak, it would inform your worships. And so the Lord bless you, preserve you, and keep you, my dear brethren, my dear brethren. [*Exit.*]

Wagner states he will finally tell them where Faustus is, but not until he points out to them their error in presuming he intended "God alone knows", an error they committed by not utilising their university training in logic. He calls them "dunces", a word that has a double significance. The word 'dunce' was derived from the name of Duns Scotus (c.1266–1308) a Scottish theologian of the Franciscan order who was responsible for founding the Scotism school in Scholastic theology. He was a meticulous ratiocinator in theological and philosophical logic, and the first to argue contrary to the teachings of St. Thomas Aquinas by concluding that certain theological truths cannot be verified by reason or visible proof and must be accepted by faith. The term "dunce" was applied to scholars who supported this school of thought, however, the significance of the word gradually degenerated to signify those who were enemies to learning, 'hair-splitting' logicians,[901] or students whose book-learning had the opposite effect and dulled their intellect.[902] Today, 'dunce' refers to those who are simply regarded as unintelligent. Wagner is implying that the two Scholars are 'book-worn' wits who are 'erroneously' accepting by faith everything that is said to them without examining it in scientific detail. Ward observes Wagner selects a scholastic phrase derived from Aristotle, i.e. *corpus naturale seu mobile*, a term that was applied in physics to define the capability of natural bodies to move or change.[903]

---

[901] *Doctor Faustus: A and B Texts*, n. 19, p. 123.
[902] Ibid.
[903] Ibid. n. 21.

Wagner demonstrates that as Faustus is a 'natural body' he is free to go where he pleases, it is illogical to presume that he knows where Faustus is at every moment. Wagner then alludes to his various 'virtues' that allow him to tolerate the two Scholars' stupidity by paraphrasing the epistles of St. James and St. Paul:

> "[…] And let every man be swift to hear, but slow to speak, and slow to anger."[…] (James 1: 19)

> "Put ye on therefore, as the elect of God, holy, and beloved, the bowels of mercy, benignity, humility, modesty, patience: bearing with one another, and forgiving one another, if any have a complaint against another […]." (Col. 3: 12–13)

However, Wagner salaciously slips and comically mentions "lechery" instead of "love", i.e. "mercy" or "charity", indicating his 'piety' is superficial and exists solely in words. Refusing to correct the Scholars with humility, he uses the situation to demonstrate his knowledge and "triumph" over them. He highlights their deficiency in logic with his little 'disputation', and is convinced they will be "hanged in the next sessions" i.e. he is drawing an allegory with the disputation examination sessions with the periodic court assizes held in England. Wagner is implying they have not the wit to approach the 'place of the gallows', i.e. they are not prepared for the torture of the examinations, and yet they will persist on this path and be 'academically hanged'.* A chilling insinuation that the universities were leading young men straight to the devil's halter. Wagner's closing remarks are then uttered derisively in the manner of a rigid Puritan, "my dear brethren",[904] and he mocks them with a parody of the eventide Family Prayer in *The Book of Common Prayer*: "The Lord bless us and keep us. The Lord make his face to shine upon us, and be gracious unto us. The Lord lift up his countenance upon us, and give us peace, this night and evermore."[905] Finally, he draws their attention to the wine that they should have observed in the first instance — he would not be carrying this libation to Faustus' study if Faustus were not there for him to wait upon! If they had used their reason, they would not have automatically presumed that Wagner did not know where Faustus was by his reply "God in heaven knows", nor would they have needed to ask him at all if they had paid attention.

In one short scene, Marlowe encapsulates the university curriculum regarding the art of disputations, and the careers that the students could hope to obtain. Wagner appears to be a servant, although it is difficult to discern if he is a hired servant who absorbed knowledge from his university surroundings, or if he is a Sizar, a student whose tuition is paid by waiting on the other Scholars. In either case, he holds an inferior position. His disputation appears ridiculous, but Wagner is making a sarcastic point. Perhaps he was insulted when the Scholars addressed him by, "sirrah", (a title referring to a servant or a person of lesser social status), and he proceeds

---

* Compare with Barbabas' lines in *The Jew of Malta*, "The sessions-day is critical to thieves, / And few or none escape but by being purg'd." [II. iii. 110–111], and also with the lines of the pick-pocket, Pilia-Borza: "Upon mine own free-hold, within forty foot of the gallows, […]". [IV. ii. 20–21]
[904] *Doctor Faustus: A and B Texts*, n. 28, p. 124.
[905] Ibid. n. 31–32.

to demonstrate that the only condition which should afford them their superiority in an ideal world is their academic skill, i.e. as orators and logicians. As he proved them inept in small mundane points of argument, they certainly cannot be great masters of dialectic and are not worthy of the status that is bestowed upon esteemed Scholars. Wagner sarcastically assumes the air of a triumphant 'graduate' and Puritan parson. If Wagner is a Sizar, they are from the same background as he; for all their higher learning, he is reminding them they are practically in the same position notwithstanding their pension and therefore do not have much to hope for socially or career wise other than a poor parish commission. They display obvious conceit in treating him as their inferior. The reference to the executioner's yard for the university is interesting — poor students are hanged if they attend the public schools, they are hanged if they do not. As he learned in his early grammar school years there is only one way to break free from the ignobility of a pauper's life: 'To flee poverty, (O Marlowe!), one must fall down from the rocky heights into the sea.'

Marlowe may also be presenting the pathetic situation of poor Scholars and Sizars through Wagner in that the sole avenue open to them for advancement was through the rigorous disputation regime, a course intended to expand the intellect, yet was actually reducing the minds of men to obsession with mere quibbles. It is significant that Marlowe did not use the technique of blank verse for this scene. He was the first playwright to firmly establish blank verse on the Elizabethan stage equalling the elegant measures of Virgil's Latin poetry, which in *Tamburlaine*, set the heroic tone befitting an Asian conqueror. In Marlowe's plays, blank verse signifies heroic deeds, daring actions, or probing philosophical thoughts, and when not used in certain areas, we observe these scenes in general portray comic, idiotic or petty situations, and moments of lunacy or despair. For example, in *1 Tamburlaine* [V. ii. 242–257] the blank verse breaks down on one rare occasion when Zabina, the Turkish Empress, discovers her husband has committed suicide. She is driven to insanity and commits suicide by dashing out her brains on the cage imprisoning her husband. Wagner in Scene Two of *Doctor Faustus* is reduced to proving his worth by engaging in a conflict of trivialities over a wine flask.

Faustus begins his conjuring in Scene Three, and the blank verse has resumed for this is an audacious moment. Marlovian scholars are amused that in contrast to the scholar of the *Faustbook* who studied magic "day and night", it takes all of one evening for Marlowe's Faustus to learn the secrets of the occult arts, as Matalene observes, " […] it is still long before midnight, though yet after dinner."[906] This short study period is generally interpreted as a further indication of Faustus' superficial study methods, i.e. his apparent tendency to skim through his books, yet we have discovered Faustus is already a famous academic, hence this 'skimming' is not without symbolic meaning. The same applies to his magic studies with Cornelius and Valdes: they have previously informed the audience Faustus is well versed in all that is required for magic, languages, minerals, astrology, astronomy, etc.. Now, all that remains for him to master are "the words of art" and the "ceremonies" — a simple matter — having already mastered the basics in his university courses, explaining how he could conjure in the short length of one evening. This is an additional covert insinuation from Marlowe, that the universities were responsible for laying the foundations of occult study.

---

[906] H. W. Matalene III, 'Marlowe's *Faustus* and the Comforts of Academicism,' *ELH* vol. 39, no. 4, (December, 1972): p. 512.

Faustus' companions mentioned a location suitable for magical experimentation, a solitary grove, but there is no indication in the text that Scene Three is set in a rural locality. Possibly, the 'grove' is Faustus' study, a quiet niche in the academic 'Garden of Eden' planted at the university. Holding his book, Faustus commences:

> Now that the gloomy shadow of the earth,
> Longing to view Orion's drizzling look,
> Leaps from th'Antarctic world unto the sky
> And dims the welkin with her pitchy breath,
> Faustus, begin thine incantations,
> And try if devils will obey thy hest,
> Seeing thou hast prayed and sacrificed to them.

[I. iii. 1–7]

Faustus describes the timeframe of his conjuring. The "gloomy shadow of the earth" indicates it is night-time, for it was believed night occurred when the sun passed under the earth, thus enveloping the land with the earth's 'shadow'. The "drizzling" constellation of Orion and the image of darkness "leaping" from the "Antarctic world" indicates it is the season of winter for Orion was considered a 'rainy' constellation when it appeared in the sky in winter at the close of day.[907] Dryden writes:

> "The *heliacal* rising of a constellation is when it comes from under the rays of the sun and begins to appear before daylight. The *achronical* rising, on the contrary, is when it appears at the close of day, and in opposition of the sun's diurnal course. [...] He [Orion] is tempestuous in the summer, when he rises *heliacally*, and rainy in the winter, when he rises *achronically*."[908]

The detail that the "gloomy shadow" of darkness "leaps" into the sky also displays that night descended quickly, an occurrence that has not happened for some time as the night "longed" to view the winter position of Orion. Hence, Faustus' declaration that the *night* is "leaping" "now" to greet Winter Orion, we deduce he is conjuring during the Winter Solstice, the shortest day of the year, an important festival day in several pagan religions.

Faustus reveals he "prayed and sacrificed" to the devils. As mentioned earlier, magicians attempted to assume the role of a holy exorcist by using the name of God and the saints to control demons, hence magic rites included prayers and fasting to obtain protection from the dark creatures they attempted to summon. Kocher observes:

> "The magician cleanses himself by fasting and prayer to God for nine days before the act of magic. [...] If he prays, it is to God, and

---

907 *Doctor Faustus: A and B texts*, n. 2, p. 125.
908 Dryden / Virgil, *Æneid*, pp. 45–46.

he never salutes the fiends but wields against them the adverse power of holy names."[909]

It is possible this perverse practise in magic, of confounding the sacred with the profane, originated with Christ's advice to His disciples in describing the means necessary to drive out demons that were particularly strong or resistant, e.g. (Mark 9:28) "This kind can go out by nothing, but by prayer and fasting."

During the Renaissance era, the practise of using holy devotions for the occult was denounced by orthodox theological teaching for any magical experiment was a service performed to honour Satan. This perception is not unexpected as the magic rites also called for some form of worship and a sacrifice offered to the spirits summoned to attract their attention and to procure their service.[910] How can one pray to God for protection, and then sacrifice to the demons? Francis Coxe describes the 'sacrifices' expected by the demons; "[...] a piece of wax consecrated, or hallowed after their own order, [...] or else it is a chicken, a lapwing, or some living creature [...]."[911] Marlowe adheres to this orthodox view and actually writes Faustus' summoning as a blatant demonic rite by literally indicating Faustus prayed and sacrificed to the devils. This did not imply that Marlowe believed in demonic spirits considering his atheistic convictions as he is simply remaining faithful to the *Faustbook*, for to diverge from the traditional perception of Faustus as a doomed reprobate would provoke undesired attention from the censors.

Faustus then hypocritically draws his 'holy' circle of protection and conjuration, calling on the God he rejected, and praising the gods of Hell:

> [*He draws a circle.*]
> Within this circle is Jehovah's name,
> Forward and backward anagrammatised,
> The breviated names of holy saints,
> Figures of every adjunct to the heavens,
> And characters of signs and earring stars,
> By which the spirits are enforced to rise.
> Then fear not, Faustus, but be resolute,
> And try the uttermost magic can perform.
> {May the gods of Acheron be propitious to me! Let the threefold power
> of Jehovah be strong! Spirits of fire, air, water, all hail! The Prince of the
> East, Beelzebub, monarch of burning hell, and Demogorgon, we ask your
> favour, that Mephistopheles may appear and rise! Why do you delay?
> By Jehovah, Gehenna, and the holy water I now sprinkle, and by the sign

---

[909] *Marlowe; Thought, Learning, Character*, p. 156.
[910] Ibid. p. 153.
[911] Francis Coxe, *A Short treatise declaringe the detestable wickednesse of magicall sciences* (London: 1561), sig. BI V. in *Marlowe; Thought, Learning, Character*, p. 154.

of the cross I now make, and by our prayers, may Mephistopheles himself
arise at our command!} [†]
[*Faustus sprinkles holy water and makes a sign of the cross.*]

[I. iii. 8–23]

Marlowe embroiders this rite with numerous details not included in the *Faustbook*, but the ceremony is consistent with the typical spells recorded pertaining to Renaissance practise of the occult. Faustus draws a cabalist circle of protection and summoning. First, he inscribes the seventy-two names of God, which would entail knowledge of Latin, Greek, and especially Hebrew, thus explaining the prerequisite for knowledge of languages.[912] Kocher writes, "In [*Doctor*] *Faustus* Jehovah's name is said to be anagrammatized because all of the seventy-two names of God are variations (i.e., anagrams) of one mystic Name, formed by the transpositions of its component letters."[913] We detect this practise derived from the legend of Solomon's signet ring featuring a mystic seal fashioned of iron and brass bearing the Divine name of God. Reportedly, this artefact was presented to him by the archangel Raphael when demons were wreaking havoc upon the construction site of the temple: the precious gift allowed Solomon not only to finish work on the temple, but to command the spirit world and all living creatures. Next, Faustus chants the "breviated" names of saints in his 'holy' invocation for protection and summoning, performed in certain incantations. Kocher notes that including the names of the saints was not a popular method with Protestant magicians resulting from their scepticism with the devotional practise of invoking the saints, although there were exceptions.[914] Kocher muses that Marlowe possibly included a play on words with "breviary", a book containing all the prayers, hymns and offices of the canonical hours.[915] However, Kocher did not determine the purpose of *abbreviating* the names. Perhaps Marlowe is referring to the Litany of the Saints, and thus Faustus has to 'abbreviate' / 'breviate' the names as the list of the elect in the Litany is extensive. This element would then have a two-fold significance in the drama; first, Faustus is planning to summon a powerful demon if he is including all the saints of the Litany in addition to the seventy-two names of God. Second, Marlowe may by adding sarcastic humour for the benefit of his Protestant audience, who equated praying to the saints with an act of idolatry. Faustus then includes the symbols of the planets, (the "erring stars"), and the heavenly bodies to draw upon their power and force the demons to rise. These mystic symbols may be inscribed on the minerals, e.g. on slabs of stone or metal, or with the various metals and elements attributed to the ruling planets of a particular demon that the magician desires to summon, hence the necessity to be well versed in astrology and mineralogy.[916]

Faustus then proceeds with the spell. Kocher notes the first half of the incantation, hailing the demons and summoning the arch-princes of Hell, is Marlowe's invention, although Erictho in

---

[†] The ceremony is originally in Latin.
[912] *Marlowe; Thought Learning, Character*, p. 152.
[913] Ibid. p. 155.
[914] Ibid.
[915] Ibid. p. 156.
[916] Ibid. pp. 151–152.

Lucan's *Pharsalia* (i.e. *Civil War,* c. 65 AD) salutes the pagan powers of the Furies, Chaos, Hecate, the Fates, Hell and its rulers during her rituals.[917] The second half of the speech is a mixmatch of traditional magic with blasphemous implications. Faustus imperiously enquires why the demons delay, thus the action is in accordance with the devil's reluctance to appear in the *Faustbook.* Apparently, a tardy apparition was an expected occurrence, for magicians often included commands to hasten the spirit's arrival.[918] Faustus sprinkles holy water and makes the sign of the cross to force the spirits to appear. In traditional magic, holy water and the sign of the cross were used to cleanse the ground in preparation for the protective circle, but here Faustus is including it as part of his diabolical ceremony.[919] Marlowe is apparently stabbing at Catholic devotions, in this instance, the use of sacramentals. Of interest, Marlowe did not write the incantation in blank verse, which we might expect at this crucial dramatic moment as Marlowe already demonstrated his ability to reshape the Latin of the Bible into a stylish format with his blank verse technique. We therefore deduce this incantation is *not intended* to be 'elegant', but rather demonstrates Marlowe's belief that certain mysterious ceremonies with symbolic gestures and rites were included in religion to "keep men in awe". Considering that the English Church was a means of establishing political dominance in his time, Marlowe apparently called Protestants "hypocritical asses" for abolishing the mystic religious ceremonies and pageantry of Catholicism that encouraged devotion and fidelity — it is difficult to 'control' believers if there is nothing to attract them to church![920] Marlowe is also demonstrating the same atheistic concept with magic rites. If religion and the service of God were the inventions of man as Marlowe professed, then so too is the occult with its mystical devil-worship and Latin incantations. We also note the lack of blank verse highlights the paradox of Faustus using the name of God that he previously rejected, and perhaps the irony that Marlowe was compelled to include this 'farcical ceremony' for the sake of the drama contrary to his atheistic belief as this dramatic incantation is exactly what the audience would anticipate any magician to perform. Plays also had their expected 'rites' and formulas to attract faithful spectators!

Mephistopheles responds to the incantation and the blank verse is resumed. The devil appears in his hellish form, and Faustus demands that he depart and return in the guise of a Franciscan friar (in accordance with the *Faustbook*):

> *Exit Devil [Mephistopheles].*
> *Faustus*: I see there's virtue in my heavenly words.
>   Who would not be proficient in this art?
>   How pliant is this Mephistopheles,
>   Full of obedience and humility!
>   Such is the force of magic and my spells.

---

[917] Ibid. p. 156.
[918] Ibid. p. 157.
[919] Ibid. p. 159.
[920] I.e. as recorded in the Baines Note: "That the first beginning of Religion was only to keep men in awe. […] That if there be any god or any Religion, then it is in the papists because the service of god is performed with more ceremonies, as Elevation of the mass, organs, singing men, Shaven Crowns, etc. That all protestants are Hypocritical asses." See Appendix Seven.

Now, Faustus, thou art conjurer laureate,
That canst command great Mephistopheles.
Quin redis, Mephistopheles, fratris imagine!
{Why don't you return, Mephistopheles, in the image of a friar!}

Enter Mephistopheles [disguised as a friar.]

[I. iii. 28–35]

Faustus is congratulating himself on a job well done and believes he gained control of the spirit world with his 'heavenly' words. He triumphantly proclaims he is a graduate in the magic arts, although we discover this is a premature declaration of success. Mephistopheles enquires of the Doctor what service he desires, and Faustus charges him to be his servant and perform whatever duty he requests, should it be to lower the moon from the heavens or to have the ocean flood the world. It was commonly believed magicians acquired these same powers through their occult arts. In Lucan's *Civil War*, it is recorded that the ancient witches of Thessaly in Greece would call the moon down to earth to aid them in their wicked spells. Mephistopheles then enlightens Faustus that he cannot simply command his service — he is bound to Lucifer and cannot comply with these demands without the permission of the Infernal Prince:

Faustus. Did not he charge thee to appear to me?
Mephistopheles. No, I came now hither of mine own accord.
Faustus. Did not my conjuring speeches raise thee? Speak.
Mephistopheles. That was the cause, but yet *per accidens.*
  For when we hear one rack the name of God,
  Abjure the Scripture and his Saviour Christ,
  We fly in hope to get his glorious soul,
  Nor will we come unless he use such means
  Whereby he is in danger to be damned.
  Therefore, the shortest cut for conjuring
  Is stoutly to abjure the Trinity
  And pray devoutly to the prince of hell.
Faustus. So Faustus hath
  Already done, and holds this principle:
  There is no chief but only [Belsibub],
  To whom Faustus doth dedicate himself.
  This word 'damnation' terrifies not him,
  For he confounds hell in Elysium.
  His ghost be with the old philosophers!

[I. iii. 44–62]

Faustus is informed he cannot control the devils by conjuring, and that the spirit came by choice upon hearing him abuse the names of God, the saints and the Scriptures. Mephistopheles confirms orthodox teaching, i.e. using holy devotions for 'protection' during the performance of magic is in reality a hypocritical act that honours the demons.

Kocher is correct in confirming that the English *Faustbook* contains no specific reference to Mephostophiles appearing by choice in answer to the incantations.[921] The *Faustbook* portrays the demons actually spurring Faustus with illicit curiosity into experimenting with magic until they eventually persuade him to sell his soul, and he discovers the name of his familiar demon when he eventually agrees to the contract. [Ch. 14] Marlowe places the onus of falling to illicit curiosity entirely upon Faustus in the A Text. However, Faustus' delusions of magic power remain constant in both mediums. In the *Faustbook* he believes he had the power to command the demons, and so too the magician in the play, and in both instances his prideful assumption is swept away when Mephostophiles / Mephistopheles corrects this misconception and relates a human cannot command a spirit by magic, a confirmed diabolical art. There is one difference — the protagonist in the *Faustbook* still retains the remnants of a conscience and is startled by the knowledge he is required to forfeit his immortal soul for Mephostophiles' service, while Marlowe's character is already a confirmed atheist who is not terrified by damnation having converted to Epicureanism that same evening, and therefore is fully intoxicated with the courageous euphoria of setting out on a new adventure with his waxen wings fully outstretched towards the fiery sun. 'Damnation' is simply a word to him, a term 'invented' to inspire fear. He "confounds hell in Elysium", i.e. he confuses it with heaven, or eradicates the Christian conception of Eternity with his pagan view of heaven. In Virgil's *Æneid*, for example, the underworld contains both hell and Elysium. In addition, we note that Dante in his *Inferno* included Limbo in the first circle of his depiction of Hell as Limbo is traditionally a place for unbaptised just souls who have only the stain of Original Sin on their conscience. It is a place and state of happiness exempt from all earthly suffering, however, the inhabitants are excluded from the glory of Heaven and the Beatific vision of God. Theologians and philosophers generally believed the just pagan philosophers were assigned to Limbo, and this is the hell Marlowe's Faustus finds attractive for he desires to learn hidden knowledge unknown to Christian scholars. Having already rejected his Creator, it is obvious he considers that the loss of the Beatific vision is not an Eternal calamity to him.

Faustus claims "Belsibub" to be his chief, which proves a strange contrast when we consider he refuses to believe in God, for one must also simultaneously reject the existence of God's enemies if God is abjured. However, the different spellings of 'Beelzebub' in the original A Text are an indication which 'master' Faustus desires to serve. Concentrating on the first syllables, 'bel' and 'sib' and the rhythm on the third, this could indicate the diminutives of the Latin 'bellus' ('beautiful'), and 'sibyl', a woman prophet of ancient times. Faustus serves the 'beautiful' art of magic and secret learning. Hence, Faustus "prays" to the Prince of pagan Elysium and the "old philosophers", and not necessarily to the Christian perception of demonic Lucifer / Beelzebub at this point in the drama. This is confirmed in the next lines when Faustus converses about "*that* Lucifer" as though Lucifer is an unknown entity to him, suggesting Faustus had renounced Christianity completely and is now turning to whom he believes is a *Middle Spirit* of the *pagan world* for his knowledge. Faustus has wiped the theological slate clean and desires

---

[921] *Marlowe; Thought, Learning, Character*, p. 159.

to be entirely re-educated in this new realm, thus explaining the elementary questions that he directs at Mephistopheles during their first meeting, which any divinity student could answer:

> *Faustus*: [...] But leaving these vain trifles of men's souls,
>   Tell me what is that Lucifer thy lord?
> *Mephistopheles*: Arch-regent and commander of all spirits.
> *Faustus*: Was not that Lucifer an angel once?
> *Mephistopheles*: Yes, Faustus, and most dearly loved of God.
> *Faustus*: How comes it then that he is prince of devils?
> *Mephistopheles*. O, by aspiring pride and insolence,
>   For which God threw him from the face of heaven.
> *Faustus*: And what are you that live with Lucifer?
> *Mephistopheles*: Unhappy spirits that fell with Lucifer,
>   Conspired against our God with Lucifer,
>   And are for ever damned with Lucifer.
> *Faustus*: Where are you damned?
> *Mephistopheles*: In hell.
> *Faustus*: How comes it then that thou art out of hell?
> *Mephistopheles*: Why, this is hell, nor am I out of it.
>   Think'st thou I, who saw the face of God
>   And tasted the eternal joys of heaven,
>   Am not tormented with ten thousand hells
>   In being deprived of everlasting bliss?
>   O Faustus, leave these frivolous demands,
>   Which strike a terror to my fainting soul!
>
> [I. iii. 64–84]

Hence, Mephistopheles quickly informs Faustus that Lucifer and his minions saw the face of God and fell from Heaven — they are not Middle Spirits, i.e. pagan entities of the elements without any hope of enjoying an afterlife.[+] God Is, Lucifer is a devil, and there is a Hell. Marlowe adheres to other theological traditions, i.e. eternal loss of the Beatific vision is infinite torture, and worse than the ever-burning flames of the Inferno. Hell is described as a state of being rather than a confined area, and this definition is also theologically correct.

[+] Empson formulated an interesting theory proposing Marlowe had originally written the character of Mephistopheles as a Middle Spirit, and that Faustus succeeds in becoming a 'spirit' thus escaping damnation although he is dissolved into the elements. Empson suggests the disapproval of the censors caused the play to be altered, accounting for the forms that survive today, i.e. with the typical Christian ending of damnation for Faustus. (See *Faustus and the Censor*.) However, Mephistopheles admits here he did see the face of God and is in Hell; therefore, he is a demon who seeks the damnation of Faustus' soul. This section in [I. iii] remains intact in the B text, hence, there is a stronger argument that Marlowe intended a traditional Christian perception of the demons in the first instance.

Now that Mephistopheles has reconfirmed the Christian concept of Eternity, salvation and damnation with his triple cry of woe, Faustus resumes his 'faulty' Calvinist theology with his 'devil syllogisms': man "*must*" sin in order to have truth within him and therefore is 'predestined' for Hell from the beginning. Faustus now shoulders the burden of his 'inescapable' fate and stoutly encourages Mephistopheles to do the same, willingly offering Lucifer his soul as he presumes it is already lost, especially having intoned his blasphemous incantation:

> *Faustus*: What, is great Mephistopheles so passionate
> For being deprivèd of the joys of heaven?
> Learn thou of Faustus manly fortitude,
> And scorn those joys thou never shalt possess.
> Go bear these tidings to great Lucifer:
> Seeing Faustus hath incurred eternal death
> By desp'rate thoughts against Jove's deity,
> Say he surrenders up to him his soul,
> So he will spare him four-and-twenty years,
> Letting him live in all voluptuousness,
> Having thee ever to attend on me,
> To give me whatsoever I shall ask,
> To tell me whatsoever I demand,
> To slay mine enemies and aid my friends,
> And always be obedient to my will.
> Go and return to mighty Lucifer,
> And meet me in my study at midnight,
> And then resolve me of thy master's mind.
> *Mephistopheles*: I will, Faustus. [*Exit*.]
>
> [I. iii. 85–103]

Faustus then muses [i.e. I. iii. 105–116] if he possessed as many souls as the stars in the sky, he would trade them all for his spirit-servant. He plans to become emperor of the world, sending soldiers over bridges constructed in the air to conquer the lands across the ocean, presumably the continent of Africa as he envisions joining this continent to Europe and making them contributories to his crown, paralleling Tamburlaine's plans to redraft the map of the world. No Emperor or king shall live without his permission, including the ruler of Germany. Scene Three concludes as Faustus announces he will live in these speculations and fantasies until Mephistopheles returns, and proclaims he has obtained all that he desired: "Now that I have obtain'd what I desire, / I'll live in speculation of this art. [...]" [I. iii. 114–115] However, what exactly *has* he accomplished or gained? At this point, his incantation did not afford him the power to control the demons as he expected, he discovered there is no basis for atheistic Epicureanism, and Mephistopheles is not yet bound to him as his servile spirit. In recognition of these particulars, we suspect Faustus entertained a secret desire more important to him than any other — *affirmation concerning the Great Eternal Plan* — is there a God, or not? At this point, he believes he received confirmation of his initial deduction according to his defective exegesis of the Bible that man "must" sin for Truth, and is consequently doomed to damnation. This is not correct as it is a sacrosanct belief a sinner may always hope for salvation and redemption, but this Calvinist dogma of predestination is the false 'rock' the demons crave Faustus to perish on.

Scene Four is a second comic interlude featuring Wagner and an impoverished knave named Robin. As expected, the blank verse is suspended for this farcical section. Wagner is searching for a personal servant, and finding Robin, the two engage in a bout of word plays and suggestive jokes. Wagner asks if Robin has any "comings in", i.e. income, and the knave replies he has, in addition to "goings out", i.e. a pun on expenses and his threadbare clothing. Wagner pities the ragged clown and remarks his starvation is at the point Robin would probably sell his soul for a raw shoulder of mutton, (which is a play on the colloquial expression for lust or prostitutes). Robin is indignant and replies, "Not so, [...] I had need to have it well roasted, and good sauce to it, if I pay so dear." The word banter continues:

> *Wagner*: Well, wilt thou serve me, and I'll make thee go like *Qui mihi discipulus*? {you who are my pupil.}
> *Robin*: How, in verse?
> *Wagner*: No, sirrah, in beaten silk and stavesacre. ‡
> *Robin*. How, how, knave's acre? [*Aside*.] Aye, I thought that was all the land his father left him. [*To Wagner*.] Do ye hear? I would be sorry to rob you of your living.
> *Wagner*: Sirrah, I say in stavesacre.
> *Robin*: Oho, oho, 'stavesacre'! Why then belike, if I were your man, I should be full of vermin.
> *Wagner*. So thou shalt, whether thou beest with me or no.

[ll. 15–25]

Wagner mimics the Scholar from the first comic scene by asking Robin to "leave your jesting", and threatens Robin that if he will not become his apprentice for seven years, he will transform his lice into "familiars", i.e. *familiar* spirits, and Robin jokes that he need not bother as the vermin are already too 'familiar' with his flesh. Wagner then offers Robin some guilders for his service, and the clown mistakes the word for 'gridirons', i.e. giant griddles used as instruments of torture. This mistake is apropos, considering Wagner has supposedly given him Dutch coins, but in reality hands him French crowns, which suggests he passed him counterfeit currency. Counterfeiting was an act of high treason in England and punishable by death.[922] The Low Countries had an infamous reputation as a centre of counterfeiting: it was in the Dutch town of Flushing that Marlowe first tried his hand at minting illegal coin in 1592. # Robin immediately recognises Wagner's coin as worthless, for each French crown is worth as much to him as

---

‡ Beaten silk: embroidered silk, or, also a pun on being 'beaten'. Stavesacre was a vermin poison made from delphinium seeds — Robin appears to be infected by lice! He first mistakes the word for 'knave's acre', once a poor neighbourhood of Poultney Street. 'Knave's acre' was also a metaphor for 'being ruined'. (Sleight, in *Doctor Faustus; A and B Texts*, n. 18–19, p. 133.)

922 *World of Christopher Marlowe*, p. 275.

"English counters", i.e. English tokens used for counting money with no material value.[923] Wagner informs him to be prepared for two devils to come for him and Robin attempts to return the 'gridirons' to release him from any obligations to Wagner, but to no avail. Wagner persistently harries the knave and finally frightens him into compliance by conjuring the two demons, Balioll and Belcher (i.e. Belial / "belly-all and "belch-er"), who chase him around the stage. When the demons exit the scene, Robin's fear dissipates and he is intrigued by this demonstration of Wagner's arts. He puns with bawdy humour on how to recognise which of the demons were 'he' and 'she' devils by their "horns" and "clefts / cloven feet" respectively, and then promises to serve Wagner if he can show him how to conjure the same spirits. Wagner appears not to acknowledge this particular request, but pledges he will teach Robin how to transform into anything he wishes, e.g. a cat, rat, or dog. Robin ponders what it would be like if he could change into a flea and "tickle the wenches' plackets", i.e. slits in skirts or petticoats, but he insists on learning how to summon the demons. Wagner imperiously silences the clown by threatening him with Balioll and Belcher, and Robin becomes submissive again:

> *Wagner*: Villain, call me Master Wagner, and let thy left eye be
> diametarily* fixed upon my right heel, with *quasi vestigiis nostris*
> *insistere*.** [*Exit*.]
> *Robin*: God forgive me, he speaks Dutch fustian.[†] Well, I'll follow
> him, I'll serve him, that's flat. [*Exit*.]

[I. iv. 72–76]

Wagner commands Robin to walk behind him as his personal manservant and disciple, with his eye forever fixed on his right heel. Robin replies that he will "follow him", presumably as Wagner's pupil — *Qui mihi discipulus!* — and promises to "serve him", a play on the expression to 'give him his just deserts' or 'serve him rightly' when the time comes.

This slapstick scene which concludes Act I first appears to have no importance apart for its comic value, however, we already discern a pattern forming when compared with the previous comic section featuring Wagner and the Scholars. Initially, the Scholars attempted to pull rank over Wagner who is their inferior, and he engages them in a petty university-style disputation to defend his pride and save face. In this scene, Wagner asserts social superiority over a poor

---

This still fails to prove the premiere date of *Doctor Faustus* was 1592. Apparently, Marlowe was first introduced to the illegal trade of counterfeiting when he met the counterfeiter John Poole while in Newgate prison sometime between 18th September and the 1st October 1589 awaiting the pending inquiry subsequent to the death of William Bradley. Poole was incarcerated two years earlier, and Marlowe later described him as a man skilled "in mixture of metals". (See Appendix Seven.) It is possible that Marlowe supervised the completion of Scene Four during the latter months of 1589.

[923] *Doctor Faustus; A and B Texts*, n. 35–36, p. 135.

* This could mean diametrically, i.e. 'oppositely', or 'completely'. Also, 'diametrally' to indicate a diameter: Wagner appears to be using an astrological term here. *Doctor Faustus; A and B Texts*, n. 73, p. 137.

** 'As if to follow in our footsteps.' Ibid. n. 73–74.

† Fustian: in this sense, bombastic gibberish. Ibid. n. 75.

uneducated pauper. On this occasion, this 'assertion' of social dominance is accomplished through the medium of poetry, not necessarily through rhythmic verse, but in the poetic ability to develop the power of language and draw upon the multiple significance of words as displayed in the various punning and double-entendres, notwithstanding their salacious and farcical tone. Notice that the Latin Wagner paraphrases, "*Qui mihi discipulus*", is taken from the opening line of a Latin poem by William Lyly (1468?–1522), *Ad discipulos carem de moribus*.[924] Lyly's poem was widely read in the grammar schools, in addition to the books on Latin grammar he compiled.[925] Robin notices the significance of the line, "How, *in verse?*" Hence, we have regressed in the comic scenes from university disputations to the mechanics of poetry taught in the grammar schools. We also note Wagner will not promise to teach Robin the full measure of his arts, insinuating that teachers often withhold the crème de la crème of their academic secrets from their pupils. Is Marlowe suggesting that the Elizabethan-style education leads to the regression of society rather than progression?

Act II opens with Faustus arriving in his study, pensively awaiting the return of Mephistopheles, and he struggles between the 'old' school of Christianity and his new-found ideal of Epicureanism:

> Now, Faustus, must thou needs be damned,
> And canst thou not be saved?
> What boots it then to think of God or heaven?
> Away with such vain fancies and despair!
> Despair in God and trust in [Belsabub].
> Now go not backward. No, Faustus, be resolute.
> Why waverest thou? O, something soundeth in mine ears:
> 'Abjure this magic, turn to God again!'
> Ay, and Faustus will turn to God again.
> To God? He loves thee not.
> The god thou servest is thine own appetite,
> Wherein is fixed the love of [Belsabub].
> To him I'll build an altar and a church,
> And offer lukewarm blood of new-born babes.

[II. i. 1–14]

As Faustus ponders on his earlier syllogisms, he finally comes to the conclusion that if he remains a faithful 'Elizabethan Calvinist' he "must" be damned, and is convinced it is useless to think of God or salvation. Immediately, he returns to consoling thoughts of serving "Belsabub", the spelling of the devil's name continues to signify Faustus' attachment to an Epicurean system of philosophy rather than his decision to follow the infernal perception of Beelzebub / Satan. 'Bel' and 'sab'-bub may be a metathetic arrangement of 'bel' and 'Saba', or 'beautiful Saba'. Saba was an ancient kingdom located in southwestern Arabia, i.e. the Biblical Sheba famous for

---

[924] Ibid. n. 16, p. 133.
[925] Ibid.

its gold, spices, and precious stones. In 3 Kings (10:10) we read that King Solomon was presented with these costly gifts by the Queen of Sheba when she travelled to his court to witness his unrivalled wisdom. This possible reference to 'beautiful Saba' indicates that Faustus' desire for 'golden' knowledge of great price from the mysterious East has not abated. At this point, Faustus hears the compelling voice of his conscience whispering in his ears to return to God, apparently drawn from Isaiah 30:21: "And thy ears shall hear the word of one admonishing thee behind thy back: This is the way, walk ye in it: and go not aside neither to the right hand, nor to the left."[926] In view of the possible allegory to 'Bel-saba', the subsequent verse in Isaiah (v. 22) is particularly apt: "And thou shalt defile the plates of the graven things of silver, and the garment of thy molten things of gold, and shalt cast them away as the uncleanness of a menstruous woman. Thou shalt say to it: Get thee hence." Faustus nevertheless decides he will not abandon his 'molten things of gold' and "go backward" to Christianity, but will follow this "god" enthroned deep within his own rapacious ego: his quest to uncover knowledge of the unknown, to which "he will build a church" and offer blood-curdling sacrificial rites. His vision to found a new sect in atheistic Epicureanism and attract converts to his 'new religion' by means of ceremonies that "keep men in awe" prevail here in this scene, although hidden under the pertinent veil of conventional perceptions regarding the satanical Sabbat, or black mass.

The Good and Evil Angels return at this point, and continue to tug at Faustus' conscience. The Good Angel speaks first and advices him to reject his magic. Apparently, Faustus heard this recommendation, and bitterly remarks, "Contrition, prayer, repentance — what of them?"[l. 16] The Good Angel replies they are "the means to bring thee unto heaven."[l. 17] The Evil Angel then negates this encouraging thought, describing these penitential tools as "illusions", and "fruits of lunacy", which turn men into fools. The Good Angel begs Faustus to think of Heaven, but the Evil Angel retorts he should think of honour and wealth. As they exit, Faustus ponders:

> Of wealth?
> Why, the seigniory of Emden shall be mine.
> When Mephistopheles shall stand by me,
> What god can hurt thee, Faustus? Thou art safe;
> Cast no more doubts. Come, Mephistopheles,
> And bring glad tidings from great Lucifer.
> Is't not midnight?
> Come, Mephistopheles!
> *Veni, veni, Mephistophile*!
>
> [II. i. 23–29]

These reflections on 'wealth' instantly reconverts Faustus to his former Epicurean plans of eradicating institutionalised Christian religion. He muses on commanding the town of Emden, a thriving port town on the German North Sea coast, an active international trade hub.[927] This may indicate his earthy desire for riches, but we also observe the town was the cradle-land of the

---

[926] Ibid. n. 7–8, p. 138.
[927] Ibid. n. 23, p. 139.

Familist, or the 'Family of Love' sect, founded in 1540 by a Dutch merchant, Hendrik Niclaes (1502?– 1580?). Niclaes promoted a pantheistic, antinomian system that renounced specific religious dogmas, creeds and rituals. He focused on the concept of a mystical union of divine love between all Christian believers. In 1580, Queen Elizabeth I attempted to suppress this sect in England and subsequently condemned their books.

Faustus then remarks there is no god that can oppose him — a reaffirmation of his atheistic principles, which Bevington and Rasmussen observe is an inversion of Romans (8:31): "[…] If God be for us, who is against us?" Faustus decides not to foster any further doubts and recalls Mephistopheles in a mocking tone inverting the Advent hymn 'O come, o come Emmanuel' to receive Lucifer's "glad tidings" (of great joy?) to his request, contorting the Angelic annunciation to the shepherds of Bethlehem.[928] We note Faustus may actually be reconjuring Mephistopheles at midnight on Christmas Eve. Although it is generally accepted Faustus has signed away his soul on that same day as he commanded the demon to return at midnight in Act I [iii. 101], (the 21st of December according to our analysis), we do not know *precisely* which midnight he may be referring to. The second comic scene with Wagner and Robin allows for the passage of time to take place, hence, this second summoning could be occurring anytime between one hour to several days from the last occasion. In the *Faustbook*, three days pass before Faustus signs his soul over to Mephostophiles, and with the addition of three days to the time Faustus first conjures in the play, we find the date is the 24th of December. Hence, Marlowe's Faustus may be signing away his soul to Satan, the Destroyer, on the night that Christ, the Redeemer, was born and at that same exact hour.

Mephistopheles enters the scene and informs his future master that Lucifer has condescended to grant his request, providing Faustus will relinquish his soul. Faustus half acknowledges he possesses a soul at this point by remarking that he already "hazarded" this invisible thing for Mephistopheles' service, for 'hazard' not only signifies 'to risk' or place in danger, but also 'to chance': we note 'Hazard' is an old English dice game. As Faustus is now uncertain where his beliefs lie, considering his vacillating conscience, he is 'gambling' with the idea he *might* have a soul, which *could* be saved, but he is unsure. He agrees to surrender his soul, but at the same time is curious to learn why Lucifer would want this intangible article that he considered a mere "trifle" previously in the drama:

> *Faustus*: Now tell, what says Lucifer thy lord?
> *Mephistopheles*: That I shall wait on Faustus whilst he lives,
>   So he will buy my service with his soul.
> *Faustus*: Already Faustus hath hazarded that for thee.
> *Mephistopheles*: But, Faustus, thou must bequeath it solemnly
>   And write a deed of gift with thine own blood,
>   For that security craves great Lucifer.
>   If thou deny it, I will back to hell.
> *Faustus*: Stay, Mephistopheles, and tell me, what good will my
>   soul do thy lord?
> *Mephistopheles*: Enlarge his kingdom.

---

928 Ibid. n. 27.

Faustus: Is that the reason he tempts us thus?

Mephistopheles: *Solamen miseris socios habuisse doloris.*

{It is a solace for the miserable to have had companions in pain;
i.e. 'Misery loves company'.}

Faustus: Have you any pain, that tortures others?

Mephistopheles: As great as have the human souls of men.
But tell me, Faustus, shall I have thy soul?
And I will be thy slave, and wait on thee,
And give thee more than thou hast wit to ask.

[II. i. 30–47]

Faustus agrees, and the demon encourages him to stab his arm and bind his soul to Lucifer that at a prescribed date the Arch Fiend can claim it. Mephistopheles insinuates Faustus will be as "great" as Lucifer if he obeys, deceitfully convincing Faustus he will be as 'powerful' as the fallen archangel and suggests he will be accomplishing the same great 'heroic' deed as Lucifer when he rebelled against his Creator and established his own kingdom: an ironic concept bearing in mind that Satan cannot create anything, including the prison of Hell, a realm created for him by God. Faustus then stabs his arm as a token to demonstrate his willingness to comply:

[*Cutting his arm.*]
Lo, Mephistopheles, for love of thee
I cut mine arm, and with my proper blood
Assure my soul to be great Lucifer's,
Chief lord and regent of perpetual night.
View here the blood that trickles from mine arm,
And let it be propitious for my wish.

[II. i. 53–58]

Faustus declares that "with his proper blood" he pledges his soul to hell. This phrase not only indicates the physical blood streaming from his arm, but also suggests he is fully cognisant of his deed and in a 'proper' frame of mind. In Medieval times, blood was classified as one of the 'four bodily humours' that determined the health and mental well being of an individual. Blood was associated with an optimistic or confident temperament. Has Faustus once again resumed his atheistic beliefs?

The fact he delays writing the actual contract and lets the blood simply trickle down his arm as his guarantee to Lucifer appears rather puerile at first, and could be interpreted as a reluctance to sell his soul. However, we observe he did "stab his arm courageously" as Mephistopheles demands and is quite willing to "assure his soul". There is possibly another explanation for Marlowe to include this bloodletting ritual. Turning to *Tamburlaine, Part Two* [III. ii], we find a similar episode when the mighty conqueror trains his three sons how to become great warriors by first teaching them to be unafraid of wounds. He stabs his arm and sits smiling as he watches them bathe their hands in his blood. His sons then request that they receive a similar wound to demonstrate their bravery. Hence, Faustus is not lacking in courage, and believes his word and his blood will be sufficient to close the deal. In this manner, he is inverting the Promise and sacrifice of Christ who redeemed mankind by the power of His Word and His blood-sacrifice on the cross.

Mephistopheles is persistent, and insists this dark covenant between them must be written:

> *Mephistopheles*: But Faustus, thou must write it in a
>   manner of a deed or gift.
> *Faustus*: Ay, so I will. [*He writes.*] But Mephistopheles,
>   My blood congeals, and I can write no more.
> *Mephistopheles*: I'll fetch thee fire to dissolve it straight. [*Exit.*]
> *Faustus*: What might the staying of my blood portend?
>   Is it unwilling I should write this bill?
>   Why streams it not, that I may write afresh?
>   'Faustus gives to thee his soul' — ah, there it stayed!
>   Why shouldst thou not? Is not thy soul thine own?
>   Then write again: 'Faustus gives to thee his soul.'
>
> *Enter Mephistopheles with a chafer of coals.*
>
> *Mephistopheles*: Here's fire. Come Faustus, set it on.
> *Faustus*: So; now the blood begins to clear again,
>   Now will I make an end immediately. [*He writes.*]
> *Mephistopheles*: [*Aside.*]
>   O, what will not I do to obtain his soul?
> *Faustus*: *Comsummatum est.* This bill is ended,
>   And Faustus hath bequeathed his soul to Lucifer.
>   But what is this inscription on mine arm?
>   '*Homo, fuge!*' Whither should I fly?
>   If unto God, he'll thrown me down to hell. —
>   My senses are deceived; here's nothing writ. —
>   I see it plain. Here in this place is writ
>   '*Homo, fuge!*' Yet shall not Faustus fly.
> *Mephistopheles*: [*Aside.*]
>   I'll fetch him somewhat to delight his mind. [*Exit.*]
>
> *Enter [Mephistopheles] with Devils, giving crowns
> and rich apparel to Faustus, and dance and then depart.*

[II. i. 59–82]

Marlowe appended a unique feature to the infamous drafting of the contract by having Faustus' blood congeal. The scholar suspects this may be an omen, but he is ignorant of its full import. He believes he commands the possession of his own soul, but he is mistaken: Man has

Free Will, but his soul ultimately belongs to God. The congealing of his blood is a sign given to remind Faustus of this theological truth, but he continues in his error and writes the deed, concluding his diabolical act by contorting the significance of Christ's last words on the cross: "It is consummated." Immediately, Faustus sees the words, "Fly, o man!" appear on his arm, i.e. a paraphrase of 1 Tim. (6:11), "But thou, O man of God, fly these things […]", yet in his consternation, this reference eludes him and he misinterprets it as a warning of his 'inescapable' damnation according to the prophet Amos (9:1–2):

> "[…] I will slay the last of them with the sword: there shall be no flight for them: they shall flee, and he that shall flee of them shall not be delivered. Though they go down to hell, thence shall my hand bring them out: and though they climb up to heaven, thence will I bring them down."

Mephistopheles distracts Faustus in his moment of delirium and succeeds in reaffirming the scholar's confidence once more with a display of his demonic powers. Faustus is entranced and questions if he will be able to raise spirits when he pleases. Mephistopheles responds in the affirmative, and Faustus replies, "Then there's enough for a thousand souls," [l. 88], paralleling his earlier exclamation that if he had a myriad of souls, he would relinquish all for Mephistopheles [I. iii. 104]. This suggests he has suddenly regained his atheistic confidence. He hands Mephistopheles the scroll, and upon securing Mephistopheles' oath to comply with his articles, Faustus formally reads the deed:

> *Faustus*: Then hear me read them.
> 'On these conditions following:
> First, that Faustus may be a spirit in form and substance.
> Secondly, that Mephistopheles shall be his servant, and at his command.
> Thirdly, that Mephistopheles shall do for him and bring him whatsoever.
> Fourthly, that he shall be in his chamber or house invisible.
> Lastly, that he shall appear to the said John Faustus at all times in what form or shape soever he please.
> I John Faustus of Wertenburg, Doctor, by these presents, do give both body and soul to Lucifer, Prince of the East, and his minister Mephistopheles; and furthermore grant unto them that four-and-twenty years being expired, the articles above written inviolate, full power to fetch or carry the said John Faustus, body and soul, flesh, blood, or goods, into their habitation wheresoever.
> By me, John Faustus.'

Mephistopheles enquires in a solemn tone if this is his contract with him, and Faustus replies: "Ay, Take it, and the devil give thee good on't." The fact that Satan requires a written surety of his soul should have raised the suspicions of the scholar, reminding him his soul has infinite value and not irreversibly damned, or the devil would not be so insistent on sealing his offer with a contract. In a sardonic twist of Fate, Faustus has signed away his soul in a petty legal deed only a few days after rejecting the Justinian code and a 'shallow' career in law with all its materialistic quibbles.

Now that Mephistopheles finally has the pact in hand, he allows Faustus to ask whatever questions he wishes. His first query focuses on the famous disputation of Hell and its whereabouts. In the English *Faustbook*, [Ch. 11.] Faustus dreams of Hell after signing the pact, and the nightmare leaves him with many doubts, causing him to question Mephostophiles on the subject for his elucidation. Apparently, the dream shakes him from his atheistic stupor and he begins to query if there is a Hell or not, although despair will not strike until a few chapters later. In Marlowe's drama, however, he questions Mephistopheles on the existence of hell simply to satisfy his academic curiosity, (since Mephistopheles already stated he had previously come from Hell), yet, Faustus is blinded by his human perceptions and cannot decipher the information the demon is disclosing. Faustus stubbornly reverts to his atheistic beliefs and continues his elementary pagan re-education — the inferno to him is a "place" invented by men:

> *Faustus*: First will I question with thee about hell.
> Tell me, where is the *place* that *men*[‡] call hell?
> *Mephistopheles*: Under the heavens.
> *Faustus*:   Ay, but whereabout?
> *Mephistopheles*: Within the bowels of these elements,
> Where we are tortured and remain for ever.
> Hell hath no limits, nor is circumscribed
> In one self place, for where we are is hell,
> And where hell is must we ever be.
> And, to conclude, when all the world dissolves,
> And every creature shall be purified,
> All places shall be hell that is not heaven.
> *Faustus*: Come, I think hell's a fable.
> *Mephistopheles*: Ay, think so still, till experience change thy mind.
> *Faustus*: Why, think'st thou then that Faustus shall be damned?
> *Mephistopheles*: Ay, of necessity, for here's the scroll
> Wherein thou hast given thy soul to Lucifer.
> *Faustus*: Ay, and body too. But what of that?
> Think'st thou that Faustus is so fond
> To imagine that after this life there is any pain?
> Tush, these are trifles and mere old wives' tales.
> *Mephistopheles*: But, Faustus, I am an instance to prove the contrary,
> For I am damned and am now in hell.
> *Faustus*: How? Now in hell? Nay, an this be hell,
> I'll willingly be damned here. What? Walking, disputing, etc.? [...]

---

‡ Italics added.

Faustus is unable to comprehend that hell is also a state of being and that the demons carry the pain of hell with them wherever they roam. Faustus alternatively considers he has lost nothing, believing he will be allowed to continue his beloved academic life as before, and therefore the concept of damnation is not a worrisome prospect.

Quickly adjourning this topic, Faustus desires to have a wife:

> *Faustus*: [...] But leaving off this, let me have a wife, the
> fairest maid in Germany, for I am wanton and lascivious
> and cannot live without a wife.
> *Mephistopheles*: How, a wife? I prithee, Faustus, talk not of a wife.
> *Faustus*: Nay, sweet Mephistopheles, fetch me one, for I will have one.
> *Mephistopheles*: Well, thou wilt have one. Sit there till I come.
> I'll fetch thee a wife, in the devil's name. [*Exit*.]
>
> *Enter [Mephistopheles] with a Devil dressed*
> *like a woman, with fireworks.*
>
> *Mephistopheles*: Tell, Faustus, how dost thou like thy wife?
> *Faustus*: A plague on her for a hot whore!
> *Mephistopheles*: Tut, Faustus, marriage is but a ceremonial toy. If
> thou lovest me, think no more of it.
> [*Exit devil*.]
> I'll cull thee out the fairest courtesans
> And bring them ev'ry morning to thy bed.
> She whom thine eye shall like, thy heart shall have,
> Be she as chaste as was Penelope,$^{\surd}$
> As wise as Saba,$^{\infty}$ or as beautiful
> As was bright Lucifer before his fall. [...]

[II. i. 143–161]

Marlowe did not include the devil's rage with respect to matrimony in this section as depicted in the English *Faustbook*. Mephistopheles discourages marriage, but not because it is a holy sacrament that opposes the Hellish kingdom. Instead, the demon describes it as a "toy", and a "ceremonial" one at that. It is a trivial rite, a 'bauble' of religion: a ritual intended to control and "keep men in awe" according to Marlowe's beliefs? Hence, Mephistopheles is attempting to shake Faustus free from the conventions of religion 'controlling' the lives of men. Notice how Marlowe uses the word "toy" in the Prologue spoken by Machevill (i.e. Machiavelli) in his subsequent play, the *Jew of Malta*: "I count religion but a childish toy, / And hold there is no sin

---

$^{\surd}$ The faithful wife of Ulysses (Odysseus) in Homer's *Odyssey*.
$^{\infty}$ The Queen of Sheba.

but ignorance." [ll.14–15.]   Mephistopheles may also be challenging *all* religio-traditional concepts of marriage, i.e. as a *heterosexual* union.   We note that in Marlow's era, it was considered immoral to have woman perform on the stage, and therefore female roles were performed by men.   Of particular interest in this case, the stage directions specifically mention a devil is *dressed as* a woman, rather than simply mention that a 'female devil' enters the scene, thus the directions *emphasise* the male gender of the actor / devil.   Hence, Mephistopheles relates Faustus is free to have any woman (or man?!) he wants in lechery.   However, we note Faustus ignores the devil's offer for the present, which will have an important bearing on the drama later as we shall discover.   For the time at hand, Mephistopheles presents Faustus with a new magic book to keep him occupied:

> *Mephistopheles*: […]   [*Presenting a book.*]
>   Hold, take this book.   Peruse it thoroughly.
>   The iterating of these lines brings gold;
>   The framing of this circle on the ground
>   Brings whirlwinds, tempests, thunder, and lightning.
>   Pronounce this thrice devoutly to thyself,
>   And men in armour shall appear to thee,
>   Ready to execute what thou desir'st.   […]

  [II. i. 162–168]

With this one volume, the devil bestows on Faustus all that he had sold his soul for: secret knowledge and wealth (both symbolised by the gold), power to control the elements of the heavens and earth, and magic to summon an army to conquer the kingdoms of men.   Faustus, nevertheless, desires more … surely, the "depths" of magic are inexhaustible?

> *Faustus*: Thanks, Mephistopheles.   Yet fain would I have a
>   book wherein I might behold all spells and incantations,
>   that I might raise up spirits when I please.
> *Mephistopheles*: Here they are in this book.
>   *There turn to them. {in same book.}*
> *Faustus*. Now would I have a book where I might see all
>   characters and planets of the heavens, that I might know
>   their motions and dispositions.
> *Mephistopheles*: Here they are too.   *Turn to them.*

  [II. i. 169–176]

Faustus becomes discouraged with this situation: he is hoping the field of magic offers at least *one* additional book!

Faustus: *Nay*, let me have *one book more** — and then I have
    done — wherein I might see all plants, herbs, and trees
    that grow upon the earth.
Mephistopheles: Here they be. *Turn to them.*
Faustus: O, thou art deceived.
Mephistopheles: Tut, I warrant thee.

[II. I. 177–182]

He believes he is swindled! How could all this knowledge be contained in one book, unless, the vast hoard of mystic and hidden knowledge he expected to receive was only a fantastic dream? Faustus is discovering that magic fails to display substantial "depths" and is proving to be wanting as in all the other subjects he rejected! He gradually slides down that slippery path to despair as the drama unfolds, now questioning his decision to delve into the realm of magic, realising he has "hazarded" his soul for naught.

At this point in the drama, a number of modern editors insert the comic scene with Robin and Rafe.[929] Robin is now a stableman and he discloses to the audience that he has stolen one of Faustus' conjuring books, (i.e. from Wagner, who originally pilfered it!) The clown has either prematurely escaped from Wagner, his former 'master', or he has completed his seven year 'apprenticeship' with him, a situation allowing for the visible progression of time in the play considering twenty-four years must elapse within a few hours. Although no longer a pauper, we note Robin's career following his 'education' with Wagner is not a major improvement. Apparently, this comic section indicates a further social regression as the previous farce alluded to the mechanics of poetry as taught in the grammar school — this scene now refers to the skill of reading at the elementary level. Robin plans to conjure with the book for his own salacious purposes: "Now will I make all the maidens in our parish dance at my pleasure stark naked before me, and so by that means I shall see more than e'er I felt or saw yet." [II. ii 3–6] He is interrupted by Rafe, a fellow stableman, who wonders what he is up to: "Come, what doest thou with that same book? Thou canst not read." [15–16] Robin informs him otherwise, and offering an example of the marvels he can perform with this book, he boasts that he can make him drunk with spiced wine, "hippocras", in any tavern in Europe without having to lighten his purse, and Rafe dismisses this as a simple feat to accomplish! Robin then promises to show Rafe how to win Nan Spit the kitchen maid for his "own use" by magic and the two scoundrels exit the stage with their scheming in progress.

Scene Three commences with Faustus bitterly regretting his decision to sell his soul:

Faustus: When I behold the heavens, then I repent
    And curse thee, wicked Mephistopheles,
    Because thou hast deprived me of those joys. [...]

---

* Italics added.
[929] This comic scene was originally placed in Act III of the A Text following Faustus' visit to Rome and combined with the comic 'silver goblet' scene. However, this creates several anomalies in the drama, which suggests a scene is missing. See *Doctor Faustus; A and B Texts* for more information.

[II. iii. 1–4]

Faustus encapsulates his repentant meditation in the first line, a reference to Psalm 8,[930] (verse 4 onwards):

> "[...] For I will behold thy heavens, the works of thy fingers: the moon and the stars which thou hast founded. What is man thou art mindful of him? Or the son of man that thou visited him? Thou hast made him a little less than the angels, thou hast crowned him with glory and honour: and hast set him over the works of thy hands. Thou hast subjected all things under his feet, all sheep and oxen: moreover the beasts also of the fields. The birds of the air, and the fishes of the sea, that pass through the paths of the sea. O Lord our Lord, how admirable is thy name in all the earth!"

Faustus contemplates his present situation in light of his recent discovery, that magic and mystical knowledge was a textually limited field as all the elements of the created cosmos could be recorded in one tome! Pondering upon the lack of profundity in magic, the subjects in Mephistopheles' book has reminded him of this Psalm: all of Creation is made by God, and lovingly placed under the dominion of mankind. How could he think of turning to magic to command the heavens and the earth, when this regal authority was already granted to him if he had remained in God's grace? How could he have rejected such a loving Creator, who not only sends a Redeemer, the "Son of Man", but also crowns mankind with its own degree of glory? Mephistopheles attempts to reason with Faustus and dissuade him from this repentant meditation, however, the dispute backfires:

> *Mephistopheles*: Why Faustus,
>   Think'st thou heaven is such a glorious thing?
>   I tell thee, 'tis not half as fair as thou
>   Or any man that breathes on earth.
> *Faustus*: How provest thou that?
> *Mephistopheles*: It was made for man; therefore is man more excellent.
> *Faustus*: If it were made for man, 'twas made for me.
>   I will renounce this magic and repent.

[I. iii. 4–11.]

The Good and Evil Angels return and begin to vie for Faustus' conscience:

> *Good Angel*: Faustus, repent yet, God will pity thee.
> *Evil Angel*: Thou art a spirit, God cannot pity thee.

---

[930] *Doctor Faustus; A and B Texts*, n. [II. iii. i.], p. 149.

Faustus: Who buzzeth in mine ears I am a spirit?
Be I a devil, yet God may pity me;
Ay, God will pity me if I repent.
Evil Angel: Ay, but Faustus never shall repent.

Exeunt [Angels.]

[II. iii. 12–17]

The Evil Angel attempts to impede Faustus' repentance by reminding him of the 'escape clause' he wrote into his contract: Faustus desired to become a 'spirit' in form and quality, not necessarily a devil at that point, but a Middle Spirit whereby he would not be doomed to Eternal punishment when the twenty-four years elapsed, but would dissolve into the elements. Faustus apparently refused to believe Mephistopheles when he described himself and his rebellious companions as fallen angels, and Faustus continued to force the 'middle spirit' issue. We learn from Mephistopheles' dialogue above that Faustus is still a man, or he would not attempt to convince Faustus he was more "excellent" than heaven. Thus, the devil has not honoured his side of the contract in this instance, rendering it null and void! Nevertheless, the Evil Angel is persuading Faustus that all agreements have been complied with, and that he is a 'spirit', a thought that is a dangerous impediment to his salvation. If he is not a 'middle spirit' doomed to extinction, he is a 'devil' unable to repent. Faustus stubbornly argues God may pity him if he repents, even if he was a devil incarnate, but this is the key problem: devil-spirits are unwilling to repent as they continue to harbour their seditious pride, and the Evil Angel drives this point home as he exits the stage. If you are a spirit, Faustus, you "never shall repent".

Faustus' mind holds fast to this parting remark, and he concludes his heart is so hardened that he cannot repent. We discover this whirlwind of despair has entrapped him for a considerable period, and he narrowly escaped committing suicide were it not for the magical pleasures Mephistopheles distracted him with, which we know only delays the inevitable, he will eventually be forced to address his spiritual predicament:

Faustus: My heart's so hardened I cannot repent.
Scarce can I name salvation, faith, or heaven
But fearful echoes thunder in mine ears:
'Faustus, thou art damned!' Then swords and knives,
Poison, guns, halters, and envenomed steel
Are laid before me to dispatch myself;
And long ere this I should have slain myself
Had not sweet pleasure conquered deep despair.
Have not I made blind Homer sing to me
Of Alexander's love and Oenone's death?
And hath not he that built the walls of Thebes
With ravishing sound of his melodious harp
Made music with my Mephistopheles?
Why should I die, then, or basely despair?

I am resolved Faustus shall ne'er repent.

[II. iii. 18–32]

Marlowe altered one detail of the *Faustbook*, i.e. where the devils prevent Faustus from repenting by distracting him with delightful music and magical scenes. In the drama, Faustus attempts to ease his despair by arranging his own inventive entertainments. The pagan pleasures magic can procure once more bolster his courage and he decides he will not repent. The particular distractions named here, i.e. the story of Alexander and Oenone, is a continuation of the Trojan War legend.[931] Accordingly, Paris ('Alexander') rejected the nymph of Mount Ida, Oenone, when he was promised Helen of Troy. Before the city fell, the archer Philoctetes mortally wounded Paris with a poisoned arrow. Oenone possessed the antidote, but she refused to cure him and later killed herself in remorse. "He that built the walls of Thebes" refers to the myth of Amphion, the ancient ruler of the same city who was a gifted musician. To build the fortifications of the metropolis, he 'charmed' the stones into place by the power of music.

Having recovered a measure of his former confidence, Faustus decides he will converse with Mephistopheles again. Perhaps he will discover additional secrets not recorded in the book previously presented to him? Faustus is still "sounding the depths" of magic and testing the worth of his infernal contract by asking further elementary questions to continue his 're-education':

> *Faustus*: Come, Mephistopheles, let us dispute again
> And argue of divine astrology.
> Tell me, are there many heavens above the moon?
> Are all celestial bodies but one globe,
> As is the substance of this centric earth?
> *Mephistopheles*: As are the elements, such are the spheres,
> Mutually folded in each other's orb;
> And, Faustus, all jointly move upon one axletree,
> Whose terminine is termed the world's wide pole.
> Nor are the names of Saturn, Mars, or Jupiter
> Feigned, but erring stars.
> *Faustus*: But tell me, have they all one motion, both *situ et*
> *tempore*? {in both location / direction and time}
> *Mephistopheles*: All jointly move from east to west in four-and-
> twenty hours upon the poles of the world, but differ in
> their motion upon the poles of the zodiac.
> *Faustus*: Tush, these slender trifles Wagner can decide.
> Hath Mephistopheles no greater skill?
> Who knows not the double motion of the planets?

---

[931] Recounted in the fragmentary Cypria, *Heroides V* by Ovid, and in Smyrnaeus' *The Fall of Troy*, Book X (fourth-century: trans. Arthur S. Way, Loeb Library, 1913). *Doctor Faustus; A and B Texts*, n. 27, p. 151.

The first is finished in a natural day,
The second thus, as Saturn in thirty years,
Jupiter in twelve, Mars in four, the sun, Venus, and
Mercury in a year, the moon in twenty-eight days. Tush,
These are freshmen's suppositions. But tell me, hath every
sphere a dominion or *intelligentia*?
Mephistopheles: Ay.
Faustus: How many heavens are there?
Mephistopheles: Nine: the seven planets, the firmament, and
the empyreal heaven.
Faustus: Well, resolve me in this question: why have we not
Conjunctions, oppositions, aspects, eclipses all at one
Time, but in some years we have more, in some less?
Mephistopheles: *Per inaequalem motum respectu totius.*
{By their unequal motion in respect to the whole.}
Faustus: Well, I am answered. […]

[II. iii. 33–66]

It is obvious that Mephistopheles presented Faustus with the Ptolemaic system of the cosmos, a strange variation from the English *Faustbook* featuring a quasi-Copernican account. This variation has raised numerous questions. Marlovian commentators have wondered if Marlowe was unfamiliar with the Copernican theory considering that the Ptolemaic system remained the preferred option, not to mention only a few astronomical textbooks available in England at that time contained passing references to this new theory.[932] However, Marlowe's ignorance of this new celestial hypothesis seems an unlikely scenario. Although not promoted textually in England, there were academics, particularly Giordano Bruno, who lectured on the new Copernican system. In fact, Faustus' first query in reference to the moon suggests he *is* asking Mephistopheles to clarify the issue: why would Faustus question the existence of 'heavens' *above the moon* when it was common knowledge according to the Ptolemaic system that *every celestial body* was above the moon? We may actually read his queries thus: 'Are there other bodies that circle the earth other than the moon, for Copernicus speculates *only the moon* orbits the earth, or, are all the celestial bodies contained in one great circle according to Ptolemy?' Faustus may also be probing if Tycho Brahe's theory may be relevant, i.e. if the moon circles the stationary earth, while the five known planets rotate around the sun, a system that in turn orbits the earth. Mephistopheles confirms that the cosmos is Ptolemaic-geocentric, and as an example, he offers the Aristotelian theory of the four elements that rise according to their cosmic gravity: the planets and heavenly bodies likewise rise above the earth each to their respective places in concentric circles. The devil also relates that the last three planets, Mars, Jupiter and Saturn, are bodies that at certain intervals travel 'retrograde', hence the term "erring stars".

Faustus is then curious to discover how the heavens actually rotate, (a question that confused astronomers and astrologers for years as no consistent or accurate numerical scheme to

---

[932] See Johnson, 'Marlowe's Astronomy,' *MLN.*

calculate the celestial movements existed). Mephistopheles explains in general terms that the movements are two-fold. The heavenly bodies appear to orbit the earth in one natural day upon "the poles of the world", yet revolve in variant motions upon the "poles of the zodiac", i.e. where they pass through the constellations of the zodiac. Faustus is annoyed with these general terms, exclaiming that every freshman, (including Wagner!$^{\sqrt{}}$), is aware of these movements, and he begins to prattle off their respective revolutions according to both "poles" or "double motions".‡ He has learned nothing extraordinary, and he attempts to extract mystical knowledge from Mephistopheles by asking if each sphere has a Guardian Angel or Intelligence to attend to their movements as philosophers proposed. The devil's curt remark, "ay", suggests he is not pleased with this dispute as it is leading to theological matters. We also detect Mephistopheles is insulted by this question. When previously explaining that the "erring stars" were not "feigned", he was also dropping Faustus new information concerning the hellish kingdom, which the scholar apparently ignored. I.e. the *names* of the three ancient 'gods' are not myths, and considering that the stars were deemed symbolic of the angels, these three 'gods' are actually demons, or 'stars in error' — we must remember the Scriptures equate the pagan gods with devils. Alternatively, Faustus concentrates on the heavenly spirits, and Mephistopheles is disgruntled that the one titbit of information he did proffer went unnibbled.

The intellectual continues his questioning, perhaps he is unnerved by the devil's succinct reaction, not elaborating beyond his one "ay", and begins to probe into the number of spheres that exist. Mephistopheles provides a disappointing answer for he excluded the crystalline heaven and the *coelum igneum* spheres, and conflated the *primum mobile* with the firmament of the fixed stars. This point is later elaborated upon in the B Text; "*Faustus*: But is there not *ceolum igneum, et cristallinum*? / *Mephistopheles*: No, Faustus, they are but fables." Johnson theorises that Marlowe is presenting an unorthodox and controversial theory that was gaining considerable momentum at that time contrary, to the idea that there were ten moving spheres, eleven with the empyreal heaven included.[933] However, we can propose a contrary argument: the "ceolum igneum, et cristallinum" spheres were *later additions* to the Ptolemaic system dating from the Renaissance period accounting for planetary precession and hypothetical trepidation, hence *these* additional spheres must be the 'new' and controversial element of the astronomical calculation that had not yet gained full recognition. Several academics were dissatisfied with these two new spheres, and consequently reconsidered theories that featured Aristotle's ancient hypothesis with only eight spheres and the empyreal heaven. Therefore, Mephistopheles' elucidation *is actually drawn from the conservative camp*. Faustus is becoming disillusioned for his 'progressive' spheres are "fables" and the information he received to this point is "freshman" material. He is also forced to reaccept Aristotle's 'devilish' theories that he adamantly rejected! Faustus is continually searching for the "depths" of magic, only to tread shallow water at every turn. He decides to venture one more query, and receives in answer, another generality that plagued the study of astronomy. Bevington and Rasmussen observe: "[... Mephistopheles'] 'explanation' is a

---

$^{\sqrt{}}$ This would confirm Wagner is a student / Sizar at the university.

‡ Faustus makes one unusual error in the Zodiac revolutions: Mars was generally believed to have a revolution of two years, not four. Commentators have concluded this may be an error attributable to Marlowe.

[933] See 'Marlowe's Astronomy,' *MLN*.

masterpiece of saying nothing, obfuscating as it does the central inadequacy of the Ptolemaic system. How to account for unequal motion of the planets was the problem that inspired the revolutionist theories of Tycho Brahe and others."[934] Faustus wearily surrenders to these "shallow depths", realising he possessed this information all along, and there is nothing new to discover. Quickly, he darts Mephistopheles a question concerning the Creation, perhaps to catch him off guard, but he is promptly rebuffed:

> *Faustus*: […] Tell me who made the world.
> *Mephistopheles*: I will not.
> *Faustus*: Sweet Mephistopheles, tell me.
> *Mephistopheles*: Move me not, for I will not tell thee.
> *Faustus*: Villain, have I not bound thee to tell me anything?
> *Mephistopheles*: Ay, that is not against our kingdom, but this
>   is. Think thou on hell, Faustus, for thou art damned.
> *Faustus*: Think Faustus, upon God, that made the world.
> *Mephistopheles*: Remember this. *Exit.*
> *Faustus*: Ay, go, accursed spirit, to ugly hell!
>   'Tis thou hast damned distressed Faustus' soul.
>   Is't not too late?

[II. iii. 66–77]

Faustus is finally realising he has compromised his life by his contract with Hell. Not only is he restricted academically more than before, but he begins to understand that 'heaven', 'hell' and 'damnation' must be true if the demons refuse to discuss the subject of Creation! He questions if it is possible to reverse his decision and extract himself from this predicament. The Angels enter the scene, and on this occasion the Good Angel has the last word, comforting Faustus with the idea that if he should repent the devils are unable to harm him. Faustus then cries out "Ah, Christ, my Saviour, / Seek to save distressed Faustus' soul!" [II. iii. 82–83]; a call to the Good Shepherd to seek out this lost penitential lamb. (Luke 15: 4–7)[935] However, he receives a sardonic answer to this plea for help when Lucifer, Beelzebub and Mephistopheles enter the stage:

> *Lucifer*: Christ cannot save thy soul, for he is just.
>   There's none but I have int'rest in the same.
> *Faustus*: O, who art thou that look'st so terrible?

---

[934] *Doctor Faustus; A and B Texts*, n. 65, p. 154.
[935] "What man of you that hath an hundred sheep: and if he shall lose one of them, doth he not leave the ninety-nine in the desert, and go after that which was lost, until he find it? And when he hath found it, lay it upon his shoulders, rejoicing: and coming home, call together his friends and neighbours, saying to them: Rejoice with me, because I have found my sheep that was lost? I say to you, that even so there shall be joy in heaven upon one sinner that doth penance, more than upon ninety-nine just who need not penance."

Lucifer: I am Lucifer,
　　　And this is my companion prince in hell.
Faustus: O Faustus, they are come to fetch away thy soul!
Lucifer: We come to tell thee thou dost injure us.
　　　Thou talk'st of Christ, contrary to thy promise.
　　　Thou shouldst not think of God. Think of the devil,
　　　And of his dame, too.
Faustus: Nor will I henceforth. Pardon me in this,
　　　And Faustus vows never to look to heaven,
　　　Never to name God or to pray to him,
　　　To burn his Scriptures, slay his ministers,
　　　And make my spirits pull his churches down.
Lucifer: Do so, and we will highly gratify thee. […]

[II. iii. 84–99]

　　　It would appear Christ fails to answer Faustus' plea, but His absence is not necessarily an indication Heaven has rejected him: the Good Angel's advice is proof of this. Commentators have proposed that in this scene Heaven is testing his faith and his desire for amendment, including his willingness to withstand the trials of Hell. Faustus fails the test and falls far short of Heaven's expectations when he sees Lucifer in his "terrible" appearance, and believes the deception that Christ "cannot save his soul" according to Divine Justice, a paradoxical answer when Christ has literally preached He seeks after the lost sheep. Apparently, Marlowe is demonstrating that the hellish doctrine of predestination according to Calvinism contradicts the New Testament and its emphasis on the salvation of hardened sinners who repent. Lucifer insinuates by the word "interest" that Faustus' sins are too great to be forgiven; the Prince of demons is not only 'interested' in his soul, but Faustus has exceeded the transgressions Christ is willing to forgive by formally *selling* his soul, and therefore Lucifer has earned extra 'interest' with their contract. The Infernal Prince continues to inform Faustus that he is acting contrary to their agreement by speaking of Christ. Although this stipulation is not strictly written into the pact as in the English *Faustbook*, Lucifer is referring to the spell Faustus used to summon Mephistopheles. We understand that in order to remain in the devils' favour it is an unspoken condition of the contract that all Christian theology, meditations and practises must be constantly abjured. Faustus is cowed into submission and he returns to his Epicurean programme to destroy Christianity, also negating his earlier remorse when he replied "when I behold the heavens" by declaring "Faustus vows never to look to heaven".

　　　Lucifer, pleased with this compliance, announces he has a pastime prepared for his 'favourite's' viewing: a pageant of the Seven Deadly Sins in their "proper shapes". This act diverges from the *Faustbooks* wherein Lucifer shows Faustus the Seven Arch-princes of Hell in their monstrous forms, but the Sins are an apt alteration. Lisa Hopkins presents a theory that Marlowe was inspired to change this detail by the Denham exorcisms of 1585–86 where Catholic priests had exorcised a demoniac named Richard Mainy possessed by the Seven Deadly Sins, who visibly displayed their presence.[936]   Marlowe may also have remembered the scriptures pertaining to Mary Magdalene, whom Christ freed from the dominion of seven demons also theologically recognised as the Seven Deadly Sins. (Luke 8:2)

Faustus remarks this proposed show will be "as pleasing unto me as paradise was to Adam the first day of his creation." [II. iii. 103–104] Lucifer retorts; "Talk not of paradise nor creation, but mark this show. Talk of the devil, and nothing else. [...]" [105–106] It is possible Faustus is referring to his 'reawakening' regarding his contract and the metamorphosis of his image to mirror that of his Infernal Prince, comparing himself to the newly created Adam, made in God's own image, who reflects on the splendours of Eden for the first time, although Lucifer disapproves of the theological nature of the allegory. We note this procession of the Seven Deadly Sins appears to be a mocking parody of the event when God gathered all the earthly creatures before Adam in the Garden to observe the names he would bestow upon them as recorded in Genesis. The blank verse is suspended for this scene. Pride enters first, of course, and is followed by Covetousness, Wrath, Envy, Gluttony, Sloth, and finally by Lechery. When they each describe their pedigrees, qualities and traits, Lucifer sends the Sins back to Hell and enquires of Faustus his opinion of this show:

> *Faustus*: O, this feeds my soul!
> *Lucifer*: Tut, Faustus, in hell is all manner of delight.
> *Faustus*: O, might I see hell and return again, how happy were
>   I then!
> *Lucifer*: Thou shalt. I will send for thee at midnight.
>   [*Presenting a book.*] In meantime, take this book. Peruse
>   it thoroughly, and thou shalt turn thyself into what shape
>   thou wilt.
> *Faustus*: [*Taking the book.*] Great thanks, mighty Lucifer.
>   This will I keep as chary as my life.
> *Lucifer*: Farewell, Faustus, and think on the devil.
> *Faustus*: Farewell, great Lucifer. Come, Mephistopheles.
>   *Exeunt omnes,* [*different ways*].

[II. iii. 166–177]

Faustus considers the Seven Deadly Sins a delightful 'spiritual nourishment' — this displays his innate evil tendencies as depicted in the *Faustbook* — but the scene of the Sins also "feeds his soul" in his insatiable hunger for *visible* confirmation of theological doctrine and philosophy, thus resolving his continuous doubts of the afterlife. It is for this reason he declares he would be happy to see hell and be able to return: he seeks *perceptible* signs of the ethereal Eternal that mankind cannot see and will only experience upon the arrival of Death. He lacks faith and seeks visible proof at every turn, a flaw in his character that is unbefitting a divinity scholar as only "a wicked and adulterous generation seeketh after a sign [...]". (Matt. 16:4) We

---

[936]   Lisa Hopkins, 'A Possible Source for Marlowe's Pageant of the Seven Deadly Sins,' *Notes and Queries* 41 (4) (December, 1994): pp. 451–452.

additionally observe that the Seven Deadly Sins actually support his former decision to delve into the myths of the pagans. The ancient Roman and Greek legends are rife with arrogant conquests, envy, strife, rapine, gluttony and orgies: the very substance the gods of Olympus were created from, the demonic "erring stars" of Mephistopheles' astronomy lesson! Faustus in this instance desires to become a partaker of this adventure by embarking on a roundtrip tour of the underworld as a new Aeneas, Orpheus or Hercules. The scene closes with Lucifer presenting Faustus with the extra magic tome he yearned for as an additional token of his favour, and he heartily accepts this gift as a vindication that magic had more to offer than all other academic fields and was worth "hazarding" damnation.

Wagner enters and opens Act III with a chorus introducing Faustus' new adventures. He has travelled to see the stars in a chariot drawn by dragons to discover the "secrets of astronomy", [III. Chor. 2.] and now desires to "prove cosmography" [7]. Faustus continues to examine the veracity of Mephistopheles' book! Wagner presumes his master will visit Rome first to enjoy "Peter's feast", i.e. the feast day of the Apostle on June 29. This is not exactly what occurs: Rome is the *last* place Faustus visits, suggesting there is a time anomaly in the text, or Faustus simply did not spend ample time viewing the heavens and decided to travel instead:

Enter Faustus and Mephistopheles.

Faustus: Having now, my good Mephistopheles,
      Passed with delight the stately town of Trier,
      Environed round with airy mountain-tops,
      With walls of flint and deep intrenchèd lakes,
      Not to be won by any conquering prince;
      From Paris next, coasting the realm of France,
      We saw the river Maine fall into the Rhine,
      Whose banks are set with groves of fruitful vines.[◌]
      Then up to Naples, rich Campania,
      Whose buildings, fair and gorgeous to the eye,
      The streets straight forth and paved with finest brick,
      Quarters the town in four equivalents.[∞]

[◌] Marlowe actually conflated two sections of the English *Faustbook* here. Following his trip to Paris, Faustus witnesses the Main River fall into the Rhine, but he did not inspect the groves as he "[…] tarried not long there but went to Campania in the kingdom of Neapolis." (*Doctor Faustus; A Critical Ed.* p. 129) Faustus espies the "fruitful vines" later when passing from Ulm to Würzburg: "[…] through the which town passeth the river Main that runs into the Rhine: thereabout groweth strong and pleasant wine, the which Faustus well proved." (*A Critical Ed.* p. 135.)

[∞] This is Marlowe's addition to P.F.'s account of Naples. P.F. simply states: "[…] the streets fair and large and straight forth from one end of the town to the other as a line, and all the pavement of the city was of brick […]." (*A Critical Ed.*, p. 129.) Either Marlowe was completing the idea of the streets as there must be intersections that quarter the city into blocks, (infrastructure cannot consist only of parallel roads leading in one direction), or he is depicting the major sections of the city that parallel the contours of the main thoroughfares, all of which fan the bay of Naples. When looking towards the east of the city, (i.e. towards Mt. Vesuvius), one can discern the "quarters" of the town that are sectioned off into large

There saw we learned Maro's§ golden tomb,
The way he cut an English mile in length
Through a rock of stone in one night's space.
From thence to Venice, Padua, and the rest,
In midst of which a sumptuous temple stands
That threats the stars with her aspiring top.
Thus hitherto hath Faustus spent his time.
But tell me now, what resting place is this?
Hast thou, as erst I did command,
Conducted me within the walls of Rome?

[III. I. 1–22]

In his rendition of the Faustian legend, Marlowe concentrated on the first part of Faustus' second journey around the world, and integrated a number of unusual variances to the voyage not recorded in the *Faustbook*. We note the first intriguing variation is Marlowe's description of Trier — Henry Jones reveals he included a partial reference to Trent.[937] This error may confirm Marlowe had an early English *Faustbook* with 'Trent' as a misprint, (that was later corrected to 'Trier' by Orwin in 1592). A minor detail, but it substantiates the theory Marlowe's play premiered at an earlier date, and also illuminates Marlowe's overall perception of Faustus' journey.

The original 1587 German Spies book contained the following description of Trier:

"[…] for that he chiefly desired to see this town because it looked so Gothic, and the monuments thereof; but he saw not many wonders, except one fair palace that was built of brick so strong that they need fear no enemy; then he saw a church, wherein was buried Simeon[←] and the Bishop Popo[≥]: their tombs are of most sumptuous, large marble stone, closed and joined together with great bars of iron […]"[938]

This paragraph configures with the original source from which this information was extracted, i.e. under 'Treveris' (Trier) in Schedel's *Weltchronik*:

'layers' "equivalent" to the "streets straight forth" encircling the bay.
§ The poet Virgil.
[937] Henry Jones, *English Faustbook; Critical Ed.*, p. 43.
[←] "A Greek Hermit (AD 1028–35) who occupied the East Tower of the Porta Negra." (Jones) Ibid. n. 1260, p. 215.
[≥] "Archbishop Poppo (1016–47) restored and expanded the proto-cathedral after its devastation by the Normans." (Jones) Ibid. n. 1262. We note there is another 'Popo': St. Poppo, a Benedictine Abbot born in Flanders. (978–1048) He helped to revive the Benedictine Rule in many of the major abbeys, including St. Maximinus of Trier.
[938] *English Faustbook; Critical Ed,* pp. 128, 214–215.

"Where there can be seen stupendous works at the palace, with what the walls in the form {and likeness} of those in Babylon, made from terracotta bricks, that are as firmly manned today♦, and no art◊ has broken them".[939]

In the English 1592 *Faustbook*, there are additional details inserted by P.F. who may have visited Trier, i.e. the bishop's palace, the number of the walls and the existence of defence trenches, (although P.F. did not specify if these trenches⁺ are dry ditches or wet moats):

"[…] for that he chiefly desired to see this town and the monuments thereof; but he saw not many wonders, **except one fair palace that belong unto the bishop, and also a mighty large castle** that was built of brick, **with three walls and three great trenches**, so strong that **it was impossible for any prince's power to win it**; then he saw a church, wherein was buried Simeon and the Bishop Popo: their tombs are of most sumptuous, large marble stone, closed and joined together with great bars of iron […]"[940]

Trier boasts of many Roman ruins and the remnants of an imperial palace. The town was also important as the seat of an ancient Episcopal see; presumably, the bishops had their separate place of residence. These facts corroborate the new additions inserted by P.F.

We propose that a simple typographical error for 'Trier' in the first English *Faustbooks* (c.1588–89, now lost) may have compounded the initial confusion between 'Trier' and 'Trent'. The English name for the town of Trier is 'Treves', and it is conceivable P.F. originally included this English name in his translation, but the 'V' type was unfortunately set as 'Λ'. Inverted type was a common printing error. Considering that lowercase V's were generally printed as 'U', the word would read as 'Trenes'. Readers with discernment might catch this fault, or, they could mistake the word as an eccentric Latin variant of 'Trent'.▼

Marlowe, if he acquired an early copy of the English *Faustbook* with this inaccuracy, undoubtedly researched geographical texts to discover which of the two towns the translator

---

♦ Or, '… are as maintained as firmly today,'.

◊ I.e 'artifices', 'artefacts' or engines of war. 'Arte' could also be the plural of 'joint': 'artus'. Hence this could also read "and none of the joints {of the masonry work} have been broken".

[939] *English Faustbook; Critical Ed.*, p. 44. "Videtur enim ibi stupendi operas palatium, quod instar Babylonici muri, ex cocto latere factum, tantae firmitatis hodie manet, ut nulla arte frangi queat"

⁺ Kocher writes; "Probably as many Renaissance strongholds had wet ditches as had dry ones, and theorists saw advantages and disadvantages in either. A dry ditch had to be as wide as a wet ditch and deeper. Depths of 30 or 40 feet and widths of 60 or 70 feet were recommended." *Marlowe; Thought, Learning, Character*, p. 250.

[940] *Doctor Faustus; A Critical Ed.*, pp. 128, 214–215. Bold text indicates P.F.'s additions.

▼ This odd misprint that could be mistaken for either city would explain why the latter editions of the English *Faustbook* vary in their spellings of Trier: Owrin (1592) returned to the German word 'Trier' to avoid further confusion, while the Windet (1608) and Allde (1610) editions contain 'Trēt' in favour of the word 'Trent'.

originally intended. Henry Jones proposes the playwright may have used Braun and Hohenberg's *Civitates orbis terrarum*, a common reference book in its day. The *Civitates* featured the *same description* of Trier as in Schedel's *Weltchronik* quoted above, but also contained the following information for the town of Trent (Tridentum):

> "Trent, a city on the boundary of the Venetia province, it is founded upon planes between mountains, with stockade walls of [hewn / polished] stone ... Streams of water placidly flow into the urban area by walls from the East [aqueducts?] ... Mountains circle the area, ... and precede all other heights, that said, the highest summit of the mountains touch heaven."[941]

Trent was also a powerful Episcopal principality similar to Trier, and had their particular tradition concerning an individual named 'Simon'. St. Simon of Trent was a child murdered by Jews in 1475 during the Easter season according to contemporary ecclesiastical investigations.

Marlowe may have found it difficult to make a selection between the two towns for various artistic reasons *and decided to combine them.*[†] Considering that the same description of Trier from the *Weltcronik* was also in the *Civitates orbis terrarum*, the image of neo-Babylonian walls combined with P.F.'s account of impenetrable trenches in the English *Faustbook* may have appealed to him when remembering his previous recreation of the moats of Babylon in *Tamburlaine, Part Two*. In one of Marlowe's university texts, Abraham Ortellius' *The Theatre of the World*, the city of Babylon is surrounded by an unnamed body of water: inspired by Plutarch's *Life* of Alexander the Great, Marlowe renamed the Babylonian moats 'Lake Limnasphaltis' after the ancient tar pits of the Euphrates basin.[942] Hence, he devised a fitting dramatic tableau for the Apocalyptic Tamburlaine considering that the Book of Revelation predicts the 'Whore of Babylon' shall be destroyed by fire with as much fury as a great millstone that is cast into the sea. (Apoc. 18.) Turning to Trent for *Doctor Faustus*, Marlowe simply continued this apocalyptic concept. With his sardonic eye, he may have noticed that the words 'Simon' and 'Bishop Popo' in the *Faustbook* were targets for punning i.e. 'Simon Magus' of simony notoriety and 'Papa' or 'Pope' as bishop of Rome, and thereby had their own unique affiliation with Trent, the site of the famous Catholic Council (1545–1563) of the Counter Reformation. It is not difficult to imagine Marlowe toying with an allegory of the Catholic Church, (condemned by Protestants as guilty of simony), symbolically ensconced within the mountainous stronghold of Trent protected with its 'Babylonian-flint wall', i.e. the Council's anti-Protestant decrees, and ready to kindle 'divine' fire to smite all opposition. The description in the *Civitates* of waters flowing from the East into Trent could have struck Marlowe as allegorically apropos: i.e. as a symbol of the eastern wisdom-waters of Eden flowing into the

---

[941] Ibid. p. 43. "Tridentum, civitas in finibus Venetiae provinciae, inter montes in planitie posita est, muris vallate lapideis ... Influit placide in urbem per muros ab Oriente aque rivus ... Montes circum se habet ...et ita praealtos, vt dicas, coelum summa montium cacumina contingere."
[†] This obviously contributed to the Trier /Trent editing confusion evident in the latter English *Faustbooks*. (See n. ▼ above.)
[942] *World of Christopher Marlowe*, pp.160, 214, 218.

Church, or rather from an atheistic view, the 'arrogant' Catholic doctrine that only the Roman Church contains the full measure of heavenly truth. We observe the 'waters' are conducted through manmade aqueducts, which may have been symbolically reinterpreted by Marlowe, i.e. that clerics in the Church purposely *invented* this creed of 'assured perfection of faith' to ensure loyalty. These images are particularly apt for *Doctor Faustus* with its undercurrents of religio-philosophical crusading. *In sum*, Marlowe retained the name of Trier in keeping with the *Faustbook*, yet slyly included a covert sarcastic reference to Trent and the Catholic Church in general for his personal aberrant satisfaction.

The second major anomaly in Faustus' voyage continues this anti-Catholic association, i.e. lines 16–18: "From thence to Venice, Padua, and the rest, / In midst of which a sumptuous temple stands / That threats the stars with her aspiring top." In the *Faustbook*, two great buildings may be directly related to Marlowe's reference of a "temple": St. Mark's in Venice, and St. Anthony's cloister in Padua:

> "[...] He wondered not a little at [...] the sumptuous church standing therein called St. Mark's; how all the pavement was set with coloured stones and all the rood or loft of the church was double gilded over.

> [...] then saw he the worthiest monument in the world for a church, named St. Anthony's Cloister, which for pinnacles thereof and the contriving of the church, hath not the like in Christendom."[943]

However, there is a separate church in the *Faustbook* with a similar description of a magnificent steeple, the Cathedral of Notre Dame of Strasbourg, the pinnacle of which was completed in 1439:

> "[...] From thence he went to Strasbourg, where he beheld the fairest steeple that ever he has seen in his life before, for on each side thereof he might see through it, even from the covering of the minster to the top of the pinnacle, and it is named one of the wonders of the world; [...]"[944]

Nevertheless, we cannot assume Marlowe is specifically indicating any of these three churches according to his flat generalisation "and the rest" : perhaps he is referring to *all* the towns Faustus visited in the *Faustbook*? Faustus praises many churches during his travels! Hence, we may deduce "and all the rest / in midst of which a sumptuous temple stands" is Marlowe's generalisation of the Catholic Church as the founding Mother of all these cathedrals of Christendom, the foremost 'temple' of the institutionalised religions of Christianity that with its authority "threats the stars with her aspiring top". It is an apt parallel with the description of Trent in the *Civitates*, i.e. "[...] Mountains circle the area, ...and precede all other heights, [...]

---

[943] *Doctor Faustus; A Critical Ed.*, pp. 129–130.
[944] Ibid. p. 134.

the highest summit of the mountains touch heaven," and Marlowe's image of the impenetrable Catholic fortress of 'Triertrent'; "Environed round with airy mountain-tops, / [...] / Not to be won by any conquering prince." *In fine,* Faustus' arrival in Catholic Rome has been thoroughly introduced in atheistic philosophical detail.

Mephistopheles escorts Faustus directly to the Pope's private chambers, and the devil proceeds to play the tour guide, explaining the great monuments Faustus can expect to encounter in the Eternal City:

> *Faustus*: I hope his Holiness will bid us welcome.
> *Mephistopheles*: Tut, 'tis no matter man. We'll be bold with
> his good cheer.
> And now, Faustus, that thou mayest perceive
> What Rome containeth to delight thee with,
> Know that this city stands upon seven hills
> That underprops the groundwork of the same.
> Just through the midst runs flowing Tiber's stream,
> With winding banks that cut it in two parts,
> Over the which four stately bridges lean,
> That makes safe passage to each part of Rome.
> Upon the bridge called Ponte Angelo
> Erected is a castle passing strong,
> Within whose walls such store of ordonnance are,
> And double cannons, framed of carved brass,
> As match the days within one complete year—
> Besides the gates and high pyramides
> Which Julius Caesar brought from Africa.

[III. I. 26–43]

This proposed Grand Tour of Rome is generally consistent with the *Faustbook,* however there are two minor alterations. First, Marlowe excludes the information the castle of St. Angelo doubles as a fortress with a secret escape tunnel for the Pope leading from the Vatican should he be in danger, but adds a new detail regarding the great "ordonnance" the castle contains. Second, Marlowe mentions the cannons of the castle are made from brass, a favourite poetic metaphor for the indestructible and invincible. If we consider the pope mentioned in the *Faustbook,* i.e. Pope Sixtus V (1585–1590), we can begin to piece together Marlowe's reasoning for these changes. Pope Sixtus faced a papacy that was in tight financial straights after the pontificate of his predecessor, Gregory XIII, and collected a considerable treasure hoard within the castle of St. Angelo by creating new taxes, increasing the number of saleable offices, and other creative financial tactics, although he distributed half of one million ducats to the poor before his death.[945] Marlowe may be referring to this great accumulation of wealth within the castle walls. "Ordonnance" not only refers to an orderly arrangement, (i.e. the designs of architecture), and

---

[945] Joseph S. Brusher, S. J., *Popes Through the Ages* (San Rafael: Neff-Kane, 1980), p. 454.

simultaneously to 'ordnance', (cannons, military supply, etc.), but also to 'ordinance', which can signify either a legal regulation or a religious rite. Hence, the playwright is criticising a pope who apparently accreted an unbelievable fortune contrary to the rule of poverty: mammon supersedes spirituality! The "brass cannons" could also be a biting allusion to the immutability of Catholic *Canon* Law and 'infallible' members of religious orders. Hence, Marlowe's simoniacal symbol of the Catholic 'Triertrent Fortress' emerges in Rome!

Faustus is elated by this proposed itinerary, and orders Mephistopheles to commence the tour:

> *Faustus*: Now, by the kingdoms of infernal rule,
> Of Styx, Acheron, and the fiery lake
> Of ever-burning Phlegethon, I swear
> That I do long to see the monuments
> And situation of bright splendent Rome.
> Come, therefore, let's away!

[III. i. 44–49]

Bevington and Rasmussen suggest Faustus' exclamation "[...] takes the form of a Virgilian journey through the underworld, no doubt inspired by Mephistopheles' account of the wonders of Rome,"[946] but we must not forget Faustus *has* actually been to hell and back in Act II following the performance of the Seven Deadly Sins, although this voyage is not performed on stage. Considering Faustus is referring to *pagan images* of the Hellish kingdom, the Devil obviously charmed a hell that he *desired to see* where "his ghost could be with the old philosophers", also corresponding with the vision of the delusional Inferno in the *Faustbook*. Bevington and Rasmussen describe Faustus' exuberant cry as an oath, although it is reminiscent of his authoritative incantation earlier in the drama: is the scholar once more deluded into believing he can command Mephistopheles with his magic? If he is, he is mistaken, for Mephistopheles did not comply with this order immediately, but persuades Faustus to relax and amuse himself with the proceedings in the Vatican. Faustus decides he is "content" with this idea, not realising he is being wound around the devil's claw and thereby becomes his tool for mischievousness in taking gleeful satisfaction that the Pope and his court are unaware of their presence. Mephistopheles charms Faustus with a spell of invisibility, allowing him to wreak havoc on the Pope's feast.

A trumpet sounds and the Pope enters followed by the Cardinal of Lorraine and attending friars. As the Pope presents the Cardinal with sumptuous dishes and the choicest wine, Faustus snatches them away to the consternation of the diners. The Cardinal believes he knows the answer to the mystery: "My lord, it may be some ghost, newly crept out of / purgatory, come to beg a pardon of your Holiness." [III. i. 73–74.] The Pope agrees, and commands that the friars prepare to recite a "dirge"⸰ to appease their spectral visitor. The Pope makes the sign of the

---

[946] *Doctor Faustus; A and B Texts*, n. 45–6, p. 164.
⸰ I.e., the Pope has ordered the friars to sing the matins prayer from the Office for the Dead, as the first word of the antiphon is 'dirige' or 'direct' from Psalm 5:9 – "Conduct me, O Lord, in thy justice: because

cross, and Faustus deals him a box on the ear, and all the court exit the stage in a tumult. The friars return, not to chant a Requiem for the 'deceased soul', but to intone an Anathema of Excommunication! Obviously, the sarcastic mocking of the *Faustbook* with its conflation of the various Catholic ceremonies did not escape Marlowe's attention:

> *Faustus*: Come on, Mephistopheles. What shall we do?
> *Mephistopheles*: Nay, I know not. We shall be cursed with bell, book, and candle.
> *Faustus*: How? Bell, book, and candle, candle book and bell,
> Forward and backward, to curse Faustus to hell.
> Anon you shall hear a hog grunt, a calf bleat, and an ass bray,◊
> Because it is Saint Peter's holy day.
>
> *Enter all the Friars to sing the dirge.*
>
> *Friar*: Come, brethren, let's about our business with good devotion.
> [*The Friars*] *sing this*:
> Cursèd be he that stole away his Holiness' meat from the table.
> *Maledicat Dominus! {May the Lord curse him.}*
> Cursèd be he that struck his Holiness a blow on the face.
> *Maledicat Dominus!*
> Cursèd be he that took Friar Sandelo a blow on the pate,
> *Maledicat Dominus!*
> Cursèd be he that disturbeth our holy dirge.
> *Maledicat Dominus!*
> Cursèd be he that took away his Holiness' wine.
> *Maledicat Dominus!*
> *Et omnes sancti. {And all the saints.}* Amen.
>
> [*Faustus and Mephistopheles*] *beat the Friars,
> and fling fireworks among them, and so exeunt.*

[III. i. 81–100]

Harry Levin observed that Faustus ironically compares the Anathema ceremony with the 'forward and backward' 'anagrammatization rite' performed during his earlier incantation.[947] The reference to "Friar Sandelo" indicates Faustus has just struck one of the friars on the head, but we

---

of my enemies, *direct* my way in thy sight." A dirge was also sung for Requiem ceremonies.
◊ This may indicate three friars return to sing the 'dirge'.
[947] Harry Levin, *The Overrecher: a Study of Christopher Marlowe* (Cambridge, Mass.: Harvard University Press, 1952), p. 120, in *Doctor Faustus; A and B Texts*, n. 85, p. 166.

notice this action occurs directly following the line highlighting the injury inflicted on the Pope, suggesting the blows may be correlated. "Sandelo" may be an allusion to 'sandell' or 'sandal', a derogatory Protestant criticism of the Franciscans. This order professed vows of poverty, however, they were often accused of violating their oath and living a hypocritical luxurious lifestyle, visibly displayed by the wearing of sandals: the only order professing poverty permitted to do so.[948] Hence, the friars in the drama may also be referring to the Pope, i.e. Sixtus V, one of the few popes elected from the Franciscan order.[949]

At this point in the drama, the original printing of the A Text features a chorus, which modern editors conclude was misplaced and therefore often reinsert this section as an introduction to Act IV. Hence, Act III in various reprints concludes with the 'Silver Goblet' comic scene featuring Robin and Rafe. Robin succeeds in stealing the cup from a tavern vintner, and the two tricksters play a series of pranks while they endeavour to conceal it from its furious owner. To frighten the Vintner, Robin proceeds to conjure Mephistopheles with the stolen book, reciting Latin and Greek nonsense parodying Faustus' incantation. In the first draft of the A Text, Mephistopheles appears onstage and throws fireworks into their midst. The sight of the devil frightens Robin into returning the stolen artefact with the cry "[…] forgive me now, and I'll never rob thy library more," (referring to the conjuring book he stole from Wagner). Mephistopheles, not pleased with this farcical disturbance caused by the clowns, turns them into an ape, a bear and an ass respectively. This may be a continuation of the "hog, calf and ass" chanting the "dirge" in Rome. However, this scene appears to be omitted, and the Text contains an alternative conclusion with an imperious speech written for Mephistopheles:

> *Mephistopheles*: Monarch of hell, under whose black survey
> Great potentates do kneel with awful fear,
> Upon whose altars thousand souls do lie,
> How am I vexed with these villains' charms!
> From Constantinople am I hither come
> Only for pleasure of these damnèd slaves.

[III. ii. 29–34.]

Mephistopheles, hearing the blasphemous incantation, albeit garbled, appears at this summoning only to discover he made a wasted trip for a team of rogues whose souls are already on the broad path to Hell. This second ending extends Faustus' journey around the world as the demon infers they were in Constantinople when the two schemers began to conjure, (however, Marlowe did not include a scene featuring the Sultan's Court in the drama).[‡] Robin is intimidated by the demon and sheepishly offers him a tester, or sixpence, to at least pay for his supper in recompense for travelling a long distance to no avail, hoping this will suffice: an ironic gesture as he has 'tested' the devil's 'patience'. Mephistopheles is insulted and before he leaves, transforms Robin into an ape, and Rafe into a dog. (The Vintner exited the scene earlier in

---

[948] *Doctor Faustus; A and B Texts*, n. 94, p. 166.
[949] *Popes Through the Ages*, p. 454.
[‡] This shall be discussed in more detail shortly with the scene featuring Helen of Troy.

fright.) The two schemers are not troubled by their predicament, Robin is gleeful he will receive many apples and nuts, and consoles Rafe that as a dog he will never go hungry as his head will never leave a porridge pot. When considering the allegorical significance of the comic sections represented in succession, we have now departed entirely from the realm of the academic world. Robin and Rafe, (and the Vintner, depending on the scene), are reduced to the level of mere brutes with only their scheming tricks and their stomachs set as their sole priorities. This outcome is a fell omen when we recall Faustus finally became satisfied with magic when Lucifer presented him with a book that contained all the information to teach him how to transform into any shape that pleased his fancy. Has Faustus plumbed all the intellectual depths and sold his soul cheap, for mere 'apples', 'nuts' and 'porridge'?

Act IV, in most modern editions, as mentioned, commences with a chorus acquainting the audience with Faustus' adventures. Now, having viewed the courts of kings and the wonders of the world, he returns home to his friends, recounting the marvels he experienced, and expounds on all the mysteries of astrology. Thus, achieving international fame and recognition, Emperor Charles V requests his presence at the Imperial court to prove the reports of his magic arts.

The beginning of Scene One in Act IV is not set in blank verse, and with just cause: Faustus has completely forgotten his former arrogant ideals to conquer the world with his magic and new atheistic ideology, and is now humbly scraping to please his Imperial Majesty. The Emperor asks, in lengthy prose, if it is possible that he may witness the power of his necromantic arts, and Faustus graciously responds in the affirmative, pledging to do whatever he can out of "love and duty". [IV. i. 16.] The Emperor then proceeds to impart his request in blank verse, a rhythm befitting his ambitious desire; a rare display of this metre in Act IV, Scene One of the A Text:

> Then, Doctor Faustus, mark what I shall say.
> As I was sometime set
> Within my closet, sundry thoughts arose
> About the honour of mine ancestors—
> How they had won by prowess such exploits,
> Got such riches, subdued so many kingdoms
> As we that do succeed or they that shall
> Hereafter possess our throne shall,
> I fear me, never attain to that degree
> Of high renown and great authority.
> Amongst which kings is Alexander the Great,
> Chief spectacle of the world's pre-eminence,
> The bright shining of whose glorious acts
> Lightens the world with his reflecting beams—
> As when I hear but motion made of him,
> It grieves my soul I never saw the man.
> If, therefore, thou by cunning of thine art
> Canst raise this man from hollow vaults below
> Where lies entombed this famous conqueror,
> And bring with him his beauteous paramour,

Both in their right shapes, gesture, and attire
They used to wear during their time of life,
Thou shalt both satisfy my just desire
And give me cause to praise thee whilst I live.

[IV. i. 19–42]

Faustus explains he cannot perform certain feats, for example, literally raising the dead, (alas, further evidence magic has proved equal to the other 'shallow' academic sciences such as medicine!) but he can conjure spirits in the shapes of those whom he desires to see. A Knight in the court mocks the scholar, first by criticising his unimpressive demeanour contradicting the grandiose stereotypes associated with a powerful conjurer, [l.12.] and now by dismissing this proposal of raising spirits from the underworld, exclaiming that if Faustus is telling the truth, he is another Actaeon transformed into a stag by Diana.* Faustus marks the taunt and replies, "No, sir, but when Actaeon died, he left the horns for you," a quip inferring horns associated with cuckoldry. [63–64] The haughty Knight exits in a scoffing huff, and Faustus proceeds with his tricks to fulfil the Emperor's request, muttering aside he will be avenged on the Knight for his ill-mannered interruptions. Mephistopheles escorts Alexander and his consort onto the stage for the Emperor's viewing. True to the *Faustbook*, he looks for the famous wart on the consort's neck, and is pleased that this one legendary tale has been proven accurate. Faustus then requests that the troublesome Knight be summoned to the court, who is duly rewarded with a pair of horns charmed onto his head in remuneration for his slighting comments. The Emperor asks for the spell to be released and Faustus complies, explaining he thought this would amuse His Majesty, but not before he imparts one last word of warning to the Knight: "And, sir knight, hereafter speak well of scholars." [IV. i. 94] The Emperor is pleased with these magic demonstrations and promises Faustus a generous reward before he leaves the court. In Act IV, we observe Faustus' descent towards destruction continues. He has forgotten his former plans for cosmic conquest and slips into his former status as a poor scholar obsequious to the elite. We notice the Knight's observation regarding Faustus' appearance suggests the scholar has not fulfilled his oath to raise the dress code for poor students to the dignity of "silk". His only assets remaining are his knowledge and magic, but these he has reduced to performing cheap tricks at the expense of the Knight. His actions mirror the slapstick antics of Wagner, Robin and Rafe.

Taking his leave of the Emperor's court, Faustus encounters a horse dealer who desires to buy his steed. Faustus agrees to sell it to him for the forty dollars offered and warns him not to ride the horse into water. The dealer exits the stage and Faustus apparently has returned to his study. He momentarily enters a phase of spiritual crisis:

What art thou, Faustus, but a man condemned to die?
Thy fatal time doth draw to final end.
Despair doth drive distrust unto my thoughts.

---

* Actaeon was a mythical huntsman who dared to claim he was a more skilful hunter than the goddess Diana. One day he happened to intrude on her privacy while she was bathing: incensed, she transformed him into a stag and his own hounds ripped him to shreds.

Confound these passions with a quiet sleep.
Tush! Christ did call the thief upon the cross;
Then rest thee, Faustus, quiet in conceit.
Sleep in his chair.

[IV. i. 139–144]

The divinity scholar committed the sin of presumption by purposely delaying his conversion and making no timely preparation to amend his life, believing that Christ will forgive him automatically at the last moment similar to the Good Thief on the cross. However, Faustus has forgotten that the thief acknowledged his sins, including the punishment he deserved, and made an Act of Faith in Christ thus confessing his purpose of amendment that merited him immediate entry to Paradise. "[…] we receive the due reward of our deeds; but this man hath done no evil. And he said to Jesus: Lord, remember me when thou shalt come into thy kingdom." (Luke 23:41–42.)

Faustus falls asleep to banish thoughts of his impending woe, and the horse dealer returns all wringing wet, complaining that Faustus duped him. Thinking the Doctor was hiding some rare quality of the horse by telling him to avoid water, he immediately did the opposite and rode the horse straight into a pond. The steed reverted to its true form … a bundle of hay. He attempts to wake Faustus, but instead, pulls off his leg, a hoax accomplished by magic. The 'cripple' wakes up and orders Mephistopheles to call the officers. The horse dealer is terrified and begs Faustus to accept forty dollars more not to call the constable. Faustus agrees, and chuckles to himself that he still had his leg and will profit handsomely from this little scheme. Considering that Faustus did not desire wealth in Act I, and recently received a handsome reward from the Emperor, he has no immediate necessity for money. "Doctor Fustian", as the horse dealer renamed him, thus continues to congratulate and amuse himself with the various pranks his 'intellect' can devise.

Wagner enters and announces the Duke of Vanholt desires Faustus to visit him. Faustus and Mephistopheles call upon the Duke, and they entertain him and the Duchess.√ Observing the Duchess is expecting a child, Faustus offers to provide whatever delicacies she desires, and she requests a dish of ripe grapes currently out of season. Faustus appears disappointed that she would be content with this trivial feat, but he complies nevertheless and sends Mephistopheles away for the desired dainty, adding that if she wanted him to accomplish a more difficult task, he would comply. When she is curious to understand how he could grant her wish, he informs her that it is summer in other parts of the world, such as India, Sheba, and the Eastern countries, thus it is a trifling matter for his spirit to fetch this fruit. The Duke and the Duchess are "beholding" to Faustus for the courtesy, and Act IV concludes as they promise Faustus a reward. This final scene is set in prose, and not in blank verse, indicating Faustus, as a servile scholar, remains in a position of ignobility as their social inferior. Of interest, we notice Marlowe stresses the details of India, Sheba, with his additional reference to the East, thus the origin of the fruit is of

---

√ This is understood from the context of the scene. It is possible this action was once included in the A Text, but was lost when the MS was fragmented at one point in time as we observe it is considerably shorter than the B Text. See *Doctor Faustus; A and B Texts*, p. 182.

significance. Faustus is also presenting his new atheistic philosophy and idealism to the Duke and Duchess, but they are incapable of appreciating all that he is prepared to present to them and they are content with mere superficial tokens. Their philosophical incomprehension and narrow academic vision prove to be a great disappointment. This is similar to Faustus' encounter with the Emperor; he obviously expected Faustus to entertain him with an audacious feat, and was duly presented with a vision depicting the glories of the pagan world, which could also allegorically represent Faustus' new atheistic principles. Nevertheless, Faustus remained in the position of a subservient commoner.

Marlowe was presenting the academic chasm in Elizabethan England between the aristocracy and those educated to obtain a living. Riggs observes the universities produced graduates learned in the various sciences that were "[...] hard to do, morally dubious and smacked of artisan labour,"[950] to fill the labour vacuum of the burgeoning British Empire. Hence, the aristocracy relied on skilled individuals who could accomplish the work deemed beneath their social standing. Marlowe cleverly depicts this social interdependency in *Tamburlaine, Part One* when Mycetes, the weak king of Persia, is surprised that Lord Meander has taken the trouble to become well versed, and therefore relies on him to defend the kingdom from Tamburlaine's attacks:

> *Mycetes*: And 'tis a pretty toy to be a poet.
> Well, well, Meander, thou art deeply read;
> And having thee, I have a jewel sure.
> Go on my lord, and give your charge, I say;
> Thy wit will make us conquerors today.

> [II. ii. 54–58]

Hence, scholars are 'toys' and 'jewels' to please the elite and amuse them, or be used in the national interest of the kingdom when the occasion arises, and thus Faustus discovers he remains forever bound by the confines of his inferior status.

Act V commences with Wagner commenting on Faustus' unusual behaviour. His master has just bequeathed to him all his worldly goods, indicating he is preparing for death, and yet is banqueting royally with the students of the university in an unprecedented manner as though death was nonexistent — a prime example of the activity of those who do not hope in nor spiritually prepare for the Resurrection: "Let us eat and drink, for tomorrow we shall die." (1 Cor. 15:32) Faustus enters with three Scholars, and the First student asks Faustus to grant them a special favour by conjuring the spirit, Helen of Troy, and thereby prove the report she was once the most beautiful woman in the world. Faustus agrees, in blank verse, fulfilling his one noble promise to aid his friends:

> Gentlemen,
> For that I know your friendship is unfeigned,
> And Faustus' custom is not to deny

---

[950] *World of Christopher Marlowe*, p. 165.

The just requests of those that wish him well,
You shall behold that peerless dame of Greece
No otherways for pomp and majesty
Than when Sir Paris crossed the seas with her
And brought the spoils to rich Dardania.
Be silent then, for danger is in words.

[V. i. 17–25]

Mephistopheles apparently summons a *vision* of Helen that passes over the stage, for Faustus orders the students not to utter a sound, which is consistent with magic spells that feature vision enchantments. The three students praise her beauty when she exits, and the First Scholar exclaims before they leave:

> Since we have seen the pride of nature's works
> And only paragon of excellence,
> > [*Enter an Old Man*]
> Let us depart; and for this glorious deed
> Happy and blest be Faustus evermore.

[V. i. 33–34.]

Faustus replies, "The same I wish to you," [35] an ironic conclusion to their visit. The students wish the 'blessings' of good fortune to Faustus, but the allusion to spiritual grace is not neglected. The audience is aware Faustus is *not* blessed and is heading straight to hell if he will not convert, therefore his reply to the students is ominous when this is taken into account: he desires them to follow his infernal atheistic path to Hell. Already, they are swayed by his vision of Helen, and the Old Man who entered during their conversation, is concerned for Faustus, who is leading many to perdition:

> *Old Man*:
> Ah, Doctor Faustus, that I might prevail
> To guide thy steps unto the way of life,
> By which sweet path thou mayest attain the goal
> That shall conduct thee to celestial rest!
> Break heart, drop blood, and mingle it with tears —
> Tears falling from repentant heaviness
> Of thy most vile and loathsome filthiness,
> The stench whereof corrupts the inward soul
> With such flagitious crimes of heinous sins
> As no commiseration may expel
> But mercy, Faustus, of thy Saviour sweet,
> Whose blood alone must wash away the guilt.

[V. i. 36–47]

Faustus responds to the Old Man's charitable warning, and is suddenly struck with despair as he momentarily rises from his spiritual torpor:

Faustus:
　　Where art thou, Faustus? Wretch, what hast thou done?
　　Damned art thou, Faustus, damned! Despair and die!
　　Hell calls for right, and with a roaring voice
　　Says, 'Faustus, come! Thine hour is come.'
　　　　Mephistopheles gives him a dagger.
　　And Faustus will come to do thee right.
　　　　[*Faustus prepares to stab himself.*]
Old Man: Ah, stay, good Faustus, stay thy desperate steps!
　　I see an angel hovers o'er thy head,
　　And with a vial full of precious grace
　　Offers to pour the same into thy soul.
　　Then call for mercy and avoid despair.
Faustus: Ah, my sweet friend, I feel thy words
　　To comfort my distressèd soul.
　　Leave me a while to ponder on my sins.
Old Man: I go, sweet Faustus, but with heavy cheer,
　　Fearing the ruin of thy hopeless soul. [*Exit.*]

[V. i. 48–62]

In the midst of his torment, the demon hands Faustus a dagger encouraging him to despatch his life without further ado: this is one of Marlowe's distinctive touches to the legend. We see an earlier example of 'honourable hara-kiri' in *Tamburlaine, Part One* when the Median Lord, Agydas, attempts to dissuade Zenocrate from betraying her betrothed Arabian Lord for the love of Tamburlaine. The incensed conqueror announces Agydas' approaching execution by having a naked dagger presented to him, and Agydas stoically decides it is a better thing to die a less painful death with honour by his own hand rather than submit to the barbaric cruelties Tamburlaine would devise for him. [III. ii.] Faustus immediately assumes he is damned, and decides it is better he should die quickly there and then to pay his impending debt to Hell and escape this mental torture than wait for the terrible death the demons would inflict upon him. Mephistopheles, naturally, desires his soul and presents him with the dagger; hence, we discover the source for the temptations inflicted upon Faustus regarding the halters and swords in Act II. The Old Man stops Faustus from committing suicide and encourages him to focus on God's mercy: grace is there for the repentant heart filled with hope. Faustus endeavours to "ponder on his sins" but he will not trust in God's clemency and Hell battles with Heavenly grace within him. However, rather than choose one or the other, he considers how he may escape death entirely and not face Eternity, and Mephistopheles immediately takes this opportunity to turn on Faustus who is showing signs of regret:

393

Faustus: Accursèd Faustus, where is mercy now?
    I do repent, and yet I do despair.
    Hell strives with grace for conquest in my breast.
    What shall I do to shun the snares of death?
Mephistopheles: Thou traitor, Faustus, I arrest thy soul
    For disobedience to my sovereign lord.
    Revolt, or I'll in piecemeal tear thy flesh.
Faustus: Sweet Mephistopheles, entreat thy lord
    To pardon my unjust presumption,
    And with my blood again I will confirm
    My former vow I made to Lucifer.
Mephistopheles: Do it then quickly, with unfeigned heart,
    Lest greater danger do attend thy drift.
        [*Faustus cuts his arm and writes with his blood.*]

[V. i. 63–75]

    Faustus quickly rejoins the forces of Hell, and this time he is resolute for his blood had not congealed the second time. He orders the demon to torment the Old Man who dared to convert him. Hence, Faustus wilfully desires to comply with his former promise to destroy those who follow Christ. Mephistopheles explains the Old Man's faith makes it impossible for him to snatch his soul, but that they can physically torment him, although they will accomplish little by doing so. Faustus then makes one last request of the demon, which has become one of the classic scenes in *Doctor Faustus*:

Faustus: One thing, good servant, let me crave of thee
    To glut the longing of my heart's desire:
    That I might have unto my paramour
    That heavenly Helen which I saw of late,
    Whose sweet embracings may extinguish clean
    These thoughts that do dissuade me from my vow,
    And keep mine oath I made to Lucifer.
Mephistopheles: Faustus, this, or what else thou shalt desire,
    Shall be performed in twinkling of an eye.

       Enter Helen.

Faustus: Was this the face that launched a thousand ships
    And burnt the topless towers of Ilium?
    Sweet Helen, make me immortal with a kiss.
    Her lips sucks forth my soul. See where it flies!
    Come, Helen, come, give me my soul again.

Here will I dwell, for heaven be in these lips,
And all is dross that is not Helena.

Enter Old Man.

I will be Paris, and for love of thee
Instead of Troy shall Wertenberge be sacked,
And I will combat with weak Menelaus,
And wear thy colours on my plumed crest.
Yea, I will wound Achilles in the heel
And then return to Helen for a kiss.
O, thou art fairer than the evening air,
Clad in the beauty of a thousand stars.
Brighter art thou than flaming Jupiter
When he appeared to hapless Semele,
More lovely than the monarch of the sky
In wanton Arethusa's azured arms;
And none but thou shalt be my paramour.
                    Exeunt [Faustus and Helen].

Old Man: Accursèd Faustus, miserable man,
          That from thy soul exclud'st the grace of heaven
          And fliest the throne of His tribunal seat!

Enter the Devils. [They menace the Old Man.]

Satan begins to sift me with his pride.
As in this furnace God shall try my faith,
My faith, vile hell, shall triumph over thee.
Ambitious fiends, see how the heavens smiles
At your repulse and laughs your state to scorn!
Hence, hell! For hence I fly unto my God.
                    Exeunt [different ways].

[V. i. 82–119]

Faustus finally selects his demonic paramour. In the *Faustbook*, the scholar philanders with numerous mistresses before he ultimately decides upon Helen, but Marlowe evidently wrote a 'chaste' role for his character of Faustus who loses all interest in satisfying his lust when Mephistopheles trivialises the sacrament of matrimony. He concentrates on other matters — until he casts his gaze upon the Grecian beauty.   Marlowe therefore considered Faustus' preference for the legendary queen particularly important, explaining why he did not include the episode of the Sultan's harem: *Faustus must have no other paramour* but *Helen*.*

When we consider the Gnostic Simon Magus legends, this obsession with the Grecian Queen is comprehensible. The Antichrist magician declared that his consort Helena, or Luna, was 'Wisdom' incarnate, the 'mother of all things' who was brought from the 'highest heaven'.[951] Thus, Faustus symbolically proclaims he has found in Helen the fullness of the wisdom and philosophy that he sought and ultimately sold his soul for. She is the epitome of all the 'eastern gold' he could acquire, for everything else is but "dross" to him. However, it is an unholy union, for his selection of the demonic Helen is an inversion of the Book of Wisdom (7:29; 8:2): "For [wisdom] is more beautiful than the sun, and above all the order of the stars: being compared with the light, she is found before it. [...] Her have I loved, and have sought her out from my youth, and have desired to take her for my spouse, and I became a lover of her beauty." W.W. Greg observed that Faustus' hope and opportunities for salvation suddenly dissipates following his union with Helen for he has shunned the appeal of the Old Man and wilfully commits the heinous sin of demonality.[952] With this last scandalous act, the Old Man recognises that Faustus is now forever accursed as he continues to reject grace and flies in the Face of God. In the final scene of the drama, Faustus bewails his fate with the students, but confirms he cannot hope for forgiveness. Hence, Marlowe specifically intended that Faustus' damnation be *irreversibly sealed* in this scene with Helen.

---

* Empson argues that this scene once existed in the drama, but was cut by the censor as a diplomatic gesture when Elizabeth I was attempting to open trade relations with the Sultan of Turkey. (*Faustus and the Censor*, pp. 62–63.) Yet, one would assume the same material would be repressed in the printings of the English *Faustbook* for the same reason if this was the case. Alternatively, there is considerable evidence suggesting Marlowe deliberately omitted the Harem Scene in both the A and B Texts — our observations pertaining to the Helen Scene mentioned above is one example. Concerning the intricate philosophical undercurrents in *Doctor Faustus*, Marlowe would have undermined his intentions by including the mockery of the Harem. Faustus yearns to study cultures from the East and learn the secrets of Eastern kings that differ from Western civilisation, it would not make sense for him to mock a culture that he has idealised. Hence Marlowe concentrated on Faustus' journey to Rome in particular; since Faustus rejected traditional Western / Christian theology and philosophy, it is logical this centre of Christendom should receive the brunt of his attacks. From the viewpoint of production tactics, we also propose Faustus' antics in the harem would be a stale joke at this point in time following the production, *Tamburlaine, Part Two*. In Act IV, Scene III, the conqueror presents to his soldiers the Turkish Concubines of his fallen foes as a reward for their bravery. When the Concubines beg him to spare their honours Tamburlaine retorts, "Save your honours! 'twere but time indeed, / Lost long before ye knew what honour meant." [86–87] It would not be a wise decision to include material in *Doctor Faustus* that could be perceived by spectators as uninventive borrowing from a previous production.

[951] I.e. in the Pseudo-Clementine Literature; see Palmer and More, *Sources of the Faust Tradition*, pp. 10–15.

[952] W. W. Greg, 'The Damnation of Doctor Faustus,' Modern *Language Review* XLI, (1946), reprint in John Jump, ed., *Marlowe* Doctor Faustus; *A Casebook* (London: Macmillan and Co. Ltd., 1969), pp. 86–88. We note this time Helen has a physical body and Faustus actually speaks to her, so she is not a charmed vision. As Mephistopheles has confirmed earlier in the drama that he is a devil fallen from Heaven and imprisoned in Hell, there are no 'Middle Spirits': therefore, a demon has come in the guise of Helen.

Theologically, a soul may yet be saved at the last moment if there is true contrition, but we propose Faustus has not accepted *any* demon for his mistress — *Satan* has come in the guise of Helen to claim Faustus as his own. When Mephistopheles assures Faustus he can bring him any woman he desires, he relates they may be as *"wise as Sheba"*, or as *"beautiful as Lucifer before he fell"*. Lucifer was the most intelligent and glorious of all the angels: the association with the legendary beauty attributed to Helen is not difficult to discern. When the students previously praised the vision of Helen, they recognised her as a *"heavenly* beauty", [V.i. 30], language reminiscent of Lucifer's angelic magnificence before the Fall, and they call her the "pride of nature's works / And only paragon of excellence" [31–32], which parallels Lucifer's state of perfection as a created spirit before his sin of pride.

Second, we observe there is an unusual reversal of genders when Faustus admires the beauty of Helen. He exclaims 'she' is brighter than Jupiter, thus casting himself in the feminine role of Semele. According to myth, Semele begged Jupiter, (or Zeus) to allow her see him in his full glory as a deity, with the result the lightning emanating from him consumed her. Faustus continues this reversal of genders when he compares himself to Arethusa, the forest nymph who fled the amorous advances of Alpheus, the river god. The goddess Artemis transformed her favourite nymph into a fountain for her protection. George Sandys notes Alpheus may be considered the "monarch of the skies" as his lineage descends from the gods associated with the sun.[953] Thus, Faustus recognises hidden masculine qualities in Helen that are not outwardly perceptible. These gender reversals may be directly related to Lucifer's appearance with Beelzebub earlier in the drama.[†] The fiend remarked that his companion is his "dam" or "dame" thus confirming his own dominant masculine attributes, not to mention his affirmation that homoerotic relationships are the norm with him, for, Beelzebub is conventionally perceived as a masculine entity. We observe that Mephistopheles previously prepared Faustus for an unconventional union by dismissing the concept of marriage as a "toy", which would include all that traditional marriage holds sacred, i.e. the union between a man and a woman.

Yet, this strange gender mutation and eradicating conventional boundaries did not conclude there. Faustus describes Arethusa as "wanton" or lascivious, suggesting, contrary to the myth, she is *not* attempting to escape an amorous relationship. Who else could be a "monarch of the sky" but the Greek goddess of the moon and the protector of Arethusa — Artemis, twin sister of the sun god, Apollo? This reference to Artemis would certainly be apropos on two levels; first, that the name of 'Lucifer'= 'Light-bearer' could also ingeniously indicate the moon as it reflects or 'bears' the light from the sun, although Lucifer's name is usually affiliated with the 'morning star', or the morning appearance of the planet Venus. Second, the reference to Simon Magus and his consort "Helena-Luna" places certain emphasis on the moon. Is Marlowe also suggesting a lesbian relationship between Faustus-Arethusa and Luciferic Helen-Artemis? If this is so, Marlowe is symbolically referring to the island of Lesbos (now Lésovs) where the Greek personal lyric was developed. From thence came several of the finest ancient poets, such as Terpander (7th century BC), who introduced the seven-stringed lyre and composed many *nomes* to honour the god Apollo. Terpander is considered the father of Greek lyric poetry and of

---

[953] *Doctor Faustus; A and B Texts*, n. 109, p. 191.

[†] It is an intriguing speculation that the actor who was cast as Lucifer may also have played the role of Helen.

Western classical music. The poet Alcaeus (c.620 – d.? BC) invented the Alcaic stanza. Sappho, (c. 7th century BC) invented the Sapphic strophe and her poetry influenced many Greek poets. However, many of her poems express her affection and love for women, thus as the Greek poet Anacreon (570?–485?BC) implied, the name of the island connoted female homosexuality. The modern terms *sapphism* and *lesbianism* are derived from these sources. Faustus therefore has metaphorically experienced the highest form of Greek lyric poetry in addition to attaining Helen's lunar 'wisdom'.

We detect Faustus experienced the gamut of every type of relationship: heterosexual, (Paris and Helen of Troy), homosexual (Faustus with Luciferic 'Helen' remasculinised as Jupiter), and lesbian (Arethusa and Artemis). Finally, through these relationships we detect a metamorphosis to a hermaphroditical state: Faustus is male, but also perceives himself as female (e.g. Semele). Lucifer is first introduced in the drama as masculine, but here in Act V he is predominantly female. Lucifer, nevertheless, as a demonic spirit is genderless for his conventional masculine attributes are symbolic of his authority as Prince of Hell. As Faustus originally desired to become a spirit in shape and quality, which technically would include the total rejection of human gender, is this relationship with Lucifer his attempt to achieve this ultimate goal? We note this strange mixture of the 'male' and 'female' element, bears a striking resemblance to the hermetic / occult philosophy of alchemy that maintained it was possible to artificially transmute base materials into a purer substance. Metals, minerals, elements and substances that were used in this pseudo-science were classified as 'male' or 'female' and symbolised in alchemical charts as the 'sun' and 'moon' respectively. When these contrasting elements were brought together in various experiments to make gold, the most valuable of metals, the result was represented by a hermaphroditical figure. Hence, the actual cause of Faustus' damnation is his wilful decision to join Satan and commit the sin of *spiritual fornication* as indicated in Scripture to finally find the 'gold' he craved. He also breaks the First Commandment and worships Satan by metaphorically praising him as being greater then God and His lightning bolts, (under the poetic metaphor of Jupiter), and thus confirms Satan in his obstinate conviction that he will not be overcome although he was cast from Heaven in this same manner as Christ relates: "I saw Satan like lightning falling from heaven." (Luke 10:18) Mephistopheles borrows the phrase "twinkling of an eye" when explaining how swiftly he can fulfil the scholars' desire in bringing him 'Helen', an interesting choice of expression. The phrase can be found in 1 Cor. 15: (51–52) when St. Paul describes the Last Judgement and the Resurrection of the Dead: "Behold, I tell you a mystery. We shall all indeed rise again: but we shall not all be changed. In a moment, in the twinkling of an eye, at the last trumpet: for the trumpet shall sound, and the dead shall rise again incorruptible: and we shall be changed." St. Paul is referring to the resurrection of the dead on the Last Day. The damned will receive corrupt bodies that are 'not changed' from their earthly filth, and the just souls will receive glorified bodies as the concupiscence of the flesh, the effects of Original Sin, will be wiped away. Mephistopheles inverts this passage, implying Faustus will be 'glorified' through Helen, but the scene presents an obverse reality. Faustus experiences Mephistopheles' rendition of the Resurrection of the Dead, for through this union with Helen, Faustus has 'been changed'— his spiritual alchemy experiment has now made him irreversibly corrupt both physically and spiritually.

This interpretation of his union with Helen explains why Faustus' attack upon the Old Man is grievous and perceptibly contributes to his ultimate damnation unlike his other transgressions, serious though they may be, i.e. his buffoonery in Rome and his trickery with the horse dealer. When he plagues the Pope and his court he is symbolically attacking Christ through his Vicar, but Christ informed his apostles that all sins may be forgiven, including those committed against Him, but this clemency will not extend to the sins committed against the Holy Spirit:

> "Therefore I say to you: every sin and blasphemy shall be forgiven men, but the blasphemy of the Spirit shall not be forgiven. And whosoever shall speak a word against the Son of man, it shall be forgiven him: but he that shall speak against the Holy Ghost, it shall not be forgiven him, neither in this world, nor in the world to come." (Matt. 12:31–32.)

The unforgivable sin committed against the Holy Spirit is the loss of faith, and a persistent refusal to reconvert to God. The Old Man appears as a symbol of Faith, and Faustus rejects his sound advice. The moment he hardens his heart in his old life of vice, the scholar ventures so far as to command the devil to maliciously attack the Old Man as he now desires to become one, in body and soul, with the Evil One. Hence, Marlowe may be demonstrating that Calvinist ideology propagating the predestination of Hell for certain souls, by *God's volition,* rather than by man's free will, is an illogical doctrine.

Now we arrive at that fateful night, December 24, twenty-four years after the signing of the first pact in Scene Two. Faustus enters the stage with the Scholars in a deeply agitated state of mind, and the first Scholar asks what troubles him. Faustus replies that he now "dies eternally" [V. ii. 4], (not in blank verse), and feverishly imagines fiendish shapes arriving to claim him, "Look, comes he not? Comes he not?" [V. ii. 5] The other Scholars believe he is ill from his "over-solitary" existence [l. 8], or from imprudent over indulgence, a curable "surfeit". [l.10] Faustus discloses it is his "surfeit of deadly sin" [11] that is now overwhelming him, a reiteration of the "surfeits" of the "golden" Forbidden Fruit of Knowledge alluded to in the Prologue. The students attempt to remind him of God's infinite mercy, but Faustus is adamant in his belief it is too late:

> *Faustus*: But Faustus' offence can ne're be pardoned. The
> serpent that tempted Eve may be saved, but not Faustus.
> Ah, gentlemen, hear me with patience, and tremble not at
> my speeches. Though my heart pants and quivers to
> remember that I have been a student here these thirty
> years, O, would I had never seen Wertenberge, never read
> book! And what wonders I have done, all Germany
> can witness, yea, all the world, for which Faustus hath
> lost both Germany and the world, yea, heaven itself —
> heaven, the seat of God, the throne of the blessed, the
> kingdom of joy — and must remain in hell for ever. Hell,

ah, hell for ever! Sweet friends, what shall become of
Faustus, being in hell for ever?
Third Scholar: Yet, Faustus, call on God.
Faustus: On God, whom Faustus hath abjured? On God,
whom Faustus hath blasphemed? Ah, my God, I would
weep, but the devil draws in my tears. Gush forth blood
instead of tears, yea, life and soul. O, he stays my tongue!
I would lift up my hands, but see, they hold them, they hold them.
All: Who, Faustus?
Faustus: Lucifer and Mephistopheles. Ah, gentlemen! I gave
them my soul for my cunning.
All: God forbid!

[V. ii. 15–38]

Faustus, now in the final grips of despair, is unable to repent. He paraphrases the biblical passage warning man to beware of the fleeting glories of the finite world, that they are not worth the Eternal price attached to them: "For what doth it profit a man, if he gain the whole world, and suffer the loss of his own soul? Or what exchange shall a man give for his soul?" (Matt. 16: 26) Faustus attempts to pray and appeal to God for mercy, but his tears, tongue and hands are held bound, a tell-tale sign he is doomed according to the traditional view that witches and wizards who sold their souls shall never show signs of repentance.[954] The demons at this point cease to threaten Faustus with torture when he shows signs of regret, for he already sealed his damnation in the previous scene, and therefore they have the power to restrict him in this manner as all opportunity for salvation is withdrawn from him by his own free will and lack of faith.

He discloses to his friends he ventured so far as to write a deed in blood confirming the forfeiture of his soul, and the time for the fulfilment of this condition of the contract is now at hand. The First Scholar asks why he did not tell them sooner as they could have sought for divines to pray for him; Faustus explains he often thought of repentance, but that the devils immediately tormented him, threatening they would tear him to shreds and claim body and soul if he desired redemption. He finally urges them to leave and save themselves. The Third Scholar offers to stay with his doomed friend with the help of God's grace and see him through to the end, but the Second prudently advises not to tempt God and to come into the adjoining room with them where they will all pray for Faustus. He begs them to pray for him, but entreats them not to come into his study regardless of any noise they may hear as nothing they can do will rescue him. They finally make their farewells and the Scholars exit the scene as the clock strikes, thus introducing one of the finest soliloquies of Elizabethan drama:

The clock strikes eleven.

Ah, Faustus,
Now hast thou but one bare hour to live,

---

[954] *Doctor Faustus; A and B Texts*, n. 31, p. 193.

And then thou must be damned perpetually.
Stand still, you ever-moving spheres of heaven,
That time may cease and midnight never come!
Fair nature's eye, rise, rise again, and make
Perpetual day; or let this hour be but a year,
A month, a week, a natural day,
That Faustus may repent and save his soul!
O lente, lente currite noctis equi!
The stars move still; time runs; the clock will strike;
The devil will come, and Faustus must be damned.
O, I'll leap up to my God! Who pulls me down?**
See, see where Christ's blood streams in the firmament!
One drop would save my soul, half a drop. Ah, my Christ!
Ah, rend not my heart for naming of my Christ!
Yet will I call on him. O, spare me Lucifer!
Where is it now? 'Tis gone; and see where God
Stretcheth out his arm and bends his ireful brows!
Mountains and hills, come, come and fall on me,
And hide me from the heavy wrath of God!
No, no! Then will I headlong run into the earth.
Earth, gape! O, no, it will not harbour me.
You stars that reigned at my nativity,

** Marlowe may have a particular motif in mind drawn from Geffrey Whitney's *Choice of Emblems* (1586) when he composed this line. It features a man attempting to leap up to the heavens with one winged arm outstretched, while the other is manacled to a stone that prevents him from rising. The emblem was printed with the following poem: 'Poverty obstructs the progress of the most gifted minds'.

One hand with wings, would fly unto the stars,
And raise me up to win immortal fame,
But my desire, necessity still bars,
And in the dust doth bury up my name:
That hand would fly, th'other still is bound,
With heavy stone, which holds it to the ground.

My wish, and will, are still to mount aloft.
My want, and woe, deny me my desire,
I show their state, whose wit, and learning, oft
Excel, and would to high estate aspire:
But poverty, with heavy clog of care,
Still pulls them down, when they ascending are.

(*World of Christopher Marlowe*, p. 243.)
The publisher of the 1604 A Text used this image as the front-page emblem.

Whose influence hath allotted death and hell,
Now draw up Faustus like a foggy mist
Into the entrails of yon labouring cloud,
That when you vomit forth into the air,
My limbs may issue from your smoky mouths,
So that my soul may but ascend to heaven.
Ah, half the hour is past! [*The watch strikes.*]
'Twill all be past anon.
O God, If thou wilt not have mercy on my soul,
Yet for Christ's sake, whose blood hath ransomed me,
Impose some end to my incessant pain.
Let Faustus liven in hell a thousand years,
A hundred thousand, and at last be saved.
O, no end is limited to damnèd souls.
Why wert thou not a creature wanting soul?
Or why is this immortal that thou hast?
Ah, Pythagoras' *metempsychosis*, were that true,
This soul should fly from me and I be changed
Unto some brutish beast.
All beasts are happy, for, when they die,[∞]
Their souls are soon dissolved in elements;
But mine must live still to be plagued in hell.
Curst be the parents that engendered me!
No, Faustus, curse thyself. Curse Lucifer,
That hath deprived thee of the joys of heaven.
                    The clock strikes twelve.
O, it strikes, it strikes! Now, body, turn to air,
Or Lucifer will bear thee quick to hell.
                    Thunder and lightning.
O soul, be changed into little waterdrops,
And fall into the ocean, ne're be found!
My God, my God, look not so fierce on me!

Enter [*Lucifer, Mephistopheles, and other*] *Devils.*

Adders and serpents, let me breathe a while!
Ugly hell, gape not. Come not, Lucifer!
I'll burn my books. Ah, Mephistopheles!

            [*The Devils*] *exeunt with him.*

[V. ii. 65–123]

[∞] Line divided as in B1 Text; as one line in A1.

The hour of death strikes, and Faustus' study is transformed to depict the chamber of Eternal Judgement, and is remarkably accurate according to theological descriptions. One of the greatest curses self-inflicted upon his life was the time stipulation he agreed to in the pact, for according to theologians, such as St. Gregory, God conceals the time of death, that the soul may remain in readiness; "We are uncertain of death, that we may always be found prepared for it."[955] Faustus, trusting in his time guarantee, conveniently postponed all preparation for his inevitable Judgement: already we have seen him presume he may be forgiven at the last moment similar to the Good Thief. Throughout his life, Faustus banished all thoughts of amending his ways while time remained, preferring to seek his happiness on earth and thereby became a habitual sinner — but now his conscience is thrown into turmoil. "When distress cometh upon them, they will seek for peace, and there shall be none. Trouble shall come upon trouble." (Ezech. 7:25, 25) St. Augustine describes this tempest of the conscience that afflicts the unprepared at their final moments, "A just punishment [...] to him who, being able was not willing to save himself, that when he is willing he will not be able."[956] St. Alphonsus Liguori would later continue this meditation when writing ...

> "[...] with what terror will the miserable sufferer whose conscience has been neglected be seized and confounded, when he finds himself overwhelmed with sins, and fears of judgement, hell, and eternity! Into what confusion will he be thrown by these thoughts, when he finds his head weak, his mind obscured and assailed by the pains of approaching death! He will confess, promise, weep; he will seek mercy from God, but without knowing what he does. And in this storm of agitation, remorse, grief, and terror, he will pass to the next world. [...] It is well said by a certain author, that the prayers, tears, and promises of the dying sinner are like the tears and promises of a man attacked by his enemy, who holds a dagger to his throat to rob him of his life."[957]

Faustus starts at every shadow, imagining the demons dragging him to Hell and bemoans the day he set foot in the university that introduced him to the occult arts. In his soliloquy he begs the stars to stand still and the sun, "fair nature's eye", to rise again and grant him additional time for repentance: an ironic request when he had time and numerous opportunities to repent while grace was yet offered to him. "Delay not to be converted to the Lord, and defer it not from day to day; for His wrath shall come on a sudden, and in the time of vengeance He will destroy thee." (Ecclus.5:8–9)

He then utters a Latin verse, Marlowe's free translation from Ovid's *Amores*: "O run, slowly, slowly, horses of the night!" In the original poem, the speaker ruefully begs the goddess of the dawn, Aurora, to delay her arrival by reminding her of the reluctance she experienced

---

[955]   St. Alphonsus Liguori, *Preparation for Death: Considerations on Death, Judgement, Heaven and Hell* [Abridged], (Illinois: Tan Books and Publishers, Inc. 1982), p. 29.
[956]   Ibid. p. 34.
[957]   Ibid. p. 37.

when forced to part from her lover and so delay the same inevitable parting with his dear Corinna.[958] Marlowe previously referred to this line by Ovid in *Dido, Queen of Carthage* when pederastic Jupiter admires his doting Ganymede,° thus there is a striking similarity with Faustus and his androgynous rendezvous with the male-female Luciferic Helen. Donald C. Baker noted that Faustus' cry to restrain the oncoming dawn in this manner betrays his lingering love for sensual and aesthetic pleasure,[959] an apt observation considering Helen also symbolises the magician's quest for pagan wisdom and culture. How fitting Faustus equates his approaching doom with the arrival of Aurora's threatening horses! He has refashioned "Wertenberge" into a second Troy, after all. "Wertenberge" became the centre of his existence when he redrafted the world map in his mind, the new *axis mundi* on which lie Heaven, Earth, and the Inferno.[960] Thus, for Faustus during his final moments, this is an appropriate symbol of the traditional centre of the world, Jerusalem, where the Last Judgement shall take place in the Valley of Josaphat, or Kidron, that separates the city from the Mount of Olives: "Let them arise, and let the nations come up into the valley of Josaphat: for there I will sit to judge all nations round about. […] Nations, nations, in the valley of destruction: for the day of the Lord is near." (Joel 3:12,14) Armageddon has descended upon Trojan Württemburg!

Faustus concludes he "must be damned", while he paradoxically attempts to "leap up to my God". He remains attached to his sins, devoid of all faith, and thus is pulled back to earth in fulfilment of the prophecy of Amos as mentioned; "[…] though they may climb to heaven, thence will I bring them down." (9:2) Faustus then sees the Blood of Christ appearing in the firmament, and he calls out, begging for a drop of Blood to save him. Jump proposes the vision fades because Faustus has once more called on Lucifer to spare him and thus he loses one last opportunity for salvation.[961] However, we propose Christ's Blood actually *appears in vengeance*. It is not a salving stream promising deliverance, but an image reminiscent of Marlowe's metaphorical weapons and streamers lifted to the heavens as an Apocalyptic prelude to an avenging battle:

<u>*Dido, Queen of Carthage*</u>:

Dido: […] only Aeneas' frown
     Is that which terrifies poor Dido's heart.
     Not bloody spears, appearing in the air,
     Presage the downfall of my empery,

---

[958] *Doctor Faustus; A and B Texts*, n. 74, p. 195.
° "As, I, exhal'd with thy fire-darting beams, / Have oft driven back the horses of the Night, / Whenas they would have hal'd thee from my sight." Dido, [I.i. 25–27]
[959] Donald C. Baker, *Classical Journal*, LV (1959), pp. 126–128, in *Doctor Faustus; A and B Texts*, n. 74, p. 195.
[960] Jan Knott, *The Bottom Translation: Marlowe and Shakespeare and the Carnival Tradition*, Daniela Miedzyrzecka and Lillian Valle (trans.) (Evanston: Northwestern University Press, 1987), p. 3, in Garrett A. Sullivan Jr., 'Geography and Identity in Marlowe,' *Cambridge Companion to Marlowe*, p. 240.
[961] *Doctor Faustus; A and B Texts*, n. 82, p. 195.

[IV. iv, 115–118]

Tamburlaine, Part One:

Tamburlaine: And when she sees our *bloody colours spread*,
    Then Victory begins to *take her flight*,
    Resting herself upon my milk-white tent.

[III. iii. 159–160]

Tamburlaine: Then, when *the sky shall wax as red as blood*,
    It shall be said I made it red myself,
    To make me think of naught but blood and war

[IV. ii. 53–55]

Tamburlaine, Part Two:

Tamburlaine:
    Hast thou not seen my horsemen charge the foe,
    [...]
    Dying *their lances with their streaming blood*,

[III. ii. 103–105]

Tamburlaine:
    Come, let us march against the powers of heaven,
    And set black *streamers in the firmament*,

[V. iii. 48–49]

This image of Christ's Blood appearing as an omen of damnation is relatively rare, but it is not contrary to theology. Scripture states and theologians write that during the Last Judgement, Christ will appear with the symbols of His Passion, particularly the cross. This will be a sign of joy for the blessed, and of woe for the damned. St. Chrysostom declared to harden sinners who will not convert; "The nails will complain of thee, the wounds will speak against thee, the cross of Christ will preach against thee."[962] Hence, the sacrifice of Christ's Blood spilled as He hung on the cross will also reproach the reprobate, especially if the sinner eats or drinks the Flesh and Blood of Christ unworthily according to St. Paul; "Therefore whosoever shall eat this bread, or drink the chalice of the Lord unworthily, shall be guilty of the body and of the blood of the Lord. [...] For he that eateth and drinketh unworthily, eateth and drinketh judgement to himself, not

---

[962] *Preparation for Death*, p. 109.

discerning the body of the Lord."[+] (1 Cor. 27,29) Now, the reprobate sacrilegiously invokes Christ's sacrifice, bringing Christ's wrath upon his head rather than clemency, and may be symbolised by this verse in the Apocalypse:

> "And the third angel followed them, saying with a loud voice:
> If any man shall adore the beast and his image, and receive his character
> in his forehead, or in his hand; he also shall drink of the *wine of the wrath*
> of God, which mingled with *pure wine* in the *cup of his wrath*,[*] and shall
> be tormented with fire and brimstone in the sight of the holy angels, and
> in the sight of the Lamb." (14:9–10)

Although Faustus did not receive the sacrament of Christ's Blood, he is unworthily invoking It without a true spirit of amendment, and therefore the Blood appears to represent God's anger, not forgiveness — especially when he seeks mercy from the Beast; "O, spare me, Lucifer!" Immediately, he sees the indignation of God as Supreme Judge:

> "Therefore is the wrath of the Lord kindled against his people,
> and he hath stretched out his hand upon them, and struck them: and the
> mountains were troubled, and their carcasses became as dung in the midst
> of the streets. For all this his anger is not turned away, but his hand is
> stretched out still." (Isaiah 5:25)

Faustus then begs the mountains and hills to fall on him, and attempts to hide beneath the earth thus recalling these verses of the Apocalypse:

> "And the kings of the earth, and the princes, and tribunes, and
> the rich, and the strong, and every bondman, and every freeman, hid
> themselves in the dens and in the rocks of mountains: And they say to the
> mountains and the rocks: fall upon us, and hide from the face of him that
> sitteth upon the throne and from the wrath of the Lamb." (6:15–16)[←]

[+] Compare with the following:

> [+] "Amen, amen, I say unto you: Except you eat the flesh of the Son of man, and drink his blood, you shall not have life in you. He that eateth my flesh, and drinketh my blood, hath everlasting life: and I will raise him up in the last day. For my flesh is meat indeed: and my blood is drink indeed. He that eateth my flesh, and drinketh my blood, abideth in me, and I in him." (John 6: 54–57) Compare with (Matt. 26: 26–28), (Mark 14: 22–23) and (Luke 22: 19–20).

[*] Italics added.

[←] Compare with the following:

> [←] "Enter thou into the rock, and hide thee in the pit from the face of the fear of the Lord, and from the glory of his majesty. The lofty eyes of man are humbled, and the haughtiness of men shall be made to stoop: and the Lord alone shall be exalted in that day. [...] And they shall go into the holes of rocks, and into the caves of the earth from the face of the fear of the Lord, and from the glory of his Majesty, when he shall rise to strike the earth" (Isaias 2: 10–11, 19)

The earth refuses to harbour him, and he appeals to the stars and the clouds, as Bevington and Rasmussen relate:

> "Faustus prays that the planets of his horoscope (whose positions at the time of his birth determined his fate) may now suck him up into a cloud, much as moisture is exhaled from the earth by the sun, where his earthly body may be violently expelled in a thunderbolt and his soul thereby freed to ascend to heaven."[963]

Faustus heaps sin upon sin by turning to astrology for help, rather than Divine Providence. He also attempts to escape his responsibility by placing the blame for his actions onto the influence of the stars. Ironically, the powers he desired to wield over the cosmos utterly fails him: the sun and the spheres refuse his command to halt their progress, the mountains and the earth will not move, and the clouds will not consume him, nor the lightning. He now perceives the futility of magic and the pagan philosophy that cost him his soul, yet he continues to cling to his ideals until it is too late to abandon them. He mourns that gift of an immortal soul, and regrets that it will not be dissolved into the elements nor transmigrate in a type of reincarnation as Pythagoras taught, thus Faustus continues to reject Christian theology although the heavy hand of God is already upon him! He has become the Evil Thief at Christ's left hand, with no fear of God at the last moment, and is therefore deserving of the Good Thief's reproach: "But the other [robber] answering, rebuked him, saying: neither dost thou fear God, seeing thou art under the same condemnation? And we indeed justly, for we receive the due reward of our deeds, [...]" (Luke 23: 39–41) Faustus at length curses himself, and especially Lucifer / (Helen?) whom he blames for depriving him of heaven. The twelfth hour strikes, and Faustus begs his body to

---

← "And the high places of the idol, the sin of Israel shall be destroyed: the bur and the thistle shall grow up over their altars: and they shall say to the mountains: cover us; and to the hills: fall upon us." (Osee: 10:8)

← "But Jesus turning to them, said: Daughters of Jerusalem, weep not over me; but weep for yourselves, and for your children. For behold, the days shall come, wherein they shall say: Blessed are the barren, and the wombs that have not borne, and the paps that have not given suck. Then shall they begin to say to the mountains: Fall upon us; and to the hills cover us. For if in the green wood they do these things, what shall be done in the dry?" (Luke 23: 28–31) Here, Christ is declaring a two-fold prophecy. First, the coming destruction of Jerusalem by the Romans in punishment for the Jews rejecting Him as the Messiah, which he had already foretold to his disciples, (Luke 19:41–44; 21: 20–36), in fulfilment of the people's wish that the guilt of Christ's death be laid upon them: "His blood be upon us and upon our children." (Matt. 27:25) All this tribulation would herald Christ's sacrifice for mankind and the dawn of His Church established under the New Testament, the time of the "green wood" and of mercy. Second, He foretells the Day of Judgement and the Last Day of the Church on earth, the "dry wood" and time of wrath. In other words, 'If these things foretell the beginning of the Church and the time of grace, what shall the latter days bring when time shall cease and Judgement draws near?'

[963] *Doctor Faustus; A and B Texts*, n. 89–95, p. 196.

dissolve into the air and his soul into drops of water — he places his last hope in the doctrine of Epicurus — and thus when he announces he will burn his books, the traditional renunciation of magic, it is too late. His plea is nothing more than an empty promise made by a condemned man with his neck in a halter who will say or do anything to escape his fate. In terror, he inverts Psalm 21, "O God, my God, look upon me: why hast thou forsaken me?", and thus implores God to turn His face away from him; "Look not so fierce on me!"√ However, he shudders at the asps and serpents that slither from the maw of the Abyss, and cannot face the approach of Lucifer. Finally, the demons carry him body and soul to Hell, and the Chorus concludes the tragic scene:

Enter Chorus:

Chorus: Cut is the branch that might have grown full straight,
And burnèd is Apollo's laurel bough
That sometime grew within this learnèd man.
Faustus is gone. Regard his hellish fall,
Whose fiendful fortune may exhort the wise
Only to wonder at unlawful things,
Whose deepness doth entice such forward wits
To practise more than heavenly power permits. [Exit.]

[V. Ep. 1–8]

Terminat hora diem; terminat author opus.
{The hour ends the day; the author ends his work.}

The Chorus recalls the downfall of Faustus was precipitated by his quest to follow those subjects defined as "deep" and worthy of his time and effort. In the beginning, he discovered every science has its limitations, including magic, as it could not provide the answers he was searching for. When he finally discovers "depth" to the occult arts it is when Lucifer presents him with a metempsychotic tome, and finally when he appears as his androgynous lover, 'Helen', symbolising all pagan art, poetry, and philosophy. The "deepness" he desires is to break the bonds of terror associated with death and the afterlife and achieve transmigration, or attain non-existence as commentators have observed. Faustus should weep and complain of attending the university with its emphasis on Greek and Roman studies! "O, would I had never seen Wertenberge, never read book!" Had he not attended the university he may not have been introduced to the philosophy that led him to reject his Christian culture: Atheism and Christianity cannot coexist, and thus he was tormented by doubts and incapable of discerning Truth. The very subjects that captivated his mind compelled him to self-destruction. The "unlawful things" of paganism, i.e. Epicureanism, transmigration, homosexuality contained in the Latin and Greek classics may only be "wondered at" as the "heavenly powers" do not sanction "practise". Is this 'Wertemberge', or the divinity course of Elizabethan Cambridge?

√ Compare with Christ's cry from the cross: "My God, my God, why hast thou forsaken me?" (Matt. 27: 46)

408

Faustus manages to break free from his lowly status by climbing the academic ranks as a Scholar, and is introduced to a new world of ideas and flattering aspirations with which the university curriculum initially inspired him, only to leave unfulfilled the noble deeds he envisioned. It is a polemical tragedy: in the real world he is forever a Scholar, a servant of the Monarchy and the State, a hero only within the confines of the university and the close circle of his few intimate friends. He sold his soul for imaginary ideals in an effort to achieve greatness, only to capture the illusive shadows of the world for a brief moment. Faustus could also claim the motto Marlowe adopted: the scholars' life fashioned him and also destroyed him.

The Genesis of the B Text

Marlowe's life following the premiere of *Doctor Faustus* was as adventurous as any protagonist portrayed upon the stage. Between the hours of two and three in the afternoon on the 18th September 1589, Marlowe was engaged in an aggressive duel in Hog's Lane with William Bradley, an innkeeper of Bishopsgate.[964] Hearing the commotion, Marlowe's friend and fellow poet-playwright, Thomas Watson, arrived on the scene and drew his sword in an attempt to separate the duellists and preserve the peace. According to the findings of the coroner's inquest, Marlowe withdrew from the fight, but Bradley attacked the bearer of the olive branch, and Watson retreated to avoid conflict until a certain ditch in the street impeded his escape. When Bradley dealt him a fierce cut, Watson retaliated in self-defence and mortally wounded his assailant with a quick thrust to the chest. Although Marlowe had retreated from the duel, he was processed as an accessory to the homicide and subsequently jailed with Watson in Newgate Prison, who is held on suspicion of murder:

> "Upon entering Newgate prison, Marlowe was manacled and taken to the lower dungeon called Limbo, 'a dark Opaque wild room', entered through a hatch from above. He remained in this dark, rat-infested hold until the gaoler came to collect his fee. If and when Marlowe paid the fee, he was moved to one of the upper cells." (Riggs)[965]

Kuriyama relates Marlowe's imprisonment may not have turned out to be completely intolerable. Considering his promptness in raising the necessary funds for his bail, which was paid on October 1st, it would appear he had the means to pay the 'fee' or bribe that would secure him more comfortable conditions and palatable food. "Only indigent prisoners suffered the direst effects of imprisonment, and Marlowe was far from indigent." (Kuriyama)[966]

Before his transfer from the confines of Limbo, Marlowe became acquainted with John Poole, a gentleman from Cheshire with connections in the Catholic underground. Poole was

---

[964] Riggs, *Cambridge Companion to Marlowe*, p. 32. See also the coroner's findings, dated 10th February, 1590 reprinted in Kuriyama, *A Renaissance Life*, p. 206.
[965] *World of Christopher Marlowe*, p. 252.
[966] *A Renaissance Life*, p. 84.

incarcerated in 1587 for counterfeiting, one of the popular subversive tactics of the Catholic rebels as it became a means of fundraising their cause and economically undermining the Protestant government.[967] Apparently, Marlowe gained Poole's trust whereby he disclosed to him the art and intricacies of counterfeiting; decisively, Marlowe realised this information would prove invaluable in the future considering his role as a secret agent for Queen Elizabeth's government. Poole was evidently responsible for Marlowe's association with Ferdinando Stanley, i.e. Lord Strange, heir to the predominantly Catholic earldom of Derby.[968] Poole, related by marriage to Lord Strange, obviously discussed with Marlowe the consequences of the execution of Mary, Queen of Scots. Riggs notes that this course of action strengthened Strange's claim to the throne and "[...] transformed Lord Strange and Henry Percy, the Earl of Northumberland, into the main rallying points for Catholic conspirators."[969] Thus, Poole offered a lucrative opportunity to Marlowe to gather intelligence, and obtain a patron:

> "[...] Lord Strange patronized a company of London actors, and numbered Thomas Kyd among his personal servants. At the time of Marlowe's release, Strange's Men were on the verge of replacing the Admiral's Men as the acting company of choice for talented English playwrights. He had, in short, all the attributes of Marlowe's ideal patron."[970]

On December 3, 1589, Marlowe was released from prison, and Watson was pardoned, the official decree being issued on February 10, 1590. Marlowe did not waste any time in seeking the patronage of Strange and his new acting company, as history displays. Circa 1590, they performed the *Jew of Malta*,[†] a tale of religious intolerance, sanctimonious hypocrisy, voracious greed and revenge: a drama that revels in the Machiavellian policies of the double agent.

In 1591, Marlowe shared a room with Thomas Kyd, which suggests he was attempting, or had succeeded to some extent, to edge his way closer to Lord Strange's circle. Of equal importance, his friendship with Watson introduced him to the social circle of the Earl of Northumberland, a fervent admirer of art and science. His preferred company included fellow academic enthusiasts and controversial freethinkers, as with Sir Walter Raleigh and Thomas Harriot. Kuriyama writes:

> "By surrounding himself with scientists, poets, a superb library, and men like Raleigh who shared his enthusiasms, Northumberland

---

[967] *World of Christopher Marlowe*, pp. 252–253.
[968] Ibid.
[969] Ibid. p. 253.
[970] Ibid. p. 254.

[†] The Prologue in the Jew of Malta announces that the Duke of Guise is dead: this indicates the play was written sometime after 23, December 1588 when the Duke was assassinated. At least one year passed following *Tamburlaine, Part Two* before *The Jew* was written, hence Riggs concludes; "Since the Admiral's Men broke up in 1590–91 and did not share their scripts with Strange's Men, *The Jew of Malta* would have belonged to Strange's Men all along." (Ibid. p. 263.)

effectively created his own university, one which fostered lines of thought and inquiry that were not openly pursued at Oxford or Cambridge. The activities he harboured and encouraged evidently included informal gatherings and freewheeling discussions of topics that interested Northumberland, Raleigh, and others in the group, including questions that may well have seemed, like those proposed by Marlowe's unfortunate Cambridge contemporary Evance, "scandalous, foolish, and opprobrious" to more conventional thinkers. These discussions [...] may have included "lectures" in which a member of the group presented arguments, which the rest responded to, or discussions of occult science and magic, or even experimental conjurations."[971]

Evidently, it was to this company that Marlowe presented his controversial arguments for atheism, and the ensuing discussions may have inspired him to develop his personal philosophy into a formal thesis.

In the latter half of 1591, or early 1592, Marlowe briefly left England for the Continent and travelled to the Dutch town of Flushing, the control of which was ceded to the English in exchange for military aid to combat the Spanish.[972] The town was a well-situated rendezvous centre for couriers and agents in the secret service, a convenient location for counterfeiters and underground printers.[973] Upon arriving in Flushing, Marlowe lodged with Richard Baines, (the same Baines who attended the seminary in Rheims), and a goldsmith named Gifford Gilbert. Apparently, Marlowe decided to put Poole's information to the test, and the three roommates experimented with minting counterfeit coin. Sometime in the latter half of January 1592, they formally launched their new endeavour by introducing a Dutch shilling into circulation. Trouble brewed when Baines developed cold feet and turned himself over to the English authorities the day following the circulation of this shilling. He also turned informant and disclosed Marlowe and Gilbert's involvement in this operation.

Curiously, the Governor of Flushing, Sir Robert Sidney, did not treat this case with the severity one would expect considering the minting of illegal coin merited the death penalty in England, particularly as the culprits admitted to minting English coinage. According to the testimonies of Baines and Marlowe to Governor Sidney, their only intention in producing the coins was to prove the goldsmith's skill, admittedly a poor justification for breaking a law of this magnitude. Nevertheless, Sidney did not question this weak motive, and excused the goldsmith whom he described as a good workman swayed by the same explanation and therefore did not originally intend to engage in a counterfeiting operation.[974] Sidney then makes light of the actual coining, describing it as an amateur endeavour that would not have succeeded bearing in mind the coins were of pewter and therefore easily detected as forged articles. However, it is obvious Marlowe and Baines intimated their connections with the secret service, and perhaps alluded that

---

[971] *A Renaissance Life*, pp. 92–93.
[972] *World of Christopher Marlowe*, p. 274.
[973] Ibid. pp. 274–279.
[974] See Sir Sidney's letter to the Lord Treasurer, Burghley, in *A Renaissance Life*, pp. 209–210. It is dated January 26, 1591, although the year was 1592.

this counterfeit operation was part of their undercover work, (which it probably was). Marlowe mentioned his connections with Lord Strange and Northumberland, and both Baines and Marlowe were "maliciously" accusing each other of planning to defect to the "Enemy or to Rome."[975] Rather than become entangled in matters that concerned the higher powers in office, it would appear Sidney decided it was a safer option to wash his hands of the affair and send the two bungling double-agents back to Lord Burghley, who by then was head of the secret service following the death of Sir Francis Walsingham in 1590. Could this incident be a covert mission that went awry considering no further mention was made of it? (For the time being.) Lord Burghley knew he had a valuable asset in Marlowe and his Catholic connections — it would not be prudent to discard him, especially as a new conspiracy to seize the throne was currently suspected that involved Sir William Stanley, a cousin of Lord Strange.[976]

When Marlowe returned home to London, he did not keep the peace for long. On May 9, 1592, he issued a series of threats to a constable and a beadle, Allen Nicholls and Nicholas Helliot, and subsequently is summoned to appear before the authorities, i.e. Justice Owen Hopton.[977] Marlowe was obliged to enter into a bond of twenty-pounds as a pledge to keep the peace towards Nicholls and Helliot, and bound to appear in the forthcoming sessions of the Middlesex County Court that October. In the interim, Marlowe concentrated on his dramatic writing.

We argue, it was during the first half of 1592, after Marlowe's mishap with the constable and beadle, and before June 23rd when the theatres were closed by order of the Privy Council, that he apparently revised certain sections of *Doctor Faustus*. This theory is founded upon textual evidence from certain plays when presented in the following chronological scenario:

- Strange's Men enjoy a long run at the Rose Theatre; the company revives the *Jew of Malta* on 26th February. Kyd's drama the *Spanish Tragedy* was also revived. These two dramas prove to be the most popular in the company's repertoire until March 3rd, that is, until William Shakespeare, Marlowe's rival, produces his first play for the stage. According to Henslowe's diary, Strange's Men perform the First Part of Shakespeare's *Henry VI*.[978]

- End of May or early June, Marlowe hears of Giordano Bruno's arrest ordered on the authority of the Inquisition in Venice: inspires him to rewrite the Scene in Rome, the Emperor's Court Scene, and other scenes in *Doctor Faustus*. The revised play, (the initial B Text?) possibly performed either early or mid June at the Rose Theatre by Strange's Men who were currently occupying the venue. Curiously we find Jeffes and Orwin in a frenzy attempting to release their famous copy of the London *Faustbook* at this time, (c. May 1592): were they trying to profit from this Faustian *zeitgeist*? (Unfortunately, they encountered difficulties with the censors, and the publication was delayed until December.)[979]

---

[975] Sidney, Ibid.
[976] *World of Christopher Marlowe*, pp. 277, 280.
[977] Ibid. p. 281.
[978] Ibid.
[979] See Appendix Eight, 'The Earliest English Faustbook Editions: Lost and Extant'.

- Shakespeare's *2 Henry VI* is then produced (date ?): certain sections apparently refer to scenes in *Doctor Faustus*. *2 Henry VI* probably performed[980] by Pembroke's Men, a new company now rivalling Strange's Men.
- Pembroke's Men play Marlowe's *Edward II* (date?): certain parts in his new play indicate he was aware Shakespeare referred to *Doctor Faustus* in *2 Henry VI*. Marlowe alludes to one of the *new scenes* in *Faustus* (from the B Text!) and perceptibly plagiarises a scene from *2 Henry VI* to inform his rival he was watching his every move!
- During the latter half of the summer, (July or August?), Robert Greene (?) writes his well-known pamphlet *Groatsworth of Wit Bought With a Million of Repentance* in which he attacks Shakespeare and Marlowe in addition to other poets / dramatists. The pamphlet is published posthumously by Henry Chettle following Greene's death on September 3rd. The pamphlet refers to the 'Machevill' Prologue in *The Jew of Malta*, to distinct sections in *2 Henry VI* and also alludes to *Doctor Faustus*.

Hence, this argument is based upon three important factors: 1) the B Text's remarkable similarity with *The Jew of Malta* in certain scenes, 2) determining if Giordano Bruno's arrest in Venice possibly inspired Marlowe, 3) and the sequence of events pertaining to Marlowe and Shakespeare's dramas mentioned above.

Beginning with the *Jew of Malta*, we find Marlowe has now progressed in his skill as a playwright with regards to his development of the interaction between characters, particularly with comic sections. Rather than segregate the comic scenes from the principle protagonists in separate 'blocks', as seen in the A Text of *Doctor Faustus*, Marlowe weaves the principle character, the Jewish merchant Barabas, into both serious and comic situations with graceful flexibility thus imbuing the drama with a greater degree of cohesion. Marlowe also experimented with the timing of blank verse oration: in the *Jew of Malta*, lengthy speech is generally reserved for moments of import or emotional emphasis as the interaction between characters is dramatically increased in velocity by the insertion of shorter periods of interlocution. Marlowe was also considering the scenic possibilities he could integrate into a drama depending on the venue available. For instance, certain stage instructions and scenic props in *The Jew of Malta* demonstrate Marlowe specifically designed this drama to take advantage of the facilities available at the Rose Theatre where it premiered, i.e. the cellar and trapdoor, the truss, and the upper gallery.[981] Barabas betrays the island of Malta by showing the Turks the underground passages to facilitate their invasion of the fortified city. [V. i. 87–95] He thereby hopes to be avenged of those Christians who dared to confiscate his wealth and property, and eventually his plans succeed when the Turks take the city (by entering through the theatre cellars) and appoint him as the new governor of Malta. However, he realises that when the Turkish army returns to Constantinople, he will be surrounded by wrathful Christians, and therefore decides he will destroy the Turks and obtain amnesty from the former town officials while retaining his post. He plans to lure the invading army into an ambush, and booby traps the 'gallery' of his castle whereby he plots to have the Turkish nobles fall into a vat of boiling oil. His construction work

---

[980] *World of Christopher Marlowe*, pp. 218–282.
[981] Ibid. pp.269–271.

on the gallery was actually written into the directions: *"Enter, above, Barabas, with a hammer, very busy: and Carpenters."* [V. v.]

In the B Text of *Doctor Faustus*, there are sections that demonstrate Marlowe revised certain comic sections in accordance with his new progressive developments in *The Jew of Malta*, i.e. Act IV where the serious protagonists, Faustus and the Duke and Duchess of Vanholt, fluidly interact with the four comic characters of Dick, Robin, the Carter and the Horse Courser. This displays Marlowe was reconsidering the 'block' format of serious vs. comic interludes used in the A Text. Of greater significance is the new detail that the Knight in the Emperor's court, now named Benvolio, appears from a window *set above the stage* — this detail is *specifically included* in the B Text: *"Enter Benvolio above at a window, in his nightcap, buttoning."*[IV. i.] We deduce Marlowe has once more taken advantage of the upper gallery in the Rose Theatre similar to the boiling oil trap in *The Jew of Malta*. Hence, if Marlowe did revise *Doctor Faustus*, these points indicate this revision was undertaken circa the premiere of *The Jew of Malta* and therefore was possibly performed by Strange's Men.

The next significant points to observe are the additions of the anti-Pope "Saxon Bruno" in Acts III and IV of the B Text, and the completely redeveloped Scenes featuring Faustus' adventures in the Vatican and the Emperor's Court. The Catholic Roman monarch and sworn enemy of Luther, Emperor Charles V, is recast as a staunch supporter of Protestantism (!) who dares to appoint "Saxon Bruno" as the successor to St. Peter's chair. The Catholic Pope triumphs over Bruno and holds him captive, but Faustus helps Bruno to escape and return to Germany. The German Emperor later praises Faustus for this brave deed. We observe a deeper divide developing in the B Text between Catholicism, portrayed by comic scenes in the Vatican, and liberal Protestantism, displayed by the Imperial court in Germany.

No historical record exits that mentions an anti-pope named 'Bruno', hence we suspect a veiled allegory was intended. The description of "Saxon Bruno" is similar to the unusual reference of "German Valdes", and therefore it is a decisive clue: this not only indicates Saxony in Germany, but simultaneously 'Saxon' according to the British term. Therefore, this anti-pope is allied with England *and* Germany! Harry Levin suggests this "pope Bruno" was included as a tribute to Giordano Bruno, and he may be correct.[982] Subsequent to his visit in England (1583–1585), Bruno travelled to Wittenberg, Saxony (1586–1588) and was warmly received at the university. Of interest, Bruno delivered an *Oratio Valedictoria* (1588) in which he praised the goddess Sophia, or Wisdom, alluding simultaneously to the Book of Wisdom and eerily to the Simon Magus legend with Helena-Sophia or "Luna" — did Bruno's *Oratio* originally inspire Marlowe's rendition of the famous Helen Scene?

> "Sophia, Wisdom itself, beautiful as the moon, great as the sun, … Her have I loved and sought from my youth, and desired for my spouse, and have become a lover of her form … and I prayed …that she might abide with me."[983]

---

[982] Harry Levin, 'Science Without Conscience,' (1952), in *Marlowe; A Casebook*, p. 147.

[983] Giordano Bruno, *Oratio Valedictoria* (1588), from Frances. A. Yeates, *Giordano Bruno and the Hermetic Tradition*, London (Routledge & Kegan Paul, University of Chicago Press 1964), in Henry Jones, *English Faustbook; Critical Ed.*, p. 6.

Bruno's reputation as an occult scholar and humanist ranked with that of John Dee, and his works were extremely popular in Europe, which also included the academic circles in England. It is possible Marlowe was indebted to Bruno for the development of his atheistic convictions, and became a devoted admirer of his hermetic studies. It is possible he was familiar with Bruno's texts, for all his Italian treatises were actually published in London: *The Ash Wednesday Supper* (1584), *Cause Principle and Unity* (1584), and the trilogy *Expulsion of the Triumphant Beast*, *The Cabala of the Pegasean Horse*, and *The Heroic Furors* (1584–1585).[984] Northumberland and the members of his freethinking academic circle undoubtedly discussed Bruno's work, thereby Marlowe could indulge his admiration for this scholar. For instance, Thomas Watson, who apparently introduced Marlowe to Northumberland's clique, simplified Bruno's occult memory system in his Latin *Compendium of Local Memory*.[985] When Bruno was arrested in Venice on May 22, 1592 and taken to the Inquisition in Rome, this news apparently spurred Marlowe to champion Bruno's liberal cause by casting him as the pontiff of Faustus' new atheistic / Protestant biased sect based in Germany. We note Faustus (Marlowe?!) in the B Text declares he will "lay his life at holy Bruno's feet". [IV. i. 64]

Finally, Marlowe's contemporary, Shakespeare, aids us in determining if the B Text is Marlowe's revision, namely with the premier of his play *Henry VI, Part Two*. Of paramount importance is the scene featuring the wizard Bolingbroke's conjuration of a spirit to supply the Duchess of Gloucester with information. When describing the optimum conditions for conjuring, Bolingbroke draws upon imagery that clearly alludes to the conclusion in *Doctor Faustus* set during the witching hour of midnight when Faustus' soul is finally dragged to Hell thus heralding the destruction of 'Trojan Wertenberge':

> *Bolinbroke*:
> Patience, good lady; *wizards know their times:*
> *Deep night, dark night, the silent of the night,*
> *The time of night when Troy was set on fire;**
> The time when screech-owls cry, and ban-dogs howl,
> And spirits walk, and ghosts break up their graves,
> That time best fits the work we have in hand.

[I. iv. 18–23][986]

Evidence that the B Text was written with a dramatic structure resembling the *Jew of Malta*, considering the facilities of the Rose Theatre, the timing of Bruno's arrest in Venice combined with the addition of the "Pope Bruno" scenes in the B Text, and Shakespeare's

---

[984] Karen De Leon-Jones, 'Forward', in *Triumphant Beast*, pp. vii–x.
[985] *World of Christopher Marlowe*, p. 187.
* Italics added.
[986] W. J. Craig, ed., *The Complete Works of Shakespeare in Twelve Volumes*, vol. vii (Oxford University Press: Reprint, Robert Frederick Ltd., 2002). References to Shakespeare's *2 Henry VI* taken from this source.

deliberate multiple reference to wizards, conjuring, midnight, and the destruction of Troy in *2 Henry VI* could not be coincidental.

To confirm our observations, Marlowe's subsequent drama *Edward II* provides one vital clue. Marlowe obviously borrowed from Shakespeare's *2 Henry VI*[987] thus acknowledging he had attended a performance:

2 Henry VI	Edward II
Queen Margaret: Not all these lords do vex me half so much As that proud dame, the Lord Protector's wife: She **sweeps it through the court** with troops of ladies, More like an empress than Duke Humphrey's wife. Strangers in court do take her for the queen: **She bears a duke's revenues on her back**, And in her heart **she scorns our poverty**. Shall I not live to be avenged on her? Contemptuous **base-born** callot as she is. She vaunted 'mongst her minions t'other day The very train of her worst wearing gown Was better worth than all my father's lands, Till Suffolk gave two dukedoms for his daughter. [I. iii. 78–90]	*Younger Mortimer*: Uncle, his wanton humour grieves not me; But this I scorn, that one so **basely born** Should by his sovereign's favour grow so pert, And riot it with treasure of the realm, While soldiers mutiny for want of pay. **He wears a lord's revenue on his back**, And, Midas-like, he **jets it at court**, With base outlandish cullions at his heels, Whose proud fantastic liveries make such show As if that Proteus, god of shapes, appear'd. I have not seen a dapper Jack so brisk. He wears a short Italian hooded cloak, Larded with pearl, and in his Tuscan cap A jewel of more value than the crown. While others walk below, the king and he From out a window **laugh at such as we, And flout our train, and jest at our attire**. Uncle, 'tis this that make me impatient. [I. iv. 404–421]
Duchess of Gloucester: No; dark shall be my light, and night my day;	*King Edward*: **Know that I am a king; O at that name I feel a hell of grief!** Where is my

---

[987] *World of Christopher Marlowe*, p. 284.

To think upon my pomp shall be my hell.	crown? Gone, gone! And do I remain alive?
[II. iv. 40–41]	[V.v. 91–93.]

However, Marlowe also alludes to an addition in the B Text of *Doctor Faustus*, i.e. the detail of an upper window where members of the nobility mock the apparel of others: "While others walk below the king and he / From out a window laugh at such as we, / And flout our train, and jest at our attire." This line in *Edward II* bears a strong resemblance to Knight Benvolio ridiculing Faustus' dowdy scholarly appearance:

> *Benvolio*: [*Aside, at the window.*]
> Blood, he speaks terribly. But for all that, I do not greatly believe him.
> He looks as like a conjurer as the Pope to a costermonger [i.e. a fruitseller]." [IV. i. 71–73.]

> [*Aside.*] Speak well of ye? 'Sblood, an scholars be such cuckold-makers
> to clap horns of honest men's heads o' this order, I'll ne're trust smooth
> faces and small ruffs more. [...] {*Referring to insignificant, ingratiating
> scholars.*} [IV. i. 164–167]

Marlowe apparently realised that Shakespeare had attended a performance and was referring to his new edition of *Doctor Faustus* in *2 Henry VI*. Thus, the sequence of performances must be as follows: (1) *Jew of Malta*, (2) *Doctor Faustus - B Text*, (3) *2 Henry VI*, (4) *Edward II*.

Finally, *A Groatworth of Wit* attributed to Robert Greene and published posthumously in September by Henry Chettle confirms *Doctor Faustus* and *2 Henry VI* were performed in the spring / summer of 1592 before the theatres were closed in June. Chettle (?) addresses Marlowe, calling him an atheist and follower of Machiavellian policy, alluding to the prologue of *The Jew of Malta*, and also to *Doctor Faustus* by his insinuation to line 155 [V. ii.], i.e. "And see, a threaten'ing arm, an angry brow":

> "Wonder not, [Marlowe] (for thee will I first begin), thou
> famous gracer of Tragedians, that Greene, who hath said with thee (like
> the fool in his heart), There is no God, should now give glory unto his
> greatness: for ... his hand lies heavy upon me, ... and I have felt he is a
> God that can punish enemies. Why should thy excellent wit, his gift, be
> so blinded, that thou shouldst give no glory to the giver? Is it pestilent
> Machiavellian policy that thou hast studied? O peevish folly!"[988]

---

[988] Greene's *Groatsworth of Wit* (Binghamton, N.Y., 1994), 80, in *A Renaissance Life*, pp. 113–114.

Next, Greene / Chettle attacks Shakespeare by lifting passages from *2 Henry VI*[**] and accuses him of being 'swollen with a self-conceit', a comparison to 'do-everything Johannes [Faustus]':

> "… there is an upstart Crow [Shakespeare], beautified with our feathers, that with his Tiger's heart wrapped in a Player's hide, supposes he is well able to bombast out a blank verse as the best of you: and being an absolute Johannes fac totum, is in his own conceit the only Shake-scene in the country."[989]

There is considerable evidence to suggest Marlowe revised *Doctor Faustus* in 1592. The sections that we may consider to be his revisions with a degree of certainty are the scenes in the Vatican, the Emperor's court, the Duke of Vanholt's Court, the following comic scene, and the conclusion as we note attracted Shakespeare and Greene / Chettle thus evincing it was perceived to be inherently novel at the time. This hypothesis, however, poses a difficult question to answer: what were the actual additions that Bride and Rowley made to *Doctor Faustus* in 1602? We acknowledge the possibility they may have enhanced certain dramatic situations, but it is also probable they were hired by Henslowe to recompile Marlowe's revised MS of *Doctor Faustus*, which possibly was fragmented due to unknown circumstances years after Marlowe's death. Already the A Text shows signs that lost important segments were not rediscovered judging by its short length. Alternatively, it is possible that Henslowe paid Bride and Rowely *as extras* in the cast — 'additions *in* Doctor Faustus' — if he was lacking a number of actors, however, this is highly speculative.

The B Text (First published: 1616)

If Marlowe was indeed responsible for revising the majority of the new sections that we now recognise today as the B Text, we gain as much information from the material he did *not* change. Overall, he was apparently satisfied with Act I as this remains intact. The Calvinist-based divinity course at the university is the guide that directs Faustus' on his way to Hell and thus this section did not require any revision, nor have any of his philosophical innuendos changed, e.g. "Indian gold", "orient pearl", "German Valdes", etc, displaying Marlowe's various ideas, examined earlier, were firmly set in his mind from the very beginning. There is a minor variation that may be viewed as pathetically humorous, i.e. when Faustus contemplates the powers a magician may wield:

[**] Queen Margaret: "Seems he a dove? His feathers are but borrow'd, / For he's disposed as the hateful raven: / Is he a lamb? His skin is surely lent him, / For he's inclin'd as is the ravenous wolf." [III. i. 75–78]

[989] *A Renaissance Life*, p. 114.

A Text	B Text
But his dominion that exceeds in this Strecheth as far as doth the mind of man. A sound magician is a <u>mighty god</u>. Here, Faustus, try thy brains to gain a deity. [I. i. 62–65]	But his dominion that exceeds in this Strecheth as far as doth the mind of man. A sound magician is a **demi-god**. Here, tire my brains to get a deity. [I.i. 59–62]

In the B Text Faustus arrogantly muses he will be greater than other 'demi-god' magicians by gaining a full 'deity'. However, Faustus fails to realise what he has related: if the potency of occult power is reliant on the I.Q. of the magician, who may become a '*demi*-god', is he only in possession of 'half' the brains to become a sound magician? A fitting addition for a scholar who reads half of his Bible verses to his utter destruction, and a unique parallel with Mephistopheles' remark that he can provide more than Faustus "has wit to ask".

A further minute alteration is actually a correction to an anachronistic error in Valde's line; "That yearly stuffs old Philip's treasury," where 'stuffs' is changed to "stuffed". Philip II of Spain died in 1598, demonstrating the acting companies amended lines when necessary, after Marlowe's death (1593).

The major change in Act I is the comic scene with Wagner and Robin. Robin is happy with his guilders, thus the allusion to counterfeit Dutch currency has been removed. Apparently, Marlowe intended to avoid presenting any reminders to the authorities of his little incident in Flushing! Robin's character has regressed, for he is quite content with the conjuring Wagner is prepared to teach him, while in the A Text, Robin insists on learning how to conjure spirits, a skill Wagner intends to withhold.

There are a number of noteworthy changes and omissions in Act II. When Faustus demands a wife, Mephistopheles voices no objection to this request nor discourages Faustus as in the A Text, but simply brings him the garish devil-woman. Faustus immediately scorns this 'beauty' and emphatically declares in the B Text he will not have a wife, which displays Marlowe was making it absolutely clear Faustus refuses all amorous relationships, until he demands Helen for his paramour.

We note there is one major omission in Act II, Scene One regarding Faustus' disappointment with the book that Mephistopheles presents to him. In the B Text, Faustus is happy with the gift, and promises to keep the book "as chary as my life." We detect a reshaping of Faustus' outlook for in the original A Text, he discovers that magic is also 'shallow' and without depth as this subject had but one book to offer. We note the book enables Faustus to wield the powers he dreamed of acquiring, and thus this change in the B Text reflecting his happiness with the gift is a logical alteration. Considering Faustus intended to fashion his Protestant-Epicurean philosophy through the occult, and is now enthused with the book in the B Text, does this reflect Marlowe's acceptance into Northumberland's academic clique and a serious consideration of his theories supporting atheism by members of the aristocracy and his colleagues?

At this point in the new B Text there is a speech by Wagner, almost identical to the Chorus of Act III in the A Text. Most editors choose to remove the speech from this section in Act II observing that Wagner's announcement of Faustus' journey to the heavens and to Rome causes an imbalance to the development of the plot.[990] Omitting Wagner's speech in the B Text leads us directly into Faustus' first earnest thoughts of amendment, i.e. "When I behold the heavens, then I repent / And curse thee wicked Mephistopheles". In the B Text, Mephistopheles is allocated an additional line when he responds to Faustus' condemnation of him: "'Twas thine own seeking, Faustus. Thank thyself."

With a few minor exceptions, the remainder of the scene is basically identical to the A Text: Faustus casts away despair for the present and concentrates on his astronomy lesson. The only addition we see to the dispute, as mentioned earlier, is Faustus confirming the number of spheres surrounding the earth. In the B Text he is surprised by Mephistopheles' conservative Aristotelian answer, and wonders if he is telling the truth: "But is there not *coelum igneum* et *crystallinum*?" Hence, the B Text reaffirms the original philosophy for the most part in the A Text, Mephistopheles did not provide Faustus with the controversial answer he was expecting. However, as Faustus' disappointment with Mephistopheles' book has been excluded, in the B Text, the astronomy lesson and the demon's refusal to explain Creation are now the sections that signal the scholar's first disillusionment with his occult career. We also note when Lucifer and Beelzebub appear with the Seven Deadly Sins, Beelzebub is allocated a speaking role and borrows several lines that were originally Lucifer's. The Pageant of the Seven Deadly Sins remains intact, the most notable difference is the reversed order of Wrath and Envy, i.e. Envy precedes Wrath in the B Text.

Following the Infernal Pageant, we encounter the third comic section with Robin and Rafe, (or Dick as he is now named). The same foolery continues with a stolen conjuring book as in the A Text, however, there is more stress placed on Robin's inadequate literacy skills — he attempts to spell out the incantation letter by letter. This corroborates our pervious observation that the various comic scenes follow a definite pattern depicting the 'regression' of the academic world, i.e. from the university disputations, to learning the mechanics of poetry in the grammar schools, and now to the petty school literacy programme re-emphasised through Robin's attempts at spelling. In addition, we note several of the jokes have been changed, but the jesting continues along the same vein, i.e. using magic for salacious purposes or to acquire beverage without having to pay for it. Altering the comic sections following the original premiere allowed companies to refresh material that had become, or, could be considered outdated by audiences in later performances and the subsequent revivals of the A Text.

From Act III onwards we observe the most extensive revisions to *Doctor Faustus*. A number of modern editors relocate the misplaced Chorus of Act II describing Faustus' voyage to the stars to Act III, as this also serves as an introduction to Faustus' journey to Rome. As mentioned, this section closely resembles the Chorus in the A Text, however Faustus' examination of the heavens is described in further detail:

---

[990] *Doctor Faustus; A and B Texts*, p. 223.

Chorus: Learnèd Faustus,
To find the secrets of astronomy
Graven in the book of Jove's high firmament,
Did mount him up to scale Olympus' top,
Where, sitting in a chariot burning bright
Drawn by the strength of yokèd dragons' necks,
He views the clouds, the planets, and the stars,
The tropics, zones, and quarters of the sky,
From the bright circle of the hornèd moon
Even to the height of the *Primum Mobile*;
And, whirling round with this circumference
Within the concave compass of the pole,
From east to west his dragons swiftly glide
And in eight days did bring him home again.
Not long he stayed in his quiet house
To rest his bones after his weary toil,
But new exploits do hale him out again,
And, mounted then upon a dragon's back,
That with his wings did part the subtle air,
He is now gone to prove cosmography,
That measures coasts and kingdoms of the earth,
And, as I guess, will first arrive in Rome
To see the Pope and manner of his court
And take some part in holy Peter's feast,
The which this day is highly solemnised. [*Exit*.]

In the first part of Scene One, Faustus obliquely informs the audience on the route he and Mephistopheles have journeyed. This section is relatively untouched, for example, the important 'Triertrent Fortress Verses' are the same. However, we suspect a later editor may have 'corrected' what they mistook to be an error during their compilation of the B Text. The additional description regarding the 'quarters' of Naples not in the *Faustbook* is removed, and the generalised passage "and the rest / in midst of which a sumptuous temple stands" now amended to reflect Faustus' visit to the eastern churches of Italy, i.e. St. Anthony's Church of Padua and the 'temple' of St. Mark's in Venice as described in the *Faustbook*. Considering our analysis of the A Text and the various allusions to Trier, Trent, and the Catholic Church, it is difficult to credit Marlowe with deleting a passage filled with allegorical symbolism in favour of returning to a simple borrowing from the *Faustbook*:

A Text:	B Text:
Faustus:	*Faustus*:
Then up to Naples, rich Campania,	Then up to Naples, rich Campania, Whose

Whose buildings, fair and gorgeous to the eye, The streets straight forth and paved with finest brick, Quarters the town in four equivalents. […] From thence to Venice, Padua, and the rest, In midst of which a sumptuous temple stands That threats the stars with her aspiring top. Thus hitherto hath Faustus spent his time. [III. i. 9–12, 16–19]	buildings, fair and gorgeous to the eye, The streets straight forth and paved with finest brick, *{Quarters: omitted.}* […] From thence to Venice, Padua, *and the east,* *In one of which* a sumptuous temple stands That threats the stars with her aspiring top. *Whose frame is paved with sundry coloured stones,* *And roofed aloft with curious work in gold.* ‡ Thus hitherto hath Faustus spent his time. [III. i. 9–11, 15–20]

Apparently, Bride and / or Rowley, or some anonymous editor, was confused by the flat statement "and the rest" and thought they were doing a service to Marlowe's memory and dramatic art by correcting this unusual deviation from the *Faustbook*. However, we suggest the A Text's rendering of this passage is definitely the preferred option with regards to its inherent imagery representing Faustus' atheistic 'eastern philosophy' crusade contra institutionalised Christian religion represented by Catholicism.

Returning to the B Text, Mephistopheles' itinerary and description of Rome is virtually intact. We find, however, one small detail that attracts our attention. When describing the number of bridges that span the River Tiber dividing the city, the number is reduced from four to two. It has been assumed this is simply an error, but if it is not, we detect a certain emphasis on the number two, i.e. the division of the city into two parts, and also the specific importance this places on the Ponte Angelo with its imposing castle:

> *Mephistopheles*: […]
> Know that this city stands upon seven hills
> That underprop the groundwork of the same.

---

‡ Compare with the London *Faustbook*: "He wondered not a little at the fairness of St. Mark's place and the sumptuous church standing therein called St. Mark's; how all the pavement was set with coloured stones and all the rood or loft of the church double gilded over." (*English Faustbook; A Critical ed.*, p.129.) Apparently, the editor of these verses in the B Text thought the gallery over the rood screen was the roof.

Just through the midst runs flowing Tiber's stream,
With winding banks that cut it in **two** parts,
Over which **two** stately bridges lean,
That make safe passage to each part of Rome.
Upon the bridge called Ponte Angelo
Erected is a castle passing strong,

[III. i. 32–39]

Rome in an allegorical sense, has replaced the seven-hilled city of Jerusalem as the location for the Last Judgement where Christ will divide the Goats from the Sheep into *two groups*, one to the left, the other to the right. However, access to the Kingdom, i.e. the Vatican representing the 'right hand', is made impenetrable by the fortified castle of 'brass cannon-law' on the Ponte Angelo. Is this an indication Marlowe was criticising the Church, similar to Christ reproaching the temple lawyers for their hypocrisy? "Woe to you lawyers also, because you load men with burdens which you cannot bear, and you yourselves touch not the packs with one of your fingers. [...] Woe to you lawyers, for you have taken away the key of knowledge: you yourselves have not entered in, and those that were entering in, you have hindered." (Luke 11: 46, 52)

This new presentation of Rome, strengthening the earlier 'Trier–Trent' tableau, prepares us for the following action within the Vatican. Marlowe recasts the Catholic pontiff, and he is now portrayed as a totalitarian Papal Tamburlaine, mercilessly wielding powers of life and death in Apocalyptic pomp:

Enter the Cardinals [of France and Padua] and Bishops [of Lorraine and Rheims], some bearing crosiers, some the pillars; Monks and Friars singing their procession. Then the Pope [Adrian] and Raymond, King of Hungary, with Bruno [the rival Pope] led in chains. [Bruno's papal crown borne in.]

Pope: Cast down our footstool.√

√ Compare with *Tamburlaine, Part One* when the conqueror ascends his throne by treading on Bajazeth, the defeated Turkish Emperor:

Tamburlaine:
  Base villain, vassal, slave to Tamburlaine,
  Unworthy to embrace or touch the ground
  That bears the honour of my royal weight,
  Stoop, villain, stoop! Stoop, for so he bids
  That may command thee piecemeal to be torn,
  Or scatter'd like the lofty cedar-trees
  Struck with the voice of thundering Jupiter.
Bajazeth: Then, as I look down to the damned fiends,
  Fiends, look on me! And thou, dread god of hell,

Raymond: Saxon Bruno, stoop,
   Whilst on thy back his Holiness ascends
   Saint Peter's chair and state pontifical.
Bruno: Proud Lucifer, that state belongs to me!
   But thus I fall to Peter, not to thee.
          [*He kneels in front of the throne.*]
Pope: To me and Peter shalt thou grovelling lie
   And crouch before the papal dignity.
   Sound trumpets, then, for thus Saint Peter's heir
   From Bruno's back ascends Saint Peter's chair.
          A flourish while he ascends.
   Thus, as the gods creep on with feet of wool
   Long ere with iron hands they punish men,
   So shall our sleeping vengeance now arise
   And smite with death thy hated enterprise.
   Lord Cardinals of France and Padua,
   Go forthwith to our holy consistory
   And read amongst the statutes decretal
   What, by the holy council held at Trent,
   The sacred synod hath decreed for him
   That doth assume the papal government
   Without election and a true consent.
   Away, and bring us word with speed.
First Cardinal. We go, my lord.

          Exeunt Cardinals.

[III. i. 89–110]

    At once we note this is not an accurate portrayal of history in several points but rather a glaring allegorical conflation attacking the papacy as a whole. This triumph of Pope 'Adrian' was inspired by the conflict between Emperor Frederick Barbarossa and Pope Alexander III (1159–81[+]): the Emperor dared to elect a rival pope, Victor IV, yet the Emperor was subsequently defeated and forced to bare his neck to the papal foot. Reportedly, Frederick

---

   With ebon sceptre strike this hateful earth,
   And make it swallow both of us at once!
          Tamburlaine gets up on him into his chair.
Tamburlaine: Now clear the triple region of the air,
   And let the Majesty of Heaven behold
   Their scourge and terror tread on emperors.

[IV. ii. 19–32.]

[+] Papal dates indicate the years of their pontificate.

declared as he knelt down "Not to thee, but to Saint Peter", indicating his acceptance of the Papacy, but not Alexander's pontificate, to which Alexander replied, "Both to me and Peter".[991] Pope Hadrian / 'Adrian' IV (1154–1159) was actually Alexander's predecessor[*] who also experienced political turmoil with Frederick, but we detect Marlowe chose this particular name as it simultaneously alludes to Pope Hadrian V (1276),[992] former archbishop of Rheims and Parma, two noted centres of the Elizabethan Catholic resistance.

King 'Raymond' is not a historical figure, but may be a sarcastic reference to St. Stephen, the first King of Hungary, (975?–1038). Converted from paganism in his youth, he became Duke of Hungary in 997. Shortly thereafter, a pagan insurrection ensued and Stephen succeeded in suppressing the revolt. When he was crowned king c.1001 he was the recipient of a royal crown from Pope Sylvester II (999–1003) who also bestowed upon him the title "Apostolic Majesty". During his reign, Stephen worked tirelessly to spread Christianity in pagan Hungary. Marlowe rendered him a second title, "Ray –mond", i.e. 'ray of the world', in keeping with the grandeur of the papal court. We note St. Stephen is feted with two feast days, one celebrated on August 20th in Hungary, and on August 16th in the Catholic world in general, drawing our attention to Mephistopheles' unusual introduction of the particular feast being celebrated at the court:

> *Mephistopheles*:
> Nay stay, my Faustus. I know you'd see the Pope
> And take some part of holy Peter's feast,
> The which <u>this day</u> with high solemnity
> <u>This day</u> is held through Rome and Italy
> In honour of the Pope's triumphant victory.

[III. i. 52–56]

Bevington and Rasmussen note the repetition of "this day" may indicate a clumsy revision by an editor, but Marlowe may have initially intended a cryptic allusion. Originally, we observed "this day" referred to the feast of St. Peter, (June 29th) in the A Text. Now in the B Text there is particular emphasis placed on Adrian's defeat of "Saxon Bruno" who dared to challenge his pontificate: the pope's victory in defending his papal authority is the particular event being celebrated. Of interest, there are *two* feast days that celebrate the establishment of the papacy, the Chair of St. Peter in Rome (January 18), and the Chair of St. Peter at Antioch (February 22), where according to tradition St. Peter first established his See before he resettled in Rome. Marlowe could be mocking this double-celebration of the papacy.

Returning to 'Pope Tamburlaine's Court', Faustus orders Mephistopheles to unleash his devilish powers on the two cardinals in the consistory whereby they may be overcome with

---

[991] *Doctor Faustus; A and B Texts*, n. 89–160, 93–93, p. 236. Marlowe's source was apparently John Foxe's *Acts and Monuments*, 2nd ed., 3 vols. (London: John Daye, 1570).

[*] In line 136, 'Adrian' describes Alexander as his "progenitor"; however, it is possible Marlowe intended Alexander to be the 'progenitor' of his fictional 'Adrian', and was not referring to historical chronology at this point.

[992] *Popes Through the Ages*, p. 368.

"drowsy idleness" as they pour over the "superstitious books" recording the decrees of the Council of Trent [III. i. 112–115]. Faustus then schemes that he and Mephistopheles will assume the shapes of the cardinals and play havoc on the court by rescuing Bruno and returning him to the Emperor in Germany. [ll. 115–121] Faustus and Mephistopheles exit the scene to commence their transformation while Pope Adrian and Bruno begin an acrimonious discourse:

> *Bruno*: Pope Adrian, let me have some right of law.
>   I was elected by the Emperor.
> *Pope*: We will depose the Emperor for that deed
>   And curse the people that submit to him.
>   Both he and thou shalt stand excommunicate
>   And interdict from Church's privilege
>   And all society of holy men.
>   He grows too proud in his authority,
>   Lifting his lofty head above the clouds,
>   And like a steeple overpeers the Church.
>   But we'll pull down his haughty insolence.
>   And as Pope Alexander, our progenitor,*
>   Trod on the neck of German Frederick,
>   Adding this golden sentence to our praise,
>   'That Peter's heirs should tread on emperors
>   And walk upon the dreadful adder's back,
>   Treading the lion and the dragon down,
>   And fearless spurn the killing basilisk',
>   So will we quell that haughty schismatic
>   And by authority apostolical
>   Depose him from his regal government.
> *Bruno*: Pope Julius swore to princely Sigismund,
>   For him and the succeeding popes of Rome,
>   To hold the emperors their lawful lords.
> *Pope*: Pope Julius did abuse the Church's rites,
>   And therefore none of his decrees can stand.
>   Is not all power on earth bestowed on us?
>   And therefore, though we would, we cannot err.
>   Behold this silver belt, whereto is fixed
>   Seven golden keys fast sealed with seven seals
>   In token of our sevenfold power from heaven,
>   To bind or loose, lock fast, condemn, or judge,
>   Resign, or seal, or whatso pleaseth us.
>   Then he and thou and all the world shall stoop,
>   Or be assured of our dreadful curse
>   To light as heavy as the pains of hell.

---

* See n.* above.

It is obvious Marlowe was intrigued with the battle for supremacy that existed for centuries between the Holy Roman emperors and the popes, in particular, the issue pertaining to papal elections. This struggle surfaced during the pontificate of Pope Liberius (352–366) shortly after the Church was liberated from three centuries of persecution by the Roman Empire with the conversion of Emperor Constantine the Great.[993] The second son of Constantine, Emperor Constantius II, was influenced by the Arian heresy and became a sworn enemy of St. Athanasius, the bishop of Alexandria, a staunch defender of orthodox teaching. Using his power, Constantius forced the bishops of the Church to abandon St. Athanasius and later threatened them with exile should they decide not to honour their allegiance and choose to defend the exiled bishop. Liberius continued to support St. Athanasius, much to the fury of the Emperor. Finally, during a council held in Milan (355), the bishops rejected the Emperor's outright demand to condemn St. Athanasius as this would be acting contrary to canon law. Constantius retorted, "My will is the canon", thus initiating this polemical period of state versus ecclesiastical authority regarding the government of the Church.

In the early 'post-Constantine' Church, the official appointment of a pope did not take place until the current emperor nominated a candidate for 'consideration'. Often, the emperor would strongly 'urge' the bishops to elect his sympathetic choice, while the bishops had their own candidate. Hence, there were many incidents of rival anti-popes appointed by emperors claming the keys of St. Peter who were not approved by the Church hierarchy. Eventually an agreement was reached whereby an emperor reserved the right to confirm the election of a candidate chosen by the bishops. Finally, Pope (St.) Hadrian III (872–882) issued a decree[994] stating the pope-elect did not have to wait for the Imperial consent before his consecration, (which may be the additional reason Marlowe dubbed his pope 'Adrian'), although the Emperors did not generally observe this decree. Hence, the current system of papal elections, i.e. solely by the College of Cardinals, entailed centuries of developmental upheaval.

In fine, "Saxon Bruno" supports his claim to the papal throne with the official nomination he received from the Holy Roman Emperor as his Imperial choice. Pope 'Adrian' is indignant with this plea, pronounces excommunication upon them, and threatens the same to anyone who will recognise the authority of the Emperor. Marlowe was alluding to the excommunication of Elizabeth I (1570) by Pope (St.) Pius V (1566–1572), who also declared her claim to the English throne null and void and absolved English Catholics from the duty of obedience to her under pain of excommunication.[995] Of interest, 'Adrian' compares the arrogance of the Emperor to a lofty steeple in the clouds, paralleling the 'steeple of the temple' Faustus mentions when he describes his travels. Immediately we detect the two opposing religious factions in the play: Faustus' Epicurean-Protestantism *contra* Catholicism. As mentioned, Charles V, the 'Holy Roman' Emperor, is recast as a schismatic supporter of Machiavellian Protestantism. 'Adrian' plans to depose the Emperor, and to honour this daring proposal, he composes an additional line to Psalm

---

[993] *Popes Through the Ages*, p. 72.
[994] Ibid. p. 220.
[995] *World of Christopher Marlowe*, p. 128.

90; "That Peter's heirs should tread on emperors,". According to Foxe's *Act and Monuments*, Pope Alexander III uttered the following lines[996] from the Psalm as he placed his foot on Frederick's neck: "Thou shalt walk upon the asp and the basilisk: and thou shalt trample under foot the lion and the dragon." (v.13)

Bruno continues to defend his cause by mentioning Emperor Sigismund and Pope Julius, another conflation of history. Sigismund, King of Hungary and Bohemia, ruled as the Holy Roman Emperor from 1411 to 1437. Sigismund did not exact the declaration Bruno claims in the drama, but alternatively was successful in convening the Council of Constance (1414–1418). The resolutions of the council ended the papal succession contentions at that time fomented by three contenders: two anti-popes, John 'XXIII' and Benedict XIII, and by Pope Gregory XII. The council established its rulings are binding for the Church, including the pope, and that similar councils are to be periodically held in the future: this may be the issue of 'papal submission' that Bruno is alluding to. The secular Emperors initially convened the early councils of the Church and therefore the issue as to whether a pope, as an ecclesiastical leader, was expected to abide by the rulings of such councils had not been formally addressed until the Council of Constance. The reference to Julius may indicate Pope Julius III (1550–1555), for Bevington and Rasmussen speculate that this name was chosen for its familiarity with Renaissance audiences.[997] However, we suspect Julius III continues the allegorical link satirising the conflict of secular versus ecclesiastical authority with church councils. His predecessor, Pope Paul III (1534–1549) saw the convening of the famous Council of Trent, but when he decided to relocate the Council to Bologna, he enraged Emperor Charles V who forbade his subjects from leaving Trent; thus the Council was abruptly adjourned when several of its members relocated to Bologna while the remainder obeyed the Emperor.[998] When Julius III was elected, he ordered all the participants to return to Trent and the Council reconvened. Bruno thus forges a connection between Pope Julius and Sigismund with their involvement in church councils, and by this example, defends his case before 'Adrian' that a pope should be obedient to the wishes of the Emperor.

Pope 'Adrian' dismisses Bruno's argument, declaring that Julius did not act properly, (i.e. not defending his papal right to defy the emperor?), and therefore pronounces his decrees null and void. 'Adrian' then states his reasons for his tyrannical dominion — papal infallibility — or rather, his erroneous application of the doctrine. He asks "Is not all power on earth bestowed on us?", and declares he cannot "err" even if he wanted to. This is a distorted perception of papal infallibility: the Church recognises that every pope is capable of sin and of committing grave errors in his personal life. Christ harshly rebuked St. Peter and called him 'Satan' for attempting to persuade Him to escape His destiny on the cross! (Matt. 16:23) And this occurred shortly after He had named Peter the foundation 'rock' of the Church, which the powers of Hell would not be able to destroy. (Matt. 16:18) Christ thereby gave him the keys to the kingdom of Heaven with the power as His vicar to bind or loose on earth rulings pertaining to the government of the Church, promising that these decisions would also be honoured in Heaven. (v.19) He later proclaimed at the Last Supper, "I will ask the Father and He shall give you another Paraclete that He may abide with you forever, the Spirit of Truth." (John 15:16–17.) Christ, the Son of God,

---

[996] *Doctor Faustus; A and B Texts*, n. 139–45, p. 238.
[997] Ibid. n. 146–148
[998] *Popes Through the Ages*, p. 442.

cannot utter a false promise; thus, the doctrine of infallibility concerns the *formal declaration* of faith and morals for the faithful to follow, and includes the power of the Church to bind or release sin. These declarations also include decisions a pope approves during a council concerning the definition of doctrine, the interpretation of Scripture and sacred Tradition, the condemnation of teachings contrary to the Faith, and the canonisation of saints. Hence, all doctrinal decisions are binding to Catholics under pain of sin or excommunication.

Although the doctrine of papal infallibility was not ratified as dogma until the nineteenth century, it was accepted for centuries according to Tradition. Later, Protestants, who could not accept that this infallibility *did not* extend to the *personal life* of a pope, utterly rebuked it. In the drama, we see 'Adrian' usurping infallibility regarding his ecclesiastical power to spiritually bind or loose as a pretext to aggrandise his secular authority, i.e. he initially excommunicates the Emperor and Bruno for their challenge to his papacy, not for any doctrinal error at this point. In fact, he increases the number of 'keys' Christ gave to Peter from two, i.e. to bind and loose, to seven thus drawing upon the Apocalyptic Seven Seals; "To bind, or loose, lock fast, condemn, or judge, / Resign, or seal," [III. i. 154–157] Note 'Adrian' concentrates on condemning and rebuking rather than on forgiveness! He ventures to include a surreptitious eighth key under his belt and therefore have the last word on the Book of Revelation by doing "whatso pleaseth us." This papal '*balteus-cum-clavis*' is an invention of the playwright, a possibly mockery of the cincture worn by monks, and also priests when they offer Mass.

When Faustus and Mephistopheles reappear as the cardinals, they deliver their solemn decree, and in the process parody the decrees of Trent condemning Reformational / Protestant teachings by denouncing the Emperor and Bruno for their opposition to pope 'Adrian':

> *Faustus*: Most sacred patron of the Church of Rome,
> By full consent of all the synod
> Of priests and prelates, it is thus decreed:
> That Bruno and the German Emperor
> Be held as Lollards° and bold schismatics
> And proud disturbers of the Church's peace.
> And if that Bruno by his own assent,
> Without enforcement of the German peers,
> Did seek to wear the triple diadem
> And by your death to climb Saint Peter's chair, ‡

° In general terms: heretics, schismatics. The term was originally applied to followers of the controversial reformer, or 'Morning Star of the Reformation', John Wycliff (c. 1330–1384). The Council of Constance (1415) decreed that his remains be disinterred and burned, which was carried out in 1428.

‡ Compare with Machevill's ('Make-evil's') prologue in the *Jew of Malta*:

> Admir'd I am of those that hate me most.
> Though some speak openly against my books,
> Yet will they read me, and thereby attain
> To Peter's chair; and, when they cast me off,

That statutes decretal have thus decreed:
He shall be straight condemned of heresy
And on a pile of faggots burnt to death.
Pope: It is enough. Here take him to your charge,
And bear him straight to Ponte Angelo,
And in the strongest tower enclose him fast.
Tomorrow, sitting in our consistory
With all our college of grave cardinals,
We will determine of his life or death.
Here, take his triple crown along with you
And leave it in the Church's treasury.
[*Bruno's papal crown is given to Faustus and Mephistopheles.*]
Make haste again, my good lord cardinals,
And take our blessing apostolical.
Mephistopheles: [*Aside.*]
So, so, was never devil thus blest before!
Faustus: [*Aside.*] Away, sweet Mephistopheles, begone.
The cardinals will be plagued for this anon.
Exeunt Faustus and Mephistopheles [*with Bruno*].
Pope: Go presently and bring a banquet forth,
That we may solemnise Saint Peter's feast
And with Lord Raymond, King of Hungary,
Drink to our late and happy victory.   *Exeunt.*

[III. i. 172–201]

We observe one peculiarity concerning the papal tiara: it is persistently referred to as belonging to Bruno. If Bruno is a rival, the crown should have initially belonged to Adrian. Is Marlowe suggesting the opposite is the case, that Adrian is usurping the papal crown? This is not unlike the development of *Tamburlaine, Part One* where the right to own a royal crown and govern a kingdom is examined in polemical detail. Tamburlaine, a shepherd-marauder without one drop of royal blood in his veins, boldly conquerors the great kingdoms of the earth and wrests from the heads of his defeated enemies their royal crowns, becoming an Imperial warrior. Tamburlaine is presented, despite his cruelty and Machiavellian tactics, as the preferred character deserving of a royal crown won by right of combat, but this conflicts with the course of aristocratic tradition — kings and their heirs will always be recognised as the true leaders of a land by birthright, even when they are deposed, thus Tamburlaine's sons will be forced to fight continually to maintain their right to rule. Returning to the papal court, we recognise these same polemics. It would appear that Marlowe considers Bruno the rightful heir to St. Peter's throne resulting from the Emperor's election, however, he has written a dashing Tamburlainic role for

---

Are poison'd by my climbing followers.

[Prol. 9–13]

Adrian, suggesting he should also be admired for daring to capture the papal crown. If Tamburlaine's sole reason for existence is rewarded by "the sweet fruition of an earthly crown", would he not endeavour to capture the only *triple* crown on earth? The name of the third crown, i.e. *triregnum* signifying "triple rule", suggests the symbolic nature of the tiara: the spiritual authority given to the pope in heaven, earth and hell by the power of the Blessed Trinity.

Continuing with Scene Two, the two impostor cardinals have resumed their original shapes, and Mephistopheles assures Faustus that he enabled Bruno to escape on a "steed, as swift as thought" that as they speak, "Flies o'er the Alps to fruitful Germany," [III. ii. 4–5.] We immediately recognise the correlation with the Machiavellian Prologue of the *Jew of Malta*: "Albeit the world think Machevill is dead, / Yet was his soul but flown beyond the Alps; and now [...] is come from France, / To view this land, and frolic with his friends." [Prol. 1–4] Apparently, Germany is also his playground, and "Saxon Bruno" his newfound friend in *Doctor Faustus*.⁻ While Marlowe may have inserted an optimistic opinion that Giordano Bruno would escape punishment or be released by the Venetian Inquisition, (for this court was not bloodthirsty as only five prisoners out of 1,565 people tried for heresy were condemned to death during the sixteenth century),[999] his prediction would not come to pass, for Bruno was sent on to Rome early 1593, and later condemned to death in 1600:

> "The charges against Bruno strongly resembled the allegations that made up the case against Christopher Marlowe. The Inquisitors accused Bruno of saying that men had existed before Adam and that Moses and Jesus had practised magic. After Pope Clement VII condemned him as an 'obstinate, stubborn, and impertinent heretic,' Bruno was bound, gagged, and burned alive at the Campo di Fiore in Rome on 17 February 1600." (Riggs)[1000]

For their next escapade, Faustus asks Mephistopheles to charm him with a spell of 'papal invisibility' in lieu of 'infallibility', allowing him to do "whate're I please" [l. 13], echoing the additional 'eighth' key the Pope cut. In fact, Mephistopheles 'consecrates' Faustus with an occult antithesis of the papal belt during his incantation:

> *Mephistopheles*:
> Faustus, thou shalt. Then kneel down presently,
>   [*Faustus kneels.*]
> Whilst on thy head I lay my hand
> And charm thee with this magic wand.
>   [*Presenting a magic girdle.*]
> First wear this girdle; then appear
> Invisible to all are here.
> The planets seven, the gloomy air,

⁻ Compare with n. ‡ above.
999 Imerti, 'The Heretic and his Trial', *Triumphant Beast*, p. 62.
1000 *World of Christopher Marlowe*, p. 339.

Hell, and the Furies' forkèd hair,
Pluto's blue fire, and Hecate's tree
With magic spells so compass thee
That no eye may thy body see. [*Faustus rises.*]
So, Faustus, now, for all their holiness,
Do what thou wilt, thou shalt not be discerned.

[III. ii.14–25]

Mephistopheles' mythological-based spell confirms Faustus in his belief that pagan philosophy and occult knowledge are the source of 'true' wisdom. First, he draws down upon Faustus the influence of the seven planets thus parodying Adrian's 'seven keys'. He then appeals to the Furies, the three Greek goddesses of the underworld that punished the wicked by pursuing them across the earth. They had snakes for hair, and blood dripped from their eyes. Although they were beings of justice, they were portrayed in literature as she-demons in later centuries. Mephistopheles also calls upon Pluto for his hellish fire, the Greek god of Hades often associated with the god of riches, Plutus, a possible continuation of Faustus' search for 'pagan wealth' or esoteric knowledge. This is an antithetical, demonic inversion of invoking the Holy Spirit, the imparter of wisdom, Who appeared over the heads of the Mother of Christ and the Apostles as flaming tongues. (Acts. 2:3–4) Hecate is included in the incantation, the goddess of darkness and the nightmarish aspects of the night: she had three heads with serpents entwined around the necks. She was also the goddess of sorcery and of crossroads. Greg notes her "tree" in the B Text may refer to an executioner's gibbet as gallows were usually located at crossroads.[1001] Possibly, Marlowe intended his audience to imagine the infamous 'Tyburn Tree', a hangman's scaffold that consisted of a horizontal triangle erected on three posts. Boas notes "tree" could be an error for "three" in reference to Hecate's tripartite nature.[1002] Thus we are aware Mephistopheles additionally inverts the mystic significance of the number three associated with a papal coronation.

On the completion of their demonic 'ordination' ceremony, Faustus and Mephistopheles sit back and gleefully wait to see the results of their trickery about to be unleashed upon the two sleepy cardinals, who have now entered the scene with the pope and his entourage. As they sit down to the feast, the two cardinals enquire of his Holiness if he is prepared to hear their sentence pertaining to Bruno. Immediately, the pope asks why they would need to do this, as they had already informed the court Bruno and the Emperor were recognised schismatics. The cardinals protest, but King Raymond attests he heard them say otherwise and saw them lead Bruno away, taking with them his crown. They once more proclaim they had not seen Bruno nor his crown, and the pope is infuriated: he threatens them with death unless they return Bruno and the tiara and condemns them to prison in shackles, cursing their souls to "hellish misery".

The feast continues, and with a few exceptions, the action is almost identical to the A Text. One of the most significant alterations includes the pope's ecclesiastical guest, who is now the Archbishop of Rheims. When Faustus snatches the various dishes from the hands of the

---

[1001]   *Doctor Faustus; A and B Texts*, n. 21, p. 242.
[1002]   Ibid.

servants, the pope threatens death to them all unless they find the culprit disturbing their dinner. The Archbishop pacifies him with the familiar sentence that it could be a soul from Purgatory that is causing the trouble in the hope of gaining his pontifical pardon. Lisa Hopkins brings to our attention Robin Chapman's analysis of this scene in his novel *Christopherus or Tom Kyd's Revenge* (1993), proposing Marlowe had drawn additional inspiration from his espionage experiences in the Secret Service for this change of character:

> "… first we have Faustus as an unseen presence in the Vatican, a spy in other words. Next comes Mephostophilis, a fellow agent from Hell, who can grant Faustus anything — at a price. Call Faustus Christofer and Mephostophilis Baines, who then serves whom and who, come to that, i[s] the Archbishop? Answer: an important papal authority from the very seminary Christofer attended. The Archbishop refers to a ghost — the Cockney name for a spy or informer is *ghost* — and says Christofer comes from Purgatory. On the face of it an unexceptionable provenance entirely suited to such a relentless spirit except Christofer once told me there were three courtyards at the seminary of Rheims which were commonly known as Heaven, Purgatory and Hell. And the English students took the air and exercised themselves at football in Purgatory."[1003]

The following excommunication ceremony when Faustus boxes the pope's ear is almost identical, except Mephistopheles notes that Faustus will receive the full brunt of the anathema, and Faustus did not call the chanting friars a "hog", a "calf" and an "ass". Of interest, the line "Cursèd be he that struck Friar Sandelo a blow on the pate," remains in the ceremony. If our earlier hypothesis regarding this 'curse' in the A Text is acceptable, i.e. that the derogate title "Friar Sandelo" may also refer to the Franciscan pope, Sixtus V, this sentence contains an entirely different inference in the B Text. The popes from whom Marlowe drew his inspiration for his 'Adrian', i.e. Alexander III, Hadrian IV and Hadrian V, were not from the Franciscan order. Thus, Adrian is unceremoniously 'made a monk' — a rare form of deposition in the early days of the Church when the enemies of a pope forcibly stripped and constrained him to put on a monk's habit, e.g. as with the case of Pope (St.) Silverius (536–537) who died in exile.[1004] Pope Stephen VII (896–897) suffered a similar demise: he was stripped of his pontifical vestments, clothed in a monk's robe, and thrown into prison where he was later strangled.[1005] It is reported that Pope Romanus (897) was also deposed in this manner, although he may be confused with Stephen VII.[1006]

Act III concludes with the familiar comic scene of Robin and Dick stealing the cup from the Vintner. Although the scene is now extended, the familiar plot remains. Robin conjures

---

[1003] Robin Chapman, *Christoferus or Tom Kyd's Revenge* (London: Sinclair Stevenson, 1993), pp. 88, 107, 161, in Hopkins, 'Marlowe's Reception and Influence,' *Cambridge Companion to Marlowe*, p. 291.

[1004] *Popes Through the Ages*, p. 116.

[1005] Ibid. p. 228.

[1006] Ibid. p. 230.

Mephistopheles to frighten the Vintner, and discovers he has summoned a disgruntled demon who complains to the "princely legions of infernal rule" [III. iii. 34] he made a wasted journey, coming all the way from Constantinople for the amusement of a worthless pair of rogues. Robin attempts to appease Mephistopheles with the offer of a tester and a shoulder of mutton for supper, (which also signifies a prostitute!), and the insulted demon turns to Dick and transforms him into an ape. Robin is pleased with this, and asks if he may carry Dick about "to show some tricks" [ll. 45–47], (presumably as a street entertainer to earn money), but Mephistopheles has other plans for Robin: "And so thou shalt. Be thou transformed to a dog, and carry him upon thy back. Away, begone!" [ll. 48–49] Robin is content, however, with the proverbial "porridge pots" [l. 51], and Mephistopheles returns to the "Great Turk's court". [l. 55]

Proceeding to the extensively revised Fourth Act, we encounter new characters in the Emperor's court, two noblemen named Martino and Frederick who prepare us for the following action. Martino assumes the role of St. John the Baptist and orders that the halls be "voided straight" [l. 3] for the arrival of his Majesty in the throne room. Fredrick enquires if Pope Bruno will attend the court, and Martino replies in the affirmative, adding that Faustus will also see the Emperor as he has planned to bring before his Majesty the "royal shapes" of Alexander the Great and his paramour by the power of his magic art. This is a decisive change from the *Faustbook* as the Emperor originally proposed the idea. When compared with the A Text, this request was one of the few sections of the Court Scene written in blank verse, symbolising the nobility Marlowe associated with the Emperor's inspiration. Now, *Faustus* is bestowed this dignity, suggesting Marlowe reinvented the character to display Faustus has indeed achieved a degree of upward social mobility by his magic and learning:

> *Martino*:
> O, yes, and with him {Bruno} comes the German conjurer,
> The learned Faustus, fame of Wittenberg,[#]
> The wonder of the world for magic art;
> And he intends to show great Carolus
> The race of all his stout progenitors,
> And bring in presence of his Majesty
> The royal shapes and warlike semblances
> Of Alexander and his beauteous paramour.
>
> [IV. i. 9–16]

We observe Scene One is almost completely re-written in blank verse unlike the equivalent scene in the A Text; however, the incredulous Knight who insults Faustus, renamed Benvolio, is allocated most of the prose thereby reflecting his uncouth behaviour.

Frederick wonders where Benvolio is, and Martino suggests he may still be in bed considering the amount of wine he drank the previous night celebrating Bruno's return. The two knights call him from his chamber, and he appears at the window still dressed in his sleep attire.

[#] 'Wertenberge' of A1 is changed to 'Wittenberg' in later printings of both the A and B Texts, possibly by an editor.

They persuade him to attend court and witness the magnificent sport Faustus plans to demonstrate, yet Benvolio, now suffering from a hangover, is not in a congenial mood and declines their invitation, preferring to watch from the open window. The Emperor and his entourage then enter the scene, and His Majesty praises Faustus for rescuing his pope-elect:

> *Emperor*:
> Wonder of men, renowned magician,
> Thrice-learnèd Faustus, welcome to our court.
> This deed of thine, in setting Bruno free
> From his and our professed enemy,
> Shall add more excellence unto thine art
> Than if by powerful necromantic spells
> Thou couldst command the world's obedience.
> For ever be beloved of Carolus.
>
> [IV. i. 48–55]

This speech continues to display Marlowe's reinvention of Faustus inspired by the scholar Giordano Bruno: he is no longer the grovelling servant awed by the aristocracy, but a beloved of the Emperor who has exceeded his initial motives for studying the occult, i.e. to command the world, by following his ideals and supporting the liberal 'pope'. Although Faustus now proclaims in response to this speech that he will serve the German Emperor and "lay his life at holy Bruno's feet", [ll. 63–64] this is not necessarily an act of servitude, but a demonstration of (Marlowe's?) loyalty to their liberal cause, i.e. Giordano's humanistic philosophy defying the orthodox conventions of society. By setting Bruno free, Faustus has earned by deed notorious distinction similar to Tamburlaine.

The Emperor then asks Faustus to fulfil the promise he made and show him Alexander the Great, (while Benvolio continues his sarcastic muttering in the background). In the B Text, the appearance of Alexander is transformed into a majestic drama recreating his historical defeat of Darius, the King of Persia: we observe a play within a play:

> *A sennet. Enter at one [door] the Emperor Alexander, at the other Darius. They meet; Darius is thrown down. Alexander kills him, takes off his crown, and, offering to go out, his Paramour meets him. He embraceth her and sets Darius' crown upon her * head; and, coming back*

---

* Compare with Tamburlaine's temporary coronation of Zenocrate as he prepares to battle with Bajazeth:

> *Tamburlaine*: […]
> Sit down by her {i.e. Zabina, Bajazeth's wife}, adorned with my crown,
> As if thou wert empress of the world.
> Stir not, Zenocrate, until thou see
> Me march victoriously with all my men,
> Triumphing over him and these his kings,

both salute the [German] Emperor, who, leaving his state, offers to
embrace them, which Faustus seeing suddenly stays him.
The trumpets cease and music sounds.

The Emperor then asks to see the famous mole and is thoroughly impressed with the demonstration, declaring: "Faustus, I see it plain, / And in this sight thou better pleasest me / Than if I gained another monarchy." Considering Marlowe's obsession with kingly rule, this statement is of import. Thus, Faustus accomplished a second astonishing feat, earning him an additional compliment from the Emperor who thereby praises him as a man of immense skill and knowledge notwithstanding the source from which it now originates. Faustus has presented convincing shadows of a famous conqueror, a man of action, whose military career was not unlike that of Tamburlaine, and thus do we observe a fascinating parallel with Faustus' illusion and the Prologue of *Tamburlaine, Part One*: "View but his picture in this tragic glass, / And then applaud his fortunes as you please." [Prol. 7–8] Was Marlowe equating the skill of a playwright with the idealistic notoriety won by epic deeds?

Faustus then directs the Emperor's attention to the sleeping Benvolio in the window who, at that moment, "sprouted" preternatural antlers. The court laughs at his predicament as he tries to draw his head through the casement without success. Benvolio furiously enquires of Faustus: "Zounds, doctor, is this your villainy?", to which he factiously replies:

> *Faustus*:
> O, say not so, sir. The doctor has no skill,
> No art, no cunning to present these lords
> Or bring before this royal Emperor
> The mighty monarch, warlike Alexander.
> If Faustus do it, you are straight resolved
> In bold Actaeon's shape to turn a stag. —
>
> [IV. i. 139–144]

He then proceeds to summon demonic dogs to attack the trapped knight, but the Emperor asks him to release Benvolio, for he has "done penance now sufficiently". [l. 156] Faustus complies as he announces in prose:

> My gracious lord, not so much injury done to me as to delight
> your Majesty with some mirth hath Faustus justly requited this injurious
> knight; which being all I desire, I am content to remove his horns. —
> Mephistopheles, transform him. [*Mephistopheles removes the horns.*]
> And hereafter, sir, look you speak well of scholars. [IV. i. 157–163]

Which I will bring as vassals to thy feet.
Till then, take thou my crown, vaunt of my worth,

[*1 Tamb.*, III. 124–130]

Following Benvolio's promise to punish Faustus for this humiliating treatment, with a wry critique scorning the scholar's unassuming "small ruff" and the disparaging comment "smooth face" mocking Faustus' servile ingratiating tactics, the Emperor declares: "In recompense of this high desert / Thou shalt command the state of Germany / And live beloved of mighty Carolus." [IV. i. 171–173.]

While Faustus' grandiose blank verse retort to Benvolio elucidating his revenge is a new insertion to Text B, this humble prose section addressed to the Emperor is almost identical to that in the A Text. His 'mistake' is not his act of revenge, for he planned to avenge himself of his foes in epic style with his occult powers, but to have demeaned himself by slipping into sycophancy at this point, for it is clear Faustus was essentially concerned with restoring his honour as a scholar-magician, rather than amuse the Emperor. However, he is hindered by the same compromising situation as any Elizabethan scholar or artist: the necessity of remaining obsequiously in the good graces of his patrons.

Scene Two is an inventive conflation of the two 'Knight's Revenge Chapters' in the *Faustbook*. Benvolio is adamant with his plan to kill Faustus for his trickery, and his two friends decide to aid him with all their soldiers. As Marlowe apparently considers revenge a daring action, it is worthy of blank verse. They hide in a grove and wait for Faustus to pass by. Benvolio reserves the right to kill his enemy while he says to Martino and Frederick they may take the wealth Faustus received from the Emperor. As Faustus enters the scene, Benvolio strikes off his head after which the knights grotesquely parody Faustus' classic description of Helen:

> *Frederick*: Was this that stern aspect, that awful frown,
>   Made the grim monarch of infernal spirits
>   Tremble and quake at his commanding charms?
> *Martino*: Was this that damnèd head whose heart conspired
>   Benvolio's shame before the Emperor?

> [IV. ii. 46–50]

While they decide on how best to mutilate his body to complete their revenge, Faustus suddenly rises up before them:

> *Benvolio*: Zounds, the devil's alive again!
> *Frederick*: Give him his head, for God's sake!
> *Faustus*: Nay keep it. Faustus will have heads and hands,
>   Ay, all your hearts, to recompense this deed.
>   Knew you not, traitors, I was limited
>   For four-and-twenty years to breathe on earth?
>   And had you cut my body with your swords,
>   Or hewed this flesh and bones as small as sand,
>   Yet in a minute had my spirit returned,
>   And I had breathed a man made free from harm.

On first inspection, this new section appears imbalanced by a major inconsistency. Commentators have observed Faustus' declaration of his twenty-four year time-stipulation to the knights implies it must be common knowledge to the characters in the drama, yet his announcement contradicts the surprise the Scholars display when he reveals the conditions of his pact near the conclusion of the drama. It is obvious Faustus was posing a rhetorical question to instil terror in the minds of his assailants: of course the knights did not know this detail! When Faustus later charms them all with horns, they decide to hide their shame and to end their days in an obscure castle, thus the secret of the twenty-four years dies with them. Hence, it is still possible for the Scholars in the penultimate scene of the play to be astounded by Faustus' disclosure of his pact.

Of paramount importance is the resurrection of Faustus, which is not included in the A Text. In both Texts, he despaired of medicine as a career when he was forced to recognise the limitations of this field as he would never accomplish the ultimate miracle of raising the dead. In the A Text, this desire is left unfulfilled, but in the B Text, this new scene once more displays Faustus discovered that magic and his pact with the devils was the only logical option as it alone fulfilled his innermost desires — his resurrection from the dead.

Faustus then conjures three demons, Ashtaroth, Belimoth, and Mephistopheles to torment the three knights who dared to assault him. As the knights are dragged away, the soldiers come out of hiding and attempt to continue the attack. Faustus charms the bushes, which immediately form a barrier between him and the forthcoming onslaught, and he calls in a troop of devil-warriors to drive the soldiers away. Faustus therefore accomplished his aspiration to raise armies to defend him when required. It is at this point that the three knights return and discover they all have horns charmed on their heads. Rather than risk being doubly-cursed by Faustus, they decide to leave him alone and retire to Benvolio's secret hideaway.

Scene Four features Faustus' scam with the Horse Courser, the plot closely resembles the A Text version, apart from a number of line revisions, and now Mephistopheles is allocated a silent role as Faustus' attendant. The Courser is cheated of forty dollars, and runs away in fright when he 'pulls off' Faustus' leg. Shortly after this latest escapade, Faustus' presence is requested by the Duke of Vanholt, and we are promptly introduced to Scene Five set in a hostelry featuring a tavern Hostess, Robin, Dick, the Horse Courser and a Carter; a new comic interlude preparing us for the revised section of the Duke's court. As the Hostess serves her guests, each one relate the unfortunate dealings they experienced with the infamous sorcerer. At this point, the tale of Faustus eating a load of hay from a carter's wagon is worked into the drama, although Faustus actually consumed the lot and did not 'return' the hay when the joke had worn thin as in the *Faustbook*. The Horse Courser then tells his woeful story how he was cheated of forty dollars, but believes he is avenged by pulling off Faustus' leg. He confesses he concealed the leg at home, not realising he is the victim of a sophisticated illusion. Robin then complains that one of the conjuror's devils had turned him into an ape, (it is obvious an editor, at one point, confused who was changed into which animal, as Dick was transformed into the simian form). Robin suggests they all retire to the adjoining room to drink, and later they will all confront Faustus and force him to account for his expensive deceptions.

The subsequent scene in the Duke's court parallels the A Text, although the Duke mentions an additional delight of an enchanted castle in the air produced for him by Faustus. The new revision to this scene features the comic characters of the tavern who decide to challenge Faustus directly at the Duke's court, (and we suspect this revised scene was originally set at the tavern as the Hostess arrives unexpectedly to serve drinks to the Duke, the Duchess and the comic characters. [IV. vi. 99–100]) As the clowns vociferously demand to see Faustus, he requests his Grace to permit them to enter as this disturbance may provide them with entertainment. The Duke grants this request, and there is comic confusion as the Carter and the Horse Courser argue whether Faustus has a wooden leg considering the troublesome outcome of the horse deal. To their horror, Faustus admits he has *regained* his limb, and the other comic characters angrily face him and attempt to exact an answer for his misdeeds, but he simply charms all their mouths shut and they are forced to wander away speechless to the amusement of the Duke and Duchess. On a sober note, this scene continues to highlight Faustus' position within the social hierarchy. With his academic proficiency, he raised his social standing, and similar to the elite, may consider the elements of the lower social spheres comical, yet notwithstanding all the favour he received from the Emperor, the Duke and the Duchess, he is nothing more to them than an educated entertainer, a 'jester' for the aristocracy.

Act V, Scene One is relatively intact: Wagner is puzzled why Faustus bequeathed to him many valuable objects as though he were preparing for death, while his feasting evinces the contrary. During the feast, Faustus proceeds to show his friends a vision of the famous Helen of Greece. The major alteration to Act V occurs in the Old Man's speech as he attempts to convert Faustus. Previously in the A Text, he concentrates on inspiring Faustus with thoughts of faith and of divine mercy, while here he exhorts Faustus to abandon magic and not to continue in his sin lest it become habitual and too late for repentance:

> *Old Man*:
> O gentle Faustus, leave this damnèd art,
> This magic, that will charm thy soul to hell
> And quite bereave thee of salvation!
> Though thou hast now offended like a man,
> Do not persever* in it like a devil.
> Yet, yet, thou hast an amiable soul,
> If sin by custom grow not into nature.
> Then, Faustus, will repentance come too late;
> Then thou art banished from the sight of heaven.
> No mortal can express the pains of hell.
> It may be this my exhortation
> Seems harsh and all unpleasant. Let it not,
> For, gentle son, I speak it not in wrath
> Or envy of thee, but in tender love
> And pity of thy future misery;
> And so have hope that this my kind rebuke,

---

* I.e. 'persevere'.

Checking thy body, may amend thy soul.

[V. i. 35–51]

This new speech confirms the theory that Faustus loses all hope of salvation and seals his damnation when he commits demonality with Luciferic 'Helen'. Faustus, had up to that time, "sinned like a man", i.e. he could still obtain forgiveness, but he "persevered in it *like a devil*", alluding to a specific sin that cannot be forgiven as he arrogantly refuses divine grace, i.e. committing the one act Lucifer publicly professes to practise in the drama: a homoerotic yet androgyny-neuter relationship with a fellow demon.

In due course, we arrive at sections that Empson[1007] termed the 'Sadistic Additions' in Act V of the B Text, i.e. where Faustus experiences excruciating mental torments before he is dragged to Hell. Following the famous Helen soliloquy, the 'Unholy Three', i.e. Lucifer, Beelzebub and Mephistopheles, enter the stage (presumably from the gallery above) to witness the scholar's final hours:

> *Lucifer*: Thus from infernal Dis do we ascend
>   To view the subjects of our monarchy,
>   Those souls which sin seals the black sons of hell,
>   'Mong which is chief, Faustus, we come to thee,
>   Bringing with us lasting damnation
>   To wait upon thy soul. The time is come
>   Which make it forfeit.
> *Mephistopheles*:   And this gloomy night
>   Here in this room will wretched Faustus be.
> *Beelzebub*: And here we'll stay
>   To mark him how he doth demean himself.
> *Mephistopheles*: How should he, but in desperate lunacy?
>   Fond worldling, now his heart-blood dries with grief;
>   His conscience kills it, and his labouring brain
>   Begets a world of idle fantasies
>   To overreach the devil. But all in vain.
>   His store of pleasures must be sauced with pain.
>   He and his servant Wagner are at hand,
>   Both come from drawing Faustus' latest will.[†]
>   See where they come.

[V. ii. 1–19]

Beelzebub and Mephistopheles sardonically echo the lines uttered by the Bad Angel in Act II when Faustus pondered upon repentance: "*Faustus*: Contrition, prayer, repentance — what

---

[1007] In *Faustus and the Censor*.
[†] Apparently, Faustus has revised his will as Wagner already mentions the document in [V. i.].

of these? [...] *Bad Angel*: Rather illusions, fruits of lunacy, / That make them foolish that do use them most." [B Text; II. i. 16, 18–19.] Now, that salvation is no longer possible (according to Marlowe's rendition of the Helen scene), Faustus 'idiotically' wastes his time with repentance, when before he could have 'made a fool of himself' with spiritual profit while the act was meritorious. Compare with the following verses from St. Paul, (1Cor.):

> "For the word of the cross, to them indeed that perish, is foolishness; but to them that are saved, that is, to us, it is the power of God. For it is written: *I will destroy the wisdom of the wise, and the prudence of the prudent I will reject.*[a] *Where is the wise? Where is the scribe? Where is the disputer of this world?*[b] Hath not God made foolish the wisdom of this world? For seeing that in the wisdom of God, the world, by wisdom, knew not God, it pleased God, by the foolishness of *our* preaching, to save them that believe." (vs. 18–21)

Faustus then asks Wagner if he is satisfied with the will, and he replies "wonderous well" [l. 21], and pledges him lifelong, faithful service. Wagner exits, and the Three Scholars enter; this section remains relatively intact. When they finally make their farewells to Faustus and exit the scene to pray for him, Mephistopheles spiritually torments Faustus for the last time:

> *Mephistopheles*: Ay, Faustus, now thou hast no hope of heaven;
> Therefore despair. Think only upon hell,
> For that must be thy mansion, there to dwell.
> *Faustus*: O thou bewitching fiend, 'twas thy temptation
> Hath robbed me of eternal happiness.
> *Mephistopheles*: I do confess it, Faustus, and rejoice.
> 'Twas I that, when thou wert i'the way to heaven,
> Dammed up thy passage. When thou took'st the book
> To view the Scriptures, then I turned the leaves
> And led thine eye.
> What, weep'st thou? 'Tis too late. Despair, farewell!
> Fools that will laugh on earth must weep in hell. *Exit.*
>
> [V. ii. 92–103]

Significantly, the leaves that Mephistopheles "turned" were *not* in a book of spells nor of magic, but the *Scriptures* — a stark reminder of the paradoxical combination of ideologies in the Elizabethan divinity course with Calvin's faulty predestination theology, pagan ideology, and the misinterpretation of the Bible resulting with the formation of 'devil syllogisms'.

The Good and Bad Angels then appear, delivering their final speeches of woe and glee, respectively:

---

[a] (Isa. 29:14)
[b] (Isa. 33:18)

Good Angel: O Faustus, if thou hadst given ear to me,
  Innumerable joys had followed thee.
  But thou didst love the world.
Bad Angel: Gave ear to me,
  And now must taste hell's pains perpetually.
Good Angel: O what will all thy riches, pleasures, pomps
  Avail thee now?
Bad Angel: Nothing but vex thee more,
  To want in hell, that had on earth such store.
      Music while the throne descends.
Good Angel: O, thou hast lost celestial happiness,
  Pleasures unspeakable, bliss without end.
  Hadst thou affected sweet divinity,
  Hell or the devil had had no power on thee.
  Hadst thou kept on that way, Faustus, behold
  In what resplendent glory thou hadst set
  In yonder throne, like those bright shining saints,
  And triumphed over hell. That hast thou lost.
  And now, poor soul, must thy good angel leave thee.
  The jaws of hell are open to receive thee,
     [The throne ascends.] Exit [Good Angel].
      Hell is discovered.
Bad Angel: Now, Faustus, let thine eyes with horror stare
  Into that vast perpetual torture-house.
  There are the Furies tossing damnèd souls
  On burning forks; their bodies boil in lead.
  There are live quarters broiling on the coals,
  That ne're can die. This ever-burning chair
  Is for o'er-tortured souls to rest them in.
  These that are fed with sops of flaming fire
  Were gluttons, and loved only delicates,
  And laughed to see the poor starve at their gates.
  But yet all these are nothing. Thou shalt see
  Ten thousand tortures that more horrid be.
Faustus: O, I have seen enough to torture me!
Bad Angel: Nay, thou must feel them, taste the smart of all.
  He that loves pleasure must for pleasure fall.
  And so I leave thee, Faustus, till anon;
  Then wilt thou tumble in confusion. *Exit.*
     The clock strikes eleven.

[v. ii. 104–137]

442

Faustus is finally permitted to see the two Angels that invisibly fought for his immortal soul, for the veil between the natural and the supernatural is drawn back during his final hour on earth. In a grotesque twist, the Good Angel's reproach to Faustus in that he should have "affected divinity" reiterates the unbalanced rationale of the Elizabethan theology course: as Mephistopheles "led" his protégé-to-be through his demonic exegeses of the Scriptures, *Calvinist / Protestant divinity is exactly what induced him to study magic.* We also observe the ironic use of the word 'affected' with the double-entendre signifying 'influenced by' and also 'to be artificially influenced'. Elizabethan Calvinism maintained those who were predestined for damnation were generally unaware of this 'fact', hence all their endeavours to attain divine grace by participating in the religious duties prescribed by the Church, were in practise, nothing more than external acts or 'artificial worship' allowed by God to maintain moral law and order on earth for the benefit of the just. In other words, the predestined reprobate, according to Calvinism, was expected to 'affect' their religion: they believed this to be God's Eternal plan.

The 'Sadistic Additions' included before Faustus' famous 'Dies Irae Soliloquy' complete the scene of his Eternal Judgement. Mephistopheles and the two Angels accuse Faustus of the sins he committed by action and omission that have reduced him to this devastating denouement. Compare this scenario with St. Augustine's description of the Particular Judgement of the soul:

> "Above him will stand the indignant Judge, below the direful
> hell, on his right his sins to accuse him, on his left devils to drag him to
> the place of torture, within him a burning conscience: whither, when thus
> straightened, shall the sinner fly?"[1008]

O homo fuge! God's Justice is poised over his head, and there is nowhere else but Hell for Faustus. The line referring to Christ's Blood streaming in the firmament seen in the A Text as a sign of vengeance and *not* mercy is removed, indicating Marlowe was ensuring this final scene of God's wrath would not be misinterpreted to suggest Faustus has any hope for salvation left. Faustus 'fits of lunacy' avail him naught, and he is dragged to Hell.

The drama concludes with a new scene depicting the Scholars' discovery of the mutilated body of their unfortunate friend and their plans for his mournful obsequies, replacing[∞] the moralising Epilogue:

> *First Scholar*: Come gentlemen, let us go visit Faustus,
> For such a dreadful night was never seen
> Since first the world's creation did begin.
> Such fearful shrieks and cries were never heard.
> Pray heaven the doctor have escaped the danger.
> *Second Scholar*:
> O, help us heaven! See, here are Faustus' limbs,
> All torn asunder by the hand of death.

[1008] *Preparation for Death*, p. 99.
[∞] In modern editions, it is not uncommon to find the Epilogue included with the new conclusion of the B Text.

Third Scholar:
The devils whom Faustus served have torn him thus.
For, 'twit the hours of twelve and one, methought
I heard him shriek and call aloud for help,
At which self time the house seemed all on fire
With dreadful horror of these damnèd fiends.
Second Scholar: Well, gentlemen, though Faustus' end be such
As every Christian heart laments to think upon,
Yet, for he was a scholar, once admired
For wondrous knowledge in our German schools,
We'll give his mangled limbs due burial;
And all the students, clothed in mourning black,
Shall wait upon his heavy funeral.   *Exeunt.*

[V. iii.]

In a twist of irony, Faustus posthumously succeeded in achieving a primary goal: dressing *all* the students in the same clothing of "skill", i.e. with the "sad" colour black associated with the dress of the poorer Scholars who completed their degrees and thereby attained 'skill', unlike the students from the more affluent spheres of society who were not expected to achieve any academic degrees to obtain a livelihood. He dressed the rich and the poor as equals. Ultimately, Faustus, as an "admired scholar", merited a decent Christian burial performed with ceremonial solemnity, notwithstanding he is publicly recognised as a reprobate lost for all Eternity.

In conclusion, the revisions to the B Text display Marlowe had regained a considerable measure of the defiant 'Machiavellian' optimism that pervaded his work written during his university days. For instance, inspired by the knowledge he was acquiring, he leaped onto the dramatic stage with his idealistic *Tamburlaine, Parts One and Two.* However, when he attempted to live and practise in the real world the knowledge he acquired at the university, he entered a duplicitous paradox, a situation reflected in the 'Anti-Tamburlaine' A Text of *Doctor Faustus.* Faustus, the poor scholar, formulates the same daring plans that parallel Tamburlaine's "high astounding terms" [1 *Tamb*. Prol. 1. 5], however, he fails to accomplish all the great deeds he envisioned, and grows increasingly dissatisfied with the occult as with his other academic subjects, discovering it cannot grant his desires. By the time Marlowe apparently revised the text in 1592, he had entered the liberal academic clique of the Earl of Northumberland and once more, the flame of renewed confidence in his controversial beliefs rekindled his artistic aspirations. Marlowe found his niche in this exclusive circle dedicated to the study of innovative, heterodox science and the search for knowledge. Faustus in the B Text is a defiant, loyal defender of liberalism with a more optimistic outlook. He accomplishes many of the deeds he solemnly vowed to achieve and is not completely disappointed with the occult as his choice of career. He is ill at ease when he discovers he must forfeit Heaven, but is quickly distracted by other pleasures. On a few occasions, he regrets he sold his soul and forbidden to enquire upon heavenly matters, but remains content with the benefits he is allowed to enjoy. He may be dissatisfied that the cosmos contains less spheres than he expected, but this is a 'fault' in Creation, and not necessarily a deficiency in the field of magic! The only compromising situation in the B Text originates with his social status: he cannot escape his plebeian roots for all his attempts to reach the light of the sun and is therefore forced to rely on his benefactors — his aristocratic patrons.

We may wonder if Marlowe had pondered upon the demise of his liberal Epicurean protagonist who achieved his goals while on earth but was ultimately doomed to infernal destruction for his choices. Did he not at least reconsider his atheistic convictions and question if he could actually lose his immortal soul to perdition by persistently adhering to his controversial resolutions? Apparently, the revision of the Old Man's reproaches from extolling the virtues of faith in the A Text, to the dangers of becoming habitually attached to sin in the B Text, displays Marlowe is aware of the theological arguments, but could not abandon his personal philosophy, which by then had become as the Old Man described "sin by custom" that had "grown into nature". This becomes hauntingly clear in Marlowe's final drama, *The Massacre of Paris* (January 26, 1593) retelling the slaughter of the Protestant Huguenots on St. Bartholomew's Day August 24, 1572. The Duke of Guise, who leads the Catholic faction, muses on his Machiavellian plans to rise in power and prestige, uttering an evocative conclusion on the sentiments expressed in *Doctor Faustus*:

> *Duke of Guise*:
>
> Oft have I levell'd, and at last have learn'd°
> That peril is the chiefest way to happiness,
> And resolution honour's fairest aim.
> What glory is there in a common good,
> That hangs for every peasant to achieve?
> That like I best that flies beyond my reach.°
> Set me to scale the high Pyramides,
> And thereon set the diadem of France;
> I'll either rend it with my nails to naught,
> Or mount the top with my aspiring wings,°
> Although my downfall be the deepest hell.
> For this I wake, when others think I sleep;
> For this I wait, that scorn attendance else.
> [...]
> For this, this head, this heart, this hand, this sword,
> Contrives, imagines, and fully executes,
> Matters of import aimed at by many,
> Yet understood by none.
> [...]

° Compare with the following lines from *Doctor Faustus*:

Prol. "His waxen wings did mount above his reach, / And melting heavens conspired his overthrow."
Faustus: "Settle thy studied, Faustus, and begin / To sound the depth of that thou wilt profess. / [...] / Yet level at the end of every art."

My policy hath framed religion.
Religion! *O Diabole*!
Fie, I am asham'd, however that I seem,
To think a word of such a simple sound,
Of so great matter should be made the ground!
[...]
Since thou hast all the cards within thy hands,
To shuffle or cut, take this as the surest thing,
That right or wrong, thou deal thyself a king.

[I. ii. 37–49, 52–55, 65–69, 89–91]

Marlowe was resolute in his decision, finally choosing the sword of atheism and risking the fate it would ultimately bring. Apparently, he did not entertain any illusions as to the Fate that may befall him: in the *Massacre of Paris* we observe not one, but two death scenes eerily predicting his future. First, the assassination of the Duke of Guise, deliverer of the above-quoted 'Faustian Resolution', by three dagger-wielding assassins, not unlike the circumstances of the ill-fated night at Deptford. Second, the assassination of the scholar, Petrus Ramus, the Protestant convert whom Marlowe had recast as *the son of a poor shoemaker* who succeeds in becoming a renowned Scholar. This death scene is strongly reminiscent of Faustus' search for academic 'depths':

Ramus: O good my lord,
  Wherein hath Ramus been so offensious?
Guise: Marry sir, in having a smack in all,
  And yet didst never sound anything to the depth.
  Was not thou that scoff'st at the *Organon*,
  And said it was a heap of vanities?
  He that will be a flat dichotomist,
  And seen in nothing but epitomes,
  Is in your judgement thought a learned man;
  And he forsooth, must go and preach in Germany,
  Excepting against doctors' axioms,
  And *ipse dixi* with this quiddity,
  Argumentum testmonii est inartificiale.
  {The argument of the evidence is inartificial.}
  To contradict which, I say, Ramus shall die:
  How answer you that? Your *nego argumentum*
  {I refuse the argument.}
  Cannot serve, sirrah. — Kill him.

[I. vii. 23–38]

Ramus refutes not the charge, and admits he "knew the *Organon* to be confus'd / and reduc'd it into a better form." [I. vii. 46–47] Accordingly, he receives the baneful dagger thrust. Although Marlowe's Faustus casts aside Ramus (aka Aristotle) for the same reasons mentioned by the Duke of Guise in that Ramus condensed logic to shallow superficialities, nevertheless, Faustus is influenced by his method and consequently abridges the Bible to his utter annihilation. Compare with the following verses from 2 St. Peter (15–16.):

> "And account the longsuffering of our Lord, salvation; as also
> our most dear brother Paul, according to the wisdom given him, hath
> written to you: As also all his epistles, speaking in them these things hard
> to be understood, which the unlearned and unstable wrest, as they do also
> the other scriptures, to their own destruction."

This destiny woefully befell Marlowe who believed he discovered the 'depths' of religion, yet refused to accept the profound orthodox theological interpretations of the Bible and trusted completely in his "arguments of inartificial evidence". For example, his incredulity on how the children of Israel could wander for forty years in the desert and not enter another country to get their bearings. Human logic dictates their journey from Egypt to the Promised Land could be accomplished obviously in a shorter period of time. Dismissing the possibility of divine intervention, Marlowe concluded Moses used his occult knowledge learned from the Egyptians concerning the workings of nature to blind the people of Israel into submission. (See Appendix Seven.) Here we detect the influence of Giordano Bruno who based his occult work on the metaphysical philosophy of Hermes Trismegistus, the "reputed teacher of Orpheus and Moses," as Riggs informs us.[1009] In all, the supposedly profound theological interpretations of the Bible, similar to organised religion, was simply another method of control. This personal philosophy would eventually cost Marlowe his life.

Sounding the Depths of Deptford

When Robert Greene / Chettle's *A Groatsworth of Wit* publicly accused Marlowe of atheism in September of 1592, his already tarnished reputation was dealt a serious blow. The pamphlet continued to fuel public fear of the rapidly growing subculture for godlessness. Rumours of Sir Raleigh's "school of atheism" obviously alluding to Northumberland's circle were creating a sensation. Atheists were considered more dangerous to the State than Catholics or Puritans since they apparently lacked any inherent religious loyalty. A rebellious faction loyal to a religious cause was easier to identify than liberal chameleons that could change their colours when the occasion suited. Although these individuals arguably made perfect double agents, the trust-factor was seriously compromised where they were concerned.

Life appeared to continue as 'normal' for a short time after this event: while the theatres were still closed due to the plague, Marlowe returned home to Canterbury where he resumed his

---

[1009] *World of Christopher Marlowe*, p. 178.

quarrelsome habits by engaging in a street brawl on 15th September with a tailor, William Corkine, whom he attacked with a stick and dagger.[1010] The case was resolved out of court in October. He then found patronage with Lady Mary Herbert of Pembroke when his friend Watson died late that September, leaving his pastoral *Aminta gaudia* incomplete for the press.[1011] Marlowe finished the project and dedicated the work to Lady Pembroke as Watson intended. By the following spring (1593), Marlowe was residing in Kent at the manor of Sir Thomas Walsingham, former patron of his friend, Watson.[1012] Marlowe dedicated his time to poetry and translation work during this hiatus in dramatic production; for instance, it was during this period he commenced *Hero and Leander*.

When the plague subsided, the theatres were briefly re-opened on 29th December 1592, and Marlowe's last play, *The Massacre of Paris,* subsequently premiered on 26th January.[1013] Large sections of text were lost, and much of what survives was obviously reconstructed from memory. As Riggs relates, "The reported text contains what the actors found to be the most memorable parts of Marlowe's *Massacre*."[1014] War and blood, assassination plots, frenzied intelligence gathering and imaginings of Machiavellian grandeur comprises the fabric of *The Massacre*: all the recognisable trademarks of Marlowe's dramatic expression. However, the season was short-lived as the plague once more threatened the city, obliging the officials to close the theatres at the end of that month. The epidemic soon spread and decimated eight per cent of the London population.[1015]

This ill-timed disaster occurred when malcontent was escalating as hardships persistently increased.[1016] The war in the Low Countries raged on, and Spain continued to pose a serious threat. The level of unemployment remained steadily high, inflation soared, and the ban on public entertainments due to the plague sealed off the amusement outlets that afforded the public diversions from the daily tensions of the world around them.[1017] In addition, the fears of sedition increased when retaliation for the death of the separatist Roger Rippon was threatened against Archbishop Whitgift and his Court of High Commissioners for Ecclesiastical Causes.[1018] The High Commission responded by arresting many sectarians, including the leaders Henry Barrow and John Greenwood.[1019] Barrow and Greenwood, and those who printed their work, were convicted of felony and sentenced to hang under the 1581 statute; 'Against Seditious words and rumours uttered against the Queen's Most Excellent Majesty'.[1020] The consequence of these proceedings had redefined the statute — ecclesiastical crimes of heresy and blasphemy were now judged as acts of treason against the State.[1021] A full-scale anti-heretic crusade was unleashed:

[1010] 'Marlowe's Life,' *Cambridge Companion to Marlowe*, p. 36.
[1011] Ibid.
[1012] Ibid.
[1013] *World of Christopher Marlowe*, p. 309.
[1014] Ibid. p. 310.
[1015] Ibid. p. 315.
[1016] *A Renaissance Life*, p. 122.
[1017] Ibid.
[1018] *World of Christopher Marlowe*, p. 316.
[1019] Ibid. pp. 316–317.
[1020] Ibid. pp. 317–318.
[1021] Ibid. p. 318.

"On March 26, the queen created a new Royal Commission to hunt down, examine and punish Barrowists, Separatists, Catholic recusants, counterfeiters, vagrants and all who 'secretly adhere to our most capital Enemy the Bishop of Rome or otherwise do wilfully deprave condemn or impugn the Divine Service and Sacraments'. The queen's Commission did not distinguish between alien religions and no religion, or atheism. Elizabethan church governance rested on the bare premise of outward conformity; the Commissioners incarcerated any parishioners who 'refuse to repair to the Church to hear Divine service', including many who held no religious beliefs at all." (Riggs.) [1022]

Simultaneously the government proposed it was a sound policy to encourage immigration from France and Holland to increase the Protestant population and thereby strengthen the economy.[1023] In March 1593, a bill was passed in Parliament, allowing foreign residents extended trading privileges, bringing further hardship upon English-owned businesses.[1024]

Consequently, the population was demoralised, and as Kuriyama explains, "[...] the emotional climate was ripe for scapegoating, and 'strangers' and Puritans, who were readily cast as dangerous others, were obvious targets. 'Atheists' — a loose term for all those whose beliefs were heterodox — were also vulnerable, [...]."[1025] Immediately following the signing of the foreign-friendly trading bill, anonymous anti-alien "libels" were found posted throughout all the streets of London in mid-April, and on the 22nd of April, the Privy Council ordered a special committee to discover the authors and printers of these seditious posters. However, a second libel was found on the 5th of May, in Broad Street on the wall of the Dutch Churchyard signed with the nom de plume "Tamburlaine". The libel consisted of a fifty-three verse poem containing a barrage of threats and complaints with lines alluding to *The Jew of Malta* and *The Massacre of Paris*, e.g. "We'll cut your throats, in your temples praying / Not Paris massacre so much blood did spill / As we will do just vengeance on you all."[1026] Obviously, an irresponsible aficionado of Marlowe's work could not refrain from incorporating some of his favourite gory scenes into his political protest, resulting in disastrous consequences for his idol. The anonymous protester attracted the queen's attention, a sizable reward was offered on May 10th for information concerning the libel, and the Privy Council conveyed the following report concerning the seditious libels to the New Royal Commissioners on May 11th:

"... there is some set upon the wall of the Dutch churchyard
that doth exceed the rest in lewdness, and for the discovery of the author
and publishers thereof her majesty's pleasure is that some extraordinary

---

[1022] Ibid.

[1023] *A Renaissance Life*, p. 122.

[1024] Ibid.

[1025] Ibid.

[1026] Quoted in Charles Nicholl, *The Reckoning: The Murder of Christopher Marlowe*, (London: Jonathan Cape, 1992), p. 41, in ibid., p. 123. Also, *World of Christopher Marlowe*, p. 319.

pains and care be taken by the Commissioners appointed by the Lord Mayor for the examining such persons as may be in this case any way suspected ..."[1027]

On May 12th, Marlowe's former roommate, Thomas Kyd, was promptly brought before the authorities for questioning. His room was searched, and a heretical document was discovered, a transcript of John Proctor's Arian tract, the *Fall of the Late Arian*. Under torture, Kyd confessed the tract belonged to Marlowe, and may have also disclosed further information concerning his roommate's controversial beliefs judging from two letters Kyd wrote to Sir John Puckering circa June 1593 following his release from prison.[1028] In the first letter, Kyd affirms the fragmented "disputation" that was discovered belonged to Marlowe, and confesses their former patron, Lord Strange, could not tolerate Marlowe's company, having learned the nature of his character and his 'conditions', obviously referring to his atheism. This may explain why Marlowe lost the patronage of Strange's Men in 1592. Kyd writes Marlowe was irreligious, intemperate, bereft of good qualities, dishonest, and "of a cruel heart". In the second letter he proceeds to describe Marlowe's shocking behaviour, i.e. jesting at prayers and the scriptures, confuting the teachings of the prophets, alleging St. John was Christ's 'Alexis', disregarding miracles attributed to divine power as the "observations of men", "attempting sudden privy injuries to men", and persuading "men of quality" to join James VI, King of the Scots, and his fellow poet, Matthew Royden.

Similar reports also proved detrimental to Marlowe. A certain Richard Cholmeley, an agent involved with the detection of recusants and a friend of Marlowe, was also a controversial individual who attracted the attention of the authorities as early as March of that year. According to an agent's report, (c. March), it was noted that Cholmeley ...

> "... sayeth and verily believeth that one Marlowe is able to show more sound reasons for Atheism than any divine in England is able to give to prove divinity and that Marlowe told him that he hath read the Atheist lecture to Sir Walter Raleigh and others."[1029]

A second report during that same month related Cholmeley attempted to seduce the queen's subjects with arguments proving the validity of atheism.

Finally, on the 18th of May, the Privy Council took the matter in hand and ordered a Messenger of the Queen's Chamber, Henry Maunder ...

> "To repair to the house of Mr Thomas Walsingham in Kent, or to any other place where he shall understand Christopher Marlowe to be

---

[1027] J. Dasent, Ed., *Acts of the Privy Council of England, XXIV* (London: Eyre and Spottiswoode, 1890), p. 222, in *World of Christopher Marlowe*, p. 320.

[1028] These two letters reprinted in *A Renaissance Life*, pp. 228–231.

[1029] Reprint in *A Renaissance Life*, p. 215.

remaining, and by virtue hereof to apprehend and bring him to the court in his company."[1030]

Two days later, Marlowe was brought in and commanded to "…give his daily attendance on their lordships, until he shall be licensed to the contrary."[1031] This signified he was to remain within the "verge of the court", i.e. within a twelve mile radius from the person of the queen, which provided him with one bonus; protection from the common courts, and therefore, from torture.[1032] In the interim, the Council continued to gather evidence. Apparently, the informant Thomas Drury was involved with this task and was responsible for the delivery of the infamous "Baines Note", as Richard Baines was an acquaintance of Drury at Cambridge in the 1570s.[1033] Marlowe's former roommate of Flushing once again emerged as an informant! The Note was handed over to the Council circa the 27th of May, with the following result: "… the notablest and vilest articles of Atheism … were delivered to her highness and command given by herself to prosecute it to the full."[1034] Considering his past criminal record, his curious escapade in Flushing, his connections with Lord Strange and the new Stanley conspiracy, his work glorifying controversial ideology and Machiavellian politics, and the incriminating evidence above … Marlowe could no longer be trusted.

On May 30th, a certain Ingram Frizer invited Marlowe to a "feast" at the Deptford residence[**] of a widow named Eleanor Bull. This locality was within the specified "verge" and was under the jurisdiction of the queen's Lord High Steward rather than the local Justice of the Peace.[1035] Frizer was a cozener and servant of Sir Thomas Walsingham, Watson and Marlowe's patron who once acted as an intermediary agent between Sir Francis Walsingham and his field operatives.[1036] Eleanor Bull happened to be related to Blanche Parry, who was once Chief Gentlewoman of the Privy Chamber and a close friend of the queen. Parry was also closely connected with Lord Burghley, head of the secret service. In fact, Lord Burghley had drawn up Bull's will: "[Burghley] knew who Eleanor Bull was and where she lived," Riggs writes.[1037] The party included Robert Poley, a ruthless veteran agent working for Lord Burghley following the death of Francis Walsingham, and Nicholas Skeres, a man once involved in a money lending scheme with Frizer who was recruited by Francis Walsingham as an auxiliary agent during the time of the Babington conspiracy.[1038]

The four men met at Bull's house at ten that morning, and the first part of the day passed pleasantly. They enjoyed lunch and a quiet stroll around the garden until about six o'clock in the evening. They returned in time for dinner, after which a quarrel broke out between Marlowe and

---

[1030] Ibid. p. 219.
[1031] Ibid.
[1032] *World of Christopher Marlowe*, p. 326.
[1033] Ibid. pp. 321, 327, 330.
[1034] Ibid. p. 330.
[**] In some accounts, the location was referred to as a tavern, but it is unclear how accurate this description is.
[1035] *World of Christopher Marlowe*, p. 332.
[1036] Ibid. p. 144
[1037] Ibid. p. 332
[1038] Ibid. p. 152.

Frizer concerning the "reckoning" of the dinner bill. Curiously, Marlowe was lying on a bed with the "front part of his body" towards the table where Frizer was sitting, with his back to Marlowe. Skeres and Poley flanked Frizer on either side of the table. It was reported Marlowe suddenly attacked Frizer following their argument, unsheathing Frizer's dagger and dealing him two severe wounds on the head. Frizer, allegedly fearing for his life (as Skeres and Poley were 'impeding' his escape due to their seating arrangement), struggled with Marlowe to forcefully reclaim his dagger, and as he was unable to regain full possession of the weapon, inflicted his assailant with a two-inch wound to the right eye in the struggle, instantly killing him.[1039]

On first inspection, this may appear to be a simple case of self-defence with a known disturber of the peace who habitually vented his spleen in duels. However, Riggs is correct when he states that certain elements do not corroborate this rendition of the events. First, the detail Frizer received two wounds to the head about two inches in length and a quarter of an inch deep that caused him to "fear for his life":

> "This is confusing. Since the scalp consists of skin and bone, Frizer's wounds can hardly have been a quarter of an inch deep, nor does Coroner Danby say that Marlowe attacked his companion with the point of his knife. The deposition rather indicates that Marlowe (or someone) pummelled Frizer's scalp with the hilt of his dagger. This was common practise in Elizabethan brawls and it had a precise connotation. Pummelling meant that you intended to hurt, but not to kill your adversary. Had Marlowe wanted to kill Frizer, he would have stabbed him in the back of the neck. Frizer's scalp wounds were the result of a beating rather than a stabbing." (Riggs.)[1040]

Poley and Skeres' reaction to the fight, or rather, the apparent lack thereof, is particularly bizarre. According to logic, one might expect them to immediately distance themselves from the area of conflict in a typical brawl, or perhaps help Frizer immobilise Marlowe and end the fight. However, they did nothing but curiously sit at the table and impede Frizer's movement, 'compelling' him to engage with Marlowe. This reeks of statecraft — was Marlowe lured to his death?

Let us presume they purposely manufactured the motive for Marlowe's attack. He was *invited* to their party after all, and naturally would be incensed when presented with the bill and told to put his hand in his pocket to pay for their fair. In all, *they expect him to lose his temper.* Marlowe pummels Frizer, meaning he is holding the blade as he beats him on the head with the hilt. Poley and Skeres then deliberately remain in their seated positions at the table, 'forcing' Ingram to 'defend' himself by grabbing the hilt of the dagger and making a sudden backward thrust over his head and sinking the blade into Marlowe's eye. The innocent-looking positions of Frizer, Poley and Skeres seated around the table, with Frizer's back towards Marlowe, fabricates the illusion it was an impromptu skirmish and therefore a perfect open and shut case of self-defence. There is also an alternative scenario: having provoked the argument with the

---

[1039] Taken from the Coroner's Inquest dated June 1, 1593, reprinted in *A Renaissance Life*, pp. 222–226.
[1040] *World of Christopher Marlowe*, p. 334.

unexpected dinner bill as the perfect set-up considering Marlowe's irascible temper, they could have pinned Marlowe to the bed during the scuffle with his head towards the table and stabbed him in the right eye. The above mentioned situation they reported would be the perfect cover-up for it would be difficult to refute their testimony on how the wound was inflicted as the right eye would be the point of entry for the blade-thrust in either scenario. Riggs writes:

> "Poley, Skerres and Frizer were used to operating in teams and had worked with one another before. They had practical experience in manipulating the law; they knew how to fabricate a trial narrative and maintain it under interrogation. These were the special skills they brought with them to Deptford on 30 May."[1041]

The mystery continues. On June 1, 1593, Marlowe was buried at the church of St. Nicholas in Deptford, the same day Frizer was judged to have acted in self-defence. The burial entry for the doomed playwright reads, "Christopher Marlowe slain by Francis Frezer, the 1 of June". Riggs observes, "The substitution of 'Francis' for 'Ingram' sufficed to conceal the murderer's identity until 1925."[1042] Marlowe apparently had no family or friends at his funeral, they were probably not aware at that time he had been killed. A charitable soul may have donated the minimal requisite of a shroud that would allow him as a human to have a decent burial.[1043]

Approximately three days after his death, the queen received a doctored copy of the infamous Baines Note.[1044] The heading was revised, purposely confusing the date on which it was delivered with the date of Whitsunday eve and the timing of Marlowe's death. Certain sections were also 'excluded', i.e. crossed out, but still legible in areas; these include the notorious sentence of tobacco and boys, the mention of the counterfeiter Poole in Newgate prison and Marlowe's proud statement he had the same right as the queen to coin, Baine's assertion he could provide a witness to these statements, and the recommendation that Marlow's mouth be permanently stopped. Riggs argues this editing was not intended to deceive the queen, for she already ordered the matter to be "prosecuted to the full" and would later read the correct time of Marlowe's death in the coroner's report around the 15th of June.[1045] In fact, the excised sections feature the articles that would be punishable according to the law; hence, they would have implicated the queen and the Council with the intrigue of Marlowe's death and therefore were conveniently 'removed':

> "The revised Note gave the queen a whitewashed version of Marlowe's death. [...] The excision of this material concealed the quarrel between Marlowe and the court, while the revised title, with its

---

[1041] Ibid. p. 333.
[1042] Ibid. p. 335.
[1043] *A Renaissance Life*, p. 142
[1044] This is also reprinted in *A Renaissance Life*.
[1045] *World of Christopher Marlowe*, pp. 335–336.

horrid blasphemies and fearful end, revealed that the hand of divine correction had come down hard on the overreacher." (Riggs.)[1046]

In other words, the circumstances surrounding his death were altered to make it appear that the Wrath of God had abruptly struck down a confirmed reprobate. Shortly thereafter on the 28th of June, Frizer was granted an official pardon. Riggs notes, "[...] this was a remarkably brief interval [to receive a pardon] for a capital offence committed within the verge."[1047]

The editing of the Baine's Note was a masterstroke of concealment blurring any links with the government, the image of Marlowe stabbed in the eye during a 'tavern brawl' had the hallmark of an ill-starred demise the heavens reserved for the damned. It soon captured the public's imagination. Similar to the historical Faustus, Marlowe's death was embroidered by contemporary writers to equal the diabolical reputation he had acquired. Of these accounts, the most famous is recorded in Thomas Beard's *Theatre of God's Judgements* (1597), which contains a highly accurate account of Marlowe's death, albeit Beard reports "[...] he even cursed and blasphemed to his last gasp, and together with his breath an oath flew out of his mouth."[1048] This rendition would influence others to inflate Marlowe's notorious end. Francis Meres believed that he had uncovered the motive for Marlowe's attack upon Frizer when writing …

"As the poet Lycophron was shot to death by a certain rival of his: so Christopher Marlowe was stabbed to death by a bawdy Servingman, a rival of his in his lewde love." *Wit's Treasury* (1598)[1049]

However, Marlowe also had admirers who wrote of him in reflective, glowing terms. George Peele called Marlowe "the muses' darling". Nashe and Chettle equated Marlowe with the ancient poet Musaeus. Ben Johnson praised his adroit use of blank verse: "Marlowe's mighty line". Shakespeare truly mourned the loss of his fellow playwright, we detect in *Richard III* (c.1593?) a veiled outpouring of rancorous grief hurled at Marlowe's attacker modelled on the famous 'Dies Irae Soliloquy' in *Doctor Faustus* with its images of God's vengeance, the gaping earth, and the cry for lightening:

Anne:
Thy deed, inhuman and unnatural,
Provokes this deluge most unnatural.
O God! Which this blood mad'st revenge his death;
O earth! Which this blood drink'st, revenge his death;
Either heaven with lightning strike the murderer dead,
Or earth, gape open wide, and eat him quick,
As thou dost swallow up this good king's blood,
Which his hell-govern'd arm hath butchered!

[1046] Ibid. p. 338.
[1047] Ibid. p. 335.
[1048] *A Renaissance Life*, p. 154.
[1049] In ibid. p. 155.

[I. ii. 60–67][1050]

Shakespeare continues to ponder upon Marlowe and his death in *Henry IV, Part One* (c. 1597?); "What is honour? A word. What is that word, honour? Air. A trim reckoning! Who hath it? He that died o' Wednesday." [V. i. 136-138][1051] His best known allusions to Marlowe, however, are in *As You Like It* (c.1599?) undoubtedly inspired by the public burning of Marlowe's translations of *Ovid's Elegies* in June 1599.[1052] Referring to a famous line in Marlowe's poetry, Shakespeare sighs: "Dead Shepherd, now I find thy saw of might: / 'Who ever lov'd not at first sight?'" [III. v. 81–82] He apparently calls Marlowe "honest Ovid among the Goths", [III. iii. 7–8] and muses through the character of Touchstone: "When a man's verses cannot be understood, nor a man's good wit seconded with the forward child Understanding, it strikes a man more dead than a great reckoning in a little room. [...]" [III. iii. 12–15] Nevertheless, it would appear Shakespeare could not credit the reports and questioned the accepted elucidations of Marlowe's death. When we continue the quote above from *As You Like It* ...

> *Touchstone*: ... it strikes a man more dead than a great reckoning in a
> little room. Truly, I would the gods had made thee poetical.
> *Audrey*: I do not know what 'poetical is. Is it honest in deed and word?
> Is it a true thing?
> *Touchstone*: No, truly, for the truest poetry is the most feigning; and
> *lovers are given to poetry* [...]. [III. iii. 16–22]

... and compare it with [III. iv. 31–33]:

> *Celia*: 'Was' is not 'is:' besides, the oath of *a lover* is no stronger than
> the word of a *tapster*; they are both the *confirmers of false reckonings*.
> [...]

... we suspect Shakespeare was suspicious that the details of the "poet-lover's" death was "falsely reckoned" at the 'tavern'. Was he struck down in a spontaneous brawl, or silenced by the powers that prevailed?

৪৩❖৪৩

A tragedy of tragedies: the education system promulgated by the Monarchy and the State fed his young mind with optimistic dreams of grandeur, encouraging him to envision the impossible, only to be dashed by the cruel realities of life. Educated beyond the confines of his class, yet limited in choice of desirable careers that were suited to his learning, the Elizabethan

---

[1050] *Complete Works of Shakespeare*, Vol. VII.
[1051] Ibid. Vol. V.
[1052] *World of Christopher Marlowe*, p. 347.

divinity course paradoxically fashioned him into a confirmed atheist and malcontent, determined to defy the restrictive boundaries and norms that society expected him to conform to. He was verily a second Faustus, who could not abandon his convictions and chose to hazard his life and soul for his proselytising crusade for Atheism. Nor was he disillusioned with this uncanny parallel; not completely satisfied with the first version of his famous drama, he felt compelled to revise it, expanding sections that clearly display he adamantly adhered to his philosophy despite the consequences. Marlowe, similar to the legendary Faustus, wrote a second 'contract' and was duly remunerated. When he chose the motto for his alleged Cambridge portrait, a prophecy became immortalised — what nourished him ultimately destroyed him.

ೞೞ❖ೞೞ

Chapter 4

The Transition Years

The popularity of the Faustian legend remained constant, particularly as the *Faustbooks* and their variants continued to be published in Europe. However, during the subsequent two hundred years, the story gradually regressed from what was once a serious subject of drama and literature into semi-farcical entertainments, and eventually demoted to the domain of the puppet theatres. While this period is generally recognised as the nadir in the Faust Tradition, it was also a time of metamorphic dormition awaiting a new generation of inspired authors and dramatists to rediscover the literary potential of the legend and fan new flames from cinders hidden beneath the ashes of familiarity.

ဆဝၶ ❖ ဆဝၶ

The next phase in the *Faustbook* phenomenon following the publication of Spies' edition commenced when George Rudolf Widman's "Authentic Life" of Faustus was published in Hamburg (1599).[1053] It was yet in the writing process during 1587 before Spies' work was printed, although Henry Jones notes Widman may have consulted a manuscript on which Spies' *Historia* was based.[1054] Widman claimed to have included material collected from the university students and the account 'written' by 'Johannes Wäiger', (i.e. Wagner). In the process of compiling this work, Widman completely reinvented the character of Mephostophiles as a benevolent Middle Spirit who unfortunately is enslaved by Satan.[1055] Faustus is portrayed as a Lutheran who according to Rose is "[…] a young man led astray by the Church of Rome."[1056] This book may have proved to be a literary favourite were it not for its daunting length and proselytising, anti-papal tone. Palmer and More describe the text as "[…] an intolerably long-winded account of Faust's career interspersed with dreary moralizing comments. […It] was apparently not reprinted until modern times."[1057]

Due to various political and cultural upheavals, the vogue for printing *Faustbooks* in Germany declined rapidly during the next seventy-five years. The ravages of the Thirty Years War (1618–1648), a conflict that erupted from the religio-political tensions of the Protestant Reformation, appears to be a major factor in the hiatus of *Faustbook* productions.[1058] When the Peace of Westphalia was finally signed on October 24, 1648, the Holy Roman Empire under the dominion of the Hapsburgs was severely weakened as the Netherlands and Switzerland were

---

[1053] Palmer and More, *Sources of the Faust Tradition*, p. 131.
[1054] Henry Jones, *English Faustbook; A Critical Ed.*, p. 7.
[1055] Ibid.
[1056] Rose, *Damnable Life and Deserved Death of […] Faustus*, p. 40.
[1057] *Sources of the Faust Tradition*, p. 130.
[1058] Ibid. p. 131.

recognised as independent states, while other territories and bishoprics were politically reorganised or ceded to France and Sweden, thus the Kingdom of France became the leading power on the Continent. This War seriously impeded the political unification of Germany, and reduced the population considerably from twenty to fifty percent in certain localities while many of the survivors were displaced refugees; the economy was in deep recession, and morale was at one of its lowest points. The first 'English Comedians' arrived on the Continent in the closing decades of the sixteenth century, i.e. travelling companies of English actors, who introduced the art of English stagecraft and the earliest English dramatic masterpieces to Germany. Shortly thereafter, dramas were on the increase, presumably as the populace sought for alternative diversions that provided an escape from the horrors of the war that surrounded them, and later from the aftermath of the conflicts that completely demoralised the various states and principalities of Germany. Faust dramas became a regular favourite, which temporarily eclipsed the popularity of the *Faustbooks*. Palmer and More also note that the general population was gradually liberated from the fevered grip of the witch-hunting frenzy experienced in earlier centuries that once heightened the intrigue associated with the occult nature of the Faust legend and contributed towards the dissemination of the *Faustbook*.[1059] Witchcraft was now scrutinised under the growing spirit of rationalism heralding the Age of Enlightenment, and the systematic slaughter of alleged wizards and witches in Europe was gradually becoming a horror of the past: Salem in colonial Massachusetts would mark the end-times of the major witch hunts in 1692.[*]

When the English acting troupes first toured Germany, they presented their repertoire of plays in the English language while only the comic sections were translated into German.[1060] Later, they translated entire English plays into German, although the integrity of the texts was severely mutilated in the process before original German works were eventually produced on stage.[1061] German actors soon joined the visiting troupes, and eventually, established native acting companies.[1062]

While an argument was presented that an early German Faust play possibly existed in the sixteenth century,[1063] there is no authenticated proof, and therefore Marlowe's drama is generally recognised as the earliest surviving dramatic representation of the legend. Consequently, scholars believe an adaptation of Marlowe's *Doctor Faustus* is the first recognised Faust play produced on the Continent in Graz (1608), considering that the acting company was English and possibly familiar with Marlowe's magnum opus.[1064] Bearing in mind the nature of these English performances with only the buffoonery translated into German, Marlowe's poetic gems and his philosophical expression were unfortunately lost on this new public as the troupes concentrated

---

[1059] Ibid.

[*] Nevertheless, witch executions continued for a number of years in Europe. The last execution in Germany, for example, occurred in 1782. (David Luke, in *Oxford World's Classics— Goethe. Faust: Part One* (Oxford: Oxford University Press, 1998), n. 93, p. 168.

[1060] *Sources of the Faust Tradition*, p. 240.

[1061] Ibid.

[1062] Ibid.

[1063] Ibid. p. 239. Walz's article 'A German Faust Play of the Sixteenth Century,' *Germanic Review*, III (1928) is recommended by Palmer and More for further reading on the subject.

[1064] Ibid. p. 240.

upon the scenic effects and comic elements to compensate for the half-translated dialogue. Nevertheless, German audiences visually comprehended and appreciated aspects of the legend Marlowe had masterfully elaborated upon that were not fully developed in the Spies *Faustbooks*, for example, Faustus' agonising deliberation in his study, and the famous chiming of the clock marking his last hour before he is dragged away by the hellish fiends. Inspired by these visual presentations, the Faust plays became popular entertainment fare as Palmer and More write:

> "We know of the following further performances during the seventeenth century: Dresden, 1626; Prague 1651; Hannover, 1661; Lünburg, 1666; Danzig, 1668; Munich, 1679; Bremen, 1688; Basle, 1696. The brevity of this list is evidence rather of our lack of definite information than of the actual frequency of performances."[1065]

Unfortunately, not a single text has survived; therefore, our primary information on these early seventeenth-century plays is derived from the diary belonging to a gentleman named George Schröder wherein the Danzig production of 1668 is briefly described, supplementing surviving theatre programmes.[1066]

Turning first to the Danzig production, we discover a new element of classicism appended to the Faust legend. This play opened with the Greek god of the underworld, Pluto, arriving from his hellish realm and summoning a number of demons, i.e. the "tobacco devil, the bawdy devil, and the cunning devil",[1067] commanding them to tempt and ensnare people on earth according to their individual vices. The next scene featured Faust in his study, abandoning the pursuit of scholastic wisdom to embark upon his magic studies, and he conjures the various devils to determine which of them he desires to serve him. Drawing upon the *Chronica von Thüringen* of Zacharias Hogel, the anonymous playwright included the detail of Faust choosing the devil that is as swift as the thoughts of man; in this case, it is the "canny" or "cunning devil". Faust demands the spirit to serve him for the familiar twenty-four years with the agreement he will forfeit his soul to the devil. The "canny devil" refuses to agree until he brings the proposal to Pluto for his infernal authorisation. The monarch of the underworld approves, thus Faust signs a contract in blood with his devil. A devout hermit attempts to convert Faust, but his warnings pass unheeded, and Faust accomplishes all manner of amazing feats; he conjures the image of Charlemagne to appear (not Alexander the Great), and of course, Helen of Troy with whom he "has his pleasure." [1068] Finally, his last hour approaches, and full of remorse, admonishes his servant, (presumably Wagner), not to fall into the temptation to study magic; a slight alteration from the *Faustbooks* wherein Faustus advises Wagner how to acquire a familiar spirit. The clock strikes twelve, and Pluto sends his minions to fetch Faust, and throwing him into the air, proceed to tear him limb from limb. The play closed with a new scene featuring Faust's torments in Hell, i.e. being eternally dragged up and down by demons with the following sentence forever appearing before him in blazing letters: "*Accusatus est, judicatus est, condemnatus est*" — he is accused, he is

---

[1065]   Ibid.

[1066]   Ibid. p. 242.

[1067]   Ibid. p. 245.

[1068]   Ibid. p. 246.

judged, he is condemned.[1069] Possibly, this new ending was fashioned from the passage in the Book of Daniel (5:26–28) featuring the vision of the hand writing on the wall inscribing the three-fold sentence foretelling the destruction of King Baltasar of Babylon: "MANE: God hath numbered thy kingdom, and hath finished it. THECEL: thou art weighed in the balance, and art found wanting. PHARES: thy kingdom is divided, and is given to the Medes and Persians."

This synopsis is an example of the basic outline upon which the early German Faust plays were constructed. However, the plays did not remain intact as classic art forms, for the texts were often changed to refresh material or to introduce new scenic effects. We note in one theatre announcement c. 1690 for a Faust play performed in Bremen, unique alterations are mentioned.[1070] Pluto spectacularly rode upon a great dragon, and a comic character named Pickelhäring was included, whose origins can be effortlessly traced to the antics of Robin, Rafe and Dick of Marlowe's classic drama. Pickelhäring apparently resorted to magic to raise some ready money and is tormented by demonic birds for his impudent daring. This play included Faust's banquet, presumably with the students or with the Duke of Anhalt as set in the *Faustbooks*, although this scene contained a novel variant in that Faust presented a great pie from which springs forth all manner of strange beings and animals for the entertainment of his guests. A unique detail was included featuring a fire-breathing raven that announced Faust's approaching death before the demons carry him off to a Hell that is "[…] adorned with beautiful fireworks".[1071] The performance concluded with a shadow-picture show retelling the action of the play and ending with a jolly masquerade.

These German Faust plays of the seventeenth century proved extremely popular, and primarily responsible for reviving an interest in *Faustbook* publishing. A Nuremberg physician named Johann Nicolaus Pfitzer revised Widman's tome, altering the biased anti-Catholic comments and republished it in 1674.[1072] Scholarly attention in the historical character and the legends surrounding him emerged at this time compliments of the Faust play *zeitgeist* as the first academic study of Faustus, *Disquisitio historica de Fausto praestigiatore* (1683), relates:

"So this magician spent his life obscurely enough and would be even less known if he had not been presented on the stage so often."[1073]

Grimmelshausen would write the following year in *Simplicissimus* (1684) explaining why the Faust plays succeeded in drawing the crowds:

"What is more eagerly acted, played and seen than the history of the accursed archconjurer Doctor John Faust, because a number of devils are always introduced and represented in all kinds of disgusting doings."[1074]

[1069] Ibid.

[1070] Ibid.

[1071] Ibid.

[1072] Ibid. p. 131. Also, *Damnable Life and Deserved Death of […] Faustus, p. 40.*

[1073] *Sources of the Faust Tradition*, p. 241.

[1074] Ibid.

Although the Faust plays remained in the general repertoire during the eighteenth century in Germany, as a genre, their position in culture became gradually undermined by the ideals of the Age of Enlightenment then sweeping across Europe. Writers, intellectuals and philosophers perceived a new springtime in the development of human knowledge that now focused on using the powers of human reason, observation and logic rather than subjective experience to raise mankind from the perceived darkness of ages past. The intellectual precursors to this movement included René Descartes (1596–1650) who rejected Scholasticism, i.e. philosophy based on accepted authorities on a subject, in favour of relying on observation and reason to prove a concept before forming a conviction on any subject, including the belief in God, maintaining that through science and mathematics mankind could understand and predict events in the physical world. He capsulated his methods in his famous sentence: "*Cogito, ergo sum*—I think, therefore I am." It was an age of scientific discovery, witnessing the breakthroughs of Sir Issac Newton (1642–1727) whose theories on gravity and the laws of motion were not surpassed until the twentieth century with Einstein's Theory of Relativity. Human reason and the power of observation were the driving forces of this period wherein the *philosophes* strove to explore the universe with new awareness liberated from the dictates of institutionalised religion believed to be responsible for the regression of the human mind and the innate quest to expand the boundaries of knowledge. There was an increasing desire for political and social change, and many intellectuals rejected organised religion in favour of Deism and its variants, i.e. the belief in God or a Supreme Being and recognising the existence of an afterlife by the use of reason, while not rigidly adhering to concrete dogmas or the complexities of Christian theology. Many deists also believed God, or the Supreme Being, remained detached from Creation once the Universe was organised and did not interact with the human race. One of the foremost exponents of the Enlightenment and the cause for Deism was the writer and philosopher Voltaire (François-Marie Arouet) (1694–1778) who summarised his criticism on organised religion and the clergy with the ominous phrase "let us crush the infamous one". Other important writers and critical thinkers of this time were Jean-Jacques Rousseau (1712–1778) and Denis Diderot (1713–1784). The German philosopher Immanuel Kant (1724–1804) proposed the motto of the age should be "Dare to Know". The optimistic Age of Enlightenment ended with the cataclysmic French Revolution (1789) and the subsequent Reign of Terror.

In Germany, this rationalist movement was spearheaded culturally during the 1730s by Johann Christoph Gottsched (1700–1766), critic, author, and reformer of the German theatre. In his famous treatise, *Versuch einer kritischen Dichtkunst* (*Attempt at a Critical Theory of Poetry for the Germans*, 1730), Gottsched promulgated the concept that literature be based on human reason. In theatre reform, he championed classic French models and strived to liberate the German stage from the garish popular productions with its clownish comic scenes that once engaged the public. Until 1740, he was the undisputed authority on German culture and expression. In response to his reforms, the actress Karolina Neuber burned an effigy of Harlekin or Hans Wurst, (i.e. a 'Pickelhäring' character), in Leipzig (1737) to demonstrate the farces that the effigy represented were now banished from the stage![1075] Palmer and More explain:

> "The educated classes of this 'Age of Enlightenment' began to turn away from the mummery, superstition and vulgarity which had come to form such a large part of the [Faust] play. The powerful influence of Gottsched [...] literary dictator of Germany, was exerted to turn the stage away from such nonsense [...]."[1076]

We note this rationalist age witnessed the last of the German *Faustbook* tradition with the anonymous abridgment of Pfitzer's edition entitled *Faustbuch des Christlich Meynenden* (*Faustbook by a Man of Christian Sentiments)*: the first dated copy is the 1725 edition, while 1797 is the last known publication.[1077] From this time onward, the Faust legend as a literary form was disseminated as popular reading material in small chapbooks, the early precursors to our modern mass media newspapers and magazines.

Although they were performed regularly, Faust plays were now regarded as lowbrow farces, however, sparks of creative genius present themselves in the innovations mentioned in the few surviving theatre announcements. For example, in the Hamburg Announcement of 1738, we learn the gruesome ferryman, Charon, is now included to interact with the character of Pluto, who remained a particular favourite:

> "[...] A great courtyard in the palace of Pluto on the rivers Lethe and Acheron in Hades. Charon comes sailing in his boat on the river and with him on a fiery dragon appears Pluto, accompanied by his whole hellish retinue and spirits. [...]"[1078]

In the scene featuring Faust's study, the Good Angel of Marlowe's drama is redeveloped as a "celestial spirit" who sings the following aria to dissuade the scholar from acting upon his rash decision:

> Faust! What hast thou undertaken?
> Oh, alas! What hast thou done?
> Hast thou all good sense forsaken?
> Thinkest thou no more upon
> The eternal grief and pain,
> And the bliss ne'er known again?
>
> Does the prick of sinful longing

[1075] Ibid. n. 9, p. 247.
[1076] Ibid. p. 241.
[1077] Ibid. p. 131. Also, *Damnable Life and Deserved Death of [...] Faustus, p. 40.*
[1078] Geissler, *Gestalungen des Faust,* Vol. I (München, 1927), pp. 222–223, in *Sources of the Faust Tradition*, p. 247.

Far outweigh your soul's delight?
Wouldst thou be to hell belonging
When thou shouldst in heaven abide?
Holdest thou the sinner's groan
Dearer than the heavenly throne?

Is there naught your mind can alter?
Oh, so gaze on heaven above
If perchance its bounteous water
May arouse in you God's love.
Let it work upon your heart
And in heaven seek your part.[1079]

The detail of the raven remained a constant; in this production, it fetched Faust's contract and carried it away. The bumbling comic character Hans Wurst accidentally witnesses Faust conjuring and is magically forced to stand still until he removes his shoes, which then "dance together merrily".[1080] Mephistopheles also allows Wurst to conjure a shower of gold. The vision of Helen in this play chastises Faust with an aria foretelling his impending doom. A number of traditional favourites were also included, i.e. the knight and the hart horns, and the horse courser with the enchanted bundle of hay culminating with the 'dismemberment' of Faust's leg. The finale featured Faust imprisoned in the courtyard of Pluto's palace where furies performed a triumphant ballet celebrating their success in seducing him to practise occult magic.

A Faust Play entitled "Unfortunate Learning" was performed in Frankfurt on the Main in 1742. The Announcement for this production records some spectacular scenes where Faust conjured before the Duke of Parma (i.e. King Charles III of Spain 1716–1788) the "[…] torments of Tantalus; the vulture of Tityos [Tityus]; the stone of Sisyphus; the death of Pompey. A woman is publicly changed into a fury."[1081] With this production, emphasis was placed on new additions derived from Greek mythology. Tantalus was the son of Zeus and king of ancient Lydia now in modern day Turkey. Highly favoured by the gods, he is invited to attend the banquets of Olympus as an honoured guest. The gods also condescended to accept his reciprocation and partook of a banquet at his palace. Tantalus kills his only son, Pelops, whom he serves as the main course at his feast in a grotesque experiment to ascertain the extent of the gods' omniscience and test their powers of detection. Immediately the gods recognised the deceit, restored Pelops to life, and imprisoned Tantalus in the region of Tartarus where he hung upon a tree and was eternally tormented by hunger and thirst. Suspended over his head were delectable fruits, yet when he reached for them, a blast of wind would blow them beyond his grasp. At the foot of his gibbet was a pool of refreshing water that would recede when he stooped to drink from it. From this myth the word "tantalise" was derived. Tityus, i.e. Prometheus, according to myth was a Titan who bestowed upon mankind the gift of fire and other

---

[1079]   Ibid.
[1080]   Ibid. p. 248.
[1081]   W. Creizenach, *Versuch einer Geschichte des Volksschauspiels vom Doctor Faust* (Halle, 1878), p. 10, in *Sources of the Faust Tradition*, p. 249.

benefits thus distinguishing the race of men as superior beings, separating them from the animal kingdom. However, as a punishment for stealing the divine gift of fire from heaven, Zeus chained him to a rock in the Caucasus where a giant eagle would come every day to rip out his liver that would immediately regenerate. Finally, Hercules rescued Prometheus by slaying the eagle. In some accounts, Prometheus is chained on a rock in Tartarus, and his tormenters are vultures. The mythical Sisyphus, son of Aeolus, king of Thessaly, was the king of Corinth. In punishment for his transgressions, Zeus sent him to Tartarus where he was eternally forced to push a huge boulder up a steep hill, only to see it roll and crash to the bottom every time he reached the summit. In addition to these mythological scenes, the death of Julius Caesar's son-in-law, Pompey the Great (106–48 BC.), the general who captured Jerusalem (c.65–62 B.C.), replaced the glorious deeds of Alexander the Great in the Faust plays. The performance concluded with a ballet and a "merry comedy".[1082]

An elaborate version of "Unfortunate Learning" was produced in Frankfurt on the Main in October 1767: although it is evident the Faust plays were now vehicles for performing diverting re-enactments of mythical and historical events, there was an imaginative rendition of the 'Old Man' converting Faust:

From an Announcement of 1767

"[…] Here follow the individual attractions, mechanical contrivances, transformations and scenes. (1) Faust's learned discussion in his study as to whether the study of theology or of nigromancy is preferable. (2) Faust's remarkable conjuration in a dark wood at night, at which appear amid thunder and lightning various hellish monsters, spirits, and furies, among whom is Mephistopheles. (3) Crispin [a comic character], in the magic circle, performs laughable tricks with the spirits. (4) Faust's personal contract with hell, which is fetched through the air by a raven. (5) Crispin impudently opens a book in Dr. Faust's library and little devils come out of it. (6) Faust's journey through the air with Mephistopheles. (7) Crispin receives from Mephistopheles a fiery rain of gold. (8) Faust, at the court of the Duke of Parma, presents various noteworthy scenes from biblical and profane history, viz., (1) How Judith cuts off the head of Holofernes on a bed in his tent. (2) How Delilah robs the mighty Samson of his hair and the Philistines overcome Samson. (3) The martyrdom of Titius [Tityus], whose entrails the ravens devour out of his body. (4) The camp of Goliath who is slain by little David with a stone from a sling. (5) The destruction of Jerusalem, surely a fine spectacle. (9) Faust will make merry with the councillors of the Prince of Parma and conjure horns on the head of one of them. (10) Shows a cemetery or graveyard with many epitaphs and inscriptions. Faust wants to excavate the bones of his dead father and misuse them in his magic, but he is urged to penitence by his father's spirit. (11) Faust is converted, but

---

[1082] Ibid.

is again seduced by Mephistopheles through various illusions, in which the mournful cemetery is changed into a pleasure garden. (12) Faust recognizes the deception when it is too late. The pleasant park is turned into an open hell and the despairing Faust, after a plaint in verse, is carried to hell by the furies amid thunder and lightning. (13) A ballet of furies. (14) Mephistopheles, to the accompaniment of fireworks, draws Faust into the jaws of hell. (15) A great finale of fireworks."[1083]

The Faust plays were steadily overpowered by Gottsched's critical influence in German literature and drama as Palmer and More explain:

> "The result was that Faust was gradually crowded from the legitimate stage and into the puppet theatre. The first puppet performance of which we know was in 1746. The last performance of the old Faust play on the regular stage seems to have been in Hamburg in 1770. On the puppet stage the play maintained its popularity, especially among the lower class, until down into the nineteenth century. [...] Most of the German scholars believe that the *Ulmer Puppenspiel* [Ulm Puppet play] represents the earliest form of the puppet play which has come down to us."[1084]

The Ulm Puppet[1085] play retained the elements that made the theatre plays popular with audiences. This particular text commences with a Prologue set in Hell. Charon confronts Pluto and declares he will be his slave no longer as the "pay" is not worth it; apparently, his boat is not laden with souls for hell as heavily as in the past. Charon advises Pluto to send his demons into the world to seduce it, or his ships will remain bereft of new citizens for the hellish empire. Pluto praises Charon's zeal for his kingdom and orders the devils to rise from their lethargy and increase their numbers by fomenting disputes, tempting merchants to prepare false weights and measures, have innocent maidens seduced, and prod the university students to indulge in alcoholic libations, swearing, magic and quarrels. The devils promise to complete their duties, and Pluto arranges to rendezvous with them in the Bohemian mountains.

Act I features the famous Study Scene where Faust deliberates on his next course of scholastic action. He first muses each scholar will find a subject suited to his talents and strengths: one student will become an artist, another an architect, one will take up the plume of poetry, others will either be good orators, philosophers or physicians. He declares students who apply themselves to the study of theology aspire to achieve honour and renown, and thus was he directed to this subject from his early days. Already he has received his degree in Wittenberg, graduating "*summum gradum Doctoratus cum laude*". However, he reveals his enthusiasm to

---

[1083] W. Creizenach, op. cit., p. 11, in *Sources of the Faust Tradition*, pp. 249–250.
[1084] *Sources of the Faust Tradition*, pp. 241, 244–245.
[1085] Reprinted in the original German in *Sources of the Faust Tradition*, pp. 251–269. An approximate date is not yet estimated for this text, although we may presume it is a representative of the puppet texts circa 1746.

learn the nature of the heavens and the various planets, and discloses his plan to appear as a theologian in public, while secretly engaging in the occult arts. Immediately, Faust hears two distinct voices, one to his right, and the other to his left. The voice on his right implores him to continue his studies in theology, or his soul will be lost, while the other voice tempts him to proceed with black magic by which he will become the most learned Doctor that ever lived in Asia, Africa, America and Europe combined. Faust proceeds to interrogate them: the Voice on the right announces it is a Good Angel sent from on High to encourage him to save his soul and thereby enjoy everlasting bliss, while the Voice on the left declares it is a Spirit sent from the Netherworld to render him the happiest of all mortals: the Good and Evil Angels of Marlowe's drama! However, there is a unique development in the plot, the Evil Angel is actually Mephistopheles. Faust exclaims; "A miracle this is, Faust, and you have every reason to rejoice: Angels from Heaven come to comfort you, and the Spirits from the Netherworld to serve you." [†] Faust, however, informs the Good Angel he already decided on the path he will follow, and concedes to the voice on his left.

Act II commences with the comic character Pickelhäring who proceeds to narrate his story. His father had recently thrown him into the streets, and he must now fend for himself in the world. In his travels, he happened across a cheap inn situated close to an isolated mountain where Pluto and his devils were holding an infernal celebration, but he manages to craftily escape from their clutches. Concluding his story, the play proceeds to Act III. Wagner enters and explains Faust granted him permission to employ an extra servant to help with the housework. Wagner espies Pickelhäring, and following a comic banter between the two, Pickelhäring accepts this employment.

We return to Faust's study for the fourth act. Faust relates that his desire to study the occult excludes all other thoughts from his mind, and he muses upon the powers magic can bestow. However, he is reminded of the existence of God and delivers a self-admonishment that his actions will anger his Creator. Wagner enters, (Act V), announcing two students have come to pay a visit, and Faust presumes they are seeking a tutor. The two students heard of his new endeavours, and actually brought Faust two magic books, describing the knowledge he may attain from them with a warning: be prudent lest their gift will endanger his soul, a paradoxical piece of advice when they are placing objects of temptation within his eager grasp. Here we detect the influence of Marlowe's Cornelius and "German" Valdes who prod Faustus into experimenting, yet are not willing to share in the risks, and refrain from participating in his incantation. The fifth act concludes with Faust reassuring the two students he will be careful, adding as they leave he intends to glean all the knowledge he can from the two volumes without losing his soul. Apparently, time has elapsed in the play when we arrive at the Sixth Act for Faust proclaims he found more than he expected in the two books, suggesting he had ample time to study them. He states he cannot be restrained from experimenting and orders Wagner to bring him the necessary items from his study to perform the conjuration, instructing him to tell all who ask of his whereabouts that he will be travelling for a few days. When Wagner exits, Faust prepares the magic circle and proceeds to call upon all the evil spirits. He interrogates them on their velocity; the first is as fast as a bird, the second has the speed of an arrow shot from a bow, but the third,

---

[†] "Ein Wunderding ist's, Fauste, du hast dich billig zu erfreuen: die Engel vom Himmel kommen, dich zu trösten und die Geister aus der niedern Welt, dir zu dienen."

Mephistopheles, is an air spirit as swift as the thoughts of men. Faust is pleased with this last answer, and inquires if the spirit will enter his service. Mephistopheles replies he must seek permission from Pluto, and Faust states he is willing to wait and orders the spirit to return with an answer by twelve o'clock the next day, thus concluding Part One of the play.

Part Two, Act I opens with Wagner complaining about Pickelhäring who is proving to be a troublesome oaf. He presents the new servant to Faust for his assessment. Faust asks Pickelhäring if he had a family, and the knave cheekily describes each member as a type of fish in suggestive or derogatory double entendres, a detail obviously inspired by Marlowe's "Pageant of the Seven Deadly Sins" where each Sin comments on its lineage. Wagner calls Pickelhäring to task for his sauciness, but Faust pardons the rogue and places him in Wagner's care to ensure he is properly trained in the duties of a servant. Wagner and Pickelhäring then exit the scene, introducing Act II. Faust recalls it is close to the appointed time for the spirit to arrive, and the voice of Mephistopheles enquires in what manner or form Faust would like him to appear. Faust replies the shape of a man will suffice; apparently, the controversial monk-figure was censored in Faust dramas at this time. The demon appears in the desired shape, and declares Faust must agree to become a citizen of Hell in exchange for his service, specifying the famous twenty-four year time-frame. Faust then asks why Pluto would desire his soul, (i.e. asking why he must agree to become a citizen of hell in return for his magic), and Mephistopheles answers with the reply that similar to mortals who have no trust in each other, so too it is with the Netherworld, and he explains their agreement must be in writing. This answer indicates Pluto suspects Faust was attempting to study magic without payment, i.e. the forfeiture of his soul, and is now closing any loophole Faust may contrive as an escape plan. Faust agrees to the conditions and prepares to write. The Good Angel returns to dissuade Faust from this action, introducing Act III. Faust hears the voice of warning, but calls upon Mephistopheles and shows him the words written on his arm in Romanesque letters "Homo fuge!". Mephistopheles ingeniously inverts the meaning: Faust must fly into his waiting arms where all power is certain. Faust writes the contract, and affixes his signature when coaxed by Mephistopheles. The Angel proffers Faust a last warning before he hands the contract over, but as expected, it is to no avail.

The enactment of Faust's numerous misadventures is condensed into two sections featuring his decision to travel to the King of Prague's court, (Acts Four and Five) and his various disputations with Mephistopheles (Act VI). In Prague, Faust conjures the vision of Alexander the Great and his consort, (including the wart on her neck), to the delight of the king. Returning home, Faust asks Mephistopheles to expound on the nature of Hell and the torments of the damned. The demon explains it is a burning Hell that consumes itself, being a place that exits, and yet is not. It is a domain of eternal pain without hope as the damned cannot see the mercy of the gods, (here he speaks poetically), nor the light of the sun. Faustus learns there is no possibility of redemption for a person in Hell who has lost the grace of God. Faustus then asks Mephistopheles what he would have done if he were created a man and in the same position, a detail drawn from the *Faustbooks*. He answers with the fallacy he would have recourse to the Commandments and thereby attain Eternity, also adding that even now he will eventually escape damnation, leaving Faust doomed to never-ending hellfire. Rather than driving Faust to despair, this 'revelation' encourages the scholar to repent, and falling on his knees, he begs God for pardon. Mephistopheles attempts to dissuade Faust from his contrition by saying that if he abides by their contract, he will make him greater then Alexander the Great or Julius Ceasar, and will bestow upon him a crown and a sceptre into the bargain. Faust rejects the offer, but finally succumbs when the demon beguiles him with Helen of Troy.

Act VII portrays Faust's final night on earth. The pseudo-theologian discloses his terrible deeds to the students and warns Wagner not to follow in his footsteps by imitating his damnable actions. The clock begins to strike and Mephistopheles torments the despairing Faust on each quarter of the hour. At the first chiming the demon declares, "*Faust, praepara te!*" "Faust, prepare yourself!", at the second he cries, "*Faust! Accusatus es!*" "Faust, you are accused!", at the third quarter he announces "*Faust, judicatus es*" "Faust, you are judged!", and finally when the bell tolls twelve: "*Faust, in perpetuum damnatus es!*", "Faust, you are damned for all eternity!" Hell opens and the devils come to claim their prey, thus concluding the Ulm puppet rendition of the legend.

৪০ৎৡ ❖ ৪০ৎৡ

Notwithstanding the public's fascination in this era with the sensational aspects of the Faust plays, there were glimmers of a promising new dawn on the horizon when the story attracted the attention of the playwright and critic, Gotthold Ephraim Lessing, a prominent leader of the new Age of Enlightenment and a founding father of German national drama. The son of a Lutheran minister, Lessing was born in the town of Kamenz on January 22, 1729. He studied theology, philosophy and medicine at the universities of Leipzig and Wittenberg. During his student days, he wrote his first drama, *Der Junge Gelehrte* (*The Young Scholar* 1748). From 1748 to 1755, he resided in Berlin where he met Voltaire, whose philosophy had a profound influence on his future work, and he also made the acquaintance of the philosopher and author Moses Mendelssohn (1729–86), grandfather of the composer Felix Mendelssohn (1809–1847). Lessing wrote the first German 'middle-class' tragedy *Miss Sara Sampson* during this timeframe (1755). He moved to Leipzig for a brief three year period (1755–1758), and subsequently returned to Berlin. In company with Moses Mendelssohn and the critic Christoph Friedrich Nicolai, he commenced the publication of a new periodical dedicated to literary criticism entitled *Brief, die Neueste Literatur Betreffend* (1759–65) (*Letters on the Latest in Literature*). Of importance, Lessing contributed many articles advocating English drama, particularly Shakespeare, as the perfect model by which German dramatists may find inspiration rather than rely on French works, eventually expunging Gottsched's dictatorial influence from German literature. Leaving Berlin, Lessing went to Breslau (Wroclaw), Poland where he secured employment as secretary to the governor from 1760 to 1765. During this period, Lessing drafted two masterpieces, *Laokoon* (1766), an essay analysing painting, poetry and sculpture, and his comedy *Minna von Barnhelm* (1767). In 1765 he once again returned to Berlin and remained for two years, eventually moving to Hamburg when he failed to obtain the coveted appointment of Director of the Royal Library from Frederick the Great. While residing in Hamburg, Lessing established a national theatre without lasting success; however, this period was fruitful as Lessing dutifully published his biweekly essays, *Hamburgische Dramaturgie* (1767–68), collectively they form an important two-volume treatise on theatrical criticism and drama. He also publicly acknowledged his interest in archaeology with his *Briefe Antiquarische* (*Letters on Archaeology* 1768–69) and *Wie die Alten den Tod Gebildet* (*How the Ancients Depicted Death*, 1769). In 1770, Lessing relocated to Wolfenbüttle and received the appointment of librarian at the ducal

468

library. He completed his popular tragedy *Emilia Galotti* (1772), and became embroiled in various religious disputes during this time. When ordered by the authorities to abandon his controversial religious writings, he produced *Nathan the Wise* (1779), a drama stressing religious tolerance by displaying that nobility of character is not constrained to any one religion. Demonstrating his interest in the origins and progression of religion, he composed his theological treatise, *The Education of the Human Race* (1780). Lessing died in Wolfenbüttle on February 15, 1781.

For twenty years, Lessing had worked sporadically on a new German Faust drama. In fact, he intimated to certain friends he had drafted two distinct texts before he decided which he would present as the definitive version. One text featured his rendition of the traditional storyline with a cast of devils tempting Faust, and a second draft depicting a solitary mischievous ore or mineral Spirit representing the Dark Side, the structure following a surreal philosophical line of development revealed in a bizarre avant-garde approach, with the result that spectators would conclude Satan had actually developed the scenes.[1086] Unfortunately, the manuscript Lessing eventually selected as the official text was lost according to his friend, Captain von Blankenburg, an officer and author.[1087] Blankenburg wrote on 14th of May 1784 that the text was in transit from Wolfenbüttle to Dresden, however, the box containing the drama never reached its destination.[1088] Blankenburg did not specify the destination, but we suspect it was en route to the publisher. Lessing's brother Karl later amended this information, stating a book dealer from Brunswick named Gebler was commissioned to take the manuscript to Wolfenbüttle.[1089] For the history of German literature, this loss was a disappointing blow. Blankenburg relates the existence of this play was announced throughout Germany and therefore the public eagerly awaited the debut of this drama that promised to be the greatest masterpiece of their time. However, Lessing's intellectual labour of love had completely vanished. Despite this tragic setback, snatches of Lessing's original ideas survive in various documents affording us a glimpse of his revolutionary perception of the original Faustian legend and early Faust dramas illuminated by his philosophy on the Enlightenment.

During his first sojourn in Berlin, Lessing attended a performance of the popular Faust play in 1754 produced by the Schuch troupe. This experience was the catalyst that inspired him to develop his interpretation of the legend, for a letter written by Moses Mendelssohn dated November 19, 1755 is the first documentary evidence suggesting Lessing had commenced his Faust drama.[1090] Four years later, Lessing presented a brief preview of Scene Three from Act II of his burgeoning masterpiece in the seventeenth *Literaturbrief* (February 16, 1759).[1091] Lessing

---

[1086] I.e. an extract from a letter written by Staatsrat Gebler of Vienna to Christoph Friedrich Nicolai, (Dec. 9, 1775), and from an extract from Friedrich Müller's (Maler Müller) account of his meeting with Lessing in Mannheim, (1777). Gebler was an Austrian politician and dramatist, (not to be confused with the book dealer to whom Lessing originally sent his MS). Nicolai was a book dealer, publisher and writer in Berlin. Müller was a poet, painter and engraver. Both extracts are reprinted in the original German in *Sources of the Faust Tradition*, pp. 279–280.

[1087] *Sources of the Faust Tradition*, p. 280.

[1088] Ibid.

[1089] Ibid.

[1090] Ibid. p. 273. (This letter is not reprinted.)

[1091] Ibid. pp. 274–277. Reprinted in the original German.

criticises Gottsched in this issue of the *Literaturbrief* for relying on French works to stimulate German theatre and suggested English drama to be a suitable alternative: Lessing was obviously preparing his *Doctor Faust* to be the epitome of this ideal.

The scene released to the public featured Faust discovering the names of the spirits of Hell and questioning them on their velocity. Lessing extended this traditional account with graceful wit and philosophical insight. Seven spirits appear to Faust and he singles one of them out, asking if it is the fastest spirit. All the devils immediately clamour they are the fastest, and when Faust enquires if they all travel at an analogous speed, they admit they do not. He questions them again, and they once more proclaim in one voice that they are the swiftest. Faust remarks what a miracle it is that among seven devils there are only six liars and declares he must learn more about them in detail. The First Spirit sarcastically replies that "one day" he will, intimating they intend to see him in Hell for eternity where he will have ample opportunity to know them all better. Faust retorts, "One day! How do you mean that? Does the Devil also preach penance?"* The First Spirit replies in the affirmative for this task of preaching penance is allocated to the 'Stubborn Ones' (den Verstockten). The demons obviously have changed their tactics in tempting the human race, realising that preaching repentance can have the opposite effect on obstinate souls who react negatively to correction, and therefore entrench their souls deeper in their life of vice. Faust asks the First Spirit its name and the nature of its velocity, yet the Spirit does not disclose its name, and suggests Faust might prefer to give an example of the speed he seeks. Swiftly, Faust passes his finger over the flame of a candle and asks the Spirit to describe what it had witnessed. The Spirit relates he saw him pass his finger rapidly through the flame, and Faust completes the answer by stating he accomplished this without burning his finger: if the Spirit can fly seven times faster than this through the flames of Hell and not burn in the process, then he will consider him worthy to become his familiar spirit. The Spirit grows silent, for it knows it cannot escape the pain of the infernal fire. Faust then taunts the Spirit for its audacious boasting as it cannot fulfil the promised demonstration, and duly notes that no sin is too small to attract a devil's attention, hinting they can be swift when they choose. Faust then turns to the Second Spirit, who informs him its name is Chil, and this in Faust's "boring tongue" would translate 'Arrow of the Plague'. Faust dismisses this entity for it is too slow for him, instructing it to go find a physician to serve. The Third Spirit states its name is 'Dilla' and explains he is carried on the wings of the wind.‡ The Fourth introduces itself as 'Jutta', a demon who travels on light beams.

Faust is exasperated as these first four display no practical use to him, however, the Fifth Spirit pacifies Faust by explaining he had questioned Satan's messengers of the physical world, but had not yet examined the demons of the spirit kingdom who are significantly faster. The Fifth demon explains he is as swift as the thoughts of man and Faust is impressed, although Faust observes human thoughts are not always quick, particularly when the subjects of virtue and truth are deliberated … how lethargic is the mind of mankind then! Faust turns away from this spirit and decides to continue his inspection by questioning the Sixth. This Spirit declares it is as fast as the "vengeance of the Avengers", and Faust inquires of the Spirit which 'Avengers' is he referring to. The Spirit replies; "The Enormous One, the Terrible One, to whom all vengeance is

---

* "Einst! Wie meinst du das? Predigen die Teufel auch Busse?"
‡ The word "Winde" = 'windlass' or 'winch' is printed, but is an obvious misspelling for "Wind".

reserved," thus intimating God, however the Spirit dares to suggest God reserves the right to avenge misdeeds simply because it is enjoyable. Faust calls the blaspheming mocker to task, and then retorts revenge is not 'fast': why is he, an erring human being, allowed to remain on earth and continue to commit sin? The demon retorts that Faust, (or any human), permitted to live in this manner, is already experiencing God's revenge, i.e. God abandons hardened sinners to their own devices if they continually reject conversion. We observe the demon conveniently focused on God's vengeance and set the subject of mercy aside. Faust balks that once more a demon presumes to preach to him, and he rejects this Spirit for it too, fails to meet his requirements. Finally, the Seventh Spirit begins to grumble, suspecting Faust will not find him acceptable. Now, Faust enquires of the Seventh Spirit how swift is he, and the Spirit answers as fast as the transition from Good to Evil. Faust is satisfied with this answer and sends the others back to Hell; "Ha! You are my devil! As fast as the transition from Good to Evil! Yes, that is fast; nothing is faster than that! Away from here, you snails of Orcus!♦ Away! The transition from Good to Evil! I experienced it, how quick it is! I experienced it!"*

Proceeding with the "Berlin Scenario" published by Lessing's brother, Karl, in 1784, we find a sketch of the missing first segments of the drama. Petsch believes this Scenario dates from the time of the *Literaturbrief* described above.[1092] The drama apparently commenced with a sophisticated redevelopment of Pluto's Prologue introduced in the earlier German plays. Lessing's Prologue is set in an ancient cathedral in Berlin with the sexton and his son ringing the bells until midnight. Beelzebub and his minions hover invisibly over the altars, and the Demonic Prince calls his court to order, demanding each devil give an account of its activities. One devil reports it set a whole city on fire, another relates it destroyed a fleet of ships by stirring up a great tempest. The third demon is rebuked for not completing its duties successfully; nevertheless, it defends its actions, boasting it enticed a holy man to become intoxicated and thereby further tempted him to commit adultery and perpetrate a murder. This discussion affords the demons an opportunity to raise the subject on how they can lure Faust to damnation, and the third devil announces he will have Faust in Hell within twenty-four hours, declaring that Faust's one weakness is his thirst for knowledge: "Too much eagerness for knowledge is a fault; and all vices can spring from a fault, if one is too attached to it."+ The devil then briefly explains his plan, although it is not mentioned in the Berlin Scenario at this particular point.

Act I takes place from midnight to the following midnight. Faust is seated in his study surrounded by books, the darkness held at bay by a single lamp. He is tormented by doubts concerning the pursuit of wisdom according to Scholasticism, ("scholastischen Weltweisheit"), and recalls an incident where a scholar reputedly summoned a devil in the form of Aristotle's *entelechie* with whom he directly discussed and resolved his philosophical questions. This

---

♦ I.e. Pluto.

* "Ha! du bist mein Teufel! — So schnell also der Übergang vom Guten zum Bösen! — Ja, der ist schnell; schneller ist nichts als der!—Weg von hier, ihr Schnecken des Orkus! Weg!—Als der Übergang vom Guten zum Bösen! Ich habe es erfahren, wie schnell er ist! Ich habe es erfahren!"

[1092] *Sources of the Faust Tradition*, p. 277. This Scenario is reprinted in the original German, pp. 277–279.

+ "Zuviel Wissbegierde ist ein Fehler; und aus einem Fehler können alle Laster entspringen, wenn man ihm zu sehr nachhänget."

particular term for 'soul' is interesting: 'entelechy' is the philosophical expression of the invisible vital principle that guides the development and function of a living being or organism. In other words, it is a substitute term for 'soul' albeit conspicuously stripped of its religious connotations. This term is apt for this scene as a devil cannot take the actual place of an immortal human soul, but can assume the shape of a person and replicate its talents and intellectual endowments. The devil would therefore appear in spirit as a human 'facsimile' and not as an actual 'soul'. Continuing with this scene, Faust admits he already experimented with summoning an entity in the guise of Aristotle, and failed many times. This first scene concludes with Faust, once more, attempting to conjure a demon.

Scene two features Faust's first successful invocation of an *'entelechie'*. A spirit rises from beneath the earth in an ethereal state of confusion as though stirred from a deep, dream-filled slumber. Faust enquires as to the identity of this spirit, but the spirit is not certain; it asks Faust for a little time to deliberate the matter, since now 'it is', or rather, exists from just then — the spirit is vaguely conscious of its current body at that point. Faust then asks who it *was*, and still in a state of blurred consciousness, the spirit inertly repeats the question. Faust rephrases his query, asking who it was formerly during its life. The spirit again echoes the question. Patiently, Faust verbally prods the spirit, asking if, at the present time under these circumstances, it can remember any of its previous "ideas". The spirit gradually becomes cognitively confident in its new environment and replies that flashes of its former thoughts are returning, adding that if Faust waits a moment he will eventually find the "thread" back to his past. Faust assures the spirit he will assist him, and once again, asks the spirit its name: the spirit is almost certain this time it is, (or was), Aristotle.

From this point onward, Lessing's brother, in general terms, proceeds to describe the remainder of this scene. Faust and the spirit engage in a detailed disputation, however, 'Aristotle' grows weary with their conversation, finding it a great effort to relive events and thought processes from his past life. He explains he cannot discuss the subjects that interest Faust while he remains in the shape of a man, and yet is unable to converse with him in his spirit form. The spirit finally asks Faust to dismiss him. Naturally, 'Aristotle' is the devil who boasted he could ensnare Faust within twenty-four hours; apparently, the devil's tactic is to artfully persuade Faust he conversed with a *human* entity completely weakened by the effects of death and who therefore cannot offer him any substantial or enduring assistance in his pursuit of knowledge. We detect the aim of this strategy is to entice Faust, and compel him to seek the aid of a powerful, immortal demon on a one-to-one basis as he already ventured to conjure a spirit. This plan succeeded, for Faust in Scene Three endeavours to summon a Demon when the fatigued 'Aristotle' vanishes. The apparition of the Demon introduces Scene Four. Attempting to dupe Faust regarding his prowess in conjuration, the fiend imperiously roars; "Who is the powerful one, whose calls I must obey! You? A mortal? Who taught you these tremendous words?"[‡] Unfortunately, Karl's description of the Berlin Scenario ends at this section. Perhaps Faust demanded the spirit to serve him, and it refuses to comply with this order unless they formulate a contract or swear a formal oath in a binding agreement. However, Faust will not flippantly forfeit his soul without considering the quality of the spirit's abilities and decides he

---

[‡] "Wer ist der Mächtige, dessen Rufe ich gehorchen muss! Du? Ein Sterblicher? Wer lehrte dich diese gewaltige Worte?"

shall have no other but the swiftest spirit as his servant and proceeds to summon all the demons, thus seamlessly leading the plot into the *Literaturbrief* Preview that Lessing had decided to print.

A friend of Gotthold and Karl Lessing, J.J. Engel, a professor at the Joachimsthaler Gymnasium in Berlin, wrote a separate account of the Prologue.[1093] Lessing had obviously revised the play at the time he described the plot to Engel, for this report includes elaborate details not featured in the Berlin Scenario.

Engel relates the Prologue opened with a desolate scene depicting the ruins of an ancient gothic cathedral. The high altar and six side altars are intact and serve as the thrones for Satan and his six demonic cohorts. Engel explains Satan's singular passion is the total annihilation of God's Creation, and therefore the Fiend selects locations once dedicated to the service of Eternal Good as his preferred haunts on earth. The proceedings of the Infernal court are audible to the audience, however, the demons remain invisible for the entire scene. Lessing obviously intended to expose the decline of religious fervour and morals with the paradoxical and eerie scene of the voice of Satan and his demons reigning on hallowed ground where God was once so honoured. Satan addresses the First Demon, demanding an account of his activities. The demon relates he saw a black cloud in the sky brimming with destructive power, and directing it over the hovel of an impoverished pious couple, he released the full force of its lightning, thus destroying all that remained of their meagre possessions. Satan is appalled with this report, remarking that by this course of action, *they* have become the "poor ones", and duly rebukes his minion: he should have tempted the couple with wealth, for if they were consumed with the desire for gold they would eventually fall into despair. Satan therefore concludes that depriving the poor of their few material possessions draws them closer to God in their desolation. He then turns to the Second Demon who relates, as he hovered over the sea, he heard a barrage of curses rising up from below, and looking down, he perceived a fleet of ships, which he successfully destroyed by causing a terrible storm, and is pleased to report to Satan all the souls on board the ships are now in his possession. The Arch Fiend is infuriated with this news for those souls were already his to begin with! We discover Satan had formulated a cunning plan for the fleet; the amoral sailors would be his ambassadors of vice, spreading immorality, greed, plunder and worldly gratification to every corner of the earth … his plans are now all brought to naught. He declares the Second Demon a traitor and sends him back to Hell. Turning to the Third Demon, Satan sarcastically asks if he too resorted to using the power of storm clouds to accomplish his destructive mission, and the devil replies he did not presume to fly that high and is not inclined to the Terrifying as he prefers to use the vice of Lust. On the contrary, Satan did not consider this a 'lowly' method, exclaiming he is a more terrifying demon to send in pursuit of souls. The Third Demon explains his technique to ensnare his prey; he becomes an incubus. He probes the thoughts of sleeping humans, in this particular case, "sleeping Blossoms",[†] and discovers their secret passions and fantasies, assuming the shape of whom they desire. Satan interrupts the euphemistic narration and impatiently gets to the point: did he manage to rob a maiden of her innocence? The demon replies he "stole" an "untouched beauty" — her first kiss — but did not drive her further into physical temptation at that point; she will certainly be theirs as he ignited a carnal flame that will

---

[1093] The document is not dated. Reprinted in the original German in *Sources of the Faust Tradition*, pp. 282–286.

[†] I.e. "Buhlerin schlummern": obviously derived from 'blühen'.

transform her into a resourceful seductress. The Arch Fiend is pleased with this report, for now they will reap victim upon victim as she spreads her flames of seduction. Although the demon had not ensnared her completely, Satan praises the strategy of his minion. The successful entrapment of souls for the kingdom of Hell is accomplished by drawing upon the weakness of humans and having *them* accomplish the dirty work of temptation, spreading evil like a plague. From the narration, we also learn the 'art' of stealing souls pivots on stirring up illicit desires in the Free Will of humans, leading them to sinful action. Satan then contrasts the missions of the first two devils with the third, declaring the former have contributed solely to the destruction of the corporeal world, while the latter employed his powers to wreak havoc in the spiritual realm, and is therefore a demon worthy of esteem. Addressing the Fourth Demon, the Infernal monarch demands a report on the deeds it accomplished. This devil replies he has nothing to report as yet, however, if his Idea could be wrought into Action, his plan would strike all other demonic strategies to the ground. He suggests the greatest, fiendish deed, were it accomplished, would be to snatch a soul favoured by God: in this instance, the demon refers to a pensive, solitary young man who rejects every human passion, except his search for wisdom. The demon remarks this is a dangerous soul to leave on earth, for if this human discovers Truth and begins to impart his knowledge to others, they will lose many souls to Heaven. Needless to mention, the introspective soul that the devil seeks to destroy is the scholar, Faust. Satan gleefully approves and asks his servant how he plans to capture this special victim, and the devil replies this will be difficult for he searched in every corner of this soul and has not discovered any weakness by which he may entangle his prey. This admission does not bother the Fiend: did this human not have a thirst for knowledge? The Fourth Demon replies in the affirmative, adding that this soul's thirst for knowledge is greater than any other mortal. Satan confirms all that is required for their success is Faust's compulsion to seek after knowledge, and he takes command of this mission as his particular project.

From this point, Engel proceeds to describe the plot in general terms. Satan is primarily engrossed formulating his strategy to tempt Faust with his lust for knowledge, and the presumption of his success in this endeavour, therefore he adjourns the council without hearing the reports of the remaining demons. The demonic band were completely unaware that the Good Angel of Providence invisibly witnessed all the proceedings and declared they shall not succeed. The Angel places Faust in a deep sleep, and concealing him in a safe location, outmanoeuvres the demons with a Phantom bearing the likeness of Faust. Throughout the play, the devils tempt this Phantom mistaking it for their target, and when they are convinced they have finally ensnared Faust's soul, the Phantom vanishes. As Engel explains, this Phantom is Faust's subconscious, which assumes his place while he sleeps, and therefore Faust experiences all that the demons impart to his double through an ethereal dream and awakes when the Phantom disappears. *In fine*, through this intervention of Angelic Providence, Faust learned Truth and Falsehood by the Phantom's experiences with the demons, acquiring all the knowledge he sought without incurring eternal death, which may have occurred if he was actually tempted and had fallen. God therefore granted a favourite soul an additional boon and Heaven ultimately triumphs as the demons' plan implodes upon themselves.

Blankenburg's brief description of the plot corresponds with Engel's account, and he provides a few additional lines for Satan and the Angel. When Satan learns Faust's single proclivity is the search for knowledge and science, he exultantly proclaims Faust's soul is his for the taking: "Ha! Then it is mine, and is forever mine, and more securely mine, than with any other passion!"[**] In the Finale when the devils believe they have captured Faust, the Angel of Providence declares: "Triumph not, for you have not triumphed over Humanity and Science: the Deity did not grant the most noblest of inclinations to mankind, in order to make it eternally unfortunate. That which you see and believe to possess was nothing but a Phantom."[√]

℠℞ ❖ ℠℞

These two sentences summarise the new possibilities that intellectuals, influenced by the Age of Enlightenment, were beginning to uncover in the original Faustian legend. Previously, Faust was rigidly cast as a scholar drawn to evil, having exhausted all legitimate avenues of education and who, as a result, turns to black magic to satisfy his illicit lust for preternatural knowledge and superhuman power. Now, Faust is perceived as a representative of the human race, an Everyman incessantly compelled to search for Truth and Knowledge. How could this yearning for intellectual fulfilment be intrinsically evil? Academia and the longing for erudition was no longer the catalyst for Faust's damnation; rather, it would become *the driving force for his salvation*. Had Lessing's play premiered, the public would have received an early introduction to a new vision of Faust transcending the legend of old. Nevertheless, Lessing's masterpiece was not lost in vain. Germany awaited a Faust drama that would excel all expectations, and soon, that anticipation would be fulfilled with the rising of a new literary sun — Johann Wolfgang von Goethe.

[**] "Ha! Dann ist er mein, und auf immer mein, und sicherer mein, als bei jeder andern Leidenschaft!"
[√] "Triumphiert nicht, ihr habt nicht über Menschheit und Wissenschaft gesiegt; die Gottheit hat dem Menschen nicht den edelsten der Triebe gegeben, um ihn ewig unglücklich zu machen; was ihr sahet und jetzt zu besitzen glaubt, war nichts als win Phantom.—"

Appendices

༄ ❖ ༄

Appendix One

Timeline of the 29 Major Faustus documents [1094]

January 9, 1483	**From the Registration Records of Heidelberg University**[1095] "Georgius Helmstetter dioc. Wormaciensis nona January" (1483). (A Georg Helmstetter of the Worms Diocese registered at the University of Heidelberg on January 9, 1483. This entry may be the Georgius Sabellicus Faustus of other documents.)
Würzburg 20, August, 1507.	**Letter of Johannes Tritheim (Trithemius) to Johannes Virdung** [1096] Faustus considered a fool, vagabond, rogue and ignorant in "good letters" by Trithemius. Apparently he declared that he was "Master George (Georgius) Sabellicus, the younger Faustus, the chief of necromancers, astrologer, the second magus, palmist, diviner with earth (agromanticus) and fire, second in the art of divination with water." Actually composed a calling card[1097] with these titles according to Trithemius. Faustus also declared with his vast knowledge and wisdom he could restore with increased beauty all the books and philosophy of Plato and Aristotle if they should ever pass from the memory of man. (Trithemius compares Faustus to Erza[1098] the Hebrew). Boasted he

---

[1094] Frank Baron's discovery in 1989 of a new Helmstetter reference has been included. Complete quotations of this abridged information from the other Faustus documents are available in *Sources of the Faust Tradition,* unless stated / cited otherwise.

[1095] From Gustav Toepke, *Die Matrikel der Universität Heidelberg* (Heidelberg, 1884–1893), I p. 370, in *Doctor Faustus: From History to Legend,* p. 17.

[1096] From Alexander Tille*, Die Faustsplitter in der Literatur des sechzehnten bis achtzehnten Jahrhunderts*, No. 1 (Berlin: 1898– 1901), [Reprint; the *Jahrbuch der Sammlung Kippenberg* Vol.s 1, 4, 8, and 9: apparently this was the source used,] in *Sources of the Faust Tradition*, pp. 83–86.

[1097] Johannes Trithemius, *Epistolarum familiarum libri due* (Hagenau: P. Brubach, 1536), pp. 312–314, in *Faust, from History to Legend,* p. 29.

[1098] According to Hebrew tradition, a priest of the tribe of Levi who was inspired by God to restore all the works of the prophets and the law given to Moses, which had been lost during the days of the Babylonian

	could also perform the same miracles of Christ whenever he wished, and in alchemy, the most learned of men. Supposedly appointed schoolmaster in Kreuznach on the recommendation of Franz von Sickengen, but was accused of "nefarious fornication" and fled the vicinity.
1509	**Extract from the Matriculation Records of Heidelberg University**[1099] **(A "Johann Faust" is recorded.)** "Nach einem Inscriptions-Verzeichnisse der philosophischen Fakultät zu Heidelberg war ein Johann Faust in Jahre 1509 bei ihr als lernendes Mitglied eingeschrieben. Ein „Johann Faust" kommt in den actis philosoph. Heidelb., tom. III, fol. 36, a unter dem Decanate des Mag. Laurentius Wolff von Speier, Baccalaureus der Theologie im Jahre 1509, als der erste unter denen vor, die am 15. Januar 1509 ad baccalaureatus gradum de via moderna ordine, quo supra notatum, admissi sunt. Er ist mit den Worten angeführt: „Johannes Faust ex Simern." Auszer ihm stehen in derselben Promotion noch 15 andere. Dem namen ist, wie einigen andern Promovirten, d vorausgesetzt, was nach des Herrn geh. Kirchenraths Ullmann Erklärung, dem ich diese Mittheilung verdank, so viel als dedit, „er hat bezahlt," bedeutet, und ein Beweis für die Wohlhabenheit dieses Faust ist. Die Via moderna ist die nominalistiche Richtung gegenüber der realistischen, welche damals als eine neue oder reformatorische beliebt war. Nach andern historischen Nachrichten, auf die wir hingewiesen haben, wird Faust auch Hedebergensis (vielleicht so viel als Heidelbergensis) genannt und tribe sich auch in der Rheinpfalz herum."

captivity. From Eusebius, *Ecclesiastical History*, tr. by K. Lane, Vol. I, V, viii, 461 (London, 1926), in *Faust, from History to Legend*, p. 85.

[1099] From Scheible, *Kloster*, Vol. XI, p. 330, in *Sources of the Faust Tradition*, pp. 86–87.

October 1513	**Letter of Conrad Mutianus Rufus to Henrich Urbanus**[1100] Faustus in Erfurt: he boasts of his feats at an inn and is called "Georgius Faustus, Helmitheus Hedebergensis"[1101] in this account. Rufus describes him as " a certain chiromanticus" (a palmist) and "a mere braggart and fool".
Entry dated February 12, 1520	**From the Account Book of the Bishop of Bamberg, 1519–1520. (By Hans Muller)**[1102] Under the "Miscellaneous" heading of the annual accounts: "10 gulden given and presented as a testimonial to Doctor Faustus,[1103] the philosopher, who made for my master a horoscope or prognostication. Paid on the Sunday after Saint Scholastica's Day by the order of his reverence."
June 5, 1528 (Journal entry: July 1528)	**From the Journal of Killian Lieb**[1104] "Georgius faustus helmstetensis[1105] said on the fifth of June that when the sun and Jupiter are in the same constellation prophets are born (presumably such as he.). He asserted that he was the commander or

---

[1100] From Tille, No. 2, in *Sources of the Faust Tradition*, pp. 87–88.

[1101] The authors of *Sources from the Faust Tradition* state in n. 13, pp. 87– 88: "The Latin phrase 'Helmitheus Hedebergensis' is unintelligible. Christian August Heumann (cf. Tille, p. 587) surmises that 'Helmithus' is a misspelling for "Hemitheus." H. Düntzer (cf. Scheible's *Kloster*, V, 36) suggests "Hedelbergensis" instead of 'Hedebergensis.' These emendations are generally accepted. Franz Babinger *(Alemania* 41, 1914), basing his argument on Kilian Lieb's report, argues for the reading of "Helmsteten(sis) Hedelbergensis," which would mean "from Helmstedt near Heidelberg." Frank Baron in *Faustus from History to Legend* states in n. 19, p. 91: "The original letter of Mutianus Rufus was copied by Heinrich Urban, to whom it was addressed. A careful examination of the manuscript indicates that the corrupted form Helmithius could have arisen because Urban was unable to decipher the letter at this point. In Urban's handwriting the difference between the letters i and s is a matter of length, and therefore one may even suspect that he was actually approximating an s as is appeared in the original letter (i.e., Helmstheus). [See also] Schottenloher, *Münchener neuste Nachrichten*, July 5, 1913 (no. 338. Also in Franz Babinger, "Der geschichtliche Faust," *Almannia*, 41. (1914), 153.".."

[1102] From Tille, No. 3, in *Sources of the Faust Tradition*, 88–89.

[1103] Of interest, the Latin spelling of "Faustus" and not "Faust" is recorded, although the account is written in German.

[1104] From Karl Schottenloher, *Der Rebdorfer Prior, Kilian Leib, und sein Wettertagebuch von 1513 bis 1531.* Goth, 1913, Friedrich Andreas Perthes A– G. (Sonderabdruck der Beiträge zur Bayrischen Geschichte). Leib's original journal is in the Staatsbibliothek in Munich, in *Sources of Faust Tradition,* p. 89.

[1105] Authors of *Sources of the Faust Tradition* (n. 22, p. 89) state Schottenloher connects this title with Rufus' "helmitheus Hedebergensis" and concludes that Faustus was born in Helmstedt near Heidelberg. See n. 22, p. 89.

	preceptor of the order of the Knights of St. John at a place called Hallestein[1106] on the border of Carinthia."
June 15, 1528	**From the Records of the City of Ingolstadt.**[1107] "(a) Minute on the actions of the city Council in Ingolstadt. Today, the Wednesday after St. Vitus' Day, 1528. (Monday 15th) The fortune-teller shall be ordered to leave the city and to spend his penny elsewhere." "(b) Record of those banished from Ingolstadt. On Wednesday after St. Vitus' Day, 1528 a certain man who called himself Dr. George Faustus (Dr. Jörg Faustus)[1108] of Heidelberg was told to spend his penny elsewhere and he pledged himself not to take vengeance on or make fools of the authorities for this order."
May, 10, 1532	**Entry in the Records of the City Council of Nürnburg (Nüremburg / Nuremberg).**[1109] "Safe conduct to Doctor fausto, the great sodomite and necromancer, at Fürth refused. The Junior Burgomaster."
1534	**Letter from Peter Seuter to Nicolaus Ellenbog.**[1110] Seuter, a lawyer in Kempton, sent a horoscope Faustus drafted for him at Heidelberg in 1490 to a friend for his assessment. "[…] I am sending this along with my horoscope, which Magister Georgius Helmstette[r] prepared for me on the basis of astrology, physiognomy, and chiromancy." (Seuter) Ellenbog was not impressed and returned the chart:

[1106] According to Schottenloher, "Hallestein" could indicate Heilenstein in Styria, which at one time, was the seat of the Knights of St. John. *Sources of the Faust Tradition*, n. 20, p. 89.

[1107] From Tille, No. 4, in *Sources of the Faust Tradition*, p. 90.

[1108] Note, original text in German, but "Faustus" is recorded.

[1109] From Neubert, *Vom Doctor Faustus zu Goethe's Faust* (Leipzig: 1932), p. 16, in *Sources of the Faust Tradition*, p. 90. The original can be found in the Bavarian State Archives in Nuremberg.

[1110] Frank Baron, 'Faustus: His Life and Legend', Website: *Historicum.net*. (November 12, 2009). www.historicum.net/themen/hexenforschung/lexikon/personen/art/Georg_Faustus/html/artikel/7114/ca/69 3f7c07ad/ See also Baron's source / reference: Baron, 'Who was the Historical Faustus? Interpreting an Overlooked Source', *Daphnis* 18, 1989, S. 297–302.

	"[…] I am returning the horoscope prepared for you by a certain Helmstetter, for I was unable to make it out fully and even less to understand it, especially since I am ignorant of chiromancy. He indicated the position of the stars with twelve houses, but he omitted the degrees of the signs (which are definitely necessary here). Nor did he show the planets with their signs and degrees. To sum up, I am unable to learn from his work, and I took care to return it to you immediately [...]."
Date of document unknown. (A prophecy made by Faust: June 25, 1535)	**From the Waldeck Chronicle.**[1111] "Dr. Faustus", the Necromancer, apparently made a correct prophesy concerning the Bishop's successful capture of the city of Münster from the heretical Anabaptist sect.
August 13, 1536	**Letter from Joachim Camerarius to Daniel Stibar**[1112] This "Faustus" a "friend" of Stibar. Camerarius asks Stibar to approach Faustus and discover what information he knows concerning the emperor: this is a possible horoscope or prophecy request.
Martin Luther (1483-1546)	**Two quotes[1113] in the Tischreden of Martin Luther:** *(1566 Aurifaber Edition);[1114] First recorded by Nicolaus Medler between October 24, 1533 and September 14, 1535.[1115] "God's Word alone overcomes the fiery arrows of the devil and all

---

[1111] From the *Jahrbuch der Sammlung Kippenberg*, I (1921), p. 322, in *Sources of the Faust Tradition*, p. 91.

[1112] From Tille, No. 5, in *Sources of the Faust Tradition*, p. 92.

[1113] *Sources of the Faust Tradition*, pp. 92–93. The *Tischreden* was originally published by Aurifaber in Eisleben (1566).

[1114] From Tille, No. 15, in *Sources of the Faust Tradition*.

[1115] *Faustus, from History to Legend*, p. 78.

	his temptations. When one evening at the table a sorcerer named Faustus was mentioned, Doctor Martin said in a serious tone: 'The devil does not make use of the services of sorcerers against me. If he had been able to do to me any harm he would have done it long since. To be sure he has often had me by the head but he had to let me go again. [...]' *(Recorded 1537; first published 1903)[1116]: Between June 18, and July 28, 1537.[1117] "Mention was made of magicians and the magic art, and how Satan blinded men. Much was said about Fausto, who called the devil his brother-in-law, and the remark was made: 'If I, Martin Luther, had given him even my hand, he would have destroyed me; but I would not have been afraid of him, — with God as my protector, I would have given him my hand in the name of the Lord. For I believe many magic tricks have been attempted against me.'"
Published 1539	**A mention in the *Index Sanitatis* by Philipp Begardi[1118]** Description of Faustus (in the past tense): No desire to remain obscure and unknown, boasted of skill in medicine, chiromancy, "nigromancy" (possible misspelling of necromancy), physiognomy, crystal gazing and other similar arts. Said to have visited "almost all countries, principalities, and kingdoms". Called himself "Faustus" and the "philosopher of philosophers". Deeds described as 'petty and fraudulent', quick to receive money for his services, and "left many to whistle for their money".
January 16, 1540	**Letter from Phillipp von Hutten to His Brother Moritz von Hutten.[1119]** Apparently, "Faustus" accurately predicted (c. 1534?) that Philipp von Hutten's expedition to Venezuela would prove unfortunate.

[1116] This extract from Walz, "An English Faustsplitter," *Modern Language Notes*, *Vol. XLII* (1927), p. 361, and Luther's *Tischreden*, no. 3601 in *Faust, from History to Legend*, p. 78. It was first recorded by Antonius Lauterbach in 1537, but was not published until 1903 by E. Kroker in *Luthers Tischreden in der Mathesischen Sammlung*, (Leipzig).

[1117] *Faustus, from History to Legend*, p. 78.

[1118] From Tille, No. 6, in *Sources of the Faust Tradition*, p. 94.

[1119] From Tille, No. 7, in ibid. pp. 95–96.

c. 1548	**From the *Sermones Convivales* of Johannes Gast**[1120] Faustus titled as a necromancer. Both names "Fausto" and "Faustus" used in this account. Two stories: - Faust spends a night at a rich monastery. A brother refuses to serve him the wine reserved for the nobles on the grounds that he does not have permission to do so from the prior. Faust leaves without notice the next day and sends a raging devil to haunt the place and cause mischief. The monks are forced to leave the monastery. - Gast's "own story": "At Basle I dined with him in the great college and he gave to the cook various kinds of birds to roast. I do not know where he bought them or who gave them to him, since there was none on sale at the time. Moreover I never saw any like them in our regions. He had with him a dog and a horse which I believe to have been demons and which were ready for any service. I was told that the dog at times assumed the form of a servant and served the food. However, the wretch was destined to come to a deplorable end, for he was strangled by the devil and his body on its bier kept turning face downward even though it was five times turned on its back. God preserve us lest we become slaves of the devil."
1549–1560	**Two extracts from the *Explicationes Melanchtoniae* (published 1594), reproducing Melanchthon's commentaries on Scripture between 1549 and 1560.**[1121] *Explicationes Melanchtoniae (Pars II)[1122]: Mention of the famous legend of Simon Magus and his attempt to fly to heaven in the presence of Nero but is thwarted by the prayers of St. Peter and is dashed to the ground. "Faustus" allegedly attempted the same feat in Venice with similar results.

[1120] From Tille, No. 8, in ibid. pp. 96–98.
[1121] Published by Melanchthon's student Christopher Pezelius. *Sources of the Faust Tradition*, n. 46, p. 99.
[1122] From Tille, No. 9, in *Sources of the Faust Tradition*, pp. 99.

	*Explicationes Melanchtoniae (Pars IV)[1123]: Comment that the devil can devise certain natural phenomenon beyond human understanding. "Faustus" while in Vienna devours another magician who is later discovered in a cave.
Zurich, August 16, 1561	**From the *Epistolae Medicinales* of Conrad Gesner. Letter From Gesner to Johannes Crato of Krafftheim.** [1124] "Faustus" described as a celebrated "wandering scholar …who died not long since." Gesner claims that the current vogue for practising the magic arts (such as astrology, geomancy, and necromancy), derived from the ancient Druids who were taught "by demons in underground places." According to his belief, these occult practises were still flourishing in Salamanca, Spain.
1563	**From the *Locorum Communium Collectanea* (1563) of Johannes Manlius. (Quotations from Melanchthon.)**[1125] Manlius transcribes the name "John" (not George). "Faustum" and "Faustus" included in the script. Says this Faustus was originally from Kundling (Knittlingen) and was a student at Cracow (Krakow) where black magic was practised openly. Boasted in Venice he would fly to heaven to provide a spectacle; the devil then raised him up, but dashed him to the ground. Faustus' death declared as occurring "a few years ago … in the Duchy of Württemberg." John Faustus on the night of his death is downcast contrary to his customary behaviour and tells his host not to be frightened that night. The house shakes in the middle of the night, and Faustus is discovered at noon the next day lying near the bed with his face turned toward his back. "Thus the devil had killed him." Some accounts of his life: recount of the tale that his dog was the devil and is compared to Agrippa, author of De vanitate atrium, who also was believed to have a familiar devil in the form of a dog. Accounts of Faustus fleeing arrest in Wittenberg and Nuremberg. Description of Faustus as a "cloaca (sewer) of many devils" (i.e.,

---

[1123] From Tille, No. 10, in ibid.
[1124] From Tille, No. 41, in ibid. pp. 100–101.
[1125] *Sources of the Faust Tradition,* pp. 101–102. Manlius was Melanchthon's student.

	possessed of many devils?) Faustus boasts that his magic was the cause of the emperor's victories in Italy, which Melanchthon refutes as lies.
1564–66	**From the *Zimmerische Chronik*. Written by Count Froben Christoph von Zimmern († 1566 or 1567) and his secretary Hans Müller († ca. 1600)**[1126] Soothsaying declared a godless and dangerous art, "Fausto / Faustus" portrayed as an example for he was "finally killed at a ripe old age by the evil one". Place of death described as "the seigniory of Staufen in Breisgau". (After 1539). Many believed the devil, whom Faustus called his "brother-in-law", killed him. A mention that Faustus' books become the property of the Count of Staufen. An account that Faustus sent a restless spirit to plague the monks in the monastery at "Luxheim" because they refused him quarters for the night.
1568	**From the Fourth Edition of Johannes Wier's *De Praestigiis Daemonium* (4th Edition 1568)**[1127] Faustus named "John Faustus". Born in Kundling, and studied magic in Cracow. Previous to 1540, he travelled Germany and performed many feats described as fraudulent. Accounts of his tricks and boasts: • Faustus is taken prisoner at Batenburg on the Maas near the border of Geldern. Baron Hermann was not present and his chaplain Dr. Johannes Dorstenius keeps Faustus in custody. In return for leniency, Faustus promises to impart some of his knowledge, which Dorstenius agrees to. Faustus is offered wine and drinks until the vessel is empty. Dorstenius tells Faustus his plans to go to Grave to have his beard shaved. Faustus promises to disclose the secret of shaving without using a razor if he is allowed more wine. The condition is accepted; Faustus advises his custodian to rub his beard with arsenic, but withholds the manner of its safe preparation. The chaplain suffers severe facial burns as a result. • Faustus remarks to an acquaintance of Wier who was "splenetic" and had a black beard: "I surely thought you were

---

[1126] From Tille, No. 13, in *Sources of the Faust Tradition,* pp. 103–104.
[1127] From Tille, No. 17, in ibid. pp. 105–106.

	my brother-in-law and therefore I looked at your feet to see whether long curved claws projected from them". • Faustus found dead near his bed in the Duchy of Württemburg with his head twisted towards his back.
1568	**From the *Promptuarium Exemplorum* (1568) by Andreas Hondorff.**[1128] **(Apparently a paraphrase of Manlius' version.)** "Such a necromancer was Johann Faustus, who practised many tricks through his black art. He had with him always a black dog, which was a devil. When he came to Wittenberg he would have been arrested by order of the Prince Elector, if he had not escaped. The same would have happened to him in Nuremberg also, where he likewise escaped. But this was his reward. When his time was up, he was in a tavern in a village of Württemberg. Upon the host asking him why he was so downcast, he replied, 'Do not be afraid to-night, if you hear a great banging and shaking of the house.' In the morning he was found lying dead in his room, with his neck twisted round."
1569	**From the *Von Gespänsten* of Ludwig Lavater**[1129] "To this very day there are sorcerers who boast that they can saddle a horse on which they can in a short time make great journeys. The devil will give them all their reward in the long run. What wonders is the notorious sorcerer Faustus said to have done in our own times."
?	**From the *Chronica von Thüringen und der Stadt Erffurth* of Zacharias Hogel.**[1130] (Written in the 17th century, but primary source is the Reichmann-Wambach chronicle of the mid 16th century, now lost.) Many accounts of Faustus — names "Fausten" and "Faust" used: (About 1550) Apparently lived at Wittenberg, but his restless spirit "Drove him about in the world" and eventually he ended up at the University of Erfurt where he rented lodgings near the "large

---

[1128] William Rose 'Forward to the First Edition,' *The Historie of the Damnable Life and Deserved Death of Doctor John Faustus: 1592* (Reprint; Indiana: University of Notre Dame Press, 1963), p. 12.
[1129] From Tille, No. 18. in *Sources of the Faust Tradition*, p. 107
[1130] From Tille, No. 26, in ibid. pp. 108–119.

Collegium". His boasting led to his alleged appointment as a lecturer of Greek. He uses his powers to summon the ancient Greek heroes of the past during one of his lectures.

At a college banquet the theological faculty and council delegates discuss the ancient poets Plautus and Terence, and express their regret that many of their comedies had been lost over time. Faustus quotes from the supposed lost works and offers to restore them with his art. His offer is refused as the objection is raised that the devil "might interpolate all sorts of offensive things" into them. The faculty also declare the works were not really needed as Latin could be learned from those which still existed.

Faustus is claimed to have spent most of his time while in Erfurt at the Anchor House of Squire N. in the Schlössergasse and entertain his guests there. One night while Faustus is in Prague, a group of his acquaintances gather at the inn looking for Faustus. One of these guests jestingly call out to him by name and implores him not to leave them. He appears at the door with his horse and says because his guests called, he wished to oblige them. He confesses his horse brought him speedily to them, but states he has to return to Prague before morning. Faustus provides his guests with whatever wine they wish by gouging out four holes in the table and closes them with plugs, which begin to pour out any wine that is mentioned. Meanwhile, his horse is tended to in the stable; however, it is continually hungry and cannot be given enough oats to satisfy it. At midnight, the horse begins to neigh until the sound shakes the whole house, and Faustus is forced to depart. He mounts the horse, which rises in the air, and he returns to Prague.

After his journey, Faustus invites his guests to St. Michael's, but there is no preparation for the banquet. He knocks on the table with a knife and "someone" enters. Faustus asks "How quick are you?" "As an arrow." This does not please him. He knocks again and a second servant enters. He asks the same question. The second servant is as fast as the wind. This also is not efficient. Faustus knocks the third time and is pleased with the reply "as quick as the thoughts of man." The servant serves a four-course meal with thirty-six dishes. All glasses and drinking mugs are placed on the table empty. Faustus tells his guests to place their mugs outside the window and they are filled with the beer or wine of their choice. The servants play music that they never heard before on "harmoniums, fifes, cornets, lutes, harps, trumpets, etc".

	The Franciscan monk, Dr. Klinge, attempts to convert Faustus and save him from the devil. Warns him of God's wrath and eternal damnation, reasons that a well educated man need not succumb to the devil for his career, and advises him to beg God for the forgiveness of his sins as God "had never yet denied anyone". Faustus replies that he knows all of this too well, but states he has ventured past the point of no return for he had contracted with the devil both body and soul. Klinge states it is still possible to retract if he calls on God for grace and mercy, be repentant and do penance, desist from sorcery and all communication with devils, and not seduce anyone. Faustus places no faith in this advice, nor the offer of Masses said for his soul: "My pledge binds me too absolutely. I have wantonly despised God and become perjured and faithless towards Him, and believed and trusted more in the devil than in Him. Therefore I can neither come to Him again nor obtain any comfort from His grace which I have forfeited. Besides, it would not be honest nor would it redound to my honor to have it said that I had violated my bond and seal, which I had made with my own blood. The devil has honestly kept the promise that he made to me, therefore I will honestly keep the pledge that I made and contracted with him." Klinge angrily tells Faustus to go to the devil and reports the incident to the Rector. The town council took steps to force Faustus to leave Erfurt.
c. 1575	**The *Chronicle* of Christoph Rosshirt,** **(containing four additional stories of Faustus' misadventures).**[1131] • Dr. "Georgius Faustus" is a lecturer of philosophy and necromancy at the University of Ingolstadt in this account. He invites guests for dinner and boasts that the wine they are drinking came from the King of England's wedding feast. By magic he transports his guests to the feast (where they are mistaken as spies), but he brings them back safely. • Faustus wishes to exchange French currency into talers with a Jewish merchant. The Jew calls upon Faustus at his inn at a later date and brings the talers, however, his customer is asleep. The Jew attempts to shake Faustus awake, and then pulls his leg, but it falls off by magic! The Jew runs away forgetting his money.

[1131] Rose, *The Historie […] and Death of Doctor John Faustus,* pp. 32–33.

	• Faustus sells some swine, but tells the owner not to drive them into flowing water. The swineherd forgets, and his herd turns into bundles of straw. • On the last night of his contract with the devil, Faustus arrives at an inn for lodgings. There is a drunken crowd there that refuses to be quiet. Faustus enchants them so they are silent and he can have his meal in peace. He is found dead in bed the next morning.
1576	**From the *Epitome Historiarum* (1576) by Wolffgang Bütner**[1132] "I have heard that Faustus, at Wittenberg, showed to the students and to an exalted man N —, Hector, Ulysses, Hercules, Æneas, Samson, David and others, who came forth with fierce bearing and earnest countenance and disappeared again, and princely personages are also said to have been present at the time and to have looked on, [which Luther did not praise.*]"
[1587]	[The Spies *Faustbook* is first published.]
1585–1597	**From the *Christlich Bedencken* of Augustin Lercheimer (3rd edition 1597).**[1133] This account states "Faust" (Faustus is not used) was born in Knittlingen, and was schoolmaster in Kreuznach under Franze von Sickingen, but fled due to accusations of sodomy. Afterwards, he "travelled about the country with his devil", studied the black arts at the University of Cracow, and came to Wittenberg, but was forced to flee. He had no permanent abode, and is described as a vagabond, parasite, glutton, drunkard, and that he "supported himself by his quackery". Lercheimer questions the account Faust owned property at the outer gate of the Scheergasse in Wittenberg, as he states there was no suburb there and no outer gate, and writes: "He was chocked to death by the devil in a village in Württemberg, not Kimlich near Wittenberg, since there is no village by that name. For he was never

---

[1132] Ibid. p. 16.

* Bracket section quoted from the *Epitome* in John A. Walz, "An English *Faustsplitter*", *MLN*, p. 361.

[1133] From Tille, No. 48, in *Sources of the Faust Tradition*, pp. 119–122. Original document in Augustin Lercheimer, *Christlich bedencken und erinnerung von Zauberey* (Edition quoted: 3rd Edition, Speyer, 1597; original edition Heidelberg 1585).

	allowed to return to Wittenberg after he had fled from there to avoid arrest." He also complains of the dubious connections made in the Spies Faust book between the infamous Faust, the famous University of Wittenberg, and with those of "sainted memory" such as Luther and Melanchthon. An account of Faust rebuked by Melanchthon for his wicked ways and warns he will come to a bad end. One day Faust threatens Melanchthon that for his abusive words, in revenge he will send all the pots in the kitchen flying up the chimney so he cannot serve his guests. However, Faust never carries out his threat. [Apparently, Faustus' presence in Wittenberg tolerated by Luther and Melanchthon for the sake of his conversion. Faustus pays no heed and the prince orders his arrest, but he escapes.[†]]
1591	**From the *Operae Horarum Subcisivarum* by Philipp Camerarius**[1134] Faustus named as "John Faustum" of Kundling, who studied magic at Cracow. (The name "Faustus" also used.) Author states Faustus' life similar to the Bohemian magician Zyto who was believed to have been "carried of by his master (i.e. the devil) while he was still alive." Wier's account of Faustus' death restated: he was found in a village in the Duchy of Württemberg with his head twisted around. Story where Faustus entertains some friends by showing them whatever they desire to see. They wish to see a vine full of grapes as it is near the end of December and thereby test his skill. He orders them to stay absolutely silent and only cut the grapes on his orders. He thereby befuddles their eyes and senses so they believe that they see the vine and grapes in the middle of the table. They each grab a bunch of grapes and await the orders to cut them off, however the vision disappears in a plume of smoke and they discover they have been holding their own noses.
1594	**From *The Second Report of Doctor John Faustus* (Author, anon.**

[†] Bracketed section: Lercheimer, *Christlich Bedencken* (3rd Ed. 1597 – Ed. Binz, Strassburg, 1888), in John A. Walz, "An English Faustsplitter", ' *Modern Language Notes* XLII (June, 1927), p. 359. Also, Walz mentions Lercheimer stated in the third edition Faustus died "sixty years ago", which would indicate approximately 1537 / 1538 as the year of Faustus' death. (Binz, p. 41, Tille, p. 93 in 'An English *Faustsplitter*', n. 18, p. 359.)

[1134] From Tille, No. 54, in *Sources of the Faust Tradition*, pp. 123–126.

	London: 1594) (Quoted from Walz.)[1135] "In the introductory statements (p. 33) we read: 'Secondly, there is yet to be seene his (i.e. Faust's) tree, a great hollow Trunke, wherein he used to reade Nigromancy to his schollers, not farre from the towne in a very remote place, which I thinke is sufficient testimony to any reasonable eare. And enquire of them which have been there, see if they will not affirme it.' *** "The Second Report [...] even gives the Latin epitaph inscribed on the marble stone on Faust's grave 'at Mars Temple, three miles beyond the Citty." But the Second Report (p. 34) also quotes Wier's statement that Faust died in a village of the 'Duchy of Wittenberg,' [Württemberg][&] and Wier is to the author of the work a great authority." *** 'First there is yet remaining the ruins of his (i.e. Faust's) house, not farre from Melanchtons house as they call at the townes end of Wittenberg, right opposite to the Schooles.'
1617	**From the *Itinerary* by Fynes Moryson (1617).**[1136] "Besides, they shew a house wherein Doctor Faustus a famous conjurer dwelt. [I.e. in Wittenberg] They say that this Doctor lived there about the yeere 1500, and had a tree all blasted and burnt in the adjoyning Wood, where hee practised his Magick Art, and that he died, or rather was fetched by the Divell, in a Village neere the Towne. I did see the tree so burnt; but walking at leasure through all the Villages adjoining, I could never heare any memory of his end."

ഇരു ❖ ഇരു

[1135] John A. Walz, 'An English *Faustsplitter*,' *MLN*, pp. 355–356.

[&] According to *Sources of the Faust Tradition*, Wier describes the place as "Ducatus Vvirtenbergici". (*Sources*, p. 107). This was often mistaken for "Wittenberg" in early sources, but is identified today as "Württemberg". Also, Walz in 'An English *Faustsplitter*' may have misspelled "Wirtenberg" as he mentions Wier's information with the correct spelling of "Wirtenberg" on the following page of his article, (p. 356).

[1136] Walz, 'An English *Faustsplitter*,' *MLN*, pp. 353–354.

Appendix Two

The Disputation of Socrates on the Nature of Opposites and the Immortality of the Soul; extract from the *Phædo* by Plato.[1137]

[...]   [Socrates]: And the same may be said of the immortal: if the immortal is also imperishable, the soul when attacked by death cannot perish; for the preceding argument shows that the soul will not admit of death, or ever be dead, any more than three or the odd number will admit of the even, or fire or the heat of the fire, of the cold. Yet a person may say: "But although the odd will not become an even at the approach of the even, why may not the odd perish and the even take place of the odd?" Now to him who makes this objection, we cannot answer that the odd principle is imperishable; for this has not been acknowledged, but if this had been acknowledged, there would have been no difficulty in contending that at the approach of the even the odd principle and the number three took up their departure; and the some argument would have held good of fire and heat and any other thing.

[Cebes]: Very true.

[Socrates]: And the same may be said of the immortal: if the immortal is also imperishable, then the soul will be imperishable as well as immortal; but if not, some other proof of her imperishableness will have to be given.

No other proof is needed, he [Cebes] said; for if the immortal, being eternal, is liable to perish, then nothing is imperishable.

Yes, replied Socrates, all men will agree that God, and the essential form of life, and the immortal in general, will never perish.

Yes, all men, he said — that is true; and what more, gods, if I am not mistaken, as well as men.

Seeing then that the immortal is indestructible, must not the soul, if she is immortal, be also imperishable?

Most certainly.

Then when death attacks a man, the mortal portion of him may be supposed to die, but the immortal goes out of the way of death and is preserved safe and sound?

True.

Then, Cebes, beyond question the soul is immortal and imperishable, and our souls will truly exist in another world!

I am convinced, Socrates, said Cebes, and have nothing more to object; but if my friend Simmias, or anyone else, has any further objection, he had better speak out, and not keep silence, since I do not know how there can ever be a more fitting time to which he can defer the discussion, if there is anything which he wants to say or have said.

[1137]   Plato, *Phædo*, Charles W. Eliot, ed., Benjamin Jowett, trans., *The Harvard Classics, vol. 2* (New York: P.F. Collier and Son Corp., 1963), pp. 101–103.

But I have nothing more to say, replied Simmias; nor do I see any room for uncertainty, except that which arises necessarily out of the greatness of the subject and the feebleness of man, and which I cannot help feeling.

Yes, Simmias, replied Socrates, that is well said: and more than that, first principles, even if they appear certain, should be carefully considered; and when they are satisfactorily ascertained, then, with a sort of hesitating confidence in human reason, you may, I think, follow the course of the argument; and if this is clear, there will be no need for any further inquiry.

That, he said, is true.

But then, O my friends, he said, if the soul is really immortal, what care should be taken of her, not only in respect of the portion of time which is called life, but of eternity! And the danger of neglecting her from this point of view does indeed appear to be awful. If death had only been the end of all, the wicked would have had a good bargain in dying, for they would have been happily quit not only of their body, but of their own evil together with their souls. But now, as the soul plainly appears to be immortal, there is no release or salvation from evil except the attainment of the highest virtue and wisdom. For the soul when on her progress to the world below takes nothing with her but nurture and education; which are indeed said greatly to benefit or greatly to injure the departed, at the very beginning of its pilgrimage in the other world. [...]

෮෧✧෮෧

Appendix Three

Wolfenbüttle Manuscript Contents[1138]

I. Here Beginneth Doctor Faustus His Vita and Historia		I.	Of his Parentage and Youth
		II.	How Doctor Faustus Did Achieve and Acquire Sorcery
		III.	Here Followeth the Disputatio Held by Faustus and the Spirit
		IV.	The Second Disputatio with the Spirit
		V.	Doctor Faustus' Third Colloquium with the Spirit, Which Was Called Mephostophiles — Concerning Also the Pact Which These Two Made
		VI.	Doctor Faustus' Instrumentum, or Devilish and Godliss Writ Obligatio
		VII.	Concerning the Service that Mephostophiles Used Toward Faustus
		VIII.	Concerning Doctor Faustus' Intended Marriage
		IX.	Doctor Faustus' Quæstio of His Spirit Mephostophiles
		X.	A Disputatio Concerning the Prior State of the Banished Angels
		XI.	A Disputatio Concerning Hell, How It Was Created and Fashioned; Concerning Also the Torments in Hell
II.	Doctor Faustus His Historia: Here Followeth The Second Part, Adventures and Sundry Questions	XII.	His Almanacs and Horoscopes
		XIII.	A Disputatio, or Inquiry Concerning the Art of

[1138] From H.G. Haile, *The History of Doctor Johann Faustus*, (Urbana: University of Illinois Press, 1965). Haile has eliminated and condensed chapters in an effort to present a hypothetical edition of the first Latin *Faust* MS.

Appendix Four

Table of Contents: the English Orwin / "P.F. *Gent.*" *Faustbook* (1592)[1139]

Page numbers as printed in the original Table of Contents.
Chapter Numbers not in original Table.

[1139]   Rose, *Damnable Life and Deserved Death of [...] Faustus.* Folio numbering from Henry Jones, *The English Faust Book: A Critical Edition.*

---

‡ This page number was not actually printed in the *Faustbook* as Orwin made a paginal error: i.e. page numbers 18 and 19 were printed twice, while 16 and 17 were omitted / skipped. Here he is correcting within the Table the number that should have been in the book.

** These chapters fall under another paginal error: Orwin reprinted the page numbers 22 and 23 twice and skipped the numbers 20 and 21. However, he does not correct the numbering in his table. (Chs. 17 and 18 should be paginated as 20 and 21 respectively.)

FINIS.

[-L4v- Blank]

⁊Ω ❖ ⁊Ω

Appendix Five

Excerpt of Chapter Twenty-one from the 1592 English *Faustbook*.[1140]

(The material featured in *Italics* here are P.F.'s additions not found in Spies. Section in **Bold** print: proposed latter insertion by printers / censors, and *not* by P.F. Gent.)

"[…] for the Sky the which we behold here when we look up from the earth, is so fast and thick as a wall, clear and shining bright as a Crystal, *in which is placed the Sun, which casteth forth his rays or beams over the universal world, to the utmost confines of the earth.* But we think that the Sun is very little: no, it is altogether as big as the world. *Indeed the body substantial is but little in compass, but the rays or stream that it casteth forth, by reason of the thing wherein it is placed, maketh him to extend and shew himself over the whole world: and we think that the Sun runneth his course, and that the heavens stand still: no, it is the heavens that move his course, and the Sun abideth perpetually in his place, he is permanent, & fixed in his place, & although we see him beginning to ascend in the Orient or East, at the highest in the Meridian or South, setting in the Occident or West, yet is he at the lowest in Septentrio or North, and yet he moveth not. It is the axle of the heavens that moveth the whole firmament, being a Chaos or confused thing, and for that proof, I will shew thee this example, like as thou seest a bubble made of water and soap blown forth of a quill, is in form of a confused mass or Chaos, & being in this form, is moved at pleasure of the wind, which runneth round about that Chaos, & moveth him also round: even so is the whole firmament or Chaos, wherein are placed the sun, and the rest of the Planets turned and carried at the pleasure of the Spirit of God, which is wind.* **Yea Christian Reader, to the glory of God, and for the profit of thy soul, I will open unto thee the divine opinion touching the ruling of this confused Chaos, far more than any rude German Author, being possessed with the devil, was able to utter; and to prove some of my sentence before to be true; look into Genesis unto the works of God, at the creation of the world, there shalt thou find, that the Spirit of God moved upon the waters before heaven and earth were made. Mark how he made it, and how by his word every element took his place: these were not his works, but his words; for all the words he used before, he concluded afterwards in one work, which was in making man: mark reader with patience for thy soul's health, see into all that was done by the word of and work of God, light and darkness was, the firmament stood, and their great & little light in it: the moist waters were in one place, the earth was dry, & every element brought forth according to the word of God: now followeth his works he made man like his own image, how: out of the earth: The earth will shape no image without water, there was one of the elements. But all this while where was wind? All elements were at the word of God, man was made, and in a form by the work of God, yet moved not that work, before God breathed the Spirit of life into his nostrils, and made him a living soul, here was the first wind and Spirit of God out of his own mouth, which we have likewise from the**

[1140] Palmer and More, *Sources of the Faust Tradition*, pp. 172–173. Empson, *Faustus and the Censor*, pp. 76–77. Henry Jones, *The English Faust Book; A Critical Edition*, pp. 125–127.

same see which was onely [only?] planted by God in Adam, which wind, breath, or spirit, when he had received, he was living & moving on earth, for it was ordained of God for his habitation, but the heavens are the habitation of the Lord: and like as I shewed before of the bubble or confused Chaos made of water and soap, through the wind and breath of man is turned round, and carried with every wind; even so the firmament wherein the Sun and the rest of the Planets are fixed, moved, turned, and carried with the wind, breath, or Spirit of God, for the heavens and firmament are moveable as the Chaos, but the sun is fixed in the firmament. And farther my good schoolfellow, I was thus nigh the heavens, where me thought every Planet was but as half the earth, and under the firmament ruled the Spirits in the air, and as I came down I looked upon the world & the heavens, and me thought that the earth was inclosed in comparison within the firmament, as the yolk of an egg within the white, and me thought that the whole length of the earth was not a span long [....]"

ॐ৪৪❖৪৪ॐ

Appendix Six

Evidence of a Paginated Precursor to Orwin's 1592 *Faustbook*

It is understood that there was a precursor to Orwin's edition according to the imprint reading, "Imperfect matter amended", however, scholars continue to speculate if Orwin's text is an actual page-for-page copy of a lost *paginated* edition. The most important piece of evidence used to support these arguments is Orwin's flawed pagination: on signature C, he has omitted 16 and 17, and incorrectly printed the page numbers as 15, 18, 19, 18, 19, 22, 23, 22. On signature L he has committed a similar error in printing the numbers 81, 80, 81, 80. However, the table of contents has been partially corrected in that Orwin lists Chapter Fifteen with the page number 16, although the number 16 was not included in the text proper. Logeman argued that the pagination errors in Orwin's book display that it is a page-for-page copy; his discussion based on the observation that while there are several errors of pagination in Orwin's book, his table of contents features the corrected page numbers. Therefore, Logeman concluded Orwin had copied a precursor free from pagination errors.[1141]   However, Henry Jones argues against this theory, for the page numbers were only *partially corrected* in the table of contents, which would suggest this paginated precursor would have contained the *exact errors* on signature C, an unlikely scenario. Henry Jones concludes:

> "Clearly the register [of contents] was made from [Orwin's edition] itself after all the text sheets were printed and it was too late to alter the text pagination; Orwin will have discovered his errors and rectified the register references where possible. Unfortunately he could not refer to the correct page number for chapters 17 and 18 (20 and 21 respectively) since his text contained no pages bearing these numbers, so here he was forced to retain the references to the incorrect paginations (23 and 23 respectively). Thus there is no case for a paginated precursor for [Orwin's text]."[1142]

Considering these details, we have an alternative hypothesis to present. It is possible that the precursor to Orwin's edition was paginated, but according to a different format, i.e. that the title page and the succeeding blank page were included, but the numbering did not commence until page 4 on sig. A2v. Orwin may have decided to number his sheets according to his own system and present a unique edition rather than rely on the numbering provided as he omits sig.

[1141] Henry Logeman, ed. *The English Faust-book of 1592: Recueil de travaux publiés par la faculté de philosophe et letters de l'université de Gand,* fasc. 24, Gand / Amsterdam, 1900, in *The English Faust Book: A Critical Edition,* pp. 41–42.

[1142] Ibid.

A1 entirely for his numbering. When the two systems are compared, we immediately see that the major pagination errors in Orwin's text configure with the pagination of our proposed precursor. We suggest that Orwin (or his compositor) simply forgot they were not copying the text upon which they were basing their edition, and eventually corrected the errors of sig. C where possible in the table of contents when they realised their mistake. For sig. L, it appears Orwin remembered his numbering would have been pp. 80, 81, but was again confused by the text he was using if sig. L of the precursor began with 81. It would seem Orwin corrected this mistake by reprinting 80, 81 on the correct side and 79 in the register of contents for the reference to the last chapter, although number 79 is not in the text. With this scenario, Logeman's theory is correct, and Henry Jones' observations are partially correct. The precursor could have been free from errors as Logeman's theory suggested, while Orwin made the corrections according to his own register and numbering system as Henry Jones relates, however, this new hypothesis featuring two separate paginal formats dismisses his conclusion that there is no case for a paginated precursor.

( ) = page numbers, (*) = incorrect page numbers, [ ]= numbers corrected

Our Proposed Paginated Precursor	**Orwin's pagination**
A1r (titlepage) (-) A1v (blank) (-) A2r (-) A2v (4) A3r (5) A3v (6) A4r (7) A4v (8)	A1r (titlepage) (-) A1v (blank) (-) A2r (-) Ch.1 A2v (2) Ch.2 A3r (3) A3v (5*) [4] Ch. 3 A4r (4*) [5] Ch. 4 A4v (6) Ch. 5
B1r (9) B1v (10) B2r (11) B2v (12) B3r (13) B3v (14) B4r (15) B4v (16)	B1r (7) Ch. 6 B1v (8) Ch. 7 B2r (9) Ch. 8 B2v (10) Ch. 9 B3r (11) Ch. 10 B3v (12) Ch. 11 B4r (13) Ch. 12, Ch. 13 B4v (14) Ch. 14
C1r (17) C1v (18) → C2r (19) → C2v (20) C3r (21) C3v (22) → C4r (23) → C4v (24)	C1r (15) C1v (18*) [16] Ch. 15 C2r (19*) [17] C2v (18) C3r (19) Ch. 16 C3v (22*) [20] Ch. 17 C4r (23*) [21] Ch. 18 C4v (22)

D1r (25) D1v (26) D2r (27) D2v (28) D3r (29) D3v (30) D4r (31) D4v (32)	D1r (23) Ch. 19 D1v (24) D2r (25) D2v (26) Ch. 20 D3r (27) D3v (28) D4r (29) Ch. 21 D4v (30)
Sig. E to K: (pp. 33–80) ↕	Sig. E through to K: Orwin's pagination is correct; (pp. 31–78) ↕
L1r (81) → L1v (82) L2r (83) L2v (84) L3r (-) Table of Contents L3v (-) Ibid. L4r (-) Ibid. (FINIS) L4v (-) (blank)	L1r (81*) [79] Ch. 63 L1v (80) L2r (81) L2v (80*) [82] L3r (-) Table of Contents L3v (-) Ibid. L4r (-) Ibid. (FINIS) L4v (-) (blank)

There are other unusual anomalies in Orwin's register of contents and text. For instance, the fact that the table of contents mentions "five complaints" of Faust while there are only four, and that Chapter Sixty-one does not feature a chapter number. Henry Jones proposes that these two anomalies may be linked: there is one chapter in Spies not included by P.F. featuring Mephostophiles mocking Faust with a barrage of satirical proverbs, which would have been inserted close to chapter Sixty-one if P.F. had included it. The "five" complaints may therefore refer to this missing chapter. Nevertheless, we observe this missing segment does not contain any of Faust's "lamentations". We suspect this anomaly referring to the "five lamentations" in the register may actually have been an error in our proposed precursor. It is possible that the compositor hastily miscounted Chapter Sixty-two *Here followeth the miserable and lamentable end of Doctor Faustus* [...]" as one of the "Complaints / Lamentation Chapters" for the register as it would have been completed at the end of these chapters on sig. K before the last "Oration" would be set on sig. L. Either this error escaped Orwin, or he simply forgot to amend the text to read "Four complaints of Doctor Faustus", as it is clear from the last reference in his own register that he recognised Chapter Sixty-two as separate on page 78.

৪১০৩ ❖ ৪১০৩

The Baines Note (c. May 26, 1593)

Features the accusations of Richard Baines against Christopher Marlowe.[1143]

ಶಿಂಬ ❖ ಶಿಂಬ

Endorsed: Baines Marlowe of his blasphemies

{A hand with index finger pointing to "Marlowe" has been drawn beside the endorsement}.

A note containing the opinion of one Christopher Marlowe concerning his damnable ~~opini~~ Judgement of re g-ligion, and scorn of God's word.
That the Indians and many authors of antiquity have assuredly written of above 16 thousand / years [ago] where as ~~Moses~~ Adam is ~~said~~ proved to have lived within 6 thousand years.

{The handwriting of these two inserted corrections is neater then the handwriting of the rest of the note.}

He affirmeth that Moses was but a Juggler, & that one Harriots [i.e. Thomas Harriot] being Sir W Raleigh's man can do more than he.
That Moses made the Jews to travel xl [40] years in the wilderness (which journey might have been done in less than one year) ere they came to the promised land to the intent that those who were privy to most of his subtleties might perish and so an everlasting superstition remain in the hearts of the people.
That the first beginning of Religion was only to keep men in awe.
That it was an easy matter for Moses being brought up in all the arts of the Egyptians to abuse the Jews being a rude & gross people.
That Christ was a bastard and his mother dishonest.
That he was the son of a carpenter, and that if the Jews among whom he was born did crucify him they best knew him and whence he came.
That Christ deserved better to die than Barabas and that the Jews made a good choice, though Barabas were both a thief and a murderer.

[1143] Public Record Office, London: Harleian 6848, ff. 185-86. Reprint in Kuriyama, *Christopher Marlowe: A Renaissance Life*, pp. 219–222. Sections in Italics are descriptions included by Kuriyama. Kuriyama presents the document in the original antiquated spelling,which I have modernised for this extract. (She reprints the infamous line referring to Tobacco and Boys as: 'That all they that love not Tobacco & Boies were fooles.') Trusting her transcription, it has been argued this line has been misread as a further attempt to slander Marlowe and that the word 'Boies' may not originally be 'Boys' but an Elizabethan variant of 'Booze'. However, we argue it is difficult to mistake an 'i' + 'e' for older English spellings of 'booze', such as 'bouse'or 'bouze', an 'i' might be confused or switched with a 'j', but to mistake it for a 'u' is less likely. Notice that this reference to 'boies' occurs after the sentence declaring Marlowe allegedly accused Christ of sodomy, it is obvious 'boies' was the intended word.

That if there be any god or any good Religion, then it is in the papists because the service of God is performed with more ceremonies, as Elevation of the mass, organs, singing men, Shaven Crowns, etc. That all protestants are Hypocritical asses.

That if he were put to write a new religion, he would undertake both a more Excellent and Admirable method and that all the new testament is filthily written.

That the woman of Samaria and her sister were whores & that Christ knew them dishonestly.

That St John the Evangelist was bedfellow to Christ and leaned always [on] his bosom, [that] he used him as the sinners of Sodom.

That all they that love not Tobacco & Boys were fools.

That all the apostles were fishermen and base fellows neither of wit nor worth, that Paul only had wit but he was a timorous fellow in bidding men to be subject to magistrates against his own conscience.

That he had as good a right to coin as the Queen of England and that he was acquainted with one Poole a prisoner in Newgate who hath great skill in mixture of metals and having learned some things of him he meant through help of a cunning stamp maker to coin French crowns, pistolets and English shillings.

That if Christ would have instituted the sacrament with more ceremonial reverence it would have been had in more admiration, that it would have been much better being administered in a Tobacco pipe.

That the Angel Gabriel was bawd to the holy ghost, because he brought the salutation to Mary.

{The next two lines are cramped and might have been inserted later. Unlike the preceding statements, they do not seem to be a report of what Marlowe said.}

~~That {illegible}~~ That one Ric Cholmley ~~hath Cholmley~~ hath confessed that he was persuaded by Marlowe's reasons to become an Atheist.

These things with many other shall be good & honest witness be approved to be his opinions and common speeches and that this Marlowe doth not only hold them himself but almost into every company he cometh he persuades men to Atheism willing them not to be afeard [afraid] of bugbears and hobgoblins and utterly scorning both god and his ministers as I Richard Baines will Justify & approve both mine oath and the testimony of many honest men, and almost all men with whom he hath conversed any time will testify the same, and as I think all men in Christianity ought to endeavour that the mouth of so dangerous a member may be stopped, he sayeth likewise that he hath quoted a number of contrarieties out of the Scripture which he hath given to some great men who in convenient time shall be named. When these things shall be called in question the witness shall be produced.

Richard Baines

{The signature is in a large quasi-italic script.}

☙ ❖ ☙

Appendix Eight

The Earliest English *Faustbook* Editions: Lost and Extant

The various London printers obviously recognised the lucrative opportunities the *Faustbook* presented and a desperate scramble ensued to possess a copy for publication, yet encountered severe difficulties with censorship requirements. In the records of the Stationers' Company there is the following entry dated Monday 7, August 1592:

> "whereas Abell Ieffes about the [22nd] day of July last did resist the search which master Stirrop, warden, Tho[mas] Dawson and Tho[mas Rente] man, renters, were appointed to make and would have made of his printing house according to the ordinance and decrees, and for that he contemptuously proceeded in printing a book without authority contrary to our master, his commandment, and for that he refused to deliver the barre of his press neither would deliver any of the book to be brought to the hall according to the decrees, and also for that he used violence to our officer in the search, it is now therefore ordered by a full court held this day, that … he shall be committed to ward."[1144]

In that same year, the following entry was recorded on Monday, 18th of December:

> "In full court held this day, Abel Ieffes, according to the direction of the lord archbishop of Canterbury, his grace, appeared and humbly acknowledged his former offence and undutifulness, craving pardon and favour for the same and promising hereafter to live as becometh an honest man, and to show himself obedient and dutiful in the Company and to the ordinances thereof."[1145]

(This entry is succeeded by the following dated the same day:)

Abell Ieffes
Tho. Orwin[**]

> Yt is ordered: that if the book of Dcor ffaustus shall not be found in the [beh] hall book entered to Richard Oliff before Abell Ieffes claymed the same wch was about May last. That then the seid copie shall

---

[1144] Records of the Court of the Stationers' Company, 1576–1602, ed. Greg and Boswell, (London: Bibliographical Society, 1930), p. 42, in *Faustus and the Censor*, p. 202.
[1145] Ibid.
[**] Actually printed in the margin of the entry.

Remayne to the said Abell as his prop copie from the tyme of his first clayme wch was about May last as aforesaid /.[1146]

While the first two of these three records do not mention the Faust book *per se*, we may still deduce the following scenario: Abell Ieffes (Jeffes) was in possession of an early English *Faustbook* translated by Mr. P.F., (now lost), and printed it in May of 1592 in partnership with Orwin, who already had has printing press confiscated the previous year.[⊠] Kocher theorises that Jeffes could have claimed the rights with Orwin "[…] as an assignee of the original Cambridge publisher as of May, 1592."[1147] However, it would appear that Richard Orliff also had a copy of the same translation by P.F. and was challenging both Jeffes' and Orwin's claim to the printing copyright. Empson observes that the printing date of a book could be used in defence as a claim to the work, although a claim may be false or unregistered in the official Stationer's records.[1148] We note there were other important issues concerning censorship of the *Faustbook*, as the archbishop of Canterbury was involved with the case against Jeffes. If we consider Logeman's argument that the extant London 1592 version is a page-for-page copy of an earlier edition, which would also have included the "amended imperfect matter",[1149] it is not improbable that Orwin and Jeffes had anticipated the material that the censors would object to, altered this offending material themselves, and rushed their copy to the press without waiting for official permission before competitors would have an opportunity to print the work. The Stationer's Company then sent the wardens during the latter half of July to search for and confiscate any illegal copies of the *Faustbook* that were printed in May prior to receiving the censors' legal approbation; however, Jeffes violently refused to comply and was taken into custody. In December, Jeffes begged the pardon of the court, presumably for printing the *Faustbook* against the rules of censorship, and promised to comply in the future. However, Jeffes and Orwin defended their printing rights of the *Faustbook*, and the court declared that if Orliff's copy was not formally registered before May of that year when Jeffes and Orwin had printed their work, the rights officially belonged to them. In the interim, the censors had found no objections to the book (that is, if Jeffes and Orwin already edited it), and it was approved for publication. Finding their work of May accepted with their amendments intact, they could now simply reprint copies of the former work featuring a new title page. Therefore, it is possible that the *extant copy* of the 1592 London *Faustbook* was not printed in May, but sometime in late December. Controversial as this proposed scenario may be, the title page actually confirms this theory:

The
Historie

[1146] Records of the Court of the Stationers' Company, p. 44., in 'The English Faust Book […] Marlowe's Faustus' *MLN*, p. 101.
[⊠] The nature of Orwin's offence is unknown. (*Faustus and the Censor*, p. 202.)
[1147] 'The English *Faust Book* […] Marlowe's *Faustus*' *MLN,* p. 101.
[1148] *Faustus and the Censor*, p. 202.
[1149] Logeman, 'The English Faust-book of 1592', *Recueil des Travaux Publiés par la Faculté de Philosophie et Lettres, Université de Gand,* Ghent and Amsterdam, (Université de Gand) fasc. 24, 1900, in *Faustus and the Censor*, p. 202.

of the damnable
life, and deserved death of
Doctor Iohn Faustus,

Newly imprinted, and in conveni-
ent places imperfect matter amended:
according to the true Copie printed
at Franckfort, *and translated into*
English by P.F. *Gent.*

Seene and allowed.

Imprinted at London by Thomis Orwin, and are to be
solde by Edward White, dwelling at the little North
doore of Paules, at the signe of the Gun. 1592.

Notice the statement "seen and allowed", which suggests *this* particular copy was printed after Jeffes admitted his error to the court in December of 1592 and was approved by the censors. The information of "newly imprinted" and "imperfect matter amended" is acknowledged collectively, suggesting the amendments were completed by Jeffes and / or Orwin, and not by P.F. As mentioned, the conjuction "and" with the translation credits is of significance as it suggests P F. translated the German book at an earlier date: if the translation was completed specifically for the 1592 printing, it is probable the credits would read ; "[...] according to the true Copy printed at Frankfort. Translated into English by P.F. *Gent.*"; thus, as previously stated, the "True Copy" referred to may be a conflation of both the Spies editions and P.F.'s original work. We also observe that the credits for his translation are set apart from the initial title information referring to the "amendments". Hence, P.F. could not be held responsible for all the insertions and mistranslations existing in the extant London *Faustbook*. Jeffes and Orwin, however, could have commenced on these editorial adjustments immediately once they had obtained a copy of P.F.'s work. If their previous work of May was approved "as is" by the censors and Jeffes and Orwin decided to recopy it for the new imprint, they could still truthfully state on the title page in December that the "imperfect matter" was amended in "convenient places" without having to disclose when these adjustments were actually accomplished.

We posit that P.F.'s original English translation of Spies' Faustbook (1587) was completed and printed circa 1589 in Cambridge, which Marlowe may have used as the basis for his famous tragedy, (i.e. the A Text of 1589). It is not a preposterous idea that this initial English Faustbook was published without formal censorship and was a more reliable rendition of the Spies original than its successors. Unfortunately, this copy is now lost — perhaps the censors were made aware of this edition, which had not been submitted for their approval, and subsequently ordered that all existing copies be seized and destroyed. Other printers had nevertheless succeeded in acquiring copies with the aim of profiting from the current Faustian *zeitgeist* initiated by P.F.'s edition and Marlowe's play. However, there is a certain three year period unaccounted for from 1589 until 1592: conceivably, publishers were as yet unwilling to edit the original translation in full compliance with the censors' demands as this would entail serious alterations that would undermine the integrity of the book as an accurate translation from the German. Alternatively, publishers may have attempted to illegally print P.F.'s Cambridge edition, but these were all confiscated: we cannot but speculate if this was the cause for Orwin's printing press to be seized in 1591. Jeffes and Orwin then formed a partnership and finally decided to alter the original material in order to be the first to have their edition printed before their competitors, but they accomplished this by anticipating what the censors would expect to be cut or altered, edited the material themselves, (e.g., the strange insertions warning all Christian readers), and printed their book in May of 1592 before receiving official approval. Of interest, this coincides with our theory that Marlowe possibly revised his tragedy, what is now known as the B Text, in May or June of the same year. Reflecting on the time and effort Jeffes and Orwin expended on the design and layout of their English edition of the *Faustbook*, is it possible they actually prepared the work as an 'official' collector's copy commemorating Marlowe's new rendition of *Doctor Faustus*?

Unfortunately, during the month of August, Jeffes was detained, his books were apparently confiscated, and his printing press seized until his case was brought to court. A certain Mr. Orliff also brought a charge against Jeffes and Orwin, declaring that the printing rights to the *Faustbook* actually belonged to him. However, as Orliff did not have his *Faustbook* registered in the Stationer's Records before Jeffes and Orwin had printed their copy in May, they were recognised as the rightful owners of the printing copyrights. In the interim, the censors had approved the alterations made to the May edition, allowing Jeffes and Orwin to reprint the book in December with a new title page reflecting the official recognition of the censors.

ଓଙ ❖ ଓଙ

Bibliography for Volumes I and II:

Adam, David. *The Edge of Glory*: *Prayers in the Celtic Tradition*. United States: Morehouse-Barlow, 1988.

Alighieri, Dante. *The Divine Comedy*. Reprint, Charles W. Eliot, ed. *The Divine Comedy of Dante Alighieri, The Harvard Classics, vol. 20*. New York: P.F. Collier and Son Corp., 1963.

Augustine, St. *Confessions*. Reprint, Charles W. Eliot, ed. *The Harvard Classics, vol. 7*. New York: P.F. Collier and Son Corp.. 1963.

Bacon, Francis:

   —*Essays or Counsels, Civil and Moral, 1625 edition*. Reprint, Eliot, Charles W.ed., *The Harvard Classics: Bacon, Milton's Prose, Thomas Browne, vol. 3*. New York: P.F. Collier and Son Corp., 1963: pp. 1–142.

   —*The New Atlantis*, Reprint, W. Eliot, Charles, ed., *The Harvard Classics: Bacon, Milton's Prose, Thomas Browne, vol. 3*. New York: P.F. Collier and Son Corp., 1963: pp. 143–181.

Baron, Frank:

   —*Doctor Faustus: From History to Legend*. München: Wilhelm Fink Verlag, 1978.

   —'Faustus: His Life and Legend'. (See Website entries below.)

Batta, András, and Neef, Sigrid eds., *Opera: Composers, Works, Performers*. Cologne: Könemann Verlagsgesellschaft, 2000.

Beach, Sarah Morehouse. 'The "Julius Cæsar Obelisk" in the English Faust Book and Elsewhere.' *Modern Language Notes 35* (January, 1920): pp.27–31.

Bevington, David, and Rasmussen, Eric eds. *Doctor Faustus, A- and B- texts (1604,1616): Christopher Marlowe and his Collaborator and Revisers*. Manchester: Manchester University Press, 1993.

Bielschowsky, Albert:

—*The Life of Goethe: Volume I, 1749–1788. From Birth to the Return from Italy. (1908)*. Reprint: Honolulu: University Press of the Pacific, 2005.

— *The Life of Goethe: Volume II, 1788–1815. From the Italian Journey to the Wars of Liberation, (1908),* Reprint: Honolulu: University Press of the Pacific, 2005.

— *The Life of Goethe: Vol. III, 1815–1832, From the Congress of Vienna to the Poet's Death, (1908)*. Reprint: Honolulu: University Press of the Pacific, 2005.

Biver, Comte Paul. O'Connor, Monsignor John. trans. *Père Lame 1855–1931*. Reprint; Illinois: Tan Books and Publishers, Inc., 1973.

Bowman, Wayne D. *Philosophical Perspectives on Music*. New York: Oxford University Press, 1998.

Bradbury, Malcolm, ed. *The Atlas of Literature*. London: Greenwich Editions: 2001.

Bruno, Giordano. *Expulsion of the Triumphant Beast: 1584*. Reprint: Arthur D. Imerti, trans., ed. Lincoln: Bison Books, University of Nebraska Press, 2004.

Brusher, Joseph S., S. J. *Popes Through the Ages*. San Rafael: Neff-Kane, 1980.

Bub, Douglas F. 'A New Solution to the "Nacht. Offen Feld" Scene of Goethe's Faust.' *Modern Language Notes, vol. 74, # 5* (May, 1959): pp. 440–444.

Burns, Robert. Eliot, Charles. W. ed. *The Poems and Songs of Robert Burns, The Harvard Classics, vol. 6*. New York, P.F. Collier and Son Corp., 1963.

Calvin, John. 'Dedication of the Institutes of the Christian Religion' (Basel: 1536). Reprint in: Charles W. Eliot, ed. *Prefaces and Prologues, The Harvard Classics vol. 39*. New York: P.F. Collier and Son Corp., 1963: pp. 27–51.

Cheny, Patrick, ed. *The Cambridge Companion to Christopher Marlowe*. Cambridge University Press, 2004.

Cicero, Marcus Tullius. *Letters and treatises on Friendship and Old Age*. Reprint, Charles. W. Eliot, ed. E. S. Shuckburg, trans. *Letters and Treatises of Cicero and Pliny, The Harvard Classics, vol. 9*. New York: P.F. Collier and Son Corp., 1963.

Clark, Martin. *Modern Italy: 1871–1982*. New York: Longman Group Ltd., 1995.

Clement of Alexandria, St. *Exhortation to the Greeks*. Reprint:. Butterworth, G W., trans. *Loeb Classical Library Volume 92*. Cambridge, MA. Harvard University Press. 1919.

Conrad, Peter. *Romantic Opera and Literary Form*. Los Angeles: Quantum Books, University of California Press, 1977.

Copernicus, Nicolaus. 'Dedication of the Revolutions of the Heavenly Bodies to Pope Paul III.' (1543). Reprint in, Charles W. Eliot, ed. *Prefaces and Prologues, The Harvard Classics vol. 39*. New York: P.F. Collier and Son Corp., 1963: pp. 53–57.

Cotterill, H. B. *The Faust-Legend and Goethe's* 'Faust'. London: George G. Harrap & Company, 1912.

Craig, W. J., ed. *The Complete Works of Shakespeare in Twelve Volumes*. Oxford University Press: Reprint, Robert Frederick Ltd., 2002.

Dalton, David. 'Goethe and the Composers of his Time.' *The Music Review, vol. 34*, #2 (May, 1973): pp. 157–173.

Dorris, George E. *Paolo Rolli and the Italian Circle in London, 1715–1744*. Hague, Paris: Mouton and Co., 1967.

Dreher, Diane Elizabeth. 'Si Peccasse Negamus': Marlowe's Faustus and the Book of Common Prayer.' *Notes and Queries, 30* (April, 1983): pp. 143–144.

Dryden, John, trans. *Virgil's Æneid*. Reprint: Charles W. Eliot, ed. *The Harvard Classics, vol. 13*. New York: P.F. Collier and Son Corp., 1963.

Eliot, Charles W. ed.:

—*Essays and English Traits by Ralph Waldo Emerson, The Harvard Classics, vol. 5*. New York: P.F. Collier and Son Corp., 1963.

—*Nine Greek Dramas, The Harvard Classics, vol. 8*. New York: P.F. Collier and Son Corp., 1963.

—*Stories from the Thousand and One Nights, The Harvard Classics, vol. 16*. New York: P.F. Collier and Son Corp., 1963.

—*Voyages and Travels: Ancient and Modern, The Harvard Classics, vol. 33*. New York: P.F. Collier and Son, Corp., 1963.

—*French and English Philosophers, Descartes, Rousseau, Voltaire, Hobbes. The Harvard Classics, vol. 34*. New York: P.F. Collier and Son Corp., 1963.

Empson, William. Jones, John Henry (ed.) *Faustus and the Censor: The English Faust-book and Marlowe's Doctor Faustus.* Oxford: Basil Blackwell Ltd., 1987.

Farrelly, Dan, ed. *Urfaust by Johann Wolfgang von Goethe in Brectian Mode.* Dublin: Carysfort Press, 1998.

Franklin, Benjamin. *Autobiography.* Reprint: Eliot, Charles W. ed., 'Benjamin Franklin, His Autobiography [1706–1757].' *The Harvard Classics, vol. I.* New York: P.F. Collier and Son Corp., 1963: pp. 3–165.

Froissart, Jean. Brereton, Geoffrey, trans. *Chronicles*, Penguin Classics (1978).

Gentili Alessandro. O'Brien, Catherine, eds., *The Green Flame: Contemporary Italian Poetry with English Translations.* Exeter: A. Wheaton and Co., Ltd. / Blackrock: Irish Academic Press Ltd., 1987.

Goethe, Johann Wolfgang von:

—*Annals; Or, Day and Year Papers (1830).* Reprint in: *The Autobiography of Goethe. Truth and Poetry: From my Own Life. Vol. II* [Books XIV-XX] London: George Bell and Sons, 1884.

—*Campaign in France 1792 / Siege of Mainz.* Reprint: Saine, Thomas P., ed., trans., Sammons, Jeffery L., ed. *Goethe: The Collected Works, Vol. 5; From My Life, Poetry and Truth (Part Four).Campaign in France 1792 / Siege of Mainz.* New Jersey: Princeton University Press, 1994.

—*Conversations of German Refugees, Wilhelm Meister's Journeyman Years.* Brown, Jane K., ed. *Goethe: The Collected Works, Vol. 10.* New Jersey: Princeton University Press, 1989.

— *Early Verse Drama and Prose Plays.* Cyrus, Hamlin and Ryder, Frank, eds. *Goethe: The Collected Works, Vol. 7.* New Jersey: Princeton University Press, 1995.

—*Faust: The First Part of the Tragedy.* Reprint: Luke, David. ed., trans., *Oxford World's Classics— Goethe. Faust: Part One.* Oxford: Oxford University Press, 1998.
— (Also) *The Tragedy of Faust (Part One).* Reprint: Eliot, Charles W. ed. *The Harvard Classics, vol. 19.* New York: P.F. Collier and Son Corp., 1963. pp. 5–202

—*Faust: The Second Part of the Tragedy.* Reprint: Luke, David, ed., trans. *Oxford World's Classics—Goethe. Faust: Part Two.* Oxford: Oxford University Press, 1998.

—*Italian Journey [1786–1788].* Reprint: Auden, W. H., and Mayer, Elizabeth, trans. London: Penguin Classics, 1970.

     —*Selected Poems*, in Middleton, Christopher, ed., *Goethe, The Collected Works, Volume 1*. Princeton: Princeton University Press, 1995.

     —*The Sorrows of Young Werther. Elective Affinities. Novella.* Reprint: Wellbery, David E. ed. *Goethe, The Collected Works, Volume 11*. Princeton: Princeton University Press, 1995.

     —*Truth and Poetry: From My Own Life.* English edition / reprint: Oxenford, John, trans., *The Autobiography of Goethe, 2 Volumes.* London: George Bell and Sons, *vol. I*, 1881, *vol. II*, 1884.

     —*Urfaust*, (See Farrelly, Dan.)

     — *Verse Plays and Epic.* Hamlin, Cyrus and Ryder, Frank eds., *Goethe: The Collected Works, Volume 8.* Princeton: Princeton University Press, 1995.

     —*Wilhelm Meister's Apprenticeship (1796).* Reprint, Blackall Eric. A, and Lange, Victor, eds., trans. *Goethe, The Collected Works, Volume 9.* Princeton: Princeton University Press, 1989.

Haile, H. G. auth. trans. *The History of Doctor Johann Faustus: Recovered from the German.* Urbana: University of Illinois Press, 1965.

Harrison, William. Holinshed, Raphael. 'A Description of Elizabethan England', *Holinshed's Chronicles.* Reprint, Charles W. Eliot, ed., *The Harvard Classics; Chronicle and Romance: Froissart, Malory, Holinshed, vol. 35.* New York: P.F. Collier and Son Corp., 1963: pp.215–383.

Hay, Denys. *Europe in the Fourteenth and Fifteenth Centuries.* New York: Longmann Group Ltd., 1989.

The Holy Bible: Douay Rheims Version. Reprint, Illinois: Tan Books and Publishers, Inc., 1989.

Homer, *The Odyssey.* Reprint: Eliot, Charles. W., ed., Butcher, S. H., and Lang, A., trans. *The Odyssey of Homer, The Harvard Classics, vol. 22.* New York: P.F. Collier and Son Corp., 1963.

Honderich, Pauline. 'John Calvin and Doctor Faustus.' *Modern Language Review 68* (January, 1973): pp.1–13.

Hopkins, Lisa. 'A Possible Source for Marlowe's Pageant of the Seven Deadly Sins.' *Notes and Queries 41 (4)* (December, 1994): pp. 451–452.

Hugo, Victor. *The Hunchback of Notre-Dame.* Hertfordshire: Wordsworth Editions Ltd., 1993.

Jantz, Harold:

　　—'Faust's Vision of the Macrocosm.' *Modern Language Notes, Vol. 68, #5* (May 1953): pp. 348–351.

　　— 'Sense in Nonsense: the Mathematics of Faust's Rejuvenation.' *Modern Language Notes, Vol. 85, # 3* (April 1970): pp. 383–385.

　　—The Structure of Time in Faust,' *Modern Language Notes, German Issue, Vol. 92* (April, 1977): pp.494–508.

Johnson, Francis R. 'Marlowe's Astronomy and Renaissance Skepticism.' *Modern Language Notes 35* (January, 1920): pp. 241–254.

Johnston, Francis. *The Wonder of Guadalupe: The Origin and Cult of the Miraculous Image of the Blessed Virgin in Mexico.* Illinois: Tan Books and Publishers, Inc., 1981.

Jones, John Henry, ed. *The English Faustbook: A Critical Edition Based on the Text of 1592.* Cambridge: Cambridge University Press, 1994.

Jump, John ed. *Marlowe Doctor Faustus; A Casebook.* London: Macmillan and Co. Ltd., 1969.

Keefer, Michael H. 'Agrippa's Dilemma: Hermetic "Rebirth" and the Ambivalences of De vanitate and De occulta philosophia.' *Renaissance Quarterly Vol. 41, 4* (Winter, 1988): pp. 614–653.

Kirchweger, Anton Josef. *The Golden Chain of Homer.* Reprint; United States: Kessinger Publishing.

Kocher, Paul H.:

　　— *Christopher Marlowe: A Study of his Thought, Learning, and Character.* New York: Russell and Russell, 1962.

　　— 'The Early Date for Marlowe's Faustus.' *Modern Language Notes 58* (November, 1943): pp. 539–542.

　　— 'The English Faust Book and the Date of Marlowe's Faustus.' *Modern Language Notes 55* (February, 1940): pp. 95–101.

Kondor, Fr. Louis, ed. *Fatima: In Lucia's Own Words. Sister Lucia's Memoirs, vol. I.* Fatima, Portugal: Secretariado Dos Pastorinhos, 2004.

Kowalska, St. M. Faustina, *Divine Mercy in My Soul: The Diary of the Servant of God, Sister M. Faustina Kowalska*. Stockbridge, Massachusetts: Marian Helpers Press, 1990.

Kuriyama, Constance Brown. *Christopher Marlowe: A Renaissance Life*. Cornwall University Press: 2002.

Lake, D. J., 'Three Seventeenth-Century Revisions: Thomas of Woodstock, The Jew of Malta, and Faustus B.' *Notes and Queries, 30* (April 1983): pp. 133– 143.

Levedahl, Kathryn Scates. 'The Witch's One-Times-One: Sense of Nonsense?' *Modern Language Notes, vol. 85, #3* (April, 1970): pp. 380–383.

The Life of Saint Patrick, The Lives of Saint Bridget and Saint Columba. Baltimore: John Murphy, 1863.

Liguori, Alphonsus St. *Preparation for Death: Considerations on Death, Judgement, Heaven and Hell [Abridged]*. Illinois: Tan Books and Publishers, Inc., 1982.

(Lucan), Marcus Annaeus Lucanus. Braund, Susan H. trans. *Civil War: Oxford World's Classics*. Oxford: Oxford University Press, 1999.

Luther, Martin:

— *Address to the Christian Nobility of the German Nation (1520)*. Reprint, Charles W. Eliot, ed. *'Machiavelli, More, Luther.' The Harvard Classics vol. 36*. New York, P.F. Collier and Son Corp., 1963: pp. 260–335.

— *Tischreden*. (Aurifaber: 1569).

Mackey, Albert. *The History of Freemasonry*. New York: Random House Value Publishing Inc., 1996.

Malory, Sir Thomas. 'The Holy Grail.' *Morte D'Arthur*. (Caxton: 1485). Reprint in Charles W. Eliot, ed. *Chronicle and Romance: Froissart, Malory, Holinshed. The Harvard Classics vol. 35*. New York: P.F. Collier and Son Corp., 1963: pp. 105–214.

Marlowe, Christopher. Steane, J. B., ed. *The Complete Plays; Penguin Classics*. Great Britain: Penguin Books Ltd., 1986.

Matalene III, H. W. 'Marlowe's Faustus and the Comforts of Academicism.' *ELH* vol. 39, no. 4 (December, 1972): pp. 495–519.

McIntosh, Christopher. *The Rosicrucians: The History, Mythology, and Rituals of an Esoteric Order*. Maine: Samuel Weiser, Inc., 1997.

Melville, Francis. Machado, Andreia trans. Portuguese edition, *O Pegueno Grande Livro da Alquimia.* Portugal: Edições Asa, 2002.

Millar, Angel. *Freemasonry: A History*. San Diego: Thunder Bay Press, 2005.

Milton, John. *Paradise Lost, Paradise Regained*. Reprint: Eliot, Charles. W., ed. *The Complete Poems of John Milton, The Harvard Classics, vol. 4.* New York: P.F. Collier and Son Corp., 1963.

Nauert, Jr., Charles G. 'Magic and Scepticism in Agrippa's Thought.' *Journal of the History of Ideas, vol. 18* (April, 1957): pp.161–182.

Oberman, Heiko A. Tr. Walliser-Schwarzbart, Eileen. *Luther: Man between God and the Devil.* New York: Yale University Press, 1989.

Ovid, *Metamorphoses.* Reprint: Melville, A. D., trans. *Oxford World's Classics—Ovid: Metamorphoses*. Oxford: Oxford University Press, 1986.

Oxenford, John, trans. *Conversations of Goethe with Eckermann and Soret*. London: George Bell and Sons, 1883. Reprint: Elibron Classic series, Adamant Media Corp., 2005.

O'Sullivan, Fr. Paul O. P. *All About the Angels*. Rockford: Tan Books and Publishers Inc., 1990.

Palmer, Philip Mason. More, Robert Pattison. *The Sources of the Faust Tradition: From Simon Magus to Lessing.* New York: Octagon Books Inc., 1966.

Paré, Ambroise. 'Journeys in Diverse Places (1537–1569)'. Reprint in: Charles W. Eliot, ed., *Scientific Papers: Physiology, Medicine, Surgery, Geology. The Harvard Classics vol. 38.* New York: P.F. Collier and Son Corp., 1963: pp. 8–58.

Plato. *Symposium.* Reprint: Waterfield, Robin, trans. *Oxford World's Classics. Plato: Symposium.* Oxford: Oxford University Press, 1998.

Plutarch, *Lives*: *of Themistocles, Pericles, Aristides, Alcibiades and Coriolanus, Demosthenes and Cicero, Cæsar and Antony. From the corrected and revised edition of the Dryden translation by Arthur Hugh Clough.* Reprint: Charles W. Eliot, ed. *The Harvard Classics, vol. 12*. New York: P.F. Collier and Son Corp., 1963.

Prévot, Rev. André. trans. *Love, Peace, and Joy: Devotion to the Sacred Heart of Jesus according to St. Gertrude.* Illinois: TAN Books and Publishers, Inc., 1984.

Richards, Alfred E.:

— 'Marlowe, Faustus, Scene 14.' *Modern Language Notes, vol. Xxii, no. 4* (April, 1907): pp. 126–127.

—'Some Faustus Notes.' *Modern Language Notes 22* (February, 1907): pp. 39–41.

Riggs, David. *The World of Christopher Marlowe.* New York: Henry Holt and Co. LLC, 2005.

Roberto, D. *The Love of Mary: Reading for the Month of May.* Reprint; Illinois: TAN Books and Publishers, Inc.: 1984.

Robertson, John G. 'The Oldest Scenes in Goethe's Faust.' *Modern Language Notes, Vol. XV, No. 5* (May 1900): pp. 270–280.

Roche, Paul. trans. *Aristophanes: The Complete Plays.* New York, New American Library, 2005.

Rose, William, ed. *The Historie of the Damnable Life and Deserved Death of Doctor John Faustus: 1592.* Reprint; Indiana: University of Notre Dame Press, 1963.

Sadie, Stanley ed. *The Grove Concise Dictionary of Music.* London: Macmillan Publishers, Ltd., 1994.

Schmöger, Rev. Carl E. ed. *The Life of Jesus Christ and Biblical Revelations: From the Visions of the Venerable Anne Catherine Emmerich as Recorded in the journals of Clemens Brentano. Four Volumes.* Illinois: Tan Books and Publishers Inc., 1986.

Scholes, Percy A., ed., *The Oxford Companion to Music.* Oxford: Oxford University Press, 1942.

Schouppe, Fr. F. X., (S. J.) *Purgatory: Explained by the Lives and Legends of the Saints.* Reprint; Rockford Illinois: Tan Books and Publishers, 1986.

Spirago, Francis, Rev. *The Catechism Explained: An Exhaustive Exposition of the Catholic Religion. (1899, 1921).* Reprint, Illinois: Tan Books and Publishers, Inc., 1993.

Steiner, Rudolf. *Goethe's Secret Revelation and The Riddle of Faust (1908–1909).* Reprint: United States; Kessinger Publishing.

Thomas, Calvin. 'The Academic Study of Faust Again.' *Modern Language Notes, no. 6* (June, 1886): pp. 85-86.

Waite, Arthur Edward. *A New Encyclopaedia of Freemasonry (Ars Magna Latomorum), And of Cognate Instituted Mysteries: Their Rites, Literature and History— Combined Two Volume Edition.* New York: Wings Books, 1996.

Walz, John, A. 'An English Faustsplitter.' *Modern Language Notes XLII* (June, 1927), pp. 353–365.

Welsford, Enid. *The Court Masque: A Study in the Relationship Between Poetry and the Revels.* New York: Russell and Russell, 1962.

Yeats, W. B. ed., *A Treasury of Irish Myth, Legend and Folklore: Fairy and Folk Tales of the Irish Peasantry.* New Jersey: Gramercy Books, Crown Publishers, Inc., 1986.

Websites:[*]

Baron, Frank. 'Faustus: His Life and Legend'. H*istoricum.net*. (November 12, 2009). www.historicum.net/themen/hexenforschung/lexikon/personen/art/Georg_Faustus/html/artikel/7114/ca/693f7c07ad/

Brian, Paul. 'Study Guide for Goethe's Faust'. Department of English: Washington State University, (1995). Revised (2000): http://www.wsu.edu:8080/~brians/hum_303/faust.html

Dillon, Rev. Mgr. George. *The Permanent Instruction of the Alta Vendita.* Dublin: M. H. Gill and Son, Ltd., 1885. Reprint E-text: www.catholicvoice.co.uk/dillon/text.htm#14

Glatz, Lawrence F. Metropolitan State College. Film: *Staufen in Breisgau: the Historical City of Faust.* http://www.lawrenceglatz.com/staufeneng.htm

'Goethe: Freemason'. *Pietre-Stones Review of Freemasonry, Short Talk Bulletin Vol. X, No. 9* (Sept. 1932). http://www.freemasons-freemasonry.com/goethe.html

Harvey, Steenie. Devilish Deeds in Staufen (2002). http://www.internationalliving.com/postcards.cfm?pcard=2379

'The Origins of Dr. John Faustus: Cornelius Agrippa' http://www.hants.org.uk/ssa/faustus/agrippa.htm

---

[*] Website URLs correct at time of research / compilation. The author does not accept responsibility for URL inaccuracies or missing sources if Webmasters change sites or addresses.

www.ingramcontent.com/pod-product-compliance
Lightning Source LLC
Chambersburg PA
CBHW050407110426
42812CB00006BA/1820